PIMLICO

207

THE CITY OF LONDON
II GOLDEN YEARS 1890–1914

David Kynaston was born in Aldershot in
1951 and educated at Wellington College,
New College, Oxford, and the London
School of Economics. He has been a professional historian for over twenty years. Since
1979 his principal interest has been the City
of London, interrupted by three excursions
into cricket history. His publications include
King Labour: The British Working Class 1850–1914,
the historical surveys *The Secretary of State* and
The Chancellor of the Exchequer, and major
histories of the *Financial Times* and of the leading
stockbrokers Cazenove & Co. *The City of London,
Volume I: A World of Its Own 1815–1890* is
published by Pimlico.

THE CITY OF LONDON

Volume II
Golden Years 1890–1914

DAVID KYNASTON

PIMLICO

PIMLICO
An imprint of Random House
20 Vauxhall Bridge Road, London SW1V 2SA

Random House Australia (Pty) Ltd
20 Alfred Street, Milsons Point Sydney
New South Wales 2061, Australia

Random House New Zealand Ltd
18 Poland Road, Glenfield
Auckland 10, New Zealand

Random House South Africa (Pty) Ltd
PO Box 337, Bergvlei, South Africa

Random House UK Ltd Reg. No. 954009

First published by Chatto & Windus 1995
Pimlico edition 1996

1 3 5 7 9 10 8 6 4 2

Papers used by Random House UK Ltd are natural, recyclable
products made from wood grown in sustainable forests. The
manufacturing processes conform to the environmental
regulations of the country of origin

Printed and bound in Great Britain by
Mackays of Chatham plc, Chatham, Kent

ISBN 0–7126–6271–5

This book is dedicated to Lucy

Golden Years is the centrepiece of a planned trilogy about the City of London between 1815 and 1986. It is a long book and yet covers only twenty-four years. Can this be justified? I think so. The late-Victorian and Edwardian City attained an international dominance and importance that it would never again enjoy – despite the optimistic return to gold in 1925, despite the rise of the Euromarkets from the 1950s, despite the revolution of the 1980s. This was the City's classic period, when arguably it was the most powerful financial and commercial centre that the world has ever seen. Such a phenomenon deserves a full-length study; all the more so when the sources are as rich as – happily – they are. The telephone was still an object of suspicion and long letters remained the order of the day, sent to an international network of correspondents eager for London's news, rumours and opinions. Much of that correspondence survives, the basis for a large part of this book.

As in *A World of Its Own*, my primary focus is the City's financial core: the Bank of England, the merchant banks, the clearing banks, the money market, the Stock Exchange. Institutions like Lloyd's and the Baltic Exchange are – however unfairly – treated more like bit-players, occasionally on the stage but usually off it. Even so, to change the metaphor, it is a broad enough army that I seek to march through the two detailed narrative sweeps of 1890 to 1902 (the end of the Boer War) and 1902 to 1914. High history (merchant bankers in their parlours settling the fates of distant nations) juxtaposes with low (coarse humour and practical jokes on the floor of the Stock Exchange); the effect may seem quixotic, even odd, but reflects a complex, multi-layered historical reality. So often the City is reduced to one-dimensional cultural stereotypes. I hope in these books, above all this book, to redress the balance and achieve something richer and more interesting.

Several great questions passed across the City's horizon during these years: among others, gold reserves, bimetallism, tariff reform, and the relationship to British industry. I have tried to treat each fully and fairly. Nevertheless, these issues mattered little to most people in the City at any one time. Instead, their physical and nervous energies were expended on the market: what was going up, what was coming down, what was making things move, what was going to happen the next day, the next hour? *These* were their real and palpable concerns – a profoundly non-teleological world view, for ultimately markets go nowhere and those operating in them live the life of a hamster on the wheel. Should we pity these prisoners of immediacy? Or envy their freedom from abstraction? Schlegel? Or Wilcox? Perhaps the answer remains Forster's, to 'only connect'.

Contents

Contents

PART ONE

Prologue

At the office, the new and very young clerk Pitt, who was very impudent to me a week or so ago, was late again. I told him it would be my duty to inform Mr. Perkupp, the principal. To my surprise, Pitt apologized most humbly and in a most gentlemanly fashion. I was unfeignedly pleased to notice this improvement in his manner towards me, and told him I would look over his unpunctuality. Passing down the room an hour later, I received a hard smack in the face from a rolled-up ball of hard foolscap. I turned round sharply, but all the clerks were apparently riveted to their work. I am not a rich man, but I would give half-a-sovereign to know whether that was thrown by accident or design.

George and Weedon Grossmith, *The Diary of a Nobody* (1892)

CHAPTER ONE

Going Underground

One may as well begin with the volley of telegrams from McNab to Scott:

> Should advise you to get 5,000 done by Trust Company Steam Loop.
> Must have positive order from you to buy at least 500 Loop shares in market Monday, to start market on . . . This necessary to insure public application and to start market. Reply.
> Unless have telegram agreeing to my former wire as to market in shares, I must withdraw from this business.
> You must agree, otherwise I drop the whole thing, as without it advertisements wasted and no public application; also no market in shares. Waiting reply.

John McNab was a young stockbroker, Dugald Scott a Manchester-based company promoter, and the date was 6 December 1890, a Saturday and thus a working day in the City. Reinforcing his four telegrams, and trusting to same-day delivery, McNab also fired off a beseeching letter:

> Honestly you ought to go at least 500 . . . Unless we can get a quotation into the papers, saying the shares at a premium, on Monday, we will never get the public on. This we can manage with practically no risk to ourselves if we combine and absolutely buy the shares. If we do not do it, the money spent on advertisements is simply thrown away. If I am to go on at all I must know that some one is going to back me up in at least starting the market in the shares. If it is not done I must give up the whole business, as otherwise I will be nothing more than a fool in this business . . . Do give this matter your assent . . .

Scott did give his assent, before the weekend was out, and by Monday morning everything was ready for the Steam Loop Company to be launched on an unsuspecting world.

It was, the prospectus declared in the pages of the financial press, a company with science on its side: 'The "Steam Loop" is an invention designed to secure to steam users economy of fuel, water, and increased power. The laws under which it acts are positive, and its action is certain. An immediate and automatic circulation is set up which returns the water to the boiler without the loss of its heat and pressure.' While as for future prospects, not least in connection with locomotives and marine boilers: 'The wide range of the applicability of the Steam Loop renders it difficult to place a limit upon the revenue which can be earned by the Company . . .' Unfortunately, times were not propitious. The Baring crisis of the previous month had seen financial catastrophe only narrowly averted; the City was still in a neurotic state; and, despite the best market-making endeavours of McNab and his allies, the issue flopped. All that was left was a bundle of invidiously revealing correspondence, the basis for what would in time become known as the Steam Loop affair.[1]

Any experienced City operator would have agreed that, if possible, telegrams and anger were to be avoided. Better by far to rely on the personal touch. On Wednesday the 10th, while McNab was still waiting in vain for a last-minute rush of country applications, the merchant banker Herbert Gibbs wrote to his brother Alban about an encouraging conversation he had just had with a friendly stockbroker:

> . . . We went on to chat about the investing public & the cheapness of Argentine securities and specially the N.E. Arg Debs with its good prospects of traffic &c. I then suggested as a happy thought that he might know of a client who would perhaps like to go in at present prices for I said I daresay we could squeeze out a foreigner & put him in on bed rock terms; I said I did not want it offered, but if he knew of anyone we would see if we could make room for him. He said he thought he did know a quite private client of theirs who knew the Plate & who went in large lines occasionally & was free from Argentine things at present. So we shall see what that brings . . .

This particular stockbroker was Arthur Hill, known as 'Consols Hill' on account of his sobriety and penchant for sound, non-speculative securities.[2]

Admirable qualities, but in themselves hardly the stuff of Capel Court, home of the Stock Exchange and a byword for matters speculative and boisterous – and sometimes more than boisterous. On Thursday the managers met specially to consider a grave report from the superintendent:

> On the afternoon of Tuesday the 9th instant my attention was attracted to smoke rising in the American market, and on going to ascertain the

cause I found that a waiter had just put out a fire caused by a quantity of newspapers burning under the seat between the American and Berwick markets. When the House was swept it was discovered that part of the floor under the seat had been burned through. Owing to the crowded state of the market I found it was impossible to ascertain who had caused it.

Cole the architect then attended, explaining that 'the fire was made of *Daily Graphics*, which contain an unusual quantity of printers' ink, and as they were heaped up the fire had no outlet and there really was a little furnace under the seat'. The managers decided the best thing to do was to write to the Committee (responsible for discipline), expressing their 'regret that, owing to the crowd and the wilful obstruction of the bystanders, their officers were unable to detect the perpetrators of this act'. The Committee met the following Monday and, clearly fortified by inside information, sent for Tom Nickalls, the leading jobber in the American market and one of the most popular men in the Stock Exchange. A straight-faced Nickalls duly attended:

> He said that the burning of the papers was a practical joke intended to dislodge him and another member from the seats in question, and that it had the desired effect. He considered that it was a very serious matter, and that he would gladly do all he could to prevent its repetition, but did not see his way to any effectual measures. The number of members engaged in such acts was too great to allow of any personal interference, or indeed to permit of the recognition of the real offenders. He doubted whether any personal appeal could have much effect, but thought it might be a good thing to issue a notice . . .

Eventually there appeared such a notice, the formulaic wording of which ('. . . a practice so obnoxious and so dangerous . . . receive the support of members generally in discountenancing . . . occasion for resort to measures . . . very reluctant to adopt . . .') failed to disguise the fundamental problem of running a club with a high proportion of overgrown schoolboys.[3] The run-up to Christmas was always a particularly uninhibited time on the Stock Exchange floor, and 1890, as the *Rialto* reported, was no exception: 'There is a good deal of larking over the raffling of various turkeys, ducks and other edibles, which included, the other day, a long string of sausages. The happy winner of the latter left his prize in the waiting-room, where it was seized by a few lively spirits. They caught a victim unawares and garlanded him round the neck with the sausages, leading him about like a sacrifice to Mammon.' But if that was standard fare, nearby, that same week, history was in the making. It was all reported in the village paper, in the facetious tone seemingly reserved for epochal events:

A representative of the *Financial Times* was despatched in the morning [of Thursday, 18 December] by his remorseless editor to make the perilous excursion and report how it felt to be drawn through a pipe by electricity for twopence. No time was allowed him to say farewell to his wife and to have one last look at the little ones . . . As he proceeded nervously towards the City station, which adjoins the Monument, he passed at the corner of King William-street – a place where the street was being taken up for the repair of electric wires, and a steadfast crowd was gazing down into the cavity, under the impression that the hole was the entrance to the new railway. One man was vainly endeavouring to book to the Elephant and Castle in the little canvas shanty which seems an indispensable accompaniment of street repairs. At the actual station there was an equal air of non-comprehension in the crowd. Every man who entered was regarded with a sorrowful interest as if he were a prisoner surrendering to his bail; and every man who came out unscathed from the ordeal by electric traction was an object of undisguised envy and admiration. The whole thing seemed to be running on the lines of a show, for the railway was not yet understanded of the people.

Our representative pulled himself together and entered. He was at once confronted by a turnstile, and had to pay his twopence before he was allowed to proceed. This made the place more than ever like a show, but the charge would be considered moderate even for a bank holiday booth on Hampstead Heath. Once past the turnstile, however, the whole world – as far as Stockwell at least – was before him. The whole City and South London Railway was open to him like a club. From the turnstile he proceeded along a passage, and found another crowd – brave souls like himself who had faced the worst. They were staring fixedly at two vast doors, like the doors of the elephants' cage in a menagerie, on which was printed in big letters, 'Caution – keep clear of these doors.' 'What is in this den,' he asked; 'the lions?' A nervous old man replied that he didn't know, but the passengers had been ordered to stop there; no doubt something would happen soon.

Presently a roaring was heard within and the doors were pushed back, disclosing an enormous lift . . . Arrived at the platform, the effect was much more pleasing than that of an ordinary underground station . . . Great interest was manifested in the permanent way, which had, in addition to the usual metals, an inner rail from which the electric power is drawn. An obliging porter announcing the fact that anybody touching that rail with his umbrella would receive a startling shock, everybody was promptly seized by a desire to do it. Until the starting of the train, our representative found ample occupation in egging various gentlemen on to the deed, but he found nobody with the requisite courage.

The engine of the electric train is small and of an unusual pattern, the driver and 'stoker' standing on insulators inside and touching little knobs instead of the recognised levers and wheels. The carriages are long and narrow like a couple of tramway cars joined, the seats running longitudinally. Entrance is obtained by a gangway in the middle of each, where a conductor stands to open and shut the gratings. On this conductor you must rely for information as to stations, since there are no windows in the carriages . . . Altogether, the journey, although it seems more like some exhibition amusement than business, is very satisfactory.

So the tube age was born; and soon *Punch* was referring to the pioneer deep-level line, running from King William Street to Stockwell three miles away, as 'The sardine-box railway'.[4] But even on that first confusing, celebratory day, there was a bad moment as one train stayed stuck in a tunnel for a quarter of an hour. Did the conversation in the carriages rise and slowly fade into silence? The mental emptiness deepen behind every face? The terror grow of nothing to think about? On all these points, the man from the *FT* was himself silent.

CHAPTER TWO

Many Cargoes

In March 1907 the thoughtful foreign banker Cornelis Rozenraad, based off Lombard Street, gave a paper to the Institute of Bankers on 'The International Money Market'. It included one particularly striking passage:

> London, gentlemen, is the principal money and gold market of the world. The Bank of England gives gold unconditionally and exchanges its notes for gold, therefore international trade can rely that all claims on London will be paid in gold, and as gold is, among all circulating mediums, the least subject to fluctuations, for this reason bills on England are negotiable everywhere, and transactions between two countries having no direct or no sufficient exchange relations are settled by bills or cheques on London.

Gold, gold, gold . . . Secretary of the Bank of England, even as Rozenraad spoke, was Kenneth Grahame, and it is hardly surprising that one of his most famous books was called *The Golden Age*, little though it touched on monetary matters. The key words in Rozenraad's passage were 'gives gold unconditionally and exchanges its notes for gold' – or the gold standard, as upheld by the Bank of England and by which sterling, the world's leading reserve currency, was ordained to be as good as gold. On this seemingly immortal relationship rested the international dominance of the City of London, king-pin in a world of unitary capital and trading flows. It was a dominance that Francis Hirst, editor of the *Economist* and a committed economic liberal, sought to encapsulate a few years after Rozenraad's paper:

> It [the City] is the greatest shop, the greatest store, the freest market for commodities, gold and securities, the greatest disposer of capital, the greatest dispenser of credit, but above and beyond, as well as by reason of all these marks of financial and commercial supremacy, it is the world's clearing house.[1]

The world's clearing house indeed – of credit, of goods, of skills.[2] Despite many fluctuations, the years between 1890, when the Baring crisis was successfully overcome, and 1914, when all the certainties vanished, were indubitably the City's own golden age. Only later did they seem to be dream days.

*

The practical as well as symbolic pivot of the whole financial system, and increasingly perceived as lender of last resort in times of financial crisis, was the Old Lady of Threadneedle Street. Above all, the Bank of England was responsible for defending the country's gold reserve and thereby maintaining the gold standard, than which successive governors knew no higher duty. This was done primarily by judicious manipulation of Bank rate – in effect, raising interest rates whenever there was a need to attract gold to London – but also by a variety of more or less open operations on the gold market. One can, though, easily exaggerate the Bank's power. For one thing, its own resources were becoming steadily smaller in relation to those of the leading joint-stock banks, and as a result the Bank often found it difficult to impose its will on the money market. For another, during this period fundamental, essentially *impersonal* forces buttressed the gold standard, not least the fact of fixed exchange rates made possible by a world of broadly open economies in equilibrium with each other. Moreover, if the Bank's powers of monetary management were limited, so too was the potential of its moral suasion, or what a later generation would know by shorthand as the governor of the day raising his eyebrows. Certainly the resolution of the Baring crisis gave a perceptible short-term boost to the Bank's authority; but over the period as a whole, the larger perception in the City was that the Bank was run along distinctly backward, old-fashioned lines and that it did not always recruit men of the highest calibre to be directors and, in turn, governors. 'It is difficult enough to get good men', conceded the Governor himself in 1891, and few informed observers would have disputed the point.[3]

Nevertheless, whatever the failings of the Old Lady, the crux remained: namely, that most of the industrialised world financed its trade through sterling-denominated bills drawn on London – and it did so because it knew that such bills, suitably guaranteed, could (in the words of Ronald Gillett, a latter-day bill broker) 'always be discounted in the London discount market at the finest rate of the day, the proceeds converted into gold and the gold taken out of the country to any part of the world'. What precisely were these bills of exchange?

Probably the best definition is that, representing a promise of payment
at a specified future date, they were able to be sold at a discount to face
value in order to obtain immediate funds; and, because they enjoyed
such ready negotiability in the London bill (or discount) market, they
were able to fulfil their underlying purpose of lubricating world trade,
solving the problem of goods not being paid for until they had arrived.[4]
There was no doubt that such bills were desirable things. 'Bills to the
average amount of 7 millions a day reach maturity', declared 'A
Practical Banker' in the *Economist* in 1891, 'and thus afford bankers
an inflow of cash, or its equivalents, of some 50 millions a
week whence to replenish their cash reserves to any needful amount at
will.' And he added that 'the rightful place for bills of exchange
amongst the liquid assets, or the readily available resources, of a bank
should, in my judgment, be next to Consols'.[5] Granted the hallowed
aura still attached to British Government stock, this was high praise
indeed.

Acting in effect as wholesalers in this extremely busy bill market
were the discount houses.[6] Here the leading players by 1890 were the
two limited companies, the National Discount and the Union Discount, the latter the result of a well-judged merger five years earlier
between the United Discount Corporation and the General Credit and
Discount Co. Then came Alexanders, which in 1891 also went limited
and thereby undertook to publish its accounts. There were also some
twenty private firms, with new entrants at about this time including
King & Foà (1886), Vaile & Carew (1888, transmuting in due course
into Allen, Harvey & Ross), and Smith, St Aubyn & Co (1891).
However, no bill on London could be acquired with certainty unless in
the first instance it had been guaranteed by one of London's leading
accepting houses, which were usually but not invariably those firms
that would be known in the twentieth century as merchant banks (the
term itself was just coming into use by 1890).[7] Barings, before its
trauma in the Argentine, had been far and away the City's leading
accepting house; but by 1892 the league table was headed by Kleinworts (acceptances outstanding running at some £5.5m), followed by
Brown Shipley (£4.5m), Morgans (£4.2m), Barings and Schröders
(£3.9m each), Rothschilds (£3.4m), and Hambros (£1.5m).[8] Accepting
was a commission business, involving a particularly nice mixture of
judgement, attention to detail and boldness; and on the back of world
trade growing for most of this period at an ever faster rate, it brought
handsome profits to what had become or were becoming the City's
great names.

A firm coming up fast after a stagnant period was J. Henry Schröder & Co.[9] Its acceptance credit clients were far-flung, but increasingly (like those of Kleinworts) concentrated in Germany and the United States, the most rapidly growing areas of the world and significantly less risky than specialising in either South America or the Far East. German clients were strongly clustered in Hamburg, whose leading nitrate importers all relied on Schröders for financial facilities. As for the States, by far the majority of the firm's clients were in New York, with important new clients featuring some of the largest sugar refiners, needing credit in order to import supplies from Cuba. Whether in Hamburg or New York, all was done by that miracle of convenience, the sterling bill of exchange, guaranteed by a merchanting firm in Leadenhall Street that was transforming itself into a merchant bank. In fact, some of Schröders' new clients were demanding formidably substantial credits: in 1891, acceptances of £648,000 were outstanding to three American sugar firms, at a time when the partners' capital comprised less than £1.2m. As commodity importing and processing became increasingly dominated by large-scale enterprises, so the stakes rose in the City of London.

There was one more leg to the three-legged stool that was the bill of exchange drawn on London. The bill had, firstly, been accepted by a merchant bank, which in effect promised to pay at maturity, usually three months; it had, secondly, been acquired by a discount house or bill broker, the wholesaler in the operation; and now, thirdly, it was sold by the discount house to a bank, which valued the bill as a self-liquidating investment. The role of these banks, whether private or joint-stock British banks or foreign or colonial banks based in London, was crucial to the whole system: not only did they invest heavily in the bill market, but they also made short-term loans to the discount houses in order that those houses could finance their positions.[10] Altogether it was a virtuous circle, responsible for financing the bulk of world trade, only some of which passed through London or had anything to do with Britain.

The bill market, however, was not the only reason why banks from all around the world, anxious to utilise idle balances as profitably as possible, were irresistibly drawn to the City. There was also the small matter of the London Stock Exchange, offering a market in sterling-denominated securities comparable to that in sterling-denominated bills of exchange. By 1890 the nominal value of the securities quoted in the Official List had risen from £3.6m in 1870 to almost £7m; there were over three thousand members, divided about equally into jobbers manning a wide range of specialised markets and brokers executing orders on behalf of private and institutional clients.[11] For banks, the London stock market offered fruitful opportunities, in the form of short-term loans to members (especially jobbers) as well as the widest possible variety of investments. For punters in general, whether banks or insurance companies or private individuals, most of these investments were in the secondary market – in other words, in well-established securities – but there were also rich pickings to be had through participating in new issues, reflecting the international dominance of the London capital market. By the late nineteenth century the City was renowned for exporting capital to all quarters of the globe, financing governments, railways, mines and all manner of economic activity. Using the unrivalled facilities of the London Stock Exchange, above all its marketability, the City's main issuing houses in this deployment of long-term capital were the merchant banks, whose issuing and accepting activities in practice neatly complemented each other. Inevitably they regarded themselves as the princes of the City – though, as they sometimes acknowledged, it could be an unruly kingdom.

*

Take a tour of the City in about 1890.[12] First stop is Herrings & Co, manufacturing chemists of 40 Aldersgate Street, where a laboratory adjoins the works at the back of the warehouse:

> This laboratory is a perfect mine of interest to the visitor thoughtfully or studiously inclined. From one large still, capable of holding 500 gallons, essential oil of almonds was gently coming over with a small stream of water. From another, oil of cloves was issuing; from a third came lavender water; while two earthenware retorts of curious shape were busy in the preparation of sweet spirits of nitre and aromatic spirits of ammonia . . . After glancing at a pretty machine engaged in the interesting operation of 'killing' mercury, we came to an enormous tank, exuding volumes of steam, and containing in its capacious depths four cwt of Jamaica sarsaparilla – a medicine much in use in certain parts – being manufactured into decoction . . .

To the immediate east are J. Maygrove, 'manufacturers of every description of silk yarns' of 29 Jewin Crescent, and John Craig & Sons, india-rubber manufacturers of 8 Wood Street, but next port of call is Ball, Beavon & Co, wholesale importers and manufacturers of musical instruments, spread over three floors at 31 Aldermanbury: 'The entire establishment is crowded with musical instruments of every kind and construction in modern use, and the magnitude of the whole collection may be in some measure understood when we say that the stock of concertinas alone amounts to 1,000 dozens.' Also in Aldermanbury are Frederick Doble & Co, blanket and rug manufacturers, but it is time to cross Cheapside and inspect Old Change Buildings in Old Change, home to Cater, Platt & Co, mantle manufacturers and cloth merchants employing 2,000 people:

> Messrs Cater, Platt & Co bring all their energies and resources to bear upon the production of ladies' and children's mantles and jackets, and abstain from any other branch of manufacture in order to ensure the highest excellence in the one department. Their manufactures are too well known at the present day to need advertisement, and their familiar trade-mark – a figure of the lamented leviathan 'Jumbo', – is admitted today in all leading markets as a sufficient recommendation for any article with which it may be associated. The trade of the house is, of course, exclusively wholesale, and its ramifications are world-wide . . .

Resisting the temptations of Paternoster Square – and in particular Vincent Wood, manufacturer of ladies' and gentlemen's abdominal and supporting belts – turn down towards the river, glancing on the way at Carter, Hedges & Co, cigar importers and manufacturers in Friday Street, and in Upper Thames Street the offices of Henry Bourn, metal trades valuer, auctioneer and accountant. The target, in King William Street just to the north of London Bridge, is the tea merchants Moore Brothers, who:

> supply the finest drawing-room tea at 2s 8d per lb; this is simply magnificent, and a treat for connoisseurs . . . Messrs Moore Brothers, in their monthly circular, very reasonably say, that after consistently pursuing their system of supplying families *direct first hand* at merchants' prices for the long period of sixty-five years, it is owing to the appreciation of their teas, and to the cheerful recommendations of their customers, that, without the enormous *expenses of sensational advertising*, they have for so many years conducted one of the largest tea and coffee businesses in the United Kingdom. It is to such firms as this that London owes her commercial greatness . . .

The tour almost over – no time to stop at Ritchie & Co, gas stove manufacturers of 3 Crooked Lane, off King William Street – it is but a short step to T.G. Hastings & Nephew, export provision merchants of 6 Rood Lane, off Fenchurch Street:

The firm deal generally in butter, cheese, hams, bacon, and kindred staple food supplies, exporting through their branch house at Rotterdam, and buying extensively in the English markets. Their export trade is of large annual volume, both from London and Rotterdam direct, to all points of South America, Australia, India, China, and elsewhere, their exportations to Brazil in these lines of provisions being larger than those of any contemporary metropolitan establishment . . .

One last stop suggests itself. At 32 Crutched Friars, just to the south of Fenchurch Street, Reynolds & Son are not only manufacturers of nautical instruments but also adjusters of iron ships' compasses. Knowing that worse things happen at sea, it is a good spot to place a final, judicious order.

All this – derived from an anonymous guide to *Modern London: The World's Metropolis* – is a reminder that, for all its ever-increasing financial importance, the City still retained in the late nineteenth century a strongly manufacturing-cum-commercial character. The point is reinforced by the City's day-census for 27 April 1891, classifying 'trades, professions, and employments' and giving figures for 'number of employers', in other words firms.[13] These included: 435 brokers, including colonial brokers, cotton brokers, indigo brokers, ivory brokers and rice brokers; 651 commission agents and commission merchants; 652 'drapers, haberdashers, mercers, &c', from silk merchants and warehousemen to shawl manufacturers and milliners; 399 with the umbrella title 'grain &c', from corn brokers to oilcake merchants; 259 'hosiers, glovers, &c'; 246 importers, including asbestos importers, cork importers, feather importers, vanilla importers and yeast importers; 207 'makers', ranging from chronometer makers and gummed-ticket makers to revolving-shutter makers and ships' bottom composition makers; 602 manufacturers, who under 's' alone included sausage-machine manufacturers, sewed-muslin manufacturers, sheep-dip manufacturers, skittle and skittle-ball manufacturers, soda engine and machine manufacturers, spring manufacturers, and starch and blue manufacturers; 2,461 merchants – hair merchants, hoop merchants, horsehair and horn merchants, and so on and so on; 631 under the rubric 'tea, coffee, &c'; 449 warehousemen; and 306 wool merchants, manufacturers and agents . . . *All* these figures, it must be remembered, were for number of employers, not employees. In 1891 up to two-thirds of all the firms in the City either made things or were essentially commercial in purpose.[14] Contemporaries tended to identify the City with the Bank of England and the Stock Exchange, but most had never set foot in the square mile.

13

This commercial world was, of course, a highly fragmented, specialised one, not easy for the outsider to understand even if he did penetrate it. Take that part occupied by the wool merchants, wool brokers and so on. When in 1890 the year's fifth and final series of London sales of colonial wool ended on 13 December, this was how Helmuth Schwartze & Co reported it:

> The fresh arrivals amounted to 122,500 bales (93,000 Australian and 29,500 Cape) . . . Scoured wools have ruled, on the average, about 1d to $1\frac{1}{2}$d lower than in October. They have fluctuated but little and have no share in the improvement of grease wools at the close. The moderate supply of crossbred sold at about 5 per cent reduction, the fall in the case of slipes being rather larger . . .

Equally arcane was the tight-knit network of commodity dealing centred on Mincing Lane. The brokers Carey & Browne were probably typical, as recalled years later by a retired clerk:

> Robert Browne devoted his attention solely to the coffee side of the business which was extensive. Substantial quantities of this commodity were sold in Public Auction; the principal sellers being the merchant banks. Considerable business was also done in Santos Coffee for shipment. In addition to what the firm negotiated, many buyers and sellers negotiated for shipment on C and F terms direct but both parties insisted on London arbitration and the contracts therefore had to be issued by a London broker. Carey & Browne were chosen and whilst the brokerage was low, this was compensated by the large tonnage which passed through their books.
> Robert Browne had expert knowledge particularly of Central American Coffees. He was accustomed to value the samples on appearance and rarely resorted to liquoring and tasting . . . It was uncanny the manner in which he could steer clear of trouble . . . [15]

Steering clear of trouble: in whatever field, whether coffee broking or manufacturing sheep dip, there was no attribute more valued in the City.
 The best way to avoid trouble was through ensuring that one dealt, whenever possible, only with safe, reputable firms; and here the invaluable helpmate was Seyd & Co, whose confidential reports were available at a price. In August 1893 a discount house asked its opinion of M. Samuel & Co of 31 Houndsditch, north of Leadenhall Street at the eastern end of the City. Traditionally the firm's activities fell into two distinct parts, shell merchanting and manufacturing on the one hand,

Japanese and oriental importing on the other; and writing about the
first part, the recent compilers of *Modern London* had been little less
than ecstatic:

> In the importation and collection of every conceivable kind and class of
> ornamental shells from every quarter of the globe, and in the manufacture
> of the same into all descriptions of useful and decorative articles, Messrs
> Samuel stand practically unrivalled . . . In the capacious basement, with
> its 6,000 feet of floor space, are stored the various kinds of shells as they
> are imported and collected. Here huge chests are piled one upon another
> in lofty stacks reaching from floor to ceiling, and these contain enormous
> quantities of shells of every species known to, and of value in, modern
> commerce. Mother-of-pearl forms a leading feature in the stock; and it
> may here be mentioned that Messrs Samuel are among our largest manu-
> facturers of pearl jewellery, buttons, and other products of the pearl shell.
> Adjoining the basement are the washing and cleaning departments, where
> all the shells are prepared for the manufactory, which latter occupies the
> three upper floors of the premises, and contains a most valuable and
> extensive plant of improved machinery. Here a skilled staff of 220 hands
> is employed, and all the various industrial processes connected with the
> production of fancy shell boxes, shell jewellery, picture and looking-glass
> frames, pearl cards, Christmas cards with shell embellishments, and with
> every kind of pearl and tortoiseshell working and button manufacture,
> are fully and most creditably exemplified. In addition to this industry the
> firm are also shell merchants . . .

However, Marcus Samuel, son of a Jewish trader from the East End,
now had other fish to fry. There was, in Seyds' report on his firm, a
faintly ominous tone:

> State their capital at £150,000, but is evidently less. They will be made
> or broken over an enterprise they are engaged in in conjunction with
> Messrs Ker Bolton & Co, Ed Bonstead & Co and Graham's in bringing
> petroleum through the Suez Canal to India in Ships converted into tanks.
> The syndicate invests £1,000,000.[16]

From shells to Shell: in spite of the scepticism of Seyds, an astonishing
mercantile transformation was on the verge of taking place.

That is a particularly dramatic example, but in a sense it was just one
of many shifts which, in the context of the continuing global communications revolution, made the late nineteenth century such a traumatic time for traditional merchanting. Three contemporary assertions
adequately make the point. 'The man who used to be the middleman is
hardly known now,' a London corn broker, William Harris, told a

parliamentary inquiry as early as 1882, adding without apparent regret that the would-be corn merchant 'gets no living out of it'. Later in the decade, the annual report of one of the City's leading textile houses, the Fore Street Warehouse Co Ltd, struck a sombre note on this increasingly vexed theme of ever-closer links between producers on the one hand and retailers and consumers on the other: 'Things are much changed now, those great retail houses go to the manufacturers and are larger purchasers than even wholesale houses can be of certain specialities.' Finally, in 1896, Richard Foster of Knowles & Foster, old-fashioned commission merchants with especially strong links with South America, offered his testimony on the basis of half a century of personal experience: 'In these days of railways, steamships and telegraphs, merchants have to work more cheaply than they did forty or fifty years ago, and they have to do more work to make an equal, perhaps a smaller amount of money.'[17] The gloom was perhaps overstated, by someone who temperamentally had an aversion to all things modern, but most City merchants would have agreed with the drift of Foster's remarks.

Individual merchants responded in individual ways – retreat, acceptance of reduced profits, new lines of business, a move to a more financial or banking role. But taking the City's commercial sector as a whole, the underlying change in this period was from the *physical* handling of goods to what has usefully been called office trade, in other words *organising* the world's as well as Britain's trade.[18] It was not only the communications squeeze on traditional merchanting that was responsible for this shift, as the Provision Trade Section of the London Chamber of Commerce implicitly accepted when in August 1885 it discussed delays on the part of the dock companies in the delivery of provisions:

> Mr Rowson [of Cotton's Wharf, Tooley Street] stated that in his case and others also, shippers systematically avoided having goods sent to London, as landing and deliveries were so irregular and uncertain, that unless delays were wanted they shipped *via* Liverpool . . .
>
> Mr Webb [of Joseph R. Webb & Co, Southwark] fully endorsed Mr Rowson's remarks, and observed that at Bristol improvements had recently been effected in a similar way that London claimed, and, as a result, there had already this season been sent to that port several shipments of over 20,000 boxes of cheese from Canada, whereas no cargo to London had exceeded 5,000 boxes. At present, if a steamer arrive on a Monday the goods may be delivered in two days or ten, and this uncertainty absolutely precludes direct shipments to any great extent in such an article as cheese.

Over the next four years, London's share of Britain's foreign trade (imports and exports combined) fell from 35 per cent to less than 32 per cent.[19] By the 1890s it was clear that London's future in physical trade lay not in bulky, low-value goods, but in a mixture of re-exports, where it still enjoyed an ascendancy over other British ports, and in high-value imported goods such as fur, feather and diamonds, where specialist expertise and marketing skills made all the difference.[20] Overall, however, it was office trade that would now give London the international edge, as the City utilised London's place at the hub of the world's telegraphic and telephone systems, as well as increasingly rapid transport. To quote the historian of this key shift:

> It became possible to conduct a global trading business from an office in the City, maintaining constant contact supplemented by rapid visits and the receipt and despatch of samples and catalogues . . . The office in London was now responsible for the details of assembling cargoes, the ship's loading and unloading, bunkering, provisioning and manning, arranging passage, handling customs, organising insurance, etc. Specialist firms emerged in the City concentrating on particular types of ships, particular cargoes or particular routes.[21]

It was not only the international shipping market that London controlled, but also the trade in most of the world's leading commodities and precious metals. This the City did partly through its communications facilities; partly through its access to high-quality, continuous commercial intelligence; partly through its adaptability and accumulated expertise; partly through its ability to continue to attract talented incomers; and partly because the increasingly complex nature of international commerce meant that there was a global need for a single centre – London, as it happened – to act as fulcrum and mediator of the whole process. The City had, in short, the necessary critical mass, human as much as technological.

An important factor in this renewed commercial dominance was a perceptible improvement in institutional arrangements. From 1875, for example, the market for the selling of colonial wool had a permanent home at the Wool Exchange in Coleman Street. A typically vigorous scene was described there some years later:

> The sale takes place in one large room . . . Selling begins at 4 o'clock. The room is constructed similar to an amphitheatre. The moment the first lot is called out the densely packed audience burst forth in one wild chorus of yells and howls. The next number is sounded and immediately

a dozen or more excited bidders leap to their feet and so on. Excitement on the Stock Exchange is tame compared with it. An Australian said: 'We call our wool sales in Sydney the dog fight, but this is the world's menagerie turned loose.'[22]

The atmosphere was almost as robust at the London Metal Exchange, established in 1882 by the City's metal merchants and brokers at new premises in Whittington Avenue, next to the new Leadenhall Market.[23] Trading, largely in copper and tin, took place by open outcry in what was known as the Ring; and the new exchange quickly established itself as the centre of the world's dealings in lead and zinc as well as copper and tin, especially after the failure in 1889 of the notorious, Paris-based attempt by the Secretan group to corner the world's copper supplies.

The signs were everywhere apparent of a more self-consciously professional approach on the part of the commercial sector. In 1875 the London Jute Association was formed, producing a series of standard contracts for worldwide use; a year later the establishment of the General Produce Brokers' Association of London led to greater uniformity of auction procedures in Mincing Lane as well as creating the machinery for arbitrating disputes between buyers and sellers; and two years later, in 1878, the founding of the London Corn Trade Association created, as in the case of jute, uniform contracts that were increasingly used internationally. Enforcing such contracts could be a demanding business – none of it glamorous, little of it in the public eye, but all strengthening the City's authority as switchboard of the world.

Corn itself was the most important of all the basic commodities, with domestically grown corn being traded in the Old and New Corn Exchanges, both in Mark Lane, and the market for imported grain being the preserve of the Baltic (not yet known as the Baltic Exchange) on the floor of the old South Sea House. The Baltic was also the City's main shipping market, and its dual role led to the creation of an explicit rival in the form of the London Shipping Exchange, formally opened in Billiter Street at the start of 1893. Not long afterwards there appeared an account, 'Where Merchants Do Most Congregate', of the new exchange, pursuing time-honoured activities very similar to those of the Baltic itself:

> At about half-past eleven – when Chartering Change is held, and at a quarter to four in the afternoon – which is the hour fixed for High Change – the floor is crowded with Members. 'Chartering Change' almost explains itself – it is the time when ship owners, freight agents and others meet to 'fix ships' and arrange rates for the conveyance of cargo.

'High Change' is a more miscellaneous gathering, which transacts all kinds of business more or less connected with ships and shipping . . .

At High Change the ship owner can meet his broker, or the merchant can arrange terms for the conveyance of his dried fruits or baled goods by the various liners. It should be said that the ship-brokers who frequent the Exchange are of various kinds. There is the 'loading broker', a man who gathers together, so to speak, the cargo of ships which are prepared to take miscellaneous goods, whose sailings he announces in good time on the Exchange. The chartering brokers, on the other hand, occupy themselves with the search for cargoes of one particular kind, such as cotton, grain, coals, iron rails, etc. They are mostly employed by the owners of what are called 'tramp ships' . . .

The London Shipping Exchange also had, on its first floor, an extremely good restaurant, something that the Baltic lacked and which no doubt filled in the time between Chartering Change and High Change.[24]

A question of intense controversy to the chartering classes in the late-Victorian City was the propriety or otherwise of forward dealing, in other words utilising the telegraph to trade in future rather than actual delivery.[25] Was such dealing an incitement to rash speculation? Or was it merely a sensible way of hedging one's bets in what was often a fluctuating market? The debate took a sharp turn in February 1888 in the context of a proposed clearing house in London for coffee and sugar – a proposal from which some of Mincing Lane's leading broking and merchanting firms withdrew their initial support. According to the *Economist*, the scheme's opponents fell into two groups. One, 'the downright opponents', were 'naturally to be found, for the most part, amongst the large, old, and conservative firms, who do not wish to see new men and new manners brought into the "Lane" by the offering of increased facilities to speculation'. The other group, aware that London had been losing much business in soft commodities to continental centres, was not opposed to the scheme in principle, but contended 'that there was not the slightest need to invoke the support of great financiers, when the whole of the capital required for so promising an investment would be furnished with alacrity in Mincing Lane itself'. These ill-appreciated financiers included most of the leading merchant banks, while from Mincing Lane itself the deputy chairman was the leading sugar broker-cum-merchant Julius Caesar Czarnikow, responsible for recruiting staff from Hamburg who knew the ways of that city's produce clearing house. Operations began on 1 May, at first in coffee only but soon in sugar also, and in its first year the London

Produce Clearing House cleared transactions in 2.26m bags of coffee and 1.27m bags of sugar. Those remained the staples, but in ensuing years it introduced contracts for forward dealing and settlement in a host of other commodities, including pepper, raw silk, indigo and even tea. Yet dealing in futures was only reluctantly accepted by the City at large, and in 1894 some of the qualms surfaced in a reprobatory article in the *Contemporary Review* on 'Market Gambling'. The author, William E. Bear, noted the vastly increased amount of futures dealing in corn that had taken place in recent years in both the USA and Liverpool, and went on:

> It is satisfactory to state that the great majority of merchants in Mark Lane set themselves resolutely against the abominable system, and regard any firm taking part in it with suspicion. On the Baltic, the importer's market in London, option dealing takes place, and the men who deal in options have their Produce Exchange [i.e. the London Commercial Sale Rooms in Mincing Lane] and Clearing-house. It is considered on Mark Lane, however, somewhat 'shady' to belong to the comparatively small clique in London who have adopted the American fashion of dealing in grain.[26]

It was clear, however, which way the trend was going, and equally clear that by providing facilities for forward dealing the City was safeguarding its international position. Perhaps significantly, the markets that dealt in futures preferred not to use that term, an American one, but instead preferred to call themselves terminal markets, deriving from the French word for time. With its inherently conservative streak, the City found reassurance in looking to the old world rather than the new.

*

A host of back-up services helped to oil the intricate machine. Take three of the confidential reports provided by Seyds between 1887 and 1890 for the private bank Frederick Burt & Co:

> R. Mackay & Co, 3 Lothbury. Company liquidators, very respectable and safe, have only liquidated respectable concerns.
> J.P. Henstead & Co, 80a Fenchurch Street. Are ship brokers in a small way established since 1870. J.P.H. having previously been in difficulties. We are not advised to take the name for much.
> J.G. Wharton, 1 Basinghall Street. Is a small auctioneer and nothing definite can be learned about him. References advisable.[27]

Among the many local services, three were especially important: accountancy facilities, legal facilities, insurance facilities. These served a wider client base than just the City itself, but without them it would have been almost impossible for the City to have functioned.

'What they *do* know isn't worth knowing!' Such was the unsentimental attitude to his shareholders of that eminent late-Victorian company director Jolyon Forsyte; and in a world of systematically concealed or distorted financial information, above all in annual reports or the launching of new companies, the role of the respectable but obliging accountant was crucial. According to the 1891 day-census, there were 701 accountancy firms operating in the City, and it was generally a rewarding occupation, not least when a company failed. Indeed, during the winding-up of the great discount house Overend, Gurney & Co, a protracted process that took no less than twenty-six years from 1867, Whinney, Smith & Whinney pocketed fees of £43,205, the equivalent of almost £2m in modern-day terms.[28] There was also useful money to be made – if, on the whole, less serious money – if one was a partner in one of the City's 2,026 firms of solicitors, especially if the firm was involved in the company promoting process, where profit margins were notoriously wide. Ashurst Morris Crisp & Co was such a firm, acting by the late 1880s for an enormous range of companies and maintaining the closest of relationships with the leading company promoter, H. Osborne O'Hagan. It was even strong enough to allow an amicable spin-off firm in the shape of Slaughter & May, established in 1889 by William Slaughter, who had worked for eight years for Ashurst Morris Crisp and whose father, Mihill Slaughter, had been a major administrative figure on the Stock Exchange. He took as his partner a young solicitor of county background called William May, and soon they too were specialising in new issue work, enjoying an especially fruitful connection with the leading international financiers Émile Erlanger & Co. 'A variety of matters turn up, something new almost every day and one comes in contact with numerous folk of all classes and degrees, rogues and otherwise, all engaged in the great mêlée of seeking wealth,' noted May a few years later.[29]

As for insurance, despite the rise of individual companies such as the Alliance and the Commercial Union, the single great focal point remained Lloyd's on the first floor of the Royal Exchange. There, following long periods of sluggishness during much of the century, there were new signs of life by the 1880s. Three figures stand out. One was Colonel (later Sir) Henry Hozier, autocratic Secretary from 1874 to 1906 at a time of mostly figurehead chairmen, and responsible for developing the system of coastal signal stations that gave Lloyd's an unrivalled grasp on the shipping intelligence of the entire world.[30] Then, on the business side, there was Frederick Marten, a marine underwriter who more than anyone pioneered large underwriting syndicates, increasing their size from the conventional two or three 'names' to up to a dozen.[31] But the most important was Cuthbert Heath, as major and innovative a figure in his field as Nathan Rothschild had been in merchant banking.[32] Born in 1859, Heath was the son of a naval officer, was educated at Brighton College, and spent two years in France and Germany studying languages. At 18 he joined a firm of insurance brokers, before he was elected a member of Lloyd's in 1880, backed by a £7,000 loan from his father. Within a year he was underwriting marine risks, but the truly seismic shift took place from the mid-1880s, when, in an opportune response to the late nineteenth-century depression in world shipping, he began to underwrite non-marine risks, something which had hardly happened in living memory at Lloyd's. Fire risks in 1885, burglary in 1889 and earthquakes in 1895 were three of the landmarks, while by the 1890s he was also pushing hard the idea of credit insurance, to protect trading firms against defaulting creditors. Like any pioneer he encountered a certain entrenched conservatism – for instance, when the Committee declined to allow non-marine underwriters to offer security to policy-holders comparable to that given by marine underwriters – but the long-term implications of what was on his part a very remunerative business were profound. Heath was a commanding, rather austere figure, possessed the highest standards, and was never to be seen in the market without the black box in which he kept his hearing aid. Moreover, unlike many pioneers, Heath had the interests of the institution to which he belonged close to his heart – something for which, in time, Lloyd's would be more grateful than it could express.

*

The Thursday in December 1890 on which the *FT*'s intrepid correspondent took the tube was a dullish, fairly typical day in the City, part of the protracted hangover following the Baring crisis. The bullion market set the tone. 'Gold is in great demand,' noted the regular circular issued by the bullion brokers Pixley & Abell, 'and dear rates have been paid to secure parcels offering.' As for the Stock Exchange itself, there was little money to be made, with the *FT*'s market report being headed 'Changes Few and Far Between':

The Stock Markets were dull and languishing all the day. There never was a real spurt of activity, and when any business was done at all, the House was as pleased with itself as a hen that has laid an egg . . . In the morning the fear of further gold withdrawals lay heavy on the market, and prices opened weakly . . . Foreigners were scarcely mentioned . . . In Home Rails, Brighton Deferred asserted its independence by gaining $\frac{1}{4}$ in the teeth of a poor traffic, when all the other stocks were declining . . . There was not much doing in Miscellaneous . . .[33]

It was, in short, a day for idle hands and practical jokes.

Elsewhere in the City, the newly rebuilt and enlarged London Commercial Sale Rooms in Mincing Lane hosted the usual crop of sales, beginning at ten-thirty with hides and suchlike. The brokers Culverwell, Brooks & Co offered 2,564 Batavia Buffalo, 740 Calcutta Buffalo, 153 Salted Cape and 1,202 Ceylon Elk; Dyster, Nalder & Co followed up with 5,400 Rangoon Ox and Cow and 3,816 Russian Horse; and Anning & Cobb, preferring skins to hides, offered 15,062 Australian Wallaby. At noon there was a mixture of tea sales and gum sales, with Marshall & French in the latter seeking to dispose of ninety cases of Gum Copal, six bags of Kowrie Dust and five bags of Angola Dust. Coffee sales took place at one, including Carey & Browne's 652 bags of Rio on ex-quay terms, and most offerings were placed at very full prices. Finally, in terms of formal sales that day at the LCSR, the brokers Thos Edwards & Sons had at four something rather special to offer: '738 Logs Honduras Mahogany, of superior quality, medium and good sizes, being the entire cargo, just landed, ex "Seier", @ Belize'.[34]

Meanwhile, both here and elsewhere, there were plenty of other markets doing their regular business. That evening's 'London Commercial Report' in the *Public Ledger* had most of the details, which were hardly sensational. In sugar: 'The speculative Beet market has been inactive, prices showing scarcely any alteration.' In rum: 'The market is quiet, but prices are steady.' In rice: 'The market remains quiet for old crop, but new crop Burma is firm . . .' In fruit: 'Raisins remain slow of sale . . .' And in shellac: 'On the spot 25 cases Second Orange sold at 87s . . .' The situation on the London Metal Exchange was not much more exciting – copper varying little in price, tin little in demand, lead quiet, spelter (i.e. zinc) easy, antimony moving slowly, quicksilver inactive – while as for the wheat market on the Baltic: 'There is more inquiry for White cargoes, especially from the Continent, and value tends towards sellers. Fine Russians for shipment are firm. Indians unchanged.'[35] This last report came from the evocatively

named *George Dornbusch's Floating Cargoes Evening List*, published
at the Baltic and available to private subscribers only.

On this particular day, the City was as usual the venue for a variety
of company meetings, reported at length in the financial press through
the method of paid advertising disguised as normal editorial matter.
The most prestigious place for such meetings was the Cannon Street
Hotel, and there the shareholders of the Exploring Co, the St John d'el
Rey Mining Co, the Demerara Railway and the North British Austra-
lasian Co gathered at different times; while at Winchester House, the
other favoured spot, there were meetings at noon of the Buenos Ayres
and Valparaiso Transandine Railway and the Santa Fe and Cordova
Great Southern Railway Construction Co, and at two of the Cordoba
Central Railway. Appropriately on such a milestone day in the history
of transport, there was also an ordinary general meeting of the Channel Tunnel Co, held at the London Bridge offices of the South-Eastern
Railway. Sir Edward Watkin took the chair. He was a man for the big
idea, and in his address he laid much emphasis on the encouraging
nature of the borings so far made, before turning to the great impon-
derable:

> With regard to public opinion – which he supposed they must all defer
> to, but which in England, as in all countries, was not always sound – it
> was a remarkable fact that, week by week, requests were received by the
> directors from all parts of the United Kingdom and Ireland for informa-
> tion as to this great undertaking . . . He had himself been on what the
> Americans called 'the stump' . . . Personally, he felt more hopeful than
> ever. He was sure that the only proper means of crossing the Channel for
> commercial and travelling purposes was by tunnel. He did not wish to
> depreciate all that had been said about bridges and tubes, but whether as
> regarded facility, cost, safety, or absence of obstruction, there was noth-
> ing in any of those suggestions to compare with the advantages of the
> tunnel . . .[36]

What was the City's view? Probably sceptical, but it would be nice to
think that among those present was the member of the Stock Exchange
known as 'Channel Tunnel' because he was the greatest bore on
earth.[37]

CHAPTER THREE

Living in Black and White

In the mid-1880s the French traveller Paul Villars, taking notes for a new book to be called *London and its Environs*, stopped for a moment at a famous spot:

> From London Bridge the prospect is superb. The River, two hundred and fifty yards wide, rolling its yellow and glittering waves along, is covered with vessels from all parts of the globe, and so packed, so pressed one against the other, that it is difficult for those going out or coming in to push their way through the crowd of boats of all kinds which dart across the narrow channel left in the centre of the stream. In fact, as far as the eye can reach, extends a forest of masts, a network of cordage, a labyrinth of yards and rigging which seems inextricable: a lace of a thousand patterns, of which the threads are ropes and chain cables . . .
>
> On the left are the Monument and the Billingsgate Fish Market, with its Italian campanile. Farther on is a great white building with colonnades – this is the Custom House. Farther down, still, the Tower; then St Katherine's Docks . . .
>
> On the right is busy Bermondsey, with its lofty chimneys, from which ascend clouds of smoke and steam, the smells of which mingle with the odours of the numerous tanneries established on that side of the Thames . . .
>
> The continued rolling of the cabs, the sound of horses' hoofs on the stones, the puffing of many steam engines, the blows of heavy hammers, the grinding pulleys, the groaning capstans, and, above all, the voices of a million of men, unite in forming a loud roaring, which is like the roaring of the sea.
>
> The noise as of waves envelopes you; you are clasped in its shadowy embrace, and lulled to sleep; the ear too rapidly struck by the multiplicity of sonorous vibrations, no longer transmits any sound. You are deafened; you feel the noise, but no longer hear it.

On the small scale as on the great, the late-Victorian City remained a world of its own, right down to its unrelentingly monochrome dress code. Herbert de Fraine, who began work at the Bank of England in 1886, recalled that code almost three-quarters of a century later:

What did we look like, outside the walls of the Old Lady? We wore the inevitable silk hat, with a strip of dull cloth, three inches wide, covering the narrow silk band. To keep it in the pink of condition, you used a curved rim-brush and a velvet pad. If you were out in bad weather, you had to pay one or more visits to your hatter during the day, where he and his myrmidons were ready to smoothe it with hot irons, for which there was no charge . . .

Trousers were worn without a turn-up, and everyone wore black boots, as often as not buttoned. Everyone without exception carried either an umbrella or walking-stick. There were several large shops round the Bank where every sort and description of stick, tens of thousands of them, from malacca cane to natural ash, were on sale.

We wore stiff-fronted shirts with stiff cuffs, and stiff white collars (not wing). We also wore tail-coats, for the short coat with the silk hat did not come in until shortly after the First World War. There was an elaborate tie with the ends of equal breadth, called a cravat, which you could build up into a formidable expanse of silk or satin, anchored in position with a gold pin . . .

As wrist-watches had not been invented, a gold-chain, varying in thickness with the owner's opulence, stretched across the waistcoat, with the watch at one end, and at the other a metal sovereign purse that held five sovereigns and had a spring to force up the small pile from the bottom as you slid off the top one.

Behold us then, pouring out into the street in what was practically a City uniform. As far as one could see in every direction were streams of bobbing silk hats. But in summer, almost as if by proclamation, silk was supplanted [from the mid-1890s] by straw, and it was as though a black carpet had been rolled up and a pale one laid down, for no clashing patch of colour was introduced by the opposite sex.

The black-coated worker stepped out into an intensely crowded street life. Costers' barrows, fixed stalls and street-sellers of all kinds took up much of the kerb space; the dense traffic of carriages, omnibuses, cabs, carts and waggons often ground to a complete halt; and such was the general grime that it was common practice to protect the snowy cuff in business hours by a half-sheet of note paper folded and fitted over the edge. Even the urbane Villars was disconcerted: 'There is nothing more curious than the appearance of the City streets. Here everyone seems to run rather than to walk. The City man goes straight forward like a shot from a cannon. He takes the shortest cuts: his minutes are valuable. Do not stop him to make any inquiry, you will not succeed . . .' The Frenchman could not have known it, but the showing of a clean pair of heels was all part of a wider code. Take that quintessential figure Walter de Zoete, a member of the Stock Exchange from 1867 to

1909, renowned for his conservatism, his phenomenal memory, and his refusal to use the telephone, on the grounds that personal contact was sacrosanct. De Zoete's advice to his son could not have been simpler: 'In the City as a young man you never walk but always run.'[1]

As for the City's buildings, the physical framework for this perpetual scurrying, the pace of change had slackened somewhat after the wholesale reconstruction of the 1850s and 1860s, at least according to *Building News*, looking back in 1889 over the past twenty years:

> Within the bounds of the City the changes have been chiefly confined to straightening, here and there widening, and in rebuilding old premises. Fenchurch-street, Gracechurch-street, Cornhill, have almost been transformed architecturally, and the neighbourhood of London Bridge has put on quite a new aspect with the completion of the line of street from Cannon-street to the Tower.

But the price of progress was its usual intolerant self, and a year earlier, in February 1888, there had been a jaunty tone to the *Statist*'s latest update:

> Antiquarians will learn with regret, while City men will rejoice over the news, that one of the oldest buildings left in the City is about to be pulled down. This is No 21, Austin Friars, which is upwards of 200 years old, and stands with its garden on part of the land that used to belong to the Augustinian Friars . . . Where the rejoicing of City men comes in is in the fact that there is to be a passage from Austin Friars to Throgmorton-avenue . . .

Two years later saw the demolition of that Tudor relic, the Sir Paul Pindar tavern in Bishopsgate, along with adjacent old houses. Were the new buildings up to the mark? 'Architecturally it has all the latest improvements,' enthused the *Bankers' Magazine* about the new building at 39 Cornhill, into which the Union Discount moved in October 1890, adding that 'it is fitted up with the electric light, has first-rate strong rooms and altogether is as airy, convenient, suitable and pleasant a building as can be wanted for the transaction of banking business'. It is doubtful, though, if it would have passed the Loftie test. W.J. Loftie, BA, FSA, was the author of an imposing volume called *London City*, published by the Leadenhall Press in 1891. His text was largely antiquarian, but in his closing pages, on 'The City As It Is', he decided to let rip:

The brief survey here attempted of some of the great thoroughfares of the City leaves an impression of sadness on the mind. London has been practically rebuilt since the beginning of the present reign, yet how little is there of good architecture to be seen anywhere. Some of the new houses would be a disgrace to any city. The designs of costly structures, covered with coloured marbles and polished granite, are often unworthy of a gin palace . . . Everywhere money has been lavished, brains have been spared. The maximum of ornament is associated with the minimum of design, and the chief modern buildings of the City are much more remarkable for their cost than for their beauty.[2]

Subscribers to Loftie's book included the Queen, the Lord Mayor and Lord Rothschild, but one suspects his words fell on deaf ears.

On Herbert de Fraine's first day at the Bank, thirty-five minutes were allowed for luncheon; and, 'a little way up Cheapside, on the right, I found a small court in which was a genuine old coffee-house with pew-seats built back to back'. No doubt on another day he tried one of Wilkinson's famous à la mode beef shops. Their menu was strictly limited – boiled beef served with soup, carrots and suchlike, all washed down by porter. Alfred Wells, who joined Freshfields as a clerk in 1889, was a keen patron: 'You entered the shop and found on either side wooden pens containing a centre table with two fixed forms, fully-dressed waiters served you, and at the end of the shop was the open kitchen with the chef. The only sweet was suet pudding and jam. These shops were so popular that at luncheon time you sat eating whilst there were three or four men at each pen waiting to take your seat when you had finished.' The experience sounds reasonably civilised, if not altogether relaxing, but elsewhere in the City a mildly horrified Villars observed feeding-time at the human zoo:

At one o'clock in the afternoon the streets are crowded with working men and clerks who hurry towards the nearest chop-houses and taverns to snatch a hasty but substantial meal . . . Standing around the counters is a crowd of men, with their hats on, hastily swallowing a few mouthfuls of food: and then, throwing down a piece of money, they rush away again, leaving their places to be filled up by new-comers as hungry as their predecessors. This manner of eating – standing, like animals from a rack – has something lowering in it, something that is repugnant to the French taste and instincts; but it is the custom, and that word explains everything . . .

There was still a significant shortage of cheap eating places in the City, and many clerks brought their own sandwiches and went out for a drink. 'Our clerks' old desks were chisled, cut about and worm eaten,' recalled Wells, 'and each contained all sorts of unconsidered trifles, and it was in these desks they placed their lunch when they arrived and generally consumed it furtively under cover of the lid.' And he added: 'The desks were never or seldom tied up and when a colleague had occasion to look for a rubber or maybe a little pounce or other office material in an absent clerk's desk, he was often assailed with an aroma enough to spoil his own lunch.' Better by far to be the son of a prosperous merchant, as the young Francis Oppenheimer discovered in the late 1880s when his father took him for the first time to the Gresham Club: 'Right across the further end of the dining room stretched a sideboard laden with the cold dishes in season: lobster, dressed crab, Dublin prawns, cold salmon, roast chicken and other birds, joints and a ham, meat pies, brawn and salads; jellies, fruit tarts and creams . . .'[3]

The needs of the inner man were rarely overlooked on the first floor of the Royal Exchange, its celebrated 'Room' recalled in the 1930s by George Emanuel:

> The Underwriters' boxes were like those in the old City Chophouses and were, undoubtedly, in the tradition of the old Coffee House in which Lloyd's had its origin. The Underwriting Room proper was shaped like an inverted 'L', the short leg being known as 'The Small Room'. In the Big Room the boxes were in three tiers with long avenues . . .
>
> The 'Brokers' Room' led off the Big Room and in it were kept the Voyage Indices, Captains' Register Atlases, Reference books etc, and here Brokers had their boxes. This room led to the Captains' Room with its big Horseshoe Bar, the favourite place for Morning Coffee . . . One could lunch cheaply and quickly at this bar, but those who had more leisure lunched in the boxes in which each habitué had his customary seat and it was an unwritten law that no one should take the seat of a regular customer . . .
>
> Perhaps the thing that impressed me most when I first came to Lloyd's in 1890 was the magnificent person in a red cloak and top hat with gold band who sat in the Rostrum and called the names of those who were wanted at the barrier to The Room.
>
> This was Walter Farrant, Caller at Lloyd's, City Toastmaster and the licensed wit of The Room. He was an imposing figure, over six feet tall, with a flowing beard that so completely covered his chest that he was never known to wear a tie – it would have been quite superfluous.

Emanuel relished the club-like atmosphere of the place, 'where cheery chat and chaff were the general order'. The same applied to the Stock Exchange, though members there did not enjoy the same physical comforts, partly because of sheer pressure on space. It is true that the erection of the New House in 1885 had almost doubled the square footage per person with right of admission, from 2.08 to 4.07, but by 1890 it was already down to 3.18 and getting less by the day. Nor was that all, as one shareholder told a meeting of a Stock Exchange proprietors in 1887. Not only were 'the acoustic properties conspicuous by their absence', so that 'he was gradually becoming deaf', but, 'if you were talking to a friend in any of the lobbies you were moved on like a Socialist in Trafalgar Square'. In short, 'the whole building was defective from its ponderous dome to its faulty water closets'.[4]

By comparison the Bank of England was blessedly uncrowded and undeafening, at least in its Cancelled Notes department, to judge by the memories of someone who went to work there in 1894:

> It was almost unbelievably soothing to sit in a quiet upper room with walls about two feet thick, looking into a soundless inner court, with nothing to do but lay out bank-notes in patterns like Patience cards, learning all about the little marks on them, crossing them up in piles like card-houses, sorting them into numerical order, counting them in sixties and finally entering their numbers in beautiful ledgers made of the very best paper, as if intended to last out the ages. The Bank all through gave an extraordinary impression of wealth, quality, permanence . . .

The writer, Janet Courtney, had been one of the first women to work at the Bank of England. She found, however, that the accumulated weight of the years cut both ways:

> The Bank was full of eighteenth-century, and even earlier, survivals, the dress of its gate porters, the 'nightly watch' going round with Guy Fawkes lanterns (I once asked them, when I met them at four o'clock on a summer Saturday afternoon, why they did this and they seemed hardly to know, except that it was an immemorial custom); the company of Guards coming in at sunset, their sentinels stationed in the courtyard; the Bank cats which a parsimonious Governor put down by docking their 'allowance'; the great bars of gold and silver in the fortress-like bullion vaults, brought in from Lothbury under guard through an archway which looked as if it ought to have a portcullis; the almost human gold-weighing machines, which spat out light sovereigns sideways and let the rest fall in a steady stream into copper vessels like coal pans – all the significant evidence of Britain's wealth and British solidarity, so picturesque, so historic, so reassuring and, in the long run, so unbearably tedious. I used to wish a bomb would explode and wreck the Bank as the only way to get out of it . . .[5]

Courtney (Miss Janet Hogarth at the time) was Oxford-educated, and like others in the City through the ages she found that a little learning could be a dangerous thing.

There were few other women employed in the offices of the square mile. At Antony Gibbs, for example, the first lady clerk did not arrive on the scene until 1889, and five years later she was joined by two others. Inextricably linked with the coming of female clerical labour was the advent of the typewriter; but though most City offices were equipped with them by some point in the 1890s, there remained a strong, continuing preference for handwritten correspondence undertaken by male copying clerks. A similar resistance to change marked the coming of the telephone. At Schröders, neither it nor women were sighted until the new century; while at the stockbrokers Heseltine Powell the intrusive ringing thing was banished to the basement. Indeed, most City offices were still, by the end of the nineteenth century, of a highly old-fashioned, rabbit-warren nature, featuring sloping desks, enormous ledgers still filled out in beautiful copperplate, and carefully attired male clerks ranging in age from 14 to 84. Panmure Gordon was one of the leading stockbroking firms of the period, but still sufficiently small for a clerk to be able to recall how 'clients would come to the office about four o'clock to study the tape and have a warm before a generous fire' while enjoying a cup of tea.[6] For all its manifest international importance, for all its plutocratic symbolism, the pre-1914 City remained obstinately in its daily round a cottage industry, with an average of fewer than ten people working in each firm.[7]

Whether an office was large or small there was always the chance of a jape. 'The practice of throwing pellets of paper about the office must be discontinued,' ran an internal notice of July 1893 posted by the Hongkong and Shanghai Bank, but it is unlikely to have had much effect. Nevertheless, despite the odd flying pellet when a senior back was turned, most firms were run with a fairly iron hand, not least the textile firm George Brettle & Co, where J.H. Mallard ruled the roost. Someone who went to work at 119 Wood Street in 1887 would later recall him soon after he was made a partner, in fearsome if not always invincible action:

> To us his manner was imperious, never speaking except to issue a command in a high haughty voice, and when he walked we felt that the god of war was stalking the boards. To talk when he was in the department would have outraged him; the result being silence, gloom and be it

added, much surreptitious humour. One morning this silence led to what threatened for a moment to develop into a first-class tragedy. Williamson, the porter, had placed in the basement an over-agitated pint of draught stout snugly corked up in a large Schweppe bottle. Presently the dreaded one came to his office bringing his silence with him. All of a sudden the cork flew out of the bottle with a sharp report and ran along the hollow boards. A voice rapped out, 'What is that?' We thought the end of the world had come, but Williamson, always smirky, replied glibly, 'It's only a rat, sir.' The imperious gentleman, in a tone vibrating with finality, thereupon issued the command, 'Then catch it. Catch it at once.'[8]

A would-be martinet was that epitome of suburban, commuting clerkdom, Mr Pooter, hero (or anti-hero) of George and Weedon Grossmith's *The Diary of a Nobody*, published in book form in 1892. Pooter spent his days as head clerk in a City firm, his evenings in domestic bliss or otherwise at 'The Laurels', Brickfield Terrace, Holloway in north London. But whatever his tribulations concerning family, servant and local tradesmen – 'I restrained my feelings,' in front of Borset the impudent butterman, 'and quietly remarked that I thought it was *possible* for a City clerk to be a *gentleman*' – Pooter's secure position was a world away from that of many City clerks. In 'Wanted: A Rowton House for Clerks', an article published a few years later, Robert White stated baldly: 'If statistics were obtainable it would probably be found that of the great army of clerks [71, 387 living in London at the time of the 1891 census] some nineteen-twentieths receive salaries of two guineas weekly, and under. We may take as typical the young man who earns thirty shillings per week, and is without a home, or other resources, in London.' Part of the problem, according to White, was that clerks, acutely class conscious, refused to go into institutions for working-class single men, and as a result there was usually no alternative to cheap lodging–houses. He went on:

> The clerk class has a first claim on the social reformer and the philanthropist. Its members are notoriously over-worked and under-paid . . . All the drudgery and but little of the rewards of commercial enterprise fall to their lot. Too peaceful to form unions and commit assaults; too orderly to assemble on Tower Hill and threaten riots; too sensitive and self-respecting to mouth out their grievances in Trafalgar Square or Hyde Park, the clerks of the metropolis have been driven by force of competition and the greed of many callous employers to the extremes of poverty. Though their pay is lower than that of the lowest class of artisans they are nevertheless expected to live well, to dress trimly, and generally to bear themselves as gentlemen.

Go into the cheap coffee-houses in the City and its environs and note the appearance of the young men who patronise them. The sort of life they are forced to live is proclaimed in the shiny black coat, the frayed collar, the shabby cuffs, and, above all, in the pale, haggard, 'washed-out' look on their faces. From the miseries of lodgings they sometimes seek relief in matrimony, only to find very frequently that their last state is worse than their first. The perpetual struggle to make ends meet and to reconcile gentility with poverty is heart-breaking. And it is the more bitter because it is concealed. In short, their privations are past finding out.[9]

Of course, it varied. In places like the Bank of England, the leading merchant banks and big insurance companies such as the Royal Exchange, there was reasonable pay and job security, as well as tolerable working conditions.[10] Even in some of the higher-class billets, though, pension arrangements, if they existed at all, could be capricious and uncertain. Elsewhere, it was a long, desperate and continuous campaign for the army of clerks. The key phrase in White's only marginally exaggerated analysis was 'force of competition'; in 1887 a chilling article in the *Chamber of Commerce Journal* had underscored the Darwinian elements:

The clerical labour market has been overstocked, apart altogether from competition, consequently the salaries of clerks are only prevented from falling by the addition of fresh branches of knowledge which were not, but are now, exacted. Few amongst the new generation of clerks have not added shorthand, and at least one language, to their qualifications. This constant demand for better men will both raise the status of the clerk and also clear the market. Fewer will attain the new level, and the transition stage from the artisan to the clerk will tend towards abolition. The lower middle classes will find that better remuneration, less of costly show, and equal status, attaches to the handiworker. Fewer will seek to realise a mistaken or unprepared evolution by migrating from the bench to the stool.[11]

That particular genie, however, was out of the bottle, and few clerks would contemplate the journey back from stool to bench, whatever the miseries of being something in the City.

This unsentimental perspective on 'Commercial Education' had resulted from a survey conducted by the London Chamber of Commerce, showing that some 35 per cent of the City's leading firms employed foreigners on their staffs. According to *The Times*, 'it is almost universal testimony of those who have responded to the questions that foreigners, and especially Germans, are employed in this country to do

33

work which Englishmen ought to perform, and would be employed to perform if they were properly educated'. The article emphasised the linguistic deficiencies of English clerks, as well as the willingness of German clerks to work for a reduced salary, in order to secure commercial experience and a London training. Moreover, even in the non-sweated category, there was no denying the thoroughly German character to some of the City's most prominent firms: at Schröders in the 1890s there were twice as many Germans as Englishmen, at Czarnikows the two Smiths on the staff were differentiated as 'grosser' Smith and 'kleiner' Smith. Resentment of German clerks led to the formation of the City Clerks' Alliance in 1890 and an attempt, more or less unsuccessful, to get the Lord Mayor to do something about the invasion. Yet it was often little fun for the Germans either. An 1887 survey of 'German Life in London' asserted that 'the plague of beggars has risen to such a height in the City that the German notice has been affixed to the doors of many City offices: "Begging is forbidden, and is punishable according to the police regulations." '[12]

In the end, it all depended – usually on birth. Take two documents. The Sassoons were acknowledged merchant princes of the City, intimate with the Prince of Wales; and in about 1890 one of them, Arthur, reported to his nephew a visit that he and his brother had just paid to the Leadenhall Street office of David Sassoon & Sons:

> We went to the office (i.e. Reuben and I) yesterday at 11 and remained there till 1, while we signed the Hebrew and Arabic letters. While we were there, Bishop called and offered some Persian opium and he said there was a margin of more than $100 between the price here and that in Hong Kong, so we thought we might as well buy a small lot and make a little money. We went afterwards to Sandown with the Prince and Rosebery in a special and were grieved to see Ladas beaten. I had a plunge on him £40 to win £70. Better luck next time!

In contrast, on 1 July 1890, Edward Clodd, Secretary of the London Joint Stock Bank in Princes Street, just opposite the Bank of England, recorded the following entry in his diary: 'My 50th birthday, spent as all my birthdays, except when they fall on a Saturday, at the Office till past 10.'[13] Clodd, a self-made man, was a well-known writer, especially on matters of rationalism and evolution, yet his diary is almost entirely mute about his life at the bank, despite the many, many hours that he spent there. And that, for the historian of the City, is the larger problem: muteness. What do we really know of the 301,000 people who, by 1891, were working daily there? Of that street-seller remembered by de Fraine, 'an old lady, plentifully pock-marked, who always sat in the same doorway with a large basket of very clean pink pigs' trotters that had a pathetically human appearance'?[14] We read *The Diary of a Nobody* and think we know, but it is an illusion.

PART TWO

1890–1902

These towering edifices with inscriptions numberless, announcing every imaginable form of trade with every corner of the world; here a vast building, consecrate in all its commercial magnificence, great windows and haughty doorways, the gleam of gilding and of brass, the lustre of polished woods, to a single company or firm; here a huge structure which housed on its many floors a crowd of enterprises, names by the score signalled at the foot of the gaping staircase; arrogant suggestions of triumph side by side with desperate beginnings; titles of world-wide significance meeting the eye at every turn, vulgar names with more weight than those of princes, words in small lettering which ruled the fate of millions of men; – no nightmare was ever so crushing . . . The brute force of money; the negation of the individual – these, the evils of our time, found their supreme expression in the City of London. Here was opulence at home and superb; here must poverty lurk and shrink, feeling itself alive only on sufferance; the din of highway and byway was a voice of blustering conquest, bidding the weaker to stand aside or be crushed. Here no man was a human being, but each merely a portion of an inconceivably complicated mechanism. The shiny-hatted figure who rushed or sauntered, gloomed by himself at corners or made one of a talking group, might elsewhere be found a reasonable and kindly person, with traits, peculiarities; here one could see in him nothing but a money-maker of this or that class, ground to a certain pattern. The smooth working of the huge machine made it only the more sinister; one had but to remember what cold tyranny, what elaborate fraud, were served by its manifold ingenuities, only to think of the cries of anguish stifled by its monotonous roar.

George Gissing, *The Crown of Life* (1899)

CHAPTER FOUR

Considering

On 14 January 1891 the National Discount Company held its ordinary half-yearly general meeting at the Cannon Street Hotel. In the chair was William Thompson, who stated that the period since they last met had 'throughout been one of anxiety, and unexplained hidden influences appeared to be at work from time to time, subjecting the market to sudden fluctuations and making any reliable forecast almost impossible'. Thompson then gave a detailed account of the City's troubles since July 1890, including the crisis month of November. After describing the nerve-racking Stock Exchange settlement in the early part of that month, he went on:

> Still men spoke to each other with bated breath afraid to repeat the rumours in the air, when on the 15th the curtain, which had shrouded so much mystery, lifted and the world was brought face to face with the astounding announcement of the difficulties of Messrs Baring, due chiefly to Argentine commitments. For a few hours a panic ruled on the Stock Exchange, reckless rumours passed current affecting the highest houses. So-called 'news' circulated with an eagerness only to be compared with the flight of vultures in the East and it was not until the public were assured that Government and the Bank of England had been equal to the crisis – that the calamity of a suspension that would have reached every financial centre in the world – reaching upon houses however solvent – was averted, that men began to look up and take courage . . .

A glorious if traumatic episode in the City's history, then, but what of the outlook? Thompson was sanguine enough: 'As very heavy liquidations have taken place and trade as a rule is sound we may look forward with confidence, but with caution.'[1] Caution should have outweighed confidence, for the City was to remain in the shadow of the crisis for several years; overseas lending almost dried up; and the world trade boom of the late 1880s was now followed by some five years of falling prices and declining activity.[2]

The bankers' immediate response was to take strength in numbers. The process of amalgamation had begun in the 1880s – one example being the creation in 1888 of what was known as 'the long firm' of Barclay, Bevan & Tritton, Ransom, Bouverie & Co, a merger between two of the City's private banks – but the crisis, with its implications for capital and liquidity, accelerated the process. In the year following November 1890, there occurred as many as twenty-four amalgamations of private banks; while in terms of the national amalgamation movement as a whole, 300 banks in 1890 were reduced to 170 by 1900. In the long term one of the most significant episodes occurred in August 1891: the Birmingham and Midland Bank, based in Birmingham, successfully negotiated to acquire the Central Bank of London, thereby giving the Midland a foothold in the capital.[3] In 1891 itself, however, the focus was on what seemed to be the death-knell for the private banks. It was a symbolic moment when in February the partners of Martins at last overcame their aversion and turned their concern into a limited joint-stock company. Not long afterwards, in June, the news came that Parr's Banking Company, still run from Warrington in Lancashire, was absorbing the venerable Lombard Street private bank Fuller, Banbury, Nix & Co and thereby acquiring a seat on the London Clearing House. This move earned a valedictory appreciation of a notable species from the *Economist*:

> There is little to be said against the private banker in this country. He has played in times past a very prominent part in its financial and commercial development, and he has conducted his business for the most part with admirable judgment and success . . . But public opinion has for some time past made a demand for the publication of accounts to which some firms like Messrs Glyn have rightly yielded, and to do so it has been found advisable to adopt the principle of limited liability with a definite share capital and reserves, an alteration which virtually converts the private bank into a joint-stock institution.[4]

Certainly the figures were sufficiently bald: there were thirteen City private banks in the Clearing House in 1870, ten in 1890, but only five by the end of 1891.[5] So too in the discount market, where, again in 1891, the third largest house, Alexanders, turned itself into a private limited company with a capital of £1m. But at least the old man, George William Alexander, born in Bunhill Row in 1802 and in the business from the age of 13, did not live to witness the unavoidable indignity, having died a week or two after the Baring crisis.[6]

Mergers and going joint-stock were not the only direct results. The wider question raised was whether it was possible to do anything about the nation's palpably inadequate reserves of gold.[7] Concurrent with much press discussion on the subject, George Goschen, Chancellor of the Exchequer, was by January 1891 in close dialogue with William Lidderdale, Governor of the Bank and still the hero of the hour, and Edward Hamilton and Sir Reginald Welby of the Treasury. With a plethora of 'schemes' in the air, Hamilton on the 8th recorded the Governor's typically trenchant views:

> He [Lidderdale] was prepared to try the experiment of £1 notes . . . but he doubted if the addition by this means of more gold in the bank cellars would be any great gain . . . The only way of increasing the spare cash of this country, the smallness of which was our real danger, was to take steps whereby the Joint Stock Banks would be made to keep larger balances; and the least objectionable manner of securing this end would probably be to require them to publish frequently their balances. Some Banks were of course much worse in this respect than other Banks: the worst defaulter was the National Provincial Bank . . . Lidderdale is prepared to go on as Governor for a third year, notwithstanding that it means a considerable private loss: he is wrapped up in the work at the Bank, and is fully alive not only to the interest but to the importance of the post. I don't think he greatly appreciates the Chancellor of the Exchequer, of whose extreme sensitiveness and at times want of courage he complains. I admitted that it was a pity Goschen was thin-skinned. 'Thin-skinned,' said Lidderdale. 'Why, he has no skin at all; he is nothing, but nerves and bones.'

A fortnight later, Lidderdale sought to stiffen Goschen's resolve: 'The Country has all along worked upon very inadequate Banking Reserves & appears determined to continue the practice.' And: 'The larger the Bank's [i.e. Bank of England's] own reserve the less Bankers like to keep *their* money unused. I know you are quite aware of this but you cannot feel it as I do & as every Governor who cares about his position for its own sake must do.' As a final rhetorical thrust, he declared that he almost regretted having helped the bankers the previous November: 'They are a stiff-necked & rebellious race each caring only for his own corporation.'[8]

On 28 January, at a banquet given for him at Leeds Town Hall, Goschen made his long-awaited speech.[9] In what was essentially a kite-flying exercise, he stressed the smallness of English bullion reserves – 'the stock of bullion at the centre of this country [i.e. the Bank of England] is 24 millions, compared with 95 millions of gold and silver in the Bank of France, with 40 millions in the Bank of Germany, and with 142 millions in the United States' – and the fact that London was the world's only free gold market and thus peculiarly exposed.

After touching on the position of the banks as revealed by the Baring crisis – 'it is a false system and a dangerous system to rely significantly upon the aid the Bank of England can give in a crisis' – he put forward his proposals, of which three stood out: that the banks should keep greater cash reserves – presumably at the Bank of England, though that was left unstated; that the banks should publish the details of their reserves more frequently; and that a fiduciary issue of £1 notes would, by taking the place of sovereigns in people's pockets, have the effect of increasing the amount of gold at the Bank of England.

Goschen's nerves were tested at once, for within thirty-six hours there appeared in *The Times* a hostile letter under the pseudonym 'W'. The writer was Bertram Currie, the leading figure at Glyn, Mills, Currie & Co and probably the most widely respected banker of the day. After confessing himself sceptical about £1 notes – 'there are few things upon which mankind are so much the slaves of habit, or so suspicious of change as in regard to the money which they are accustomed to handle in their daily transactions' – he made his central point:

> The banks who are invited by the Chancellor of the Exchequer to increase their cash reserves will naturally inquire to whose custody such reserves are to be intrusted. Is it seriously proposed that they should largely increase them for the benefit of a rival establishment, whose competition they already feel with increasing severity?

The Old Lady, in other words, was a competitor in everyday banking life as well as a saviour in times of crisis; and Currie ended his letter by calling on the state to refrain from interference, leaving the banks and the Bank of England to get on with co-operating as best they could and in their own way. Still, 'W' might be the exception not the rule, and that same day, the 30th, a perhaps over-optimistic Hamilton noted that 'so far the Goschen proposals have not been badly received'. Nor, on 4 February, was Lidderdale downhearted when he reported to Goschen on the response of the City as a whole:

> No one supports the view that Bankers' balances are large enough. No one has seriously objected to frequent publication of skeleton accounts.
> No one cares much about the £1 notes . . . There is some apprehension of compulsory percentage of reserve – the usual grudge against doing anything which would help the Bank – as expressed by Currie – & an inclination to patch up the matter by good resolutions or expressions of assent to the proposition that larger reserves ought to be kept.

In the privacy of his diary next day, Hamilton was a shade more pessimistic, asserting that 'no one is in love with £1 notes, because they won't recognise them as a means to an end'; though he reckoned that such was the 'consensus of opinion as to the inadequacy of the present balances kept by the London Banks at the Bank of England' that the banks, 'being unable to stand up much against this opinion, will probably consent to publish their accounts more frequently'.[10]

Soon afterwards, the whole issue went underground, resurfacing in early May on the occasion of the City Corporation's rather belated post-crisis banquet in Lidderdale's honour, held at the Mansion House. The Governor took the opportunity to reiterate his remarks of about a year earlier concerning the need for the banks and the Bank of England to be what he called 'rowing in the same boat'. After a heavy-handed reference to how 'it would be for the common advantage of bankers and the country if the rowers would take their time a little better from the stroke oar', he went on:

> The more I see and learn of the complicated and interdependent finance of this country, the more strongly do I feel that the one thing most needful is a general recognition of the fact that the maintenance of a sufficient and proper reserve for national wants is the concern in their various degrees of all banks, and not merely of the Bank of England alone.

The next speaker was Goschen, emollience itself: 'You pulled a strong oar last November, Mr Lidderdale, and you were seconded by fine rowing in the rest of the banking boat.' The Chancellor did add, however, that he agreed 'entirely with what has fallen from Mr Lidderdale, that we must look to see how, by hook or by crook, we can strengthen the reserves of this country'. Once again, the banqueting tables had hardly been cleared before Currie was firing off a letter to *The Times*. In it he asserted not only that the banks had responded to Goschen's Leeds speech by significantly strengthening their cash reserves, but also that the Bank of England had used these increased reserves precisely 'in the way which the other banks foretold – by lending them freely to the customers of these banks'. There ensued an acrimonious exchange of correspondence between Lidderdale and his critic, with few words minced and honours about even. 'That the Bank should desire to increase the balances of its customers is natural and laudable', wrote Currie at one point, 'but how the public, other than the holders of Bank Stock, are to be benefited, I fail to see.' To which Lidderdale responded: 'Somebody who once was sick wanted to be a

Monk, but changed his mind on recovery. Similarly, the Bankers increased their balances after the Leeds speech . . . but this soon became too much for their virtue.'[11]

Lidderdale was perhaps his own worst enemy. Hamilton soon afterwards reported a suggestive conversation with him, in the context of the Russian government having announced its intention to withdraw up to £4m of its gold deposits in London:

> It was the impending withdrawal of this large amount of gold that made the Bank of England, somewhat to the surprise of the outside world and to the inconvenience of the Treasury, raise their rate ten days ago to 5 per cent. The rise, Lidderdale said, had been attended with great success, for no less than 4 millions of gold were on the move towards this country. What he was afraid of was that, the moment the gold arrived, down would go the rates & out would go the gold again. However he had been preaching at the Joint Stock Banks again; & he believed that they would cooperate in keeping up the rates.[12]

The key words were 'preaching' and 'again', while the entry as a whole reflected the Bank of England's abiding problem of making Bank rate effective, granted the far superior resources of those slowly wakening giants of the late nineteenth century, the joint-stock banks. Still, Lidderdale could at least derive satisfaction from the fact that most of the big London joint-stock banks had agreed to monthly publication of their balance sheets, though not the weekly basis that he and Goschen would have preferred. That, undeniably, was something gained – but whether the Bank and the banks would really row together, in the second half of 1891 and beyond, was altogether more doubtful.

*

'None of the three members of the Stock Exchange who celebrated the beginning of the New Year by getting hammered was a notable man. Mr Robert Henry Traill was a small punter, whose operations were all understood to be on his own account. Mr Henry George Thomson was a small jobber in the Brighton market, and Mr Maltby, who went under yesterday, was an eccentric jobber of the peripatetic kind.' Thus the *Rialto* on 10 January 1891, at the start of one of the City's more difficult years. To be hammered on the Stock Exchange was a painful ordeal – 'Gentlemen, Mr X begs to inform the House that he is unable to comply with his bargains,' the waiter on the rostrum would announce to a hushed audience after the hammer had come down thrice –

and in the course of 1891 as many as thirty-seven members failed, more than in any year since the 1870s. The general tone of this post-crisis year was set by Alexander Wallace, a director of the Bank of England and one of the two dominant partners in the East India merchants Wallace Bros, established in 1862 but with roots going further back. He wished, he told his firm, 'to impress upon all that the sun does not always shine, that the best ships have to face storms and that credit which has taken 50 years to create may disappear in a night; it is such a delicate thing'. Or, in short: 'We must be as careful of our credit now as if we were still creating it.'[13]

The merchant banker Herbert Gibbs would have heartily agreed, not least during three vexed days later in January 1891. On the 19th he wrote to his brother Vicary:

> The Market has been full of rumours & we have been freely talked about . . . The story was that we were under contract to finish the Arg. N.E. [the Argentine North Eastern Railway, which Antony Gibbs & Sons had unsuccessfully brought to the London market three years earlier], that we had not been able to sell a third of the Stock and we could not finish the railway, that we had been selling large blocks of Consols & Mexicans. We authorised Akroyd [Jack Akroyd, of the stockbrokers Cazenove & Akroyds] to say that we were not under contract to finish, that we had only a small interest in the line, part of which we had sold, that we hadn't sold any Consols, that we hadn't got any Mexicans & finally that we & our friends intended to finish the line for our own interest & profit if the report of our engineers was satisfactory which we had every reason to suppose it would be . . .

Akroyd seems to have convinced the jobbers of the soundness of Antony Gibbs (though the firm was in fact making thumping losses at this time), but the next day Herbert, notoriously short-fused, heard that the Hongkong and Shanghai Bank had refused to take drafts to the value of £12,000. As he told Vicary, he at once stormed off, with his brother Alban, to see the bank's London manager, Ewen Cameron, who admitted that he had done this on his own authority:

> I told him of the Bank of England, the National Discount and the other half dozen leading Discount Houses with whom we have had and have now large sums of money. I also told him that his informants were all ignorant people and that I was astonished that an institution of the importance of that Bank should give currency to idle rumours without attempting to get them confirmed.
> I told him to put the matter before his Directors and tell them that in

the opinion of A.G. & S his conduct had been (I do not wish to use a strong expression) mischievous . . . I was civil in manner . . . I was in a cold fury. I think I said his conduct was disgraceful, I am sure I implied it.

On the 21st, Herbert wrote to another brother, Harry, telling him that he had seen a director called Deacon, that he had got it off his chest, and that Deacon had been very apologetic. Moreover, later in the day, 'I met Deacon & Keswick [chairman of the head office, Hong Kong] at the Club and after a pleasant luncheon I said a few words to the latter, on the duties of Bank Managers &c . . .' Still later in the day, Herbert reported, Deacon tried to get Cameron to write a letter of apology, but the impenitent manager refused. And: 'In consultation with Father we determined not to say anything to Lidderdale or anyone else about the matter.' All in all, Herbert concluded, it had been a harrowing episode: 'I passed a more or less sleepless night owing to the H & S Bank affair, not from worry but rage (which does not affect the liver) . . . If I had been fat I might have had a fit perhaps, but as I am not I feel all right again, or shall do after a night's rest.'[14]

Meanwhile, as an anonymous member noted on the 24th, business on the Stock Exchange itself was almost non-existent: 'Tone? Well, there is none. Like Mrs Harris, it is only talked of. Brokers come into the House to get quotations and to flee from the tormenting letters or visits of sorrowing clients. When prices fall the ingenuous British public rage. Brokers then seek an Alsatian refuge within the House, where little now goes on beyond horse-play.' Singing as well as horse-play, he might have added, as there took place the following week a revealing vignette about the *mores* of Capel Court:

> The Stock Exchange gave itself up with unction on Thursday to the congenial task of roasting a member who had meted out severe measure to a clerk whose moral delinquencies he had spotted. The formation of a Vigilance Society of one in the Consol Market was not appreciated by the House, and all its wit, sarcasm, and draughtsmanship was called into play at the expense of the moralist. The most favoured hit was a parody of 'The Bogey Man':

> 'Sh-, 'Sh-, 'Sh-,
>   He is the moral man.
> So keep away from Charing Cross,
>   He'll catch you if he can.
> His purity's astonishing,
>   He never said a d – n.
> He wears a costume in his bath,
>   He's such a moral man!

Still, with markets in such a depressed, nervous condition, for all the high jinks on the floor, there was a serious question to be asked whether the much-vaunted jobbing system was pulling its weight. The *Economist* thought not, arguing in late February that too often jobbers failed to provide genuine marketability, a view refuted by the *Rialto* a week later:

> The fact is, that the whole of the case against the jobbers is founded upon exceptional circumstances. It is undoubtedly the fact that in such securities as Gas, Water, and other purely investment stocks, the dealers will only make very wide prices, or will refuse to deal until they know which way the broker is, and only then if they know another broker with whom they can undo the bargain. In these cases the jobber is a middleman pure and simple, and to that extent an anomaly. But even then he is not without use. What would be the result if there were no jobbers? Would it not be found by holders of such securities that the difficulty of finding buyers was increased twofold? . . .
>
> In free markets, where the volume of business admits of a close price, the value of the jobber is so evident as to be scarcely worth defending. Take the case of Consols, Colonial stocks, or Railway Preference stocks amongst investment securities, and suppose that a Trust estate, in process of being realised, necessitates the sale of an odd amount of stock. It is obvious that, without the existence of the jobbers, it may take days, or weeks even, before a purchaser is found for the exact quantity . . .

But whatever the merits or demerits of the jobbing system, a subject of recurrent debate, there was no doubt that jobbers as a class were socially inferior to brokers; and it was in 1891, almost a century after the foundation of the modern Stock Exchange, that the first old Etonian became a jobber, in the person of C.T. ('Pubbles') Barclay.[15]

Harry Paxton was a more typical dealer. One of the many hearty, extrovert jobbers who made up the American market, he had been a member since 1878; and now, on the last Saturday in March, after an intensive training programme on the sands at Yarmouth, he was due to meet a clerk called Cuthbertson in a challenge walking match on which large sums had been laid. Cuthbertson was a well-known athlete, whereas Paxton weighed almost nineteen stone. The agreed route was from Piccadilly to Croydon, and the start, amidst some publicity, was to be outside Hatchett's Hotel at half-past seven in the morning:

> Mr Paxton, who is very tall and of powerful build, wore a dark jacket, blue serge trousers, and cricket cap. Both gentlemen at once took their places in the road. Mr Ralli cried, 'Are you ready?' and, silence implying consent, he said 'Go.' And away they went, some riders and drivers preceding, others following them, and a swarm of people running alongside. As the moving mass turned down St James's Street a policeman cried, in astonishment, 'What's all this?' ... Mr Cuthbertson, walking with an agile, springy step, at once shot ahead. Mr Paxton seemed to work as hard with his shoulders as with his nether limbs, and, though his long stride was really carrying him onward at a good pace, he did not appear to be making much headway. This was evidently the impression of the riff-raff in the street, who were unaware that the heavy man had a time allowance of 23 minutes in the walk to Croydon, and who indulged in a number of derisive observations, one man expressing his critical judgment by crying 'A pound to a penny on the little 'un!'

Cuthbertson continued to pull away – 500 yards by the time his opponent got to the Horse Guards, out of sight by Westminster Bridge. On Brixton Hill the heavyweight's 'long and strong stride stood him in good stead', but by Streatham Station, the halfway point, the difference was almost eleven minutes. Meanwhile, outside the winning-post, the Greyhound Inn in Croydon with its 'curious old horizontal beam stretching across the street', there gathered a crowd of jobbers, brokers and others. Cuthbertson, 'walking in splendid style', was flagged in at 9.17, and attention turned to his opponent:

> Mr Paxton pluckily walked on, energetically working both legs and shoulders, as he traversed the road between Streatham and Croydon. He seemed resolute and hopeful, but got rather disconcerted as he entered Croydon by some of the cries intended to encourage him. Applause from friends was cheering enough, but exclamations of 'Go it, Packy!' from local *gamins* who had happened to hear his familiar designation, were rather trying to the dignity of a member of the London Stock Exchange, and at this point Mr Paxton did not display his usual amiability. His excellent prospect of succeeding in his task was, however, a capital emollient. With the company assembled at the Greyhound his success seemed doubtful ... He had but four minutes. Then there was a cry of

'He comes,' caused by the rush onward of some local people full of excitement; but instead of the stalwart form of the Stock Exchange heavyweight there appeared a youth of professional demeanour, who, it was afterwards ascertained, had availed himself of the pace being made by others to test his own prowess. At last, when his time seemed all but up, the genuine champion appeared. He had before this doffed his jacket, and, attired in only a white jersey and blue trousers, strode in with a proud consciousness of triumph suffusing his countenance, and with an increasingly vigorous swing of the arms. He was greeted with a deafening cheer by his many friends assembled. His arrival was within 1 minute and 18 seconds of his time allowance, and he thus won his wagers, which are understood to have been heavy in amount . . .

Perhaps 'Packy' really needed the money, because the previous year he had dropped a cool £7,000 in a bet with his fellow-jobber Tom Nickalls over the outcome of the University Boat Race.[16] Either way, it had been worth the sweat.

Two months later, in May 1891, the *Economist* (which had not troubled to notice the walking match) looked ahead to the imminent Queensland loan on the London capital market. 'It will not do,' it declared with typical coolness, 'for the colonies to count as part of their inheritance that their credit, or the price of their stock, should constantly improve.' A reference to Queensland's present 'labour difficulties', and in particular the existence of 'camps of riotous men in numerous parts of the colony', merely added to investor discouragement. Against that background, as well as the City's generally less than animated spirits, the issue was badly undersubscribed the following week. The *Economist* now warned Queensland not to take the rebuff as 'especially personal', and in its austere way even suggested a silver lining: 'Possibly the rates of wages in Australasia will suffer by a partial cessation of borrowing, but the trade of that important section of the empire will be far from suffering in consequence. It has been no unmixed advantage to render borrowed money too easily come by, as has been the case at the Antipodes in recent years.' Thus the City and its commentators regulated the rhythms of economic life down under, and it was perhaps no surprise when a few months later the Queensland Premier, Sir Thos M'Ilwraith, launched a fierce public attack on the house responsible for bringing out the recent loan: 'I believe the Bank of England did not behave to the Colony of Queensland in the way that an honest Bank ought to have done.' Specifically, he accused the Bank of having broken its promise to see the colony through its current financial difficulties. This was a charge wholly denied by

Lidderdale – 'there is not the slightest foundation for saying that we undertook to find all the money not provided by the Public' – but the upshot was that Queensland, and in time other colonies both in Australia and elsewhere, increasingly looked to different issuers. The man they found was a remarkably skilful, hard-working and high-minded stockbroker, Robert Nivison, whose firm of R. Nivison & Co, usually acting in conjunction with the London and Westminster Bank, came to dominate a whole chunk of the London issuing machine.[17] He enjoyed a strong market following; he had the ability to tap into a wide range of investors, whether via other brokers or his own personal contacts; and, should an issue not 'take' in the first instance, he provided a loyal after-market service, seeking to place stock when and as he could. The self-made son of a Scottish colliery manager, and possessed of a keen sense for the nuances of pricing and distribution, Nivison was a first-rate, non-speculative operator and represented the other side of the Stock Exchange coin to what one might call the 'Packy' syndrome.

Someone on the Paxton rather than Nivison side of that coin, though probably without the big man's redeeming qualities, was young Bill Playne. His father was a mill-owner and his mother one of Beatrice Potter's older sisters; Beatrice spent part of the summer of 1891 staying with them at Box House in Minchinhampton, Gloucestershire. 'I am going out to ride with the "accomplished young ruffian" this morning,' she wrote to her future husband Sidney Webb, and went on:

> We are on friendly terms – both desperately anxious to be agreeable to one another and with a certain personal liking – but with a very whole-hearted contempt for each other's point of view – which shines through our bland amiable manners now and again. I fear I gave a little shock to his self-complacency, quite accidentally. He was asserting that no arguments could shake his Tory principles, that they were based on *good sound instinct*, when I remarked 'We should not wish to convert you, my dear Bill, you are not up to our standard.' It was a perfectly involuntary remark – said in the kindest of tones – but he turned scarlet and looked quite surprised and perplexed.

Playne was poised to begin his career in Capel Court, a place conspicuous for its absence of male socialists, let alone the blush-making female variety. Instead he would find there an almost self-consciously masculine, extrovert, right-wing code into which he could slip as easily as the proverbial glove, a code nicely captured by a snippet the next year from the *Rialto*:

No less than three members were in the London Rowing Club eight that has just been beaten so ignominiously by a French crew on the Seine. All three are jobbers – and a nice job they have made of it! The result of the race has hurt the feelings of the House very much, and in the Brighton Market the account of the race was stuck up surrounded by a black border . . .[18]

The Brighton market was part of Home Rails, its leading jobbers were Laing & Fletcher, and the stocks it dealt in comprised the Caledonian, South Eastern, Chatham, Metropolitan and Sheffield railways as well as the line from London to Brighton, one much used by members of the House. There was nothing quite as solid, reassuring and thoroughly untheoretical as a British railway line, and a special lustre attached to those who manned its markets.

The American market, mainly concentrating on US railroads, was also rather special, though distinctly less respectable. The jobber E.S. Woolf was not a member in the 1890s, but much of his vivid recollections of the pre-1914 American market applied also to that decade:

It was a market unlike any other . . . We worked hours which today [1963] seem fantastic . . . When the House closed at 4 we retired into Shorter's Court for the Street Market. This lasted until the New York Stock Exchange closed at 8 p.m. our time. Even on Saturdays we were on the Street from 1 o'clock until 5 p.m. . . .

When I first started jobbing there was no kind of shelter over the Court. When it rained or snowed, there was a cry 'Up the Court!' and we sheltered as best we could under the archway leading into the Court. In winter, office boys waited at the exits of the Stock Exchange with our coats and galoshes . . .

There were about 200 dealers at the time, and in the House the American Market was unique. At the centre stood a solid block of jobbers who undid the bargains which their colleagues, who stood on the outside, had made with brokers. When a bargain was done, the dealer wrote it on a slip and passed it to his partner or clerk in the centre market. When business was active it was often a struggle to force one's way in. The dealers in the centre wrote changes in prices on slips and passed them out to their partners who were making bargains with the brokers. This solid block of dealers would never allow anyone who was not in the Market to pass through their ranks, and if anyone tried, there was a cry of 'Louisville!' and the intruder had a rough time. The Market was in two halves – in one nearly all the railway companies were dealt in, in the other steel, Southern Pacific, and a few other shares.

On the whole it was a very friendly and jovial Market . . . However, the leading firms had high opinions of themselves and could at times be extremely unpleasant and rude. The great men of the Market were

50

flamboyant and lived on a scale that is inconceivable today. They nearly all had loud voices and loud manners. They made a lot of money but spent it all . . .[19]

From the mid-1880s cable communication between New York and London allowed the American market very quickly to supersede the Foreign market as the main centre of arbitrage – in other words, exploiting minute price differentials between different financial centres – as well as making it generally imperative for the Yankee dealers as a whole not to leave the City while Wall Street was still open and sending over almost instantly received prices. In October 1891, after earlier attempts had failed, members of the market made a sustained effort to procure accommodation inside the House after four o'clock, gravely informing the Committee that:

> the present absence of accommodation, and the subsequent exposure of respectable members of the House to the inclemency of the weather in Shorter's Court and in Throgmorton Street, and to the ignominy of standing shoulder to shoulder in the open street with the most disreputable characters, together with the additional disgrace of being subject to interference by the police, formed altogether a disgrace to the Stock Exchange, and a public scandal.

The Committee was probably not unsympathetic to these arguments, but unfortunately for the weatherbeaten jobbers, their memorial with 116 signatures was no match for a counter-memorial with 1,070 signatures got up by other parts of the House. The counter-memorialists argued, forcibly and effectively, that it would not in practice be possible to confine dealings to American securities after four o'clock – and that if official facilities were given to the American market, this 'concession would practically result in an extension of the general hours of business, already long enough in busy times, and almost needlessly long when there was little doing'. The Committee did allow itself a 'long discussion' on the question, but the eventual 13:0 vote, 19 present, was conclusive proof that, in a self-governing institution, it is numbers that count on such occasions. Still, the failure of the campaign did allow dealings in the street to continue in a vigorous, unfettered way, open to non-members as well as members, and arguably none the worse for that.[20]

Striving to make their voices heard above the hubbub and poor acoustics inside the House were the often hapless waiters – summoning members to clients, to the telephone, and on occasion to the Committee. In May 1891 the managers of the Stock Exchange, answerable to the building's proprietors and responsible for these waiters, elected a trio of them 'on the understanding that if during a month's trial their voices did not prove satisfactory . . . they would not be confirmed in the appointment'. Their names were Vaughan, Nutting and Barfield; and early in August, after a trial that had in fact lasted for two months, Rogers the superintendent gave his report: 'Vaughan is in every way satisfactory. Barfield unfortunately has a weak voice, but in other respects I find him most useful and intelligent. The third man, Nutting, I consider altogether unsuitable.' Accordingly, only Vaughan's appointment was confirmed, but two months later Barfield's was too, and his uniform ordered, after Rogers reported 'that his voice had improved lately'. That left only the third man, and a few weeks afterwards, 'an application by D. Nutting to be compensated for wear and tear of clothes while on trial for a waitership was refused'.[21] The date was 4 November and that meant only one thing: the annual incendiary tendency had come round again, and there would be no peace for the virtuous until the last firework had been lit on the floor of the London Stock Exchange.

*

In mid-November 1891, Hamilton of the Treasury dined at the Bank:

> I had talk with sundry Directors about the Chancellor of the Ex-chequer's currency scheme; the main features of which are (1) to increase the central store of gold by extracting gold from people's pockets and substituting therefor one pound notes . . . and (2) when that central store has been increased, to give the Bank Charter Act some elasticity, which will dispense with the rude necessity of breaking the law [i.e. by peri-odically having to suspend the Act in time of crisis] and will give the Directors a discretionary power on payment of a high rate of interest to issue excess notes. Notwithstanding that the measure has the cordial approval of the Governor himself, the majority of the Court appears to be very lukewarm about it, if not hostile to it. It is a case of 'laissez nous faire'. 'We have got on well enough up till now, why not leave us alone?' The unfortunate part of it is that Goschen admits that he is not very 'sweet' upon the plan himself. He thinks his own judgment has been a little warped by the views of Lidderdale, Welby & myself.

In fact, Lidderdale informed Goschen that fifteen directors were in favour of the revised plan and eleven against; but it is clear from individual letters to the Governor, written during October, that most of those opposed were extremely hostile, typified by H.R. Grenfell's emphatic protest 'against the idea that Bankers should rely either on the Government or the Bank to protect them from the results of their own want of perception'. A future governor, the merchant Samuel Gladstone, took an even stronger line: 'So long as speculation exists, and over-trading is possible, we may expect times of panic and pressure, and Mr Goschen's proposal would have as much effect on foreign exchanges as King Canute's orders had on the waves of the sea.' There was also concern about the practicability of small notes, Edward Howley Palmer referring sententiously to 'the danger and risk to the working classes of the forgeries which existed so extensively when they were last in circulation.' As for those reckoned in favour of the scheme, fairly typical of their lack of warmth (with few exceptions) was the seasoned verdict of Benjamin Buck Greene: 'Though, on the whole, I should perhaps prefer that matters remained as they are, yet I cannot but approve the object the Chancellor has in view in proposing to establish an independent and tangible reserve of gold from which to meet any temporary, though rare, emergency . . .' There was, in short, an understandably wan tone as Lidderdale reported back to Goschen on his soundings: 'Do you expect enthusiastic support from the Bank to anything? We are not a very youthful body of men, though wonderfully youthful in spirit, – considering.'[22]

Inevitably, much would turn on the response of the bankers themselves, for historical reasons not represented on the Court of the Bank of England. After Goschen's Leeds speech they had mostly lain low, waiting for more definite proposals to be formulated. The notable if pseudonymous exception had been Currie, and few would have been surprised when, early in November, at a meeting of the Institute of Bankers, his right-hand man at Glyns, A.S. Harvey, broke cover. After acknowledging without reservation that the Bank of England had acted correctly over the Baring crisis, he went on:

> The effect that this crisis has had upon us as bankers has undoubtedly been, that we have been subject to a vast amount of criticism; criticism which, to some extent, has resulted in intensifying the prudence which, so far as I can see, bankers have generally been conspicuous for exhibiting; and I dare say on the whole, the criticism will be beneficial to all of us. But I think I may venture to say, that if we want anything, it is rest. I think bankers should be left alone for a little while. From several quarters, not excepting the highest quarters, we have been exposed to criticism for which we are as devoutly thankful as people generally are when they are criticised . . .

'A very shrewd, hard-headed fellow' was Hamilton's estimate of Harvey (once of the Treasury himself), and in such a gathering Harvey's words would strike a sonorous chord; it was also apparent that Lidderdale commanded less than unanimous support to his immediate rear: poised to pounce from the Opposition benches was Gladstone, ever ready to denounce what he liked to call 'quackery'.[23] Altogether, it was little wonder if Goschen, never the most resolute of men, was starting to waver.

Nevertheless, he stood and delivered ably enough on 2 December to a meeting of the London Chamber of Commerce held at the Merchant Taylors' Hall in Threadneedle Street. About 750 were present, including many leading bankers, and the well-known private banker Sir John Lubbock took the chair. 'The end which he has in view is admitted by all to be of paramount importance: it is the means – the £1 note issue – which is regarded with some suspicion and doubt,' Hamilton noted anxiously in his diary that evening. Press reaction the next day was mixed. Among those broadly in favour was the *FT*, which did however criticise Goschen on the grounds that 'there was throughout the address a tone of appeal for support from the banking interest which, though no doubt flattering, was perhaps rather overdone'. It was a point Lidderdale took up. 'I think,' he wrote to Welby on the 3rd, 'the Chancellor should insist upon his proposals being considered from the point of view of Public advantage, not of individual inconvenience.' And he added, with his words underlined: 'Let the Bankers justify their opposition.' Hamilton, meanwhile, continued to gauge response. By the 4th he had 'seen a certain number of City people', including the Rothschilds, and was having to admit that 'they certainly don't jump at the Currency scheme'. Three days later he was somewhat less downbeat: 'The reception accorded to Mr Goschen's scheme is not on the whole unfavourable: there is no enthusiasm for it no doubt, but the great thing is there is no serious outcry against it.'[24]

Shortly before Christmas the situation turned decisively. On the 17th, *The Times* came out strongly against the scheme; within hours Gladstone was denouncing it as a charter for speculation; and by the 19th Hamilton was starting to bow to defeat: 'Goschen's currency scheme gains no support; & it looks as if its abortion is inevitable. The "Times" did its best the other day in a leader to dig a grave for it; and I am afraid all that can be looked for now is a decent interment.' Operating powerfully behind the scenes, and seemingly inspiring a whispering campaign against Lidderdale, was Currie. 'As far as I could gather before I left London,' he wrote to the Shadow Chancellor, Sir

William Harcourt, on about the 17th, 'the feeling of the Bank directors and of the authorities generally, was not encouraging to the scheme of Goschen.' Currie insisted that the idea of £1 notes was doomed to unpopularity ('Fancy asking a hansom cab-driver for change for a £1 note') and took his customary tart line on the question of reserves: 'Mr Lidderdale is very eloquent upon the burden and cost to the Bank of maintaining the reserve, but, as I have ventured to point out to him, the dividends on Bank Stock continue to increase, and the rate of profit, as shown in a recent article in the *Economist*, is double that of any other Bank.' Harcourt took the bait, and in his usual forthright way wrote to Hamilton on the 21st:

> I don't find that the City at all share your admiration of Lidderdale. Indeed since it has been apparent that his confident predictions as to the favourable issue of the Baring settlement are not well founded his reputation has fallen as quickly as it rose. I have had letters from persons whom you would recognise as being of the highest authority who regard the recent scheme as a mere Bank of England job to increase the profits of the Bank of England . . . From whatever cause it may arise it is clear to me that at present Lidderdale's authority will anything but strengthen currency proposals in the City.

Harcourt's second sentence was an intriguing one, a reference to how long, in falling markets, the Baring liquidation was taking, thereby keeping the guarantors uncomfortably on the hook. Hamilton, as Harcourt knew he would, passed on the gist of his letter to Goschen, who in turn replied to Hamilton on the 27th:

> I am not surprised at what H. has heard. The Bankers have been sore with Lidderdale almost from the first. He lectured them & has rather boasted of the language he told to them. The City is ungrateful . . .
> The 'high authority' may be Bertram Currie. The guarantors are beginning to be uneasy, & people think that Lidderdale has been too sanguine.[25]

It was a perceptive assessment, but the episode cannot have fortified the Chancellor's resolve.

The early weeks of 1892 merely confirmed that he would not be putting his proposals before Parliament. 'That the central gold reserve of the country needs enlarging is true', conceded a negative editorial in the *Bankers' Magazine*, 'but the right method of augmenting it is by steady accumulation, and not by tampering with the system on which our currency is based.' On 21 January a general meeting of the London Chamber of Commerce to consider Goschen's scheme was at best inconclusive; soon afterwards, a questionnaire sent out by the Institute of Bankers to its fellows, about half of whom were City-based, produced a three to one ratio against the proposals. Hamilton was usually prepared to yield to the City's superior understanding in monetary matters, but by late January he felt himself little less than a prophet spurned:

> Natty R. has become more & more hostile to Goschen's currency scheme; & he won't argue the case quietly. He insists that the proposals are rotten in principle & would not work. I suppose I am prejudiced; but I confess I am much struck with the total absence of substantial or even plausible objections to the scheme. Indeed, I think the best objection I have heard yet raised to the introduction of the £1 note is that you could not toss with it as you can with a sovereign ... Some day people will think themselves very foolish for having rejected the scheme: they may face a much more disagreeable & penal measure; and they may see it rushed through.

A Rothschild would never toss a sovereign for England, but Hamilton should not have been so surprised by the City's deep-seated conservatism and failure to put an intellectual spin on its instinctive, even atavistic objections. 'The sovereign is a general favourite,' the long-headed Harvey had written to him in the course of 1891, adding presciently that 'patriotic fervour would induce the nation to surrender its gold coins, but I doubt if abstract financial considerations will'.[26] On this the sentiments of the City and of the public were as one, grinding down between them the suddenly rather ill-appreciated custodian of the nation's central store of gold.

It was an irony of the situation that the proposals had intended to introduce a greater degree of elasticity in the working of the Bank Charter Act, which was precisely what many City bankers had demanded in vain back in 1844. Now, however, such was the hallowed aura of Peel's masterpiece, that most bankers considered it tantamount to heresy to suggest remoulding it. Nevertheless, out of the chequered reform process following the Baring crisis there had come two major changes to the banking system.[27] Firstly, it had given a further push to the amalgamation movement, especially through the effect of monthly published balance sheets heightening competitiveness awareness between banks, and this in turn produced a more concentrated system that was easier for a central bank to attempt to control. Secondly, in the course of the 1890s the general level of bankers' cash reserves did increase appreciably. Moreover, the failure of the plan to introduce £1 notes had the important if unintentional consequence of focusing attention in a less distracted way on the whole question of the central reserve. During the 1880s there had been little disposition to challenge Bagehot's conclusion that there was no realistic alternative to a single-reserve system; but it was a significant straw in the wind when the *Bankers' Magazine* asserted in March 1892 that instead of banks concentrating all their reserves at the Bank of England, 'we shall have to revert to the older methods – to causing each bank to maintain an adequate cash reserve of its own'. Or, as the inveterate Currie privately put it some months later, 'the time for living under the patronage of the Bank of England seems to be passing & the other Banks would act wisely in recognising this fact & in making provision for future troubles before they arrive'.[28] Over the next two decades the question of the reserve and its whereabouts would not go away, and it came to symbolise the shifting balance of power not only between the Bank of England and the rapidly growing joint-stock banks (capital of over £50m by 1891, compared with £35m ten years earlier, and almost a thousand more branches), but also in some sense between an entrenched City establishment and a group of unwelcome, muscle-flexing upstarts from the provinces.[29] In the spring of 1892 the Institute of Bankers heard a paper on banks and banking in 1891 given by James Dick of the North Eastern Bank, Newcastle upon Tyne. The ensuing discussion was led by Harvey of Glyns, and to his highly rational mind the central conclusion reached by Dick's paper was crystal clear:

> It comes to this: that banking has undergone a system of combination and centralization, that there has been an extension everywhere of the joint stock principle, that there has been a real invasion of London – we London bankers, with old associations and traditions, have been invaded by a vast horde of country bankers. They have a right to come, and I hope they will have a welcome, but there is no doubt that they have come.[30]

CHAPTER FIVE

Misunderstood

' "How long is this to last?" is a question which every City man carries just now on the tip of his tongue. No one thus addressed mistakes its meaning. It refers to the utter prostration of financial enterprise in the City.' So W.R. Lawson began his survey of 'The Financial Outlook in 1892', in large part an outlook still darkened by the understandable 'loss of speculative appetite on the part of the public' in the protracted wake of the Baring crisis. As for other consequences of that crisis:

> The present generation cannot hope to see another firm enjoying a tithe of the influence and the world-wide connection which were sacrificed at the fall of the Barings. One or two great houses survive, which, in their own way, may be quite as pre-eminent, but their sphere is different, and it requires all their energy to hold it. When an ordinary gap occurs in the financial ranks it is soon taken possession of by surrounding competitors, but a huge chasm, such as yawns in Bishopsgate Street, cannot be filled up in a day or even a quarter of a century. For all practical purposes it is a permanent void in high finance.

Lawson's assumption that Barings was a permanently spent force was not shared by everyone. As early as January 1891, Hamilton noted that young John Baring, son of the unfortunate Revelstoke, had 'really got his nose to the grind-stone', adding: 'If he sticks to it, he will probably be a leading City man one day, & may live to see financial prestige restored to the name of Barings. According to all accounts, the new house is doing well & has lost but few of its old customers.'[1] Nevertheless, things in the City would never be the same again, and certainly there would be no return to the old Rothschilds–Barings duopoly. Over Argentine state loans, for example, Morgans from the 1890s claimed equal rights with Barings; while generally in the highly prestigious field of issuing for foreign governments, the post-crisis tendency was for the burden of responsibility to be shared by several houses, in other financial centres as well as in London. Often this burden-sharing was disguised for the sake of appearances, but increasingly it was the reality.[2] And though Barings in the event was to stage a remarkable recovery, especially from the turn of the century, the days of being Europe's 'sixth great power' had gone for ever.

*

The conclusive bursting of the speculative bubble in 1890 had other lingering effects. Early in March 1892 the Stock Exchange Committee considered a complaint from Edgar Draycott of 1 Pembury Road, Clapton.[3] He accused his broker, W.W. Daw of 88 London Wall, of having dealt on his behalf but then refused to disclose details of from whom he had bought, to whom he had sold, and dates and times. Both men attended, Draycott, as usual for a non-member, acknowledging that he would accept the Committee's verdict as final:

> Mr Draycott said that he was a servant to the London and North Western Railway Company, and he complained that when he demanded the information, Mr Daw wrote to him a letter containing threats of denouncing him to the directors of the company unless he withdrew from his demands. He – Daw – charged him with making false representations: of defrauding the company, and concluded by saying that he had saved him from bankruptcy and disgrace, which was utterly untrue as he – Draycott – had freehold property.
>
> Mr Draycott here handed a letter from Mr Daw dated 2nd February 1892 and Mr Daw said that he had not carried out his threat but had put into the fire the letter which he had intended to address to the London and North Western . . .
>
> Mr Daw explained, and justified the contents of his letter to Mr Draycott, saying that whatever professions Mr Draycott might now make as to his solvency, in September 1890 he owed him £24, which amount was increased to £63, which he could not pay. At that time he – Draycott – was a bull of Mexican Rails, at 68, which he said he would like to take up, but as he could not pay him £60 which he owed him, he – Daw – closed the account at 48, notwithstanding his threats. By this time Mr Draycott owed him about £150 and on the 27th of November, his account shewing this debit was sent to him. Mr Draycott came to him the next morning with a piteous statement as to his inability to pay, of his intention to commit suicide, and of the illness of his wife, &c. He – Daw – feeling sympathy for him, did what he could to calm him, and told him that if he would only remain quiet he would manage his account for him, if he would pay him as far as he could. The result was that the balance debt rose from £290 to £350, and towards the end of 1891 he eventually closed Mr Draycott's account . . .

Daw explaining that he had done this after discovering that Draycott was a clerk, and therefore by Stock Exchange rules not entitled to be dealt for by a member, the discussion then turned to Draycott's transactions (208 in all) and Daw's failure to supply details. The railway clerk expressed a particular grievance about the lack of information concerning Mexican Rails. Whereupon:

> Mr Daw was asked to refer to his books, upon which he said that he was unable to produce the names of the dealers in the case of Mexican Rails. He said, that some years ago he had unfortunately consented to underwrite some shares in a water company, which had been wound up, and the liquidator trying to implicate him as a promoter, he had been unfortunately involved in some legal proceedings, which lasted for a long time before they were abandoned. These proceedings were so vexatious, that he became seriously ill, suffering from brain fever, and it was long before he recovered. Having in mind the suffering he endured, he had destroyed his old books and had given instructions to his clerks, never to keep any old books in future . . . He charged Mr Draycott with a knowledge of the fact that the books containing the particular entries he required could not be forthcoming and with founding his present complaint upon that knowledge.
>
> Mr Draycott denied this accusation and persisted in his demand for particulars. He was asked why he could not himself give dates and other details, and also for a specific answer to the inquiry why he had delayed making his demand until the present time? In reply, Mr Draycott could only say that he had his suspicions – he could not say why having suspicions, he continued to employ Mr Daw and had actually increased his account with him.

On which unsatisfactory note, the parties withdrew; and, after a long discussion, the Committee decided that Draycott had failed to furnish evidence of bad faith on Daw's part. The Chairman, however, told Daw 'that the Committee regarded the destruction of his books as a most unjustifiable act and one which they could not pass over without giving expression to their severe displeasure'. In a case in which neither party had been reluctant to raise the emotional temperature, perhaps it had been an appropriate act of arson.

Draycott was the type of petty operator who more usually would have taken his custom to an outside broker, in other words not a member of the Stock Exchange. These outside brokers advertised extensively in the financial press (members were not allowed to, in effect as a form of quality control). None paid for as many column inches as George Gregory & Co of 4 Tokenhouse Buildings, Lothbury, with branches in Piccadilly, Regent Street, Brighton and Hastings. 'Altogether, the immediate outlook is most promising', declared its fortnightly circular in mid-May 1892, 'and investors and speculators alike are at present afforded most favourable opportunity of selection from among the pick of securities certain of an immediate advance in value.' This pick included selected Home Rails as well as all Grand Trunk stocks – 'in several past issues we have warned friends not to go short of these' – while in general Gregory made its principles clear to would-be principals: 'We continue to direct constant attention to every class of investment or speculative business . . . Cover in protection of clients' operations may be deposited either in the form of cash or any marketable security. The fullest information cheerfully and promptly given in response to all inquiries.' The question of cover was crucial: all outside brokers insisted on it, whereas most member firms of the Stock Exchange eschewed it, on the grounds that it savoured too much of the bucket-shop, that disreputable place where punters betted on the latest tape prices all day long.[4]

Most outside brokers were a lot closer to the bucket-shop than to a large, flourishing concern like Gregory. Take, for instance, Frederick Moore & Co, based at 4 Copthall Chambers and adjudicated bankrupt in the spring of 1892.[5] Moore had originally been a clerk in his stepfather's stockbroking office; he had started his own firm in the summer of 1890, with two partners and a total capital of £230; office organisation had been minimal; the partnership had been dissolved in acrimony; markets had continued to slide; and now, soon after being declared bankrupt, Moore found himself in Carey Street being examined by the official receiver:

> I see that you owe Mr Roberts [presumably an inside broker] £110. He is the petitioning creditor I think is he not? – Yes.
> How did that debt come into existence? – Through speculation in stocks with him.
> Did you instruct him to buy certain stocks? – Yes.
> In anticipation of a rise? – I instructed him to sell Brightons and buy Milwaukees.
> Was that a speculation of your part? – Yes.
> Purely? – Yes.
> And it resulted in this loss? – Yes.
> How did Mr Paddon's claim arise? – No cover was paid on that and therefore it was not due really. Mr Wreford came down to the office and asked me to open 2,000 Grand Trunks for his cousin Mr Samuel Paddon. Mr Wreford was working on commission with us at the time. He came down and I said, 'Very well, they will be done at the next price on the tape

in the afternoon.' Then I asked what cover I should have and he said, 'Oh, I will see Paddon tonight and get the cover.' Of course he never came and the stock went up and Mr Paddon thought fit to close, and closed the difference, but I never admitted having it open . . .

A belated show of defiance on Moore's part, but ultimately it was a pretty squalid, small-beer world that he and many other brokers inhabited – a world from which the main avenue of escape was down rather than up.

Union between firms was rarely an available route, and the 1890s produced not even a hint of a stockbroking equivalent to the amalgamation movement that was transforming the structure of banking: that would have to await a world war or two. In the banking amalgamation movement itself, though, a further milestone was the announcement at the end of May 1892 that Parr's was to merge with the Alliance Bank, effectively taking it over. Parr's had won its seat in the London Clearing House only the previous year, and now it was attracted to the Alliance on account partly of its very fruitful Stock Exchange connection, partly because, being a joint-stock bank (established in 1862), the Alliance's premises in Bartholomew Lane were more spacious than those of the Lombard Street private bank Fuller, Banbury, Nix and Co which Parr's had recently acquired. The announcement was on the whole favourably received, though the *FT* did have a grumble about the unwieldy name chosen for the new bank, to be called Parr's Banking Company and the Alliance Bank, Limited. The manager of this verbal hybrid was John Dun, a front-rank representative of the invasion of provincial bankers.[6] He was in his late 50s, the son of a Scottish composer and music teacher; he had won many glittering prizes in his Edinburgh education before joining the Bank of Scotland; after fifteen years he had become manager of Parr's in Warrington, from where he presided over its steady growth through amalgamation with other northern banks before it came to London in 1891. In London itself, he was already a well-known figure through his thoughtful papers to the Institute of Bankers on such subjects as 'Bi-metallism Examined' and 'The Law of Value'. He was, in short, no lightweight, though his admitted passion for golf suggested that he was a human being as well as an upwardly mobile meritocrat.

At the heart of the City establishment which joint-stock bankers like Dun aspired to penetrate were the well-established merchant banks, those dispensers of universal credit and, for the fortunate few, long-term funding. Among them was Hambros, which in March replied in the negative to Hope & Co's invitation to participate in a Transvaal government loan to be floated on the Dutch market: 'The loan you refer to would not find any takers upon our market; partly upon political grounds, and partly on account of the utter apathy displayed at present by our investing public.' The reply reckoned without the abiding clout of Rothschilds, which over the next two months persuaded Pretoria that, despite the recent unhappy history between Britain and the Transvaal, it would be possible to raise money for railway construction purposes on the London market. The amount was agreed at £2.5m, the coupon at an attractive 5 per cent, the issue price at a cautious 90; and in early July the *FT* reported, rather suggestively, the City's reaction:

> The Loan has been well received here, and is now at a premium of three and an eighth . . . At the same time, it would be idle to conceal that the market would have been better pleased had the railway schemes on which the money is to be expended been specified, and had the gentle art of the *réclame* been made less use of while the terms of the subscription were still unknown. At the same time, such feeling as has found expression in Stock Exchange circles has not been turned to the detriment of the new Loan, the terms and prospects being regarded as sufficiently attractive and satisfactory to override these minor considerations.[7]

Put another way, profit was a more powerful motive force than prejudice, while it remained wise not to refuse a Rothschild offering.

Still, even the sovereignty of New Court had its limits, as an interesting sequel to the flotation showed. On the 12th, a week after the *FT*'s commentary on the loan, a satisfied Natty Rothschild wrote to Cecil Rhodes assuring him that Rothschilds would not allow the Transvaal government to spend the proceeds of the loan in such a way as to thwart Rhodes's own ambitions in southern Africa. 'Naturally,' he added, 'we shall never let them think that we are acting at your suggestion.' The next day Rothschilds wrote to Kruger himself a letter that was a classic of its kind:

> As Your Honour is aware, the Loan was applied for a great many times over, and the quotation remains firm in the market at about 4% premium. Nevertheless we are more convinced than ever that it would have been dangerous and unwise to have issued the loan at a higher rate than 90, and feel sure that the success is due to the price of issue which tempted investors, who otherwise would certainly have kept aloof.

Then came the business part:

> As we have every confidence in the wisdom of Your Honour's Government as well as in the future prospects of the Transvaal we did not hesitate to give our name and influence to the operation, and we sincerely hope that not only will the large sum of money raised be used with the very greatest prudence and economy but also that all expenditure will be subjected to a strict and efficient control, so that, in the future we may have every reason and justification to be perfectly satisfied with the action we have just taken.

In particular, New Court wanted Pretoria not only to be compelled to account to it for all expenditure, but also to leave the money deposited there until it was required. To New Court's surprise, however, Kruger declined to accept these terms; and Rothschilds felt it had little choice but to climb down as graciously as it could.[8] The client relationship remained, but in this case it was one marked by trust and goodwill on neither side.

Rothschilds was perhaps right to pitch the price low, though, for during the summer there was such lack of business on the Stock Exchange that an almost paralysing ennui prevailed. True dog days were reached in August, as the *Rialto* began a diary column entitled 'Capel-Court Day-By-Day'. The week beginning 15 August had a memorably mindless quality to it. On Monday: 'There has not been such a rowdy day for a long time, dealing being completely abandoned in most departments in favour of throwing hard paper balls about.' On Tuesday: 'The paper-ball nuisance . . . is becoming worse and worse daily. The most heinous offenders are certain promising lads in the Home Railway department, who were so successful at the game this morning that they sent a broker home with a damaged eye.' On Thursday: 'Within half an hour of the start brokers were reading newspapers upon the forms, and the jobbers were wandering aimlessly about the floor gazing mournfully upon them.' There was just as much time to be killed the following week – the clock over the door of the American market becoming the favourite target of paper balls – while by the first Tuesday in September, such was the listlessness in the Trunk market, traditionally a hive of speculative activity, that 'the dealers stood in a ring most of the day with a string across it to watch people trip'. September saw no improvement, and on the last nominally working day of the month, 'in almost every department members were to be seen all day sitting about on the forms tossing for pennies, reading the newspapers, or deeply immersed in the latest from

Mudie's'.[9] Psychologically as well as physically it could hardly have been a less healthy existence; and it was no wonder if, over the years, the House did not always send out the most rational signals to the investment community at large.

One aspect of Stock Exchange irrationality was the way in which the climate of the moment affected the tone of the markets. Take 2 September 1892: 'Among the adverse factors in the earlier hours were execrable weather, and the announcement of the suspension of the London and General Bank . . . But in the afternoon the sky cleared, and a less pessimistic spirit prevailed.'[10] Not even the sun coming out, however, could alter the fact that the London and General had failed; and since it was banker to the Liberator Building Society, and a host of related property companies, all of which like the Liberator now collapsed, the 2nd marked the start of a major City scandal, the Liberator itself being based in Budge Row off Cannon Street. At the centre of the tangled affair was Jabez Spencer Balfour, a Liberal MP and known in his pomp as Spencer Balfour.[11] An energetic, aggressive, quick-talking man, he was the son of temperance lecturers and had helped to form the Liberator almost a quarter of a century earlier, building it up into a formidable organisation. His great mistake had been to switch its resources increasingly into the property market, as opposed to orthodox lending to individuals, at a time (the 1880s) when property prices were generally falling; the upshot was the systematic misappropriation and manipulation of the Liberator's deposits, and ruin when the money market tightened one further screw in 1892.

This was more than the usual behind-the-back assets-shuffling fraud, as the *Economist* would emphasise three years later, after most of the dust had settled:

> Balfour's conduct stands out in a peculiarly despicable light, from the fact that it owed its success mainly to his posturing as a philanthropist with strong religious convictions, and as a politician whose one desire in life was the regeneration of the masses. Himself a shining light of liberationism and temperance propaganda, he was cunning enough to secure the co-operation of men of mark in the pulpit and on the platform as co-directors, while throughout the length and breadth of the country Nonconformist ministers were, no doubt quite innocently on their part, made the means of bringing vast amounts of money into the Balfourian net.

Balfour had fled the country in December 1892. According to the memoirs of the late-Victorian company promoter H. Osborne

O'Hagan, he did so against his will and because 'he was urged by his City friends to make himself scarce', for 'they feared his being tried and convicted'. Because they also feared courtroom revelations? On that O'Hagan is silent. In the event he was soon tracked down in the Argentine, but then fled to the Chilian/Bolivian border, before finally entering British custody and being tried towards the end of 1895. By then he was a semi-forgotten figure, such was the pace of financial events in the mid-1890s, and his sentence to fourteen years' penal servitude aroused little general interest. Those who did not forget were the Liberator's thousands of depositors, mainly elderly and of modest income. A relief fund was established under royal patronage, and the last word goes to a supplicant letter from a schoolmistress who had invested her all in Balfour's uplifting creation: 'This trouble with its sleepless nights of racking anxiety has so crushed me – some days are dragged through in agony – my future is dark enough, I know not in the least what will become of me. I can only sob out in the night (the only time I can allow myself the luxury of crying), "Oh God, I have worked so hard, and looked forward to my little home, with my books, so longingly, save me, oh save me from the workhouse . . ." '[12]

By the 1890s, religion and the City on the whole mixed uneasily, unless perhaps the faith was Anglicanism of the least threatening, most suet-pudding variety. Generally it was off the agenda, though just occasionally older passions could still be stirred. Near the end of September 1892 there took place at Guildhall the annual, usually non-contentious ritual of electing a new Lord Mayor. The senior alderman in point of rotation was Stuart Knill, the son of a self-made fruit broker and wharfinger. On account of his faith, he was soon under fierce examination from the Court of Common Council:

> His answer was 'No!' to the question whether he had attended the service that day at St Lawrence, Jewry. (*Hisses, cheers and uproar.*) He was a Catholic, and he attended St Mary's, Moorfields. He thought it right for every man to attend divine service in the place of worship to which he belonged. (*Cheers, and cries of 'No'.*) The next question was, would he attend Christ Church, Newgate-street, on Easter Tuesday? His answer was 'No'. He should attend the services of his own church, but if he was elected Lord Mayor (*cries of 'You won't be'*) he should appoint a *locum tenens* to attend the service. He could not now pledge himself to attend at Paul's Cathedral on the occasion of the Festival of the Sons of the Clergy, and take the chair at their dinner at Merchant Taylors' Hall. So far as he was at present advised (*Loud uproar*) . . .

Mr Alderman and Sheriff Renals: Gentlemen, you must give the Alderman a fair hearing. (*Cheers.*)

Soon afterwards, following further noisy exchanges, an alderman called Beaufoy Moore formally protested against the election of Knill, receiving 'loud and prolonged cheers' before he went on:

> He was not there to say anything of the Alderman's personal character, for he believed he was an honourable gentleman. So they all were, he hoped. But he objected to his being nominated for the office of Lord Mayor on the ground that the Alderman was a Roman Catholic – ('*a bigot*') – and that he owed allegiance to the Pope. A great deal had been said about the liberty of conscience and the freedom of religious thought, but when the Roman Catholics were in power the country had to tolerate a despotism of which the country might well be ashamed. The freedom they now enjoyed was gained for them by the blood of their ancestors – men who were carried on the hurdle and burnt at the stake. (*Cheers, and 'Waste of time'*) . . . Mr Alderman Knill had declared that he would not fulfil the duties of Lord Mayor according to ancient custom. He could already see the fires of Smithfield rekindled, the thumb-screws and other instruments of torture brought from their resting places to furnish amusement for the herds of Jesuits at the Mansion House . . .

In the event, a Protestant candidate was put up against Knill, but the Court of Aldermen (a much smaller body than the Court of Common Council) gave the vote to the senior alderman amidst a renewed storm of hissing and hooting as well as the inevitable cry of 'No Popery'. The *Financial News* the next day applauded Knill's election as 'a triumph of intelligence and fairness over bigotry and prejudice', adding that Knill's opponents 'can scarcely have remembered – perhaps they did not know – that the Corporation of the City of London has for ages been the champion of religious liberty'. But then, the *FN*'s own founder, proprietor and guiding spirit was Harry Marks, whose father was head of the Reformed Congregation of British Jews.[13]

*

In May 1892, almost a year and a half after the unsuccessful flotation of the Steam Loop Company, one of its promoters, Dugald Scott, sought, before Mr Justice Wright at Guildhall, to recover the money he had paid his stockbrokers Brown, Doering & McNab during that fraught operation. Scott made the claim largely on the grounds that, instead of purchasing shares for him in the ordinary way, the broking firm had covertly transferred to him its own shares in Steam Loop; and, in the course of the case, McNab's imploring telegrams and letter of 6 December 1890 were made public knowledge. The judge dismissed Scott's claim, but it then went to the Court of Appeal early in August, leading to a forthright condemnation by Lord Justice Lindley and his colleagues of the whole process of artificial market-making.[14] Inevitably much adverse press comment was aroused, with the Stock Exchange Committee being urged in the strongest terms to take firm action against the practice. The Committee room beckoned for Philip Brown and Walter Doering, still partners, and their former partner John McNab.

On behalf of Doering as well as himself, Brown pleaded ignorance of what McNab had done and called on the Committee 'to deal with the culpability of each member of the firm individually, and not with that of the firm in its entirety.' McNab then read a long statement exonerating his former partners from any share in the market-making negotiations and asked the Committee to withdraw the case against them. As for the case against himself, he 'regretted that an expression in one of his letters, that unless something was done they "would never get the public on" had been misunderstood.' And, he 'recognised his imprudence, but denied his guilt'. After hearing further evidence, the Committee voted eleven to five that all three had brought themselves under the operation of rule 16.

Confirmation was, for legal reasons, delayed until 5 September, and before then McNab had received a letter of support from a senior member of the House, R.H. Bristowe:

> My belief is that you had implicit faith in the Steam Loop Company, in fact you were infatuated with it. You gave almost the whole of your time to it, put money into it yourself and induced friends to do so also, but did not mean to act dishonourably or do anything wrong. You no doubt acted foolishly and did what you know was usually done, either by promoters themselves or by others when a company was being brought out. You bought and sold shares previous to allotment to bring the notice of such company before the eyes of the public. Of course had the company been a success and the shares had risen you would have acted properly and committed no crime, but unfortunately the company has not been successful, the shares are unmarketable, everybody is dissatisfied and you have committed a fraud . . . My opinion is that the Committee cannot and ought not to punish you severely; they ought to think for themselves and do what they think is just and right irrespective of the judgment of the Court of Appeal . . .

McNab, from his home at 57 Gypsy Hill, SE, sent the Committee this letter, along with an impassioned plea of his own:

I appeal to your sense of right and justice: is it fair to condemn me when you know the practice has always been an admitted and recognised one in Stock Exchange business? Am I the first man in the history of the Stock Exchange who has been party to starting a market in shares of new concerns? If I were, I would say by all means make me the last, but as I am not – as you all know – I ask you, is it justice, to ruin me, by publicly branding me, as a man who has been guilty of 'dishonourable and disgraceful conduct', because I did what I believed to be a perfectly legitimate and legal piece of business? How many members of the Stock Exchange are there, who ever thought the practice of making a market in shares, illegal? I venture to assert, not many . . .

These letters failed to do the trick, however, and the previous month's resolution was confirmed in the case of all three, followed a fortnight later by a near-unanimous vote that they be expelled.

The penultimate stage of an inexorable process was reached on 3 October, as the Committee read McNab's appeal-for-clemency letter, quite without the faintly truculent note of his earlier effort:

The confirmation of this decision means my ruin for life. I am entirely dependent upon my own exertions to make a livelihood and further I know no other business and have absolutely nothing to fall back upon. Also I am at an age at which such a decision must utterly blast for me, every hope and chance in life.

Now at last the quality of mercy was exercised, and the sentence of expulsion was reduced to three years' suspension – but with Brown and Doering then each receiving an extra year on account of having threatened to take legal action against the Committee, whereas McNab in this respect at least had 'loyally submitted himself' to the conditions of his membership. Still, for all this relative leniency, McNab may have reflected with some bitterness on the underlying reason for his punishment, a reason that he was perceptive but tactless enough to give in the first of his written apologia: 'Is it that the disgrace and dishonour attaches itself to me because the honour and prestige of the Stock Exchange has been (so to speak) dragged in the mire through the action in the Appeal Court? In that case, I can only offer you, gentlemen, my deepest apologies . . .'[15]

CHAPTER SIX

A Family Party

'I tried to talk City a little, but we did not get far. We agree in rejecting Bimetallism! – perhaps that is our only point of agreement.'[1] So reported Sidney Webb in March 1892 to his future wife Beatrice, one of whose older sisters was married to Daniel Meinertzhagen VI, a partner in the merchant bank Huths. Sidney was staying with the Meinertzhagens and it is unlikely that, in his awkward conversation with Daniel, he related his own experiences in the square mile, as a one-time clerk in the office of a small colonial broker. Still, to agree on bimetallism was something, for during most of the 1890s that arcane subject remained, as it had since the mid-1880s, high on the political economy agenda, even if not always uppermost in the daily thoughts of busy practical men.

Against a long-run background of falling prices and a more or less depressed world economy, the basic premise of bimetallism was that the introduction of a double monetary standard – silver as well as gold – would check the fall in silver prices. This would make it easier for countries not on the gold standard to import goods, thus benefiting trade as a whole. The argument made an obvious appeal in Lancashire, heavily reliant on the cotton export trade with India, while in the City it was a highly charged, even emotive question, granted the widely held assumption that the return to the gold standard in 1819, though enforced on a reluctant Bank of England, had in practice laid the foundations of London's nineteenth-century prosperity and international dominance. Over the years the bimetallists and their gold standard opponents brought up armies of statistics to help wage their unyielding campaigns, but there were also gut instincts at work.[2]

These instincts represented an immovable force. Hamilton acknowledged as much in May 1892 after a bimetallic deputation, largely comprising Lancashire merchants, had been received in Downing Street: 'How is it possible that bimetallism should make way against the rooted mono-metallic convictions of every influential City man, bar two – H. Gibbs & H. Grenfell? It may be all very well in theory;

but it is absolutely impossible in practice.' Hamilton exaggerated the absence of bimetallic support in the City, but his central point was in tune with that of the *Bankers' Magazine* the following month, in the context of an impending, American-inspired international conference on the silver question: 'In this country we are strictly monometallic on a gold basis, and we cannot believe that any suggestion will be made to our Government for any change in that respect. Such a suggestion would certainly not be acceptable in banking circles here.' By the end of the summer, however, a decision as to where that conference should be held was becoming urgent, as was the question of who should be the British delegates. 'We cannot put ourselves in the position of receiving a report more or less Bimetallistic signed by a majority of British Commissioners', was the clear view of Gladstone on 21 August, soon after beginning his fourth term of office; and in this he was backed to the hilt by his Chancellor, Harcourt, who had lost little time in stressing to Hamilton his unequivocally monometallist views, unlike the recent electoral flirtation with bimetallism on the part of Salisbury and Balfour. A comfort was the support of a third Liberal believer, Bertram Currie, who had agreed to be a delegate, albeit reluctantly, telling Gladstone that 'no good can come out of the conference'.[3]

Who would be the City's other representative? Currie helpfully marked the Treasury card: Everard Hambro was 'an intelligent man of business' but had not 'given much attention to the silver question'; Sir John Lubbock's name carried less weight in Lombard Street than in the columns of the press; Henry Raphael, the merchant banker and arbitrageur, understood the subject and had 'the reputation of being a strong man'. None of the names seemed quite right, and by 31 August Hamilton was noting that 'Harcourt is going to insist on a Rothschild going to the Conference', adding: 'He says they can't refuse. "England owes something to the Rothschilds; but the Rothschilds owe a great deal to England." ' Currie was unimpressed – 'Lord Rothschild bears no doubt a name of weight but that is about all' – though in the event it was Natty's younger brother Alfred, recently retired as a Bank of England director, whom a suitably flattered New Court put forward. 'Alfred is most anxious to meet your views,' Natty wrote to Harcourt on the 31st, 'and help you in your "dilemma". Although he would very much prefer London he will consent to go to the Hague if you wish it.' Harcourt replied the next day:

Pray express to Alfred my sense of his kindness . . . The name of Rothschild will carry a weight which no other could command in the monetary world. I have not the advantage of knowing Alfred's opinions on these subjects but I take for granted that he is a good sound staunch monometallist (what Mr Gladstone calls a 'sane man') who will uphold to the death the single gold standard . . . If there were any doubts or hesitations on this point I am sure you would let me know . . .

Natty in turn replied on 2 September: 'Alfred is perfectly on all subjects particularly so on Bimetallism.' Presumably the missing word was 'sound', but in any case Alfred himself wrote to the Chancellor on the same day: 'As regards my views on the great question of the day, I can give you at once the assurance that you could have found no stauncher supporter of Monometallism than myself.' Alfred still hankered after London, but as Harcourt put it to him a few days later, 'I confess I am not particularly anxious in these days of contagion to infect the City of London with a horde of wild bimetallists.' By early October the venue had been definitely decided – not The Hague, but Brussels – and Alfred now took it in his stride: 'The selection of Belgium certainly augurs well; it was there that the great Duke of Wellington raised the standard of England to the zenith of military glory, and you may rest assured, my dear Harcourt, that as regards my own humble efforts, they will be strenuously devoted towards maintaining our financial standard to which England owes her overwhelming mercantile supremacy.'[4]

Henry Hucks Gibbs, writing to a fellow-bimetallist two days later, was unimpressed by Harcourt's deliberate weighting of the British delegation as a whole, though he took sardonic pleasure in the choice of the new Iron Duke: 'Things look ill. Our fat friend has pickeyed us . . . Alfred Rothschild!! Well! he will have the satisfaction of having found the man of all those East of Temple Bar who knows least of the matter & has the most decided opinion.' Over the next few weeks, perhaps to relieve his frustration, Gibbs engaged in vigorous debate on the whole question with the equally combative Harcourt. 'The truth is that Bimetallism is only another form of Protection just as diphtheria is a variation on scarlet fever,' was typical Harcourtian understatement, while as for his overall position:

I desire London to remain what it is, the Metropolis of the Commerce of the World to which all nations resort to settle their business. This I believe and I think all those who have practical knowledge of the money market (with the striking exception of yourself) believe to be owing to the soundness of our monetary system, London being the only place where you can always get gold. It is for that reason that all the exchange business of the world is done in London. Though I have no objection to currency dialectics which are an amusement like double acrostics I confess in dealing with such great interests I lay more stress on practical results.

After stressing the great increase over the past twenty years in the volume of trade, the national wealth and so on, Harcourt directed his final gibe against someone who had recently been Conservative MP for the City: 'I am not such a reckless radical as you are – I don't desire Revolution even in precious metals.' Soon after, on 14 November, Gibbs exploded:

> The money market! There is your error! You take the money market to comprise the whole of the Commerce of England; and therefore listen only to Bankers Home and Foreign – of whom Currie and Alfred Rothschild are good examples – who think (some of them) that they and their class have an interest in the maintenance of the present system. It would be not unnatural if the Rothschilds & the Banking interest generally should look upon the Money Market, and the dealing in Bills of Exchange, and in Foreign Securities, as the Be-all and End-all of Commerce. It is their own particular 'leather' . . . I am on the other side. I look upon those things as the handmaids, the very useful handmaids, of Commerce . . .

Claiming that not all bankers were in fact hostile to bimetallism – even that Natty Rothschild was 'not afraid' of it – Gibbs made a last rhetorical thrust: 'You have chosen your side. You have elected to march with the Drones, and against the Working Bees. I take the other side, and – I shall win.'[5]

On 17 November, with the Brussels conference imminent, Harcourt gave a dinner to the British, Indian and American delegates. Afterwards he kept behind the four British monometallist delegates (two City, two non-City) 'and gave them their final instructions'. The phrase was that of Harcourt's son and private secretary 'Loulou', who in his wonderfully gossipy diary revealed the last-minute dispositions:

> A. Rothschild has a plan of his own which he wishes to develop and with which he means to startle assembled Europe but will I expect only succeed in boring them. However happily we do not know what the plan is and are not responsible for it. B. Currie is a brutal monometallist and means to treat all bi-metallists with very scant courtesy and wants to 'have it over' & get back to England as soon as possible.
>
> Their private instructions are to discuss no abstract questions, to be civil to any definite plan for bi-metallism but to disagree, . . . & generally to give a civil attention to the currency faddists.

Was Alfred really going to be so staunch as he had promised? Two days later 'Loulou' recorded his father trying to still his doubts:

> Chex [i.e. the Chancellor of the Exchequer] went to see Alfred Rothschild to beg him to be moderate and conciliatory at Brussels. Alfred was in a great state of excitement & most anxious to show & explain to Chex his 'plan' which is to be propounded on the authority of the House of Rothschild but Chex firmly declined to know anything of it . . . I expect A.R. & B. Currie will fight tremendously at Brussels.[6]

There was nothing more Harcourt could do. He had picked his team, and if they failed to play for him he had made sure that his back was protected.

The conference began on the 22nd. Within three days Loulou Harcourt was noting a visit from Natty Rothschild, who had professed himself 'much alarmed at what he calls the "crash in silver" which he says will take place if the Monetary Conference breaks up without doing anything and he threatens the failure of many City houses including Gibbs'. Harcourt senior remained unmoved. Meanwhile, in Brussels itself, Alfred's right-hand man at New Court, Carl Meyer, was with him, and he reported to his wife the interminable round of the international conference: 'We have endless small meetings, discussions, visits, &c. The worst of it is that Alfred won't go to see anyone & always sends others which with some of the swells produces a certain friction and coolness. As usual the French are the most disagreeable but our worst enemy is Bertram Currie . . . who is jealous of Alfred and tries to thwart his plans.' That was on the 27th, and the next day Currie, in a thoroughly bad mood throughout these weeks, listened with ill-disguised impatience as Alfred outlined his compromise plan designed to prevent the conference from sundering. Although distancing himself from the bimetallic position, he proposed an international agreement for purchasing silver, in order to keep up silver prices. It was never really a runner. On the 30th, Currie wrote to his wife that Ernest Cassel, the acute international financier, was in town for a day or two: 'He takes a very sensible view of the silver question, and has had nothing to do with the Rothschild proposal.' Or, as Welby at the Treasury noted the next day, 'we are much amused at the Rothschild proposal'.[7]

Alfred himself wrote Harcourt a letter on 5 December, from the Hotel Bellevue, which was a virtual admission that the plan was dead. Harcourt's reply – shown in advance to Natty and Leo Rothschild, who said that Alfred's trouble was that he was 'so excitable and nervous' – took the line that the failure of the conference had at least demonstrated 'that the Bi-metallic theory is generally repudiated' and 'that there is no material for an agreement upon subsidiary measures for the support of a silver currency'. In short, 'this result may be regarded as a *settler* for Bi-metallism'. Nevertheless, Harcourt declined to hand Rothschild and Currie their demob papers, saying, 'you know as well as I do the importance of *the form* in these international transactions'. And, with a conscious historical echo: 'I pray you therefore have patience yet for a little time and then you shall return bringing back "Monometallism with Honour".' Even as Harcourt wrote, Alfred's proposals were being formally withdrawn, it being clear that there was no support from either the French or the American delegates. 'He has done his best,' Harcourt with rare tact wrote to Natty on the 7th, 'but the situation was hopeless from the first. Since the days of the Tower of Babel the world has made up its mind not to agree. A monetary compact is as impossible as a Tariff concordat or a disarmament project.'[8]

The conference slowly wound to an inconclusive halt, and a week before Christmas one of the last speeches was given by Currie. 'It was,' a less than admiring British delegate told Harcourt, 'spoken over the head of the Conference for English instruction – appealed to Bimetallists to return to their senses & consider the question closed – offered a remedy for increasing the Bank of England reserve – and finished up with some satirical remarks . . .' Still, the great thing for Currie and those who thought like him was that the world had apparently been made safe for monometallism; and when Loulou Harcourt jotted down on Christmas Day an entry conveying the fearless digestion of youth ('A magnificent turkey from Natty Rothschild full of great foie gras – excellent'), he would have had no worries about unwonted silver coins popping out of Christmas puddings.[9]

*

At the start of 1893 a young man arrived in the City. The senior partner of Schröders, John Henry Schröder, was childless and approaching his late 60s; so he recruited from Hamburg one of his nephews, Bruno Schröder, who had been expecting to pursue his commercial career in the local family firm of Schröder Gebrüder after a full apprenticeship in London, the USA and South America. Instead, no doubt attracted by the long-term prospects suddenly opened to him, he found that his future lay in Leadenhall Street. It was the shrewdest of choices, and from the start Bruno was expected to succeed John Henry, sooner rather than later. After only a few days he was discovered examining the bills that had come in for acceptance – the very heart of the firm's business. On its being pointed out to him that only one or two confidential employees had access to these bills, he replied that his uncle had given him permission to see them. Bruno was quiet, hard-working and thoughtful, but also imbued with a streak of commercial boldness; and when, not long after coming to the firm, he first met one of Schröders' most important clients, the very senior Caesar Czarnikow, he reduced the older man to silence by telling him, entirely justifiably, that future developments in the sugar market meant that Czarnikow required an appreciably larger line of credit.[10] A private firm like Schröders was liable to stand or fall by how deftly it solved the succession problem, and it was a great thing to have at hand an international pool of well-trained young men.

On the very Monday, 2 January 1893, that Bruno began to enter his inheritance, so a white newspaper turned pink. The *Financial Times*, Lidderdale had informed Welby in December 1891, 'is considered a more respectable paper than the *Financial News*'; but over the next twelve months that would have been thin comfort to the *FT*'s owner-manager, Douglas MacRae, as he struggled in depressed markets to mount a sustained challenge to the commercially more successful *FN*. The decision to give the pages of the paper a pinkish tint (as opposed to the bold salmon pink of modern times) was to prove one of the great marketing strokes of the age, signalling from all those railway bookstalls of late-Victorian London that the *FT* was a very special paper; at the time almost the only other coloured publication was the *Sporting Times*, popularly known as the 'Pink 'Un'.[11] Respectability *and* a dash of colour: that, over the years, has been the magic formula for success in the City.

The *FN* remained content to rely on the colour of its prose style, as in the first paragraph of a new Saturday column called 'Round the "House" ' beginning on 11 February:

> A weary, wretched week has ended, and that is quite the best thing it has done. It has witnessed the third settlement of the 'Happy New Year', which has been so uncommonly like those of the unhappy last year that, but for the calendar before us, it would have been difficult to tell the difference. The Stock Exchange sinks deeper and deeper into the doleful dumps, and the coming question for its members is 'How the Poor Live'.

Among those who had already failed in 1893 was Walter Daw (presumably not to Edgar Draycott's regret), but material suffering was not confined to members of the Stock Exchange. Later in February, Herbert Gibbs wrote to his father, Henry Hucks Gibbs, in very meaningful terms about the implications of the fact that, though the firm's financial position was improving, the capital of the partners was still 'not commensurate with their liabilities':

> Alban tells me that his private income from Directorships, marriage settlements &c amounts to about £1,500 a year, and if, as I would suggest, his expenditure did not exceed £4,000, his withdrawals would be reduced to £2,500. He is giving up his place in Scotland, and has reduced his stable arrangements, and the question now is whether his household expenses should be reduced. He seems inclined to doubt whether it would be wise to change nearly all his servants, which this proposal undoubtedly involves, and he fears the notice that it may attract . . .

Herbert himself had reduced his expenditure from over £4,000 in 1890 to a modest £2,500 by 1892 – some £120,000 in modern money values – and it was with a certain bitterness that he referred to the need 'to prevent those partners, who are endeavouring by economy to increase the capital of the House, from being discouraged or prejudiced by the expenditure of others'.[12]

The Gibbs family almost certainly did not deign to notice the London and Scottish Banking and Discount Corporation, floated in March 1893 to a chorus of disapproval led by the *FT*, which called it 'this wretched concern' and pointed out that not a single banker was on its board of directors. The new bank was based in Lombard Street, and included in its prospectus was the preposterous claim that in addition to ordinary banking business it would 'embrace the very lucrative branches of Discount, Advances on Stocks, Title Deeds, Approved Securities, &c, from which profitable business, by their Charters and Regulations, many of the leading Banks are debarred'. The issue was undersubscribed but did obtain £29,000 from a gullible public; little business ensued; and in 1895 the bank went into liquidation. The leading spirit behind the London and Scottish was Edward Beall, a City-based solicitor who had gone bankrupt in 1892, but not before winning the sobriquet of 'the Black Prince' on account of his splendid coach drawn by four fine horses; eventually, in 1899, he appeared at the Old Bailey charged with having published a false prospectus and defrauding the shareholders. Among those cross-examined was Leonard Barker, a clerk:

He became associated with Beall in 1889. In 1892 he received a letter from Beall's office enclosing him a memorandum of association, and asking him to sign it. Witness was then ill in bed in Southsea. He signed the memorandum of association as required and sent it back to Beall's office. He also signed other documents. Witness knew nothing whatever about the company . . . He was afterwards appointed assistant cashier, his salary being £2 a week. Witness had not had the slightest experience of banking business before . . .

Or, as Beall had put it to another clerk, who had been appointed cashier despite disclaiming any knowledge of cashiering or keeping books, 'Oh, you will get on all right.' Rufus Isaacs, a new QC who in an earlier life had been hammered on the Stock Exchange, led the princely defence. Despite his best efforts, including the argument that the London and Scottish had been a genuine business against which old-established banks had made a dead set, Beall was found guilty and sentenced to four years' penal servitude. 'A notorious figure is removed – for a space, at least – from the City,' declared the *FT*, which back in 1894 had added to its investigative credibility (generally the preserve of the *FN*) by exposing in detail the fraudulent nature of the whole enterprise.[13]

It was the *FN*, though, that in the spring of 1893 recorded a small piece of Stock Exchange history: 'The first coloured clerk has made his appearance in the House this week, and has proved a source of much amusement to the members. He has been greeted with a serenade, in which the old plantation ditty, "Down where the darkies are a' weeping", has been the pièce de résistance . . .' The report did not specify, but the serenading may well have been led by Charlie Clarke, the acknowledged wag of the House. If so, it was only preparation for a much more important piece of showmanship that awaited him soon afterwards, namely his leading part in the Stock Exchange's mass demonstration on Wednesday, 3 May against Gladstone's hated Home Rule Bill. The occasion was a protest meeting at the Guildhall, for representatives of the City as a whole, and Clarke spent the morning marching up and down the House like a sandwich man, displaying on his back a big poster announcing the meeting and distributing hand bills to all and sundry. Towards the end of the morning a copy of the Bill was brought into the Stock Exchange on a bamboo pole and solemnly set alight, prompting a loud chorus of 'God Save the Queen'. Thereupon, according to the *Rialto*:

The singing of the National Anthem constituted the signal for departure, and at once the procession began to form. Drapers'-gardens led off, preceded by two enormous Union Jacks and bearing the Irish flag in their midst. They were followed by the Shorter's-court contingent, while Capel-court brought up the rear. It is estimated that from 1,500 to 2,000 persons took part in this triumphal procession, the majority of them being decorated with the emblem of the Union. Some consternation was excited during the course of the proceedings by the discovery that the Union Jacks had been 'made in Germany', but patriotic fervour ran too high to be damped by such a trifle. At intervals along the procession, poles, surmounted by Union Jacks, were carried, and Mr Charles Clarke proudly bore aloft the charred fragments of the Home Rule Bill. Crowds of curious, and for the most part sympathetic, spectators lined the route, and joined heartily in the lusty singing of 'Rule Britannia', with which the processionists freely indulged themselves. To the tune of this national Chant, the leading files passed under the portals of the Guildhall, but it was noticed that the rear ranks, probably through some misunderstanding, seemed to prefer the popular ditty known as 'The Man who Broke the Bank at Monte Carlo'.

Inside the Guildhall, the report went on, as well as more singing of 'Rule, Britannia' and 'God Save the Queen', there was much 'artistic whistling by members of the Stock Exchange, political speeches by Mr Chamberlain and others, and performances by the London Military Band'. Altogether it was a proud day for Charlie Clarke – a man with a face rather like that of Buster Keaton, a notably hot temper, and sufficient independence of mind that, as an amateur playing for Surrey, he had been the first wicket-keeper in first-class cricket systematically to stand back to fast bowling. In his working life he was a jobber in Trunks, the market devoted to the stocks of the Grand Trunk Railway of Canada; and the events of the day merely cemented his already considerable popularity. A few weeks later fellow-members presented him with a set of sleeve-links, decorated with the Union Jack, in recognition of his services.[14]

*

Ireland was a symbol of British imperial unity, but the City had few vital economic interests at stake there. In many other parts of the world it was a different story, and the words of the *Economist* some years later had a wider, resonant truth: 'London is often more concerned with the course of events in Mexico than with what happens in the Midlands, and is more upset by a strike on the Canadian Pacific than by one in the Cambrian collieries.'[15] A handful of quickfire case-studies between the autumn of 1892 and the end of 1893 illuminate the global point.

Take the Ottoman Empire, an excellent example of a watchful City that had been badly burnt by the Turkish default of 1876.[16] Thereafter new British investment almost dried up (being replaced by French and German), but the City still retained a strong degree of influence through its representation on the Ottoman Public Debt Administration, established in 1881 to oversee Ottoman government finance on behalf of European bondholders, largely British and French. The alternate President of the Administration's council was Vincent Caillard, who in November 1892 used his annual report to launch an appeal to British investors back home. 'It is surely time,' he wrote, 'that English capitalists should forget old sores and begin to turn their eyes once more to a country so interesting as Turkey; so full of possibilities, and lying close to their doors . . .' Caillard's particular pitch was the attractiveness of supplying capital for railway construction, but the City was unimpressed. 'It is all very well to speak of forgetting old sores, but it can hardly be forgotten that the bankruptcy of Turkey was of an exceptionally flagrant kind . . . The less that is said about the financial honesty of Turkey the better it will be for her.' The *Economist*'s verdict accurately reflected opinion, and the paper was especially critical of how Caillard had been signally uninformative about Turkey's present financial situation, not least the ominous fact that payment of official salaries had fallen badly into arrears. Beyond the negative economic judgement – pretty well-founded as it transpired – lay a personal factor: though Caillard was a plausible financier who had gone to Eton and enjoyed excellent connections in the City, his penchant for intrigue meant that he was never quite trusted. Perhaps at some level there was also a growing feeling that the Near East as a whole meant trouble and was better avoided in terms of new commitments. A few months later, in April 1893, the Stock Exchange took it badly when King Alexander of Serbia, a boy of 17, declared himself of age, arrested his regents and ministers, and appointed a cabinet of his own. 'A good deal of anxiety was felt at first,' the *Rialto* reported, and 'as one member shrewdly remarked, "When the big burst comes for the European war, it will begin in just such a pottering way." '[17]

A country of even keener interest to European bondholders was Egypt, under British occupation since 1882. Running the show there as a more or less enlightened despot was Lord Cromer, a younger brother of the Lord Revelstoke who had been largely responsible for the Baring crisis. He was helped to collect taxes and control expenditure by Alfred Milner, whose largely laudatory survey of *England in Egypt* received an equally laudatory review from the *Statist* in January 1893: 'It is a wonderful proof of the recuperative energy of Egypt herself, of the docility of her people, and of the practical skill of the British agents in financial matters, that the credit of Egypt has been raised so high . . . The re-organisation of the finances was the most essential work that lay before us, and it has been admirably done.' As for the future, the *Statist* saw no likelihood of early withdrawal: 'Reforms have been effected because they have been insisted upon by England; they would soon be lost if British supervision were withdrawn.' Servicing Egyptian finances was, from the City's point of view, a highly lucrative activity; and not long afterwards, on 15 March, Hamilton of the Treasury recorded a visit paid to him that afternoon by Sir Elwyn Palmer, financial adviser to the Khedive:

> He has come over from Egypt about the conversion of the Domains Loan. The Rothschilds, who are the administrators of the loan, are, he thinks, opening their mouths rather wide about commission. They offer to bring out the new $4\frac{1}{4}$ per cent loan firm at 100, & to give the Egyptian Government 98. He wants the Chanc of the Exchequer to try & induce them to lower their terms . . . I told him I was no judge, though 2 per cent commission did seem rather high: that Sir W. Harcourt is not likely to interfere, & that it might be well to think once, twice, & thrice before he broke off with our friends in New Court.

The next day Hamilton took Palmer to see Harcourt – '& as I expected Harcourt declined point blank to interfere'.[18] Sir Elwyn was forced to button it, and the Rothschild hold over Egyptian borrowing was further strengthened.

Harcourt was a regular visitor at Natty Rothschild's country home at Tring, as was also a former chex, Lord Randolph Churchill; and one Sunday early in 1893 there occurred a remarkable scene, as described by Loulou Harcourt: 'He [Churchill] attacked Rhodes & S Africa & Mashonaland most bitterly, said the country was bankrupt & Rhodes a sham and that Natty knew it and Rhodes could not raise £51,000 in the City to open a new mine etc. All this was to Natty's face and made him furious – so much so that he went out of the room for a few minutes to cool himself.'[19] The relationship between Rothschilds and Cecil Rhodes has been the subject of much controversy, based largely on fragmentary evidence, but certain aspects seem clear: that Rothschilds was consistently suspicious of Rhodes's more grandiose imperial ambitions in southern Africa; that, up to the mid-1890s anyway, it was equally consistently committed to Rhodes as a businessman; and that, as a businessman, Rhodes was *not* the most successful or far-seeing of the South African mining magnates (or the Randlords, as they would become known), which meant that Rothschilds of necessity cultivated strategic alliances with rival magnates.[20] By the early 1890s the critical question as far as South Africa was concerned was whether the development of deep-level mining was going to rescue the gold-mining industry from the geological impasse into which it had run by 1890. Writing to New Court from Johannesburg in March 1892, the invaluable Carl Meyer was certainty itself: 'I have no hesitation in saying that in my opinion these fields have an enormous future before them and that the country altogether will for the next 10 or 20 years offer greater scope for European capital than South America and similar countries.' After describing Kruger as 'a queer old Boer, ugly, badly dressed and ill-mannered, but a splendid type all the same', Meyer added somewhat over-optimistically that 'the relations between the old Boer party and the new mining industry population are getting much better than they have been hitherto'. New Court took the hint, and the upshot was not only the Rothschild imprimatur on the Transvaal loan later that year, but also enhanced support for deep-level activity on the part of the Exploration Company, essentially a Rothschild-backed vehicle that provided mining finance. Its managing director was the leading international mining engineer Hamilton Smith, an energetic American who in January 1893 wrote for *The Times* a thoroughly bullish 'special report' on 'The Witwatersrand Goldfields'. Paying tribute to 'the active and energetic set of men who now have this industry in hand', he gave every impression that the sky was the limit, metaphorically speaking of course.[21]

In the event, though there was to be a glittering future for deep-level mining, neither Rhodes and his Consolidated Gold Fields, nor the Rothschilds, nor even Hamilton Smith, were to be the main men as it came to fruitful maturity. That privilege belonged to Alfred Beit and Julius Wernher, joint senior partners of Wernher, Beit & Co.[22] Both men were German, both by the early 1890s were middle-aged, and both had made their reputations in South African diamond mining before basing themselves permanently in London. Wernher was a fairly orthodox operator – hard-working, somewhat cautious, and with a well-bred, upright bearing that made him popular in the City – but Beit was something else, being that relative rarity, a genuinely creative financier. Years later Frank Harris recalled interviewing him towards the end of the 1890s:

Beit's manner was nervous, hesitating: he had a tiny dark moustache and a curious trick of twirling at it with the right hand, though he seldom touched it; the embarrassed nervousness of a student, rather than the assurance of a man of affairs accustomed to deal with men; but the nervousness was chiefly superficial, due perhaps to weak health, for as soon as he began to talk business he came to perfect self-possession . . .

'Well,' said Beit, 'I was one of the poor Beits of Hamburg; my father found it difficult even to pay for my schooling, and . . . I had to leave before I had gone through the *Realschule*. Of course, in Hamburg at that time everyone was talking about the discovery of diamonds in South Africa . . .'

There followed a detailed account of how, after two years in Amsterdam learning about diamonds, Beit had made his initial fortune in Kimberley, through property speculation as well as dealing in diamonds. But he was, Harris emphasised in his memoirs, more than just a man of money:

> Like many Jews, he had a real love and understanding of music; and he admired pictures and bronzes, too, though he was anything but a good judge of them. At bottom Beit was a sentimentalist, and did not count or reckon when his feelings were really touched . . . Of all the millionaires I had chanced to meet, Beit was the best. He had a great deal of the milk of human kindness in him, quick and deep sympathies, too, sympathies even with poverty, perhaps through his own early struggles . . .

Rhodes offered a crisper, less generous verdict on his sentimental fellow-magnate. According to him, 'all that Beit wanted was to be rich enough to give his mother £1,000 a year'.[23]

Whatever his motivation, it was Beit who in 1890 became convinced of the long-term potential of deep-level gold mining and bought the properties on the Central Rand that in time became the great deep-level mines – mines such as Jumpers Deep, Nourse Deep, Glen Deep, Rose Deep, Village Deep and Geldenhuis Deep.[24] By February 1893 he was ready to float Rand Mines, which in effect acted as a holding company for all the individual deep-level mines and was the pioneer of what became known as the group system of mining, allowing significant economies of scale. Beit ensured that his own firm kept a controlling interest in Rand Mines, but he was astute enough to give substantial shareholdings to the Rothschild brothers, to consulting engineers like Hamilton Smith, and to Ernest Cassel – a policy that not only kept potential enemies sweet, but also ensured that Wernher, Beit & Co itself did not have to put all its own resources at risk. Beit was well aware that deep-level mining was an extremely capital-intensive process, that lead times were long before the gold started to flow, and that there remained considerable scepticism about the efficacy of deep-level methods. It would be another year and a half before South African gold-mining shares really began to boom on the London Stock Exchange, but even in the spring of 1893 the incipient signs were there. 'If Connie Nickalls persists in driving through Throgmorton-street in a hansom cab he will upset some of the markets,' warned the *Financial News* in April, adding pointedly: 'Of course, in these days the toffs of the Kaffir Circus cannot be expected to walk even round the corner; but the toes, if not the dignity, of the open-air markets must be respected.'[25]

If South Africa was a growth stock, the diametric opposite applied to Australia, for some thirty years a favoured borrower on the London capital market but now in deep economic trouble.[26] The Queensland loan flop of 1891 was a sign of chillier times, and in May 1893 the suspension of many Australian banks prompted a recriminatory mood in the City strongly tinged with *schadenfreude*. Particularly lacking in compunction was the outburst of the house journal of the London Chamber of Commerce: 'The colonies have found themselves unable to bear the burden of unproductive public works encouraged and indulged in, for years back, at the dictation practically of the popular vote.' And again: 'We learn once more that money is an indispensable commodity and that the nation which has it, and keeps it, remains strong. The Australians thought they had reached the time when they could do without us. They will find the mistake of this belief, and also that they are still controlled by the London money market, whether they like it or not.'[27] The state of play could hardly have been put more plainly. In the short term most of the Australian banks that survived were the ones with a London base and strong City links; over the medium term it became clear that the price of any further borrowing from London was strict financial orthodoxy, repudiating the dangerously free-spending tendencies of a youthful democracy. Australia's touring cricketers even had the decency to lose to England in the summer of 1893, though it was probably not a deliberate act of contrition.

The City also waved the big stick when it came to negotiating the post-1890 debt settlement of that honorary white colony, the Argentine.[28] The crunch year was 1893, and the *Economist* set the tone in February by brusquely dismissing complaints of ill–treatment on the part of Buenos Aires:

We certainly have no desire to act as apologists for the financial houses that ministered so freely to Argentine extravagance. In pursuit of gain, they have done much that is to be deplored and condemned. That, however, does not alter the fact that the debts were voluntarily contracted, and it is idle to speak as if the nation were rather to be pitied for having been permitted to borrow so freely than blamed for having incurred too heavy obligations.

The so-called Rothschild Committee – comprising Natty himself, Walter Burns of Morgans, Everard Hambro, Charles Goschen of the Bank of England, Vicary Gibbs, and George Drabble of the Bank of London and the River Plate – acted on behalf of the bondholders. A settlement with the Argentine government was finally reached in June, known as the Romero Arrangement after the Argentine Finance Minister, and ratified six months later by a justifiably reluctant Argentine Congress. Inevitably the settlement's terms were complex, but in essence it was a trade-off: on the one hand, giving the Argentine the breathing space of five years of reduced interest payments; on the other, tying the Argentine increasingly closely to the London capital market, with a concomitant insistence on a deflationary economic orthodoxy, which in turn led to the Argentine rail network passing virtually into British control. In London, press as well as bondholder reaction was almost entirely favourable to the settlement. 'Perhaps the most satisfactory feature in the whole matter,' crowed the *FT*, 'is the fact that the various issuing houses have succeeded in enforcing the rights of their clients on an equitable basis.' And, quite unblushingly, it went on: 'In particular, Messrs J.S. Morgan and Co, in fighting for and establishing the priority of the loans which they only consented to issue on condition of that priority, have done splendid work for the maintenance of London as the financial centre of the world.'[29]

Still, in the City's eyes one thing even more underpinned its international dominance – the supremacy of the British navy. In 1889 the government had laid down the celebrated doctrine of the Two Power Standard, demanding a navy stronger than that of the next two largest combined, but already by the end of 1893 that doctrine was coming under practical pressure. The City had little faith in the super-patriotism of a Liberal ministry led by Gladstone, and a fortnight before Christmas there took place at the Cannon Street Hotel a well-attended meeting, under the auspices of the London Chamber of Commerce, 'for the purpose of considering the state of our naval defences'. The LCC's President, Sir Albert Rollit, took the chair, arguing that the meeting wanted 'not only security but a sense of security, and also that confidence which was the very basis of our commerce'. Rollit's sentiments were fully endorsed the next day by the *FT*, which laid heavy stress on the large naval expenditure of France and Russia and hoped that 'the resolutions in favour of making our naval defences adequate "regardless of cost" . . . will not be without their effect on the government'.[30] 'Regardless of cost': even in Cobden's heyday the City had never been Cobdenite; and at this stage it was wholly qualmless, whether in terms of domestic finance or the nascent international arms race.

*

Time, on 17 June 1893, stood still:

> It is an unwritten law of the Stock Exchange that members, if they wear any head-gear in business hours, must confine themselves to the decorous 'chimney-pot'. Heavy and oppressive it may be, but it imparts a certain dignity even when worn, as it generally is, on the nape of the neck; and anybody entering the 'House' in a 'bowler' soon finds the tattered brim dangling over his collar, while the remainder is serving as a football elsewhere. But there is a point at which wearing a tall hat ceases to be a virtue, and that point was reached on Saturday, with the thermometer registering 90 in the shade. Accordingly one member boldly appeared in a straw hat. A furious uproar resulted, and the question was eagerly debated whether the offender should be tried by a Court-martial of the Committee, or should be summarily lynched by being suspended for two years on the scaffolding in the old building. Being a big and muscular man, he survived, and presently half-a-dozen straw-hats appeared, followed by others in quick succession. In view of this revolutionary departure, Consols should be sold.

Pioneers, oh pioneers, but two months later, during another heat-wave, the *Rialto* was reporting that 'the cool and comfortable "straw-yard", which was at first barely tolerated, is now accepted as a thing of course, and it is beginning to be recognised that the absence of a waistcoat does not necessarily imply moral or financial degradation'. Still, an American-style blazer remained beyond the pale, and one day in August it was so hot that members resorted to cooling themselves with penny fans.[31]

Perhaps, towards the end of a trying summer, the penny variety was all they could afford. 'The Australian Banking crisis seems to be tided over; but everybody in the City complains that there is absolutely no business going on.' So Hamilton noted in June, and during much of July the tone in Capel Court was deeply apprehensive. Among those hammered was W.B. Moore, for over thirty years a jobber in the Brighton market: 'The seat on which he has sat for so many years, snuff-box in hand, looks strangely deserted now. It was to this vacant seat that the whole market turned with sympathetic gaze when his name was declared.' By Saturday 22 July, according to William Keswick of Mathesons, the tone was improving. 'There has been here serious depression on the Stock Exchange and great anxiety owing to rumours of the difficulties of many eminent houses,' he wrote to the New York office of Jardine Matheson, 'but in a great measure these have now passed and no grave trouble is now regarded as probable.' Two days later the well-known brokers Sutton & Co were hammered, speculations in Eries having gone so badly wrong that the partners owed £100,000 to fellow-members.[32]

It was, as Keswick implied, not only on the Stock Exchange that nerves were taut. A month later, Brown Shipley described to Brown Brothers in New York a recent, highly revealing episode:

> Mr Drabble (Chairman of the London & River Plate Bank) called on us & said that what with bills already in their portfolio & others on the way his Bank saw that they now hold on BS & Co £170,000 *all drawn by one House*, & that before telegraphing anything to Rio about it, he thought that we might prefer that he should give us an opportunity of reopening the Line. We thanked him for his courtesy & at once offered to take up £50,000 at a rate to be agreed upon between us today. He accepted the offer & the rate has now been fixed @ $4\frac{1}{4}$ % per ann.
>
> It was all very pleasantly & amicably arranged & we do not think that the incident has done us harm in any kind of way. But it emphasises the fact that a very big line of Credits granted to any one House – however good – is liable to cause inconvenience in unexpected ways, whenever want of confidence is the prevailing attitude of men's minds.
>
> There has been an epidemic of that lately, & it has been never absent for long since the Baring collapse in 1890, & we are liable to feel the effects of it whensoever any one of the Foriegn Exchange Banks is led to think that they have too much of any particular firm's drawings upon us, to be placed readily in the London Discount Market.

Clearly the bill market was in almost as anxious a state as the stock market, but some allowance has also to be made for the fact that by the 1890s Brown Shipley was an accepting house with an ageing partnership which no longer inspired the confidence it once had. 'Is not line Brown Shipley & Co, London, too large?' asked a cable in September 1893 from J.S. Morgan & Co in London to Drexel, Morgan & Co in New York. And: 'We have no information specially and we do not doubt entire solvency but credit seems to be decreased both here and abroad.'[33]

Jumpy markets inevitably focused attention on the value or otherwise of the London Stock Exchange's unique jobbing system; and in September 1893, amidst growing complaints about lack of marketability, the *Economist* put 'The Utility of the Jobber' under the critical microscope:

> Roughly speaking, half the members of the Stock Exchange are jobbers, so that the outside world supports some 1,500 men, with an average of about two clerks apiece, purely for the purpose of securing a continuously free market; that is to say, we expect, with the help of the jobbers, to be able always to buy or sell officially quoted securities readily, and at a reasonably close price.
>
> Unfortunately, we are liable to be disappointed. Only in those markets in which there is an even stream of buying and selling, and only as long as that stream flows can a broker be sure of having a close price made. In out-of-the-way departments in which business is restricted and apt to run in one direction only, such as Home Railway Preferences, Bank shares, and most of the Miscellaneous securities [i.e. mainly home industrials], the jobber either makes only a very wide price, or refuses to make a price at all, saying that it is entirely a matter of negotiation, that the broker must open his book to him, and that he will see if he can 'get on', that is, find a broker who wants to deal 'the other way' . . . And the same thing happens all round the House in times of violent fluctuation either way. Even in the American and Mining markets, which the continuous flow of speculative business renders the freest in ordinary times, the jobbers are apt to refuse to make close prices when anything like a panic or a bear squeeze is developed. They do not see why they should be landed or caught short, and accordingly mark prices up or down against the public, and often in the course of the recent downfall refused to make prices at all, or only made them quite preposterously wide . . .

So, did the *Economist* actually advocate the abolition of the jobbing system? Not quite, making the familiar point that the spread of securities quoted in London was so much wider and more diverse than in New York or Paris that brokers unaided by specialist dealers, in effect wholesalers, would be unable to do their business. But it insisted that 'if the jobber is merely an expensive encumbrance, he will vanish,' adding that brokers increasingly met on an informal basis to match bargains between themselves.[34] Implicitly, it seemed, the long-run Darwinian logic was towards the abolition of single capacity.

Brokers themselves hardly basked in praise during the 1890s. 'One broker cannot know about all stock, and even if he did in a way do so, his knowledge of most cannot but be superficial. He is apt to be swayed by the opinions current in the market at a given time, and these opinions rarely coincide with investors' interests.' That was the unflattering verdict in 1892 of the *Investors' Review*, edited by the tough-minded A.J. Wilson. The *Statist* took a similar line two years later when it fielded the real-life query of 'a gentleman (not in business)' as to whether he should 'operate from a distance' or 'go into the City and talk to his broker' before choosing his investments. The answer was unequivocal:

> Stay right away from the City. In the City you will be confused by the noise and rattle, you will talk to a broker who is in a great hurry, and cannot give you a quiet ten minutes, to a broker who is under the influence of the last tip he has heard going round the market, or the last bid he heard before leaving it, who, in nine cases out of ten, will advise you to do what everybody else is doing, which perhaps is precisely the opposite to what you should do; or who will recommend a purchase of some other stock in which friends of his are interested.

Fertile of tips, barren of analysis, most late-Victorian stockbrokers had the saving grace of not taking themselves too seriously as professional men. Or as Joseph Braithwaite (of Foster & Braithwaite) liked to growl: 'Stockbrokers are not prophets, neither are they sons of prophets.'[35]

Towards the end of 1893 brokers, jobbers and the whole murky, populous world spinning off from Capel Court – touts and half-commission men, outside brokers and speculators – were agreed that the tone of things was at last improving. 'A change of feeling,' noted the *Rialto*'s House correspondent on 24 November, 'is becoming apparent, not only in the Stock Exchange, but all over the City – people giving up talking so much of what they have lost, and beginning to speak about how they may best regain it.' A few days later Loulou Harcourt attended one of Natty Rothschild's house-parties at Tring, with fellow-guests including Lord and Lady Suffolk, Lord Newport and his daughter, and N. Boulatzell from the Russian Embassy. Thursday the 30th was given over to shooting, though Natty himself sat it out: 'We got 800 Pheasants before luncheon and 1,100 by the end of the day. I was shooting very well. There were Kangaroos, little Japanese deer, Egyptian geese and wild Turkeys jumping out of the woods all day.' In a happier mood the Stock Exchange was also frolicking in the week before Christmas, though as the *Rialto* reported, all in a good cause:

Larking has been the order of the day throughout the markets, and the sensation of the session was the display of ballet-dancing, skirt-dancing and clog-dancing by a couple of agile members at four o'clock in the Trunk market. This is an annual event, a collection being taken in aid of a Children's Christmas Dinner Fund. This time a very creditable performance was rewarded by a peculiarly lavish contribution of coppers, the extensive dancing area being simply paved with pence.

There were no prizes for guessing who was the champion cloggie, named by the *FN* as Charlie Clarke. Still, business was business: the outlook remained at best uncertain, and as the year ended a deathless snatch of conversation was overheard in Shorter's Court:

Hungry Broker (*scenting a possible £12 10s*): 'Do you want to make a bit over the new year? Buy yourself 500 Milwaukee.'

Client: 'But I was just thinking of selling 500.'

Hungry Broker (*eagerly*): 'Well, not so bad either!'[36]

One stockbroking firm poised to take advantage of any permanent upturn was Pember & Boyle, with its offices at 24 Lombard Street, on the first floor above Alexanders the discount house. A new partnership deed came into operation at the start of 1894, with the five junior partners taking only 28 per cent of the profits but each having something distinctive to offer by way of all-important 'connection'. F. Chetwynd Stapylton had traded on his own during the 1880s, thereby building up a useful network; Owen Bevan was related to the Bevans of Barclays Bank; Charles Campbell's brother was Colin Campbell, a future director of the National Provincial Bank; Francis Anderson's father was a director of Alexanders; and Theodore Althaus had come to the firm through the good offices of Natty Rothschild, having been private tutor to Natty's son Walter. As for the two leading partners (on 36 per cent each), George Pember was a well-respected broker who had been a member since 1867; while though Cecil Boyle had disappointed his many admirers from Clifton College days by pursuing such a humdrum occupation as stockbroking, he still had some excellent connections. One was Gaspard Farrer of the small but select merchant bank H.S. Lefevre & Co, who later in 1894 wrote a letter of encomium to one of his main correspondents on the other side:

Cecil Boyle, partner in a stockbroking firm here of good standing, & a great friend of mine, called on me yesterday to say that he was starting for New York in a few hours, so there & then I scribbled him a line to you . . . He has been prosperous, & ought to have been very prosperous, but his actions are guided by generous impulses rather than cool judgement.

Farrer explained that Boyle's present mission was to seek to defend his clients' interests in relation to Reading Railroad bonds; and he added that Boyle was 'as straight as a die & a good sort – & you would like him'.[37]

Sir Horace Farquhar was an altogether more controversial City figure.[38] He was born in 1844, the fifth son of a Scottish baronet; beginning his business career in the City, in the well-known East Indian house of Forbes, Forbes & Co, he subsequently entered Scott's Bank, based in Cavendish Square, where he became its most active partner and introduced into it the presence and capital of his close friend the Duke of Fife. By the early 1890s, still a bachelor, he was accepted in the highest society. Eddy Hamilton stayed in September 1893 at Mar Lodge, Braemar as a guest of Fife, and among those present was 'of course' Farquhar – to whom, Hamilton noted, 'Fife's marriage [to a daughter of the Prince of Wales] has made no real difference as regards his footing here and at Sheen, although in order to be a little independent he rents part of the Mar Forest (the Geldie) to which he goes for one or two nights in the week.' Hamilton spent one night with him there, and 'Horace talked to me a good deal about his disappointment last year.' Namely: 'He had set his heart on a peerage, and the Duke of Devonshire had submitted his name to Lord Salisbury for the dignity on the ground of his services to the Liberal Unionist party . . . At the last moment Lord Salisbury put him into the batch of Baronets in lieu of Peers.' Perhaps Salisbury had been influenced by the taint attached to Farquhar outside his work as a private banker. In particular, Farquhar had deemed there to be no conflict of interest between being on the one hand a director of the British South Africa Company, a chartered company, and on the other hand Chairman of the Exploration Company, actively seeking mining concessions in Matabeleland and Mashonaland. Still, as far as Scott's itself was concerned, a major development was at hand – its absorption, like so many private banks, by a big joint-stock bank, in this case Parr's. The announcement was made on 23 February 1894, along with the news that Farquhar was to join the board of Parr's.[39] It was hardly the ermine, but cemented his reputation as a City man of some significance if doubtful propriety.

A week later a small item appeared in the financial press that a stockbroker called Montague Spier was lying gravely ill at the Covent Garden Hotel after shooting himself in the head. On 10 March he was moved to St Thomas's Hospital, and died there on the 18th. He was 43, his offices had been at 6 Hercules Passage off Threadneedle Street, and he had lived with two sisters in the Harrow Road. At the inquest, evidence was given by his cousin, a solicitor, to the effect that Spier had come to see him early in February saying that he owed £1,500 to one of his clerks, Radford, and that he had no prospect of repaying the money, speculations having gone badly wrong. He had talked to his cousin of going to visit an uncle in Bournemouth to see if he could borrow the money, but in the event did not do so. Two letters were produced, written by Spier from the Covent Garden Hotel on 27 February, shortly before he pulled the trigger. The first was to his other clerk, T.J. Ives of 39 Alfred Street, Bow:

> With the few hours of life that still remain I believe I can see clearly and duly estimate the correctness of my judgement, and I still believe I was right as to the value of Italian stock, Coras, and North British, also Louisville; but I confess to feel doubtful about some of the others. I have still faith in Italy [Spier had apparently been a bull of £50,000 Italian stock], and also that the frugality, industry, and self-sacrifice of the Italians will enable them to easily surmount their financial troubles.

The other letter was to Radford himself:

> The step I shall have taken by the time you receive this will be the means of enabling you to recover (by the insurance money) what I have lost through speculation. I know quite well you will bitterly regret my acting thus, and I feel equally sure you would have taken every possible means of preventing my present action had I given you the faintest means of suspecting my desperate intention. For the pain and grief my death may cause you and others I earnestly crave your and their forgiveness, but, rightly or wrongly, I see no other quick and certain way of repaying the loss, and for that reason I decide to pay with the forfeiture of my life. With sincerest wishes for your happiness and welfare and for your complete restoration to health, yours in deep misery and despair, M.H. SPIER.[40]

The jury found a verdict of temporary insanity, but the unfortunate man seems to have been thoroughly clear-eyed about the fact that he had insured his life for a grand.

*

One of Goschen's last achievements as Chancellor was the Bank Act of 1892, under which the Bank of England found itself being distinctly 'squeezed' by the Treasury in terms of how much the government paid for the day-to-day conduct of its financial business.[41] Inevitably this attack on the Bank's income created strains. By August 1893, following a visit to Threadneedle Street, Hamilton was sounding an ominous note: 'The Bank will, I see, need to be carefully handled: they have not got over (what they consider to be) the hard bargain which we drove with them last year, and there is not a single Director who is politically friendly towards the Government.' To perform this careful handling, there could not have been a worse Chancellor in situ than Sir William Harcourt – Liberal, abrasive, and spoiling for a fight with what he regarded as one of the last great unreformed vested interests. In the opposite corner was Lidderdale's successor as Governor, a rather unimaginative, obstinate merchant called David Powell. A month later Hamilton was on holiday in Scotland, listening to Farquhar's laments, when he received a Harcourt special:

In your absence I have fought a great fight with the dragons of the Bank parlour.

I sent for the Governor who came supported by that valiant champion Deputy Governor Wigram. After some polite beating about the bush we came to close quarters on the rate of interest on Ways & Means advances.

I blandly threw out a $\frac{1}{2}$ per cent above the rate on deficiency advances which at the present discount rates would have been $2\frac{1}{2}$ p.c.

The two pundits looked at one another in blank dismay and revealed the fact that they had come with instructions to ask $3\frac{1}{2}$ p.c.; thereupon I poured upon them the vials of my wrath; I showed them that such a rate had never been paid when the Bank Rate was 4%; I asked them with indignation how they dare behave in such a way to a customer who kept an average balance of £5,000,000 in their hands; I told them point blank that nothing would induce me to listen to such an exorbitant demand and I said it would become my duty to enquire what 'other persons' there were in the City of London who might be ready & willing to accommodate HM's Govt at a reasonable rate. I said I had hitherto been unwilling to open a Govt account elsewhere than at the B of England but that such demands might make it necessary to look in other quarters for reasonable accommodation. This was quite enough to indicate the proximity of New Court to Threadneedle St and they trembled at the notion of the Ch of the Exch dealing with Jews less extortionate than themselves. After I had exhibited this bug bear sufficiently I was prepared to dismiss them with the question whether I was to take their proposal as an ultimatum upon which the ferocious Powell hinted that I might write and suggest 3% and they would give it anxious consideration.

These two gentlemen who looked for all the world like the picture of the money lenders at Windsor then retired. The valiant Wigram looked daggers – but used none.

I accordingly wrote a polite note splitting the difference which has been graciously acceded to, they endeavouring to cover their retreat by alleging 'the change in the condition of the money market' as the reason of their climbing down . . .

Harcourt by now had the bit thoroughly between his teeth and a few days later wrote again to Hamilton about 'the scandalous conduct of the Bank which I shall not forget', accusing it of having, despite his best bargaining efforts, 'practically robbed the public of $\frac{3}{4}$% on £2,000,000'. Therefore, 'I shall have as little dealings as I can help with these gentlemen in the future . . . We have been made thorough fools of . . .' And, in a postscript, Harcourt declared with apparent sincerity that next time he really would borrow from Rothschilds '& show up these Bank gentlemen to the public for what they are'.[42]

The same gentlemen had, earlier in 1893, considered a report on the Bank's internal administration. 'It has long been manifest,' it asserted, 'that there are two main obstacles to economy in the Bank's administration; the first, common to banking business generally, is the irregularity of the work, which is subject to periods of considerable pressure and slackness, not only within the year but within the day; and the second, the employment, for some of the duties in the Bank, of a class of persons not always well fitted for such duties.' An example given was the work of sorting old notes in the Bank Note Office, the report being 'strongly of opinion' that the work was 'more fitted for women than for men or lads'. The next year the Bank did take on women clerks in the cancelled notes department, a move that caused something of a sensation in the City and many a tedious joke about 'old' and 'young' ladies of Threadneedle Street. One of the report's three authors had been the Bank's chief cashier, Frank May, who controlled almost as a personal fiefdom the cashier's department, employing over half the Bank's staff of over a thousand and responsible not only for the management of the note issue, but also the Bank's discounts and advances as well as its regular operations in the gilt-edged and money markets. 'Mr May,' a profile a few years earlier in the *Bankers' Magazine* had asserted, 'is said to despise what is known as popularity, and, still more, the insincerity of word and manner sometimes laid to the charge of men who flinch from what may be their strict, although unpleasant, duty to their fellow-workers.' It was later to be said that May's 'military stiffness' had been 'much resented' outside the Bank, but on that matter the typically deferential profile was silent.[43]

The more critical retrospective tone was occasioned by a scandal, which was the discovery of 'certain irregularities', as the recurrent phrase went, in the chief cashier's office. A sub-committee comprising Lidderdale, Benjamin Buck Greene and James Currie reported to the Committee of Treasury on 8 November 1893, revealing that for several years past it had been May's practice to make large unauthorised advances. The chief cashier did not seek to justify himself and resigned almost forthwith. The next day Powell wrote to Hamilton: 'I am sorry to say there have been irregularities in Mr May's "office" which we were obliged to notice but there is no reason for publishing this fact.' Perhaps Powell and his deputy Clifford Wigram hoped to avoid an interview with the dreaded Harcourt, but a meeting was arranged for the 11th at the Treasury, with Hamilton among those present:

> It appears that May had renewed advances without the express sanction of the Governors, and had likewise made loans to people on insufficient security. One of these advances had been made to his brother-in-law nominally, but in reality to himself. Harcourt spoke his mind out very strongly & perhaps in rather too hectoring a tone. He thought the Governors would have done better in the interests of commercial morality, had they dismissed May summarily, and had they taken proceedings against him.

Hamilton then added his own thoughts and some further information:

> What struck one most was that there must be some very weak spot in the management of the Bank to have made it possible for May to act in the way he had, without being detected sooner. What had evidently been May's principal cause of ruin was his son's being in a firm of speculative brokers, through whom May had speculated on his own account with the result that he had on his own admission been completely cleaned out.[44]

For Harcourt the whole episode was a wonderfully opportune stick with which to beat the Bank, and by Monday his son was noting that 'Chex has written a very strong letter to the Governor . . . telling them that he entirely disapproves of their action in trying to hush up May's "irregularities" and suggesting that they should at once set the Public Prosecutor to work.' However, 'Welby & Hamilton think the letter too strong and *ultra vires* so it is withheld for the present.' So they did, Welby having written to Harcourt that day to suggest that it would be better if his letter took 'rather the form of advice, at all events in the first instance, than of censure, a criticism which perhaps many at the

Bank would not be slow to make'. For the moment, Harcourt held his fire. The next day Loulou recorded a further twist:

> The Bank business gets worse, the more one hears of it. It appears that May advanced Bank money to Crump the City Editor of the 'Times' without security & when the Trust Co's began to topple over May told Crump he must repay the loan. Crump replied 'You can't squeeze blood out of a stone. I am stone broke & have not a penny in the world.' May said he must raise the money so Crump went to the Proprietor & Editor of the Times & they dismissed him on the spot without a pension.[45]

Many investment trust companies, products of the late 1880s boom, had indeed perished amidst the protracted fall-out from the Baring crisis; while as for Crump, his name was not to feature in the official history of the Thunderer.

By early 1894 rumours of the exact nature of May's misdemeanours were starting to surface in the public prints, along with broader attacks on the Bank itself. An especially well-publicised blast ('A Paralytic Bank of England') came from the pen of A.J. Wilson in his *Investors' Review*:

> Little of the true condition of the Bank can be known until daylight is let in on its accounts. The Bank publishes no balance-sheet – nothing whatever except the meagre weekly returns. There is no outside audit of its books; its stockholders have no control whatever over the management. Under the charter shareholders are supposed to meet and elect directors and governors at stated periods, but this power has dwindled into mere routine or pantomime. The 'House List', as it is called, is always elected as a matter of course, so that the board is really co-optative. It is thus, in great measure, 'a family party'. The son follows the father, the nephew the uncle, or a lucky marriage brings with it a seat at the board. At best tradition prevails, and the new director is never a banker, rarely a man trained in the hard school of competitive business.

That was published at the start of January, but *The Times* on the 8th took a less critical line, deciding it was:

> ... absurd to adopt towards the Bank the attitude of a preacher denouncing the abomination of desolation. There is no call for Habakkuk Mucklewrath masquerading as a critic of modern finance ... We see no advantage in assuming, as some assume, that the Bank is governed mainly by noodles. The Bank directors are not gods, but they are not blackbeetles either.

Chancellor and Governor, meanwhile, were resuming their difficult relationship, and on the 12th Powell and his deputy were treated to another ear-bashing from Harcourt, who wanted to know 'what changes in the system of the management of the Bank are in contemplation' and to discuss whether the Bank should provide fuller public information about the nature of the securities it held.[46] Perhaps this time one of them was tempted to pull out a dagger.

An important effect of Wilson's critique, and others, was to bring out into the open again the whole question of who ran the Bank.[47] Back in January 1891, Hamilton had asked Lidderdale 'whether he favoured the idea of a permanent Governor. He said, on the whole "No". It was difficult enough now to get good men to serve as Directors, and if you deprived them of the chance of occupying the *chair*, which to many was a coveted distinction, you would probably get even less good men to enter the Bank.' It was hardly, from one of the most capable governors of the century, a ringing endorsement of the calibre of the current direction. A more outspoken critic was Bertram Currie, who wrote privately in February 1893 that 'the old type of director has become extinct, and they are now recruited from iron-masters, ship-builders, brewers, – in fact from every class except bankers'. By early January 1894, Currie's thoughts were focusing on the Committee of Treasury, traditionally far more influential than the Court of Directors itself. 'He thinks it essential,' Welby reported to Harcourt, 'that the Governor's Council should be enlarged, & that the Octogenerians always excepting Greene should be shunted.' Nor was Currie alone in desiring this major reform. Hamilton, by 25 January, discovered that Everard Hambro, supported by Charles Goschen (the former Chancellor's younger brother) and some of the junior directors, were proposing to change the Committee of Treasury from an ex officio body of past governors to one elected from the general body of directors. 'It is believed,' he noted, 'that the present ex-Governors are too averse to so radical a step to admit of its being taken.'[48]

Henry Hucks Gibbs was one ex-Governor decidedly averse. On the 27th he wrote to Powell to express his opposition. Without attacking Hambro personally, he identified him as the representative of 'Directors below the Chair' – that is, those who had not yet had a turn as governor – and poured scorn on them as a group:

> Some have shown more interest in the daily working of the Bank than others; but not a tithe of the active interest which used to be taken by their predecessors of 20 years ago.

As a body – I hope I may say it without offence – they have neglected their own duties; and now they propose to assume ours . . .

Gibbs, a seasoned controversialist, then gave what one can only call the grand bum's rush to the nascent reform movement:

Whence has all this agitation arisen? There can be no doubt I think that it grew out of the unhappy misconduct of Mr May, and of the comments of the press to which that gave rise. Now I must say, Mr Governor, that it is wholly beneath the dignity of the Court that any of its members should be influenced by the ignorant comments of the Press.

It would scarcely be more indecorous if they themselves were to influence such comments.

Powell made sure to circulate Gibbs's letter, and on 1 February the Court voted against Hambro's initiative, by an unspecified margin. The decision was too much for that thrusting young meritocrat the Earl of Leven and Melville, who had been a director since 1884 but now resigned.[49]

So, reform was officially off the agenda, but debate continued for a while longer, especially in the *Bankers' Magazine*. The February issue contained an article by 'A Banker' on 'What the Bank of England Ought to Do', asserting 'it is clear that the system of drawing the directors from the different branches of English trade and commerce, though probably right in the past, has now become obsolete'. The author wanted more merchant bankers (as opposed to merchants) on the Court, citing Sir Mark Collet (of Brown Shipley), Gibbs, Goschen (of Frühling & Goschen) and Hambro as good examples of a trend to be encouraged. But as to the thornier question of whether the Court should have on it bankers as such, like Currie or Sir John Lubbock, he was less sure: 'Circumstances are certain to arise in the course of time where the interests of the Bank of England and those of the private banks represented by these gentlemen will not be identical, and this consideration would counsel caution before adopting this new departure.' Presumably the possibility of a *joint-stock* banker on the Court was beyond contemplation. What about the question of the top man? 'The system of leaving the management in the hands of one director, who is elected governor for two years, and who, by chance, may know least about banking, is so absolutely out of date that nobody is likely to defend it.' However, 'A Banker' preferred the prospect of a permanent manager to that of a permanent governor, who 'might easily become too strong to be controlled by the board'. The following month, a leading article in the *BM* returned to the whole theme, and on one key aspect, that of the Court's composition, was refreshingly unequivocal: 'The only persons disqualified are the bankers of the country, who are excluded by a private and traditional rule of many years' standing . . . Such a rule condemns itself.'[50]

None of these matters, of course, were raised on 15 March when the proprietors attended the regular half-yearly general court, held in the Bank parlour. Instead, Powell laid great stress on the measures that had been taken to ensure that the May 'irregularities' could not be repeated (irregularities that he was still unwilling to elaborate on), and wound up with some mildly defiant remarks:

> I suppose that no body of directors has ever gone through a more trying time than we have in the last six months – trying in more senses than one – for the work here has been incessant. Things had to be found out, and there was naturally a feeling of suspicion thrown over the whole establishment . . . It is very satisfactory to us to know that you have still confidence in us in spite of what has happened. I do not think the fault rests altogether with the directors, there may have been some fault in the system; but the directors have always had the best interests of the Bank thoroughly at heart, and they have tried, and will always try in the future, to do their best.

Powell himself stayed at his post for another year, because his deputy Wigram was seriously ill; and at the end of that year, in March 1895, his old adversary received a surprise – and fruitless – visit, as recorded by Loulou: 'The wife of the Governor of the Bank of England (who looked like a Regent St prostitute) came to see Chex this morning to ask that some "honour" should be given to him on his retirement from the Bank . . .' Harcourt's reply is, disappointingly, not recorded.[51]

The fundamental issue remained: to what extent was the Bank still a private body, to what extent had it become a public institution? In practice, this conflicting balance of interests tended to be played out in the money market, and on 6 October 1893, a day after Bank rate had changed and a month before the May scandal broke, the *Financial News* squared up to the question:

> The Bank of England is trying to serve two masters. One of these masters is the body of its own shareholders, whose dividends depend upon the amount of discount business done by the Bank, and who do not like to see their prospects injured by the successful competition of the open market; and the other is the vast interest of British credit, represented in the City mind by the amount of gold in the Bank's vaults. The

policy of the directors, as exemplified in their latest exploit of reducing the minimum official rate to 3 per cent, is too obviously the policy that animated Mr Facing-both-ways in Bunyan's allegory. They want to get some of the business which now drifts into other channels, and they do not want to encourage withdrawals of bullion by foreign customers. As usual in similar attempts, they have adopted a compromise course which is not at all certain to achieve either of the desired ends . . .

The *FN* went on to analyse the Bank's conflicting relationships with the government and its own shareholders, and concluded by calling in strong terms for the Bank's responsibilities to be more clearly defined.[52] That, however, over twenty years after Bagehot had addressed the subject, was something that few people inside or outside the City yet had the vision or will to attempt to do – not least in the 'company of merchants' itself, to use Ricardo's scornful but in some ways still apposite phrase.

CHAPTER SEVEN

'Ware Bombs!

On the last day of January 1894 the *Pall Mall Gazette* announced in flaring type that Gladstone was about to resign. When news of this reached the Stock Exchange, business came to a temporary halt, as members broke out in loud, enthusiastic cheering. Then, the cheering over, 'they began to bid lustily for stocks at a sixteenth under the market price, to express their feelings without adding to their holdings'. For the moment the rumour proved false, but it refused to go away. On 14 February Natty Rothschild paid a visit to Harcourt, 'evidently wishing' (Loulou wrote) 'to "fish" about the Gladstone reports'. However, 'Chex turned Natty off on to the subject of the revival of trade & business in the City . . .' At last, early in March, the G.O.M. did go, and the *FT* appreciated the choice of Lord Rosebery (as opposed to Harcourt) as his successor: 'A Radical, yet an Imperialist, he is fully in touch with the progressive spirit of the times, but not with the advanced fanatics who would rush headlong to perdition.' He was also, the paper did not add, linked by marriage to the Rothschilds and had a certain City reputation. Nevertheless, the *FT* did go on: 'On all accounts the speedy advent of the Conservatives to what is likely to prove a long spell of power is to be looked for. From a financial point of view the change is one that will be heartily welcomed, for it will doubtless help to hasten the long delayed revival of public confidence.'[1] With those sentiments few figures of substance in the City would have disagreed.

A direct outcome of the lean years since 1890 was the row over the provision of tape facilities to outside brokers. It began in October 1893 when the Stock Exchange Committee's relevant sub-committee considered a memorial from members 'respecting the indiscriminate supply of the telegraph tape prices', in other words by the Exchange Telegraph Company to non-members, with the ETC not only supplying these up-to-the-minute prices, but also collecting them in the first place from the floor of the House and renting out its tape machines to outside brokers, newspapers and clubs. One of the memorialists, appearing in person, 'narrated facts within his experience with a view to show that the bucket-shops who took cover without doing any bargains against the orders they received could afford to go through the form of making prices with very short margins, even in the most speculative securities, and thereby succeeded in attracting a good deal of business which would otherwise be entrusted to members of the Stock Exchange'. The memorialists in effect wanted the ETC banished from the House, and their petition was followed up in November by what one paper called 'quite a mass meeting on the borders of the Mexican Railway market'. The ETC was defended by its managing director, Captain Davies. His main thrust to the sub-committee was that his company supplied tape facilities not to bucket-shops but to genuine brokers. Moreover, on the basis of an inquiry he had commissioned, he produced figures about the value of the business that subscribing outside brokers brought to the Stock Exchange: 'The answers were to the effect that 294 Stock Exchange men did business for and with these outsiders, and that over 53 millions of stock had been dealt in over a certain period. One outsider had 20 Stock Exchange men to do his business, another 15 . . .' Davies also argued that his antagonists were overrating the importance of the tape itself: 'It must be remembered that the universal use of the telephone provides the means of obtaining prices that outsiders never before possessed.'[2] It was a valid point, but by this time there were too many members whose standard of living had declined alarmingly and for whom the whole question of the tape had become little less than a bee in their collective bonnet.

Matters came to a head on 4 April 1894 when the sub-committee received a list of subscribers from the ETC and decided who could remain on it. Seventeen banks and financial houses were to be allowed to retain their machines, as were twenty-one newspapers; but eighty-seven outside brokers, or fronts for them, were to have their facilities removed. The ETC was hardly happy with this major drop in its income, but since it was only on sufferance that its representatives entered the House in order to collect prices, it had little alternative but to comply. Press reaction to this attempt to banish the tape was almost wholly unfavourable. Reflecting the accuracy of the Captain's analysis, the *FN* reported that, though some of the clients of the big outside brokers 'miss the familiar clicking of the instrument to whose fascinations they have long been captive', nevertheless, 'they are gradually becoming accustomed to the black board which has now replaced it', with 'the quotations being telephoned through by some agent of the outside broker'.

No one stood so boldly outside the Stock Exchange's would-be ring-fence as George Gregory, king of the outside brokers and a man of undeniable energy and lavishness. Later in 1894 he gave an interview to the *Star*, revealing that he now got his prices by phone from the Stock Exchange, before transferring them on to his personal tape machines. Or in his own, inimitable words: 'Let the Committee identify my agent, and suspend him, I will have another, I will have 20 others, within the hour. As long as there is a Stock Exchange, and as long as there is a tape supplied to members, I will have my prices. Why, there is many a member of the Exchange who is not making £250 a year. Do you see any difficulty, then, in getting all the information you want – at a price?'[3]

The territorial imperative ran deep – or, to put it less kindly, an inherent tendency on the part of a closed institution towards adopting restrictive practices. Take the memorial signed in June 1894 by thirty-two dealers in the market for brewery stocks and shares. They complained that Ricardo & Robertson, for many years past jobbers in English Railway preference shares and debenture stocks, had been circularising brokers with an offer for sale of £25,000 Ind Coope debenture stock. Frank Hurst and Thomas Kitchin attended the Committee on behalf of the objectors; Charles Robertson defended:

Mr Hurst said that the recognition of such a claim as that contended for by Messrs Ricardo & Robertson would probably lead to some inconvenience. For example, amongst the principal stocks dealt in in the Breweries market were the Guinness stocks, of which Lord Iveagh was the chief holder. Supposing something was to happen which would lead to one of those stocks suddenly changing hands, would it be open to a syndicate of Consols dealers to deal in it? If so, the Guinness market as at present existing would probably cease to exist. He would ask where would the brokers be, if there were no jobbers to make prices? . . . What the jobbers in his market wanted to know from the Committee was, how far was it permissible for a jobber to deal out of his legitimate market? . . . The object of the memorialists was not so much to complain of Messrs Ricardo & Robertson, as to elicit an expression of opinion from the Committee as to whether it was legitimate for a firm of jobbers to hold themselves out as dealers in a particular market, with liberty to deal also in the securities of a market other than that in which they have been openly and notoriously dealing . . .

Mr Robertson said that he did not pretend to confine his operations to any particular securities. He considered that as a Stock Exchange dealer he was at liberty to purchase any Stock Exchange securities which might be offered to him in any market anywhere, just as any member of the public might buy it, although his speciality was Railway Debentures and Preferences . . .

Mr Kitchin said that having regard to the principle of separate markets for separate securities, Mr Robertson's claim struck at the root of the practice of the Stock Exchange from time immemorial.

The Committee delayed its decision for a week, but then voted eighteen to one against interfering. A week later that resolution was confirmed, while a proposal that it should nevertheless declare that it did not consider the transaction 'to be in harmony with the custom and usages of the Stock Exchange' was defeated by thirteen to nine.[4] Clearly there was a gut feeling that it would indeed be preferable if jobbers stuck to their particular markets. But against that, still more powerfully, there was a realisation on the Committee's part that to attempt to enforce demarcation lines ultra-rigidly would not only open many cans of worms but also fail to take account of the fact that jobbers lived in a world where individual markets rose and fell according to larger economic circumstances. It was, one might say, a reluctant economic liberalism.

The question was not a philosophical burden for most jobbers. On 7 June, for instance, the afternoon was dominated by a tug-of-war, a member having brought in a thick cable for the purpose:

The struggle was supposed to be between the Home Railway Market and the American Market, but as a matter of fact everybody in the neighbourhood joined in promiscuously. After a tough fight, which was prolonged by the fact that one end of the cable was for about five minutes tied to an immovable form, the American Market was declared the winner. Some members waxed very indignant over the introduction of this horse-play during business hours, and described the whole thing as a trick. It was about 2 o'clock that the tug-of-war took place, and while the whole market was in confusion several brokers seized the opportunity to plant several lines of Caledonian Deferred at about $43\frac{3}{8}$, the buyers finding to their disgust, when the fooling was over, that the market had really fallen to $42\frac{7}{8}$. These irritated members suggest that the settling-room [in the basement] should be set apart by the Committee as a play-ground except on settling-days.

The key element in the success of the Yankee jobbers was that immovable force, Harry Paxton, and he may well have been to the fore in another episode a month later:

'An Anarchist in the House!' was the cry in the Stock Exchange on Thursday afternoon, when a seedy-looking individual, wearing a bowler and a red tie – symbolical of the worst passions – found his way in at the Shorter's Court door and penetrated to the very heart of the American market. With wild exclamations of ' 'Ware bombs!' and 'Down with Anarchy!' the members hustled the stranger into the street, dishevelled and gasping. The Stock Exchange was saved.

For sheer intensity of feeling, though, nothing surpassed what occurred on 2 November, in the wake of a high-minded campaign, led by Mrs Ormiston Chant, against the favourite music-hall haunt, in Leicester Square, of all right-minded members of the Stock Exchange:

> A violent demonstration was made against Mr A.L. Leon in the 'House' yesterday. Mr Leon is a member of the County Council and of its Licensing Committee, and, in these capacities, worked and voted against the renewal of the Empire Theatre licence. The jobbers in the American market – and, indeed, the jobbers generally – sympathised with the Empire, and they showed their sympathy by hooting Councillor Leon most vigorously . . .

According to another account, the members of the American market 'rose upon him in fury' and 'he fled through the Brighton market, pursued by a hooting and howling mob, and was glad to escape at last by the Consol door'. Arthur Leon himself was a major jobber in Yankees, where Leon Bros did a highly profitable arbitrage business; but this in a sense merely compounded the crime, as did the fact of the Liberal sympathies of both partners.[5] Or, put another way, moralising and Stock Exchange mores was never a combination that sat easily.

But if the American market was as rumbustious as ever – not least on Guy Fawkes Day, with fireworks let off, revels led by the incorrigible Tootie Brander, and a squib fastened to the coat-tail of an unsuspecting broker – there was no doubt that in the closing months of 1894 all eyes were increasingly turned to the South African mining market, otherwise known as the Kaffir Circus. In September, following a record gold return from the Rand in August, the *Economist* reported sceptically on 'Witwatersrand Mining Progress'. It argued that 'continued purchase by continental operators' was causing such a high level of Rand share prices, and that that level was 'too high, in view of the fact that in many cases the outcrop deposits are being rapidly exhausted'. Besides which, 'the deep-level claims have, for the most part, yet to be proved'. The mood of the market, however, was progressively more bullish over the next few weeks, partly through the educational efforts of the leading American mining engineer John Hays Hammond.

Basing himself in London during the autumn, he systematically canvassed the support of the main brokers and jobbers dealing in Kaffirs:

> After many meetings with the heads of these firms I devised a plan which helped materially to convince mining investors of the attractiveness of deep-level shares. I made diagrams which indicated clearly the number of claims being mined on the outcrop areas. I showed that the yield per claim averaged $250,000, with a profit of about $90,000.
>
> On the same diagrams, immediately below the skeleton drawings of outcrop companies, I outlined on a proportionate scale the deep-level companies. In size the latter were eight or ten times as large as the former. The diagrams not only included the estimates I had made of the cost to sink shafts to reach the reefs, but also showed the time required and the comparatively enhanced costs of mining upon the deep-level areas. These diagrams were then hung with my compliments in the offices of stockbrokers dealing in South African shares.[6]

Unblinded by science, these brokers now went to their missionary work with a zeal.

No firm or bank gained more from the ensuing boom than the struggling *FT*, for whom it meant increased circulation and increased advertising revenue, especially from publishing the prospectuses of new mining companies. When Ada Blanche the next year sang 'Golden Africa' – at the Empire in Leicester Square, of course – it could have been the theme song of the City's pink paper.[7]

Everyone was eager for a slice of the Kaffir action. The well-connected financier Sir Edgar Vincent, for example, was currently based in Constantinople as Governor of the Imperial Ottoman Bank.[8] His London manager, Robertson, was doing his bidding and wrote to him on 6 November 1894:

> I received your telegram this morning and bought immediately
>   1000 Primrose @ $5\frac{1}{4}$
>   2000 Johannesburg Consolidated Investment Co @ $1\frac{11}{16}$.
> I took the liberty to exceed your limit of 157 as there were strong buying of these Investment shares last night and today.
> I hear a good deal in favour of the Deep Level properties generally, particularly of
>   Randt Mines
>   Geldenhuis Deep
>   Consolidated Deep.
> Of course Randt Mines are between 16 & 17 & therefore at a high price. Still the prevailing view is they will go much higher.

I read all the literature about these mining properties and certainly it looks as if large profits will be made out of them.

Three days later Robertson was writing again, to tell him that he had executed his order to buy a further 5,000 South African gold-mining shares, mostly Johannesburg Consolidated and New Primrose. Robertson happened to have a mining engineer friend in Johannesburg, so his chief no doubt felt himself handily placed on the inside track.[9]

By mid-November a boomlet was becoming a boom. 'I hear that one firm of brokers in the Kaffir market have been so busy of late,' the *FN*'s House correspondent noted on Saturday the 17th, 'that they have had to employ two staffs of clerks, one working all day and the other all night. In the case of another firm, I know that the clerks were kept at work all Tuesday night, and up to five o'clock on Wednesday morning, Warnford-court, where the offices of the principal dealers are situated, being illuminated from dusk till sunrise.' That particular nocturnal marathon was occasioned by the fortnightly settlement, and on the 24th the *Economist* wrote sternly of 'The Disabilities of the "Kaffir" Market', wanting to know 'how it is that the House, to which "Kaffirs" have brought so large an influx of business, at a time, too, when it was greatly needed, does nothing to facilitate transactions in South African securities'. The paper was disturbed on account of both investors and members:

> We are quite unable to understand . . . why the Stock Exchange Committee refuses to recognise, or rather ignores, Kaffir securities. It is true that they have not been issued publicly in the way which it approves; but then just the same may be said of many other securities – as, for example, many Foreign Government securities and most American railway shares, &c – which enjoy the privilege of a quotation in the 'Official List' and all that is thereby implied . . . The quotations in the so-called 'Official List', we know, are not worth much in most cases; but the 'markings' of business done do possess a positive value, and perhaps in no department would they count for more than in the 'Kaffir Circus', which abounds in dark corners, devious ways, and doubtful transactions . . . As they are not officially recognised, South African securities are not admitted to the Stock Exchange Clearing House, and hence an enormous amount of work is entailed in the 'making-up', or 'passing of names', at each settlement . . .

The chances are that the reason for the Committee's aloofness lay precisely in the 'dark corners' and 'devious ways'. In similar vein, the *FN*'s House correspondent had referred a few months earlier to how 'the Kaffir Circus appears to be composed of such heterogeneous elements that ordinary English rules do not seem to apply to it'.[10] In short, there were influential elements – in the Stock Exchange itself, in the City at large – that would have been perfectly happy to exist without the whole vulgar and noisy South African roadshow, a phenomenon that in their eyes exemplified cosmopolitan finance at its very worst.

The week beginning 26 November was tumultuous, focusing on the fortnightly settlement, when once again 'the clerical staffs of the principal brokers were at work all Tuesday night, and there was a perfect pandemonium in the checking room on ticket-day, the clerks fairly climbing over each other in their rush to get their business over'. A mass migration was also under way on the floor of the House, reaching its apotheosis on Thursday the 29th:

> The wail of 'Ichabod! Ichabod!' passed over the American market, when it was found that several of the leading dealers had girded up their loins and departed for the Kaffir Land of Promise . . . Tom Nickalls has gone, with his brother H.P., and Mr Paxton has gone with Mr Romaine in joint-partnership. Tom Nickalls seemed to revel in the excitement of the Mining market, which reminded him of old times; but presently he was found seated again in the American department. His fellow-members gathered round him and cheerfully chanted, 'Tommy's Come Marching Home Again, Hurrah!' but it transpired that he had returned only for a breath of fresh air and a few minutes' relaxation on a seat. It is reported that his parting remarks were: 'Well, boys, I've discovered how to lose £50 every quarter of an hour; but I've got a thundering book now that will bother 'em!' Mr Paxton's introduction to the Kaffir market was very ceremonious, members forming a double line the whole length of the House from the Yankee to the Kaffir markets, along which he had to pass; but when he got there he was apparently mistaken for a football. When Tom Nickalls had been half-an-hour dealing in the Mining market he saw 'Packy' approaching, and exclaimed bitterly: 'I wish these new jobbers would not keep coming to our market!'

The Kaffir boom was officially started; and the joke going the rounds was that the big white bear at London Zoo, whose death had recently been announced, had died by his own paw.[11]

CHAPTER EIGHT

Frightfully Busy

It makes one hot even now on a cold day to think of the time when, as a clerk, one tore off coat, waistcoat, collar and tie in order to run the faster in the Settling Room beneath the Stock Exchange, 'passing names' in connection with that mad gamble. A rugby football scrum was child's play to the continual struggles; and, after the most violent excitement had subsided, there were always fights to be settled before one went upstairs to work the whole night through.

That was how, almost twenty years later, the broker-cum-journalist Walter Landells recalled the Kaffir boom of late 1894 to late 1895; and indeed, over the years the boom became one of those phases of City history that almost ranked with the South Sea Bubble in terms of mythological status. It was a boom that, among many other things, highlighted the way in which the City of London was, by the late nineteenth century, the unique financial and commercial global centre.[1] The stock market may have had inadequate settlement procedures for Kaffir shares, but much more important was the fact that it offered ready marketability in the leading mines, competitive facilities for enabling speculators to carry over accounts from one fortnight to another, and a system of arbitrage with other financial centres (most notably Paris when it came to Kaffirs) that made London the hub of a truly international securities market. Behind the stock market stood the London money market, lending short-term in large sums to the leading jobbers and brokers engaged in the boom. The City's many syndicates and investment groups (such as Sir Edgar Vincent's Eastern Investment Co) were also borrowing freely. These had been set up to exploit the boom, sometimes by floating companies but mainly by buying large blocks of shares on a rising market and hoping to unload them shortly before that market peaked. In terms of information flows, varying from the fairly reliable to the ultra-unreliable, not only were most of the gold-mining companies themselves controlled from London, but also based in the City were the leading firms of mining engineers as well as a rapidly expanding financial press; and finally, in terms of what became of the gold itself, it is easy to overlook the fact, amidst the glamour of the Randlords and their machinations, that London was the world's leading bullion market, besides providing refining facilities not available in the Transvaal until well into the twentieth century. The Kaffir boom could not have happened without a marked increase in the value of gold production on the Rand itself, from £5.18m in 1893 to £7.84m by 1895; but London was ready and, for the most part, willing.

It has been estimated that the net British purchase of Rand shares during the boom was some £40m, and the prevailing mood that inevitably accompanied such a figure was nicely caught in October 1895 itself by the financial journalist S.F. Van Oss: 'In clubs and trains, in drawing-rooms and boudoirs, people are discussing "Rands" and "Modders"; even tradesmen and old ladies have taken to studying the *Mining Manual*, the rules of the Stock Exchange, and the highways and byways of stockbroking . . . In short, we are in the midst of one of those eras of feverish speculative activity.' Many of the securities most actively dealt in were of a low denomination, thus appealing to a new, less wealthy type of punter; staffs of Stock Exchange firms often doubled in size during the boom; and quite a few partners did extremely well for themselves, such as Foster & Braithwaite's R.H. Savory, acquiring a handsome property at Chertsey in Surrey. Inside the Stock Exchange itself, the events of this tumultuous year, directly mirrored in the proliferating numbers of the Kaffir Circus, made a profound impact. Hubert Meredith – who did not enter the House until 1906, but clearly talked to a lot of older members before writing his book in 1931 about Stock Exchange history – specifically attributed changes in market manners to the boom of 1895. Prior to that date, the House 'adhered strictly to old-fashioned etiquette', by which 'each broker dealt with a particular firm of jobbers in each market', so that 'if a broker came into a market and found his particular jobber absent, one of the other jobbers in the market would endeavour to find the missing dealer'. This, according to Meredith, all changed in 1895 with 'an influx of new members who had no old traditions behind them'. In fact, it is difficult to be sure who these Kaffir jobbers were: many of course were migrants from the American market, but some at least seem to have been freshly admitted naturalised Germans, prompting the *City Times* to note sullenly in February 1895 that a phrase like 'What for price you make für Croesus?' was becoming typical in the Kaffir market; while according to the *Evening News* a few weeks later, the dominant firms in that market were Hyams Bros (not long after,

changing their name to Higham), Beazley & Mitchell, Adolph Hirsch
& Co, and Pollack & Bamberger. As for the broking firms that
specialised in Kaffirs, none was more powerful, nor probably made
more money, than L. Hirsch & Co. 'It was connected with various
Transvaal mines as London Agent,' a knowledgeable merchant banker
recalled in 1911, 'but the great bulk of the riches of the firm came from
marketing Kaffir shares in Paris through the instrumentality of Baron
de Gunzberg.' Most merchant banks more or less eschewed the Kaffir
boom – with, it must be said, the notable exception of Rothschilds –
but among the brokers now dealing proactively in Kaffirs was Henry
Ansbacher of Spielmann, Ansbacher & Co, a fledgling firm quickly
acquiring a grasp of the angles.[2]

One place and one man epitomised the boom. The place was a new
'club for financial men' in Angel Court, off Throgmorton Street.
Formally called the City Athenaeum, it was known to everyone as the
Thieves' Kitchen, and its proprietor was Ernest Wells, hoarse-voiced,
immaculately dressed and nicknamed 'Swears'. 'In the interval after
lunch and from the closing of the "House" onwards until it was time
to go West for dinner, the "Club" would be noisy with the rattle of
dominoes . . . And what sums used to pass across the domino tables at
the end of the game!' So wrote the *FN* many years later, adding that
brokers' clerks would run to and fro executing the commissions of
their masters sitting in the Kitchen. An early member of the club, but
never of the Stock Exchange, was Barney Barnato, perhaps *the* man of
1895, whose visiting card was overprinted with the convivial statement, 'I'll stand any man a drink, but I won't lend him a fiver.' His life
was already the stuff of legends: born Barnett Isaacs in the East End in
1852, and completely uneducated, he had made his fortune on the
diamond fields of Kimberley, where quick wits counted for everything,
breeding nothing. Now, like the other diamond magnates, he was
concentrating mainly on gold mines, and at this stage his chief financial vehicle was Johannesburg Consolidated Investment, which in the
twelve months up to February 1895 issued 623,000 shares.[3] Unlike Beit and Wernher, he was not a serious businessman committed
to the long-run development of South African gold mining; instead,
with his ready tongue and ability to move share prices, he acquired
during the course of the boom a strong Stock Exchange following,
which believed with some justification that if Barney flourished in his
shameless booming of selected stocks then there would be lucrative
pickings for them too. Against that, what did it matter if he dropped
his h's?

Golden Years

*

The *FN* on 8 December 1894, just over a week after Tom Nickalls and Harry Paxton had made their momentous switch from Yankees to Kaffirs, assessed the Circus's mood:

> The old jobbers in the Kaffir market are not at all anxious to do business on the eve of the holidays, and are rather disposed to take a rest with even books. Not so the newcomers in the market. These ardent spirits are as keen as ever to do bargains, and several of them have done very well during the week, the frequent fluctuations in De Beers, Jumpers, Rands, and a few other specialities having afforded them excellent opportunities for quick turns. There is still a good deal of jealousy between the newcomers and the old brigade; but this will not last. There is likely to be business enough for everybody before long . . .

True enough, and on Monday the 17th, after the day's dealings, there was a strong Kaffir presence up west:

> Mr Leo Harward's Sports Dinner was a very interesting and enjoyable event, and reflected great credit on the Savoy Hotel and its excellent *chef*. The company numbered 45, including Messrs Concannon, 'Charlie' Marks, McKenna, Barnato, Sharpe, and, by no means least, Mr Tom Honey, in whose honour the now famous song of 'Honey, my Honey' was originally written. Full justice was done to the Château Talbot and the magnums of Moët and Chandon, and some very straight tips were given and some heavy wagers were laid on the Pritchard fight . . .

There was no slacking over the following week, and on Christmas Eve itself, reported the *Economist*, 'although the arrangements in connection with the settlement were in full swing, an excited crowd of dealers and brokers blocked the way in Throgmorton Street long after the House had closed, bidding for shares for the new account'. It proved to be a hectic settlement, with the Stock Exchange's clearing house working, with a staff of forty, right through Christmas Day to complete its business. Still, back office problems did not impinge all that much on the actual Kaffir jobbers, operating on the front line, and on the 27th another six dealers left the American market – to 'go over to the majority', in the words of one less than gruntled observer.[4]

Then came 1895, a golden year, or so it seemed for much of the time. '*On dit*,' noted the *FN* on 12 January, 'that Mr. B.I. Barnato has bought the lease of Lord Dudley's house in Park-lane, and will make his future home there, close to the site of Mr Beit's new residence.' The following week saw the mid-January settlement, described by a *Statist* reporter who had been 'invited to personally witness some of the discomforts of a busy broker's office':

> With difficulty could we force our way into the outer section of the office, which was besieged with a crowd of clerks, busy on the evening of Tuesday in endeavouring to trace tickets to reach an eventual deliverer of shares. A large staff of the firm's clerks in the interior of the office were trying to reduce chaos to order by sorting a multitude of tickets, preparing transfers for the signature of vendors, and usual clerical work of a routine character. All hands were physically worn out . . .

Clearly to blame for this state of affairs was the Stock Exchange Committee, 'mostly composed of gentlemen who, in the vernacular, have "made their pile", are advanced in years, and have notions of their own that operations in anything outside securities of a high and dry character ought rather to be impeded than assisted'. A week later, however, the same paper recorded with satisfaction that the clearing house was at last opening its doors to some of the leading South African securities, including Buffelsdoorn, Glencairn, Johannesburg, Consolidated Investment, Langlaagte, May Consolidated, Modderfontein and Randfontein shares; but in the same issue, the *Statist* warned its readers against putting their all into new and untried gold mines, asserting that 'when one sees the large dealings going on in African Consolidated Land, Southern Geldenhuis, Graskop, Lower Roodeport, Ottos Kopje, and the like, one is afraid the public later on will have cause to regret their investment'. Did any of this worry Packy? Certainly not on 1 February, when 'a foreigner of strange appearance made his way into the "House" and sat down in the Spanish market, apparently much interested in the proceedings'. Whereupon, 'by the combined efforts of the waiters and Mr Paxton, he was forcibly removed, with some slight detriment to his personal appearance, but otherwise uninjured'.[5]

By the middle of March, with Kaffir prices still rising inexorably, Barney Barnato was back from a brief holiday in Monte Carlo – a great City favourite at that time of year – and was personally directing operations during after-hours dealings in Throgmorton Street. 'Was there ever a spectacle illustrating the race for gold more drastically than the seething, shouting, maddened crowd in the South African street market? And how long can this mad boom last? We feel inclined to say just as long as our French neighbours continue to send buying orders.'[6] Almost certainly there was much truth in this analysis by the

Citizen, emphasising the continental dimension to the Kaffir boom. But wherever buying orders were coming from, come they did in phenomenal quantities, and the week beginning 18 March proved to be one of the more remarkable in the Stock Exchange's history. It began late on the Tuesday afternoon, when four members were arrested in Throgmorton Street during after-hours dealings, taken to the police station in Moor Lane, and charged with obstruction, disorderly conduct and resisting the police. Many other members gathered at the police station to protest, led by Harry Paxton, towering head and shoulders above everyone else. The following morning, at the Guildhall Police Court, one member was fined £10, another £5, and Mr Alderman Phillips 'said it was quite clear to him that the police were quite right in endeavouring to clear this thoroughfare'. Reaction that Wednesday was swift:

> The accusations brought by the police against the Kaffir crowd caused bitter feeling in the House, and the word was passed around to 'turn out' in force after four o'clock. Throgmorton Street at a quarter past four was simply impassable, although about thirty constables and three inspectors were on duty . . . Several times a rush was made by the crowd, carrying constables and inspectors off their feet. At about twenty minutes past four several empty cabs passed along, but the drivers refused to take fares. Mr Paxton, however, took possession of one, and, with Mr Leo Harward, drove up and down Throgmorton Street, to the great delight of the crowd, who cheered vociferously. On the second return of the vehicle an inspector boarded it, but withdrew when Mr Paxton ordered him off. It was not until 6.30 that Throgmorton Street resumed its ordinary aspect. No arrests were made.

The next morning, at a regular meeting of the Stock Exchange Committee, attention was drawn to these disturbances; but, 'after discussion, further consideration of the matter was deferred'.

In fact, the climax was at hand, for at five o'clock that Thursday afternoon the hugely popular Packy found himself under arrest. The police took him away with difficulty, through a crowd of turbulent dealers, as their comrade 'courteously acknowledged the salutations by raising his hat'. Charged with disorderly conduct, he was released after an hour or so. The next morning the outsize jobber appeared before Mr Alderman Bell at the Guildhall Police Court, again packed with members. Inspector Stark explained the circumstances of the arrest:

> There was a large crowd of about 600 or 700. The crowd was generally disorderly; they were shouting, hooting, and hissing the police. It was a

narrow thoroughfare, with scarcely room for two lines of vehicles. It was impossible to pass through one side of the street. Witness saw Paxton and a number of other members of the Stock Exchange round him. He was in the middle of the thoroughfare. Just then some vans and empty cabs came through. Paxton shouted out at the top of his voice, 'Who pays for those cabs?' He repeated that several times. Then there was cheering by the crowd, and witness requested Paxton to desist from shouting and causing the disorder.

The Clerk: What did you say?

Witness: I said, 'Stop this, and pass along, please.' Paxton then said, 'You are paying for these cabs.' He was very excited, and I said, 'I shall take you into custody for being disorderly.' There was a great rush, and he was carried away from me about two yards. Superintendent Mackenzie came up, and he took hold of Paxton, who kicked him on the leg . . .

More edifying evidence followed before Bell summed up. He declared that Paxton and his fellow-members had turned Throgmorton Street 'into a bear garden', that they 'had no more right to the place than any other person in London', and that the police must be upheld. He declined, however, to punish Paxton, and the defendant 'left the court in the company of his friends, who, on getting outside, cheered heartily'.

Later that day the Stock Exchange Committee voted by twelve to four 'to caution members against countenancing by their presence the scandalous disturbances which take place in Throgmorton Street after the closing of the House'. Writing to his correspondent in Melbourne, the merchant banker Harry Gibbs retailed the episode, accused the police of having been 'very rough', and added that Paxton had been described to him as 'an enormous man with a face like an elephant'.

Over the next few months, after-hours dealings in Kaffirs did continue, but there were no more outright confrontations; and soon the events of March 1895 became fixed in the collective memory as the Battle of Throgmorton Street. A last word on them goes to the protagonist himself and one of the thin blue line, in an exchange related by Charles Duguid in his history of the Stock Exchange published in 1901: 'It is told of Mr Paxton, who frequently refers jocularly to his experiences at the police court, that quite recently he playfully pushed his huge form against a policeman, saying, "Out of the way, I'm bigger than you." "Yes, sir," was the constable's respectful, ready reply, "I know you are. I saw you measured, you know, sir!"'[7]

*

Although never an occasion for pitched battles, the bimetallist issue was something that stubbornly refused to go away. In May 1894 the bimetallist-minded International Monetary Conference was held at the Mansion House and addressed sympathetically by Arthur Balfour, who expressed the view that City opinion was 'beginning to incline in their favour'. Soon afterwards, when the President of the London Chamber of Commerce, Sir Albert Rollit, used the LCC's annual meeting to refer to the bimetallist movement as an attempt to replace the gold standard by 'a currency of cowries and brass farthings', he was reprimanded by an 'aggrieved' East India and China trade section and compelled to state that he had been speaking in a personal capacity. By November the President of the Institute of Bankers, Thomas Bolitho, was calling, in his inaugural address, on fellow-monometallists to stand and be counted: 'A large number of persons, some of them of undoubted standing in this city (perhaps influenced by a feeling of despair), have become converts to the bimetallic faith. This can hardly be a satisfactory state of things to those of us who still adhere to monometallism, and it might be wise to take some steps to remedy it.'[8]

The issue was also returning to the political agenda, and in January 1895 Chamberlain sounded out Goschen as to whether the Conservatives might commit themselves to proposing a new bimetallist conference, presumably comparable to the one at Brussels. Goschen, however, replied that the existence in the City of a 'fanatical' monometallic clique – backed by the London press, including the *Economist* and the *Statist* – meant that bimetallism was not a viable electoral issue. Still, perhaps the City *was* shifting. 'I dined last night at Alfred Rothschild's,' noted Hamilton on 14 February, and those present included 'Harry Chaplin [a prominent Tory politician], who declared that he should win on bimetallism in 5 years' time. He felt sure he had now Natty Rothschild on his side, who has long been wobbling. The brothers – Alfred & Leo – did not deny it . . .' On St Valentine's Day itself, there was a strong Stock Exchange presence for the first night of Oscar Wilde's *The Importance of Being Earnest*. Did City ears cock when they heard Miss Prism's advice? 'Cecily, you will read your Political Economy in my absence. The chapter on the Fall of the Rupee you may omit. It is somewhat too sensational. Even these metallic problems have their melodramatic side.' Or perhaps Capel Court's finest agreed with Cecily: 'Horrid Political Economy!'[9]

Early in April the controversy began to come to the boil. Addressing the annual meeting of the Bimetallic League, held on the 3rd at the

Mansion House before 'a large attendance of members and friends', Balfour sought to reassure the City that bimetallism in no way threatened its prosperity:

> London's financial supremacy depended upon three facts: – First, our insular position as a nation rendering us less liable to risks of war than other less favoured countries; (2) through many generations the bankers of this City had proved themselves men whose credit could be relied upon; and (3) the fact that England was the greatest manufacturing country in the world. Not one of these facts was endangered. London, as the financial centre of the world, must gain, rather than lose, by anything that placed our currency upon a sounder basis than at present. (*Applause.*)

Two days later, at Glyn Mills at 67 Lombard Street, Bertram Currie assembled over twenty leading lights, mostly from the City, in order to form what became known as the Gold Standard Defence Association. They included Bank of England directors, such as those close friends Everard Hambro and Hugh Colin Smith; merchant bankers like Daniel Meinertzhagen of Huths, Henry Tiarks of Schröders, and Herman Kleinwort; and clearing bankers like Francis Bevan of Barclays and R.B. Wade of the National Provincial.[10]

On 20 May the GSDA presented its monometallic memorial to the Chancellor of the Exchequer, still Harcourt in what were the dying days of the Liberal government.[11] Merchant banks to sign up included Brown Shipley, Frühling & Goschen, Hambros, Huths, Kleinworts, Robert Benson, Raphaels and Schröders. Notable absentees were Barings, Morgans and Rothschilds. A few days earlier Natty had sent a decidedly disingenuous reply to Currie's request, stating that he did not propose to sign on the grounds that 'the movement abroad in favour of bimetallism appears to have quite died out now'. Currie himself lamented the fact that 'there are so few Bank of England signatories'. Both the clearers and the discount houses were, however, very well represented on the memorial. Two days after presenting it, Currie gave a full-scale speech at the London Institution in Finsbury Circus. He played down the current commercial depression as very different from the mid-century disasters he had known as a young man in the City; asserted as usual that an international agreement on silver 'belongs to the region of dreams and not of realities'; described his fellow-adherents to monometallism as 'considerable in numbers and not wholly unprovided with the world's goods'; and concluded by cautioning Balfour and his party, likely to be in power very soon, not to tamper with the gold standard:

The benefits to be derived from such a course are speculative and imaginary, while the possible dangers are real and palpable, sufficient to appal the stoutest heart and shake the nervous and disturb the slumbers of the most solvent trader in the City of London.

It was no surprise when Harcourt on the 27th replied to Currie in the most approbatory terms: 'I concur entirely in the opinion expressed in your Address that the experience of well nigh a century has proved that our present system of Currency is suited to the wants of this great Commercial Country and that to depart from it would be disastrous to the trade and credit of the United Kingdom.'[12]

Sir William was still in office on 22 June to field yet another missive from Henry Hucks Gibbs: 'Here you have our counterblast. I wonder if you will find time to read it!' The enclosed bimetallic memorial included a typically Gibbsian passage:

We think, with great respect, that in view of general and widespread depression in the Textile, the Coal, the Iron, the Shipping, and other great industries in the Kingdom, with a Parliamentary Committee sitting even now to inquire into the condition of the Unemployed; and with Agriculture grievously affected, and in many districts well nigh ruined, it may be well for the Memorialists [i.e. of both persuasions] to remember that it is upon the welfare of her Commerce and her Industries, even more than on her banking interests, that the prosperity of a country, and its people, ultimately depends.

Gibbs also emphasised that in the list of bimetallism's supporters were 'included not only Merchants and Bankers in the City of London, but representatives of nearly every Industry in the Country, besides well known leaders of the Working Classes . . .'[13] Undoubtedly there were some leading City figures and institutions among the memorial's signatories: Sir Samuel Montagu; the Hongkong and Shanghai Banking Corporation; two partners of David Sassoon & Co; Baron Émile d'Erlanger; Hugh Matheson and William Keswick of Mathesons; Lidderdale; Edward Howley Palmer, another former governor; the leading stockbroker Andrew Hichens; and, perhaps attracted by the 'bi' aspect, Sir Horace Farquhar. Even so, not only was there a significantly 'eastern' weighting, but also there was not quite the same depth of solid City names as on the rival list – names such as Smith, Payne & Smiths, Alexanders and Robarts, Lubbock, as well as most of the leading merchant banks below the big two. Rothschilds and Barings (and indeed Morgans) continued to stay aloof from memorialising, though Thomas Baring did sign for the bimetallists in an individual capacity. All in all, despite his obvious prejudice in the matter, Harcourt's assertion to Currie that the monometallist memorial bore 'names amongst the most weighty which could be found to represent the judgement of the Merchants and Bankers of the City of London' was broadly correct – though perhaps one should add that it was a judgement that was coming to place greater weight on the financial than the commercial.[14]

Crucially, and for all his personal bimetallist sympathies, Salisbury appointed Sir Michael Hicks Beach, a diehard monometallist, as his new Chancellor. By November 1895, the Institute of Bankers' new President, the Hon Dudley Ryder of Coutts in the Strand, was able to claim that the monetary question had receded since 'this time last year'. He referred specifically to 'the greatly increased production of gold' as well as the government's ultimate unwillingness to move in a bimetallist direction, whatever the views of some individual ministers. The following March the highly able Henry Raphael wrote in confident vein to the secretary of the GSDA: 'Bimetallism is only a form of discontent, when trade is bad & the country not prosperous. The reverse being now the case, I have for months past not been anxious about the excited activity of our adversaries . . .' Practical City man had, it seemed, triumphed completely. Or, as another merchant banker, Robert Benson, later in 1896 assured the Oxford economist Edwin Cannan, the GSDA had 'behind it $\frac{9}{10}$ths of the firms whose acceptances facilitate the trade of the world'. And he added, with an assurance that it would have needed a Cambridge economist to dent: 'There are no economic phenomena with which these men are not conversant.'[15]

*

Kaffirs were not the only gold-mining shares to flourish during 1895: there were also Westralians, following the discovery of gold at Coolgardie in 1892 and at Kalgoorlie in 1893, both in Western Australia.[16] A series of scams characterised the early financial history of Westralian gold mining, beginning with the outrageous episode of 'Fingall's Folly'.[17] The Eleventh Earl of Fingall was an impecunious Irish peer who on a trip to Australia in 1894 teamed up with an opportunist financier called T. Hewitt Myring; together they acquired the Londonderry reef twelve miles south of Coolgardie. Some phenomenally rich quartz from a surface pocket of the reef was sent over to England to be publicly exhibited, and amidst much enthusiasm the Londonderry

Gold Mining Company was floated in London at a massively capitalised – the *FT* said overcapitalised – £700,000. That was in November 1894, and two months later shareholders were told that the mine was currently cemented and sealed, but would soon begin operations. Perhaps the shareholders should have been on their guard, since the Chairman was Colonel North, the notorious 'Nitrate King' at his height in the late 1880s, but it seems they were not. The first week of April 1895 proved traumatic for anyone who did put his trust in the Colonel. On Monday the 1st, according to the *FT*'s daily account of dealings in the Mining market, Londonderrys were 'slightly easier at $1\frac{11}{16}$ '. On Tuesday the shares slumped, down to 1 before closing at $1\frac{1}{16}$. 'Various rumours were rife as to the cause of the decline. It was stated that there had been a disagreement among members of the pool recently formed to support the market, and that it had resulted in selling from New Court. A difficulty as to the Paris quotation was also talked about.' Londonderrys hardened slightly on Wednesday, closing at $1\frac{1}{4}$. 'There are still various rumours as to the cause of the slump, but nothing authentic has transpired.' On Thursday the shares were 'distinctly flat at $1\frac{1}{16}$', before the denouement arrived on Friday:

> The further slump in Londonderrys has today been the sensation of the market. The shares were heavily offered as soon as business commenced, and the price steadily declined to $\frac{9}{16}$. The cable from Lord Fingall, appearing in the early editions of the evening papers, was soon ascertained to be the cause of this startling movement . . . The price closed $\frac{11}{16} - \frac{3}{4}$ The grounds for the dissatisfaction which led to the disruption among the inner circle, two days ago, and consequent sales attributed to New Court, are now evident.

Fingall's telegram was a miniature masterpiece:

> Regret in the extreme have to inform you that rich chutes of ore opened very bad indeed. Does not appear to be practically anything important left. Continuing exploration work, but the aspect of affairs is very discouraging; please telegraph at once your wishes.

The telegram was dated Coolgardie, 1 April, 5.15 pm. It must have reached London by Tuesday at the latest – and yet the Londonderry board did not formally meet to consider it until Thursday afternoon – and in turn did not release it to the press until Friday morning. North had in fact already been unloading shares during March, especially in Paris, but clearly there were more left to unload coming into April. Not surprisingly, the delay in the telegram's publication gave rise to considerable ill-feeling; as the *FT* put it in a leader on the Saturday, 'between Monday and yesterday we regret to say that there has been a sufficient amount of lying committed by those connected with the mine to justify London being punished by the same fate as that which destroyed Sodom and Gomorrah'.[18] In all, it had been a spectacular example of dirty work at the crossroads. Nevertheless, hope sprang eternal, and later that month a big strike at Kalgoorlie meant that Westralians would be ready to take up the speculative slack should the Kaffir boom falter.

For the moment, there were no signs of this. A fairly typical day in the Circus was 22 April, and something of the flavour of the boom, ever onwards and upwards, comes through in the daily report on the Mining market that the outside brokers J.V. Turner, Lupton & Co, of 5 Copthall Buildings, inserted in the financial press as an advertisement for its services:

> There was every reason to justify the very general belief that yesterday, besides being the first day of the week, and also the day before the carry-over, would consequently be one of quietude. In times such as these, however, when the markets are beyond the control of the professional element, all such calculations have a knack of being upset, and yesterday was a case in point. Dealings in Kaffirs were on an extensive scale, the chief feature being some of the deep-level mines . . . Nourse Deep advanced $\frac{3}{4}$, to 6d. Goldfields Deep were up $\frac{1}{2}$, to $6\frac{11}{16}$. Roedepoort Deep improved fully $\frac{9}{16}$, to $4\frac{5}{8}$, while other upward movements included a gain of 1 in Heriot, to $10\frac{7}{8}$. Modders rose $\frac{1}{4}$, to $14\frac{1}{4}$, while this gain covered the movement in Crown Reef to $10\frac{3}{8}$, and Consolidated Deep to $5\frac{7}{8}$ . . .

Dealings continued after hours 'in the Street', where according to the *FT* 'the efforts to deal produced a hideous Babel, the excitement being such that it was difficult for two parties interested in the same share to get in contact'. Even the experienced Rothschilds were impressed, the three brothers telling Loulou Harcourt the next day, at lunch in New Court, that 'the quantity of genuine business being done in the S. African Gold Mining Market is now enormous'.[19]

George Cawston was one member definitely not missing out. His new offices in Warnford Court were described by the *FN* early in May as 'very much up to date, being furnished with a direct telephone to Paris for the convenience of the continental operators in Kaffirs, and fitted up on a scale of convenience and luxury quite unrivalled'. Soon afterwards, on 9 May – following a fortnightly settlement that had revealed a considerable bull account still in existence, with high carry-over rates being charged in order to shake out the weaker operators and so-called 'ragged brigade' – there was held an important social occasion, also recorded by the *FN*:

> The farewell dinner to Mr B.I. Barnato, at the Criterion on Thursday evening, was a very pleasant and enjoyable affair. Over 200 sat down to table under the presidency of the Lord Mayor, who was in excellent form, and proposed the health of the guest of the evening in his most felicitous style. Mr Barnato responded in a very humorous speech, largely autobiographical; and the rest of the evening was devoted to music and tips, the chief item in the musical programme being the song of the Colorado millionaire from 'The Shop Girl', the appropriateness of which was at once recognised.

Sir Joseph Renals had been a controversial, only narrowly elected choice as Lord Mayor the previous autumn, on account of his reputedly close connections with various companies; but he had a happy turn of phrase, paying the compliment to Barnato that 'whether appearing as of old, on the dramatic stage, or in the latest field of finance, he remained the same old comrade still'. Barney himself, after amusing anecdotes about early days of diamond mining and the Rand, was in expansive mood:

> The credit of the Cape was now absolutely next to that of Consols, and South Africa was undoubtedly the country of the future . . . The gold-mining industries he was personally responsible for represented over £20m, and in many of these concerns he had returned the shareholders all their capital. He was proud to say that he had never issued a prospectus, so that he was pleased to find that so much confidence existed in his name alone. (*Cheers.*)[20]

The great man was off to South Africa, and among those present in Piccadilly to cheer him on his way was the elephantine Packy.

In this buoyant climate, Loulou Harcourt spent some time in the City, fixing things up first for a friend, then himself, and in the process obtaining some juicy gossip:

> 23 *April*. I lunched in New Court with Natty, Walter [Natty's eldest son], Leo and Alfred Rothschild . . . I arranged with Leo to get a clerkship in a Stockbroker's office for Jack Bradburne.
> 30 *April*. Went to see Roger Eykyn [a leading stockbroker] in the City

this morning as to the investment of £12,000 which Chex has given me in lieu of part of my allowance . . . I arranged to put £6,000 of it in L & SW Ry ordinary Stock to qualify me for a Directorship and Eykyn is to draw up a scheme for the investment of the other £6,000. He told me he could get me a directorship of the L & NW Ry any day I liked but I said I thought I would wait for the *South* Western which would on the whole suit me better.

14 May. Went to see R. Eykyn in the City about L & NW and L & SW Ry directorships for myself – both of which he thinks I have a fair chance of obtaining. He showed me a sale note of 400 Johnnies shares [a Barnato stock] of Rosebery's who he tells me has been gambling tremendously lately in stocks, S African mines etc and lost a *great deal* of money. This may account for some of the Insomnia.

5 June. Went to see Roger Eykyn at his office in the City about the P & O directorship which he thinks I can get. He has seen Sir T. Sutherland who is favourable . . .[21]

The sequence is an instructive insight into how things got done, and Eykyn was clearly one of those stockbrokers who made it his business to be on nodding terms with everybody who was anybody.

May saw a temporary reaction in Kaffirs, but by June the boom was back in full swing; on the 15th of that month Julius Wernher complained to Eckstein & Co (the famed 'Corner House' in Johannesburg, with which Wernher Beit was in highly effective partnership) that the Kaffir market as a whole had become 'so big and so cosmopolitan that it becomes more hopeless than ever to prophesy'. To return to the City became the aim of many who had been compelled to leave it during the dull years earlier in the decade, and on 8 July the Stock Exchange Committee considered a rather poignant application for readmission from one George Gray:

> I first came to the Stock Exchange as clerk to my father and uncle in 1851, was admitted a member in 1863, and continued one till last year, when in consequence of business I resigned, in order to make an application to the Benevolent Fund for assistance to go to Canada, where it was represented to me I could make a living by photography. I was grievously disappointed when I got there. I tried to get employment otherwise, but found so many younger men looking for situations that there was no chance for me. Having heard that business had sprung up again here, I returned home on 5 June and believe if I can be reinstated in the Stock Exchange I shall be better able to get a position as clerk than if I had not the entry to the House.

The Committee, however, found itself unable to entertain Gray's application. It was a minor episode that, inevitably, made little or no impact amidst the general euphoria – a euphoria summed up by a no-literary-bars-held paragraph on 'The Boom from the Street' that appeared on 13 July in a publication called, naturally, *South Africa*:

Your City man is nothing if not natty; his tall silk hat is always so brilliantly glossy that in time of need it might well be used as a mirror, and life is full of dust and ashes in his eyes if he has not a sweet flower as a button-hole. As a rule he walks along smartly enough and with a purposeful air; but in a time of boom he rushes. His voice loses its wonted sweetness and soft modulation, and instead of the sober stillness of the City the voice of the jobber is heard in the street, the glossy hat is oftentimes forgot in the excitement of rushing out to buy the latest tip, or to learn what new developments have taken place. The ordinary steady stream of business-men becomes a very flood, and the Babel of voices rises higher and higher. Every here and there one sees little knots of men, chatting most eagerly together, when, perhaps, they are joined by one who, with 'becks and nods and wreathed smiles', holds forth about his pet speculation, whether it be some Transvaal land, a new Rhodesian flotation, some well-established mine on the Rand, or some other mine that parodies a well-known name of which he carries the latest information in his pocket. Anon the street grows fuller till the pavements overflow into the roadway, and men work eagerly with book and pencil. Now the names of various mines are bandied about the street, and men shoulder and jostle one another in their eagerness to join the fray. And all the while the sun is blazing down upon them; the thermometer is standing at over eighty in the shade, and still the crowd increases . . . All want to be in the swim. Every day brings fresh tidings of fresh developments and new strikes, of projected flotations. The Rand, which was a bare patch of veld, is now a flourishing city, giving up, at the call of pick and dynamite, 200,000 ozs of gold from Dame Nature's choicest treasure-house. Such are the links that bind the farthest corners of the world. More gold is found in Africa, and Throgmorton Street is filled with frantic crowds of jobbers, and the Kaffir Circus is turned upside down; while in every village of the kingdom bright eyes look eagerly for the post that brings the golden-clad *South Africa* to tell them of the profits they may make, if they will but note the many good things that are about during the progress of the boom.

Soon afterwards the Tories returned to power, and the Stock Exchange's euphoria was merely compounded. Years later, in his biography of Loulou's father, the veteran Liberal journalist A.G. Gardiner recalled the context in which the landslide 1895 election had taken place, and it is difficult to gainsay his rather sour verdict: 'Speculation had seized the public mind to an unprecedented degree, and the Stock Exchange had become the centre of the national life. The riches of the

Rand . . . had created a feverish excitement in the public mind that penetrated every part of the country . . .'[22]

*

1895 was not without its *haute finance*. On 17 April the signing of the treaty of Shimonoseki brought to an end the Sino-Japanese War, leaving China with a massive indemnity to pay, estimated by early May at up to £50m.[23] Over the previous twenty-one years China's regular loan-maker had been the Hongkong and Shanghai Bank, and on 11 May the bank's London manager, Ewen Cameron, informed Sir Thomas Sanderson of the Foreign Office that he wanted to raise £15m immediately in London, with a further £35m to be raised in due course. 'He seems to think it could be floated,' minuted Sanderson. Two days later Cameron paid no fewer than three visits to the FO, during the third of which he showed to Sanderson the memorandum of a recent conversation between his stockbroker – Harry Panmure Gordon, the renowned China expert – and Natty Rothschild. Following two conversations of his own with Rosebery (still Prime Minister), Natty had told Panmure Gordon that, in the interests of China, it would be a mistake to achieve a diplomatic triumph over France and Germany by bringing out the loan on a solo basis. Instead, Natty proposed (in the words of Sanderson's own memorandum):

> That the loan should be divided in equal parts between the three countries: that Rothschilds would join the Hongkong & Shanghai Bank in bringing out the English portion. That if any attempt were made by France & Germany to exclude us, the British market should be closed to the loan.
>
> Mr Cameron said this was contrary to his plan of a loan brought out in England alone. He had understood from me that the Government were not opposed to his plan.
>
> I said that was also my understanding; but I had told him we could have nothing to do with it. If he succeeded he would have achieved a triumph. But the best advice we had been able to get was that a loan of so considerable an amount as China would require could not be floated on the mere security of an engagement in the contract to an English firm. I told him in strict confidence that that was the opinion not only of Lord Rothschild but of Mr B. Currie. If it could not be done, we must take the next best alternative, and Lord Rothschild's proposal was such as we could openly write for . . .
>
> He said he would consider carefully with his friends what they should do.

Despite this opposition from the Rosebery–Rothschild axis, Cameron continued to push for an entirely English loan with the Hongkong Bank receiving exclusive government support. To no avail. On the 20th, the FO was unequivocal that it expected him to ally with New Court in the matter. 'I readily admit the pre-eminent position held by the great firm of Rothschilds in the financial world,' an aggrieved Cameron replied the next day, 'but I maintain that this Bank is quite capable of carrying through any business connected with the Chinese Loans.' The letter was, though, only a gesture, and on the 22nd Cameron fell into line more or less graciously.[24] In the end, he well appreciated, his bank was playing a longer game.

It soon emerged that the French had broken away to form a financial alliance with the Russians; and though over the next few weeks the Anglo-German group battled away under Rothschild leadership, victory went to St Petersburg, where on 6 July it was formally announced that a £16m loan, guaranteed by Russia and issued in Paris by a French syndicate, would be made on China's behalf. 'Russia has won the toss,' commented the *FT*, 'and gone in first on a good wicket, with France as a partner to make the boundary hits. But we are to have our innings after the turf is worn...' There would indeed be future Chinese indemnity loans – on who knew what sort of wicket – and perhaps lessons would be learned from the first. 'This is England's opportunity. It will not remain open long. Have we a statesman who can see it and seize it?'[25] That was what a fairly young banker called Charles Addis, working for the Hongkong and Shanghai in Shanghai itself, had written to his father shortly before the signing of the peace treaty. The events of the early summer showed that England did not have that statesman; but they also showed, perhaps more important, that in the context of keen international rivalry for influence in China it would no longer be possible for the FO to pretend that loan-raising finance existed in a virtuous void. Henceforth the worlds of finance and diplomacy were entwined – increasingly so over the next twenty years, and not only in China.

There was a significant coda to the story of the first Chinese indemnity loan. On 2 July, shortly before the ratification of the £16m Russo-Chinese loan, the prospectus appeared in London for a £1m loan to China.[26] The formal issuer was the Chartered Bank of India, Australia and China, but the man behind it was Cassel, emerging as the City's foremost international financier. The detailed background to this loan is shrouded in mystery; but it seems clear enough that Cassel over the previous few months had been working closely with the FO, and that once it became clear that the Rothschild-led initiative was doomed to failure, then there was official encouragement for the much smaller Cassel loan as a way of maintaining British face. 'The Chinese transaction has doubtless given you great satisfaction,' Cassel's main American banking friend, Jacob Schiff of Kuhn, Loeb, wrote to him in August, adding that 'it is only a pity that the Russians and Frenchmen intervene so that you now control only the smaller and not the larger loan'.[27] Cassel was someone whose activities historians have struggled to trace precisely, not least because of his temperamental disposition to operate as far as possible as a loner.[28] 'A partner,' he once remarked, 'is a man who can commit you to things and I don't mean ever to be committed to anyone.' There was quite a lot to be said against this self-made German Jew (and many said it): little sense of humour; few social graces; and the thinnest of skins when it came to any slights, real or imaginary. But there was much to be said on the other side, and one of the best pen pictures of Cassel comes from another German, Saemy Japhet, who was based in the City from 1896 and became a relatively close associate:

> He hid an innate modesty under what seemed coldness, and however kindly and almost affectionate he could be to those who were far below his own station in life, he could be very distant, even haughty towards those whom he suspected of snubbing him. He never gave them a second chance. As he was a true friend, in the same way he was a good hater; he never forgot an insult.
>
> His leading characteristic was his power of concentration and his directness. His 'yes' was 'yes' and his 'no' was 'no'. All who had dealings with him, whether they came to a successful end or not, were struck by the straightforwardness of his methods. He was a good listener, never interrupting, but his answers came out at once, well-formulated, clear, logical and full of common sense. Where others hesitated he acted, and many a proposition was already approved – or rejected – long before others had grasped the essential points. His perception was quick as lightning. He used to think of the smallest details while doing the biggest things.[29]

These were the City's golden years, and most of them were golden years for Ernest Cassel too.

*

Cassel completely avoided the Kaffir boom, still raging by August 1895. 'Within the recollection of the oldest member of the Stock Exchange there has been no speculative movement at all comparable,'

declared the *Economist* on the 17th, adding that it 'shows as little sign
of abatement as ever'. The solicitor William May noted in his diary on
the 23rd: 'Frightfully busy in the office – new work chiefly mining
companies are simply flocking in and for vacation it is wondrous. Very
few people are really *en vacances* this year as they don't like to miss the
boom while it lasts.'[30] Barney Barnato was by this time back in London, pulling strings with obvious pleasure. In the course of the month
he revealed his plan to bring out what he grandly called the Barnato
Bank Mining and Estate Company – in theory a holding company for
his various ventures, in ill-disguised reality a gambling machine.[31] The
FT was swept along by the prevailing mood, and on the 28th it offered
a generally favourable verdict on 'Barney's Bank', about to come out
with a capital of £3½m:

> The functions of the Company will be to act as financiers and stock-
> holders. We need hardly point out that with Mr Barnato as the moving
> spirit the institution will have every chance of getting into good things in
> South Africa. He is not likely to give the cold shoulder to the bank
> bearing his name, and we must confess to a feeling of envy towards the
> successful applicants for shares at the issue price.

Barney himself was always available for interview, and on Saturday
the 31st the *City Recorder* (one of 1895's many short-lived publications) carried some characteristic pronouncements:

> When will the prospectus be out?
> Prospectus! I never issued a prospectus in my life. There will be no
> prospectus, but the Barnato Bank will be in existence on Monday certain.
> You have delayed its coming out, have you not?
> Yes, in the public interest. When I arrived and found how the specula-
> tors had run the thing up I would not allow it to appear until I had
> examined everything, and found that all was in perfect order. Of the
> many things I have brought out, not one company is standing at less than
> 50 per cent premium, and some are at 800 per cent premium; consequent-
> ly, it would scarcely do for me to make a mistake with my pet scheme,
> and the biggest of all.
> Fifty to eight hundred per cent is pretty good.
> Yes. But I hope to go one better. It will startle a good few of the
> old-fashioned City bankers. Such confidence as has been reposed in me I
> certainly don't think has been equalled.

Elsewhere in the interview he boasted that he was 'followed and
backed by the best bankers in London, and practically by the whole of

the Stock Exchange', so presumably the best bankers were not the old-fashioned ones.[32]

Monday, 2 September was, according to the *FT*, 'Saint Barney's Day':

> We have reason to believe that business was done yesterday in other stocks than 'Barney's Bank', but it was very difficult to discover it . . . In the market the morning scene was wonderful, and the excitement intense. Brokers had orders at limits based on one or other of the conflicting rumours as to the price at which the market would open; but the work of these was simple compared with that of the brokers who had orders to buy 'at best', and who had to fight their way through a crowd to get the opportunity of asking a jobber to make a price . . .
>
> About the concern the public knows comparatively little, except that Mr Barnato has given his name to it, and that that name is associated with successes of the most brilliant kind. There is nothing succeeds like success, it is said, and yesterday's market is a notable example of the weight of this aphorism. How many million pounds sterling 'Barney' may be worth is a favourite subject of discussion in and about the Stock Exchange. The estimates vary in the most picturesque way, but on all hands it is agreed that he is a millionaire as many times over as is necessary to enable him to make a success of even bigger things than he has yet taken in hand – and some of these are big. There may be bigger yet to come . . .

It was the very zenith of the Kaffir boom, after almost a year of bucketing along regardless, and the market was now being flooded with a vast quantity of watered stock based on gold-mining properties that for the most part were either marginal or undeveloped.[33]

On 14 September the *Economist* noted that 'the settlement in mining shares which has taken place within the past few days was about as little like the usual condition of things in the Stock Exchange during the "dead season" as it is possible to conceive'. On 1 October, Hamilton referred in his diary to 'the extraordinary boom in S. African gold shares, than which people can talk or think of little else, and out of which many are making their kills'. But the turning-point came on 3 October, a Thursday, when massive sales in Paris led to prices slumping in London. In both the Paris and London markets, according to the *FT*, 'sales produced the greater effect from the fact that the Jews were again absent [following the Day of Atonement the previous Saturday], the day being one of their special celebrations, and thus a great deal of sustaining power, which might otherwise have been forthcoming, was wanting'. Over the next week the relapse in prices continued more or less unabated, with the *Statist* on the 12th blaming 'the refusal of the London banks to take such bills drawn upon the London branches of Continental banks as had a financial appearance', an acceptance that much of the protracted Kaffir speculation had been Paris-led. The Circus continued to have the jitters until the 18th, when some of the leading South African houses quietly, and Barnato Bros noisily, agreed to take up stocks they had issued and for which no buyers could be found in the market. 'Barney to the Rescue' was the *FT*'s headline, with the paper praising Barnato for having 'loyally and pluckily supported the market' and seeing his bank as the target of a systematic, very determined bear raid. Subsequently, it was stated that Barnato had laid out £3m in supporting the shares in which he was specially interested; and the *Economist* commented darkly that 'if this be the case', then it proved 'that the market had got into a more serious condition than had been generally supposed'.[34]

Soon afterwards, on 7 November, in the closing days of his controversial mayoralty, Renals returned various unspecified favours by giving Barnato an official Mansion House banquet as formal recognition of what he had done to avert a catastrophe in the stock market. It was, Hamilton exclaimed that day, a dinner 'to thank this gentleman for supporting his own over-valued speculations and to advertise him more than he is already advertised'. He went on: 'It is said that it has been a costly affair – this dinner I mean – to Mr "Barnie" himself. I call it down-right prostitution of civic hospitality. Fortunately all respectable people with very few exceptions declined their invitations.' Hamilton was right, and it was a thin turn-out (though including Carl Meyer) to hear Renals and Barnato pay mutual compliments.[35] The City, in short, remained sceptical about the merits of the Randlords and their loyal acolytes in the Kaffir Circus.

*

Meanwhile, another drama – wholly private and unreported – had been going on. Richard Meinertzhagen, second son of Daniel Meinertzhagen of Huths, was 17 years old and due to leave Harrow at the end of the year. Daniel wanted him to follow family footsteps, Richard's deepest desire was to go to university to study zoology, and on 6 October son wrote to father:

> Money is not everything and I hate the City. If I can get a good degree in zoology I shall yet be a credit to the family. I know that both you and

mother think I am no good but neither of you really know me or have seen my serious side. You know, Father, I do get things done, I think a lot and am not a complete ass nor have I earned the epithet 'black sheep' which has been bestowed on me. If I cannot do zoology may I do geography? A financial future has no attraction for me. I would sooner be penniless and doing congenial work than a millionaire living in and loathing the City.

Daniel remained adamant, and Richard wrote again on 4 November, saying that 'the idea of entering Huths fills me with loathing'. To which Daniel replied on the day of Barney's banquet:

You have been well educated and enjoy a certain standard of living which is high. You must always try and live up to that standard and keep your place in the world. I think you should give the City a chance for you cannot enjoy life without money . . . After all, you have commerce in your blood and I can help you a great deal in the City. In the scientific world I should not be of any assistance to you. I am quite sure that if you worked hard in the City for a few years you will never regret the many advantages which would accrue.

At last, on the 9th, the would-be zoologist gave way:

Money! I would sooner be a penniless scientist with successful research to my credit than be a senior partner in Huths, my soul blighted by gold and ripe to die of cancer in the stomach at the age of 55. Alright, I'll start in the City but the day I'm 21, if I hate it, you must let me go.[36]

CHAPTER NINE

Baiting the Swim

Another victim of the Mine 'slump'. An inquest was held yesterday concerning the death of Frederick Oliver Heath (38), a member of the Stock Exchange, who was found with his throat cut in a train at Gros-venor-road Station on Tuesday. It was stated that he had been unable to sleep for the past three weeks owing to trouble caused by heavy monetary losses . . .

Heath slit his throat on 19 November 1895; it was clear that the recent market support operation by Barnato and others had failed to reverse the sharply downward trend in a notoriously overvalued sector. Gloom was not confined to the City. The new play at the Criterion was *The Squire of Dames*, including a scene where Miss Zoe Nuggetson, an American heiress, presses Mr Kilroy to marry her. He explains that she is too rich, to which she replies, 'We could speculate.' According to the *FN* on the 23rd, 'when this remark was made the other evening, after the collapse in the stock markets, a subdued but audible groan was heard from various parts of the stalls.'[1]

Far worse, though, was soon to afflict those interested in Kaffirs. The ill-conceived Jameson Raid at the end of the year plunged the Circus into a state of crisis, marking a long step on the road to eventual war between Britain and the Transvaal, with all the attendant consequences for the South African mining industry. Rhodes was certainly implic-ated in the Raid, Beit probably, with a question mark hovering over other Randlords. The general view on the Stock Exchange seems to have been one of accepting that the Uitlanders had legitimate griev-ances, and admiring the pluck of those involved, but deploring the probability that the Raid should (in the *FN*'s words) 'be the means of bringing upon investors further losses and disappointments'. There was, at this stage, little rational assessment of whether the policies of the Kruger government represented a fundamental obstacle to the future development of the gold-mining industry. Instead, immediate attention focused partly on share prices, partly on the outrage of the Kaiser's impudent telegram to Oom Paul; when a Stock Exchange

132

member called Hermann Moritz took to the floor of the House and showed where his allegiances lay by giving a crowded audience a spirited rendition of 'Rule, Britannia', he was heartily cheered when he came to the word 'slaves' at the end of the final chorus.[2]

Moritz did his party piece on 13 January 1896, and the next day there took place a notable set-piece occasion, encapsulated by the *FT* as 'Barnato at Bay':

> Seldom has the City of London manifested greater interest in a public meeting than was shown at that of the shareholders of the Barnato Bank. Although the meeting was not arranged to take place until mid-day, many persons secured seats as early as 9 a.m., and a number of shareholders were unable to obtain admittance at all. The Great Hall at Cannon-street was crammed almost to suffocation . . .

Barnato's speech lasted a full hour, and in the course of it he offered an upbeat assessment of the bank's assets, declared that he could sympathise with the grievances behind the Jameson Raid but not with the action itself, and expressed regret that the shares in his bank, currently standing at $1\frac{11}{16}$, had initially gone to a £4 premium, against (he insisted) his wishes. The tender-hearted Barney then looked ahead:

> In my humble opinion, when the clouds are the thickest there is always a little sunshine behind them. We are not going to see as dark days; we are going to see brighter times. We have a grand future, if it is administered properly. The gold is not taken away; the mines are there, and there has been no earthquake in South Africa . . . The strength I have had before I have today, and I hope I shall retain it for years to come. To show the great belief I have in this institution, and also to show the faith of my colleagues, we hold in the Barnato Bank two-thirds of the capital. (*Cheers.*) If you want faith, there is faith. If you want confidence, there is confidence.

Finally, the peroration:

> I am absolutely your guardian and your trustee, and I shall do all I can for the best interests of your property. (*Cheers.*) If I fail I cannot help it; I am only mortal, but I have done my best. In conclusion, I can tell you this, that the name of the Barnato Bank will not die out whilst the name of Barnato Brothers lives. I have every hope, and I trust that I shall be able to support these words – that the Barnato Bank will be one of the most successful of the many successes I have made in South Africa. (*Loud and continued cheers.*)

Altogether it had been a tour de force, well received on the Stock Exchange, where Barnato Bank shares closed on the 14th at $1\frac{15}{16}$. Yet, for all his bold assertions, Barnato himself was now on a rapid downwards slide, his resources battered by the £2m or so he had been compelled to pour into the market, his assets far stronger on paper than in reality. He still retained a loyal following in Capel Court – on returning at the end of July from a trip to South Africa, he was met at Southampton by some thirty members who had travelled down specially to greet him – but by the end of 1896 his cherished bank was in liquidation. And as the *Citizen* had presciently wondered aloud in February that year, 'who will live in Mr Barnato's house in Park-lane when it is finished?'[3]

Barnato's fortunes were in striking contrast to those of Wernher Beit which, under the capable leadership of Julius Wernher (possessed of a more robust constitution than Beit), used 1896 to reposition the firm in the context of the collapse of the Kaffir boom and the protracted political after-shocks of the Jameson Raid. 'I am not one of those people,' Wernher once remarked, 'who create fortunes by genius or new combinations, and lose them again and win them again. I only walk well-known paths, but I walk steadily . . .' By May 1896 he was looking to limit his exposure on the Rand, writing to a colleague that 'a reduction in the Transvaal will be useful'; and over the next few years Wernher Beit steadily diversified its investments. Nevertheless, with the firm's cluster of deep-level mines poised to come on stream, and Geldenhuis having already done so in 1895, Wernher was determined that Rand Mines should not 'suffer for want of capital'. In December 1896 the holding company issued £1m 5 per cent bonds, with the majority being placed privately, including to Rothschilds and the Exploration Co. Wernher was also determined that, in any future bull market, Wernher Beit should control the destiny of its shares rather more effectively than it had managed during the frenzy of 1895; and it was probably at about this time that his firm, along with other leading mining houses, initiated the system that the Stock Exchange Committee was to quiz a leading Kaffir jobber about in 1903:

> Mr Higham was asked whether it was not a fact that many of the outside firms, Messrs Wernher, Beit & Co, the Consolidated Gold Fields of South Africa and others were not what was known as 'the Shop' in various stocks, exercising a controlling interest over the market in these stocks. He replied that this was so, but that these outside firms would not make a price like an inside jobber, but the broker would have to disclose which way he was when approaching them.

The so-called shop was a phenomenon that rarely surfaced in contemporary accounts of the Stock Exchange, but it was basically a method of limiting the omnipotence of the jobbers and, used with increasing effectiveness after the turn of the century, seems to have been mainly confined to the Mining market.[4] Seeking to ensure that the power to determine prices lay *outside* the House, no shop could succeed without a regular supply of tame brokers – and of these, there was never any shortage.

The year 1896 was not an easy one for the Kaffir Circus, but on 24 February it enjoyed one afternoon of lustre when the jobber W.A. Nickalls, a brother of Tom, introduced two of Jameson's troopers into the House. He did so without permission, but his defence to the Committee was heartfelt: 'Having fought against the Boers in '62 and being imprisoned myself, I naturally feel very enthusiastic about the present state of political affairs in the Transvaal.' And, in person, he added that he had met 'the two young men in question quite by chance at the club at Angel Court', presumably the Thieves' Kitchen; and that, 'after some chaff', he had consented to their request to let them see the inside of the House. Nickalls's punishment was a fortnight's suspension, too little in the eyes of some members.[5]

Over the next few months other, more significant aspects of the Raid reverberated in the City, including the enforced resignation of Rhodes as managing director of Consolidated Gold Fields, a move that signalled a fresh assertion of City authority over the company. The British South Africa Company was also affected, with Rhodes and Beit both being compelled to resign from the board. 'Poor Horace [Farquhar] has been badly put out about the Chartered Company business,' noted Hamilton on 7 May. There were still some flurries of intense market activity in Kaffirs, but on the whole the market did not prosper, not least because during the second half of 1896 it became the established conventional wisdom – owing more to febrile invention than detached analysis – that deep-level mining on the Rand was not going to be as successful as had generally been assumed. There was also the larger political situation, and when Barnato in October sent Kruger a placatory gift of two marble lions, the jaundiced view in the Circus was that 'a "stoney" bull and a cheerful-looking bear would have been more appropriate supporters for the President's roof-tree'. No wonder that Tom Nickalls had returned by the autumn to the American market, a move that he can hardly have regretted the following spring as Anglo-Transvaal relations hit yet another rocky patch. 'There is a very general feeling in the City that trouble is brewing in South Africa,' reported the *Citizen*'s resident Stock Exchange columnist in March 1897, and for once the City had got it right, even if the time-scale remained uncertain.[6]

*

Where had all the gold bugs gone? The short answer was, to a part of the world blessedly free of a septuagenarian Boer in his Groote Schuur. The Westralian boom, which had begun during 1895, was given added impetus by the South African traumas.[7] By the autumn of 1896 there were some 260 securities actively dealt in in the Stock Exchange's Westralian market (compared with some 360 in the Kaffir market); and their names included such enticing gold mines as Bayley's Reward, Bird-in-Hand, Empress of Coolgardie, Faith, Gleeson's Success, Golden Australia, Hannan's Golden Dyke, Hit or Miss, Just in Time, King Solomon's, Nil Desperandum, Sam's Wealth of Nations, and World's Treasure. Like their Kaffir counterparts, very few of these securities enjoyed the implicit sanction of an official quotation, and usually the method of their flotation left much to be desired. To quote the *Statist* in April 1896:

> What is perhaps the most unpleasant feature about West Australian promotions is the list of companies offering entirely undeveloped, or but little developed, properties at extravagant prices, having regard to the amount of work done. In great part the extravagance of the prices arises from the greed of the intermediaries in contracts.
>
> Promoters still resort to the practice of issuing companies in what is termed a private manner; in other words, without essential facts being made public. Here and there circulars appear, but they have not the character and weight of a definite prospectus statement . . .

The *Economist* similarly complained about how 'it is impossible to trace the operation from the local-vendor stage to the utterly disproportionate basis upon which investors are asked to subscribe', while the *FT* agreed, asserting that 'on the Westralian, as on all mining fields – especially new ones – there has been a great amount of misrepresentation by unscrupulous experts, vendors and promoters'.[8]

Two of these promoters were peculiarly scruple-free: Horatio Bottomley and Whitaker Wright.[9] Bottomley was now in his mid-30s, the son of an East End tailor's cutter. His main venture to date had been the Hansard Union, a printing and publishing company that crashed within two years of its launch in 1889, amidst justifiable charges of swindling and gross over-capitalisation. Bottomley, however, put up a superb defence in the resulting lawsuit and lived to fight another day. His friend O'Hagan at this point solemnly warned him to stay away from company promoting, but to no avail; between 1893 and 1897 he promoted some twenty West Australian mining and finance companies, all but one of which failed to last more than a few years before inevitable liquidation, the direct result of Bottomley holding back for himself and the vendors the lion's share of the initial cash subscription. It was the invariable policy of a supremely self-confident financier, memorably drawn by Frank Harris:

> Bottomley was a trifle shorter even than I was, perhaps five feet four or five, but very broad and even then threatened to become stout. He had a very large head, well-balanced, too, with good forehead and heavy jaws; the eyes small and grey; the peculiarity of the face a prodigiously long upper lip . . . He was greedy of all the sensual pleasures, intensely greedy; even at thirty he ate too much and habitually drank too much. To see him lunching at Romano's with two or three of his intimates, usually subordinates, with a pretty chorus girl on one side and another siren opposite, while the waiter uncorked the fourth or fifth bottle of champagne, was to see the man as he was.

Yet, as Harris also said, he knew almost no one who had Bottomley's 'invincible good humour' – a quality that was to stand him in good stead over the years.[10] We have, unfortunately, a less vivid picture at this stage of his fellow-promoter Whitaker Wright, ultimately the more important City figure. Wright was by now in his mid-50s, a North Countryman by origin, and had spent much of his life making and losing fortunes in American mining. By the mid-1890s his two main vehicles were the West Australian Exploring and Finance Corporation and the London and Globe Finance Corporation. Both were holding companies for speculative share operations, though in Lake View Consols he possessed a genuine gold-producing mine, if dangerously starved of working capital. A large man with a fluent tongue and a head for figures, Wright knew that the Westralian boom marked his last chance for a bite at the really big cherry.

On the floor of the Stock Exchange itself, the Westralian market never quite attained the outsize aura of the Kaffir Circus, but nor was it a place where staider members of the House felt entirely comfortable. One of the younger jobbers learning the ropes there in 1896 was Vivian Nickalls, one of Tom's rowing boys. Towards the end of January he was the victim of a time-honoured hoax, as extensive dealings took place in Boulder United and he made a large, apparently very profitable book in them, before 'the truth was gently broken to him, by the posting of a notice that the settlement in Boulder United would take place "some day" ', whereupon the champion oarsman 'put on a spurt in his best style, and disappeared speedily from view'. Over the next few months the boom reached its apogee, with the *Citizen*'s House correspondent declaring on 23 May that 'no words of mine can describe the excitement and the crowding of the "Kangaroo" market during this last week' and adding that 'almost half of the Kaffir market has migrated, and, in fact, jobbers from all quarters of the House are now scrambling for orders in Australians'.[11]

The partners of Antony Gibbs followed the Westralian market closely during 1896 and kept up a regular correspondence with Frank Keating of Gibbs, Bright & Co in Melbourne. 'I think the public will rush WA shares almost like they did Kaffirs this time last year,' was the wholly orthodox view of Harry Gibbs in mid-May, adding that 'we certainly ought to be able to make a lot of money in arbitrage when there is a boom on'. Easier said than done, and by late June there was already a certain nervousness evident about the conduct of mutual arbitrage business. London rather than Melbourne was the leading market for most Australian securities, so a special responsibility attached to the Antony Gibbs end of the operation; and with Keating less than satisfied by the service he was getting from Bishopsgate, Vicary devoted much of 14 July to a long letter of explanation and justification:

> You comment on our knowing nothing beforehand of a boom which took place in Mt Lyell & Mt Lyell South . . . It is impossible to say when a boom is going to occur in a particular mine. However, I think that when any indication of a move is going on in London, in any particular mine, we might profitably communicate the fact to you, then if you think it well, we or you could operate. We have talked to Williams in this sense & have told him to be more active in keeping us posted with any tips that he can collect.

The reference was to the stockbroker responsible for the firm's mining business, and Vicary added that 'Essex the small red-headed clerk of Williams is told off specially to attend on us, which he does very efficiently, being sharp & industrious, but he never proposes any new business or very rarely.' Vicary then turned to his own firm:

> I may as well mention here that this branch of the work is closely and regularly followed by Herbert, Harry and myself, and that as a rule we have consulted and talked over the operations on this side, tho' of course

from time to time it has been necessary for one or other of us to act off his own bat. Barker also who, as you know, follows the work with zeal and accuracy, keeping all the stocks on hand daily before us, entering all your limits, advices and suggestions and managing everything with an almost inhuman freedom from error. I certainly do not consider that there has been any neglect or inattention, either by partners or clerks, indeed arbitrage has taken up more of our time than its present importance warrants.

You have naturally singled out occasions when the market has continued to rise rapidly, directly after we have sold, but probably a counter list could be prepared where prompter realisations would have been more profitable.

Whether this defence convinced is unclear, but it seems that Williams took the hint, for barely a week later Vicary was writing to Keating about their having successfully anticipated the recent rise in Lake View Consols: 'Our informant was the jobber Young (brother-in-law of Williams our broker), who as you know is interested in many Australian mines and has his own sources of information.' And on the last day of the month, Vicary happily informed Harry: 'Lake View Consols: we made about £400 on this spec.'[12]

All the world loves a spec, and Whitaker Wright had plenty of them up his sleeve. By the autumn of 1896 his master-plan was to merge his two finance corporations and, in the ensuing reconstruction, acquire for himself a few hundred thousand shares, thereby usefully supplementing his £6,000 salary as managing director. In November he addressed his shareholders through an open circular widely advertised in the financial press:

The position of the united Companies is now so strong that your Directors feel that, in future, they can afford to issue only 'going concerns', in which the original subscribers will be able to secure handsome premiums for their shares, or, at least, substantial dividends on their investments; in short, that your consolidated Companies, under the title of the LONDON AND GLOBE FINANCE CORPORATION, will become an issuing house second to none in the City of London. At any rate, your Directors look forward to the future with *unabated confidence*.

The following February, at the Cannon Street Hotel, shareholders met to decide formally on amalgamation, and Wright favoured them with a few words:

In regard to the scheme itself, it was not worth while discussing whether it should be modified or not, because it must be accepted in toto or not at all. It was exactly in accordance with the memorandum of the company, which, like the laws of the Medes and Persians, was fixed and unalterable . . . If the consolidation scheme were carried through, they would carry over practically £300,000 or £400,000, which they believed would be increased to half-a-million . . . They had other businesses on hand which would net half-a-million more, and they ought from the enterprises which would be going concerns during the year to net a profit of another half-a-million, so that if the shareholders imagined their stock was being watered by this consolidation they were labouring under a great mistake. (*Applause.*)[13]

The very thought was shameful, and the shareholders unanimously agreed to amalgamation. In the reconstruction that followed, Wright took the opportunity to add new names to the London and Globe's board, and in particular he enticed as Chairman the Marquis of Dufferin and Ava, former Governor-General of Canada, former Viceroy of India, and ultimate guinea-pig director of the era. It cost a few bob – perhaps as much as £10,000 – but the London and Globe's prestige rose sharply.

And Bottomley? In April 1897, four years after his acquittal, he informed the shareholders of the Hansard Union that he intended to transfer to trustees almost £$\frac{1}{4}$m for the relief of the shareholders, after they had suffered so much following the Union's collapse. Among the audience at the Cannon Street Hotel, purely as an interested observer, was O'Hagan:

> He made a wonderful speech, as was his wont, and was cheered to the skies. So far as I could make out, only poor shareholders who had lost their *all* were to be benefited, and certain trustees were appointed to hold the funds, and to ascertain and deal with deserving cases. I do not know whether an announcement was ever made as to how many shareholders were benefited . . .
>
> Eventually it seemed to me that friends of Bottomley were appointed trustees, and I think the funds transferred consisted of but little cash and a lot of securities, but of what value I cannot say. How many people were benefited from this fund I do not know, but Bottomley obtained what he wanted, a huge puff advertisement.

As a propaganda move it worked brilliantly, typified by the *FT*'s remarkable leader the next day, one of the less happy moments in that paper's history:

> Today not only those who benefit by his manly, and we may even say princely, generosity, but those who read of yesterday's proceedings will

need little argument to convince them that whatever faults or failings can be charged against the Hansard Union, or those connected with it, Mr Bottomley has completely exonerated himself and his colleagues from any charge of bad faith or dishonesty, and that his spontaneous regard for his fellow-sufferers entitles him to the complete rehabilitation of his character in the public mind. We trust that Mr Bottomley's career henceforth may be made pleasanter by reason of the troubles he has so successfully combated, and join in the fervent wish which found expression in yesterday's meeting, and which today will be shared by the larger world who will read of it, that Mr Bottomley may have a long life of usefulness and uninterrupted success before him. Such examples of generous commercial rectitude are all the more welcome because they are so infrequent.

His reputation so wonderfully vindicated, O'Hagan's analysis surely being correct, Bottomley now prepared to launch on the world the West Australian Market Trust; and, in an interview with the *FN* towards the end of May, we hear the authentic voice of a self-made man shamelessly, splendidly on the make:

What will be its main object?

Well, it will by degrees acquire large and, perhaps, controlling interests in many of the best things in the West Australian market; it will advance money on approved shares; it will carry over stock from account to account; and, generally, it will act as a financial institution at the back of the Westralian market . . . Everyone connected with the market agrees that there is immense scope for such an undertaking, and that, judiciously and energetically managed, it should be a great power for good. At any rate, that is the conclusion I have arrived at after a very thorough investigation, and I shall take the position of chairman of the Trust. It should be very pleasant and interesting work, and ought not to seriously interfere with other aims I have in view.

And have you any assurance that a scheme of this kind will meet with support?

Assurance! Since it became known that I had taken the matter seriously in hand I have had numerous offers of support, and am constantly being asked for advance particulars.

Is it known that you will be chairman?

Yes. A month ago I was advised by most of my friends to keep in the background. They now make it a *sine quâ non* that my name should be identified with the undertaking. Several of the big men in the 'House' have offered to take large lines of the shares; so I must go ahead and justify their confidence.

And when is the company to be publicly issued?

In about ten days or a fortnight.

And you are, of course, hopeful of a very successful issue?

I am certain of it. Just at present, for reasons which must be obvious, I have no intention of associating myself with a failure.[14]

*

'Leo Rothschild has promised me a bicycle as a present if he wins any race this week, and as he has been losing so far Natty Rothschild today said that if Leo did *not* win a race he (Natty) would give me a bicycle instead.' Thus an expectant Loulou Harcourt in June 1895 during Ascot week, and two days later: 'Leo Rothschild won the last race today so I get my bicycle from him and when he came tonight to join our "bike" ride with the others he told me to buy the best Humber I could get & send the bill to him!' Over the following winter the nation pedalled away in ever greater numbers, and in April 1896 the *FN* summed up 'The Cycling Boom':

> For some time past the cycling industry has been making enormous strides; the manufacturing companies have been unable to keep pace with the orders, and their shares have been steadily rising in value, in anticipation of the splendid dividends which are in many instances assured. There is at present no indication of any slackening down of popular enthusiasm with regard to cycling . . .

The paper added that, 'quite recently, a new company was brought out with the special object of dealing with the whole of the Humber output in this country'; and, 'although no attempt was made to make a market, the shares went to a premium, and the large capital required was over-applied for'.[15] That flotation, however, paled into insignificance when, early in May, there appeared the prospectus for the Dunlop Pneumatic Tyre Company. It was the wonder of the day – capitalised at a vast £5m and featuring not only the Earl de la Warr as Chairman but also the Duke of Somerset and the Earl of Albemarle as fellow-directors. The Dunlop shares were massively oversubscribed, and shortly afterwards the *FN* commented that 'the whole promotion has been handled with great skill and boldness . . .'[16]

The man behind this spectacularly successful and highly lucrative promotion was Ernest Terah Hooley, who basically had bought the existing Dunlop company for £3m and then sold it to the public for £5m, though of course having to meet certain advertising and other expenses in the process, not least in securing his guinea-pig directors. Hooley was a Nottingham lacemaker-turned-stockbroker; by 1895 he had become actively involved in the cycle boom; and from the spring of 1896, soon after floating Raleigh, he based himself in London, occupying an extensive suite of rooms on the first floor of the Midland Grand Hotel at St Pancras. He was a teetotaller who in an earlier life had been deacon and organist at the Baptist church in Long Eaton; while Frank Harris recalled him as 'well dressed and always polite without a particle of "side", too earnestly busy to show any conceit', as well as having 'a perfectly open mind for any and every scheme' and being 'an optimist to the fingers' tips'.[17] It was a good time to be an optimistic company promoter. Money was cheap in 1896 (Bank rate at 2 per cent for much of the year), the Kaffir boom had made great fortunes but run out of steam, the Westralian boom did not have quite the same all-consuming nature, and from a speculative point of view the cycling craze could not have been more opportune.

What, though, made Hooley run? According to the memoirs of H.F.M. Weston-Webb, a Nottingham yarn merchant who had known him from youth, he was not motivated by personal greed, but took risks 'because he "loved a deal", and he rushed in where others would fear to tread'. He was also, Weston-Webb insisted, generous, had a sense of humour, and possessed 'extraordinary quickness of thought, especially where figures were concerned'. Hooley, moreover, had the City pretty well taped. Describing its lawyers and brokers as 'easy game' and 'dazzled by a successful man' (in a book published in 1924 and engagingly entitled *Hooley's Confessions*), he reckoned that they were 'nearly all greedy for business, but quite willing to be satisfied with their legitimate fees, leaving their commercial hero to take the lion's share of the swag'. And after noting that brokers tended to be 'too busy operating on the Stock Exchange to follow their client's big operations', he added: 'When the crash comes they mostly take their physic like men, although they may have lost their own money as well as their clients'. They are real sports, and I raise my hat to them, but often think how strange it is that such clever people should be such – well, I won't say what.'[18]

Prior to the Dunlop coup the market in cycle shares was mainly confined to Dublin and Birmingham, but during May 1896 its centre of gravity shifted to Capel Court, where according to the *Citizen* 'any broker now is more likely to know the price of "Components" or "Dunlops" than "Berthas" or "Milwaukees" '. Several of the leading jobbers in the Miscellaneous market speedily learnt to specialise in cycle shares and were accorded the nickname of the 'windbags' by fellow-denizens. A series of usually profitable flotations came their way over the ensuing months, including several masterminded by Hooley, one of which was the conversion early in June of Singer Cycles into a public company. It was capitalised at £600,000, its directors included the Earl of Warwick and the Earl of Norbury, and acting as London brokers to the issue was the firm of Alistair Hay & Co. In the event the Hooley connection led to a row between the Hon Alistair Hay and his two partners, who accused him of having put payments from the commercial hero into a private bank account without inform- ing them. The case eventually came to the Stock Exchange Committee, at which point:

> Mr Hay was questioned as to the personal promise made to him by Mr Hooley of a payment of £5,000 on account of services specially rendered by him. He explained that the promise was made to him upon the first occasion of his meeting Mr Hooley. It was after a dinner party about the end of May. He – Hay – did not attach very great importance to the promise, because it had been made after dinner. It was repeated sub- sequently, but now it was repudiated . . . Mr Hooley's motive in making the promise was to obtain his – Hay's – introduction to influential people to serve on the board of the Singer Cycle Co.

The case as a whole was a complicated one, involving breaches of faith all round and eventual suspension for Hay, but it did provide an interesting, contemporaneous glimpse into Hooley's methods.[19] By the autumn the cycle boom was showing signs of faltering, though Hooley brought the Swift Cycle Company to the market in October (with Lord Churchill as Chairman) and saw its shares four times oversubscribed; before the end of the year he felt able to spend £70,000 on acquiring the Papworth Hall estate in Cambridgeshire, from where he enter- tained freely and which he sensibly put into his wife's name.

There was one other killing that autumn, to round off Hooley's *annus mirabilis*. On 23 October the shareholders of Bovril met in order to authorise the sale of the concern to him, a sale justified by J. Lawson Johnston in the absence of the Chairman, Lord Playfair: 'We are not financiers – Mr Hooley is; and we must conclude that the business plus Mr Hooley will be capable of much greater things than it possibly could be without him.' The usual vainglorious Hooley prospectus appeared a few weeks later, endorsed by the *FN* on the grounds that 'Lord Playfair and his colleagues are not the men to associate them- selves with an inflated undertaking' – in other words that there was no question of over-capitalisation; and a full subscription was achieved, though with far less ease than in the Dunlop case. For Hooley, who had bought the company for £2m and relaunched it with a capital of £2.5m, there were post-costs profits of about £300,000, as well as unspecified gains from insider dealing, not least when Bovril shares jumped up sharply following the shareholders' meeting. For Bovril itself, the boons were less than obvious: gross over-capitalisation (despite the soothing words of the *FN*), leaving the company hobbled for several years by the problem of servicing its capital. In a sense, for all its immediate pay-off, the episode marked the beginning of the end for Hooley. By 1897 his star was on the wane, and that May his flotation of Schweppes – old company bought for just over £1m, new company sold to the public for £1¼m, the Earl of March as Chairman – was at best only a partial success from his point of view, involving exceedingly heavy promotional costs to prevent the issue flopping. For the new company, its board too trusting of this Napoleon of finance, the legacy was again one of over-capitalisation putting a severe brake on future expansion. 'I bought a business as cheaply as I could and sold it again for the biggest price it would bring. Some people might say that by this method I robbed the public of millions of pounds, but nevertheless I did not do anything against the law.'[20] With a disarming defence like that (in *Hooley's Confessions*), what need for the prosecution?

The other main company promoter in the cycle boom – sometimes as a rival to Hooley, more often as an ally – was an equally unscrupulous character called Harry Lawson.[21] Little is known about his background, apart from the facts that he was born in the City in 1852 and that his father was a brass turner, but from the late 1870s he was a bicycle pioneer, promoting companies whenever and wherever he could. He was also a pioneer of motor cars, emerging in the mid-1890s as the man determined to keep control of a nascent industry, so far as he could, in his hands alone.[22] His initial financial vehicle, first registered in November 1895, was the British Motor Syndicate, which early in 1896 brought to the market the Daimler Motor Company, the first of its intended manufacturing subsidiaries. 'If you could send me something along just to liven the prospectuses up, I should be much obliged,' Lawson jotted on 1 February to his consulting engineer Frederick Simms; soon afterwards Daimler was launched, with the typical Lawson assertion that 'this new industry is, in the opinion of the Directors, likely to cause a revolution equal to that achieved by the most sensational invention ever brought before the public, even including the steam engine'. True enough, but as the *Statist* pointed out the disturbing fact was that of the capital of £100,000 now being sought, only £60,000 was working capital, the rest going to the British Motor Syndicate: 'Any intending investor in this Daimler Motor should ascertain what this £40,000 is really paid for. Is there an established manufactory, or is it only for patent rights? We offer no opinion as to the oil motor itself, but the finance appears to us to require looking into.' Sufficient investors stilled their qualms, and in May, almost simultaneously with Hooley's big Dunlop issue, Lawson not only organised an exhibition of motor cars at the Imperial Institute, visited on its opening day by the Prince of Wales, but successfully floated the Great Horseless Carriage Company. Two-thirds of its capital of £750,000 was set aside to acquire the patents of the British Motor Syndicate, one-third for working purposes; and it was claimed that a four-storey fire-proof factory had been acquired in Coventry. 'Such a sum is certainly not excessive when the possibilities of the industry are considered,' noted the *FN* of the working capital, in a generally supportive editorial; but the *Statist* pulled no punches, making fun of the fact that the prospectus was '20 by 15 inches as to size, and profusely illustrated', and sarcastically recording that 'only the modest (!) amount of £500,000 in cash or shares is the purchase consideration'.[23] From a strictly financial point of view, the auguries were poor for a time when Parliament might at last allow powered vehicles to travel at more than 4 mph without the need for a man with a red flag.

That happy day dawned in November, and there started to appear daily in the financial press a full-page, generously illustrated advertisement about 'The Coming Revenue of the British Motor Syndicate, Limited'. The run from London to Brighton on Saturday the 14th was the centre-piece of the motoring celebrations – an event sceptically described by the *Economist* on the day itself as 'apparently designed much more with the view of attracting capital from the public for one or other of the motor-car companies which have been launched, or are "upon the stocks", than purchasers for the vehicles themselves'. It was, indeed, basically a Harry Lawson venture, and at the dinner that evening at the Hôtel Métropole in Brighton, with the Earl of Winchelsea in the chair, it was Lawson who was toasted and who made a long speech. 'I am pleased to tell you,' he said, 'that every one of my own cars and the patent cars of the British Motor Syndicate arrived in Brighton quite safely.' But, with the BMS poised to refloat for a putative £3m, compared with an original capital of £150,000, would the City buy it? During the week following the Brighton run, it was reported that 'motor carriages have been very much in evidence around Throgmorton and Broad Streets, and a large number of Stock Exchange men turned out to see them working, and the dealers in the Miscellaneous market were prominent and seemed satisfied'.[24] Lawson, in short, was drumming his message home.

The prospectus appeared at the end of November, claiming that the BMS controlled 'almost the entire motor car industry in this country' and boasting amongst its directors the famous cricketer Prince Ranjitsinhji, described as 'owner of Indian patents'. The tone of press comment on this unblushingly opportunistic reconstruction was set by the *Economist*, which described Lawson as having 'the reputation of great shrewdness, and a distinct capacity for looking after the main chance'. The *FT* was particularly scathing, asserting that 'Mr H.J. Lawson evidently regrets the loss of that red flag', since he 'continues to emphasise the necessity for its existence by sending out motor-car prospectuses which require a special danger signal of their own to precede them'. And: 'It is with difficulty that we can restrain our mirth sufficiently to discuss the prospectus of the British Motor Syndicate in the manner demanded of those who write upon financial subjects in the City.' The paper, though, controlled its mirth sufficiently to offer a detailed, devastating analysis of a venture that was intending to allocate £2.7m to the vendors (headed by Lawson himself) and assign only £300,000 as working capital. And:

> Why, may we ask, are all material figures suppressed? Why is there no showing by a respectable accountant who vouches for their accuracy? Mr Lawson may be offering the public the chance of a lifetime, but why in the name of common sense hide his light under a bushel, if he is so doing? Modesty of this sort is not appreciated in the City . . . A pictorial supplement accompanies the prospectus, of a character that may amuse a child, but will certainly do little to convince a would-be shareholder . . .

Lawson's flotation never recovered from this and other attacks, and by mid-December the editor of the *Citizen* was demanding to know 'whether the motor-car movement has altogether fizzled out'. Further Lawson promotions in the early part of 1897 fared poorly, and in May the *Economist* flatly asserted that 'whatever incipient vitality the motor-car industry may have possessed seems to have been entirely extinguished by the expedition to Brighton and back', adding that BMS shares had become practically unmarketable. Or in the words of the same journal some months later, in the context of the shares of both Daimler and the Great Horseless Carriage Company at a severe discount and both companies struggling for life, 'very few company promoters have equalled Mr Lawson in glowing promises, while fewer still have been associated with so many ventures that have signally failed in the matter of performance'.[25] Further financial misadventures lay ahead, and it was little surprise that on his death in 1925 no obituary appeared in *Autocar*.

Did it matter that by far the most important financial intermediary in the early history of the British motor-car industry was a crook?[26] The answer is surely yes, for quite apart from the specific matter of shortages of working capital adversely affecting pioneer producers such as Daimler, the Lawson saga marked the beginning of what would be an uneasy, mutually mistrustful relationship between that industry and the City. The industry, not unnaturally, feared being ripped off again; the City, just as naturally, perceived the industry as full of unprofitable 'lemons' and was reluctant to subscribe or encourage the subscription of further capital. The analogy with the electrical industry, following the catastrophic 'Brush boom' of the early 1880s, is painfully obvious. How different it would have been if, say, one of the leading merchant banks had perceived the implications of the transport revolution that was at hand and acted as responsible financial midwife. Less ambitiously, it would even have made a perceptible long-term difference if influential City figures had pushed for an environment in which ambitious company promoters like Hooley or Lawson found it harder to wreak such damage. That, however, was not consonant with the whole business thrust of the City in the nineteenth century, a thrust aptly summed up in the timeless phrase *caveat emptor*, let the buyer beware. In February 1896 the Institute of Bankers heard a paper by an outsider on the state of the Companies Acts and proposed amendments. The chair was taken by Richard Biddulph Martin, banker and MP; and he started the discussion with an affirmation of abiding City verities:

> I am one of those who have often said here, and have always repeated, that the less legislation we have in things mercantile the better. We think we are able to take care of ourselves just as well as the Government can take care of us. What we want is reasonable means of carrying out our transactions, and not an interference with how these transactions should be carried out . . .

What did this freedom from interference mean in practice? Many years later, writing with admirable candour, the stockbroker Cecil Braithwaite recalled the untroubled world of the 1890s:

> In these days it was quite customary for say half a dozen men to get together and form a company. No prospectus was produced till many days after dealings had commenced, and the procedure was as follows.

The broker appointed by the promoting group went into the market and told his friends that he was bringing out a company to exploit, we will say, a gold mine. He – the broker – explained what the company was, and let his friends have some shares, with probably a call of more. He then arranged to have the shares bid for in order to attract attention, his friends in the market having 'Bated [*sic*] the Swim' among their friends. At this stage the company was not even registered. If the operation was successful, and a good market was established, a prospectus was then advertised, and nominally the public had a chance of subscribing. I say nominally, because if the shares already stood at a good premium, the public had very little chance of obtaining any. A special settlement was then applied for, which unless there was opposition generally went through. If the efforts of the group in the market failed to make the shares go, and be popular, often nothing more was heard of it . . .[27]

Was this an appropriate milieu for would-be borrowers in the world's leading capital market? South American republics hardly thought so in the 1820s, nor Central American ones in the 1870s, and now at the close of the Victorian age it was the turn of British industry to begin to question the complacent, convenient assumptions of the City of London.

*

Booms came and went, but nothing affected the sobriety of the money market report. 'Money was in fair demand today,' intoned the *FT* at the end of business on 14 November 1895, but almost certainly all sorts of arcane dramas were being played out that particular Thursday, including at the bill brokers Smith St Aubyn:

> *Settling Day.*
> A very big day and we were very short all the morning. About three o'clock Mr Daniell [the Government broker] came in & lent us £100,000 at 1% for a month. Believing this to be the long expected Japanese money the writer shot out & bought 5 laks of Rs per Page at an average price of 60.18.2 . . .
> Later in the day discounted McIver 22^m [i.e. thousand] Feb bills all nice names @ $1\frac{1}{4}$ for cash. Fine work!

Friday and Saturday were just as strenuous:

> By far the hardest day we have had for many months. £230^m called . . . After the greatest exertions & aware that I could not afford to risk anything I went to the Bank for 50^m. Not a shilling anywhere at 2.30 and

over £400^m on each side of the book. Discount varies between $1\frac{3}{16}$ and $1\frac{2}{8}$. Having no Stock prevented us getting Money from Stockbrokers.

Money was again very much wanted and at one time it looked like the Bank. Eventually however we got in money and finally at half past one we took 50^m fine running February from McIver at $1\frac{1}{2}$.

'The Bank' was of course the Bank of England, and early in 1896 a letter from Brown Shipley to Brown Brothers, responding to a recent remark from the New York end 'that you hope that we will make our discount account a "live" one at the Bank of England', further reflected the brooding presence of the Old Lady:

> With every desire to avail ourselves of facilities, our working with the Bank of England must be done with some circumspection. Every transaction of this kind comes under the scrutiny of the Committee of Directors in daily waiting & among these are some of our keenest competitors. Unless & until other Firms of *our standing* do it, we should be sure to expose ourselves to adverse criticism if we did it, without some such obvious reason as that with which the Venezuela scare lately supplied us.

Albert G. Sandeman was Governor for two years from the spring of 1895. A wine merchant with no very clear banking expertise, he still controlled an institution whose lightest word could make or break.[28]

In fact, the Bank of England was an increasingly competitive force in banking at large by the mid-1890s. The determining context was partly the Goschen settlement of 1892 having squeezed its regular income, partly the long period of cheap money (Bank rate at 2 per cent from February 1894 to September 1896) further reducing income, and partly a wish to do something to redress the balance in relation to the ever vaster resources and thus potential muscle power of the joint-stock banks. The main form that this new competitive attitude took was much increased discounting by the Bank's provincial branches, which during most of the 1880s had run at a loss but during the first half of the 1890s returned handsome profits of up to £80,000 pa.[29] In May 1896 Beckett Faber of the Leeds bank Beckett & Co complained to the Central Association of Bankers that the Bank's instructions to its provincial agents had become ' "Get business at fair rates if you can, but get business" ', and he went on:

> We do not complain about fair competition but this is fostered by free money costing the lender nothing at all. How can we country bankers who pay well for our deposits meet such competition as this? Our loans

are taken from us; our bills no longer exist in our cases and our current accounts are 'touted' for . . . The time is already arriving, if it has not already arrived, when the Bank of England must choose whether to be the banker for the Government or a commercial bank. It cannot be both . . .

At the meeting of the Association a few days later, Faber's views were strongly supported by other country bankers; but talk of the banks keeping their own independent reserve was swiftly dispelled by other, City-based bankers, including Felix Schuster of the Union of London, who successfully argued that a more prudent course was discussions with the Bank. On 3 June the Association held its annual dinner, and among those present were Sandeman, the Deputy-Governor, Richard Biddulph Martin, and a country banker called Rowland Hughes, Liverpool manager of the North and South Wales Bank. Hughes noted: 'Martin twitted the Bank of England upon its new departure in competing against its neighbours. He charged the "old Lady" with having adopted the role of the "new woman".'[30] Almost six years earlier the resolution of the Baring crisis had apparently presaged closer union between the Bank and the banking system, but things were not quite working out that way.

In the course of his three days in the City, Hughes took the opportunity to have long conversations with the sub-manager of the City office of the London and Westminster Bank and Whitburn of the bill brokers Reeves, Whitburn & Co, eliciting from them a series of opinions that owed much to inside information, something to prejudice and nothing to verbosity. These opinions he faithfully recorded verbatim:

> *R. Raphael & Sons.* 'They are quite undoubted. The senior is not dead. The announcement you saw of the death of "Raphael" referred to a relation of theirs – a stockbroker.'
> *Baring Bros & Co Ltd.* 'They are all right & doing very well; there is no danger of a repetition of their trouble.'
> *Credit Lyonnais.* 'They are very good; I regard them with more favor than either the Deutsche Bank or the Comptoir D'Escompte (the latter I don't care for) & I think all the better of them because they are not concerned in industrial enterprises.'
> *Lazard Bros & Co.* 'They have large means, but it should not be forgotten that their estate is all out of this country. They are very able people.'

Hughes also saw Sir Samuel Montagu. 'I may tell you,' he told Hughes, 'for your own information, that we have a capital of at least

£1,000,000. Some people give us credit for having more than this.'
Lofty words, but there ensued a rather sparky dialogue:

> L/M [i.e. Liverpool manager] reminded Sir Samuel that some time ago
> they offered us French Treasuries at $1\frac{3}{8}$, but in response to our counter
> offer of $1\frac{1}{2}$ they increased their rate to the latter figure.
> L/M pointed out that it was desirable they should in any offers they
> made to us quote the very best rate in the first instance, as we did not care
> to haggle about rates.
> *Sir Samuel*: 'On the occasion you refer to we were able to increase the
> rate because the exchange next day favored it.'[31]

Almost half a century earlier Montagu had made his way from Liverpool to London, becoming a great City name if never a warm
favourite, and it is unlikely that he was best pleased by this
particular country banker.

The week after Hughes's fact-finding visit, Messrs Barclay, Bevan,
Tritton, Ransom, Bouverie & Co of 54 Lombard Street issued a
circular announcing the creation of Barclay & Co, Ltd, an amalgamation of twenty private banks and capitalised at £6m. All but two of the
twenty were situated outside London, with a heavy bias towards the
eastern side of England, and the family ties between the partners of
these banks were extensive, with (historically at least) a distinctly
Quaker character. 'The Directors,' announced the circular, 'have been
selected from among the existing Partners, and the local management
will remain in the same hands as heretofore, the private character of
the Banks being thus preserved.' It was a claim made in implicit
contrast to existing joint-stock banks, and to a large extent it was
fulfilled, as Barclays over the next thirty years maintained a notably
decentralised structure, putting a banking premium on local knowledge.[32] Reaction at large, to an announcement that caused a considerable stir in the City, was probably summed up by the assertions of the
Bankers' Magazine that 'the spirit of the age cannot be resisted' and
that, for good or ill, 'amalgamation is the order of the day'. The
following February, at the Institute of Bankers, the theme of 'Bank
Amalgamations', not just the Barclays one, was addressed in a paper
given by the London and County Bank's F.E. Steele, from its head
office at 21 Lombard Street. Following his generally sanguine assessment, the ensuing discussion featured some altogether grumpier remarks from Harvey of Glyn Mills:

> Years ago I remember talking to an old private banker, who has since
> been absorbed, and he said, 'Perhaps we were not very wise, but we never

failed to support all private trade in the locality with which we were associated.' I think the private banker did that, and I think, moreover, when you consider the mechanism of the joint stock bank with its travelling inspectors, and the elaborate machinery by which it is managed, that there cannot but be a want of elasticity. I take it that the more you organise, the more you must sacrifice elasticity. The more you eliminate the personal equation, the more you destroy the personal influence, the more you substitute rule and precept for personal knowledge, to that extent you reduce the area of usefulness and limit the sphere of real service.[33]

The larger debate would run and run. It was hardly surprising if many in the City disliked these new joint-stock creations, for not only did a high proportion of their leading figures come from the provinces, but the very way in which they were organised seemed to undermine the personal basis on which the City had traditionally conducted its business.

The middle of May 1897 saw Rowland Hughes back in London. The bill broker Whitburn gave his usual crisp judgements, including on two major institutions. The first was the London and Westminster Bank, by now, some sixty years after its controversial beginnings, becoming a pillar of the City. 'They are,' said Whitburn, 'the only Bank in London who keep a bonâ fide reserve of gold. They have had for years £500,000 in gold locked up in their vaults and I have not heard of its being disturbed. It is the first Bank in London after the Bank of England.' His other assessment was of that venerable pillar itself: 'The feeling is general in the City that there is a want of competency in the management of the Bank of England. What they require is a strong man with a large salary who would be above suspicion. They do some very queer things there . . .'[34] The Governor by this time was Hugh Colin Smith, who in his favour was not a wine merchant – but instead, a wharfinger.

Was Smith the man to nurture a new spirit of concord between Bank and banks? Apparently so, to judge by events during Hughes's three days in London. First, Beckett Faber reported on the outcome of the delegation to the Bank that had arisen out of his protest letter of the previous year. It had comprised two London joint-stock bankers, two London private bankers and two country bankers, and according to Faber the Governor (who may have been Sandeman rather than Smith) 'promised to give instructions to their agents not to compete unduly with their neighbours'. Then, at the dinner of the Central Association of Bankers, Smith (in the words of Hughes) 'made a short but effective

speech to the effect that he personally regretted that they did not see
more of their Banking friends, & said that another thing he regretted
was the isolation of the Bank of England except when bad times came'.
The Governor's conciliatory sentiments were endorsed by J. Herbert
Tritton, a director of Barclays and honorary secretary of the London
Clearing House, who in his speech 'expressed a hope that something
might arise out of the Governor's speech which would lead to a better
understanding amongst Bankers'.[35]

Hopeful words, but in practice peace failed to break out in 1897, as
it took several years for the Bank's theoretical policy of drawing in its
competitive horns to be translated into action, above all in the provinces. This may have been because Smith's competitive instincts got the
better of him over the remaining almost two years of his governorship,
but perhaps more plausibly it was a case of the men on the ground
finding it more convenient to make their own policy. If so, a key figure
was undoubtedly Ernest Edye, in overall charge of the branches from
March 1897, producing from them an annual average profit of
£145,400 in his first seven years, almost double what it had been
over the previous nine years. 'This business has grown up,' wrote
Edye in 1904 in a typically combative retrospective report, 'in spite of
what I may, at least, term lack of encouragement on the part of the
Court – which is rather depressing. One Director, for instance, has
more than once expressed his opinion that Branch Deposits had better
be invested in Consols . . .' Such sentiments were anathema to Edye,
who, especially in his early years in charge, seems to have
sought business without apparent compunction. However, as he frankly admitted:

> The other Bankers, keeping accounts with the Bank of England, view
> with extreme jealousy any activity in the Bank's Banking operations –
> more particularly in the provinces, where the bulk of business in any
> individual place being less than that of London, particular operations are
> more easily identified. Bankers know that in the total 'private deposits'
> [i.e. of the Bank of England] their own deposits bulk very large, and from
> their point of view it is not unnatural that they should think it unfair that
> the Bank, holding their money free of interest, should compete with them
> in discounts, advances and the general Banking facilities which attract
> Drawing accounts.

Resentments, in short, were being stored up – and would
linger long after Edye's competitive drive had been forcibly
suppressed.[36]

Palpably short of competitive drive, in City matters anyway, was Richard Meinertzhagen, by January 1896 in reluctant situ at 12 Tokenhouse Yard:

> I was installed in a small windowless room and was given all sorts and conditions of Bills of Lading, Accounts, Letters of Credit, Acceptances and Cheques which I did not understand and did not want to understand. I loathed the whole business and was miserable . . . Moreover, I had to wear a black coat, London trousers and a top hat every day. I never felt so out of place. Nobody seemed to pay much attention to me, in fact for days nobody would come near me or try and explain things I had no wish to understand. The whole business seemed to be making huge loans of cash on coffee crops in Brazil and Costa Rica, on furs from Russia, on wool from Australia and the Argentine, and seeing to a whole mass of correspondence from Bremen, Hamburg and other business centres in Germany relating to the shipment of raw material from outlandish places to London. I spent much of my time with an atlas looking up the many places from which these world-wide letters came and making a list of those which I intended to visit some day.

The 17-year-old's misery was compounded by the presence in the City of his cousin Bill Playne. 'He was tall, of magnificent physique, a fine horseman and boxer,' but, 'I saw through Bill, for, beneath the out-ward geniality, virile good health, and amusing companionship, there was another side to his character'; and when the older cousin tried to get the younger fixed up with a prostitute, and Meinertzhagen refused, Playne 'had the most profound contempt for me as I did not share his views on sex'. On another occasion, Playne came into Huths 'brand-ishing a telegram and exclaiming: "Just my bloody luck, read this." The telegram read: "Your father is better and is now out of danger." ' After eight dismal months Meinertzhagen was sent by his father to Göttingen, from where he wrote at the end of September: 'I shall never make a City man, but learning German will be useful to me whatever I do.' And he went on: 'I want to see the world and not moulder away in a London fog. How can I justify my life to the Almighty if I have frittered away my time trying to make money, whereas if I can say I have done something to benefit humanity, I might get a good mark.'[37]

To outsiders, though, the money-making experience could seem thrilling. Part of the attraction derived from a reluctance over the years to explode the popular myth that jobbers on the Stock Exchange were somehow omniscient, possessing the gift of rapid, authoritative insight denied to other mortals. The truth about these extrovert and noisy but strangely inarticulate men was altogether more humdrum. It comes through strongly in a trio of snippets from the *Statist* in 1896:

> *15 August.* 'What do you think of Bryan's speech?' [of the American presidential candidate on the silver question] everybody was asking his neighbour in the American market on Thursday morning. Very clever and unexpectedly moderate was the general verdict pronounced on it . . . It was comical to observe how nonplussed the jobbers were at the opening, and how slow to commit themselves. It was at least five minutes before anyone would venture to make a price, even in plain stocks like Milwaukees, Louisvilles, or Denver Preferred. They stood waiting for each other, and it was with great difficulty that business was started even in a small way.
>
> *5 September.* It was perhaps a mercy that the telegram announcing the death of Prince Lobanoff [Russia's Foreign Minister] appeared in only one morning paper – the *Daily Telegraph* – which does not happen to have much vogue on 'Change. Three-fourths of the men in the House at Monday's opening knew nothing of the Kieff sensation, and even in the Foreign market it was not generally credited till confirmed by Reuter. When it did get known, many had to ask who Prince Lobanoff was; and a jocular reply, that he was only the Czar's brother-in-law, helped to still the troubled waves.
>
> *12 September.* The psychological moment in Capel Court happened about a quarter-past twelve o'clock on Thursday, when the Government broker, entering the Consol market unexpectedly, got up on a bench and announced that the Bank rate had been raised to $2\frac{1}{2}$ per cent. The Consol men were so completely taken back that they cheered the announcement, and they only recovered their senses when a smart man offered Goschens down to 112 . . . Meanwhile, every other man was remarking to his neighbour, 'Quite an event, isn't it?'

The real position was neatly defined by Lawrence Jones, a merchant banker who came to the City just before the First World War. He wrote in his memoirs: 'The idea that stock-jobbers have secret sources of information and know what a Poincaré is going to say next Sunday before he says it, and mark the prices of their wares up and down accordingly, is of course moonshine. They take the same interest in public affairs as the rest of us, no more nor less, and have the same sources of information, which is usually the press . . .'[38]

Perhaps, though, the Stock Exchange Committee had inside information when it came, towards the end of 1896, to appointing a member to be its new secretary. On 3 December the chairman of the special sub-committee 'called attention to the paragraph in the notice inviting applications which stated that the candidate must be between the age of 30 and 50, and stated that an application had been made by E.C. Grant, the official assignee, who was over the age of 50'. After discussion it was unanimously resolved that Grant's application could not be considered. The official assignee was responsible for ensuring the equitable distribution to creditors of a defaulter's assets, a not unimportant job, and two days later Ernest Grant was penning a letter strong on reproach if shaky on logic:

> May I appeal against the decision of your Sub-committee? . . . Admitting, as I must, that I am four months over the strictest interpretation of the words adopted, I am at the same time only 50 in the ordinary parlance, and I was well under that age at the time the vacancy was first mooted. The experience I have acquired during 18 years, of what I can only characterise as continuously unpleasant and painful duties, varied at times by a pressure and strain which has taxed my physical capacities to the utmost, should give me an advantage equivalent to several years in age over a candidate who has not had similar opportunities . . .

All in vain: a shocking example of ageism, but fifteen months later Grant was dead, his funeral at Aylesford in Kent being attended by the deputy Chairman.[39]

Maybe it was becoming a young man's game, to judge by the rising temper of the House in February 1897. On the 15th the Committee considered a letter from R.W. Blumenthal 'complaining of the annoyance to which he had been subjected in the market, which culminated when he was subjected to personal violence'. Names were mentioned, and names attended:

> In answer to questions, Mr Sanderson stated that there had been a good deal of play in the market, but that it was in the nature of good-humoured fun: that several other members had been subjected to similar treatment and that the whole market was concerned in the affair.
>
> Mr Walker admitted pulling Mr Blumenthal's coat, but said he did not tear it.
>
> Mr Phillips admitted that he was one of those concerned, but stated that he did not hold Mr Blumenthal for the purpose of sawdust being thrown over him.
>
> Mr Jackson said that he was not concerned in the affair, as he had himself just been put over the screen and was outside arranging his collar at the time, but that he did not wish to dissociate himself from the other members complained of.

At which point Blumenthal, who before the meeting had received a letter of apology from the four musketeers, appealed to the Committee to take no further action in the matter, and only a mild punishment ensued. All around was continuing discord, as the *Citizen* related on Saturday the 20th:

> A good deal of horseplay and other things have gone on this last week, and the row between Mr Percy Joseph and Mr Le Mare was not an altogether edifying spectacle. I expect that when Mr Joseph thought over the day's business – probably in an easy chair after dinner with a cigar in his mouth – he wished that he had not ventured a second time into the Eastern market during the afternoon to try to deal in £1,000 North British. His methods are sometimes very annoying to jobbers, and consequently he cannot at all times do his business as well as his bringing-up makes him wish to. Mr Paul Schweder has had several rows, and as this is nothing unusual I only refer to it because they have been more numerous than is commonly the case, but it was certainly hard luck on him to be called 'a dirty Polish Jew', and I was glad to see that Mr Edward Mocatta should take exception to this term, the last word of which was said in a tone of disdain for the race which should not be used anyhow on the Stock Exchange, where so many good examples are prominent members.[40]

'. . . anyhow'!

Richard Meinertzhagen was back in London by about this time. His father had arranged for him to join the highly respectable stockbrokers Laurie, Milbank & Co, which he did as a clerk in May 1897. 'I loathed the whole business, did not understand the work, nor did I wish to understand it,' was Richard's usual biddable attitude, even though his father Daniel 'did his utmost to raise my enthusiasm by asking large firms to give me orders on which I received fantastic commissions'. For instance: 'On one occasion, old Charles Goschen asked me to go round and see him. We had a pleasant conversation which ended in him asking me to buy him £75,000 worth of a South American investment. I did so and got a commission of over £80.' It made not a halfpenny of difference, as he recorded in his diary later that summer: 'I do not think I can stand this life much longer. I am wasting my life and my youth. A stuffy office, no exercise, complete slavery and a future ruined by an atmosphere in which gold is the sole aim.' The end of this wretched phase came with merciful swiftness. The following February his elder brother Dan died suddenly of appendicitis, and both his father and Frederick Huth Jackson pushed for Richard to take Dan's prospective place in Huths; but his mother insisted that he was unsuited, Richard himself remained adamantly against, and instead the berth went to his younger brother Louis, leaving Richard free to hunt for bigger game than sordid commissions.[41]

Did the soul of Bertram Currie nod mutely as young Meinertzhagen made his great escape? Who knows? The hammer of the bimetallists was operated on for cancer in December 1895, but was back in the City by the end of the following month. In August 1896 he found out from his doctor that his cancer had returned, and at once he wound up his affairs at Glyn Mills and said farewell to Lombard Street. 'From the moment . . . that the sentence was pronounced,' his widow would write in a memorial letter addressed to her dead husband, 'you steadily faced the near prospect of death, and ceased to feel any interest in the business that had hitherto engrossed you.' A renowned and sardonic atheist, he was now, in the words of his widow, 'most desirous to do all that he could to make amends for his neglect of religion in the past', and that autumn he was received into the Catholic Church. Currie died on 28 December 1896. His old admirer Sir Edward Hamilton wrote in his diary a warm appreciation – 'I shall always regard him as the longest-headed man in the City of his day' – that ended, however, on a melancholy note: 'He was a striking instance of the irony of wealth. His wife was a hopeless invalid & he had only two children, one of whom died and the remaining boy is sickly; while he was himself overcome by the direst of all complaints. How little can riches do to redress such a balance!' Many public tributes were paid, including of course from Gladstone, but the last word on a notable career belongs to Currie himself, on whose lips there was often the following favourite jingle:

> A City banker born and bred,
> Sufficient for my fame,
> If those who knew me best have said
> I tarnished not the name.[42]

*

England's leading urban novelist of the late nineteenth century was without doubt George Gissing, and in *Born in Exile*, published in 1892, there takes place a striking conversation between the impoverished intellectual Godwin Peak and a refined young lady called Sidwell Warricombe. She cites Charlotte Brontë's preference, as expressed in *Villette*, for the busy City over the indolent West End, but he disagrees:

'That term, the West End, includes much that is despicable, but it means also the best results of civilisation. The City is hateful to me, and for a reason which I only understood after many an hour of depression in walking about its streets. It represents the ascendency of the average man.'

Sidwell waited for fuller explanation.

'A liberal mind,' Peak continued, 'is revolted by the triumphal procession that roars perpetually through the City highways. With myriad voices the City bellows its brutal scorn of everything but material advantage. There every humanising influence is contemptuously disregarded. I know, of course, that the trader may have his quiet home, where art and science and humanity are the first considerations; but the *mass* of traders, corporate and victorious, crush all such things beneath their heels. Take your stand (or try to do so) anywhere near the Exchange; the hustling and jolting to which you are exposed represents the very spirit of the life about you. Whatever is gentle and kindly and meditative must here go to the wall – trampled, spattered, ridiculed. Here the average man has it all his own way – a gross utilitarian power.'

'Yes, I can see that,' Sidwell replied, thoughtfully. 'And perhaps it also represents the triumphant forces of our time.'

He looked keenly at her, with a smile of delight.

'That also! The power which centres in the world's money-markets – plutocracy.'

Events of the next few years hardened Gissing's loathing of the City, and he spent the second half of 1896 writing one of his most remarkable novels, *The Whirlpool*, published the following spring. It is, among many other things, a study of rampant greed and commercialism, as well as the fear and misery that accompany them; and a key figure in the early stages is the company promoter Bennet Frothingham, whose highly speculative Britannia Loan, Assurance, Investment and Banking Company crashes as he commits suicide. The novel's central character is the Gissing-like Harvey Rolfe, who on the morning of the smash reflects philosophically: 'After all, it promised to clear the air. These explosions were periodic, inevitable, wholesome. The Britannia Loan, &c, &c, &c, had run its pestilent course; exciting avarice, perturbing quiet industry with the passion of the gamester, inflating vulgar ambition, now at length scattering wreck and ruin.' But later in the day his mood darkens, and he writes to a friend about his intention to leave London and go to the country for a few days: 'I feel as if we were all being swept into a ghastly whirlpool which roars over the bottomless pit.'[43] Though flawed by the author's lack of flesh-and-bones knowledge of the square mile, the novel persuasively placed the City at the heart of a much larger argument about what later generations would call the state of the nation.

Gissing must have had Hooley at least partly in mind, though earlier in 1896, soon after the Jameson Raid, he wrote prophetically to a friend: 'The late troubles in S. Africa are of course due entirely to capitalist greed. I cannot see any hope for peace, so long as these men of the money-market are permitted to control public life – as they now practically do.' One of those greedy capitalists, and a hero of the Stock Exchange, was Barney Barnato, though not himself implicated in the Raid; and in 1897 his career moved to a Frothingham-style conclusion. On the last day of May, he was the subject of a letter sent to Sir Edgar Vincent in Constantinople by one of his London representatives: 'I imagine that his indisposition must be DT's . . . A Cape telegram says he is better. I am afraid if anything goes wrong with him that the shares of his Companies, such as Barnato Consols, Johnnies, Buffels &c will suffer.' Soon afterwards the afflicted, increasingly melancholic Barnato left the Cape, hoping to be back in London in time to give a party on Jubilee Day, 22 June, at his grandiose new Park Lane house where he had yet to live. He never did, jumping overboard when the ship was south of Madeira. News of his death reached the Stock Exchange on Tuesday the 15th, when Tommy Marks of the brokers Marks, Bulteel, Mills & Co moved swiftly by going into the market and buying up shares with which Barnato was connected and thereby stopping, on behalf of Barnato Bros, any possible slump. Barney's funeral took place the following Sunday at the Jewish Burial Ground in Willesden and there was an impressive City turn-out, with mourners including Alfred Beit, Sir Joseph Renals, Harry Paxton and Douglas MacRae, as well as the great Surrey cricketer George Lohmann, who had strong South African connections. Absent was a survivor of the infamous Renals banquet, Carl Meyer, who on hearing the news wrote to his wife: 'Poor Barney! What a tragic end to the career of a gigantic humbug but an amusing one.'[44] That, in the end, was the City's verdict on the meteor that had passed across its firmament.

Jubilee decorations abounded everywhere, and the procession of the cortège down a packed Edgware Road made an incongruous sight. The next morning, the 21st, almost all the members of the Stock Exchange assembled on the floor of the House under the leadership of Charlie Clarke; and, according to the *FT*, 'if the musical rendering of the National Anthem was not exactly musical, it was the result of heartfelt sentiment'. There was plenty of Jubilee gossip, including Hooley's self-publicising gift of gold communion plate to St Paul's Cathedral;

while Gissing that Monday jotted down a characteristic entry in his commonplace book: 'The hideousness of the streets. Nothing obvious but huge stands reared on speculation.' On Jubilee Day itself, the Queen passed through the City after the service at St Paul's in the morning, and *The Times*, at this high noon of British imperialism, described the scene in preparation for a frail old lady:

> All the way along Cheapside there were festoons and garlands hung from Venetian masts, while innumerable flags lent colour to the dingy fronts of the houses, and imparted an air of festivity and rejoicing to the scene. The Mansion-house was tastefully decorated with evergreens, and blue-embroidered drapery . . . Over the Bank of England had been erected an ambitious allegorical painting by M. Legros, intended to symbolize Great Britain, Labour and Commerce; but the decorations as a whole from St Paul's to the Mansion-house were not remarkable for originality, or, indeed, for anything except brightness and variety. It may safely be affirmed, however, that never in the long course of its history did the City look gayer or more picturesque than yesterday. The presence of thousands of ladies in the daintiest and most elegant of summer dresses was in itself more effective than any decoration that could have been devised . . .
>
> No more striking contrast can be imagined than that which the neighbourhood of the Mansion-house presented to its normal everyday appearance. The roadway in Cheapside was perfectly clear, and that seething whirlpool of traffic in front of the Royal Exchange which fills with amazement all who look upon it for the first time had disappeared. One saw instead the brilliant uniforms of the soldiers composing the 5th Brigade, whose commander, Colonel Barrington Campbell, of the Scots Guards, galloped backwards and forwards . . .
>
> During the long interval which elapsed between the time of taking their places and the arrival of the first part of the procession the spectators had abundant opportunities for looking about them, and to those for whom associations have a charm there was no lack of interesting material for observation and reflection. It is using no figure of speech to call this spot the heart of London, and of the Empire.[45]

CHAPTER TEN

Gone off Pop

'The Chanc of the Exchequer has written an able and lucid mem^{n} containing his views on the proposals of the American delegates,' noted Hamilton on 31 July 1897 in the context of a visiting mission led by Senator Wolcott banging the old drum of an international bimetallist agreement. 'He points out the objections to all of them, so far as the Imperial Gov^{t} is directly concerned, with the exception of the suggestion that the bullion reserve of the Bank of England be kept in silver to the extent of $\frac{1}{5}$th as allowed by the Act of 1844 . . .' Hicks Beach had taken suitably monometallic advice from the Bank, the Rothschilds and Hamilton himself, but the rub, uncommented on by Hamilton at the time, lay in 'the exception'; and when, in the middle of September, an article in *The Times* and a statement at the General Court made it clear that the Governor of the Bank, Hugh Colin Smith, had agreed that the Bank should, under certain conditions and in accordance with Wolcott's proposals, hold one-fifth of its reserve in silver, a fresh storm broke over monetary matters.[1]

Hamilton recorded it on the 16th: 'The reception of the announcement, which is regarded as an imprudent flirtation of the "Old Lady" with bimetallism, shows how exceedingly sensitive the great City world is about any suspicion of tampering with our currency system.' Significantly, he went on: 'The retention of a moderate amount of the white metal in the Issue Department is the least harmful of the proposals of the American Delegates; but the game would certainly not be worth the candle.' Four days later the *FT* almost surely reflected mainstream City opinion when it declared that the Bank had 'no business to be coquetting with bi-metallism at her time of life', adding that though it might be 'a perfectly innocent flirtation', nevertheless 'no one wants to hear the dear old lady "talked about" at all in such a connection'. Then, on the 22nd, a meeting of London's Clearing House bankers considered the question. Parr's proposed a resolution 'disapproving of the Bank of England agreeing to hold that proportion [i.e. one-fifth], or any other proportion whatever, of silver against the note circulation', and the resolution was passed 'with practical unanimity', the sentiments of the bankers being conveyed to the Governor.[2]

A surprising exception to the unanimity may have been Sir John Lubbock, who had succeeded Currie as President of the Gold Standard Defence Association and seems to have sought compromise. 'I have been annoyed to hear that Sir John held a brief apparently for the Bank at the Clearing House meeting,' Robert Benson wrote the next day to George Peel, secretary of the GSDA. Benson also canvassed the idea that it might be necessary to call for the heads of Gibbs and Grenfell, that inveterate bimetallist duo, as directors of the Bank, but then dismissed the notion: 'We don't want to force matters to the point of Gibbs & Grenfell's resignation. The former I fear has not long to live [another ten years] & is a loveable man. As to the latter a letter I have received this morning calls him an impostor & a guinea pig. I don't quite agree. He is . . . ugly if you like. Henceforward let the Times *print him small.*' And: 'I feel sure that there must be a division of opinion at the Bank which we may leave for the present to fructify.' Benson's analysis was probably correct – according to him, many of the directors had been 'entirely ignorant of the Governor's action', that of 'a wharfinger & not a banker' – but arguably the larger truth lay in the calm assertion of the *Bankers' Magazine* in October that even if the one-fifth proposal did 'come to a practical issue', improbable though that was, 'we may depend on the care and prudence of the Bank to see that the banking business of the country incurs no injury thereby . . .'[3]

Still, even if a storm in a teacup, storm it was, and in mid-October Hicks Beach received a numerously signed monometallic petition from City merchants, bankers and others, as well as a counter-memorial from the Bimetallic League. 'Natty Rothschild declines to sign the mono-metallic memorial,' observed Hamilton, 'on the ground that as his Firm was consulted by the Government it should stand aloof. This is not much of a reason. I suspect he is mainly influenced by his intimate relations with the bimetallic First Lord.' The allusion was to Balfour, but Hamilton perhaps did Natty an injustice, for on the 16th the latter sent a letter of warning to Balfour: 'I think it right that you should know how astonished I have been to find, that an intense feeling has been raised in this city against any concessions being made here in London to the bimetallist party. The idea that the Bank of England might keep a portion of its reserve in silver has raised quite a storm of indignation.'[4] This may well have been a decisive intervention, and a week later the government made plain its wholesale rejection of the Wolcott proposals.

On 1 December a good sprinkling of monometallists, still flushed by victory, gathered at the Institute of Bankers to hear the inaugural address of its President, Colonel Robert Williams MP of William Deacon's, 20 Birchin Lane. Williams took exception to a letter by Professor H.S. Foxwell that had been read aloud at the bimetallic conference held in Manchester on 12 October, in which (according to Williams) this economist had attacked as essentially self-interested the opposition of London bankers to the recently proposed policy concerning the Bank's reserve. The President then considered the wider issue:

> If the mere undertaking of the Government of the Bank, in certain unlikely conditions, to keep one-fifth of its reserve in silver, is enough to send an ominous shiver throughout the City, what might have been the effect of the knowledge that our Government were seriously considering the far-reaching propositions laid before the Conference? This country has enjoyed an unexampled career of prosperity for the last three-quarters of a century under (I do not say because of) our present system of currency. This system has become so much a matter of course to the vast majority of those engaged in commerce here as to appear a law of nature. I can hardly doubt that if alterations were seriously attempted it would cause such a storm of bewilderment and panic as would compel the strongest Government to abandon the most perfect bimetallic scheme ever conceived.

The vote of thanks was given by a leading member of the GSDA, J. Herbert Tritton of Barclays, who took the chance to tackle Foxwell head on:

> We move in wide circles, and we are in touch with men and affairs. I ask you, is a professor in touch with men and affairs? No, he is not as a rule; but we bankers are, and we speak with knowledge, and we speak with effect, because we are in touch with the affairs of the world, and because we know we have the backing of the very large proportion of the educated opinion of this country on the side which we urge.[5]

It was a rare outburst on the part of practical City man, whose relationship with the academy would never be an easy one.

1898 saw a revealing tailpiece to the monetary debate. Five years earlier the Indian mints had been closed to silver, against the wishes of the Bimetallic League; now, after a period of stabilisation, the question arose of whether India should follow the example of most of the civilised world and adopt the gold standard.[6] The arguments were complicated, but the clear wish of the government of India (not shared by the Manchester exporting interest) was to do so. However, on 25 March Lord George Hamilton at the India Office warned the Viceroy that 'our Lombard Street friends are terribly sensitive upon a..ything relating to the dispatch of gold from this country' – a warning, in other words, that the City's enthusiasm for the gold standard was muted as regards India. The following month the Fowler Commission on Indian Currency was appointed, prompting the City to get up a well-signed petition in May complaining that too many of its members had been taken from the official class, whereas it 'should have been composed to a larger extent of men with thorough practical knowledge of Indian trade and with the effect of movements of bullion on the Commerce of this and that Country'. However, the petition did more than that, as the monometallist Welby (by now retired from the Treasury) explained on the 13th to a like-minded correspondent. He related a City conversation earlier that day with his friend Lawrence Chalmers of Brown Shipley:

> He [Chalmers] told me that he had seen the petition, and that it had two main points. 1. remonstrated against the narrow constitution of the Commission & 2. regretted that the instruction was so limited, ie that the Commission c[d] not take up opening the Mints or bimetallism. They got the Gov of the Bank (ass!) to sign first – not if you please as Gov but because he owns a convenience or something of that kind in Tooley S[t]. Then why does he sign first? Both Lubbock & Tritton signed – with Gibbs & all the Heretics.[7]

The official mind still wanted India on the gold standard, but Lombard Street, it seemed, was cooling by the hour.

That same day, 13 May, the GSDA's Peel wrote a key letter elucidating what was a complex situation:

> The Bimetallists, of course, wish to oppose a Gold Standard for India & to replace India upon a silver standard. Once that is done, Bimetallism is alive again & enters into the sphere of practical politics, in the calculations, at least, of the Bimetallists.
> The Monometallists are divided. Some wish for a gold, and some for a silver standard, for India. Both of these two latter classes express their views freely & do their best to influence public opinion. Members of both are upon the Gold Standard Association for we can belong to either class while strenuously opposing Bimetallism.

The opposition to a Gold Standard for India is somewhat accentuated at the present moment by the proposals of the Indian Government which include the withdrawal of a certain amount of gold from the London market. Many bankers are not prepared for such a drain of gold.

Three days later, with the GSDA in some danger of breaking up, Peel sought to reassure an irate Welby, for whom the action of Lubbock and Tritton had been beyond the pale:

The real fact is that, what with the speeches of Lord Salisbury and Mr Chamberlain [in the context of an apparently threatening situation in the Far East], the existence of a war [between the USA and Spain], of a high bank-rate [4 per cent], and of dear bread, many leading men in the City think that a drain of gold to India at this time would cause a panic . . . I cannot think that, taking into account the reality of this feeling and the vast nature of their obligations, there is anything unreasonable in their request [i.e. to broaden the terms of the Fowler Commission] and that there is any connection at all between this action and a tendency towards Bimetallism.[8]

All of which meant that a gold standard for India was no longer a runner. Nevertheless, the apparent alternative of a silver standard did *not* triumph. Instead, the eventual outcome was what is best described as a gold-exchange standard, by which the sovereign was made legal tender there and sterling thus reigned supreme over the rupee; while back home the City was protected from sudden major outflows of gold (in addition to those it already had to cope with) and the GSDA held together.

In May 1901 that body, having fulfilled its function, was formally disbanded. Thereafter bimetallism was little more than a historical curiosity, something to be studied by Brenda Last in her ill-fated economics course in Evelyn Waugh's *A Handful of Dust*. It had foundered partly because of long-term economic factors – above all, industrial revival and vastly increased gold production – but also through hitting the rocks of City resistance, which in practice put the movement beyond the bounds of feasible politics, whatever the individual sympathies of Conservative ministers. It was a resistance based to only a limited extent on an objective, thorough assessment of the merits and implications of rival policies. Rather, to quote the bimetallist Hermann Schmidt writing in the *Bankers' Magazine* in 1895, 'the objection of so many bankers to a change of standard is probably attributable to the innate conservatism of their class, which dislikes all change'. Or, as another bimetallist, Herbert Gibbs, put it to Senator Wolcott in March 1897, when the American still had high hopes of his mission to England, 'a Banker is an animal by nature cautious and it is exceedingly difficult to get him to say anything, except in favour of existing conditions whatever they might be'.[9] These bankers of the late-Victorian City were fortunate men, who saw the existing order of things as natural, ordained and likely to last for, if not all time, at least their prosperous lifetimes.

*

By the autumn of 1897 Harry Paxton was back in the American market – 'very much in favour of Wabash "B" bonds', the *Citizen* reported on 9 October, 'a big buyer of Central Pacifics' a week later – but to judge by the weekly gossip columns of the same paper, pride of place amongst Yankee jobbers now went to an equally extrovert figure. 'Wires come pouring in and dealings often go on in the Street up to as late as 5.30. Mr Tootie Brander is always to be found at work, and has apparently been receiving good orders from a large outside operator with whom he is generally to be seen refreshing himself at Messrs Moore Brothers after the day's work is over.' That was at the end of July, while three months later as the nights drew in: 'Mr Tootie Brander's new overcoat has been one of the features of the Street market, and he seemed pleased it was so much liked!' In February 1898 he was still a feature: 'Mr Tootie Brander has been booking bargains almost faster than usual, and it was very pretty to see the way he picked up a small line of Union Pacifics from the arbitrage dealers the other evening at $34\frac{5}{8}$ after they had refused to sell them to him nearly $\frac{1}{2}$ dollar higher.'[10] The jobbing equivalent of a delicate late cut, it was a reminder that there was more to the craft than a loud voice and sleek overcoat.

By the 1890s the Stock Exchange possessed an emblematic quality, nicely reflected in the new melodrama that opened at Drury Lane in September 1897. Called *The White Heather*, and written by Cecil Raleigh and Henry Hamilton with a palpable eye on the main chance, it was described by *The Times* as 'particularly rich in spectacular effect – an immense piece of theatrical mechanism rather than a play'. It included several scenes 'which may each be called a triumph of sensationalism', one of which showed 'the interior of the Stock Exchange with its horse-play and its excitement culminating in the "hammering" of a prominent member', who promptly 'falls dead under the shock'.

And, 'all the characteristic manners of the Stock Exchange are exhibited in this scene with a ruthless fidelity; and the public reward the
enterprise of the management with unstinted applause'. The clapping
and cheering first-night audience included many members in the stalls
and dress circle, with an abundance of clerks in the pit; over the next
few weeks it became almost de rigueur in Capel Court to sport a sprig
of white heather in one's buttonhole. It was even rumoured that
members appeared on the stage itself from time to time as supers. That,
though, was a privilege denied to the Stock Exchange's waiters: when
the suggestion was made that they might like to earn a few shillings on
the side by appearing in exact copies of their resplendent uniforms, the
managers firmly quashed it.[11]

But the real drama that autumn was the great Cripplegate fire in
November. It began just before 1 p.m. on Friday the 19th in Hamsell
Street, on the premises of the mantle manufacturers Waller & Brown,
and soon spread all over the Cripplegate area – a rundown district
that, as part of the Barbican, lay outside the City walls and was full of
narrow streets and six-storey warehouses and sweatshops stuffed with
the most inflammable materials. The *City Press* the next day rose to
the challenge:

> The rapidity with which the flames enveloped huge warehouses was
> amazing . . . The heat was excessive some distance off; and, though it was
> broad daylight at the time, the huge tongues of flame that now and then
> leaped high into the air tinged the clouds above with a ruddy hue which
> was observable in all parts of the City . . . Various rumours were afloat
> as to injuries which were sustained by some of the girls who were working
> in the warehouses, and in this connexion we have to record the prompt
> action of a young fellow named James Vaughan, in the employ of Messrs
> William Wood & Co, portmanteau manufacturers, of Edmund-place.
> Vaughan was made aware that several young women were in danger on
> the top floor of one of the burning warehouses, and very pluckily he
> carried some eighteen of them – several having fainted – across the roofs
> to positions of safety . . .

No one died, but about a hundred buildings were damaged, of which
at least half, according to the *City Press* a few days later, were 'either
absolutely burned down or burned out'. Premises totally destroyed
included, in Hamsell Street alone, those of the brace manufacturers
Ramsay & Co, mantle manufacturers Phillips & Abbott, ostrich-
feather merchant J.H. French, tie makers H. Pentony & Co, and
merchants and shippers Lethem Bros & Mellin. How had the fire

started? The chief witness at the subsequent inquest held in the old
Council Chamber at the Guildhall was Alfred Brown, principal of
Waller & Brown:

> At the time he was up stairs on the third floor with two of his
> forewomen. He did not occupy the whole of the house, but only the first,
> second, and third floors. At the moment when his attention was first
> called to the fire he was looking at the cutting order book. The fire
> appeared to him to come right up the ventilation shaft. He looked down
> the shaft, and saw a quantity of smoke . . . There were some thirty hands
> on the premises, all women and girls. He got them out on to the parapet,
> and, with the exception of two or three, who went into hysterics, they
> behaved very well. They were all safely conveyed from the parapet to an
> adjoining warehouse . . . He had been in business for 12 years, and was
> insured for £8,000 . . . So far as he knew, nobody had been smoking on
> the premises prior to the outbreak of fire. He was smoking between
> half-past ten and eleven o'clock in his office. Nobody else was allowed to
> smoke, and he did not think that any of his hands would have lighted
> their pipes before leaving the building [i.e. the male hands, who ate lunch
> out]. When he finished his morning pipe he did not put it in his pocket,
> but on his desk.

As other evidence was heard, attention focused on Brown's apparent
sang-froid as his warehouse crashed about him, as well as a rumour
that, a few days before the fire, he had offered his entire stock at 40
per cent under cost price to a firm of mantle manufacturers in Manchester; but in the end, after an examination by accountants had
shown the solvency of Brown's firm, the jury decided that, though the
fire had been wilfully caused, it had been done so by some person or
persons unknown.[12] It was an unsatisfactory end to London's largest
fire since the Great Fire of 1666.

The same month a letter from Brown Shipley, definitely inside the
City walls, to Brown Brothers reflected the increasingly pressing
general problem of how to find new blood to transfuse the closed,
often rather neurotic world of merchant banking partnerships. It followed renewed pressure from New York to revitalise the London end:

> We have no hesitation in saying at once that if we knew of a man
> possessed of good means, the requisite ability & experience, & favour-
> ably known to people in London & in the United States, who wished to
> join our Firm, we quite see that it would be for the benefit of all
> concerned that we should admit him. But the fact is that we do not know
> such a man at present & we feel sure that to make any conspicuous effort
> to find such a man would do us more harm than good. Moreover . . . we

should have to make everything clear to an outsider (if there is to be any prospect of working harmoniously with him afterwards) and we might do all that & *yet* meet with a refusal of the invitation after all.

J.S. Morgan & Co was also now searching, after the death of Walter Burns in November left open the position of senior partner in London, amidst a feeling on both sides of the Atlantic that this time it should be filled by an Englishman; Morgans' quest proved protracted but at least it met with eventual success, which was more than could be said for the half-hearted efforts of Brown Shipley to find a suitable outsider, in other words non-family. One firm did not even try, arguably all the more culpably in that it had at hand a ready-made recruit who over the years had climbed through the ranks at New Court. Hamilton, from his vantage point as an intimate of Natty and the others, recorded the rather sour outcome shortly before Christmas 1897:

> There is considerable excitement in Rothschild circles about the retirement of Carl Meyer from his post in the firm. He has been a clever *aide* to the firm, being a good linguist and having a great aptitude for calculations. Latterly, having feathered his nest well, he wanted to be less tied; and, fully expecting that he could dictate his own terms, he threatened to retire unless his position was improved. Hence to his surprise, he was taken at his word: it being thought by the brothers that he was getting a little 'too big for his boots'.[13]

The underlying crux, however, was the obstinate refusal of the Rothschilds to take a non-Rothschild into partnership, despite Meyer's outstanding abilities and the fact that he was in his prime. This was a fateful choice, and Natty, for all his many merits, made the wrong one, rashly staking everything on the prowess of the rising generation of Rothschilds.

It was probably in the winter of 1897/8 that Harry Paulet, soon to become the sixteenth Marquess of Winchester, was in a railway compartment with Ernest Cassel, returning to London one Monday morning. Cassel was opening his post, Paulet recalled, 'when suddenly he said, "My ship has come home". I asked him what he meant and he told me that the Rothschilds had declined financing the construction of the Assuan Dam, and the Government had accepted his offer.' Cassel was right to recognise this as a turning-point in his career, for his initiative, in marked contrast to Rothschild caution, gained him not only further riches but also intimacy in the counsels of the Foreign Office (which saw the dam as crucial to the future of the Egyptian economy) and a general recognition that he was the pre-eminent City financier of his age – in short, it transformed him from somewhere near the top of the first division to global superleague.[14] The contract for the construction of the dam was signed in February 1898, and four months later the National Bank of Egypt was created to further Egyptian economic development, with Cassel again the master influence. Sitting on its board was Carl Meyer, by now very much Cassel's man, though not in the quasi-feudal sense that had so irked him at New Court.

The same year, 1898, also saw the Rothschild star on the wane in the Far East, two years after the second Chinese indemnity loan had given the Hongkong and Shanghai Bank the chance to reimpose its local authority as far as the Foreign Office was concerned. 'The Chinese don't seem to be jumping at our offer,' Hamilton noted in January about the proposed third indemnity loan, adding: 'The Rothschilds have not been consulted, which is a great mortification; and in order that there may be an appearance of their being "in it", Natty R., I hear, says that he tendered his advice and it is being acted upon.' The loan itself proved a difficult one to land, amidst an accelerating international scramble for all things Chinese, but the Hongkong and Shanghai's Cameron ('a very intelligent straightforward man', according to Hamilton) pursued it tenaciously and won the day by the end of February. Soon afterwards, Hamilton found himself being 'pressed' by the Rothschilds to get Hicks Beach to 'move' the Bank of England 'about issuing as well as inscribing the new Chinese loan'. It was an ill-disguised ploy to undermine the Hongkong and Shanghai, and Hamilton commented: 'This he will not do. The Bank would take great exception to it themselves; and as the institution is regarded abroad as a semi-state bank, it would be certain to be said that, notwithstanding all our protestations, the Government were really standing behind the financiers.'[15]

Even so, Rothschild influence was far from being extinguished by 1898. In February, against the background of a rapidly emerging conventional wisdom that if only there were 'good government' in the Transvaal then working costs in the gold-mining industry could be drastically reduced, Rothschilds co-operated closely with the Colonial Office in ensuring that the Transvaal government found itself unable to float a projected loan on the London market. During the summer, Natty Rothschild effectively dictated the terms of Brazil's controversial £10m Funding Loan, involving harsh deflationary medicine for that country's economy as the only alternative to what he posited as 'the complete loss of the country's credit' and even 'the extreme of foreign intervention'. And in September, at a meeting held at New Court, it was almost certainly Rothschilds who brokered the agreement seeking to ensure that British syndicates on the hunt for Chinese railway concessions should act in a complementary rather than competitive way with each other.[16] In short, the house remained a considerable force so long as Natty himself was still in harness.

At the other end of the City spectrum stood the bulky financier with the reassuring Northumbrian burr, the object of Gaspard Farrer's beady, prophetic eye in December 1897:

> The London and Globe under the direction of Mr Whittaker [*sic*] Wright has made an immense sum during the last few years, speculating in Australian mines, and has, I believe, at the present moment in addition to its mining properties, £1,000,000 Sterling put away in Consols and other securities of a similar nature. Consequently Mr Wright has plenty of means and plenty of following, for the time being. I am afraid I am a sufficient sceptic to believe that both the parent Company and its offshoot the British American Corpn will, in a few years, reach the same ending to which all other similar Companies have attained. For the present all is 'couleur de rose' . . .[17]

Wright's empire by now included at least two highly productive West Australian mines – Lake View and Ivanhoe – but the trouble was that he was an inveterate manipulator, with a particular penchant for elaborate share-dealing and asset-trading between his various companies. During the winter of 1897/8 his fertile brain was operating on peak form, and creations included not only a rash of speculative mining companies but also two new holding companies, the British America Corporation and the Standard Exploration Company, to supplement the existing London and Globe Finance Corporation.[18] In January 1898 a 'crowded attendance' assembled at Winchester House for the meeting of British America, not long after it had been successfully floated for the palpably superfluous purpose of acquiring the London and Globe's mining rights in British Columbia and the Yukon. It was chaired by the Marquis of Dufferin, the first time, he said, he had addressed 'a body of shareholders in his capacity as a City man'. The former Viceroy gave a typically accomplished performance. 'Like the skilled diplomatist that he is,' noted the *Economist*, 'he has displayed conspicuous ability in making rough places plain, and in glossing over apparently difficult points in such a way as to impress the average shareholder with the conviction that things are really much better than they look, and that "everything is for the best in the best of all possible" enterprises.' Unfortunately, according to the same journal, the British America was essentially a scam (though it did not use the word), its real purpose being to put money into the hands of London and Globe shareholders (alone allowed to apply for shares) and create a new set of fat fees for Wright and his directors. Wright himself remained unperturbed. He had his tame guinea pigs safely in his pocket, much of the financial press also, and underwritten by all sorts of profitable share options he was becoming a country gentleman on the grand scale. The estate he acquired was at Witley, near Godalming in Surrey, where he built the subaqueous billiards room which, through G.M. Young's inclusion of it forty years later in *Portrait of an Age*, would become the symbol of a whole plutocratic era.[19]

Horatio Bottomley, Wright's great rival, had his own country pile in Sussex ('The Dicker'), but preferred horse-racing as a rich man's pastime. In July 1897, as part of the process of floating his West Australian Market Trust, he invited all those interested in the market (mainly jobbers) to a grand luncheon at the Cannon Street Hotel, where he outlined his altruistic motives in providing the market with adequate financial facilities, comparable to those provided by the Randlords for the Kaffir market. The venue was still the same when, just before Christmas 1897, Bottomley addressed the Trust's shareholders and, in a stirring peroration, made much of having captured for the Trust the former engineer of the London and Globe:

> Ladies and gentlemen, I have said that the whole of the City of London is nothing more than a sport, and I am sure the simile does not apply to anything more than the history of the West Australian market. I remember the history of it very thoroughly. It is only about three years old. I remember very well when, so to speak, the flag first fell and the race began. I remember how some of my young sprinting friends of the West Australian market started off at such a pace that one could see they would soon come to grief. I can remember how month by month others fell back or were badly thrown; some, I regret to say, were fatally wounded; but I am also sure that in those days no group had to sustain a heavier weight than that which was imposed upon myself and those who worked with me in those times. Well, ladies and gentlemen, we have plodded on; we have ridden a consistent, and, I believe, those who know us will say a straight and an honest race in connexion with West Australia; we have given full room and berth to all our opponents, with the result that for some time past, far away and in front of the rest of the field, we have been running a neck-and-neck race with one other group which I will not

further particularize. But I do say this, ladies and gentlemen, that now that we have secured their first jockey in the person of my friend on my right, I am certain – knowing the cattle we have in our stables, knowing the form of our opponents to the ounce – I am certain that with Charlie Kaufman up, the West Australian stakes are at your mercy. (*Loud and continued cheering.*)

But if Bottomley had the populist flair, Wright had (relatively speaking) the staying power. In the early months of 1898, Bottomley puffed as hard as he could one of his 'cattle' – Northern Territories Goldfields of Australia, a company without obvious merits – and bought heavily for the rise; but in April a major bear attack, led by Wright, carried the day, and confidence began to wane among Bottomley's followers.[20] Wright's empire was based on something, Bottomley's on very little, and even in the corrupt world of mining finance that still made a difference.

Business in the summer of 1898 was pretty flat – not even enlivened by the opening in July of the Waterloo and City Railway, the beloved 'Drain' of future generations. But for one ambitious banker these were weeks of supreme importance. Edward Holden was the son of a Lancashire calico bleacher and, at the age of 50, had risen from an apprenticeship at the Bolton branch of the Manchester and County Bank to general manager of the London and Midland Bank.[21] During the 1890s it was Holden who was largely responsible for the Midland's ambitious programme of amalgamation and branch extension, applying to the task enormous energy and self-belief as well as formidable negotiating skills. The Midland's first great phase of expansion climaxed in 1898, as Holden sought to achieve his largest amalgamation to date, with the City Bank. A letter of 7 August was typically clear-minded:

> Among the advantages of the amalgamation, I may mention: a) We shall have the largest Reserve Fund of any Bank in the Kingdom except the Bank of England. b) The sum carried forward is increased by £20,000. c) There will be a considerable addition to the profits of the Bank. d) The prestige of the Bank in London will be materially improved. e) We have secured most desirable Bank premises [in Threadneedle Street] for Head Office which would have cost us £200,000 if we had secured them under any other circumstances.

Holden might have added that only three banks held more Stock Exchange accounts (i.e. those of members) than the City Bank, which also conducted a flourishing acceptance business with foreign and colonial banks; this merger placed the Midland right at the heart of the City. The negotiations were taxing in the extreme – 'am heartily sick of it', Holden admitted at one point – but eventually a price of just over £2½m was agreed. The merger made the Midland into indisputably one of the leading joint-stock banks, in terms of deposits (£31.9m) lying behind only the National Provincial (£49.3m), the London and County (£43.5m) and Lloyds (£37.7m). It also made Holden into a major City figure. 'I have worked day and night and sacrificed everything in order to make this Bank one of the first in the kingdom,' he wrote in November 1898.[22] Surrounded by City men for whom the cult of the amateur was part of their upbringing, this self-made Lancastrian was only just beginning his sternest battles.

*

Hugh E.M. Stutfield was a member of the Stock Exchange well known for his contributions to the more thoughtful journals of the day, and in March 1898 he published in the *National Review* a piece called 'The Higher Rascality'. The title was taken from Ibsen's most recent play – in which the financier Gabriel Borkman refers to 'the morals of the higher rascality' – and Stutfield's underlying contention was that 'finance, rather than trade, is now the recognised royal road to wealth, and the cult of Midas, the successful company-monger, is a natural phase of modern Mammon-worship'. Then, with Hooley and his ilk firmly in mind (though no names were mentioned), he went on:

> The enormous extension of the joint-stock system, the scientific development of the *haute finance*, and the perfection of modern methods of market manipulation, have placed a most dangerous power in the hands of skilful wire-pullers, and they are not slow to use it. Somehow or other, sooner or later, a check must be put on the depredations of those men who may be termed the vampires or blood-suckers of the commercial world. For the trust or company-monger pure and simple, who is neither producer nor distributor, but is content to make his own dirty profit out of the ruin or impoverishment of other people, is nothing but a blood-sucker, in that he benefits nobody but himself. True commerce is, like charity, twice blest; it advantages both buyer and seller and, through them, the entire community; but wherein does the world at large benefit by our dog-eat-dog fashion of financial cannibalism, the stock combinations and share-splittings and re-shufflings, the rigs, corners, creations of sub-trusts and baby companies, and all the other devices of up-to-date market jugglery? Are they not simply 'the law of the beast' working in the

mercantile world, the modern counterpart of primitive 'tooth-and-claw
rivalries' that existed before company-mongering was invented?

Stutfield concluded by expressing the fear that such gross individual
misconduct, taking the form of 'the abuse of money-power', would
lead to the establishment of Socialism, 'than which no graver calamity
can befall the human race'.[23]
At this stage the author had little to say about the responsibility or
otherwise attaching to the institution to which he was proud to belong,
but no such reticence afflicted A.J. Wilson, who in the 24 June issue of
his *Investors' Review* launched a full-scale broadside entitled 'Is the
Stock Exchange Rotten?' Seeking to explain the current stagnation in
Capel Court, especially in speculative dealings, Wilson took the line
that this was in large part 'the direct offspring of stock market habits
of business'. He claimed that the 'fair and honourable traders' who
comprised the majority of members were 'at the mercy of the dishonest
and unscrupulous minority'; and argued that Capel Court's invariable,
all-purpose defence – to the effect that most swindles did not *originate*
in the Stock Exchange – was inadequate:

> Equally true is it, however, that these swindles are nearly all effected by
> means of the facilities this great market affords, often in defiance of its
> own rules, to the outside thief. Is it any wonder, therefore, that the people
> whose pockets have been rifled by 'dealings for the coming out', 'dealings
> for the special settlement', 'pocket orders', fraudulent simulations of a
> market demand, &c, &c, for this and the other trash or dishonest
> concoction, should blame the instrument by which these rascalities are
> effected far more than the scoundrels who play upon it?

It was, Wilson went on in two splendidly trenchant paragraphs, the
hypocrisy that was almost the worst aspect:

> All this and much more goes on under the decent forms of regular and
> legitimate business. A broker who is a member of the Stock Exchange
> may take part in foisting a swindle on the public, but he must not
> advertise his name in the newspapers, except on prospectuses. That is a
> capital crime . . . Most other rules of the Stock Exchange may be set at
> defiance, or dodged with impunity, but this one must not be violated, for
> fear of confounding a most respectable body of men with keepers of
> 'bucket shops'. The forms of bargaining, according to prescribed rules,
> must also be adhered to; that not only promotes discipline, but salves the
> conscience should the substance of the transaction be a fraud, or a thing
> on nodding acquaintance with fraud. By the rules of the 'House', dealings

in letters of allotment are not recognised, but the rule is ignored in practice, and is, indeed, rendered nugatory by that other rule, in virtue of which bargains of any sort cannot be annulled except on proof of fraud or wilful misrepresentation. By the same rule, quotations in the Stock Exchange Official List are forbidden to the shares of a company which has not been floated upon a prospectus publicly advertised; yet some of the worst and most brutally callous swindles of the past and of the present day have been perpetrated by the aid of the machinery, and with the active assistance of members of the Stock Exchange in complete contempt of this rule – witness the 'boom' and collapse of the Barnato companies. Share lists compiled in derision are taken as genuine, and the rule that two-thirds of the number of shares offered to the public must be genuinely allotted is, by this and other means, made a dead letter. Companies with a foreign domicile which exempts them from British law, whose share registers cannot be inspected, and whose meetings are held abroad, can be laid before the public here, through the Stock Exchange, with perfect ease.

To add to the facilities in these and other ways given to unscrupulous members of the Stock Exchange – driven perhaps sometimes into dishonest ways by stress of hunger – to bring the institution into disrepute, and injure the honest majority, the utmost care is taken to shield the whole body of its dealings from public criticism, and still more from actions-at-law by wronged 'outsiders'. The affairs of defaulters are wound up inside the Exchange, without public interference or criticism, and we fear in these proceedings the interests of the public are not unfrequently forgotten. Transactions which might bring scandals; robberies of securities, frauds, participation in plots to defraud, the invasion of the province of the broker by the jobber, and *vice versâ* – all such things are, as much as possible, hushed up for the sake of that 'respectability', which is of the essence of the game.

In fine, such was the modern sophistication of inside cliques and syndicates that the writer 'would as soon think of deliberately putting his hand into the fire as of perpetrating "a time bargain on open account" on the Stock Exchange in any security, so fully persuaded is he that the odds are bound to be against his success'.[24]

Wilson could fairly claim the moral high ground. Back in 1875, while on the *Pall Mall Gazette*, he had knowingly turned his back on a fortune by refusing to use his knowledge of the intention of Disraeli's government to buy a large stake in the Suez Canal Company; he founded the *Investors' Review* in 1892; and a contemporary was to describe him as 'the knight, without fear or reproach of City Editors'.[25] However, with a very few honourable exceptions, led by Wilson's paper and the *Economist*, the probity of the financial press (and financial editors generally) left an enormous amount to be desired in the 1890s.[26] 'That the City has a large number of "reptile" journals, which will praise – and for that matter also condemn – anything as long as they are paid for it, is by this time well known to any one who is not a tyro in finance,' stated the *Nineteenth Century* in May 1898; and not long afterwards 'A Financial Journalist', writing on 'The Art of Blackmail' in the *Contemporary Review*, flatly asserted that 'the price of a venal City Editor ranges from £100 up to £5,000 as a first payment, with a bonus on all subsequent "business" – such bonus taking the shape either of a number of shares or hard cash'.[27] It is arguable that to resist such temptations needed the qualities of a saint, and there were never many of them in the City.

Against this background, of a rising tide of criticism of all things to do with company promoting, the Stock Exchange and the financial press, came the Hooley revelations, the event of 1898. Having in the space of three years promoted twenty-six companies, only a handful of which were not now in serious financial difficulties or bust, Hooley was declared bankrupt in the summer. The patrons of the Palace Theatre saw Miss Julie Mackey perform a mock-lament on his post-Dunlop predicament:

> What a shame he didn't stop
> After his three million 'cop'
> 'Schweppes' soda' proved a useful 'prop'
> Now, like the corks, he's gone off pop!

Hooley's evidence before the London Bankruptcy Court began in late July, focusing at an early stage on the celebrated Dunlop promotion of May 1896 that had made his name and, as it seemed, fortune:

The Official Receiver: Did you make any payment to those gentlemen who went on the board?

The debtor: Am I obliged to answer that question?

The Official Receiver: Did you make any payment to Earl De La Warr for becoming a director of the company?

The debtor said he should not answer the question unless compelled to do so.

The Registrar: I can quite understand your feeling in the matter, but you must answer the question.

Mr Beyfus [acting for Hooley]: The position of the debtor is a very uncomfortable one, he feels it is a very delicate matter.

The Registrar: This is a public matter, and private feelings must be put aside.

The debtor: I paid Lord De La Warr £25,000. (*Sensation.*)

The Official Receiver: Was that paid to him, or was he to share it with any other directors?

The debtor: I paid him £50,000, of which he was to have £25,000, and the balance was for the others.

The Official Receiver: How was the remaining £25,000 divided?

The debtor: The Duke of Somerset received nothing. Lord Albemarle received only £12,500. He ought to have had half, but I don't think he knew what the half amounted to. (*Loud laughter.*)

Hooley then explained how he had ensured the enthusiasm of the fourth estate for pedalling Dunlops:

> He gave what he termed 'Press calls' on shares. That term was applied to calls on shares at par given to persons connected with the Press. In order to deliver the shares he was compelled to purchase them in the market at 27s 6d each, and the 'Press calls' diminished his profits by £63,500 . . .
>
> He paid a sum of £500 to Mr Jennings, who was on the editorial staff of the *Financial News*. He considered that the articles in that paper were the cleverest that he had seen . . . He denied that a cheque for £10,000 made payable to Mr A.J. Benjamin as broker on behalf of Mr Marks [Harry Marks, editor and proprietor of the *FN*] was in respect of articles that appeared in the *Financial News*; it represented a deal in shares.

Despite these vexing costs, Hooley conceded that he had netted somewhere between £100,000 and £200,000 from the Dunlop promotion.[28]

Delays in the proceedings then ensued, first through Hooley's being ill and then because other circumstances compelled postponement until November; but *The Times* in August produced an interim leader on Hooley's startling revelations designed to make Lord Dufferin blush:

> Till now, the name of a peer or a man of great family upon the 'front page' of a prospectus has been valuable, because the public has not ceased to regard these persons as men of scrupulous honour, who would not give their names for secret 'consideration'. We seem to be changing all that. Whether it is that the City is anxious to buy the West-end, or that the West-end is anxious to be bought by the City, every 'boom' is nowadays accompanied by the ugly phenomenon of men of high social position accepting directorships in doubtful or over-capitalized companies. The world now knows that it has been the practice to make secret payments to these people, as the price of their names. Probably Mr Hooley paid

more than anyone else, but he did not invent the system. He found it in existence, and he developed it. Let us hope that these scandalous exposures will work to cure, both by opening the eyes of investors and by bringing home to those who bear great names the truth, so often forgotten, that *noblesse oblige* – nay, that the very basis of social honour is social confidence, and that to shake the latter is to bring the former into serious danger.

A different approach was taken by W.R. Lawson, a former editor of the *FT* who had become a member of the Stock Exchange in 1895 and made a small fortune (mainly through bear operations) while continuing to wield a versatile, authoritative pen. 'Company Promoting "À La Mode" ' appeared in the *National Review* in September:

> Doubtless the City has sins enough to answer for, and it contains many undesirable citizens, company promoters, and what not. It is by no means guilty, however, of all that is laid to its charge during the periodical agitations raised against it when plungers like Mr Hooley come to grief. The promoting fraternity would have a poor life if they depended entirely on what they could reap within the City bounds. Mr Hooley said frankly and truly in his examination that London contributes a very small percentage of the subscriptions to new companies, not a tithe, in fact, of what comes from the provinces. Its share in the Dunlop and Bovril reorganisations was particularly small, and its losses through them are less than those of some third-class provincial towns. Its greater intelligence and calmer temperament enabled it to resist the glamour which dazzled the provinces . . .[29]

Lawson, in short, laid the blame firmly on the greed and gullibility of the general public.

As for Hooley, further evidence followed early in November. The name of Harry Marks continued to crop up, and in all he seems to have received from the promoter a grand total of £31,110 in cash and shares. Hooley at one point was pressed to explain one of the larger payments, in connection with a Harry Lawson cycle flotation, which for £25,000, of which a third was to go to Marks, he had agreed not to oppose:

> He did not give the money to Mr Marks to abstain from writing in the *Financial News*. He would not say whether the payment was in virtue of a preconcerted arrangement. As a fact Mr Marks did about this time cease to publish unfavourable comments. The only reason why he gave Mr Marks this money was that Mr Marks was a friend of his. (*Laughter.*)

Even the name of the *FT*'s Douglas MacRae was mentioned, in connection with a cheque for almost £2,000, though Hooley added to further laughter that MacRae was 'the honestest man of the lot'. However, Hooley's evidence went well beyond the financial press. From the wider point of view his most damaging revelation was of a donation of £10,000 to the Conservative Central Fund as the price for his election to the Carlton Club and, he hoped, an eventual peerage. Though the Party offered to return the money, the damage was done.[30]

'The now famous Mr Hooley' (in Hamilton's phrase) had in fact almost half a century of relative obscurity ahead of him, but his place in the history books was secure. Even before the bankruptcy proceedings ended, the Lord Chief Justice, Lord Russell of Killowen, took the opportunity of his address at the Law Courts on Lord Mayor's Day, on the occasion of the new Lord Mayor taking the customary oath of office, to inveigh against 'fraud which is rampant in this community, fraud of a most dangerous kind, widespread in its operation, touching all classes, involving great pecuniary loss to the community . . . fraud blunting the sharp edge of honour and besmirching honourable names'. Inevitably, Stutfield also had his say, contributing a perceptive, well-measured piece ('The Company Scandal: A City View') to the December *National Review*. If Hooley-style abuses were not to be repeated, the public must be educated, for 'the confidence investors display in the honesty as well as the ability of financiers to make money for them is quite touching in its *naïveté*'. Stutfield did not exonerate the Stock Exchange, but blamed 'a small minority' of members for making false markets and called on the Committee to take firmer action, above all to prohibit dealings before allotment. He also warned that 'the power and importance of the Stock Exchange are so great nowadays that the due performance of its functions is a matter almost of national concern, and if some of its members do not mend their ways we may witness some day the appointment of another Royal Commission and, possibly, the establishment of some form of Government control over its proceedings'. Stutfield then addressed the wider implications of the whole Hooley episode:

> The opponents of company law reform lay great stress on the danger of impeding enterprise by too stringent legislation. They seem to overlook the fact that the dishonesty fostered by our existing limited liability system is a still more serious drag upon industry: firstly, owing to the squandering of vast sums on promoters' swindles; and, secondly, by deterring the public from embarking their money in undertakings which, though possibly speculative, are yet perfectly legitimate and useful. One

is always hearing complaints in the City of the difficulty of obtaining capital to develop good properties. The joint-stock frauds of the last few years have rendered investors over-suspicious; they cannot distinguish what is honest from what is fraudulent . . .[31]

The pity was that few others in the City recognised, let alone accepted, the exercise of quality control by its financial intermediaries as crucial to a flourishing economy. Instead, a seductive mix of 'animal spirits', *caveat emptor* and promoters' slush funds continued to carry all before it, as the City's establishment – the Bank of England, the great joint-stock and private banks, the merchant banks, the most reputable stockbroking firms – looked on more or less unconcerned.

CHAPTER ELEVEN

Where's the Conductor?

In December 1898 the Chairman of the London Shipping Exchange (E.H. Forwood) wrote to the Chairman of the Baltic (Septimus Glover) about 'the proposed idea of seeing whether some arrangement could not be arrived at' with a view to the members of their respective bodies 'joining together and building an Exchange worthy of the City of London':

> Ever since I have been in London – some twenty-eight years or more – I have found it irksome to have to attend so many Exchanges in order to be able to carry on my business; I also have found it very costly in as much as I have to subscribe for my clerks being members both of the Shipping Exchange and the Baltic. Now, if anything could be done to concentrate the trade of the City under one roof it would prove a great boon to the City commercial world, especially seeing now that everybody has to get through more work in a day than was the case in the past. I have for two years studied all the different sites in the City and the only site which would give the area necessary for such a General Shipping Exchange I find to be in Jeffrey's Square [to the east of Bishopsgate] . . . I would point out to you that owing to traffic etc the Mansion House is virtually out of the City Community, and between that and the Baltic [still in South Sea House, just to the west of Bishopsgate] is mainly taken up by the financial world, and therefore the bulk of your members are located more in the direction of Jeffrey's Sq than the Baltic . . .

Eventually a new, consolidated Baltic Exchange would emerge from this initiative, but for the time being the members of the Baltic continued to do their business in South Sea House. A couple of years before Forwood's letter something of their daily round was described in *Chambers's Journal*, a reminder not only that there was more to the Baltic than shipping pure and simple but also of the City's abiding commercial character whatever the temporary excitements of a free-booting financier:

> Wheat, of course, is the chief market of all, and its power is such that it often exerts an indirect influence over articles which have to all appear-

ance only the remotest connection with it. Often the price of wheat affects, not only that of maize and of barley, &c, but also to a more or less appreciable extent that of linseed and cottonseed, owing to the cake products of these articles being used for [animal] feeding purposes. And the freight markets are directly influenced by the state of the grain markets; when the latter are brisk, chartering proceeds with a swing; and conversely, when grain is stagnant, there is little demand for tonnage, and rates of freight generally fall . . .

Near the entrance to the room is the freight market, where current rates from Odessa, from the Danube, from Alexandria, from the River Plate, are discussed, and where expressions such as 'laydays', 'cancelling dates', 'deadweight capacity' are heard all around. In the centre of the room, linseed is the prevailing topic, and one can learn the price of 'spot Calcutta' or 'May-June Plate'. The same brokers will tell one the current value of 'November-January cottonseed', or of 'July-August brown Cawnpore rapeseed'. At the farther end of the room, wheat and feeding stuffs reign supreme. The prices of 'No. 1 Californian' wheat on passage; June-July 'Plate' maize; May-June 'Azof' barley; and March-April 'Libau' oats become familiar to the ear. One learns that the months refer to the periods during which the produce must be shipped; that the mysterious expression which sounds like 'siff' means c.i.f. – say cost, insurance, and freight; that 'rye terms' are more favourable to a buyer than *tale quale*; that produce is often sold before it is shipped, and sometimes before it is grown; that f.a.q. means 'fair average quality', being a guarantee which obviates the necessity of showing samples . . .

'The Baltic' affords the opportunities so important to a commercial man, of transacting a maximum of business with a minimum of time and trouble. A merchant can sell a cargo of produce for shipment at some future period, and can then proceed to another part of the room and charter a steamer against the sale . . .

On Mondays, Wednesdays, and Fridays, members may be seen in large numbers at the Corn Exchange in Mark Lane, where the brokers meet their country clients, and exhibit samples of grain which they have for sale. And every afternoon there is an exodus of those members engaged in the oilseed and cognate trades to the Royal Exchange, where sellers and buyers come into free contact with one another. 'Going on 'Change' is a daily duty which is rigorously observed, whether or not it is likely to be productive of business.[1]

*

Horatio Bottomley was on the rocks by 1899. In January, at the Cannon Street Hotel, he met the shareholders of his Westralian Market Trust. The headlines were familiar – 'Mr Bottomley Describes the

Business on Hand: A Prosperous Career Predicted' – but in fact he had had to reconstruct the Trust, which had ceased to pay dividends. Bottomley in his speech conceded that the Trust's progress had been 'somewhat rudely interrupted', but even on this occasion his natural buoyancy got the better of an intended sobriety:

> We have learned a great many lessons from the experience of the past, and whatever may be my own inclinations to go ahead I am held very firmly in check by the responsible and mellowed colleagues – (*laughter*) – who sit around the Board and are determined that we shall not get into any trouble again. They may keep me back as much as they like, but they cannot prevent the Market Trust earning dividends (*hear, hear*) . . .

During most of the year, however, the share prices of Bottomley's various mining companies continued to slide; and by 1900 he was no longer a major City figure. The rest of his career was chequered indeed, most famous (or infamous) for his involvement in the mass-circulation paper *John Bull*. In 1922 he was at last convicted of fraud and went to Wormwood Scrubs. There he was visited by the padre, who found him stitching mail-bags and said, 'Ah, Bottomley, sewing?' To which he replied, 'No, reaping.' On another occasion he was spotted in the exercise yard by Hooley, also in prison for fraud. 'Buck up, B!' called out Hooley, but by this time a thoroughly punctured Mr Toad had little fight left in him.[2]

Whitaker Wright also had a fraught 1899, though the outlook seemed rosy enough in April when one of his main West Australian companies, Lake View Consolidated Mines, published a cable announcing the discovery of an enormous additional amount of gold in the mine. The price of Lake View Consols rose rapidly, amidst a fresh burst of speculative enthusiasm for Westralians, if somewhat muted in the case of Bottomley's ventures. But for Harry Gibbs, writing at the start of June to Keating in Melbourne, there was an unsatisfactory tinge to this latest Westralian boom:

> It certainly looks as if the great output of gold from the Colony, coupled with the forcing up of prices by the cliques, has at last induced the Public to come in & gamble, & when the London Public once begin to gamble, it isn't the worthlessness of a stock that will prevent it from rushing up to almost any figure . . . A nasty feature is the way in which great mines like Great Boulders & Lake Views seem to suppress or publish cables just as it suits them. I think the two mines I have named are the most audacious offenders in this respect. This tends to frighten the Public, very naturally.

Soon afterwards, in July, Wright received a cable from his mine manager at Lake View that a new, very rich pocket of ore had been struck;
armed with this information, which naturally he kept secret, he did all
he could to intensify the bull movement. By mid-August Lake Views
had reached their all-time height of 28, but thereafter their price
declined. On 6 September the fall was from $23\frac{11}{16}$ to $23\frac{1}{8}$, attributed by
the *FT* to 'the circulation of the statement that a considerable decline
in the return for August is to be anticipated owing to the smelters being
unable to take ore on account of being full up with the supplies of
other companies'. A denial by the company gave a firmer tone by the
end of the next day; but as the *FT*'s Mining market report ominously
noted, 'it is stated that the mischievous story put about yesterday
emanated from an unscrupulous speculative clique, bent on getting the
shares to a lower price'.[3] It was now a fight to the death between the
squire of Witley and a very professional bear clique.

F.W. Baker was another City-based company promoter who specialised in gold mines.[4] During the mid-1890s he had floated various
Rhodesian as well as Westralian enterprises, most of them worthless,
and by 1899 his main vehicle for any future efforts was the Venture
Corporation and Exploration Co. The Venture's consulting engineer
was T.A. Rickard, an American of high principles who in March
reported on the Independence mine at Cripple Creek, Colorado. The
mine was generally known as Stratton's Independence, after the former
carpenter W.S. Stratton who had pegged his lucrative claim eight years
previously; and Rickard estimated that the mine, though a peculiarly
difficult one to evaluate in terms of the value of its unexposed ore,
could produce $2m of gold a year for at least three years. Baker was
desperate to buy, but would the former carpenter sell? Another mining
engineer, John Hays Hammond, tells the story:

> Stratton was invited to come to London at the company's expense to
> meet the board of directors. He proved no more tractable in England than
> in the States. As a last resort, it was decided to give him a banquet. At the
> appearance of the first course, they offered him five million dollars [the
> equivalent of £1m] for his mine. He promptly turned it down.
>
> As the dinner proceeded, the price rose to five and a half millions.
> Stratton showed some sign of interest, but was still unwilling. When the
> figure reached six millions, his eyes opened wider and he began to pinch
> himself. But his head had started wagging in the negative and he could
> not seem to stop it.
>
> Except for the price, the contract was ready for his signature. At six and
> a half millions the pen was placed in his hand. But he said he liked his
> mine; he couldn't bear to part with it.

In desperation seven and a half million was written in and his fingers were firmly closed around the pen. Still unable to believe his eyes or his ears, he affixed his signature.

When I met him some time afterwards, I asked, 'What would you have done if I'd offered you a check for five million dollars for the property before you had been approached by the Venture Corporation?'

'I'd have jumped at it!'

The London flotation of Stratton's Independence took place in May 1899, with the board including not only Stratton (of Colorado Springs, Colorado) and Baker (of Copse Close, Wimbledon), but also the Earl of Chesterfield, presumably an expert on Derbyshire pits. The trouble was that, by the terms of the agreement, the Venture Corporation was committed to buying from Stratton no fewer than two million £1 shares at £2 each (Hammond's account may even have underestimated the extent of Stratton's windfall). For this to be a profitable exercise for Baker and his associates, they would then have to be able to sell the shares at as much as possible over £2; so, until the Venture had, by instalments, bought the 2 million shares, Stratton was to retain complete authority over the workings of the mine. It was an agreement predicated, from the Venture's point of view, on achieving a prolonged bull market in the shares – a state of affairs that demanded maximum publicity for a series of wholly fictitious telegrams from the mine about the latest wonderful crushings or spectacular new ore discoveries. This was expensive to arrange but necessary, and for a year or more Baker by a virtuoso display managed to keep the price above £2. In short the mine became, in Rickard's subsequent regretful phrase, 'the sport of flamboyant finance', and in time a *cause célèbre*.[5]

Three weeks after the Strattons flotation, Parr's Bank led a consortium that brought out a £10m loan on behalf of the Japanese government. There was a curious story behind the choice of Parr's, a clearing rather than a merchant bank. Manager of its Lombard Street branch was Allan Shand, a thoroughly upright, old-fashioned banker, who once said of Gladstone that 'he is my religion as well as my philosophy'. In the 1870s he had been the Yokohama manager of the Chartered Mercantile Bank of India, London and China, as well as advising the Japanese government on the establishment of English-style central banking. He had then returned to England in 1878, working for the Alliance Bank until it merged with Parr's in 1892. His links with Japan remained close, in particular with Korekiyo Takahashi, who as a boy had worked under Shand and who now, as Deputy-Governor of the Yokohama Specie Bank, oversaw his government's negotiations in London.[6] 'There is next to no doubt that it will be largely subscribed,' declared the *Investors' Review* on the eve of the loan being issued early in June. For its part, though, Wilson's paper argued that the Japanese financial position was 'by no means so satisfactory at the present moment as seemed to be indicated in the statement issued to the underwriters' and accused the Japanese government of being 'at the end of its tether, and can no longer juggle with figures and show a surplus where a deficit exists'. There followed a notably condescending passage:

> With the outcome of the war against China came an awakening of the Japanese mind to a consciousness of higher things before undreamt of, and this awakening took the customary form. The country decided at once to double the land forces, and promulgated a highly expensive naval plan which was to be spread over several years. The people, reckoning that they were quite as clever as the cleverest in Europe and the United States, decided to emulate the rather outworn civilisations with the view of superseding them ultimately in the arts of peace as well as of war, thereby making Japan the centre of the commercial world . . .

In the event, the issue was an almighty flop, less than a tenth being subscribed for, with the rest going to a mixture of the Japanese government, the Bank of Japan and the underwriters. Market conditions had not been propitious (largely because of the threatening war in South Africa), but two major lessons stood out: that the standing of Japan was not yet very great in the City; and that any future issue would need some merchant banking muscle applied to it. The man responsible for marshalling the interests of the underwriters in a difficult after-market was the flamboyant stockbroker Harry Panmure Gordon. Eventually, in September 1900, he tried to persuade the great Pierpont Morgan, head of J.P. Morgan & Co in New York, to place on the American market £4m of the stock still held by the underwriters: 'I took all my books and papers to Mr Jack Morgan [Pierpont's son, who spent most of his summers in England] and I showed him everything, and if he had been a Partner of my Firm he could not have more what I call inside knowledge.'[7] Pierpont, however, declined the offer, and Japanese credit continued to languish in the outworn West.

Pierpont himself had by this time solved (or thought he had) the problem of finding a resident senior at J.S. Morgan & Co in London. It was a search that took over a year, and there is some evidence that Morgan during 1898 made an approach to Barings with a view to achieving a grand, albeit improbable merger of the two Morgan

houses, Barings, and Kidder Peabody of New York.[8] But at last the
search ended, and the chosen one was not a recognised City figure
but an ambitious, intellectually able civil servant in his late 30s.
'C. Dawkins, whose appointment as financial member of Viceroy of
India's Council is just made public, came to see me today. It is great
promotion for him; but I expect he will be found equal to the work.'
That was Hamilton in October 1898, but three months later Clinton
Dawkins, still in London but about to travel to India, was in a state of
high agitation as he wrote on successive days to his mentor Sir
Alfred Milner, High Commissioner in South Africa, currently staying
in London:

> *19 January.* I have a favour to implore of you. I *must* see you tomorrow,
> as an extraordinary and most important proposal has been made to me,
> possibly entailing an entire change in my life.
> *20 January.* Have seen [Everard] Hambro who gave me the warmest
> assurances about the character and position of the business, and the
> character of Mr Morgan. In his opinion my share of the profits (which
> were to be guaranteed up to £25h [i.e. £2,500]) are more likely to be £50h
> than in the neighbourhood of the minimum. My position would be that
> of a Full Partner and Head of the London house.

Between the two letters Dawkins had seen Pierpont Morgan, whose
force of character and powers of persuasion were considerable. By the
end of the month a partnership agreement had been signed, to come
into force from April 1900, with Morgan having allowed Dawkins a
year in India to help to deal with the currency question there. Dawkins
'retires on the strength of a fabulous offer made to him by Morgans',
noted Hamilton early in July 1899 as news leaked out, and two days
later Dawkins himself wrote from Simla to his old friend Cecil Spring
Rice. He explained that both Balfour and Chamberlain had 'pressed'
Morgan to 'take an Englishman'; mentioned that Goschen, Welby and
Milner had all advised acceptance of Morgan's offer; and, on a more
personal note, added that 'my hair is getting grey, and if my figure is
not much altered still I puff when I play tennis'. Two months later he
blithely envisaged to a perhaps dubious Spring Rice his future life in
London: 'No, I will not get bloated, at least I will try and not get
bloated. But you may reckon for certain on a den with dirty pipes and
old books into which no finery shall be admitted.'[9]
City reaction to this surprise appointment was encapsulated in a
letter to Brown Brothers in New York from Sir Mark Collet of Brown
Shipley:

If Mr Morgan, with the exceptional position he holds & with the advantage of having Mr Hambro (himself an able man who knows the London *business* community more intimately than most) to enquire, look out & suggest without in any way committing himself, has failed to find a man of Mercantile & Banking experience, and he has had to be content to fall back upon a capable Treasury official, who has his work to learn, is it surprising that we have not been successful?

At least Collet the merchant banker recognised that there was a problem to be solved, in contrast to the City's leading private banks who so often in the nineteenth century simply buried their heads in the sand, a major cause of their continuing precipitate decline in relation to the joint-stock banks. For example, Smith, Payne & Smiths of 1 Lombard Street performed, in the course of 1899, a plausible imitation of an ostrich in its response to an entirely sensible initiative on the part of Smith, Ellison & Co of Lincoln to bring together the various Smiths banks, London and country, into one tightly combined group. The senior partner of Smith, Payne & Smiths was Samuel George Smith II, a septuagenerian who so refused to countenance the thought that when the Lincoln partners called at his Belgrave Square home to discuss their proposed amalgamation scheme, he refused to see them and instructed his butler to show them out. 'He is often now in an impossible frame of mind, and argument is useless', observed one of the Lombard Street partners. The attitude was in sharp contrast to the thrusting joint-stock banks, as told to Rowland Hughes on one of his investigative trips to London in May 1899. A main source was the joint general manager of the National Provincial Bank. First on the subject of female shareholders: 'We now accept these without question, and we make no difficulty about married women shareholders.' And then on the London City and Midland Bank: 'We have it from an apparently reliable source that one of their friends boasted the other day of having secured forty accounts for them and for which service he received £2 2/- in each case.'[10] Holden's name was not mentioned, but it was he who embodied the visible future of British banking.

Another informant was the bill broker Whitburn, who gave Hughes the latest on the Bank of England: 'I hear from all sides that at the Branches they have adopted an aggressive and an irritating policy. I suppose they have too much regard for the power of the London Banks to go on similar lines here.' Towards the end of June, against this background as well as general anxiety about the diminished level of gold reserves at a time of potential danger, the whole question of reserves returned forcibly to the agenda. First the Central Association of Bankers and then the Committee of the London Clearing Bankers voted to set up committees on the subject.[11] The implications were clear. The great joint-stock banks had, by virtue of their enormous balances, become the dominant force in the money market and now naturally wished for a tangible expression of that power. Gold reserves provided a stick with which to beat the Old Lady – and would do so even when the Bank toned down its competitive policy, especially in the Edye-influenced provinces.

In August the organ of mainstream banking opinion, the *Bankers' Magazine*, noted how in recent weeks 'the practicability of establishing a bullion reserve on a definite system has been the chief theme of discussion in banking circles', explaining that two main schemes had been submitted:

> The first contemplates a co-operation between the joint-stock banks and the Bank of England in conserving a bullion reserve furnished by the public and private banks and held apart from the current balances with the central institution. The other proposal is of a more complicated character. Under it a reserve of ear-marked bullion would be controlled by a combination of bankers, and independent of the Bank of England.

Insisting that the initiative taken by the joint-stock banks was essentially disinterested, that 'they desire to create a visible stock of the precious metal to bear a proportionate correspondence with the general banking commitments of the country', the *BM* plumped for the more radical alternative – a standing reserve 'withdrawable only by the associated banks, and held apart from the uncontrolled discretion of the Bank of England'. The *BM* was happy, however, to have this 'central store of gold' *physically* held at the Bank of England. Was it a runner? In the same issue, the *BM* printed the text of a Mansion House speech given by Hicks Beach less than a week after the Central Association's decision in June. Two sentences stood out: 'It might be a question whether an increased reserve should be held at the Bank of England or whether a separate reserve should be formed elsewhere. Might he venture to say that in his belief combined action was of the essence of the matter?'[12] Or put another way, even if the new reserve was physically located in the vaults at Threadneedle Street, it was doubtful if the notion of its being 'withdrawable only by the associated banks' quite came under the Chancellor's rubric of 'combined action'.

'The market looks exceedingly healthy, business being extremely active . . . If the activity continues, we see every probability of a great boom when, as hitherto, the public will go mad.' That was the opinion in February 1899 of the cautious Lionel Phillips of Wernher Beit, writing to H. Eckstein & Co in Johannesburg, as Kaffir shares flourished in response to deep-level mines coming increasingly into production. A few weeks later the *Citizen*'s columnist observed an interesting scene in what had become a vigorous Street market: 'On Tuesday evening Mr Uzielli "let himself go", as whilst standing in the middle of the market he bid loudly for 1,000 Goldfields at $8\frac{5}{8}$, and a like number of Chartereds at "over $\frac{9}{16}$", but I could not help noticing that as soon as some came on offer he dried up, and the price soon shed a fraction in each case.' There was, however, to be no repeat of the memorable Kaffir boom of 1895, for it became steadily more clear, as spring turned into summer, that there was a very real chance of war in South Africa. It is true that in the middle of June 'a well-known jobber' accepted 'a wager of £5,000 to £600 that there will be no war between Great Britain and the Transvaal or between this country and any other Power during the next six months'; but most readers would have agreed with the *FN* that it was, on the jobber's part, 'a very sporting bet'.[13]

The prospect of war between nations is never agreeable to cosmopolitan men of *haute finance*, and Carl Meyer, who earlier in the year had toured Egypt with Cassel ('a little dictatorial'), was no exception. During August, operating from his new City base at the National Bank of Egypt, he wrote almost daily to his wife, on the 25th noting: 'Markets rather lower. New Court selling heavily on less satisfactory Transvaal telegrams . . . Lord R. had a dose of Jingoism this morning from Beit but I persist in believing that a modus vivendi will be found FOR THIS TIME – though I admit Kruger is trying the Govt's patience very severely and as I said before there is smell of gunpowder in the air which is dangerous.' On the 28th, two days after Chamberlain's public warning to Kruger that the sands were running down in the glass, he was still hopeful: 'I persist in believing that Kruger will at the last moment cave in . . . The City has only been slightly affected by the acuteness of the situation but will become more nervous should an EXPEDITION be sent out . . .' As for the mood in the Kaffir Circus itself, the *FT*'s Mining market report for 5 September summed it up: 'The generality of the dealers at the close still inclined to the opinion that war would be averted by the Boers giving way, though most of them seemed less pronounced in this judgment than hitherto. They were, at the same time, rather disposed to welcome a conflict, as the only likely means of clearing the situation.' The atmosphere in the City remained turbid for the rest of September, amidst mounting press hysteria and a perpetual volley of rumours. Harry Gibbs reported to Vicary on the 26th how his wife had received a letter that morning from someone called Critchley, apparently to the effect that General Buller did not think there would be a war. And Harry went on:

> When Hodgson [the stockbroker] got into the train this morning, he was as usual 'absolute for death', so I told him confidentially what C had written, & he was quite knocked edgeways, as he viewed it as an undoubted 'Tip' & a very important one, as though Buller & C might be wrong, yet it indicated a current of feeling in 'exalted quarters' which make for peace, & that probably Buller knew Chamberlain's mind. I pointed out that very likely Buller had only said to C, 'I don't believe they will fight', half in joke, but H formed a theory that Chamberlain knows that Krüger wants to have a large English force sent out, so that he may tell his people that they can do nothing in presence of 'force majeure' . . . H & I agreed that we should find Consolidated Goldfields down to $5\frac{7}{8}$ this morning, & H said he should buy 500 & hold them for a £4 profit. He asked if he should do the same for us, & I said he might at $5\frac{7}{8}$, & he did it at that price before 11 a.m.[14]

It was probably a profitable spec, as markets enjoyed a day or two of temporary buoyancy, but by early October few doubted that, at last, war had become inevitable.

Perhaps the clinching moment came on Tuesday the 3rd, as Bank rate was suddenly raised from $3\frac{1}{2}$ to $4\frac{1}{2}$ per cent. The financial journalist Charles Duguid, in his history of the Stock Exchange written not long afterwards, described an occasion more sullen than exultant:

> The state of war had not then been actually reached, but heavy ship-ments of gold were being made to South Africa, and the day before Consols had fallen as much as $1\frac{3}{8}$ to $102\frac{5}{8}$, a lower point than any that had been touched for five years. The unexpected announcement of the ad-vance in the Bank Rate was made in the usual way in the Consol Market, but scarcely any one heard it. The Kaffir Market knew nothing of the alteration until a waiter was seen changing the figures above his stand. There was a sudden silence; he felt every eye upon him, and, as he nervously fumbled, an angry, impatient shout broke from the eager crowd.

Just over a week later, at three o'clock on the afternoon of the 11th, the Boer ultimatum expired. War had begun, and again Duguid's pen did justice to the scene:

> Two great flags – the Royal Standard and the Union Jack – were unfurled from the bench in the Rhodesia Market, drawing all the members present to the spot. The singing of the National Anthem suggested itself. 'Where's the conductor?' yelled a voice. Mr Charlie Clarke made his way to the front and mounted the bench, walking-stick baton in hand. The dead silence which followed the clearing of throats might have proved suggestive even to a less witty member, recalling the similar silence which ensues sometimes after settlement days, when the waiter mounts the rostrum with his hammer. It inspired Mr Clarke to make one of the most effective remarks ever heard within the Stock Exchange. 'Gentlemen!' he cried, having dealt the three dread blows. 'Mr Kruger has not complied with his bargains!' The effect was electrical; roar after roar of laughter and applause greeted the sally . . .

According to another account, it was a penny hammer that Clarke used, at what was arguably, for good or ill, the Stock Exchange's all-time supreme moment.[15]

'It was such a very cheerful war. I hated its confidence, its congratulatory anticipations, its optimism of the Stock Exchange. I hated its vile assurance of victory.' Such indeed was the prevailing mood in October 1899, caught by the incorrigibly dissenting G.K. Chesterton. Can one, though, go all the way and agree with J.A. Hobson's famous verdict, pronounced soon after the event, that the Boer War was 'the clearest and most dramatic instance of the operation of the world-wide forces of international finance'?[16] There is no doubt that Britain had formidable economic interests at stake in South Africa – not only gold, but also trade in general;[17] nor that, as far as the gold-mining industry itself was concerned, it had become an *idée fixe* that 'good government' in the Transvaal could get working costs down to 22/- a ton, six shillings less than they were in 1898 and the sure route to higher dividends;[18] nor indeed that by this time the attitude of the Randlords was generally warlike. Take Julius Wernher, temperamentally a moderate. 'I never thought it my business to conquer the Transvaal for England,' he remarked in 1898, but by August 1899 he was characterised by Carl Meyer as having been 'bellicose all the time'.[19] Was there also some connection made, in the City and in the official mind, between London's continuing role as the world's only free gold market, the less than happy state of the bullion reserve, and the perceived need to ensure in the long term a regular supply of gold from South Africa? The connection or otherwise has been much debated, on remarkably slender evidence, and it is only instinct that tells one that there was some such connection.[20] South Africa meant gold, gold had become the very pivot of the City's existence, and to deny the connection surely goes against the grain.

Yet it would be still more foolish to deny the dimension of political autonomy involved in government policy. Two key assertions were made by Salisbury, dragged into war by Chamberlain and Milner almost against his better judgement. Justifying the conflict, he said it was in order to teach the Transvaal 'that we not the Dutch are boss'; and this, he emphasised, was a sufficient justification even if it involved fighting 'for people whom we despise, and for territory which will bring no profit and no power to England'.[21] Nor was dislike of the Randlords confined to aristocratic statesmen. On 8 September, just over a month before hostilities began, Harry Gibbs wrote to Keating in Australia:

A Cabinet Council was held today, but nothing is known of what happened. I still don't believe in War – though to read the leading papers, one would think that the Boers had at least occupied the Isle of Wight or massacred every English speaking person in the Transvaal! If we honestly said we were going to war to annex the Transvaal & avenge Majuba Hill, I shouldn't mind, but to fight in order to secure a 5 instead of a 7 years franchise & things of that kind for Messrs Neumann [a reference to Sigismund Neumann, a Randlord recently hobnobbing with the Prince of Wales] & other German Jews, seems to me quite criminal. If the mining speculators etc don't like the Boer laws, let them leave the country; they have all made pots of money in it, in spite of the 'cruel oppression'.

Natty Rothschild was more ambivalent in his attitude to the Randlords. He laboured long and hard, but to no avail, to prevent war.[22] He failed not because others in the City were more successfully manipulating the politicians, but because the politicians were – for a variety of reasons, some of them economic – prepared to go to war, knowing that they had public opinion behind them.

It was a popular support in which, when all was said and done, the City was firmly in the vanguard. On Monday, 16 October, there assembled at the Guildhall the massed ranks of the square mile, in an atmosphere in which patriotic fervour far outweighed economic calculation:

The proceedings were announced to begin at half-past two, but the audience assembled long before that hour, and by half-past one the hall was almost filled by a cheering mass of people . . . For an hour before the meeting began the Guildhall rang with cheers, and with deafening choruses of patriotic songs. Again and again the National Anthem, 'Rule, Britannia', 'Soldiers of the Queen', 'See, the conquering hero comes', and half-a-dozen other stirring songs were sung with tremendous energy, the excitement being fomented by the waving of the Union Jack and the Royal Standard by some persons in the body of the hall.

The Lord Mayor (Sir John Moore) made the first speech:

> Our Government received from the Government of the Transvaal an ultimatum (*loud groans and laughter*) – I wish to goodness Mr Kruger could have heard that groan. (*Laughter.*) This ultimatum came in the midst of negotiations then proceeding between the two Governments, and came before the proposals of our Government had been received by the Transvaal. ('*Shame*'.) The ultimatum was of the most extraordinary kind. (*Laughter.*) It dictated to her Majesty that we shall not move our own troops (*laughter*), in our own ships, to our own ports, in our own country. (*Laughter.*) It also demanded that troops which, since a mentioned time, had already been landed and taken their position in South Africa should be immediately withdrawn, and it required an answer in 48 hours. (*A voice, 'It got it!'*) And this, too, under a threat of war. (*Laughter.*) This small State in South Africa sent that message to the Queen of the first Empire in the world! (*Loud cheers.*)

Seconding the resolution supporting the government's policy, Sir John Lubbock stressed the grievances of the Uitlanders, and he was supported by Samuel Gladstone, the Governor of the Bank of England. One of his predecessors, A.G. Sandeman, now President of the London Chamber of Commerce, then declared that 'the merchants of the City of London and of Great Britain are very adverse to having their affairs unsettled by war, but when the occasion arises, when the necessity is seen, as in this case, they rise as one man'. At which point: 'The Lord Mayor put the resolution to the meeting, and it was carried amid great enthusiasm, one man only holding up his hand against it. He was alleged to be a German, and as he appeared to be suffering from over-excitement he was conducted out of the building.' Other speeches followed, including by William Lidderdale – who sounded a regretful note, but saw no alternative and called for 'a merciful victory' – and John Hichens, Chairman of the Stock Exchange. Hichens was a civilised man from a civilised family, friendly with the eminent painter G.F. Watts. If he had his doubts he concealed them, for at this juncture there was no consideration more paramount than the rabidly nationalist mood of the institution he headed:

I do not believe that there is any body in England more patriotic and loyal than the Stock Exchange. Indeed, some of the very few Little Englanders to be found among us have told me at times that we are a body of jingoes. I do not know that I rightly understand what a jingo is, but if a jingo is a man who refuses always to believe that his country is in the wrong, if a jingo is a man who is determined, as far as in him lies, by his vote and by what influence he has, that England shall have an effective Army and an invincible Navy – then, gentlemen, I think the Stock Exchange without shame may accept the name of jingo, and confess that if it be a sin to covet honour for their country they are the most offending souls alive. (*Cheers.*)[23]

CHAPTER TWELVE

Not All, Not All

On 1 November 1899, three weeks into the Boer War and with much exaggerated fears starting to be expressed about London's gold supplies now that South African mines were being shut down, Lord Hillingdon of Glyn Mills gave his inaugural address as President of the Institute of Bankers. He noted that, whereas twenty years previously the Bank of England had been easily pre-eminent in terms of its deposits (over £38m, with the National Provincial coming second on just £26m), now the Bank of England's £43m was surpassed by the National Provincial and the London and County, with two or three other banks poised to overtake. Hillingdon, with an implicit nod to the recently formed bankers' committees, then considered the implications:

> We have now to face a situation in which the Bank of England has admittedly lost a certain power of control in many ways. In many quarters, for instance, as you will have seen from the papers, there has been some anxiety as to the amount of our national reserve of gold, as this has not increased in anything like the same degree as the development of our credit. The Bank of England is, of course, the custodian of this reserve, and how far it is desirable to assist, and how we can best assist in augmenting this is a problem worthy of the keenest thinkers in the City . . . We should always bear in mind that we are not starting, as it were, with a clean slate, but are living and doing our business under a system which has worked fairly well for more than half a century. In that system the Bank of England has played a great part, and laid us as bankers, and the commercial community generally, under many obligations, and it is, in my opinion, certain that it must continue to play a prominent part in the future.

Hillingdon's assessment was very much that of a City insider, the eminent private banker instinctively unwilling to upset the existing order of things.

In sharp contrast was the perspective of John Dun of Parr's, who in seconding the vote of thanks to Hillingdon lamented the general failure to take action so far over the question of the inadequate bullion reserve, attributing that failure to 'a deal of apathy in the British mind'. However, Dun pointed out with satisfaction that 'many bankers, feeling that they ought not any longer to hang upon the skirts of the Bank of England, have begun to provide independent reserves for themselves – they have locked up bullion, sovereigns, and Bank of England notes in their strong room, so that when a period of pressure does occur, the strain should not be exclusively on the Bank of England'. And he went on:

> Whether it may be possible to form any scheme whereby there should be combined action on the part of leading banks independently of the Bank of England to carry such reserves further and put them upon a more systematic footing, I do not know. That is a matter which is open to discussion among the leading men who administer the London banks. I will not enter further upon that question, but something must be done, and I think the big banks are the people to do it . . .[1]

Everyone accepted that there was a problem, but whether the leading joint-stock bankers were capable of coming up with a solution that was financially and politically acceptable – financially to their shareholders, politically to the rest of the City and its influential friends – was another matter entirely.

For the moment it seemed they were not. The bankers' committees failed to produce a report, and early in 1900, in his speech to the Union Bank of London's shareholders, Felix Schuster conceded that the question of increased gold reserves could not be systematically dealt with until after the war. Nevertheless, the question remained on the agenda, and in April 1900 a paper on 'Banking Reserves' produced a surprisingly frank discussion at the Institute. It was led by Dun, who in effect revealed why the twin initiative launched the previous summer had been a damp squib:

> It is a fact which is no longer a secret that many – I cannot say all, because we do not know – but many, and I think I may say most, of the large Joint Stock Banks, have accumulated in their own vaults, cash reserves beyond their daily requirements for till money. That is an admirable thing. That we should be able to fall upon some scheme whereby such private reserves on the part of the larger banks should be regulated, is another matter, and a very, very difficult matter indeed. The banks may be, and are, very friendly, but there is a good deal of latent jealousy, and not very latent competition amongst them, and Bank A would not brook that Bank B or Bank C should know the amount that it possesses deep

down in its vaults in the shape of gold coin to meet an emergency. Therefore, I fear, although the subject is one on which I should like to preserve quite an open mind, I fear that we cannot fall upon a general scheme whereby the maintenance of such reserves can be regulated.

Inevitably the other main contributor to the discussion was Schuster:

What we require is co-operation, and not legislation. More harmonious working together, although we compete with one another; more harmonious working towards one common end is absolutely necessary, not only between outside bankers, but between us and the Bank of England. In every foreign country, I believe, the State Bank has on its Board representatives of all the other great Joint Stock institutions in the banking world. The State Banks are practically managed, or supervised, by those whose special experience lies in the banking line. I hardly think that such a thing is practicable here – I would not advocate it for a moment – that is not in my mind; but I should think some means could be devised by which the Bank of England, instead of holding itself rather aloof from other banks, should periodically meet us and tell us what their views of the situation are, and that we should from time to time discuss a common policy, and act harmoniously with one another, instead of acting in the dark, as we are doing now, quite unaware of what may be in the minds of the Bank of England . . .[2]

In short, put less tactfully, the time had come for the company of merchants to accept, at last, the City's foremost joint-stock bankers as first-class citizens.

*

Once the Boer War began in October 1899, the prevailing mood in the City was little short of euphoric, reflecting a belief that, none too soon, a long-standing boil was about to be speedily lanced. Even the sober-minded Lionel Phillips of Wernher Beit caught the mood, on the 27th telling an Eckstein partner in Johannesburg that 'we are all greatly excited and eager for news from the seat of war'. News soon afterwards of a military reverse caused prices to tumble, but by the start of November William Keswick of Mathesons was assuring his correspondent in New York that 'when our forces arrive there is likely to be a concentration in the Transvaal that will speedily tend to the restoration of peace'. Such remained the conventional wisdom until the dark days of December, days encapsulated in a clutch of *FT* headlines. On the 12th: 'A Dismal Day: The Stormberg Reverse and Dear Money

Depress Prices'. On the 14th: 'Another Dismal Day: Prices Flat on the War News and Dear Money'. On the 18th: 'A Heavy Slump: News of Buller's Check Demoralises Markets'. And on the 20th: 'Another Black Day: Heavy Liquidation All Round the "House" '. A laconic but worried Gaspard Farrer informed his Montreal correspondent two days later that 'we have had lively times here' and explained: 'The fact is nobody anticipated these reverses and nobody was prepared; business as you know was extended and extending instead of having been curtailed and kept well in hand; the real trouble at the moment is the Government's requirements . . .'[3] It was starting to dawn on the City that this was going to be a protracted – and therefore expensive – affair.

Following considerable speculative losses at the tail-end of 1899, business in the Stock Exchange ground almost to a halt during the early weeks of 1900, leaving ample opportunity for ever more fervent displays of patriotic zeal. All sorts of wheezes – smoking concerts, raffles, the sale of members' doggerel – were resorted to in the cause of war charity, while particular enthusiasm attached to the hundred or more members and clerks about to set out to fight. Most of these clerks had their places kept open by their firms, but the *Daily Mail* reported (probably erroneously) on 15 January that one firm had told two of its clerks this would not be possible. 'It is needless to say,' the report added darkly, 'that the partners in this firm are not of English extraction.' No name was given, but it soon became common knowledge that the culprits were Kahn & Herzfelder, and when Maurice Herzfelder arrived in the Kaffir Circus later that day he found the House in an ugly mood. An eye-witness described the upshot: 'A hostile crowd pressed close to him, and he found himself being pushed with increasing violence from one side of the closing circle to the other. Soon, he was on the floor, and, perhaps regrettably, several members thought fit to kick him about the body and in the face, as he lay in a bruised and bleeding state.' The firm made a formal complaint to the Committee, but two days later Kahn stated that his partner was still too 'ill and dazed' to attend; and after Herzfelder had in due course written to the Committee 'to the effect that owing to the suddenness of the cowardly attack, the pressure of the crowd and his consequent bewilderment, he was unable to furnish the names of any of the persons who assaulted him', the Committee contented itself with posting one of its anodyne notices about disorderly conduct. The episode was even raised in the House of Commons, but the Home Secretary played the deadest of bats, stating that 'the Stock Exchange is a private place, and it is the duty of the authorities of the Stock Exchange to take whatever proceedings are necessary to preserve order therein'.[4]

If only a limited number felt that assault and battery on a German Jew stained the honour of the House, condemnation was more widespread when it emerged the following month that Guy Nickalls was before the Committee on a serious charge. The son of Tom, who had died the previous year amidst regret and tributes, he was himself a highly popular member famed for his prowess on the river, above all a notable series of triumphs at Henley. 'A day spent on the river sculling, or learning to scull,' Guy wrote in a Stock Exchange anthology on sport, 'is by no means a day wasted, as it will teach one many virtues and keep one from many vices.' Now, in February 1900, he was accused as a broker of having transgressed Stock Exchange rules, not only through writing to people he did not know (including a Miss Wade of St Leonards-on-Sea) in order to bid for some recently issued Vickers Sons and Maxim shares, but also by bidding only 10s premium for those shares when they were quoted at over £3 premium in the market. Despite plentiful protestations of innocence and misunderstood intentions, the result was suspension for five years. The *Economist* did not regard the punishment as unduly severe. Guy thereafter gave up hunting for the cheaper pastime of beagling; did several stints at Yale as rowing coach; worked for the advertising agents Walter Judd; and played many games of tennis, invariably crying 'Let it settle, let it settle' if an opponent caught the ball before it bounced. He died in 1935, and his posthumously published autobiography, *Life's a Pudding*, was as good humoured as the title, entirely passing over its author's ignominious exit from Capel Court.[5]

One way and another, it was a somewhat febrile City that the government had to deal with as it prepared, early in 1900, to raise £30m with which to fight the war. Hamilton conducted preliminaries on the Treasury's behalf, while the Governor's chair at the Bank of England was occupied by Samuel Steuart Gladstone, senior partner of the East India merchants Ogilvy, Gillanders & Co and a first cousin of the great man. 'Unfortunately very self-opinionated, and will have his own way,' was the unflattering estimate of one leading bill broker, but it was probably a just verdict. On 6 February he reported to Hamilton that 'the prevailing opinion' in the City was 'in favour of an addition to Consols', as opposed to the creation of a separate stock; and it soon became clear that this was also the Bank's own opinion, backed by Rothschilds and the Government broker J.H. Daniell, largely on the grounds of the unrivalled liquidity of Consols. The advantage of a separate stock, though, was that it would appeal to a wider public, something Hicks Beach naturally wanted, and two significant City figures supported that alternative. One was Cassel, who saw Hicks Beach on the 6th and objected to Consols partly because (in Hamilton's summarising words) 'there were large *bear* accounts open, and the speculators might put down the price against us as soon as they got wind of a large issue'. The other was Revelstoke, who as John Baring had succeeded to the title of his ill-fated father three years previously. Senior partner of Barings, and striving hard to restore the house to something like its old eminence, he wrote a letter to Hamilton on the 19th that fully suggested a return was being made to the high table of policy-making:

> You know my views on the subject; but I should like to express to you once more how earnestly I hope that a decision will be taken not to issue Consols, and that no advice tending to a *low* price of issue will be listened to.
> I am aware that the general 'City' opinion is against an issue at any price approaching the present one of Consols; but you will I am sure realise that a great deal of advice has most interested motives . . .
> I am told that John Dun – the manager of Parr's Bank – was sent for to the Treasury last week, & that the first thing he did on receiving the message was to send for Jefferson [Harry Jefferson, of Wedd, Jefferson & Co] & to ask him 'what he should say'.
> This Jefferson is by far the biggest dealer in the Consol market. He is said to be heavily short of Consols . . .

By the end of February the decision was made to go for a separate stock, and Hamilton on the 26th, after a visit to Threadneedle Street, even persuaded himself that the Bank was 'coming round to the idea of a special war loan in lieu of Consols'.[6]

Then, early on 1 March, a Thursday, came the news that Ladysmith had been relieved:

> The Stock Exchange had the news at five minutes to ten, and members dashed straight into the House before going to their offices. Each new-comer as he entered the excitable swing-doors asked wildly if the news were true, and hands were shaken all round as the report was confirmed . . . Five minutes before eleven Mr Charlie Clarke was seen to be extremely busy, and the whole House turned in the direction of the Consol Market. There was a sea of upturned faces and not a hat to be seen. There could hardly have been fewer than 5,000 men present as the first note of the

National Anthem boomed solemnly from the knot round Mr Clarke. The voices were at first in almost perfect unison, but in the other verses the tenors and altos took up their parts. Then at the tip-top of his voice the conductor called for cheers. Cheers for Buller, for White, for the Colonial and the British troops. It was a stirring scene, and as the markets returned to work, such as it was, they sang 'Rule, Britannia'. Later in the day the House went mad. Flags were waved, football played, members with supposed pro-Boer tendencies roughly but good-naturedly handled . . . One member took his post-horn into the House and gave selections all the afternoon, winding up his day by conducting a chorus of 'Soldiers of the Queen', and then tearing round the House on the sturdy shoulders of six human horses, who finally landed him – a panting heap – among the Westralians. Various processions filed round the Stock Exchange, inside and outside, during the day, at the end of which many members had entirely lost their voices.

There were some strange stories next morning. One broker confessed that he was strolling about the West End in the early hours, and, feeling tired, dropped into a cabmen's shelter, where he promptly fell asleep. He was awakened by the entry of a stranger, and turned half round to remonstrate against having his rest broken, when he found it was another member of the House. Another member failed to reach home, but found himself in the lamp-room of a suburban station, although he had not the remotest idea of how he had been spirited thither. Many members had lost their hats in the grand scrimmage of the afternoon, and no fewer than twenty-one were collected and placed on view in the Stock Exchange cloakroom with a view to identification. But perhaps the strangest story came from Waterloo. A Stock Exchange man who was found asleep on one of the seats in the station, discovered four first-class tickets in his pocket, all for the same place. How they could have come there is still a mystery. The only conclusion his friends could arrive at was that after taking the first ticket he must have met someone who invited him to toast the victorious Generals, and that he took another ticket afterwards, forgetting about the first, the performance being thrice repeated.

That was Duguid's account soon afterwards, while Sidney Webb at the time wrote to Beatrice: 'All day long, in the City, there appears to have been a pandemonium of joy and shouting . . .'[7]

The news was a marvellous fillip to the prospects of the imminent war loan, but the enthusiasm seems barely to have infected Gladstone at the Bank. Writing to Hamilton on the 2nd, in response to a draft prospectus, his mainly technical letter ended on a thoroughly sour note: 'In conclusion I feel regret that the loan is not to be raised by an addition to Consols and would have preferred a terminable 3% annuity at par to a $2\frac{3}{4}$% one at a heavy discount and I hope that in pricing the price of issue the Chancellor will not aim too high.' Also in the band of doubters was Natty Rothschild, who was being overriden not only in his wish for Consols but also in the notion that the issue should be backed by a Rothschild-led guarantee, a plan that Hicks Beach shortly rejected. Writing to Hamilton from Tring Park on Sunday the 4th, he referred with foreboding to 'a financial Maggersfontein' (one of the Boer War disasters) and went on:

> It is no use living in a fool's paradise. The operation will have to be very carefully managed and everything done to insure success. The Germans are already trying to place a large loan and will no doubt offer very tempting prices to under-writers here and in America . . . The Chancellor told me he would send for me when he is ready. I am always at his disposal so please wire me to New Court when I am to call on your Chief.

In fact, Natty and his brothers were in the process of being moved sideways in the consultative process. A memorandum written by Hamilton on the Monday revealed who was entering centre stage:

> I had a talk with Sir E. Cassel last night. (He returned from Rome on purpose to render assistance.)
> He agreed cordially with me that it would be better to dispense with a guarantee altogether, if possible. If the price was fixed at (say) 98, he believed that the loan would be certain to go; and it would be much more dignified for the Government to appeal direct to the public who would respond.
> At the same time there could be no harm & it might be a satisfaction to the Chanc of the Exchequer to sound a *few* big persons as to what they would be good for – he would be responsible for 2m himself.
> The Bankers might be summoned by the Governor on the eve of the issue, and their co-operation invited.[8]

In essence Cassel's plan was adopted, though the eventual price was $98\frac{1}{2}$, a full point above what most City people had been pressing for.

On Friday the 9th, just as the prospectus was published, the City's leading bankers were summoned to meet not just the Governor but (on an idea of Hamilton's) the Chancellor himself. Gladstone remained malcontent to the last. He disapproved of a personal appeal to the bankers, telling Hamilton that 'in my humble opinion their patriotism is a mere matter of price – make that attractive enough and there will be no danger of the loan not being subscribed'. That was to no avail, but he had more success with his other main grumble, which was to insist that a suggested addition to the prospectus, stating that applications could be made to the London Clearing House banks as well as to the Bank of England, be taken out. 'I hope it will not be pressed,' he wrote. 'It is not necessary & therefore undesirable: please leave this paragraph alone & turn a deaf ear to the suggestions of other Bankers.' Hamilton modified the wording, but it hardly mattered, for the issue proved a roaring success and was massively oversubscribed. 'Scores of clerks,' reported the Chief Cashier at the Bank itself, 'are here every night until 10, 11, 12 and even $\frac{1}{2}$ past one o'clock.' A satisfied Hamilton noted in his diary on Friday the 16th: 'The loan, which the Stock Exchange with their love for slang have nicknamed "Khaki", was closed on Wednesday evening. It was subscribed more than 11 times over . . .' Arguably, City anxieties about overpricing had led to the loan being underpriced, as Revelstoke against the trend had feared. Hamilton, however, preferred to turn his attention to the question of allotment: 'Cassel who dined with me this evening thought that we were giving the big folk too much and not allotting enough among the small applicants. We can easily remedy this.' His word was becoming law, and it was not only for Egyptian reasons that Hamilton a few weeks later referred to 'the jealousy with which the Rothschilds regard Cassel'.[9]

It was all academic to Cecil Boyle. In November 1899 he had brought a charge of incivility against waiter G.H. Smith, causing the Stock Exchange managers to investigate the matter; but, it transpiring that 'the incivility was in tone and manner more than in words', Smith was let off with a reprimand and caution. Soon afterwards Boyle went to South Africa with his yeomanry, the Queens Own Oxfordshire Hussars; there, 'when French made his splendid ride to Kimberley, Captain Boyle acted as one of his gallopers, and entered the town almost side by side with the victorious general'; and in April 1900, in battle near Boshof, he was killed, the second member of the Stock Exchange to fall during the war. For his old admirers, it was a redeeming moment:

> Dear hero, you, of school's ideal day,
>   Ranging the Clifton close in far-off years,
> A king and captain of our battling play,
>   Once more your form appears.
>
> Life's business came, you passed into the stress
>   Of gainful rivalry, and 'Lost!' we cried;
> 'Buried in honoured affluence and success
>   His promise and our pride.'

> Then struck the stern hour of an Empire's need,
>   And you were forward to obey the call.
> Forward, high heart, to follow or to lead,
>   Or, if God willed, to fall.
>
> And you have fallen, and it is achieved –
>   Duty and victory and a gallant end;
> Not all, not all our love and faith conceived,
>   But nought we would amend.

Or as the *Rialto* put it more prosily, in words curiously reminiscent of Pember's commendation over twenty years earlier: 'Cecil Boyle was an English gentleman. Can any higher tribute be paid to his memory?'[10]

Within weeks of this hero's death, news reached London, on the evening of Friday, 18 May that Mafeking also had been relieved. 'The war has been hateful to us from the outset but the pluck and example of that little garrison is legitimate grounds for pride and enthusiasm.' That was the reaction of Gaspard Farrer, but relatively few in the City shared that sense of hatefulness, least of all on Mafeking Day. A memorable Saturday – and for the City, the high point of the war – was described by the *FT* in its daily stock-market report:

> So far as business was concerned, the Stock Exchange might just as well have been closed today, but it provided a useful purpose in providing a gathering place for some 5,000 City men who had gone crazy over the news of the relief of Mafeking. A huge crowd of members and clerks had assembled soon after ten o'clock, and found that the whole of the markets had been lavishly decorated with flags, which the crowd proceeded to generously supplement until the House was one blaze of bunting. Not only were the walls and pillars covered with flags, but almost every member or clerk had a Union Jack of his own to wave. The excitement was in excess of even that aroused by the relief of Ladysmith, and the wild cheering might almost have been heard by Baden-Powell in South Africa. A few minutes before eleven Mr Charlie Clarke announced that on the stroke of the hour photographs would be taken of the House, and asked members to stand steady and cease cheering at the time. Two groups were taken by the London Stereoscopic operator, one of the Consol market and one of the Trunk market, the idea doubtless being to join them together in panoramic style. The photographs are to be sold, and the proceeds are to be devoted to the relief of the people of Mafeking ... After the photographs had been taken 'God Save the Queen' was sung with fine enthusiasm, followed by 'Rule Britannia', 'God Bless the Prince of Wales' and 'For He's a Jolly Good Fellow', rousing cheers being given for Baden-Powell, Roberts and the Queen. The House then degenerated into a somewhat riotous condition, members marching about in cheering

columns, waving flags and blowing trumpets, while the note of the inevitable coaching horn was heard over all. It was obvious that nobody wanted to do any business today, and that it could not be done even had any foolhardy jobber attempted it. . .[11]

*

As the summer wore on it became uncomfortably clear that the Boers were not going to curl up, close their eyes and think of Capel Court. Everyone knew that more money was going to be needed to wage the war, and successive diary entries show Hamilton caught between an anxious financial adviser and his deliberately calm political master:

> *19 July.* John Baring (Revelstoke) was strong today not only on the expediency but also on the necessity of our borrowing at once and borrowing an outside figure. The uncertainty about our requirements is doing much harm in the City . . .
> *20 July.* I had a talk with Beach this morning as to making an early announcement of his borrowing intentions. Similar representations to those made to me yesterday by Revelstoke had already reached him & the First Lord. But he was not to be moved: the City might all go to the devil as far as he was concerned: he was not going to make an announcement a day earlier than he chose.

Gladstone was still Governor, and on the 23rd he wrote solemnly to Hicks Beach: 'I deprecate the issue of a further War Loan on the lines of the previous one, for it could only now be made at a considerably worse price than the former issue . . . I do not hesitate to say that an issue of Consols would be more popular with the City and the public than any other form . . .' The next day the Bank, already lending the government some £8½m, formally declined to lend a further £½–1m, thereby forcing Hicks Beach's hand; also that day, Hamilton conveniently found himself in Threadneedle Street. After 'a talk with the Bank people' – still adamantly pro-Consols, anti-Khaki – he went on to New Court, and later in the afternoon 'got hold of Sir E. Cassel'. This time, to Hamilton's relief, the two great authorities were in agreement: both Rothschilds and Cassel insisted that Consols were out of the question and instead plumped for Exchequer bonds. Their word proved decisive, as Gladstone's advice was again spurned.[12]

A complicated week ensued as rival priorities vied with each other.[13] One was the government's need for money, the other was the Bank's need for gold in order to bolster its flagging reserve; and it quite quickly became government policy that the best way to square this pressing circle was to ensure that a substantial proportion of the new loan was placed in America, which would have the almost automatic effect of attracting considerable quantities of gold to London. The policy owed little to any initiative by Gladstone at the Bank, while Hamilton by the 31st saw it as the lesser of two evils:

> I have had talks today with Revelstoke and Dawkins (who has become manager of the great American house of Morgan here) about the taking up of some of the Bonds we want to float, in the United States. I don't much like the idea. It looks so much as if we had come to the end of our borrowing tether, and had to go cap in hand to America to enable us to carry on the war. On the other hand, there are threats of tight times here; and the only way of preventing excessive tightness is to get gold. So there are direct advantages to be attained by our negotiating with our Anglo-American friends.

In the end it was agreed to an advance placing in America of just over half the £10m issue. Hamilton reflected on 2 August that this was something that ought to be stated in the prospectus. However, 'the Bank of England are averse to this, and think we can arrange the matter by closing the list as soon as the sum required has been applied for'.[14]

Hamilton's concern was amply justified, and in due course the *Statist* told the story of a sore episode in relations between Chancellor and square mile:

> He has certainly not dealt very fairly with the City. He brought out the loan on one of the most unfavourable days of the whole year. It was known by very few on Friday afternoon [the 3rd]. It was publicly announced on the Saturday morning preceding the August Bank Holiday, when the Stock Exchange was closed, and when, owing to the great heat that had prevailed previously, everybody that could was anxious to get away for a few days. The list was opened at 10 o'clock on Tuesday morning. Fifty minutes later it was closed, when it ought to have been known to everybody concerned that the day after the Bank Holiday the trains would all be late, and intending applicants would therefore not be in a position to apply early. As for the provinces and the Continent, they were entirely shut out. Lastly, the Chancellor of the Exchequer, in announcing the loan, did not state that more than half of it was already disposed of. Surely that was a material fact that ought to have been made known to intending subscribers. If the British Government holds back such a material fact as this, how can we expect anything better from the private promoter?

The atmosphere in the City that Tuesday morning (the 7th) was red-hot, as Natty Rothschild fired off an angry letter to Hamilton:

> I have given myself a great deal of trouble about the Exchequer bonds and have written and telegraphed all over the World. I had some applications to send in but was coolly informed at the Bank that the list was closed.
>
> If this is to be the policy of Her Majesty's Govt in large transactions, closing the list the day after a Bank Holyday and precluding Banks and other large institutions from subscribing when they have been taking a great deal of trouble to collect subscriptions, I do not think that in future anyone will care to trouble themselves to work for the Chancellor of the Exchequer. The list should have been kept open all day.

Not surprisingly, the language at New Court, as Carl Meyer reported to his wife later that day, was 'the reverse of complimentary'; while elsewhere, 'others threaten lawsuits against the Treasury – in fact, there is a h--- of a row and the papers will be full of it tomorrow'. So they were ('the Government has gone in for stag hunting before the grouse shooting has begun' was the *FT*'s wry comment), but Hamilton took the larger view: 'We have got our money easily subscribed; and the London market is relieved at not having to find the whole of it itself.'[15]

Of course, what really rankled at New Court was the muscling in of the Morgan houses on an important British government issue, an eloquent testimony to their ability to offer a high-class transatlantic distribution service. It was with the purr of a cat that has got the cream that Dawkins, barely three months in the City, wrote to Milner on the 16th:

> I have been lingering on at Brook's with Eddy Hamilton & Haldane, finishing up my first large deal with the British Govt.
>
> You may have observed that we placed half, really more than half of the new ten million loan in the US.
>
> The Treasury were quite right in their general policy, and the gold we are bringing over will avert what would have been a 7 pc Bank rate and considerable trouble. But, of course, the Treasury went hopelessly wrong in details owing to the colossal stupidity of the Bank . . .

Dawkins then explained how the Bank had struck out from the draft prospectus the crucial 'material fact' and how Hicks Beach had 'weakly consented', thereby 'exposing the Govt to violent abuse'; and later in his letter he could not resist groaning, 'But the Bank of England! If that old institution is not reorganised on some better basis it will bring us into trouble yet.'[16]

If Dawkins was starting his City career on an auspicious note, the company promoter H. Osborne O'Hagan spent the summer of 1900 seeking to finish his with a culminating triumph. After many months of patient negotiation on his part, the flotation took place in July of Associated Portland Cement Manufacturers (1900), Ltd, described by the *Economist* as 'a big "combine" of cement undertakings' (no fewer than thirty-four firms and companies) 'situated mainly on the Thames and Medway'. The prospectus was published on Saturday the 14th, offering almost £7½m of stock and shares to the public, and on that first main day of pre-allotment dealings 'an active business was done in Associated Portland Cement Manufacturers, the Ordinary shares being in demand at ½ premium, the Preference at ¼ premium and the Debentures at 4½ premium'. But in the same day's *FT*, there was an ominous headline: 'Peking: The "Massacre" Rumour Repeated: Still Nothing Direct or Official'. Then, over the weekend, the *Daily Mail* released the text of a telegram purporting to come from its special correspondent at Shanghai, a generally lurid account of the Boxer uprising in Peking, ending with the memorable words, 'overcome by overwhelming odds, every one of the Europeans remaining was put to the sword in most atrocious manner'. This report was published by *The Times* on Monday morning. It eventually transpired that the telegram was a fake but, as O'Hagan claimed to know immediately, the damage was done:

> It was taken as a properly verified announcement by *The Times*. The panic created was so great that all securities on the Stock Exchange depreciated, and for some days it was practically impossible to sell anything.
> Such a panic had not been known for years. The cement prospectus had yet three days to be before the public, and it is hardly necessary to say that it greatly influenced the applications for shares and debentures. The Stock Exchange 'stags' and 'bears' became bold, and during these few days offered the shares at ½ and even at ¼ premium in thousands, and so long as the prospectus was before the public I had to buy them regardless of consequences. Then the lists were closed, but not before all Stock Exchange applications were withdrawn, and when we came to tot up the position it was apparent we should be short about two and a half million of cash to complete the purchases and provide the working capital required.

In fact the impact was more delayed than O'Hagan's account would suggest – Monday the 16th saw 'a steady flow of buying orders' for Associated Cements – but in broad terms his recollections of an acutely vexing week were accurate. 'The cables from China are most conflicting,' Carl Meyer wrote to his wife that Wednesday, adding that 'the

City, needless to say, is beastly and likely to remain so'; while that evening the Miscellaneous market report of the *FT* (a paper friendly to O'Hagan) noted with disapproval how, in relation to the new issue, 'some of the dealers are indulging in premium snatching in hopes of being able to replace the shares on allotment', in other words the traditional tactics of the stag. O'Hagan's frantic buying managed to keep the price of the ordinary shares up to $\frac{15}{16}$ premium by the end of the week, but the following Tuesday they were down to $\frac{3}{16}$ premium, 'it being stated in the market that applicants for shares will get all they applied for'. In the event O'Hagan, far from retiring, spent much of the next two decades seeking to retrieve the company's fortunes. In his own words: 'It struck me that I more than anyone was responsible for the mess. I had a strong opinion that a *débâcle* would spell ruin to some of those who had joined us, and perhaps throw a slur on men who held their heads high in the City. I felt that all question of profit or loss must be left out of consideration.'[17] Undone by circumstances beyond his control, O'Hagan represented the acceptable face of late-Victorian company promoting.

The ill-fated flotation was also not helped by the South African situation – on 18 July, markets were adversely affected by 'the news that De Wet had broken through General Rundle's cordon, and this it is thought may cause a considerable prolongation of the war' – but for some the continuing hostilities represented an opportunity rather than a hindrance. Soon afterwards the Stock Exchange Committee considered a communication from a Major Hamilton of the 6th Dragoon Guards, writing from the Pretoria Club, Pretoria:

> Would you kindly inform me what I ought to do in following matter? Before leaving for SA I met an old brother officer, Capt C.A. Osborne, who is now on the Stock Exchange, and hearing how war news affected the gold mines I arranged to send him wires of war news, and should that news arrive before it was made public, he was to act upon it. Capt Osborne finally wrote me, and sent me a code saying 'Now to business, if I received a wire "Pay cheque to Coutts" I buy you 500 Consolidated Gold Fields deferred, on the other hand if you wire pay cheque to Cox [another West End private bank], I sell the same amount. Let me have a line confirming this.' I confirmed this agreement, and sent two wires which arrived after the news was known in England, and Capt Osborne informed me were not acted upon. I then joined General Beach's column for the relief of Kimberley. The matter was of course kept very secret, but in my opinion was sure to be successful, so I wired four days before we left Orange River, 'Pay cheque to Coutts, wait fortnight,' meaning you will not hear the news for about a fortnight. When I reached Kimberley I

again wired 'Hold on' as I knew we should take Bloemfontein. At the end
of about a month I received a letter from Capt Osborne enclosing an
account from Messrs Wagg & Co for 150 'Matebeli Gold Riefs' bought
at about 8. I wrote saying there must be some mistake, as I had never
heard of 'Matebeli Gold Riefs'. I enquired about them when I got to
Johannesburg, and found they were not a Transvaal mine at all . . . Capt
Osborne is an old friend of mine and I simply want to know what is fair.
I have received an account for about £50 from Messrs Wagg & Co. I have
left the letter of agreement at Bloemfontein with my heavy luggage . . .

The Committee replied to Hamilton that it was 'unable to advise him
in the matter referred to'; and there seems to have been no question of
taking disciplinary action against the Captain, who doubled for the
brokers Helbert Wagg as an unauthorised clerk and half-commission
man, in effect touting for orders and if successful receiving half the
commission.[18]

Osborne was a busy man that summer, to judge by a letter at the end
of August from Harry Gibbs to his brother Herbert. The subject was
the Camp Bird gold mine in Colorado:

This is a mine we have this morning taken an interest of £15,000 in. We
took £10,000 through Capt Osborne of Helbert Waggs, & £5,000
through young Hugh Smith of Rowe Pitmans [i.e. Lancelot Hugh Smith
of the brokers Rowe & Pitman] . . . The mine from the reports seems very
large & good, it is at Cripple Creek, about 200 miles from Stratton's
Independence. The names of the people in it weighed with me & Alban,
& the amounts they have taken. Beit has taken £350,000, Hambro
£100,000, Morgans £100,000, Marks Bulteel [brokers, traditionally
specialising in Kaffirs] £200,000, & Robinson [J. B. Robinson, the
notoriously unpleasant Randlord] £300,000.

Camp Bird, which had not yet produced any gold, was another promotion by the Venture Corporation, and this was indeed a powerful
syndicate. A fortnight later, writing to his cousin John (also a partner),
Harry Gibbs was still in a buoyant mood, though anxious to guard
against any last-minute snares:

As to 'Camp Bird' what I feel about it is, that as we are in on the same
floor as Beit, Robinson, etc, we may safely conclude (their interest being
infinitely greater than ours) that the arrangements they make are the best
possible under the circumstances. The only thing that strikes me on
reading your letter, is that it now looks as if the syndicate would have
1,000,000 shares between them *less* whatever shares are sold to realise
the purchase price of £1,350,000. I understood that the idea was to issue

1 Capel Court entrance, 1891.

2 *Saturday, 19 May 1900 at 11 a.m.: Mafeking has been relieved, and Charlie Clarke,* centre, *prepares to lead the singing of the National Anthem.*

3 *The floor of the House, 1902.*

MAX · COWPER

4 *A member is hammered, as markets plunge in March 1907.*

High jinks in October 1908: 5 OPPOSITE *throwing the tape over the handrail;* 6 ABOVE *'ragging' scenes.*

7 Throgmorton Street, 1905: ten years after 'the Battle'.

to the public in six months time with a Capital of £1,000,000. One does not exactly see therefore how the syndicate are to avoid a heavy loss, which of course is not contemplated. I therefore sent for Osborne – he however was out of town, & in his place there came a sort of head clerk, who said that Capt Osborne had left a slip with him in case there should be enquiries about the change of policy in The Camp Bird . . .

Shortly afterwards a large Jew arrived, whom I divined to be Wagg himself – he said he could explain matters, but as I found he (like his clerk) was wholly ignorant of the business, I am forced to believe that the object of his visit was to inspect our private room which he informed me he had never before seen, though he had been 30 years in the City.

The 'large Jew' was indeed Arthur Wagg, senior partner of Helbert Wagg since 1866 and not renowned for his stringent intellect. On this occasion, after failing to explain matters, he stated feebly that 'he really didn't understand "latter-day finance" '; and so Gibbs sent for Lancelot Hugh Smith of Rowe & Pitman, and 'he did explain the matter'.[19]

Camp Bird proved to be an excellent mine, not too heavily overcapitalised at the outset, and a largely profitable venture for those involved. Indeed, there even seemed a strong possibility, during the autumn of 1900, that the leading South African mining houses were about to shift their centre of gravity across the Atlantic. Hays Hammond (the mining engineer) 'had a meeting with a lot of the South African people', Harry Gibbs reported to Herbert, '& told them he didn't think there would be any more sensational finds of gold in the Rand, that one knew pretty nearly what was there, & that they (the SA lot) had got about the best of everything already, & he advised them to turn their attention to the Cripple Creek mines, which they certainly seem to be doing with a vengeance'. But although Camp Bird came off, the shift failed to happen. 'The projected transference of African money to American mines will *not*, I think, take place. There has been division and discussion, I believe, in the African camp on the matter, but the decision is as I say.' So Dawkins correctly informed Milner at the start of November, almost certainly in the wake of a highly negative report by Hammond on the prospects for Stratton's Independence, the other main mine in the Venture Corporation portfolio. The report was commissioned by a Rand group that had lent heavily to Venture Corporation, struggling since the flotation of Stratton's the previous year to keep the price up, and Hammond found that Stratton himself had been systematically stripping the mine of its richest ore and doing little or nothing about development work. Only the favourable parts of Hammond's report were published in November, and the share price was kept up for a while longer. But eventually, in the course of 1901, the truth started to come out, as amidst much acrimony the share price collapsed. Baker of the Venture Corporation blamed Stratton for sending consistently false information about high crushings and suchlike, but his protestations of injured innocence carried little conviction. In the seasoned words of the leading mining journalist J.H. Curle, in the 1902 edition of his authoritative *The Gold Mines of the World*, 'the history of this mine is very typical of the wretched way in which our gold-mining industry is carried on'.[20]

In 1900 itself, as the Boer War continued its increasingly weary course, a highlight came on 29 October. Through crowded streets, the City Imperial Volunteers, a body of almost two thousand with a heavy weighting of clerks, made their way from Paddington Station to the City headquarters of the Honourable Artillery Company, via a service at St Paul's to celebrate their safe return from South Africa. 'Business Paralysed' was the predictable headline of the *FT*, but its Monday evening stock-market report gave an interesting slant on the day's proceedings:

> It would be simply hopeless to attempt to convey to the minds of those who were not in town the frenzied excitement with which the City, in common with the rest of the Metropolis, welcomed the return of its gallant Volunteers . . . For once in a while, however, the Stock Exchange did not catch the infection of the public demonstration; there has been no waving of flags within its precincts, no Inferno of penny 'hooters', and no 'long tiddling'. Gorgonzola Hall has simply been deserted as regards attendance and dull in tone . . . According to our information the House has not been very much inclined to associate itself with the festivities, not because it fails to recognise the gallantry of the City regiment, in which, of course, it has a strong muster of brave representatives, but apparently because the recent outbursts of patriotic fervour have been lacking in restraint and dignity . . .[21]

*

For Whitaker Wright the closing weeks of 1900 were the most stressful of his career, but they followed an already challenging twelve months.[22] Late in 1899 he was the victim of a relentless bear attack, as it emerged that he had been duped by his mine manager into bulling

Lake Views; the following summer he exacted temporary revenge on the bears, running up the price of another West Australian mining counter, Le Roi No 2, and squeezing his enemies hard; but by the autumn of 1900 he was again on the rack, as it became increasingly feared in the City that he had overextended his resources, especially through the London and Globe's commitment to build the Baker Street and Waterloo Railway (what was to become the Bakerloo line).

There ensued in December a battle royal on the Stock Exchange, with Lake Views the main target of persistent bear attacks. By Monday the 10th, according to the *FT*, there was 'talk of a syndicate having been formed to advance the price against bears'; a week later, at the London and Globe's annual meeting, held in a 'crowded' Great Hall at Winchester House, Wright as managing director defiantly apologised for the absence of a dividend:

> The majority of you who have investments of various characters know that there are always cycles in finance. For several years there is an upward tendency in all markets and you cannot go wrong. At another time – and this year it has been occasioned, as you know, by the war in South Africa, and political unrest generally – you might as well attempt to dam a river with a bar of sand as to stop depreciation. (*Hear, hear.*) . . . We do claim that this company, from its commencement to the present time, has acquired more good properties for you than many exploration companies of a similar character. A certain clique at the present moment are trying to mark down your securities on the Stock Exchange, but they are not selling them, and one of these days you will see a reaction which will carry them up to where they belong.

Lord Dufferin in the chair received his usual generous applause and paid his usual handsome tribute – 'never have I seen any man so devote himself, at the risk of his health, and at the risk of everything that a man can give to business of the kind, as Mr Whitaker Wright' – but even he had sufficient command of finance to know that the issue would be resolved not by rhetorical flourishes but in the marketplace. Late on the 17th, after the meeting, some leading jobbers offered Lake Views by the thousand and, the *FT* related, 'so successful were these workers for the fall that in almost half an hour they succeeded in depressing the price to the extent of about £3'. Over the following week Lake Views fluctuated wildly, and the market swirled with 'ugly stories' about 'some "ratting" having occurred' in the much talked of, but never precisely identified, syndicate that was supposed to keep up the price of the shares.[23]

Events moved swiftly after Christmas, with the Stock Exchange's end-December settlement. On the 28th, a Friday, it became clear that the London and Globe, after frantic buying of over 60,000 Lake View shares during the previous fortnight, was unable to meet its obligations; and the next day, thirteen Stock Exchange firms were hammered, involving twenty-nine members, most of them brokers who had bought shares for Wright on the mistaken assumption that he was backed by a powerful syndicate that would be able to pay for them at the settlement. 'The very hand of Barker the waiter,' Duguid wrote, 'shook like an aspen leaf as, amid death-like silence, he announced failure after failure.' Inevitably a rash of vindictive attacks broke out against Wright, which the *FT* deplored, though not denying that his financing had been 'reckless, indiscreet and blameworthy'. For Dufferin the London and Globe's default was a crushing blow, a humiliating end to a noble public career, and he died in 1902 a broken man. There rang in his ears the cruel schoolboy jibe: 'Why was Whitaker Wright? Because he took a Dufferin.'[24]

The question remained, for almost a year and a half after the collapse of Wright's empire, whether his downfall had been caused by the mysterious bull syndicate treacherously pulling the rug from under him. Many in the City believed so, and eventually in June 1902 there took place a legal action by the London and Globe against five Stock Exchange firms and two individual members, the so-called 'Stock Exchange Syndicate'. It transpired that the syndicate had indeed lent the Globe almost £½m to help it over the mid-December settlement, but that it had not made any similar commitment for the end-December settlement, and that any suggestion at the time that it had was the result of rumours deliberately spread in the market by Wright, desperate to keep prices up and apply a squeeze against the bears. The Globe lost its case and the following February its managing director did a runner, first to Paris and then New York, from where he was extradited. Wright was accused of large-scale fraud, and his trial began at the Old Bailey on 11 January 1904. It lasted twelve days, during which Rufus Isaacs led for the prosecution and exposed in detail the astonishing financial juggling and malpractice with which Wright had conducted his business. In the summarising words of one City man recalling the trial years later:

Entries from one company to another – shares to the value of over £1½m being transferred from the Globe to subsidiary companies a day or two before the balance sheet was issued, only to be sold back a day or two after – loans raised in various ways at exorbitant rates of interest for a few days, explaining the substantial amount of cash in hand showed by the Globe Corporation in its balance sheet . . .

At the end, Wright was sentenced to seven years' penal servitude. Half an hour later he was dead, having swallowed a tablet of cyanide of potassium. As his body was taken out the watching crowd doffed its hats in silent admiration, recognising that, whatever his sins, a giant had passed; and on a country tombstone the words were inscribed, 'Lord of the Manor of Witley'.[25]

CHAPTER THIRTEEN

This Cosmopolitan Crew

> I went down yesterday to Mentmore for a night. According to an arrangement made a year ago, there was to be a Rothschild gathering at Mentmore to see the 19th century out. I think we mustered 24 in all – R. [Rosebery] & his 3 unmarried children, the Crewes, Natty & his two sons, the Leos & their three boys, the Arthur Sassoons . . . Rosebery after dinner proposed 'prosperity to the House of Rothschild' in a touching little speech, which elicited tears from Natty & Leo.

Three weeks later, Hamilton and everyone else were adjusting to a new century without Queen Victoria. The news from Osborne came on a Tuesday evening, and as one member-journalist recorded, there followed an awkward morning on the Stock Exchange:

> The House was open at the ordinary time, in fact, members assembled earlier, and also in larger numbers than usual – a leading member said to me that he never remembers to have seen the House so full at eleven o'clock in the morning. It was not for nearly 20 minutes after this time that the committee room waiter was sent down with the message that it had been decided to close the House at once, and the old familiar cry of 'Closed' was immediately made by the waiters at each entrance . . . It is said some few deals were made in the West African market [popularly known as the Jungle market, and flourishing during the winter of 1900–1] on Wednesday morning, and I also heard someone say that a deal in Consols had been negotiated, but in every market dealers simply looked on, and talked in hushed whispers. One gentleman went into the Yankee market, and asked the price of Milwaukees, and promptly got his hat smashed for daring to think of business, whilst one dealer who could not refuse a pet broker, told him to say no more about it, but put some Louisvilles he wanted to deal in down to him at anything he thought fair – he did not mind taking a risk, but he obstinately refused to attempt to deal. A wild rush was made out of the House, and long before twelve o'clock the street was practically empty.

On Saturday, 2 February the funeral cortège passed through London, from Victoria Station to Paddington Station via St James's Park and

Piccadilly. One of the Stock Exchange's oldest members, Thomas Fenn, viewed the procession from a window in his club. He then returned to his home in Down Street, sat in his armchair and quietly died. A freemason for many years, he had been a leading member of the United Lodge of Prudence – the Stock Exchange lodge – and the *FT* recalled him as 'a great authority on the law and practice of the Order'.[1]

*

For two other active freemasons, February 1901 marked the start of something big. After school at Marlborough and a year in New Zealand, Harry Wrightson had spent seven years working in the City for his cousin Ernest Cooper, an insurance broker. Since 1898 he had been an underwriting member at Lloyd's, and now he was poised to launch out on his own account. He wrote to his mother on the 12th:

> I have at last squared up a partnership with a man at Lloyd's.
> He is a man of the name of Matthews, aged about 45, Ernest Cooper made all arrangements and now it is only the details to be decided.
> I have not known the man previously but Ernest thinks very highly of him.
> He has been manager of a big firm here and left voluntarily at the end of last year thinking that he could do better for himself. He has done all the travelling for the firm so knows all the shipowners and ought to have good connections.
> It will mean putting our backs into it, but I think we ought to be able to make things go.
> He wants to combine chartering business (chartering and selling vessels for people) and I will look after the insurance brokerage part, then in two or three years I hope that we may also have an underwriting department and bring Robert in to look after that, as by that time he ought to know something about the business.
> Matthews I think can get the business but he wants more capital so my being able to put something into the business will make a lot of difference . . .

J. Woodrow Matthews was the other freemason. As a boy he had started in a shipping office in his native Devon, before coming to London and joining the shipping firm of W. Lamplough & Co, where he became manager of their Lloyd's department while still in his 20s. The partnership of Matthews, Wrightson & Co was announced on 18 February, taking effect from the start of the year. The firm flourished, and in 1903 not only did Harry's elder brother Robert become a partner but the firm initiated the first syndicate at Lloyd's entirely devoted to non-marine business, taking on a stage further the pioneering approach of Cuthbert Heath.[2] It had been a classic marriage: between an old hand and a new hand, between practical experience and money, between two serious-minded men.

It was, like most events in the shipping and insurance world, not a marriage that impinged on the Bank of England, the banks, the money market and the Stock Exchange, that financial core of the City. Finance's main concern in the early months of 1901 was the government's heavy borrowing requirements in order to wage the war.[3] On 23 January, the day after the Queen's death, Barings wired to Baring Magoun in New York: 'Very important negotiations should not be suspected. We recommend caution, specially Rothschilds. Chancellor of Exchequer very anxious negotiations to be kept private.' The context was the intention of Hicks Beach to issue £11m of Exchequer bonds, once again using Morgans and Barings in both London and New York, with a substantial American placing. 'We will not be popular here, but it is the only way of getting a good price *and* of helping the gold situation here,' Dawkins wrote to Milner on the 25th. The first part of that assessment was certainly correct, for on the same day Hamilton was visited by Granville Farquhar, brother of Horace and senior partner of Steer, Lawford & Co, 'a firm of eminently respectable stockbrokers'. Farquhar argued strongly for an issue of Consols, not least on the grounds that this was necessary if they were to recover their former prestige and supremacy as *the* British government security; and he went on (in Hamilton's subsequent account to Hicks Beach):

> Though any further issue in anything else but Consols would be unpopular, because the market is so stuffed with the short securities, what would be still more unpopular would be resort to the American Market. Nothing had given so great offence to the City for years as the allotment of those Exchequer Bonds last August in the United States. They (the Stock Exchange) would have much preferred the grave inconvenience of a 7 or 8 per cent Bank rate whereby gold would have come. That would have been temporary; whereas it was feared that permanent injury had been done to the London market by last year's arrangements. What had to be faced sooner or later was that New York would 'cut out' London; and nothing had 'put on the hands of the clock' (as he called it) in that direction so decidedly as these arrangements under which the example was set by the British Finance Minister. As a matter of fact, it was known

that almost the whole of the Bonds issued to the American firms had come over here now, which made the City more sore because they were 'stuck' with the Bonds and foreigners had bagged the commission . . .

Farquhar's views were broadly echoed by Daniell the Government broker, and by 5 February the Chancellor, though still adamant against Consols, was more or less admitting to Dawkins that he was unable to decide what to do. 'I don't believe it is possible to obtain a really disinterested opinion from City men,' Hamilton confided to his diary the next day, but it was also on the 6th that Hicks Beach came to the conclusion that there was no alternative but to seek guidance from the most traditional source. 'I am inclined to put the thing straight to the Bank people,' he wrote to Hamilton. 'If they assure me that they believe the market here will take the bonds, and can themselves help *largely*, if necessary, to secure this, then I w^d try a free issue here. If they can't, then US.'[4]

Hamilton over the following week recorded the outcome:

> *8 February*. The Chanc of the Exchequer went to the Bank today; & we settled about the loan. The whole of it is to be issued here, being put up to open tender without a minimum, and though the City authorities don't believe we shall get more than 97 . . . I should not wonder if we did rather better. Revelstoke & Dawkins, representing Barings and Morgans, were quite nice about our declining their offer; and indeed their offer did not come up to the terms we hope to get in the City.
>
> *11 February*. I hear the Exchequer Bonds have been subscribed for more than twice over, in spite of the prophecies of the croakers that the London market would not find the money. I am glad we have kept clear of America on this occasion.

The City as a whole was also pleased that there had been no repeat of the previous summer's manoeuvre, but the *FT* on the 13th was less than enamoured by other aspects of the latest war loan. It declared that 'a subscription of less than $2\frac{1}{2}$ times over' for an issue offered on attractive terms was 'not overwhelming'. It pointed out that 'the average price obtained is only £97 5s 4d, as compared with £98 2s 10d for similar bonds last November'. And it sounded a warning note: 'The public has shown that it does not like borrowing by pinches in the case of a big war; that it does not like the form of security changed every time, and that it does not like the principle of tender. We trust the Treasury will learn these lessons, but we imagine its great pride is that it has succeeded in "muddling through".'[5] By mid-March peace negotiations had collapsed, and it was obvious that there would soon be opportunity for further muddle and acrimony.

The new loan was to be for £60m, ensuring that it would be the last of the year. City opinion, as relayed to Hamilton at the end of March and beginning of April, was unanimous in favour of an issue of Consols, with a strong preference for a fixed price. 'We must try & get the general investor in,' he summarised as Cassel's view, adding that 'an issue by tender [i.e. as opposed to fixed price] leads to so much cornering, & to favouring of syndicates'. So Consols at a fixed price it was, but £60m was a huge amount, enough to make Treasury and Bank distinctly nervous, especially at a time of considerable strain on the money market. At this stage the determining factor was the presence in Britain of the world's most renowned financier. Hamilton, as usual, is the invaluable guide:

> *17 April.* Mr Morgan came to see me yesterday. Dawkins brought him to pay his respects on the Chanc of the Exchequer. He impresses one at once as a strong man; but the appearance of his nose, poor man, is a terrible drawback to his company. He is quite open to a deal in connection with the new loan.
> *Same day (later in the entry).* In view of the immensity of the sum the Chanc of the Exchequer has practically approved the placing of 10 millions firm with Morgan and twenty millions with Rothschild. I think we shall be able to get $94\frac{1}{2}$ for our Consols.
> *18 April.* After seeing Cassel & Dawkins as well as Natty Rothschild & Daniell, I came to terms for the Government . . . I believe $94\frac{1}{2}$ is on the whole good; and that as 30 millions have been placed the other 30 will be greedily subscribed for. In the City there is always a 'sheep-like' tendency to follow the lead.
> *19 April.* Consols have fallen. So the terms accepted yesterday are turning out good. The City people won't 'get fat' upon the loan.

Half the £20m placed firm with Rothschilds in turn went to the Bank of England, while a further £2m went to Cassel, who as ever had his finger closely on the City pulse. 'I have done my best', he wrote to Hamilton on the 18th, 'to impress upon the Rothschilds that the banking element should be taken care of . . . If there should be a strong demand and the bankers are left out there will be a great deal of ill feeling which may easily be avoided.' The next morning Hamilton passed on this opinion to the new Governor, Augustus Prevost, who replied almost at once:

> Curiously enough just as your letter of today arrived Lord Rothschild had only left the Bank a few minutes.

We had a thorough discussion on the very matter about Bankers & Joint Stock Banks to which you refer and came to the conclusion that there would be no advantage in including them in the amount taken firm. One of the great difficulties is what Banks to include & where to draw the line: they will subscribe if they want the Loan just as willingly as they would join in the amount taken firm.

'A member of a declining firm which is doing no good, and he has never shewn any grasp', was how a member of the discount market had recently described the new Governor; and even if Prevost did feel any love for the joint-stock banks, which he presumably did not, he was hardly the man who was going to dissuade Natty in this particular matter.[6]

By Monday the 22nd, with the public portion of the loan starting to go live following the publication of the prospectus, it was, the *FT* reported, 'freely rumoured on the market that a syndicate composed of certain prominent London, New York and Continental financial houses (the names of Rothschilds, Morgans, Sir Ernest Cassel and Wernher Beit and Company were mentioned) had made themselves responsible for the moiety of the loan'. Such rumours were like a red rag to Granville Farquhar, who from his office at 3 Drapers' Gardens despatched to Hamilton a grand remonstrance suffused with the xenophobic strain of anti-Semitism shared by many, outside as well as inside the Stock Exchange:

> When the British Government issues a National Loan we do not expect in the *English Circles* in the City that the German Jew element are alone to be considered. With such people as Alfred Beit, Bischoffsheim [Henry Bischoffsheim, for whom Cassel had once worked], Cassel, Carl Meyer in, and 10 millions to America, no wonder that the premium is a vanishing one, and that the feeling amongst all Banking Circles is wonder and indignation at the way things are managed . . .
>
> Is it to be wondered at that they are furious at finding every dirty German Jew in, and themselves left out? You will find Horace [still on the board of Parr's Bank] just as strong as I am about this, and I have heard but one opinion in and outside the Stock Exchange, and that is that the whole affair is disgraceful.

On Tuesday the market's best guess was that the £30m publicly available had already been subscribed eight times over; while the next day Consols fell to $94\frac{1}{8}$, their lowest point since 1890, and the premium on the new scrip finished $\frac{1}{8}$ down at $\frac{7}{16}$. 'It was,' according to the *FT*, 'asserted by some that the decline had been brought about by unloading on the part of the syndicate to whom the thirty millions was allotted by the Government, and this rumour, whether correct or not, provoked a good deal of dissatisfaction.' Probably on Wednesday evening, this time from his home at 24 Park Street off Grosvenor Square, Farquhar sent Hamilton another, undated blast, reiterating his most deeply felt grievance. It was scandalous, he insisted, that 'this cosmopolitan crew' of Cassel and the others should have been given such 'a huge plum' to the exclusion of English merchant and joint-stock banks. Moreover, from the moment they 'had it in their power to sell the stock at a premium', they 'poured it in the market by the million'. How, he asked, did that help the issue? And he went on:

> But there is worse behind. There is a very large Firm of dealers in Consols who were bears to the tune of some £2,000,000 to £3,000,000. They have lost no opportunity for months past to sell Bears, & to work the price of Consols down in every way in their power. The reward to them for this unscrupulous & unpatriotic conduct has been, that through the instrumentality of one of the participants in the £30,000,000 (I have name of the man they job it through), this Firm replaced the whole of their Bear and are computed to have made £600,000 to £800,000 by the transaction. I have never in my 26 years of City Life, heard such vehement condemnation on all sides of this business. Both out and in the Stock Exchange. Can you wonder that people are furious that the unjust should reap such a reward? With ordinary care such an extraordinary dirty transaction should have been impossible . . .[7]

Whether Hamilton again replied is unclear, as is the identity of the fortunate jobbing firm, but it can hardly have made comfortable reading for the patriotic, highly conscientious civil servant.

Less than a fortnight later, on 5 May, the impugned Meyer was in cynical vein. 'I hear the West end is gambling like mad in Yankees,' he wrote to his wife, 'so the crash is sure to come.' While the next day, less flippantly: 'City cheerful and the Yankee market still booming, for some particular shares – no collapse yet but all the serious people here regard the situation as fraught with great danger.' Among those particular shares was Northern Pacific Common, which opened at $114\frac{1}{2}$ and closed almost twenty points higher. Also on the 6th (a Monday), Morgans in London received two telegrams, the first in the morning from J. Pierpont Morgan at Aix-les-Bains: 'Buy all you can up to 20,000 shares NP common without materially advancing price for your account.' The other, in the afternoon, came from Morgans in New York: 'Strictly confidential &c. Most important you or friends should not sell any NP common at any price without consulting JPM.'[8]

The background to these mysterious communications was that there had begun on Wall Street a titanic battle for control of the Northern Pacific Railroad, with J.P. Morgan & Co on the one hand, and Kuhn, Loeb & Co on the other, representing the rival railroad interests. The battle – severe but inconclusive – was essentially an American story but with dramatic implications for London, by far the principal external market for American securities. By the 8th the price of Northern Pacifics was fluctuating wildly on both sides of the Atlantic, far too wildly for an old campaigner like Meyer: 'I am NOT making any money as it is much too dangerous to operate in the Yankee market in either direction – so I sit quite still and await events.'[9]

The following day, Thursday the 9th, proved one to remember. 'Panic Stricken Yankees: The Market Demoralised by the Northern Pacific Deadlock: Sensational Break in the Street': the *FT*'s headlines were matched by its report:

> The American market has spent one of the wildest days in its history, and although the dealings here were the mere echo of what is happening on the other side, the violence with which prices fluctuated – amounting in the Street to nothing short of a panic – was an eye-opener even to the oldest members of the House . . . The first real signs of trouble occurred just after the New York opening. Advices from the other side indicated that the fight for control was still raging in earnest; Northern Pacifics were reported to have touched 1,000 [dollars] on Wall Street – one operator, in fact, put the figure at 5,000, but he was evidently a wag. This information caused renewed uneasiness, and Northern Pacifics rapidly dropped to 125 [having at one point earlier in the day been 138½]. . . The worst, however, was yet to come, for soon after the commencement of dealings in Shorter's Court there was a general rush to sell . . . A little later the tide turned; Northern Pacifics were bid up to 140, and most other shares followed with equally rapid recoveries, but the sentiment continued highly erratic until the finish, and it was impossible to follow all the lightning-like changes that occurred.

According to the *FN*'s market reporter, the shares of Northern Pacific Common 'oscillated in a manner that was devoid of intelligibility'; while the same paper provided an atmospheric sketch – perhaps deliberately low-key – of the late afternoon City scene:

> New York 'panic stricken', which the tape reported about 5.30, was not noisily reflected in the unwonted silence which prevailed in the Street on this side. A huge crowd stood patiently in Shorter's-court, and covered the intervening space between the court and the Bartholomew-lane end of

the Street, extending in the other direction as far as Copthall-court. But it was not noisy. People talked in low voices and, save for an occasional shout from the recesses of Shorter's-court, the predominant sound was the steady drip, drip, from the umbrellas erected in all directions to keep off the fast-falling rain.

Of business there was little or none in Americans. The all-absorbing desire of the crowd was simply to discuss the situation, and to be astonished with the occasional tit-bits from the other side – such as the quotation of 1,000 for Northern Pacific Common, which appeared on the tape as the record of 'New York, 11.45' at about 5.40 p.m. There were tales of London men who had 'made fortunes since three o'clock'; but they did not meet with general credence, as may be imagined; though the dealers did not deny that they had never before seen such a state of things.[10]

It was hardly surprising if there was a certain incoherence and lack of consistency in the various reports, not least because by the latter stages most of the jobbers simply closed their books, making it almost impossible for observers to gauge the real picture. At the end Northern Pacifics were quoted a nominal 135, a misleadingly unremarkable rise of $5\frac{3}{4}$ for the day.

On Friday the American market behaved more normally, but the shadow loomed of the next Stock Exchange settlement, due the following week. Camped in London by Saturday was Pierpont Morgan, who wired his New York office at 8 p.m.:

> Arrived tonight. Have had interviews leading members London Stock Exchange including R. Raphael & Son Panmure Gordon & Crews [i.e. Crews, Lichtenstadt & Co]. They say situation very serious even go so far as say unless some relief before Monday 9.30 a.m. panic anticipated and will follow which will cause bankruptcy many houses and of which effect will be disastrous more than Baring Bros of 1890.

Because of the extraordinary situation on Wall Street – in effect, the creation of an artificial corner in Northern Pacific stock – the underlying position in London was that some of the main Yankee dealers found themselves heavily over-committed and in no position to deliver the actual stock. According to one estimate, they had unwittingly sold the rival bidders some 150,000 shares more than actually existed. Over the weekend they called on the Stock Exchange Committee to grant a moratorium, thereby enabling those who were short of stock to postpone indefinitely the time of delivery. First thing on Monday morning, at a special meeting, the Committee agreed to do so, the motion being carried without dissent, after personal representations from R. Raphael & Sons, Leon Bros and others. The *FN* the next morning accurately mirrored the City's response to this well-nigh unprecedented intervention:

> Some objection has been taken to the action of the Committee; but it is almost universally approved. On theoretical grounds one may regret that the Committee has found it necessary to interfere with the free higgling of the market as between buyer and seller; but practical considerations over-rule all such punctilios. We believe one or two bulls of Northern Pacific complain bitterly that they have been deprived of the opportunity to fleece the bears to the uttermost, and were the circumstances normal we should agree that they had been hardly dealt by. In an ordinary struggle between bull and bear the latter obtains and deserves little sympathy. But the bears whom the Stock Exchange Committee has made haste to protect are in many, if not most, cases 'innocent' bears, in one form or another. If the arbitrage houses did not supply shares there would be an end to the American market in London.

As usual unable to share in the general enthusiasm for the soft option was the *Economist* – 'Are the magnitude of the transactions involved to be taken as a reason why the parties concerned in them are to be exempted from the penalties which the case of misadventure would attach to smaller operators?' – but there is no doubt that the moratorium, which in the event lasted for five weeks, was a key reason why the drama did not turn into a crisis.[11]

However, it was not the only reason, as was clear from some pointed remarks in the June issue of the *Bankers' Magazine*:

> Some of the members of money-lending establishments appear to have lost their heads over the unprecedented position created by the 'corner' in Northern Pacific stock. When settling-day arrived, although bankers as a rule grasped the situation, and were generous in the matter of advances, a few concerns, instead of assisting in the relief of the Stock Exchange, stubbornly refused aid except where long connection and powerful influence rendered such proceedings impossible. Money was drawn in from all quarters, and a huge sum obtained from the Bank of England. With such ample supplies available, it would have been easy for all the banks to have been generous in their treatment; instead, they strengthened themselves and allowed the Stock Exchange to find a way out of its own difficulties. That it did so is now history, and it was enabled to come through the ordeal by the spontaneous 'open-handedness' of the Morgans and the Rothschilds and of certain of the foreign and colonial banks.

'An interesting study in human nature – not always edifying, though sometimes ludicrous,' was how Gaspard Farrer on 24 May described the whole episode; but the day before, in front of the Stock Exchange Committee, one of the Raphael partners was full of gratitude as he 'detailed his efforts to get Messrs Morgan & Co and Messrs Kuhn & Loeb to assist in the settlement of the account and read a letter from Lord Rothschild'. Yet for Raphaels itself, one of the City's leading arbitrage houses, it had been a chastening experience, as a confidential report a year later made transparently clear: 'It came as such a shock to the market that a firm of such standing and repute was doing a business that was capable of landing them in such an awkward position, that their eyes are now open to contingencies that they never dreamed of before the unfortunate incident occurred.' But the effects lingered, even by late 1904, when Kleinworts next reported to its New York correspondent on the standing of Raphaels: 'The great reluctance to purchase this name has to a material extent passed away. At the same time it is generally considered that there is not the same amount of money there that there used to be. This is as you are aware due to their Northern Pacific entanglement.'[12]

Still, Raphaels lived to fight on – unlike at least one jobber in the American market. Vivian Nickalls, younger brother of Guy, had migrated to Yankees at some point after his ragging at the hands of the Westralian market back in 1896. In his own autobiography, he told without self-pity the story of how he came unstuck:

> At that time I was dealing with my father's agents, Prince & Whitely, in New York, and when prices went soaring up they kept advising me to sell Northern Pacific and buy Union. Actually if I had done just the opposite I should have been worth half a million by June!
>
> One fatal day two or three brokers came and bought some thousands of Northern Pacific from me, and hoping to get them back in New York, as I had done previously, I cabled to my agents there. However, Harriman [the railroad magnate] had 'cornered' them and there was not a share to be had! They went up to 1,000 in New York, whereas I had sold them at 135–40, and they eventually allowed us to get in at 175. Unions, with which I had been plastered, I offered down 25 points from 133 in fifteen minutes, got level, and sold a bear, which I bought back in the Street at 95. I went home that night 'broke to the wide'!
>
> I then went to see my uncle, Sir Patteson Nickalls [a prominent jobber], and Bob Young [likewise], told them my plight, and said that I must hammer myself, as if I did so in the middle of the account I could pay 20s in the pound. After a meeting they pointed out that if I took this course there would be twenty other failures and that they therefore proposed to see me through.

Eventually Sir Patteson, Walter Chinnery [a leading jobber in Yankees] and Bob Young took hold of my account, and the market found some thousands of pounds on condition that I did not go back to the Stock Exchange for two years. A lot of thanks were due to those friends who helped me, though if they had not done so the market would have been in a far worse plight as many small firms would have been hammered. Actually most of the firms concerned had made quite a lot of money out of me previously and would have suffered more severely at the time if they had not come to my assistance.

I then found myself stranded with £300 – which was all they had left me – and very little prospect of obtaining more! I decided therefore to take a trip to New York to visit Messrs Prince & Whitely, from whom incidentally I had to collect £100, and so at the end of May I sailed in the *Oceanic* . . .[13]

It had been a bad year or two for the Nickalls brothers, and Vivian like Guy never returned to Capel Court. Instead, a future beckoned of transport riding in South Africa, a disagreeable year selling insurance in Dorking, and (again like Guy) coaching rowing in the States. And the title of *his* memoirs? *Oars, Wars, and Horses*, of course.

*

The Northern Pacific episode was not an entirely creditable one but nor was it, at the London end anyway, a scam. For that, in 1901 as most years, it was necessary to look to the shadowy world of mining finance. Take the case of the Paringa Copper Mines Company. In May it offered the jobber Arthur Hawes the call option of 100,000 shares, with Hawes being obliged to secure a quotation on the tape by the end-June account. He subsequently sold the shares to another recently elected jobber, James Bett, though without telling him that the option had lapsed; and a special settlement was granted in July. In the autumn Bett took Hawes to the Committee, where it was perforce revealed that Paringas were a wholly artificial one-man market under the control of Hawes. The upshot was that jobber being charged with three offences – deceiving Bett, making an artificial market, making use of the Exchange Telegraph Company to record prices in that market – for which he received a three-year suspension. As for Bett, he got two years for helping to create an artificial market.[14] His basic tactical mistake had been to draw the matter to the attention of the Committee, which as a purely reactive body, much preferring to let sleeping dogs lie, had no alternative in this case but to take action.

These two jobbers were only passing bit players in the great City drama, unlike Matheson & Co of 3 Lombard Street, which was the London house of Jardine Matheson and, at this stage in its distinguished history, the uncomfortable object of some attention.[15] The episode causing the blushes had been summarised in April 1900 by the *Engineering and Mining Journal*, a largely reputable organ based in New York:

> We are continually recording the promotion of companies in London to operate mines which prove very soon after flotation to be of comparatively little value. The latest example of this is the Panuco Copper Company, Limited, which was formed in the spring of 1899 to take over the mines of that name which are situated in the State of Coahulla, Mexico. This company was floated by Matheson & Co of London, who control the Rio Tinto [the famous Spanish copper and sulphur mine] ... At the time of flotation the mines were valued at £375,000, of which £208,000 was paid in cash, and now the properties are deemed to be of practically no value at all. Considering the eminence of the issuing house and of the mining experts employed, this promotion is by no means a hole-and-corner affair ... London is full enough of untrustworthy promoters to make both the shareholders and mine owners tremble in their shoes as they walk its streets, and if we are to lose confidence in Matheson & Co who, though not always infallible in their judgment, have as a rule done well for their following, it will be a bad thing for those who wish to bring legitimate mining propositions to the moneyed classes in England.

Some 200 shareholders, led by an architect from Newcastle, sued Mathesons and its senior partner William Keswick, who was also MP for Epsom. They claimed not only that they had been misled but also that the firm had received a secret commission from the vendors of Panuco; and when judgement was delivered in July 1901, it did not go in favour of Lombard Street. 'This way of doing business is not quite expected from an eminent house,' declared the London correspondent of the *Engineering and Mining Journal*, adding to the pleasure of his American readers that 'the incident has caused the majority of investors to doubt if there is such a thing as a straightforward mining promotion business in London at all'.[16]

In fact, especially in relation to two of the most important mining areas, South Africa and West Australia, mining finance was starting to change – away from short-term promotion and speculation, towards long-term production and development.[17] The change was particularly dramatic in the Westralian sphere, in the immediate wake of the financial demise of Bottomley and Wright; and, from its London head office, exercising an increasing influence over Westralian mining was the mining firm Bewick, Moreing & Co. One of its new partners was the rising American engineer Herbert Hoover, who headed for Kalgoorlie in late 1901. The stockbroker Francis Govett was also on the ship.[18] He had led the City opposition to Wright during the second half of 1900 and was now the newly elected chairman of Lake View Consols as well as another part of Wright's former empire, the Ivanhoe Gold Corporation. Govett was in his 40s and, after reading law at Oxford, had gone straight into the family firm Govett, Sons & Co. Hoover recalled their relationship:

> He was a man of wide outlook and of high integrity, with all the loyalties and formalism of Englishmen of his class. He had no previous experience at all with mines. After he had been in Kalgoorlie a few days he came to me and stated that he was in a complete fog. He said it was all Greek to him . . . He asked that our firm take complete charge of these two mines, reorganise them technically and financially . . .

And, Hoover added, following equally dubious management elsewhere, 'in time several other West Australian groups came to us for management'.[19] Overall it was by no means a change from pure black to pure white – Bewick Moreing itself almost certainly continued to exploit its prime access to inside information – but what was clear was that the old rip-roaring, nakedly exploitative era was over.

In the South African mining market, the mood by November 1901 was bullish, as at last the end of the war seemed 'in sight'. When Sir Patteson Nickalls (a vocal Liberal as well as Vivian's jobbing uncle) was reported to have chaired a pro-Boer meeting in Maidstone, he was given a hot reception on his next appearance in the Kaffir Circus. For the next three months Kaffirs boomed, so much so that by February 1902 the *Westminster Gazette* ran a feeling piece called 'Where to Breathe in the House'. By this time the square footage per person of those entitled to admission to the floor of the House was down to a claustrophobic 2.36, and as usual it was the clerks who took most of the blame for the prevailing congestion, being accused of loitering and sundry other offences. In February, following a decision to restrict firms to two authorised, three unauthorised and four settling-room clerks, the Committee voted that unauthorised and settling-room clerks were henceforth to 'wear a distinctive badge in the lapel of their coats'; in due course five firms were asked 'to submit designs in three sizes with a statement as to the price at which they would be prepared to supply 4,000 in white metal or in silver, the top to be of blue for unauthorised and crimson for settling-room clerks'; the order went to Sidney Smith of Upper Street, Islington, whose successful tender was £304. In fact the villains of the piece were probably not the clerks, who for the most part performed valuable duties on behalf of larger firms, but rather the abundant, seriously undercapitalised small-time jobbers; but apart from increasing entrance and annual membership fees (up by 1901 to 250–500 guineas and 20–40 guineas respectively, depending on class of admission), it seemed impossible to do anything about such a numerous, potentially powerful group.[20]

Soon the Kaffir boom faded, as it became obvious that the war still had some way to go and the British government prepared to raise a new, £32m loan.[21] In his preliminary soundings Hamilton found that the City was almost unanimous in its preference for a Transvaal Guaranteed Loan rather than a further issue of Consols – 'they say that there are still a good many Consols undigested', he noted in February. By mid-March the matter was starting to come to a head, as a less than reverent Dawkins reported to Milner in South Africa:

> Beach sent for Rothschild on Tuesday [the 18th].
> Natty was violent for a Transvaal loan. Consols wd be most unpopular, wd not get people to take them, wd proclaim to all the world that the Govt felt the end was not in sight, wd depress Govt credit & markets for a long time, &c.
> Then Beach sent Hamilton to me, and I went as strong for Consols as the Jew had gone against them . . .
> Since seeing Hamilton I have discovered there is a peculiar inwardness for Natty's strong line. He took a lot out of the last Consol issue & has still got them on his hands at a loss. We took the same amount, but are out at a slight profit.
> I shall let Beach know this inwardness.
> It is a pity he himself knows nothing of the City, or he [would] be less bothered by threats that he will lose his friends & that people will not 'come in'.
> Friends don't exist in this kind of thing, and the very big houses *dare not* be left out.

Hamilton's account of Natty's interview with Hicks Beach was similar, the diarist adding that Natty 'never does himself justice when he is called in' and, what was becoming a hobby horse, 'I believe it is impossible to get an unprejudiced opinion from a City man on a financial matter.' Hamilton's diary provides the authoritative version of how a difficult situation was resolved, not without some more of the ill feeling that throughout had characterised the war loan process:

2 April. Cassel came to see me yesterday. He has just returned from India. He has, I expect, the longest head in the City; and he at once recognised the difficulties about a Transvaal Loan [i.e. while the war was still continuing]. Indeed he could not see how anything but Consols could be defended.

7 April. The Chanc of the Exchequer saw both Cassel and Natty this afternoon. The former is for Consols; the latter for guaranteed Transvaal loan.

9 April. Consols are gradually winning the day.

11 April. Mr Pierpont Morgan [just arrived in London] expressed himself willing to help in the matter of the Loan, if he was wanted to do so. But it must be Consols. I would rather do without him this year. American assistance is not appreciated much in the City.

12 April. The Bank people came this morning. The feeling in the City may be summed up thus: They hope for a guaranteed Transvaal loan but *believe* it will be Consols. Mr C. Goschen who accompanied the Governor said that, while from a City point of view he should recommend a guaranteed loan, yet if he were Chanc of the Exchequer political & parliamentary considerations would influence him decidedly in favour of Consols.

14 April. Mr Morgan came again this morning; and after a certain amount of haggling he said he would take 5 millions firm at $93\frac{1}{2}$.

15 April. I went down to New Court this morning, and told Natty R. that the Chanc of the Exchequer's price was $93\frac{1}{2}$. He did not like it but he knew Morgan had agreed to it & so he had to acquiesce. I went on to the Bank, & settled the terms of the prospectus. The Rothschilds undertook to place the remainder of the half – that is, £16,000,000 less £5,000,000 taken for America. £2m goes to the Bank & £2m to Cassel: the remainder [i.e. £7m] will be left to the Rothschilds to dispose of, though we have stipulated that the Joint Stock Banks should be invited to co-operate . . . I met Mr Morgan at dinner this evening at Lady Kaye's. He had been annoyed at having been met with a refusal by the Rothschilds, when he applied for an allotment for his *London* house.

17 April. The Consol Loan has been a great success. It has already been subscribed many times over. The Chanc of the Exchequer now says he gave it away too cheap; but I believe he got the best price he possibly could in a rising market [in the context of renewed expectations of an imminent peace], about which there is always much risk.

Hamilton's diary only touches on the minor spat on the 15th between Rothschilds and Morgans, in effect Natty's symbolic, rather petty revenge. In fact, Dawkins that same day formally complained to Hamilton ('Mr Morgan does not desire to press the point'), Hamilton on the 16th asked Prevost at the Bank to do something about it, Prevost reluctantly agreed to cede to J.S. Morgan & Co a quarter ($£\frac{1}{2}$m) of its own allotment, and finally Dawkins (still on the 16th) thanked Hamilton for having arranged a participation but said that Morgans could not possibly take it, being 'in an issue that has already gone to a premium'.[22] All in all, it seemed as if the moral as well as financial upper hand was starting to pass across the Atlantic.

By the final week of May there was little doubt that, at last, the end of the war was nigh. 'The Kaffir market remains in an expectant attitude . . . The general impression is that good business is in store on the consummation of the long-looked-for event.' That was the mood on Wednesday the 28th, the eve of yet another mining scandal. The *FT*'s Mining market report on Thursday evening told the story:

> 'Geduld Deep' which were today put on the market at about $2\frac{1}{4}$ were run up at one time to $2\frac{5}{8}$, but fell back almost as quickly to $2\frac{1}{8}$, and thus finished their first day with a small relapse . . . These shares came in for some satirical comment, and it was considered that the title might prove misleading as tending to the inference that the property of the Company is on the southern boundary of that of the Geduld Proprietary Mines, whereas it actually comprises a small block at the extreme south of the farm of which the latter Company owns practically the northern half, and there is no connection whatever between the two undertakings.

Put another way, Geduld Proprietary Mines was an important deep-level property on the Johannesburg Main Reef, Geduld Deep was a spurious venture situated nearby, and the two had been linked by a series of deliberately planted paragraphs in less reputable quarters of the financial press; shortly after their prospectusless introduction to the market the shares of Geduld Deep became practically worthless and unmarketable. Later in the year, the deluded shareholders called on the Stock Exchange Committee not to grant a special settlement; but, perhaps guided by the *Economist*, which called it a 'childish appeal', the Committee allowed the settlement, notwithstanding the disreputable circumstances. Back in May, however, most eyes were on the larger issue. A small item in the *FN* on Saturday the 31st caught the optimistic mood:

> There doesn't seem much to complain of in the Concentration Camps now. According to the return for April, out of the 112,733 inhabitants there were only 298 deaths – equivalent to 2.6 per 1,000, say 32 per 1,000 per annum. English factory towns often get as high as that.

The next day the War Office released Kitchener's telegram announcing that he had signed peace terms with the Boer delegates, and in the evening a copy was posted at the Mansion House, causing much enthusiasm. Also that Sunday, King Edward VII wrote to Cassel, his financial adviser: 'You will have doubtless heard that Peace is signed, which is the greatest blessing that has been conferred on this country for a long time! "Consols" are sure to go up tomorrow. Could you not make a large investment for me?'[23] Cassel's reply does not survive, but it is unlikely that he advised the King to take a punt instead on Geduld Deep.

PART THREE

A Commercial Civilisation

She rose superior, above all, on the happy fact that there were always gentlemen in town and that gentlemen were her greatest admirers; gentlemen from the City in especial – as to whom she was full of information about the passion and pride excited in such breasts by the objects of her charming commerce. The City men *did*, in short, go in for flowers. There was a certain type of awfully smart stockbroker – Lord Rye called them Jews and 'bounders', but she didn't care – whose extravagance, she more than once threw out, had really, if one had any conscience, to be forcibly restrained. It was not perhaps a pure love of beauty: it was a matter of vanity and a sign of business; they wished to crush their rivals, and that was one of their weapons.

Henry James, *In the Cage* (1898)

CHAPTER FOURTEEN

Figures, Figures

At eight o'clock the roar of the City has gathered strength and fulness, approaching the din of noonday. At nine o'clock every man, woman, and child in the Metropolis seems to be going somewhere. Crowds bubble intermittently from the underground stations. 'Buses in endless procession converge upon the Bank. The pavements are black with people. The scene from the Mansion House steps beggars description. You look upon a very maelström of men. They are not only 'going' to business! They seem to be rushing there! . . .

You saunter into Cornhill. It seems almost quiet after the bewildering spectacle in front of the Mansion House. Here it is easier to study individuals who appeal to the fancy. An oldish man, tall, and slightly stooped, with very long white hair, and a frock-coat a couple of sizes too large for his gaunt, spare figure, glides along the pavement like one who would not willingly attract attention. His chin almost touches his necktie. You can see his shirt-front through his straggling grey beard. In one hand he carries a small black bag. The other grasps a cotton umbrella, midway between the handle and the ferrule. He is a man with whom the world has not gone well – probably a clerk over whose unlucky head juniors have passed. His lethargic air is in sharp contrast with that of a vigorous-looking man, of aldermanic girth, who takes to the road in his eagerness to push forward. His fat hands are very white. His back is very broad. His frock-coat fits him without a wrinkle. There is plenty of energy and resolution in his walk. Nobody will get in front of him in business or anywhere else – if he can help it. He turns into a side street, and enters one of those great buildings in which mercantile men of all sorts have offices. At once you know his trade. He is a commission agent . . .

In every part of the City carriages and cabs bowl past frequently. Some men try to hide themselves in a corner of their hansom . . . A very different type of man sails through Leadenhall Street in a handsome phaeton. His sallow, clean-shaven face is a curious blend of cynicism and good nature. He wears a soft hat and a tweed suit. Any of his clerks is more expensively dressed. He is a magnate in the City. But, lolling rather self-consciously in his splendid carriage, he is utterly insignificant-looking. Sometimes the laggard charters a hansom he can but ill afford. You know him by his anxious look. He is impatient of all obstructions.

His heart is envious of the ease with which a disembodied spirit could transfer itself to a counting-house stool. For the psychological moment is close at hand when the master frowns upon vacant desks . . .

London Bridge! It is the climax, the apotheosis, as it were, of all thus far seen. So crowded is the canvas, so full of movement, it dazes one. Life sweeps over the bridge like the rush of the sea by the sides of a ship – always Citywards. In thousands they advance, leaning forward, with long, quick strides, eager to be there! Swiftly they flash past, and still they come and come, like the silent, shadowy legions of a dream. Somehow they suggest the dogged march of an army in retreat, with its rallying point far ahead, and the enemy's cavalry pressing on its rear. Looking down upon the swarming masses, with the dark sullen river for a background, they fuse into one monstrous organism, their progress merges in the rhythmic swaying of one mammoth breathing thing. Stand in the midst of the mighty current of men! A wearied, languorous feeling creeps over you, as face follows face and eyes in thousands swim by. It is the hypnotic influence of the measureless, the unfathomable, the you-know-not-what of mystery and elusiveness in life, stealing your senses away.

During an hour these multitudes in drab march past to the relentless City, to barter what they have of value for their daily bread. The monotony of the endless parade is overpowering, numbing; and minute by minute the railway station, not a stone's throw away, yields up fresh battalions for this sublime muster of citizens. Within the station itself is being enacted a scene which is an impressive combination of order and disorder. A train rushes alongside a platform. In a twinkling its passengers are thronging to the exits. A few seconds more and the place is clear. The empty train disappears to make way for another, whose impatient whistle is already heard. Again a crowd of passengers melts, and another springs up in its place. The train is again shunted, and the metals it vacates are speedily covered. And so proceeds like clockwork the arrangement – so simple and so intricate – for the mobilisation of the army of business men who pour in one wonderful phalanx across the noble bridge.

For a full hour it continues. Then, as the clock points to ten, there are gaps in the ranks. The tide of life suddenly slackens. The reinforcements grow weaker. Traffic once more moves freely in opposite directions; for the invasion of the morning is consummated. Business has begun.

This spirited rendition of 'Going to Business in London', by P.F. William Ryan, was one of many such genre sketches that comprised *Living London*, an enormous anthology compiled by George R. Sims and published in magazine form from 1903. At the other end of the day, we have 'Midnight London', as penned by Beckles Willson:

At the Mansion House and the Bank there is a little crowd waiting for the last omnibuses westward; and a few flying figures in front of the

Royal Exchange indicate that the last train of the Central London underground railway will shortly depart on its journey from the Bank to Shepherd's Bush. On all hands are dark vistas of streets, silent as the tomb; tall empty buildings, which a few brief hours ago were, and in a few hours more will be, thrilling with life and with the world's commerce.

A squad of City sewermen are flushing the thoroughfares which surround the 'Old Lady of Threadneedle Street', turning the hose on the marks and débris of the 1,300,000 pairs of human footsteps and 100,000 vehicles which are said to enter the London square mile daily. Some of them have been sailors in their time, and as they work at their midnight task they sing in unison a song like that the mariners sing at the capstan bars. Of course, it might be 'Yo ho ho, and a bottle of rum', and I wish for Mr Stevenson's memory it were; but it sounds more like the latest music hall ditty chaunted *adagio*.

Sailors! Ah, that suggests that there are soldiers inside the Bank – a red-coated squad of them have marched from their western barracks just before sundown to guard the millions in specie and bullion which are enclosed within those massive, grey walls – more sombre and sepulchral now than ever they seemed by daylight.

As we tread the sombre City streets, not so hushed maybe as you might suppose, because nearly all night long they are traversed by heavy vans bound for the docks, goods stations, carrying depôts, or the markets, but yet, for all that, grim and gloomy enough compared with the daytime, one notes an occasional window lit by gas or electricity, which bespeaks some anxious merchant, cashier, or manager who, pen in hand, is trying to steal a few hours from inexorable Time . . .[1]

*

By 1901 there were only some 27,000 people resident in the City, compared with 51,000 twenty years earlier; but the total working population was up from 261,000 in 1881 to 332,000 by the new century. John Cadogan, just started with the stockbrokers Edinger & Asch, was a recent recruit to the daily workforce:

Of course in those days we had to commute by Underground or horse-drawn transport. The 'smart boys' had their own hansom cabs and senior members their private broughams. A lot of people used to walk from Charing Cross Station along the Embankment to their offices and back again in the evening. The Rothschilds used to give a brace of pheasants to bus drivers on the Mansion House–Bank of England route, so that just before Christmas their whips were adorned with the Rothschild racing colours. But all this died with the advent of the internal combustion engine. The motor car was referred to as the 'sparrow starver', as when the horses went the sparrows too disappeared from the City.

Still more workers used the overground railway, many of the less well off having migrated east to live in Essex, served up to nine o'clock by cheap trains into Liverpool Street. Meanwhile the tube network was developing, with the Central London Railway open from 1900, at this stage only running west from Bank. 'People are already beginning to grumble at the crowds in the twopenny tube rendering travelling uncomfortable and vexatious!' noted Carl Meyer within weeks of the official opening by the Prince of Wales.[2] Meyer was a faithful patron of the new line, as was its financial godfather, Sir Ernest Cassel, but a fact of twentieth-century life would be the impossibility of commuting to and from the City without a degree of discomfort.

Whatever one's station in City life, it was crucial to be turned out correctly. When, one Saturday morning at the Mincing Lane commodity brokers Lewis & Peat, a partner's son arrived wearing a soft collar, instead of the regulation stiff collar and morning dress, he was peremptorily sent home by the senior partner, Andrew Devitt, with the encouraging words, 'Come back when you are decently dressed.' In November 1900 a leading journalist, R.D. Blumenfeld, experienced the sartorial code second-hand:

> Some people carry their prejudices rather far. I sent a reporter today to see a City banker on an important matter. He saw him, but also sent me a note – he is a personal friend – suggesting that in future I might like to take into consideration the fact that reporters should conform to custom by coming into the City attired in a manner more in keeping with the dignity of their calling; meaning that they should not wear bowler hats and brown boots.

Perhaps the reporter should have visited Austin Reed, the first branch of which (called Reed & Sons) had opened at 167 Fenchurch Street a few months earlier. Branches followed in St Mary Axe and Cheapside, and in 1911 the first West End branch. Reed had a keen nose for marketing, concocted striking window-displays, and specifically targeted the younger City man, unlike the rest of the City's retail traders in menswear. He offered shirts in three different sleeve lengths; white stiff collars in quarter-inch sizes; and each summer made a speciality of straw hats at 3s 6d each, the Fenchurch Street branch selling 8,000 in May 1908 alone. Some observers, though, thought standards were slipping. 'Members sometimes appear in light-coloured, even flannel, suits,' wrote Duguid with a tinge of regret in his history of the Stock Exchange published in 1901. It was a tone shared by Blumenfeld, who by February 1908 was experiencing the conservatism of advancing years:

> We are becoming somewhat negligent in dress. Down in the City today, where I talked with the Hon Claude Hay [a stockbroker as well as an MP], I noticed that he wore a soft collar, such as golfing men often wear, and brown boots. Also, he had no gloves. Many men, more than usual, go about the City in bowler hats nowadays, which shows the trend of the times.

Still, there *were* limits – limits more rigidly enforced on the Stock Exchange than anywhere else, with the possible exceptions of Lloyd's and the discount market. Fred Cripps (an elder brother of Stafford) came down from Oxford in 1906, joined the brokers Henry Pawle & Co as a clerk on a half-commission basis, and soon afterwards became a member:

> Even in summer I always wore a tail-coat or a short black coat, pin-striped or check trousers, with white- or buff-topped patent leather boots – and, of course, a top-hat. In my early days on the Stock Exchange, I thought it would be rather amusing to try to flaunt tradition. I had just acquired a light brown suit, so I wore this to Throgmorton Street. Directly I was spotted there was a rush to seize me and frog-march me. There was quite a fight between my friends and the opposition: I was not long in getting out of this frivolous wear into black clothes.[3]

Cripps himself was very much a hunting, sporting, clubbable extrovert (*Life's a Gamble* he called his memoirs), so it is unlikely that this momentary aberration was held against him.

Tradition also held sway when it came to that pivot of the day's routine, lunchtime. When the members of the Baltic were temporarily evacuated to the Great Eastern Hotel at the turn of the century, the railway's catering department proudly provided 'The Baltic Menu' – namely, grilled sole and boiled salmon (1s 6d), saddle of mutton (1s 2d), roast beef (1s), asparagus (8d), pudding *du jour* (4d). At Simpson's, the well-known chop-house in Bird-in-Hand Court off Bucklersbury, an enormous cheese was exhibited and diners had to guess its exact weight, height and girth, the prize being champagne on the house. Even at the Throgmorton, the largest restaurant in the City, built in 1900 by Joe Lyons along self-consciously palatial lines – full of carved wood, marble, onyx and alabaster, with not a sanded or sawdusted floor in sight – the reassuring claim was that one could get a cut off the joint for tenpence the same as at any other City restaurant. Just as satisfying, and significantly cheaper, was the tried and tested alternative to which the 16-year-old Laurance Mackie resorted when he began at Schröders in Leadenhall Street in 1905:

> I had lunch in a pub called Mooneys Irish House where the assistants were all Irish. I'd read my newspaper at the counter and I would have a half pint of draught Guinness, an extra-crusty roll, butter and a piece of Cheddar cheese. That was a lovely lunch and the whole lot cost 5d; 2d for the Guinness and a 1d each for the bread, butter and cheese. It was quite adequate, but I had to lie to my mother a bit because she was always so anxious that I should have a good lunch. So I used to invent all sorts of lunches.

There were, however, two significant developments by this time. One, from about the late 1880s, was the fairly rapid growth of the tea-shop, suitable not only for the emerging class of women workers in the City but also for boys less bold than Mackie and men tired of pub and eating-house. The ABC became a familiar landmark and served as a genuine boon. The other positive development was the increase in staff restaurants at the major banking and insurance houses. But wherever one chose, lunch was important. P.G. Wodehouse, for example, a clerk at the Hongkong and Shanghai Bank between 1900 and 1902, has Mike Jackson, the hero's friend in *Psmith in the City* (1910), taken out on his first day by a friendly cashier. After going down 'obscure alleys' they reach a chop-house: 'Mr Waller ordered lunch with the care of one to whom lunch is no slight matter. Few workers in the City do regard lunch as a trivial affair. It is the keynote of their day. It is an oasis in a desert of ink and ledgers . . .'[4]

Psmith's City was very different from the City of that equally indomitable fictional figure, Jorrocks, the Surtees hero of the 1830s. During the Victorian era City floorspace increased by at least one-half, from roughly 50 million to 75 million square feet; even more tellingly, of every five buildings standing in the City in 1855, only one remained in 1901.[5] Emblematic of a larger, irresistible process was the wholesale change wrought on the north side of London Wall. Traditionally occupied by small-time traders, this area to the east of Moorgate was transformed in the early 1900s into a cluster of huge, undeniably impressive office blocks, most notably Salisbury House, Electra House (headquarters for the Eastern Telegraph Company) and London Wall Buildings (where Wernher Beit based itself in resplendent offices). At the same time Jeffrey's Square, home of the Cheeryble Brothers in *Nicholas Nickleby*, was being systematically demolished to make way for the new Baltic Exchange, open for business from 1903. In 1905 the Liverpool, London and Globe Insurance Company, prominently sited on the corner of Cornhill and Lombard Street, was rebuilt with added height and grandeur; that same year the fruit and sweet stall in Change Alley was closed down by the authorities, following the death of its proprietor Joseph Isaacs (known to the City as 'Joe') at the age of 90. Not long afterwards saw the end of Crosby Hall, a medieval palace to the north of Leadenhall Street that had been a restaurant since the 1860s. The house was dismantled and moved to Chelsea Embankment; new offices were erected; and 'the last of the City gardens', with its pond, its summerhouse and its picturesque thorn and fig trees, was no more.[6]

It was in this sort of twilight mood that the elderly Henry James, commissioned to write a book on London, spent some time in the City in 1907 taking notes:

> 23 *August*. Good and 'pretty' this noon the *mouth* of Walbrook, beside the Mansion House, with the narrow slightly *grouillant* dusky vista formed by the same with the second-hand book shop let into the base of St. Stephen's (*plaqué* over with a dirty little stucco front) and the rather bad spire above – very bad, rough masonry and *mean* pinnacle. Interior (all alone here this cool summer noon) very much better than poor smothered outside (smothered in passages and by the high rear of the Mansion House) gives a hint of – very fine *quadrille*-panelled with old grey plaster rosettes and garlands – Dome – quite far and high, and today, with the florid old oak pulpit and canopy, the high old sallow sacred picture opposite, the 18th century memorial slabs, the place is quite the *retreat*, with the vague city hum outside, as they all get it, of the ghostly sense, the disembodied presences of the old London.
>
> 24 *August*. Here I come suddenly on delightfully placed old St. Dunstan's in the East. I never chanced upon this one before – just out of Eastcheap, on the way to the Tower, and beyond (south) the little St. Margaret Pattens. High 'fine' Gothic tower and spire, and built as it is on the steep hill down to the river the little old disused and voided churchyard is raised on deep southward substructions under the south wall of the church and employed as a small sitting-place for the specimens of the grimy public – *such* infinitely miserable specimens – who are dozing and gnawing bones (2 tramps under the south wall together doing *that*) in it now . . . Come back of course – get in. All these city churches have their *hours* on notices at doors. Make record of these.

Two years later, in the autumn of 1909, James spent two more days in the City. On the second of them (1 October), he passed the morning in St Paul's, taking detailed notes on the memorials in the crypt, and then in the early afternoon walked to the Cripplegate area:

In the old churchyard of St. Giles to look at the bastion of the old City Wall – 'restored' alas, after fire in 1897, but massive and quaint. The large churchyard, with separated (business) passage through it, in itself interesting: with strong and sturdy aspect of tower from it; with so fresh green of turf and plants that have replaced all the burial-stones, after this wet summer. No city churchyard has held its own better, more amply; with hideous workhouses and offices pressing hard, it seems still to bid them stand off – keep their distance civilly, and respect a little the precious history of things.[7]

That was the final entry in the notebook and the nearest he got to writing *London Town*, potentially the last great prose evocation of the City.

James, of course, never worked there. Someone who did, but managed to escape, was Thomas Burke. Writing in the 1930s about the City he had known around the turn of the century, he offered a quite different perspective:

There were still numbers of dens below ground in which ill-paid clerks worked for small firms under all-day artificial light. There were dusty garrets up four pairs of stairs in which six or seven people worked together. Light, in its narrow alleys, was so hard to come by that they tried to trap it by means of sheets of glass projecting from each window. Many of the side-streets, which housed hundreds of offices, were as slummy as a court of King's Cross or Haggerston. The general impression left with me, after the short time I spent there, was of fustiness, superannuated gloom, and cramp; plus, of course, the tight-lipped commercial spirit which took no account of these things so long as it could do business . . .

Wherever one looked the scene was colourless. The buildings had a tone peculiar to the City, for which there is no name. It wasn't black or brown or dun or drab. It was not so definite as the tone of mud or the tone of cobwebs or manure. It was such a tone as you might get from wet smoke mixed with Army-blanket fluff and engine smuts. Every street was riddled with courts and alleys, where this tone was thicker, and each of these courts and alleys was a rabbit warren . . .[8]

*

How did one get a berth in one of the 40,000 or so firms (quite apart from joint-stock banks, insurance companies and investment trusts) that comprised the Edwardian City?[9] The short answer was, seldom by formal qualification (least of all by university degree, even in the Bank of England), sometimes by linguistic prowess, and usually by personal connection. A five-minute interview for a fifty-year career was about the going rate. Take the case of Albert Martin, for whom a long City career lay ahead. In 1899, as a 14-year-old, he was interviewed for the job of office boy at the stockbrokers Cazenove & Akroyds and given some sums to do. He performed so well that he was told by Swinny Akroyd that he was 'too good for us'. Martin, however, insisted that he wanted the job and was given it – his first task being to empty the chamber pots kept by the Akroyds in the partners' room.[10]

Hours were long, though not ferociously so. At Kleinworts, one of the hardest-working outfits in the City, the stipulation was ten o'clock until work was finished or six o'clock, whichever was the later. But there was also, everywhere in the City, compulsory Saturday working, when clerks rarely left before the middle of the afternoon. In many firms (mainly less well organised than Kleinworts) the working day began at half-past nine or even nine. As for clerical pay, it varied greatly according to age, experience and duties, as well as type of firm. We tend to know about the higher-class firms – such as the stockbrokers Heseltine Powell, whose twenty clerks and office boys had an average annual salary of some £225 by the turn of the century, or Kleinworts, where by 1910 almost two-thirds of the seventy-three men employed were earning above the Income Tax threshold of £160 per annum, a threshold that barely a million in the whole country had crossed – but in many, many firms in the City pay was worse and prospects uncertain.[11] Pensions still tended to be paid on an informal basis, if at all, and the long-serving clerk who died in harness remained a reality as well as a tradition. In short, to be something in the City was not necessarily that gilt-edged proposition that many on the outside assumed it to be.

Office atmosphere varied as much as remuneration. 'Ten years ago,' wrote Walter Landells in 1912, 'it was no uncommon thing to enter an office in which four different jobbers occupied as many corners of the room and shared the services of a single clerk-and-office boy, who spent most of his time smoking cigarettes and arguing questions of high topical interest with another over the way or across the passage.' At the other end of the scale was the Bank of England, employing an army of clerks for whom monotony was the price of security. Somewhere in the middle was the Hongkong and Shanghai Bank, accurately depicted in *Psmith in the City* as overstaffed, fairly relaxed and full of young men who had just left public school. In the words of one of its clerks, better qualified than most: 'I entered London office in Lombard Street in 1905 from the Westminster Bank; the change from a formal ordered strict regime to the undergraduate atmosphere of the Hong-kong Bank was very pleasant though rather startling . . . about half of us were reasonably serious over our work . . .' The higher the propor-tion of German and German-speaking staff, the more industrious the atmosphere was likely to be. The classic case was Czarnikows, leading produce merchants and brokers based at 29 Mincing Lane, where to be a Smith on the books was still to run the risk of being known as 'grosser' or 'kleiner' Smith. The founder, Julius Caesar Czarnikow, continued to make everyone jump to his unpredictable beat; C.F. Worters ran the spot department along implacably rigorous lines; and the accountant was grim by nature and Grimm by name, though at the successful end of the tense half-yearly ritual of balancing the books he would solemnly take out his charges for a glass of port. A more jocose atmosphere prevailed at the accountants Haydon & Haydon of 16 Union Court, Old Broad Street, where the young Cyril Bird started as an articled clerk in 1900:

> We were a small firm. Our Aduit Clerks were an old man of seventy and his son, and our general shorthand writer and typist, a Mr Martin, was a very stout and completely bald man of about fifty who in his spare time and also in office hours ran a mail hair-restoring business which paid him far better than did Haydon & Haydon . . .
>
> Our Managing Clerk, a Mr Biddle, who took me under his wing, much resembled King Edward VII of which he was inordinately proud . . .
>
> Our office boy was the star turn. Mr Flaxman Haydon once severely reprimanded him for not showing in an important client. 'I want to see all clients,' the old gentleman told him. A few days later, Archibald Ferguson knocked at the door of the Private Office. 'A gentleman to see you, Sir,' he said, and ushered in an itinerant match and bootlace vendor. Archibald got his marching orders.

The partners in this thoroughly English firm were Flaxman Haydon, who 'knew little or nothing about Accountancy' and whose 'great ambition was that his only son should follow in his footsteps', and his brother Harry, who 'dabbled unsuccessfully in song writing'.[12]

But even at Haydons, as the office boy found out, there were limits; and, in the City at large, most firms and companies, certainly the more important ones, were run along stern, strongly hierarchical lines. At the Capital and Counties Bank in Threadneedle Street, Edward Merri-man was for thirty years an autocratic chairman who induced many a tremble with his quill-penned letters. At the Bishopsgate office of the Liverpool merchants Balfour, Williamson & Co, Robert Balfour terri- fied errant clerks by asking in all apparent seriousness if they had not mistaken their vocation and would be better employed as dustmen. At Kleinworts, the five senior managers commanded almost as much awe as the rather remote partners. At Rothschilds, Alfred de Rothschild was reported by Carl Meyer in 1905 as 'becoming more unbearable than ever to the staff and treats men of 30 years service like office boys'. At Barings, some years earlier, the 1845 regulations were re- printed, with an added paragraph 'drawing attention to the slovenly way in which some of the Junior Clerks post their books, and to the great number of mistakes made in the Office'. And at the Union Discount, a letter to its staff from the manager implied a degree of putative control that extended well beyond 39 Cornhill:

> Subordination being absolutely necessary for the good order of an establishment where so many persons are employed, you are required to pay strict obedience to your superiors in office, and you are expected to be civil and obliging in your deportment to the public and to your fellow clerks.
>
> Your salary should be prudently and judiciously expended. Remember that if you omit carefully to regulate your expenditure you will become involved in pecuniary embarrassments, disqualify yourselves for any office of trust, and render yourselves unfit to be employed in the Com- pany's service.
>
> I must call your particular attention to the rules which prohibit clerks from becoming security for any persons, either in or out of the Office, from entering into bill transactions of any kind or dealings with profes- sional money lenders and from taking part in gambling transactions of any description.
>
> I desire also most seriously to impress upon you that you are held responsible for your conduct as well when absent from the Office as when employed upon your duties here. You are therefore warned against contracting habits of dissipation, and you are strictly enjoined to be careful in the selection of your companions and to maintain for yourself a respectable character in all the relations of life.

Such paternalism had its merits, including often a genuine concern for the individual clerk and his problems; and arguably it was a concern that was reciprocated. Did the staff of the London City and Midland Bank willingly subscribe to 'a magnificent set of silver' presented in 1902 to 'the popular managing director and his wife' (Mr and Mrs Holden) on the occasion of their silver wedding? Did the clerks of the commodity brokers Carey & Browne accept with gladness the gift from Robert Browne of a cigar or two with the accompanying request to smoke his good health after lunch on Sunday?[13] To believe they did is not to think any the less of them.

Most of a clerk's work took place inside the office – opening and date-stamping the inward mail, clearing the partners' out-trays, attending to all sorts of callers, sending out price lists to clients, working through the day's transfer and certificate piles, copying letters without perpetrating smudges, and a hundred and one other tasks, depending on the business involved – but for some of the younger clerks there were also the daily 'walks', which, in the words of Mackie, 'meant taking a selection of demand drafts which had come in with the mail round to the offices of the different drawees, and later calling back for the corresponding cheques drawn on clearing banks'. And: 'These cheques we had to make sure of getting back to the office in good time to be paid into our own clearing bank. In order to save time, we found out all the short cuts, even if these sometimes led through private premises – necessity knows no law!' This clerk worked for a merchant bank, but for his equivalent in one of the clearing banks the daily venue was the Bankers' Clearing House – an insignificant building hidden away in a court leading out of Lombard Street, but doing an annual business of some £10bn or more. In his piece for *Living London* on 'Money London', Charles C. Turner described the process:

> The scene is remarkable. A stream of 'walk clerks' is continually arriv-ing, each man carrying a portfolio which in most cases is securely chained to him. As each arrives he hurries to one of the desks and gets the amount of his load credited. Subsequently the cheques and bills are entered against the various banks on which they are drawn.
> The 'walk clerk' has a double journey to make, that from his bank to the Clearing House, and the return journey. In the latter case his portfolio may contain a big draft on the Bank of England . . .[14]

'Walk clerks' tended to be not only young but also well built, though in practice cases of bag-snatching happened less often than one might have expected.

Inside the office, there remained in the new century a generally grudging attitude towards the introduction of new technology. Before 1914 there were no typewriters at Mullens the Government brokers or Gilletts the bill brokers; they were only slowly introduced at the Bank of England; and at the commodity brokers Lewis & Peat, Andrew Devitt insisted that all contracts (one to the seller, one to the buyer, one to be posted into the large contract book, each of them identical) be laboriously written out by hand. As for telephones, though they were widely installed by the 1900s (at the Bank of England in 1902, at Linklaters in 1907), a residual mistrust was felt even at a progressive firm like Schröders, where Baron Bruno allowed one only on condition that the firm's number was omitted from the telephone directory, on the grounds that incoming calls would be a distraction from business. More susceptible to new technology were the clearing banks:

> Towards the end of 1901, strange rumours began to circulate to the effect that machines had been invented, capable not only of listing the amounts of cheques, but also of casting the items accurately. One afternoon the news spread through the Office that one of these machines had arrived and was installed in the Country Clearing Department. Crowds of anxious enquirers proceeded without delay to inspect it, and, upon arrival in the room where it was said to be, found a strange-looking contrivance on one of the desks, while a member of the departmental staff explained how it worked. Upon close examination, it was found that some wag had promoted a very ancient coal-scuttle from the floor to the desk. The scuttle had a hole in its base and into this had been inserted a paper-roll borrowed from Lloyds Bank, who already possessed a real machine. But the affair soon reached the ears of the Chief Clerk who immediately came up and closed the exhibition. However, our own machines shortly afterwards arrived and much of our most uninteresting work was abolished.[15]

So recalled one old hand from the Lombard Street office of the London and County Bank; it would depend on perspective whether the key word was 'anxious' or 'uninteresting'.

Telephones, typewriters and adding machines tended to lead to the employment of women; and though they were usually paid less than men, many employers were determined to resist for as long as possible. Seminars on 'Managing Change' were not exactly the style of the Edwardian City, least of all at Price, Forbes & Co, a firm of insurance brokers and shipping agents which in about the mid-1900s decided, no doubt reluctantly, to install a telephone switchboard:

> Miss Coombs was young and pretty with beautiful Titian hair. She also possessed an attractive voice, and Mr Thomas Forbes, to whom the employment of women in the City was a startling precedent, was determined the attractive voice should be heard only through the medium of the switchboard. Moreover, the presence of a single woman – in both senses – in an office full of men was considered to be so full of danger, not only to her own modesty but to those traditions the City fathers held

dear, that it was further resolved the lady's charms should only be admired through glass. A kind of glass case was therefore erected about her, and the staff were forbidden, under threat of dismissal, to communicate with her except over the telephone in the normal course of their duties.

It was at first intended that this should be a temporary appointment. Miss Coombs was on loan from the telephone company and she was to move on elsewhere to demonstrate her skill to others interested in installing the system. But she became so captivated by her novel situation and the kindness she received that she decided to apply to Mr Riesco [the office manager] for the post of permanent telephonist. However, he informed Miss Coombs that this was not possible as he had been instructed by Mr Thomas Forbes to select 'the oldest and ugliest' he could find, a duty he scarcely approached with enthusiasm. How Mr Thomas Forbes was persuaded to change his mind nobody can vouch, but the outcome was that she became the first lady member of the staff.

Nevertheless, the romantic aspect of this glazed princess led to just that state the partners had laboured to avoid. Exactly by what method the happy man, Mr Hammond (who looked like Beethoven), penetrated the fastness of that glass cage is a mystery which so far he has declined to reveal. Other than by telepathy or by sending signals with a handkerchief in the naval manner it is difficult to imagine how his advances could have been conveyed. When asked many years later to provide the answer to this enigma, Mrs Hammond smiled and said, 'He must have used his eyes' . . .

She remained four years with the firm before being obliged to retire owing to ill health. But by then the female foot had been wedged firmly in the door and it was not long before it was flung open wide. In 1909, another lady, Miss Cox, was engaged as a filing clerk and she was followed shortly by Miss Wingrove, who also found a husband in the office. Then there was a celebrated Miss Burfield who while ostensibly never deviating from the strict code of behaviour laid down by Mr Thomas Forbes, was continually breaking the point of her pencil and asking the 'man of the moment' to sharpen it.

Soon, Marchant – once the only typist – and C.J. Johnson, his assistant, were being assisted by growing numbers of 'typewriters' as they were sometimes called. Generally, the whole character of the office underwent a marked change . . .

It was not until the war, though, that at Price Forbes as elsewhere the floodgates really opened. Before 1914 there were no women at Mullens or the Hongkong and Shanghai, and only two at Schröders, while at Kleinworts the first female typist had to work with a screen surrounding her desk, since one of the partners would consent to her being employed only if he never had to see her.[16] The City remained a male bastion inhabiting a male culture exuding male pride and male prejudice.

Justifiably resentful was Ruth Slate – a feminist, a socialist and an internationalist, that rarest of combinations in the square mile. She came from Manor Park in East London, her family background was Methodist, and her father was an irregularly employed commercial clerk. In 1902, still in her teens, she got a job at Kearley & Tonge, large wholesale grocers in Mitre Square, where she started as a clerk in the salesroom. 'Although it has a bad name throughout the City for overworking its employees, I manage to get on very comfortably there,' she wrote in her diary the following year. But by May 1907 she had reached a crisis:

> I have written very little, or nothing, in my diary, about business, but a climax has come, and the course of my life may be altered by it. I have not written previously, because I knew if I started I should want to say so much, moreover it would be difficult to express the disgust and indignation I daily feel. The whole system is so abominable, and so unjust – its influence so crushing – that I wonder it does not bring about revolt; but the crushing, I suppose, prevents that . . . The firm is universally spoken of as a firm of 'sweaters', and the experience proves the name truly given.
>
> Numbers and numbers of office staff, male and female, have been trying to get the small increase in salary which in most cases, including my own, has long been overdue. Yesterday we were told it is vain to ask and that if we are not satisfied we had better look for something else . . .
>
> In addition to the unjust treatment, there is the terrible depression to which I so often fall a prey, in consequence of being in the department for dealing with all questions of competition. The meanness of tactics adopted for the baffling of tradesmen and their ultimate undoing, is beyond description. The unfortunate managers, whose business is to flog them up well, and be flogged themselves by Head Office for not being drastic enough, all come into our little office before Mr Bray, who is certainly a splendid 'bully'. But to listen to this bullying, day after day, makes the heart sick.[17]

Slate wanted to leave the firm and train to become a deaconess; but in the course of the summer she decided not to and, for another seven years, continued to work for Kearley & Tonge.

Walter de la Mare, though definitely not a socialist, was similarly heartsick. For eighteen interminable years (1890–1908) he compiled statistics and sales charts for the Anglo-American Oil Company at Dock House, Billiter Street. At last he got his release, through a government grant engineered by Henry Newbolt, and in old age

declared (in his biographer's words) 'that he had never found his Oil
life on a single occasion inspiring the smallest passage or slightest
character-sketch in his writing; it did not enter his dreams, he said, and
hardly crossed his mind again'.[18] But for a more representative clerk
with literary ambitions, one should turn to Sydney Moseley. He was
born in London in March 1888; his father, a violinist, died when he
was a baby; his mother was left with seven children and tried to make
ends meet by opening a small millinery shop. In 1902, on his way to
school, the young Sydney bumped into a former classmate who had
recently secured a position in the counting house of Waterlow & Sons
of 85 and 86 London Wall – described in that year's Post Office
Directory as 'manufacturing, export, law and general stationers,
parchment dealers, engravers, lithographers and printers, photo-
graphic art printers, photo lithographers, account book makers, railway ticket makers and printers, cardboard makers, cheque printers,
bank note and postage stamp engravers, envelope makers, die sinkers,
tracing paper and cloth makers, trade marks registration agents, writing and copying ink makers and bookbinders' material dealers'.
Sydney's chum told him that there was a vacancy, and although Sydney
had that very week passed the Royal Society of Arts general examination and was keenly looking forward to a more advanced education,
the thought flashed across his mind of earning some money to help his
mother. She wept when he told her, but managed to find a pair of long
trousers for the interview:

> Whether they fitted me or not [Moseley wrote many years later], and
> how I looked when I called on the highly conservative Mr Sykes in
> London Wall I do not know, for the impassive kindly old man gave no
> sign. He conducted me to the Counting House – the main artery of the big
> firm. I was engaged. I was asked how much I wanted; I didn't know, of
> course, but I was offered and gratefully accepted eight shillings a week.
> That very day I skipped school and went to work. At a long, large desk,
> one of several others, I was soon at work with a remarkable trio. Mr
> Almond, 'boss' of the desk, was a model of the 'How to Get On' type –
> ever punctual, ever quietly working, ever correct – Heaven help us,
> *punctiliously* correct! And what beautiful handwriting! Waterlow's were
> supreme as lithographers. There was a special department for that; but
> Mr Almond wrote all his ordinary letters as if they were copy for a
> lithographic plate.
> Occupying a corner of the long desk was dear old Buddimore, sweetly
> Irish to the backbone. He wore a frayed top hat and a frayed top coat (the
> only one in the Firm to do so, and the poorest paid). Buddimore was a
> pleasant looking man, with a striking black moustache. He was for ever

working on his ledger – never uttering a sound – never wasting a moment. But somehow he could never manage to arrive at work on time; he was always two or three minutes after nine – a heinous offence, for nobody else failed to be at his desk punctually in this too well-ordered Victorian office.

At one o'clock sharp, Buddimore would carefully lay down his pen, blow his nose violently, take from his desk the *Daily Telegraph*, adjourn with it to the lavatory, come back and open a newspaper packet containing a hunk of bread and a piece of cheese. These he ate while reading. Just on the stroke of two, he would clean the desk, blow his nose violently for the second time, wipe his moustache carefully and be ready with his pen just as ever-punctual boss Almond arrived with heavy, quick tread.

On my side of the desk was the tall, staid, aesthetic looking George West. He had the appearance of a tragedian dressed in black, and confirmed this impression by turning his head away from his work and muttering mysteriously under his breath. The vigilant Mr Almond was contemptuous of his two aides; and now he had me to add to his troubles!

What typically Dickensian characters they were! What a picture the Master could have drawn of that staid, respectable group of middle-class, white-collared British clerks in the heart of the City of London. No swish of petticoats in that office! No wasteful moments! Each man kept to his job, always conscious of the eye of the short, stocky secretary of the company, north-countryman R.G. Smythe, seated in a raised glass edifice from which he could survey all thirty men and youths over whom he quietly but rigorously reigned.

As for the new recruit, his diary tells the story:

1 October 1903. The work is very monotonous – calling out 'Requisitions' all the time ... just figures, figures! Today Mr Almond, my boss, told me I was promoted to do two large senior accounts.

24 December 1903. And now the great day arrives at work. I mean my rise. It is only 2s 6d. Not much, but good in comparison with the other rises. I started with 8s. Now I will get, with my new rise – the second I have had – 12s 6d a week, and Mr Almond advised me to ask for another rise in middle of next year! He gave me Christmas present of 2s 6d and encouragement, saying I must not think I am going backwards.

27 December 1903.

Daily time-table

Arise .... 7 a.m.
Prayers .... 7.45 a.m.
Walk in garden .... 8 a.m.
Start for business .... 8.30 a.m.
Arrive home from work .... 7 p.m. (alternate weeks 8 p.m.)
Study .... 8–9 p.m.

```
Supper ....................................................... 9.30 p.m.
Fresh air ................................................. 9.45–10 p.m.
Rest .......................................................... 10 p.m.
```

9 March 1904. My 16th birthday, but feel sad, because Mother still in hospital and also Spurs lost replayed Cup Tie with Sheffield Wednesday . . . The monotony of calling out Requisitions is driving me mad.

10 April 1904. These disturbed nights make me miserable . . . Some of the boys tell me of their sexual practices, and I warn them about the dangers of this, having read about it in the physical culture magazines and books . . .

13 June 1904. Mother is dead . . . She will surely go to Paradise. She was only 54.

5 August 1904. Was told today I have been selected (on trial) to pay the wages to the Counting House and Great Winchester Street staffs at Waterlow's. Fine, eh? Progress!!

12 August 1904. Today I paid the staff wages at Great Winchester Street. At first a little anxiety – I thought I had blundered – paid out too much – but, thank God, all turned out all right.

31 August 1904. That terrible sex urge! After warning boys of its dangers, I have to watch myself.

30 January 1907. I'm jiggered if I know how it's going to end . . . Will I be a 30s a week clerk, an ordinary fellow with a wife and children to keep – or (as I hope) a brilliant speaker, writer, singer.

7 January 1908. Another attack – now frequent – of sheer hysteric wilfulness. Absolute horror of doing any work, which, indeed, has no interest for me . . . If I were able to settle here in this Counting House, I could easily get somewhere. But this sort of life is impossible. I am tied and there seems no way of escape into the open. It is maddening.

25 November 1908. A new crisis at Waterlow's. It is ridiculous leaving things to fate. Things do *not* shape themselves; *we* shape them. French complains to Emerson re bad figures and Emerson reports to Smith. Smith gets very ratty and tells me I'd better look out for a job.

3 December 1908. The Climax again. Leave out from Day Book a figure of £2,000. The Bosses – Sir Philip and Edgar Waterlow – have to be told. Ashamed! The vultures waiting to pounce . . .

At last, in May 1909, Moseley did leave Waterlow's ('no gift, but – firm handshakes and hearty goodbyes'), taking a job selling insurance for the Equitable that lasted until early in 1910, when he migrated to the literary uplands of the *Daily Express*. 'Figures, figures . . . damn them!' he would write in old age. 'They haunted me for years after I left London Wall. They haunt me still.'[19]

CHAPTER FIFTEEN

Merchants and Others

We are in the London and India Docks warehouse in Crutched Friars. On all sides of the big courtyard are offices, storehouses, and lifts. Also there are direction boards pointing to various salerooms. One leads to the 'Shell Room', another to the 'Fur Sale'. The one we will be guided by points to the 'Crude Drug Department'. If we are members of the trade, we are at once admitted to a room containing samples of drugs which will be sold by auction on the following day. This sample-room contains much that is mysterious and instructive. There is the dried juice of aloes in gourds, and even in monkeys' skins; and there is sarsaparilla from Jamaica. We see cinchona, camphor, and strophanthus, a deadly poison from Africa. There are drugs in horns, and in barrels; bottles of musk, sold by the ounce; a parcel of musk skins; bales of ipecacuanha; gums, myrrh, eucalyptus, sandal-wood, and turmeric.

At other warehouses of the Company are periodical sales of ivory. There are even sales of birds' skins. The drug sale takes place in the Commercial Sale Rooms – the great Exchange for foreign and colonial produce. On any day the Commercial Sale Rooms present a busy scene. Hundreds of brokers and merchants in the fine marble hall, standing in groups before the handsome fire-place, overflowing into the vestibule and street, are talking, bargaining, and recording transactions in pocket-books.

Dealing in a wide range of goods – among others tea, sugar, coffee, cocoa, wines, spirits, raisins, dates, rice and spices – the London Commercial Sale Rooms in Mincing Lane remained a vital part of *Living London*. In June 1899, a few years before Turner's sketch, they hosted London's largest ever coffee sale. It was organised by Carey & Browne; it lasted three days; and the 13,121 bags of coffee put up for sale included 4,879 bags of Costa Rica coffee, 3,082 bags of Guatemala, 2,130 bags of Salvador, 287 bags of Nicaragua, and eight bags of what were called Sweepings.[1]

The inner history of the LCSR is largely a mystery, but we do have the memoirs of Gordon D. Hodge, who began his career as a sugar broker in 1903:

The Commercial Sale Rooms was a public company, and it was controlled by a manager whose name was Engelhardt. He acted in a very dictatorial fashion, and was universally disliked. There were many members of the Commodity Markets who used the Rooms, but the Sugar Market was the largest, having about 200 out of a total of 1,500 members. The Sugar Market was the noisiest market and made most of the fun. A few days before Christmas the sugar fraternity started to sing carols, which were eventually taken up by all the other markets, and there was nothing whatever the manager could do about it. On the 5th of November, soon after 3 p.m., crackers and fireworks were exploding in all parts of the Rooms. The manager on this particular day of the year always found some engagement which took him home directly after lunch.

This manager was ensconced in a big mahogany desk or rostrum which weighed over a ton, and on one side it had a door, which, when opened, revealed a staircase; there were about six steps to reach the desk. On one occasion when he was at lunch about twenty of the younger men turned the desk around, so that the door and staircase were next to the wall. When the manager came back from his lunch he was bewildered, and, as the rostrum could not be moved, he arranged for a small table and chair to be put near to his original desk. On the table was put some blotting-paper, ink, and pens, and there he sat irate and glaring at every one who passed him.

In fact London was the world's leading market in neither coffee nor sugar, but in both commodities it did a large business; while in the sugar-beet market, having handled less than half a million bags in 1888, by 1910 it was handling over 31 million.[2]

Turner's piece on commercial London also encompassed the Corn Exchange in Mark Lane, the Coal Exchange in Lower Thames Street, the Wool Exchange in Coleman Street, the Fruit Sale Room in Monument Buildings (from oranges to mangoes, bananas to persimmons), the Hop Exchange in Southwark just to the south of the river, the Hudson's Bay Company with its warehouse in Lime Street full of valuable skins ready for the annual fur sale in the middle of March, the Shipping Exchange and the Baltic (about to merge), and the Underwriters' Room of Lloyd's on the first floor of the Royal Exchange, 'always full of excitement and bustle'. It omitted, however, the textile quarter between Wood Street and St Paul's Churchyard, where business continued to be done on a scale seldom appreciated by contemporaries. At Cook's of St Paul's so large was the staff that at the turn of the century as many as 300 juniors 'lived in' in Stamford Street across the river, while at I. and R. Morley, on the corner of Wood Street and Gresham Street, over 800 were employed. A house history of Morleys, published in 1900, was full of detail: over 2,000 letters usually arriving by the day's first post; electric lighting everywhere in the vast building; and excluding the counting-house, the shipping, export and packing rooms, a total of twenty-one departments, including silk hose, children's socks, merino underwear, fancy woollen hosiery, haberdashery, umbrellas, ties, bandannas (as they still called handkerchiefs at Morleys), blankets, shirts and collars. To take only the collars department:

> A prodigious number are kept in stock. Here may be seen over 600 patterns of linen collars alone, each with a name of its own. The great bulk of the collars sold in England, however, are the stand-up collars pinched down at the corners. Paper collars, which once had a certain vogue, are now seldom seen. They got a bad name, partly because, clever as the imitation was, they could be seen not to be linen, partly because the button-holes were apt to break.[3]

Serving the home as well as foreign market, the City's textile merchants and warehousemen remained king-pins of the British textile industry for another generation.

In general, improved communications, as well as increasingly reliable grading and sampling methods, f.a.q. ('fair average quality') standards and rigorous arbitration meant that the primacy of the Mincing Lane auction sale began to be challenged. In particular, the 'spot' basis of trading started to give way to trading done on a c.i.f. basis (involving a sale of as yet unshipped produce). Nevertheless, with its usual conservative streak, the City was reluctant to consign the auction sale to history, and it remained an important part of the overall trading system at least up to 1914, with as many as sixty commodity auctions sometimes taking place in Mincing Lane in a day.[4]

Inevitably, these were not years of uniform commercial growth for the City. On the Wool Exchange the 1.68m bales sold in 1895 represented a peak, as wool-producing countries thereafter increasingly marketed their own wool direct; while although the Coal Exchange still attracted up to five or six hundred merchants and traders for its thrice-weekly sessions, one observer noted in 1907 that 'the smaller markets held at the terminii of the great coal-carrying railways have robbed it of its unique position'. On the whole, though, the trend was the other way. Above all, London continued to exercise a global dominance over office (as opposed to physical) trade – a dominance accentuated from 1901 when the advent of wireless telegraphy made even a ship at sea subordinate to control from the square mile. As for futures trading, where indeed the future lay despite the City's misgivings, this continued to spread – partly through the somewhat half-hearted efforts of the London Corn Trade Association, but above all through the London Produce Clearing House, its efforts helped by German legislation, first in 1896 and then in 1908, inimical to future transactions. Hodge recalled the LPCH as being 'controlled and managed by an outstanding Prussian, who rejoiced in the name of Schultz', and there is little doubt that in this period it became an international byword for efficiency as well as willingness to introduce new contracts wherever feasible, including for grain, nitrates, maize, cotton, fruit, rubber and copra in addition to coffee, sugar and other commodities.[5]

All the time the telegrams continued to hum around the world – by 1903, an average of 2.4 a minute into and out of the Baltic Exchange alone. What were the implications for that traditional City prince, the merchant? Profound, according to the *Statist* that same year. After reviewing the transport and communications revolution of the nineteenth century – railway, steamship, telegraph – it went on:

> One of the consequences of the beneficent inventions to which we have been referring, and of other inventions which wonderfully heightened their value, is that the great merchant of former times has become unnecessary, and therefore is rapidly ceasing to exist. In the old times it was so uncertain when goods would be received that it was absolutely essential to keep large stocks always on hand; therefore great merchants with very immense capitals grew up, owning vast warehouses in which valuables of all kinds were stored for gradual use. The railway and the steamship lessened the need for these great merchants; the telegraph abolished the need altogether, for since an order to buy can be sent to any part of the world in a few hours, and the order can be executed so quickly, and the goods can be carried in a week or 10 days from the United States, in four or five weeks even from Australia or China, it is obvious that it is no longer necessary to incur the cost of keeping vast stocks in expensive warehouses. Gradually, therefore, the great merchant has been dying out. A well-trained, intelligent, enterprising clerk, without capital to speak of, can now compete with the millionaire if he can induce a house in good standing to open credits for him . . .[6]

The article might further have argued that, whatever the size of his capital, the merchant as such was becoming redundant; that, as relations between producer and retailer became ever closer, there was less and less need for the merchant as intermediary in the whole process. Certainly, that was the ultimate logic of the communications revolution. And, since it was a revolution that had been under way for over half a century, it was hardly surprising if, by the early twentieth century, the merchants of the City were responding to it in various ways and with varying degrees of effectiveness.[7]

One response was incorporation, though there remained an innate reluctance to cede family control, a reluctance exemplified in the textile sector by Morleys and Cooks. Another response was specialisation, typified by Edward Johnston, Son & Co in the case of Brazilian coffee, Blyth, Greene, Jourdain & Co in the case of Mauritius, and Goad, Rigg & Co in the case of hair.[8] A quite different response was diversification, forming what were in effect investment groups, defined by their historian as 'an entrepreneurial or family concern whose name and reputation was used to float a variety of subsidiary trading, manufacturing, mining or financial enterprises, invariably overseas and often widely dispersed'.[9] India, China and the Far East was a particularly favoured part of the world, and City-based investment groups operating there included Mathesons, Wallace Bros, Harrisons & Crosfield (moving presciently into Malaysian rubber plantations in the 1900s), and Marcus Samuel (whose Shell Transport and Trading Company was launched in 1897 with the help of seven other Far Eastern trading houses). In Latin America, two significant operators were Balfour Williamson (its head office in London from 1909) and Knowles & Foster (best known for its Rio Flour Mills Company). Other investment groups operated in other parts of the globe, but the great advantage of the investment group as such was that, if properly managed, it allowed London-based family control, albeit sometimes watered down by the judicious employment of outside experts. Rather like the British Empire, much hinged on the relationship with the man on the ground; but technologically speaking, the balance of power lay ever more at the centre.

This may not have been entirely advantageous, though it is almost impossible to offer the general evaluation of mercantile performance in this period that would enable one to judge. Apart from the fact that the British share of world trade slipped from 26.6 per cent in 1890 to 23.7 per cent in 1910 but still remained the largest of any country, we are left with little more than snippets. We know, for example, that in the textile sector the once leading firm of George Brettle & Co continued as an important player but had become a thoroughly conservative organisation; that in the rapidly expanding field of oil transportation, Sir Marcus Samuel of Shell allowed himself in 1903 to be more or less gobbled up by Henri Deterding of Royal Dutch; and that in the

immensely profitable global grain trade, British merchants came a
poor third to Bunge & Born and Louis Dreyfus & Co, neither of which
was primarily City-based. Against these snippets there are impressive
examples of diversification, but one should also bear in mind the
contemporary verdict of a City banker, Francis Steele of Parr's, during
a discussion at the Institute of Bankers in 1900 on 'Our Commercial
Supremacy':

> During the last four years I have kept a memorandum book of facts, for
> the truth of which I can vouch, showing the mistakes made by merchants
> who export to the East – not isolated mistakes, but mistakes of policy
> pursued in spite of repeated warning – such blunders, for instance, as
> quoting in sterling, instead of in currency; want of knowledge shown by
> export houses as to native wants; instances of what I might call insuffi-
> cient scouting before attack; in other words, want of study of markets as
> a preparation for dealing with them; such mistakes as sending patterns in
> bulk, instead of in selection, as if patterns, like projectiles, were effective
> in proportion to their impact . . .[10]

One source goes beyond generalisations, and at last gets one close up
to some of these City merchants. This is the information books kept
with characteristic attention to detail by Kleinworts, sometimes for the
firm's own accepting purposes, sometimes as confidential credit
ratings to be conveyed to Goldman, Sachs & Co in New York. Stressing the abiding City criteria of liquidity and general uprightness, these
assessments may not always have been accurate, but are wonderfully
suggestive and free of cant.[11]

They begin with Ricard & Freiwald, metal merchants of 115 Leadenhall Street who were seeking trade finance from Goldman Sachs:

> *26 April 1900.* Very enterprising firm & have seen many ups & downs –
> lately they have made money, much more than would have been possible
> if they had not speculated heavily. The business they *say* they will propose
> to you involves no risk, but no doubt it will be followed by others. We
> advise you to be careful in the matter of credit. Very possibly Ladenburgs
> [of New York] have found a hair in the business.

F. Lenders & Co, commission merchants of 29 Great St Helen's, were
assessed first by Kleinworts, then by others giving their confidential
estimates to Kleinworts:

> *10 August 1900.* A prominent firm in the grain trade, doing a large
> business and they are considered perfectly good for their engagements.

Opinions differ about this firm very much – some say they speculate heavily, which in other quarters is strenuously denied – certainly not a name for open credit.

Louis Dreyfus & Co, 28 October 1904. Lenders lives in good style and spends his money fairly freely. We look upon them as having perhaps £70,000 to £80,000.

Wm H. Pim jun & Co, corn brokers, 29 October 1904. Lenders are considered on the Market to be first class people . . . They made considerable amounts in South Africa during the late war and must be worth well over £100,000.

Seyd & Co, 31 October 1904. First class energetic people, undoubtedly doing well. Capital must be fully £150,000 or more. Lenders is a shrewd business man.

Seyds, 30 January 1908. Hear this firm has lost a great deal of money & care is necessary in dealing them.

On the same day as that warning, a circular stated that F. Lenders & Co was to be formed into a limited company, with a capital of £150,000 and no public issue of shares. Three months later, however, the company went into voluntary liquidation.[12]

Many of the assessments were about character as much as capacity, and that certainly applied to Samuel Weiss & Co, merchants of 27 Mincing Lane:

Carey & Browne, 7 August 1907. Believe they are going on much the same as ever. There was a rumour that they had been bears of Cloves in which case they must have made money. Weiss always seems to us however to be very cautious.

S. Figgis & Co, colonial brokers, 22 April 1910. We run market risks with them for moderate amounts. Do not like young Weiss – too big for his shoes. They do a large & speculative business in Cloves.

Dalton & Young, colonial brokers, same day. Should say they were too speculative & want careful watching. The son is a very objectionable individual – swollen head.

Carey & Browne, same day. The business seems to have quite altered since the son came along: he is anxious to teach us all our business. Know nothing of means. Do almost nothing now with them.[13]

So much in a family business depended on what happened to the capital if a senior partner retired or died. Wm Caudery & Co, merchants of 1 Fenchurch Avenue with sizeable interests in Burma, was typical of many firms:

Whiteman verbally, 19 February 1903. Our firm was never in a better position & our capital is *considerably more* than in 1885 (i.e. than

£50,000). Old Mr C. is still alive & visits the office daily, but being an old man, arrangements have of course been made to have everything ship-shape in the event of his death. I am his son in law.

Whiteman verbally, 19 November 1903. The responsible Capital in the firm is now quite £100,000 and we are stronger than ever before. The reason of our requiring such large credits is the length of time it takes before the teak is actually marketed here and paid for, the time between felling of the timber, floating the logs down the Creeks and Rivers to our Mills on the Coast, sawing, shipping, the voyage here, landing & delivering occupying quite 18 months if not more.

October 1904. W. Caudery is dead, Will proved for £102,000 – goes to his two daughters in equal shares.

Seyd & Co, 6 May 1905. The credit of the firm is in no way altered, but is considered first class.

London Joint Stock Bank, 15 June 1906. Caudery left the bulk of his fortune to his daughter who did *not* marry Mr Whiteman. They believe the money was tied up rather tightly & cannot be employed in the business.

Whiteman verbally, 4 July 1906. Denies the above. Mr C. left his money in equal parts to his two daughters. There never was any question of withdrawing the money from the business.[14]

But wherever the assessments came from, the great value of these information books is the way they give *authentic* City standings at any one time. Take David Sassoon & Co Ltd, merchants of 12 Leadenhall Street and veritable City princes in the eyes of most outsiders. The firm was founded in Bombay by David Sassoon, who in 1858, six years before his death, sent one of his sons to England, where he opened branches in London, Liverpool and Manchester. By the 1870s three of the sons had become well ensconced in the highest reaches of Victorian society; the nerve-centre of the firm's operations shifted from India to London; and though the firm continued to conduct an enormous business with India, China and the Middle East, the seeds had been sown of a long-term decline. In 1901, with the second generation dying out and the third more interested in politics and society than business, the firm incorporated as a private company, without a public issue. Kleinworts watched and sounded out the situation closely:

1 June 1906. The general opinion among the Eastern Banks is that this firm is perfectly good but at the same time they regard them as a more or less declining firm . . .

London Joint Stock Bank, 19 December 1907. Believe them to be quite good but after they turned their business into a limited company they did not enjoy the same credit as formerly.

National Bank of India, 3 September 1908. The firm does not seem very active of late years.

Chartered Bank of India, Australia and China, same day. Of course they do not possess the same standing as before they became a 'Limited Company' but he [the manager] was of opinion that Sassoons, outside the money in the business, would protect their name. No fears need be entertained.

David Sassoon's second son was Elias, who in 1867 split from his brothers and set up his own firm, E.D. Sassoon & Co, in Bombay and Shanghai. By the 1860s it had opened an office in the City, and it was soon competing hard – and on the whole successfully – with the other Sassoon firm. Revealingly, control remained in Bombay, but there was a significant presence at 9 and 11 Fenchurch Avenue. Kleinworts on 1 June 1906 admiringly noted its progress:

All the Eastern Banks look upon this firm as quite A1. They are very keen energetic people reported to possess a capital of between $1\frac{1}{4}$ to $1\frac{1}{2}$ millions – spending very little money. They possess considerable property in Hong Kong & other Eastern centres & do a very large trade in opium. The Banks buy their clean drafts to a large extent.[15]

E.D. Sassoon & Co was, in short, precisely the kind of pennywise firm with which Kleinworts liked to do business.

If the traditional merchant was under pressure, representatives of the leading merchant houses remained powerful City figures. Over a fifth of the directors of the main London-based joint-stock banks were, between 1890 and 1914, merchants and ship owners; the proportion rose to over a quarter in the case of the principal Anglo-foreign banks, such as the London and Brazilian Bank, the Bank of Australasia, and the Hongkong and Shanghai Bank. As for the Court of Directors of the Bank of England, about half of those who sat on it during this period were merchants; and it was from that half that, by accident or design, most of the governors were drawn, one of the Edwardian governors reputedly using his room at the Bank to receive his travellers with their samples. Many in the City – above all leading joint-stock bankers, but also some of the leading merchant bankers – took a pretty dim view of the 'company of merchants', believing it to be amateurish, insular and generally mediocre, if an unavoidable necessity. Among them was Herbert Gibbs, who wrote to his father (Lord Aldenham, the former Henry Hucks Gibbs) in October 1902. The context was the possible refusal of the Bank of England to advance £1m on Antony

Gibbs's nitrate business, despite the position of Gibbs as long-established customers of the Bank. 'I want to convey the idea,' Herbert explained in a note accompanying the draft of a letter for the aged Aldenham to send to the Bank, 'that the Governors are charming fellows & that I would leave them in charge of a roast chestnut business with the most absolute confidence but that the same rules do not quite apply to the centre of the Commercial centre of the world.'[16] Almost certainly there were some who would have felt he was being too kind.

*

'I am celebrating this very day another anniversary of my appearing into this odd world. I suppose I ought to be more cheerful. I am happy enough in the City, but there is *not* enough to do there . . .' So Clinton Dawkins complained to Milner in South Africa on 2 November 1900, not long after he had started at 22 Old Broad Street. The following spring, with Dawkins waving before Milner the prospect of a partnership at Morgans if he wanted one, he elaborated on his feelings:

> Much of the work is interesting. In connection with it comes the whole question of transforming the banking arrangements of this country. To put it briefly: if the rapid rate at which we are surrendering our foreign investments so reduces our invisible exports and dividends that they do not cover the excess of imports can we continue the free market for gold?
> Per contra; much of the work is dull, and it is intermittent.
> But it is a jealous mistress. The City does not involve long hours or much fatigue. But it means incessant presence and attention. You never know when you may not be called upon. You would not like this after the continuous excitement and prestige of high office.
> Coming from India – and striking a dull moment – I hated it at first. I like it now.

By November 1902, returning to London from an American trip, Dawkins had entirely changed his original tune:

> I came back to find considerable bustle in Old Broad Street, not all of it of an agreeable character. But the rough must be taken with the smooth. The bustle is steadily increasing there, and it is enough to absorb one's whole energies the deeper one becomes involved. However Sundays in the country are a great resource.

Or as he wrote the following March, again to Milner and in words that retrospectively had an ominous ring to them, 'we are driving away in the City'.[17]

One of Dawkins's initial problems was adjusting to the distinctive culture of merchant banking, far less bureaucratic than the higher reaches of the civil service, far more based on personal relationships, trust and instinctive decision-making seldom formally rationalised or articulated. It was a culture still wedded to the family-based private partnership rather than the joint-stock form of organisation, its terms of reference were essentially private rather than public, and it placed a deliberate emphasis on eschewing anything that smacked of the flash, the modern or conspicuous consumption. 'A little uncommon without being swagger' was Vicary Gibbs's approving response in 1894 to his new-born nephew being called Ronald. Small staff sizes were a vital part of this culture – at the turn of the century, some thirty-five at Schröders, forty-eight at Hambros, seventy-one at Barings.[18] Was it also a culture that engendered a deep-lying and damaging business conservatism? Certainly it is tempting to argue that case, not least on the basis of missed opportunities by merchant banks in this period: arbitrage and foreign exchange; industrial finance; South African gold mines; Chinese loans.[19] There was also a palpable sense in which the City's senior merchant banks, fortified by the shared experience of having survived the Baring crisis, now grouped themselves into an exclusive club, reluctant to admit outsiders and intensely respectful of each other's spheres of influence.[20] 'It is understood, of course, that the preserves of Brazil and Chile will be respected as belonging to our noble friends in New Court': Revelstoke's caveat to Alfred Mildmay in 1902, in the context of Barings forging a continental alliance for the purpose of new South American loans, was hardly redolent of tooth and claw. The system of underwriting, now virtually mandatory for state loans, further strengthened the club by offering mutual insurance.[21] It was, on the face of it, a cosy existence, arguably made possible by the fact that, offsetting the private partnership structure and relatively small capital at their command, many merchant bankers possessed tentacles which reached deep into where the City's real money was: the joint-stock banks, the insurance companies, the investment trusts. Directorships were the crux, including of course of the Bank of England, still off limits to clearing bankers; and in this period a major joint-stock bank like the London and Westminster (the London County and Westminster from 1909) had at varying times on its board partners from Arbuthnot Latham, Brown Shipley, Frühling

& Goschen, Hambros and Huths.[22] If a merchant bank enjoyed an unimpeachable reputation, and if it had the right connections, there was usually little difficulty raising large sums of money very quickly.[23]

In practice, it was not quite so *gemütlich*. This was a period of enormous business opportunities, and no merchant bank could have stayed in contention unless it took at least some of them. Analysis of the balance sheets of Barings and Schröders shows how, between 1895 and 1910, these merchant banks became increasingly 'bank-like' in their conduct of business, relying not just on their own capital to back their acceptances but also on ever-increasing volumes of deposits and client balances.[24] 'We have a desire to get more into the general banking business,' a partner of Morgans in London wrote to the Paris firm of Morgans in 1907, 'and to accomplish that end we should be quite willing to consider a reduction in the charges we have hitherto made to our clients, provided that by doing so we could secure a considerable increase in Banking accounts.' Moreover, a host of new-comers had been entering the merchant banking arena, total number of firms rising from thirty-nine in 1890 to sixty-six by 1897. A few of these new entrants were actively interested in issuing, but for most the great attraction was accepting – profitable but, by the 1900s, increasingly competitive, with the competition coming from not only rival merchant banks but also joint-stock banks and foreign banks with a base in London. Among those listed as 'merchants', but in fact merchant bankers, were Dennistoun, Cross & Co of 37 Threadneedle Street. In about 1904 Kleinworts tried to nail them down on behalf of Goldman Sachs:

We have been told that the money withdrawn from the firm after the death of Mr Seller a few years ago [1901], has been replaced by fresh capital put in by the Dennistoun family, yet we are somewhat sceptical on this point. Should it be true the resources of the firm should remain in the neighbourhood of £200,000 ... The policy of the firm during the latter years of Mr Seller's lifetime was most eccentric, this was no doubt to a great extent due to his poor state of health. They have been known at times to effect a wholesale cancellation of credits without any sufficient reason & in a similar manner to blossom forth a few months later with the greatest activity & eagerness to do business. This same policy seems to prevail now ... The magnitude of the amounts purchased by your good selves, which is only a portion of the amount that passes through our hands, will shew you that they are engaging in business to a greater extent than their means appear to justify, & should this firm make a heavy loss at any time it would probably cripple them severely.[25]

Reputations only partly depended on figures, which anyway were usually kept top secret. Nevertheless, inasmuch as they can be prised out, they have their own interest. In terms of capital towards the end of the period, Kleinworts and Schröders were clear leaders, with over £4m and £3m respectively; while of other merchant banks, probably only Antony Gibbs, Morgan Grenfell (as Morgans became in 1910), Barings, Hambros, Rothschilds, Lazards and Brandts had a capital of at least £1m.[26] As for profits, probably the most reliable runs are for Barings and Schröders, which between 1893 and 1903 made an average annual net profit of £142,000 and £98,000 respectively, between 1904 and 1913 of £342,000 and £318,000 respectively.[27] To get those figures into some perspective, the profit of £208,000 that Schröders made in 1905 was the equivalent of some £9½m by the early 1990s. In the case of both merchant banks, the sharp rise in the second half of the period was a direct reflection of the growing volume of world trade, its annual rate of growth rising from 3.1 per cent per annum in 1893–1904 to 4.1 per cent in 1905–13.[28] Acceptance figures told the story (even though rates were being squeezed because of competition). At the end of 1903, the league table for outstanding acceptances was Kleinworts (£8.6m), Schröders (£6.7m), Morgans (£5.3m, a 1901 figure), Barings (£3.8m), Hambros (£1.9m) and Rothschilds (£1.2m), with Brown Shipley's not available. Ten years later the top two were unchanged, but there were changes below: Kleinworts (£14.2m); Schröders (£11.7m); Barings (£6.6m); Brown Shipley (£5.1m); Hambros (£4.6m); Brandts (£3.3m); Rothschilds (£3.2m); and Morgan Grenfell (£2.8m).[29] What one cannot conclude, however, is that Kleinworts and Schröders emerged in this period as the City's foremost merchant banks. Quite apart from the whole question of the issuing side of the business, there remained larger imponderables such as personal wealth, political influence, social standing and general City clout.[30] In the City as elsewhere, league tables give only part of the picture.

Dawkins, trying to entice Milner in February 1901, had no doubt who the big three were:

> Let us glance at the general position.
> Old Pierpont Morgan and the house in the US occupy a position immensely more predominant than Rothschilds in Europe. In London J.S. Morgan & Co now come undoubtedly second to Rothschilds only.
> Taken together the Morgan combination of the US & London probably do not fall very far short of the Rothschilds in capital, are immensely more expansive and active, and are in with the great progressive undertakings of the world.

Old P. Morgan is well over 60, and no human machine can resist the work he is doing much longer. Behind him he has young Morgan, under 40 with the makings of a biggish man, and myself.

The Rothschilds have nothing now but the experience and great prestige of the old Nattie. The coming generation of the Rothschilds est à faire pleurer.

Therefore provided we can go on and bring in one or two good men to assist the next 20 years ought to see the Rothschilds thrown into the background, and the Morgan group supreme.

In London the resuscitated Barings are the only people nearly in the same rank with us. In the US they are nowhere now, a mere cipher, and the US is going to dominate in most ways. The Barings have nobody but Revelstoke, a man commonly reputed to be strong, but a strange mixture of occasional strength and sheer timidity. He has no nerve to fall back upon.[31]

One should not place undue reliance on the judgements of Dawkins – at this stage he had been in the City for less than a year – but unlike most operators he was at least willing to commit his impressions to paper.

Other City men, with rather longer experience, agreed that Rothschilds was a declining force. 'Absolutely useless & not remarkable for intelligence' was Cassel's crisp verdict later in 1901, while according to Revelstoke two years later, 'they refuse to look into new things . . . and their intelligence and capacity is not of a high order'. Even Hamilton, a loyal friend to the firm, admitted as much, noting in 1905 that though Rothschilds 'have a sort of prescriptive right to be consulted by the Government', they were 'being rather left behind in the great race'.[32] Though it was still accepted that the firm spoke for the City on the great issues of the day – despite the firm's isolation from large parts of the City – this perception of decline was almost certainly accurate.

In most eyes the main responsibility for the firm's increasingly manifest timidity rested with Natty, though Cassel remarked to Hamilton in 1902 that it was Alfred 'to whom the brothers defer' and the problem was that 'he would hardly take anything up now that had not the British Government guarantee behind it'. Natty himself worked hard, and had plenty of common sense if not brilliance; but, undeniably, his gruff manner did not inspire confidences:

An interview with Lord Rothschild had to be amazingly rapid . . . He came in, placed a watch on his desk, and intimated that the interview would last five minutes, or three, or even less. In that space of time he absorbed in his right ear – on the other he was deaf – an extraordinary grasp of what was said to him, made one or two shrewd comments, and then dismissed you to stalk off to some other room to listen to another proposal in the same manner. In this way he got through an extraordinary amount of work.

That was perhaps Natty on a good day, to judge by the experiences of two stockbrokers. One was Fred Cripps, who knew Natty socially a little and would go once or twice a week to New Court in search of business. 'One waited in an ante-room before being ushered into the presence; and then one filed through as though it were Buckingham Palace.' Inside the partners' room, 'big and splendid', Cripps on one occasion was asked by Natty the price of Rio Tinto shares. 'When I had given my answer, he said: "You are wrong by a quarter of a point." ' To which Cripps replied, ' "Why did you ask me if you already knew?" ' The impudent young man then expected an explosion, but in fact 'there was just an awful silence in the room', and, 'I was utterly crestfallen, and under cover of the stifled hush I rapidly retreated.' The other broker was Alfred Wagg, still feeling his way in the City and, towards the Rothschilds, as instinctively canine as his father Arthur:

> Lord Rothschild sat at a desk at the end of the room. As I approached – the last of some dozen brokers who had probably all bored him by telling him a list of prices which he already knew – he sat facing the door sideways to his desk, puffing a huge cigar. I had barely got the first word out of my mouth, when he whisked his chair round and began writing. Nothing left for me to do, but to retreat, feeling like a whipped hound.

Natty undoubtedly had his merits, as Balfour rather touchingly acknowledged after his death in 1915: 'I was really fond of him; and really admired that self-contained and somewhat joyless character. He had a high ideal of public duty and was utterly indifferent to worldly pomps and vanities. Moreover he was perfectly simple.' But, from a business point of view, he was seriously flawed – by his offputting manner ('Lord R. still on milk and biscuits and objecting to being asked about his health,' noted Meyer after a New Court lunch in 1901), by his residual dislike of the underwriting system that in turn made him intensely reluctant to bring out new issues, and above all by an almost paralysing fear of taking any unnecessary risks. 'He does not like trusting his own judgment,' Hamilton observed in 1904.[33] It was a sad comment to have to make on a grandson of Nathan Rothschild.

But, as Dawkins intimated, the real problems came with the next generation. Neither of Natty's sons (Walter, born 1868, and Charles, born 1877) took to finance with any relish, and Walter in particular was an almost perpetual worry to his father.[34] His great passion was zoology. 'I spent an interesting little turn this afternoon in Walter Rothschild's famous Museum,' Hamilton wrote during a weekend at Tring in 1896. 'It competes with, and in some respects excells, the collection at the Natural History Museum. One of the newest specimens he has is of two fossiled turtles.' The only aspect of the City that does seem to have attracted Walter, during weary hours at New Court, was private speculation on the stock market. By July 1902 a worried client wrote to Joseph Rosselli of the brokers Nathan & Rosselli from a hotel on the continent:

> I must say I have been very much perplexed to account for the slump. It is evidently unnatural. I hesitate much to write this but you know whenever Mr Nathan has asked for a portion of a loss I have always been able to let you have it. Now however I am placed in this position I cannot possibly ask my people to pay any money just now as there would be a fearful row just now especially as the annual balance sheets are just being made out. Therefore I must ask you to speak to Mr Nathan & tell him I hope to be home again in 3 weeks when I will make some arrangements with him, & ask him to wait till then. It is most repugnant for me to have to write this but I assure you I cannot arrange matters otherwise, or I would do so at once with pleasure. Meanwhile I hope prices will be much better on my return.

Things did not improve over the next few years, and by early in 1907 Walter was supposed to be making monthly payments of £200 to Nathan & Rosselli to clear his debt. A year later Lord Balcarres recorded in his diary a somewhat exaggerated version of the outcome:

> Walter Rothschild is on the verge of bankruptcy. Papa has already paid his debts once or twice: now, he has speculated, he has expended huge sums upon a rather indifferent book about extinct birds, and they say that a lady friend has absorbed many shekels.
>
> Anyhow poor fat Walter has raised money on the post-obits of papa and mamma. The former is furious: most of all that for the first time in history a Rothschild has speculated unsuccessfully. It is a great blow to the acumen of the family. They say that a meeting of the Tribe will be summoned at Frankfort or Vienna, or wherever the financial headquarters are, so that Walter may be tied up more severely in the future . . . Personally I rather like him. He has certainly this much which is

interesting – namely a clumsiness of person, voice, and gesture which is quite unique.[35]

His debts approaching a million pounds, Walter now left New Court: a relief to himself but no reassurance for the long-term future of N.M. Rothschild & Sons.

The firm's traditional great rival was more fortunate.[36] Ned Baring's son, born five years before Walter, was the subject of a telling entry in Hamilton's diary in 1901:

> Cromer came to see me this morning . . . He came to speak about John Revelstoke, who had had without much choice to take the chairmanship of the Royal Com[n] sitting on the London Port, and to whom the work had caused very considerable loss owing to its involving so much absence from the City. Revelstoke, Cromer said, was anxious to get right to the front in the City – and so he will – and nothing would help him more than a Privy Councillorship, if his Royal Com[n] work could be held to justify it. We must see what can be done when the Report is out.

Revelstoke, already a director of the Bank of England, did get his privy councillorship, and he did rise to the front in the City. He was honest, industrious and did much to restore the position of Barings; but with his self-importance, his distaste for most of mankind and his vestigial sense of humour, he was not someone to whom people readily warmed. 'He has the mind of a haberdasher who reads the social column in the *Daily Mail* every morning before retailing second-hand trowsers and "Modern Society" and Browning on Sunday afternoons,' was the harsh verdict of one contemporary.[37] A far more attractive character was Gaspard Farrer, who came to Barings from H.S. Lefevre & Co in 1902 while still retaining a partnership in the latter merchant bank.[38] He was humane (apart from the usual anti-Semitic prejudices of the day), honourable and had a gift for figures, which he applied with especial relish to American railroads, in which he was much involved for many years. Typically, in a dictum uttered late in life, he took the line that, while statistics mattered in evaluating a company, 'the really most important issue . . . is the character of management, its efficiency and honesty'. Between them, Revelstoke and Farrer went a long way to giving a more competitive edge to Barings during the 1900s. 'The old practice here was to sit and wait for applicants,' Farrer wrote in 1905 to Hugo Baring in New York in relation to the accepting business, adding that 'of recent years we have reached out to encourage old friends and get new ones, and the results so far seem highly satisfactory'. But in the end, Farrer's creed was a conservative one, as he had spelled out to an impatient Baring some months earlier:

> Your remarks about confining our business to financing securities guaranteed by the British Government are true enough and very natural, but I hope you will bear in mind, and bear in mind continuously, that our *credit* is the only asset which the firm of Baring Brothers & Co possesses, that and character which is part and parcel of credit. We cannot hope to vie with these nimble Jews in point of brains and sharpness, and are not in it for weight of metal in comparison with the rich men of this country and the multi-millionaires of the United States. I have always told John that for his lifetime and mine we must be content to work slowly and build up the business to its former pre-eminence, and if I am content to do that, I am sure anyone of your name should be willing to follow the example. I think only one who has been brought up outside the business like myself can realise how fatal a single mistake would be. Through the efforts of those who have been working here since 1890, mainly through those of John and Francis [Baring, recently retired], a great advance has been made, and everywhere people are disposed to be friendly, but I know that the least lapse into speculative finance, even if successful, would immediately raise a storm of criticism. Forgive me for writing this appalling lecture . . .

Farrer could hardly have written a more cardinal text for the Barings ethos in the twentieth century (until the fateful February 1995). As a coda, one might add his request to his Liverpool office in 1905 for information about a local merchanting firm: 'We are particularly concerned to ascertain whether they are prudent, understanding their business and attending to it, also whether one may feel confident that they would sell the shirts off their backs sooner than fail in their engagements.'[39]

The third of Dawkins's big three was of course J.S. Morgan & Co itself.[40] The firm came out of the Boer War with much enhanced prestige, following its intimate involvement in the transatlantic dimension of British government loans. Over the next decade it concentrated increasingly on issuing rather than accepting business, partly on the grounds that competition for acceptance business was reducing commission rates to the point where it was no longer a sensible deployment of capital. But it was also a reflection of the firm's unrivalled American connection, at the highest level of *haute finance*, as well as the personal preferences of the London partners. In the early 1900s, however, the problem was the London partnership. Jack Morgan was always destined to succeed his father in New York; Walter Burns junior was fairly described by Dawkins in 1900 as, 'though quite capable', nevertheless 'young, fat & lazy'; and Dawkins himself was not quite the dream ticket he imagined himself to be. Essentially, he saw his time with Morgans as a necessary and rather irksome money-making prelude to his entry, later in his 40s, to the world of politics; and even while with Morgans, he spent a large chunk of his time away from the office chairing the Committee on War Office Reorganisation, winning a knighthood, but not a reputation as a City heavyweight. He also viewed the City in too cerebral a light, underestimating the time-honoured importance of instinctive money-making skills, often allied to a judicious blend of self-deprecation and conviviality. 'It is only once in a Blue Moon that I ascend to the smoking-room of the City Club after lunch,' he wrote in one of his high-minded dispatches to Milner.[41] In the event Dawkins's failings did not do Morgans permanent damage, but served to illustrate the risk of high-level recruitment of someone not trained in the sordid world of commercial finance.

Montagu Norman's City credentials by contrast could not have been more impeccable.[42] His grandfathers were George Warde Norman, a long-serving director of the Bank of England, and Sir Mark Collet, a Governor in the 1880s; his father was Frederick Henry Norman, a partner (and then director) in Martins Bank. Norman himself (born 1871) was educated at Eton and Cambridge before going to Martins in 1892, moving after two years to Collet's firm, Brown Shipley. During the second half of the 1890s he spent much of his time in the States, acquiring an intimacy with American business methods. On his return to London he became a partner in Brown Shipley at the start of 1900. There soon followed active service in the Boer War, and in turn illness, and it was not until 1903 that Norman began properly to establish himself at Founders' Court. Brown Shipley was a merchant bank that had become entrenched in increasingly conservative ways during the late nineteenth century, its main business being the granting of acceptance credits to American customers of Brown Brothers in New York.[43] Norman swiftly emerged as the leading figure among the new generation of partners, broadening the acceptance business to include Europe and the Empire as well as the United States, but doing his best to discourage his fellow-partners from doing overmuch foreign exchange business, on the grounds that it encouraged speculation. In general, if not the man to raise Brown Shipley to the top of the merchant-banking league, he gave the firm a degree of renewed vitality. 'A sort of merchant' he described himself to the wife of Charles Ashbee, and in truth the main interests of his life lay outside the City. In 1904 he acquired Thorpe Lodge on Campden Hill and transformed it into a house owing much to the ideals of William Morris. He read widely in philosophy, theology and psychology, endeavouring (in the words of his first biographer) 'to work out a coherent view of life which would allay the restlessness of his mind and meet a need which his work did not satisfy'.[44] In 1906 he grew a beard, in 1907 he became a director of the Bank of England, but for several more years the search for a spiritual equilibrium continued to preoccupy him.

A different agenda obtained in the partners' rooms at Kleinworts and Schröders.[45] Herman and Alexander Kleinwort (the founder's sons) ran the family firm as a forceful duopoly until 1907, when their nephew Herman Andreae joined the partnership. The business dominated the brothers' lives and they resisted as much as possible City distractions and outside interference. The story goes that on one occasion Alexander accompanied the Governor of the Bank of England to the door of 20 Fenchurch Street, with the words, 'You look after your Bank, and I will look after mine.' The ethos was somewhat similar at Schröders, where the duo in effective control by the early 1900s was Bruno Schröder (Baron Bruno from 1904) and Frank Tiarks, son of Henry. The ageing Sir John Henry Schröder remained, however, a significant force in the background until his retirement at the start of 1910. 'Certainly not! You are not to mention it to him. Bruno is to work for *me*.' John Henry's response when Schuster of the Union Bank sought to recruit Bruno on to his board was matched by his refusal to allow Tiarks to become a director of the Bank of England, the unequivocal argument being that it was a waste of time. Baron Bruno and Tiarks made a remarkably well-suited pair:

> The differences between them were at once obvious. Frank Tiarks was gifted with an unusual facility of words while Baron Schröder was essentially ineloquent. The Baron was a man who was courteous by nature and though he was proud of his position in the firm of which the name was his personal property and of which he owned ninety per cent of the capital after his uncle's retirement, he always consulted Frank Tiarks and his other associates so that the manner of their reply could not fail to be a response to the courtesy of the question and the whole tone and process of intercourse was that of courtesy and formality.
>
> Frank Tiarks was the happy extrovert and the practical man. He was extraordinarily quick and also extraordinarily adroit when it came to solving a practical difficulty or getting out of an awkward situation. He was endowed with unusual physical vitality which expressed itself in a ready and characteristic laugh that infected others with a sense of the enjoyment of work.

Baron Schröder was an old-fashioned banker, who talked the language of banking and who attached its proper importance to the daily work of bread and butter business out of which would arise naturally and easily the occasional and exceptional great transactions. Daily co-operation with the Baron in this work and the extreme familiarity with the regular business coupled with his practicality and gift for quick expression tended to give the impression that Tiarks's judgments were all snap judgments. Nor can it be denied that he had no gift for reasoning from principles and that his judgment had something of the shallowness of the merely practical. . .

I do not think that it can ever have occurred to anyone that Baron Schröder could let him down. This sense of dependability was joined to the impression he gave that no confidence would be misused. He was a great gentleman and beyond doubt one of the very small company on whom depended the good name of London in the world of finance . . .[46]

The memoirist was Henry Andrews, husband of Rebecca West. He worked at Schröders between the wars and his description was largely applicable to that pre-1914 era when the two men were hitting their stride.

For both Kleinworts and Schröders, accepting was the cornerstone of their respective businesses and the field in which they increasingly dominated the rest of the City's merchant banks.[47] Both firms had intimate, long-established connections with Germany and the United States, and were thus plugged into the world's most dynamic economies; both firms showed excellent judgement of clients and would-be clients, with a cautious streak exemplified by Kleinworts' dictum of June 1907 that 'we prefer to be on the safe side and would rather lose a good connection here and there than incur the risk of being involved in a heavy failure with the feeling that we had been warned', in the context of instructing its New York agent to cancel a credit granted to a firm of tanners after hearing that that firm stood to lose $1\frac{1}{2}$m through skins being ruined during processing; and yet, at the same time, both Kleinworts and Schröders showed themselves consistently willing to defy merchant banking convention by maintaining notably lower ratios of capital to acceptances than did their main rivals, a calculatingly risk-taking policy, placing the highest possible premium on judgement, that enabled them to expand their businesses to a spectacular degree. Inevitably, some grumbled, and there was the occasional alarum. 'They are of course perfectly good, but just now the market is very full of the name,' commented Brown Shipley in 1897 of bills endorsed by Kleinworts. Four years later, in a report to Goldman Sachs, Kleinworts itself felt in a position to raise a mildly censorious eyebrow: 'The losses of the Lewisohns [New York commodity brokers] and the United Metals Selling Co on copper must be very heavy and consequently the large amount of the concern's bills on London, principally on J.H. Schröder & Co, who are reported to have accepted enormous amounts, are giving rise to some little comment. We hear that some of the Banks have lately declined the name of Schröder . . .' Perhaps inevitably too, it was at Barings, for so long before 1890 the City's unrivalled accepting house, that resentment was felt most keenly. 'Personally I am glad to think,' Cecil Baring at Baring, Magoun in New York wrote in 1900 to his elder brother Revelstoke in London, 'that Baring's credits are not to be got as easily as Kleinwort's and Schroeder's, because I am vain enough to think that the good-will represented by our name is in a different class from that represented by the above named and their like.'[48] The sourness may have been understandable, but there were few prizes for offended dignity in the keenly competitive acceptance world.

There were many other merchant banks and bankers. A house on the up, though lacking the Kleinwort imprimatur in a report to Goldman Sachs in 1905, was Émile Erlanger & Co:

> An old established & generally reputed wealthy firm but we have no knowledge as to what their actual business is. They style themselves Foreign Bankers but we do not come across them in business & we are under the impression they are principally occupied with financial schemes & company promotion. The nature of their business is much too speculative & unknown to render their acceptance desirable & we recommend you to completely avoid the name in the course of your exchange business.

Baron d'Erlanger was based as much in Paris as in London until his death in 1911, but his son, also called Émile, was now the firm's most active figure. It was indeed involved in a whole range of 'financial schemes' and in 1897 made its first London issue, for the New Cape Central Railway. 'I had learned,' the younger Émile later wrote, 'that if you took a business to an issuing house you could lay claim to a fair initial commission but that you lost all right to any commission on any business arising out of the first.' During the Edwardian period Greek finance was a particular speciality, usually in liaison with Pericles Freme of the stockbrokers de Zoete & Gorton.[49]

Erlangers may not have been everyone's cup of tea, but it was probably less unpopular than Speyer Bros, part of a German-American network whose London operation was headed by Edgar Speyer. Born in Frankfurt in 1862, he settled in England in the late 1880s and over the years became (at least in some quarters) one of the City's great hate figures – partly because of what a partner of Morgans called his 'over-bearing manners'. Still, Speyer's business manners were probably better than those of Walter Cunliffe, in his case ranging from the bluff to the outright bullying. A large man with a walrus moustache, his family background was the discount market, and in 1890 he and two brothers founded the firm of Cunliffe Bros, concentrating mainly on accepting. Asked how he knew which bills to approve, he would reply as a true City man, 'I smell them.' Two of his brothers-in-law were at various times directors of the Bank of England, and in 1895 he became a director himself. His main initial contribution there seems to have been to make the life of Kenneth Grahame a misery, so much so that in 1908 the Secretary of the Bank abruptly resigned his position, apparently after being provoked into saying to Cunliffe, 'You're no gentleman.'[50]

Yet Cunliffe was the exception, and surely a more representative merchant banker of the period, certainly a more sympathetic figure, was Daniel Meinertzhagen of Huths. 'He was of an almost shy disposition, painfully so with strangers, and he had a horror of pompous intellectuals for they just bored him. He regarded philosophy as moonshine . . . When away from his bank he preferred absolute relaxation, devoid of mental effort . . .' Not surprisingly, his son Richard added in a finely drawn portrait, 'he fled from the house' when the Webbs one day brought George Bernard Shaw to his country house in Hampshire. There were other salient characteristics. He 'liked being on good terms with everyone'; he 'was a fine classical scholar' but 'had little interest in science or natural history'; his 'conception of honesty was almost puritanical'; he 'lived entirely in the present' and 'never talked of the past or thought of the future'. He was an authority on mezzotints, 'his hobbies were fishing and shooting'; at meals he 'demanded punctuality and conventional dress'; and, 'though my father had hundreds of acquaintances, his intimate friends were few and none of them was connected with his business'. There was one thing, nevertheless, on which Meinertzhagen and Cunliffe might have agreed, and that was the response of Revelstoke in 1909 when asked by a friend if he could suggest a career in the City for his son: 'It is almost a platitude to say that I consider that character and power of application count for more in the City – or indeed in most careers – than brains or brilliant abilities.'[51]

*

'Lombard Street under Foreign Control' was the typically melodramatic title given by W.R. Lawson to an article in the *Bankers' Maga-*

zine in March 1901. Estimating that over half of London's 160 banks (excluding 'small bankers, discount brokers and money changers') were foreign or colonial, Lawson argued that the foreign element of the banking system was 'now so strong as to be practically in control' and that 'it has more influence over the foreign exchanges than all the joint stock banks, or even the Bank of England itself'. He even asserted of that element that 'through the foreign exchanges it may, under the peculiar working of the Bank Charter Act, give any desired turn to the money market'. Lawson's tone may have been somewhat hysterical – Lombard Street as 'that sacred spot' now 'assuming a distinctly foreign aspect' – but his analysis was pertinent. In particular, it was in the realm of exchange business, which 'the ordinary London banker knows little or nothing about', that foreign bankers were stealing their march: 'They stay on with some of the foreign banks domiciled here, and help to draw the threads of foreign exchange more and more out of the slack hands of British bankers. London simply provides accommodation and appliances for them. It has very little share in the actual work of foreign exchange – the most interesting of all forms of banking.' Lawson would have conceded that there were some City firms known as 'foreign bankers', most notably Samuel Montagu, that had long specialised in foreign exchange; but his general point concerning a traditional ignorance and eschewal of the business was largely if not uniformly true in relation to both merchant and (especially) clearing banks. As a remedy, he called not only for professionalisation – 'monetary science as a whole is much more earnestly and systematically studied abroad than it is in this country' – but for a fundamentally new approach: 'If London is not to become a mere rendezvous for foreign bankers doing cosmopolitan business, its own branches must take a leaf out of the foreigner's book and become as cosmopolitan as he is.'[52]

This 'cosmopolitan business' practised by foreign banks with a branch in London had two other main strands apart from foreign exchange dealings.[53] The first was arbitrage in securities between London and leading stock exchanges elsewhere in the world. The second was an acceptance business, creating sterling bills of exchange in order to finance the foreign trade of businesses back home. Typically, the London branch of the Deutsche Bank would accept the bills of German clients and then sell those bills in the London market. It was a business that fully recognised the continuing primacy of the sterling bill of exchange, and thus the London bill market, but inevitably put those foreign banks into direct competition with the City's recognised accepting houses, who drew their clients largely from outside Britain.

We have some contemporary individual assessments. The Guaranty Trust Co of New York (later Morgan Guaranty) opened a London office in 1897 at Plough Court, just off Lombard Street, mainly to place bills from New York in the London market; five years later Kleinworts commented to Goldman Sachs that 'the market seems to be getting a little too much of the acceptance of the Guaranty Trust Co', that indeed 'there appears to be a somewhat strong feeling against the Guaranty Trust Co at present'. In 1903, commenting on the London branch of the Yokohama Specie Bank, the same source suggested a more widespread prejudice: 'In view of the feeling in this market towards Foreign Bank acceptances generally we do not think those in question will be very enthusiastically received.' Above all, the continental banks were disliked. 'They . . . are fearful poachers & will stick at nothing in order to get business', declared Sir Samuel Montagu to Rowland Hughes in 1897. A fuller, less harsh 'inside' assessment was delivered nine years later:

> The Deutsche Bank and the Crédit Lyonnais stand quite in the first class, and but for the fact that they are foreign Banks – and so tabooed by the Bank of England – their acceptances rank with the very best paper. The Disconto Gesellschaft approaches the above two pretty closely. As to the Dresdner Bank, they do not enjoy at all the same favour. Some few years ago they were supposed to be very much tied up with sugar speculations, and to be pursuing an ambitious but somewhat risky policy . . . Since then, however, their capital has been very much increased and the position improved . . .
>
> This description of the Dresdner Bank would equally apply to the Swiss Bankverein, which, under an able and somewhat rash Manager, has also been going ahead rather too fast.[54]

Morgans in London was right to keep Morgans in New York fully posted, because these banks were undoubtedly part of the big picture. By 1905 Deutsche was one of the five largest acceptors in the bill portfolio of the bill brokers Gilletts, along with Schröders, Kleinworts, Barings and Huths; by the eve of war the acceptances of Dresdner, Deutsche and Disconto-Gesellschaft were in the same league (£12–15m) as those of Kleinworts and Schröders.[55]

Nevertheless, 'and so tabooed by the Bank of England' is a telling phrase. In 1901 Leo Heart had made the same point, writing to the *Bankers' Magazine* in response to what he regarded as Lawson's overstated piece:

It is indeed a source of satisfaction to the English merchant banker – to whom really the foreign banks constitute competitors – that the Bank of England – fearing the possibility of litigation in foreign courts – does not take the acceptances of these powerful foreign banks – neither as discount nor as security for loans – except when bearing the endorsement of two English firms . . . The discount market and all connected with it are mindful of this restriction . . .

It was not only a penchant for rate-cutting that made the acceptances of foreign banks unpopular in the bill market; it was also the set of constraints identified by Heart, with the lead firmly taken by the Bank of England, seeking to erect something of a ring-fence around firms whose *principal* centre of operations was London. Moreover, a larger point to be set against Lawson's fears had already been made in 1900 by Felix Schuster of the Union Bank of London, at an Institute discussion on 'Foreign Competition in its Relation to Banking': 'If it is from the purely parochial point of view as bankers, whether this competition may decrease our dividends or earnings for the moment, perhaps the competition does us a little injury; but, looking at it from the broader point of view, I think the coming to London of these foreign banks, and their opening of branch offices, it is a distinct advantage to the country, and to our trade at large.' The presence of these banks, in other words, appreciably broadened the range and depth of facilities offered by London. Still, as Schuster had the grace to acknowledge later in the discussion, 'the competition is not so much with British bankers, as we understand the term, but it is chiefly with the merchant banker'.[56] That recently designated breed, he might have added, could never quite enjoy the luxury – unlike the clearers – of not having to live on their wits.

*

Clearing (or commercial) banking itself was becoming ever less private, ever more joint-stock. Lombard Street's last wholly private bank, Brooks & Co, was absorbed by Lloyds in 1900; that same year the death of the recalcitrant Samuel George Smith II paved the way to what was in effect a takeover of Smith, Payne & Smiths (and the other Smiths banks) by the Union Bank of London in 1902; in 1903 the Union of London and Smiths Bank absorbed Prescotts Bank, where once George Grote had been senior partner. Avebury's own bank, Robarts, Lubbock & Co, survived for the moment (eventually absorbed into Coutts & Co in 1914) but was not a dynamic force, any more than were two banks, Glyn Mills and Martins, that had gone some way but not all the way towards shedding the private form of organisation: in both these last cases there were succession problems and a lack of full-time, focused leadership. Glyn Mills, moreover, squandered the opportunity of developing a defensive block of private banks. 'In my opinion,' Martin Ridley Smith of that famous banking dynasty acknowledged to the Institute of Bankers in 1903, 'private banking has not proved equal to the largely increased wants of the community, and it has naturally enough, therefore, been superseded by larger and more powerful institutions.' Few more powerful than the Union of London, for whom Schuster, also present, insisted that 'every endeavour in our case is being made to preserve all the old traditions in every way', adding tactfully of the partners of the old private firms that he was so busy absorbing that, 'I hope that they will be useful, and that they will always justify their existences, not alone in business, but in their social position also.'[57]

All the leading joint-stock bankers kept a watchful eye on the various league tables. In terms of branches, Lloyds was ahead in 1897 with 248; by 1913, after a period of phenomenal countrywide expansion, the London City and Midland led with 725. In the case of both banks, there was a shift from Birmingham to London as the centre of operations. In terms of deposits, the top six at the end of 1903 were: Lloyds (£54.5m); National Provincial (£50.4m); London City and Midland (£45.4m); London and County (£44.1m); Barclays (£34.6m); and Union Bank of London (£33.9m). Ten years later the leading trio were London City and Midland (£93.8m), Lloyds (£91.5m) and London County and Westminster (£85.4m); there was then a large gap until National Provincial (£67.9m) and Barclays (£60.8m); and a further sizeable gap to Union Bank of London (£41.3m) and Parr's (£41.2m). By this time the Midland and Lloyds both had deposits greater than either the Deutsche Bank (£79m) or Crédit Lyonnais (£89m), the leading commercial banks of Germany and France.[58] As for specific City clout, at least of one type, an interesting measurement is the number of accounts held by members of the Stock Exchange: easily top in July 1901 was Parr's (858), followed by London Joint Stock (731), London City and Midland (643) and London and Westminster (617). Tying on fifth with 342 members was the curious pair of the Bank of England and the London and County Bank, popularly known as 'the farmers' bank' until its merger with the London and Westminster later in the decade.[59]

Could the leading joint-stock banks have done more than they did with the formidable resources at their command? It has been persuasively argued that, with some exceptions, the day-to-day running of them was in the hands of mainly lower-middle-class managers, but that real power was vested in boards comprising mainly merchants and merchant bankers as well as former private bankers; and that, as a direct result, it was the traditional City elite, with its strong representation also at the Bank of England, that continued to rule the roost, assigning to the joint-stock banks merely the subordinate role of providing the cash credit to service the global activities of the 'merchant' fraternity.[60] Daniel Meinertzhagen of Huths, for instance, was also chairman of the London Joint Stock Bank (tenth largest in 1903 in terms of deposits), but his central orientation remained the pursuit of accepting business at Tokenhouse Yard. It is reasonable to assume that this distribution of power partly explained the tardiness of the joint-stocks banks to move in a serious way into the sphere of issuing foreign loans, though some in the City also felt that it denoted a lack of aptitude. When Émile d'Erlanger was involved in the late 1890s in an issue by the Chilean government of Treasury bills, he asked the stockbrokers Panmure Gordon to help him place them. Panmure Gordon in turn asked d'Erlanger that the bills should be domiciled at the London and Westminster for repayment, and this d'Erlanger arranged. 'Some few months later I called upon the Manager of the Bank on some business, whereupon he said "What terrible news about your Treasury Bills!" "What news?" I said, "I have received none." "Why," replied he, "have you not read in this morning's press about the bombarding of Santiago?" ' In fact the London and Westminster man had confused Santiago de Cuba (being bombarded by the USA) with Santiago de Chile. And when d'Erlanger told Willy Koch of Panmures the story, 'he only said, "Thank the Lord, Émile, they are such fools, otherwise where would be your business?" ' Herbert Gibbs fully shared this condescending attitude towards the joint-stock banks, despite their liberal sprinkling of well-known City figures. In October 1902 he took the line to Alban that it was better to stick with the Bank of England, despite its disappointing behaviour, rather than move the firm's account elsewhere: 'I rather feel that the Board of the Bank of E are all more or less friends of ours & would not talk against us in troublous times, & that the Boards of the other Banks are much less well known to us & contain some very tag raggy sort of people I think.'[61]

By the turn of the century the English banking system was starting to be criticised for its lack of ambition and its determination to confine itself largely to deposit banking, and was being compared unfavourably with the less specialised systems that prevailed on the continent.[62] Taking comfort from the recent turmoil in the German money market, William Cole of the Maidstone branch of the London and County Bank drew an obvious lesson in an article published in the *Journal of the Institute of Bankers* in October 1899:

> German banks have always ... taken a much larger and more direct interest in the commerce of their country than is the custom here, and at times with great profit to themselves. But careful observation of the plight in which they have lately found themselves ought to convince us that, in the long run, at all events, there is nothing that pays better than conducting business on sound banking lines as understood in this country ... The German banks try to foster and assist the industries of their land, and end by becoming shareholders and speculators in industrial companies. British banks, on the other hand, look only to their own stability; and by doing this they are, in the end, doing more for the cause of industry than their German rivals.

It was a historic fault line, one that would persist as generations of mainly home-grown bankers resisted the temptation to become so-called 'universal' bankers – a concept of banking that, in the challenging terrain of industrial finance, would have meant taking long-term stakes in industrial companies and issuing their securities. At an Institute meeting in January 1900, John Dun of Parr's flew a provocative kite for his fellow-bankers:

> With regard to the practices of foreign banks, we are aware, of course, that the banks abroad undertake transactions which are not considered ... sound and proper transactions for banks to undertake in this country. Perhaps the one that transgresses our traditional ideas most is that of acting as promoters of commercial enterprises, as, in fact, promoters of companies for the purpose of furthering commercial enterprise. Great care, great forethought, would require to be exercised if any such business were entertained by our English banks. I think we are capable, as a class, of giving that care. I think we are capable of using all precautions. It only requires the investigation, the honest, the laborious investigation, of the undertaking, of the enterprise, that has to be launched, and then the bank might undertake the work of promotion. This, of course, is very heterodox, very heterodox indeed. I do not recommend it, but it is to be thought of.

The report of the discussion does not say whether there was a hushed pause, but Schuster for one was openly sceptical. After noting that the

Deutsche Bank's capital was almost £10m, he went on in words (including an allusion to the gold reserves question) with which most of his peers would have firmly agreed: 'I do not think an English bank, with much smaller paid up capital, and, having much larger deposits repayable on demand, could with safety go into this business . . . We have almost a national duty, because the currency is almost in our hands here. I speak with due respect to the Bank of England, but it is not alone in the hands of the Bank of England . . .'[63] A City initiative to put Hooley and his ilk out of business would have to come from elsewhere.

Whatever his views on industrial banking, Felix Schuster was becoming by the 1900s one of the giants of the City.[64] 'He occupies a high position in the banking community, being a very intelligent and shrewd man,' wrote Hamilton in 1902, while even Herbert Gibbs conceded that he was 'clever & enterprising enough'.[65] Significantly, his background was more 'City' than that of most of the leading joint-stock bankers. The family firm of Schuster, Son & Co, cotton merchants and foreign bankers, had traded in London since the early nineteenth century; and Schuster himself (born 1854) had, after being brought up in Frankfurt and doing his early training there, been based in London since 1873. After fifteen years working at Schusters in Cannon Street, for most of them as a partner, Schuster's life was transformed when the Union Bank of London bought out his firm and he became a director of the bank. In 1895 he was elected Governor, and for almost thirty years he ran the bank – both day-to-day *and* high strategy – with an iron hand, the very model of the professional joint-stock banker. In July 1902, following the somewhat stressful negotiations that led to the Union Bank's takeover of Smith, Payne & Smiths, he wrote to one of the partners of that bank a personal letter that conveyed something of his banking credo. After declaring that his aim now was 'to further the interests of the combined institution . . . not merely from a money making point of view, but mainly with the desire of making the Institution as you say the strongest & most respected Bank in London & in the Country', he went on:

> As long as I have been in charge of the affairs of the Union Bank I think I may fairly claim that the Dividend has always been only the second consideration in my thoughts – my chief aim has always been to maintain its position & to establish between the Bank & its clients a personal relationship & feeling of good will which is usually not associated with a joint stock concern. That policy I believe has been successful – the

dividend I always tell my people will take care of itself as long as we keep free from doubtful or speculative business . . .

None the less, Schuster believed passionately in the intrinsic merits of joint-stock banking; and in an address he gave in 1904 to the Students' Union of the London School of Economics, on 'International Commerce and Exchange', his peroration included a personally revealing passage on the rise and rise of the phenomenon:

> It is too often thought that these large undertakings are mere huge machines. No greater mistake could be made – behind all the machinery must be human life and energy, must be the living active brain, and the greater the advance of science, the greater will be the need for well-trained, well-educated minds, not only in what are called the learned professions, but also for those engaged in commercial pursuits. There will be openings and careers for those who are willing to study, willing to learn and go on learning as they grow older, willing, above all, to work.

A meritocratic profession for an increasingly meritocratic world was, in short, how Schuster saw joint-stock banking. It was typical that he should have taken the time to speak at the LSE, for during this period he emerged as the unrivalled intellectual among joint-stock bankers – 'a financier and economist of conspicuous ability', as the *Bankers' Magazine* put it for once without exaggeration.[66] At a time when most joint-stock bankers preferred to keep their heads below the parapet, leaving the expression of 'opinions' to their betters, Schuster was one of two outstanding exceptions.

The other was Edward Holden of the London City and Midland.[67] 'He talks political economy as easily as some men talk horses' noted the *Toronto News* in 1904 during a visit of his to North America. Such facility was little recommendation in some City eyes, and in 1901 the bill broker Whitburn offered his concise verdict to Rowland Hughes: 'Holden is able, & his Directors think a lot of him. He is on good terms with himself.' This remarkable banker had already achieved much, and over the next decade he would have even more to be pleased about, as the Midland swallowed up bank after bank and its reputation grew apace with its rapidly extending branch network. Holden himself became Chairman in 1908, but retained his position as Managing Director. Snatches of correspondence from these years reveal the man. To an automobile manufacturer: 'I have, as you are no doubt aware, bought one of your cars [a Lanchester]. I gave £850 for it, and it is not worth £50. The man who is responsible for the design and the building of the car ought to have a rope put round his neck, and a heavy weight attached to his feet, and be thrown into the River Thames. Your concern will never be any good if this is the kind of car which you turn out.' Or to his manager at New Street, Birmingham: 'I am tired of hearing Mr Docker [Dudley Docker, an important client] criticise the furniture in your Office. For heaven's sake get the old things cleared out and have something new and up to date in their place.'[68] It is Holden's detailed working diary, however, that gives a full picture of him in formidable daily action:

> *4 June 1902.* Sir Weetman Pearson. I strongly pressed upon Pearson the necessity of curtailing his expenditure as all the show that he was making was perfect nonsense.
>
> *22 June 1904.* Faudel-Phillips, Sir Geo [an alderman and former Lord Mayor as well as a director of the bank]. Saw Sir George and pointed out to him that we had not been treated fairly at the Lord Mayor's Dinner. He said he would enquire into it.
>
> *20 January 1905.* Saw Mr Schuster who complained to us that we were doing the accounts of the Bank of Cincinnati at one under Bank Rate. He also complained generally about other things. I told him I would have Dinner with him.
>
> *20 March 1906.* Saw Mr Lewis of the Chartered [Bank] who came to discuss terms. They wanted the call of £200,000 at any time. He would give us Bank Rate, and £10,000 free balance. I told him we make a considerable loss by his paying in one day and drawing out another; that the money was so bad that we could not use it at the Bank, and that it generally lay on balance there until they wanted it. We suggested he should use the Brokers more, and use the money, as we did not care about it because there was such a loss on it.[69]

'We' may well have included Samuel Murray and/or J.M. Madders, two of the three joint general managers appointed when Holden became Managing Director in 1898. Both men seem to have been present also on 12 April 1907, when Holden's diary recorded the supreme example of his personal rule. Seeking to settle some of the main positions below him at the Threadneedle Street head office, he conducted a series of characteristic interviews, starting with W.H. Hillman, who was to become a joint general manager:

> Mr Holden said: Well now Mr Hillman, we have had this matter before the Board today, and they have appointed you to succeed Mr Pollock at the salary agreed upon, viz £1,350 . . . You will not be worried like you are downstairs. It will be three nice years for you because the work is very

interesting, and we have always said of you that whatever else you are, you are careful, and we told the Directors today very properly that you were a gentleman of large experience, that you had had charge of four or five Branches of the City Bank, and we wanted to see you in that position because we thought that, having regard to the respect in which you are held by the Staff of the City Bank, this appointment would do a great deal towards keeping cemented that particular section of the Bank. Now it was hinted by a Director that you might not take this position because he understood you were not well; and I said I thought Mr Hillman would be much better from a health point of view in this position than in his present position. Now we want you to be broad in your views of this work. You will have two gentlemen under you, who are senior responsible men, and you need not trouble with them about little things such as £250 or £500. Do not interfere with them there. Your work will be more to watch the larger things. The Office downstairs we want carefully watching . . . Fix your attention on the big things and come up, and discuss them with me. You will always find me ready to discuss them with you.

Mr Hillman replied: I have to express to you my great gratification and thanks for this appointment. I can only say I will do my utmost.

Less content with his lot was the next interviewee, A.D. Rutherford:

Mr Holden said: We have had this matter before the Board today, and they have appointed Mr Hillman to succeed Mr Pollock, because they think he is fairly entitled to that position. Now that leaves the door open for you. You are now the Assistant Manager. I had a conversation with you some time ago about this appointment and the Directors have now appointed you to be the senior Manager, that is, you will be the senior in every respect in that Office, and they have agreed that the salary shall be £1,000 to start with. Does that satisfy you?

Mr Rutherford: I thought they would have done a little more.

Mr Holden: If I were you, I would not raise that point because they had before them the figures before the amalgamation, and you have not done so well since, so don't let me have to go back. You have the appointment.

Mr Rutherford: Yes, thank you very much.

Then came Frederick Hyde, originally with the Derby Commercial Bank before it was taken over by the Midland and a particular protégé of Holden's:

Now Mr Hyde, you know Mr Pollock is going, and the Directors have appointed Mr Hillman to succeed him. That leaves a vacancy downstairs. Now of course, I have got you and I have got Mr Woolley. As I pointed out to you before, Mr Woolley has experience which you have not got.

Keep that before you. Mr Woolley is equal to – or senior to – you in service. You are in the position that you understand the Threadneedle St Office, and therefore we have recommended the Board that you should go into that management as junior Joint Manager with Mr Rutherford; and the Accountant will be Mr Woolley who will be amenable to discipline. You will practically have the same salary, and this does not mean that you are really going to outstrip him in the future. We say nothing at all about the future. When I am gone, and Mr Madders has gone, and Mr Murray the only one, we say there will be positions there, but we say nothing about them. All we say is that you are the Manager downstairs, and Mr Woolley is the Accountant, and Mr Woolley has something which you have not got, and that will be taken into account. Then there are other good managerships out in the Country, but you have a knowledge of the Head Office here, and it will depend upon you. No promises are made for the future.

Mr Hyde: I quite understand.

Mr Holden: Now I have to take you to task. I have heard criticisms about you, and they are that Mr Hyde does not keep himself as smart as he ought to. Now I tell you that so that you may know that eyes are on you, and you must watch that point and study it because I had to defend you. I had to say that it is not always the man with the waxed moustache that is the best man. Then there is another thing. I don't know that I am a very good example to talk about this, but I can see where I fail, and while you were in your position as Accountant with a Staff under you, you have had to be the bull-terrier. But now they will seize any fault they can find, and it is that he is too rough with the men. You may have taken that from me, but that has always been my great fault. I am getting toned down as I get older, and I want you to profit by my experience. Your policy therefore must be to go gently and quietly. Whatever you have to do with your customers, let it be the gentle and the quiet policy. Wherever you can, play up to these London gentlemen . . . If I had to do it again, I should be as amiable as I possibly could . . . We have recommended the Directors to start you at £625, that is £50 this year. Is that satisfactory?

Mr Hyde: Quite, for the present.

Mr Holden: Now you have got in the saddle, and you can spend that extra £50 on improving your appearance. Now remember the future is with you. You are entering now upon the most difficult part of your life. You are now going under the light that will glare upon you and show up all your defects. Your title will be Joint Manager of Threadneedle Street.

Holden's final *tour de force* that day was with Edgar Woolley, a year older than Hyde. After outlining the position and Woolley's new duties, he stressed that he had told Hyde that he must keep steadfastly before him one thing, that he must 'never cut Mr Woolley'. Holden went on:

Now we give you the same salary as Mr Hyde has. We raise it from £575 to £625. Now I think you are very lucky. A young fellow like you commencing with such a prospect and a salary of £625. How old are you?

Mr Woolley: Forty now. Not quite so young as I used to be.

Mr Holden: Now Mr Murray, this man is a disappointed man, and therefore foolish. He has shown it in his face. Now I tell you Mr Woolley, you have got to work and study, and you will be the Accountant of Threadneedle St and Head Office, and be responsible for the whole of that Accountancy . . . Now are you perfectly satisfied to start on these conditions? No promise for the future.

Mr Woolley: You said the positions were equal, at the present time.

Mr Holden: Now just hear him. Please blot out Mr Hyde altogether. I will not have him discussed any more. I am not going to have you interfering between us and Mr Hyde. Supposing I sent you to Bradford to be the Manager there. What would you say to Mr Hyde then? What would he have to do with it? I have told you I am not going to be bound in any shape or form as regards you and Mr Hyde . . . I know this, that if I were either of you and had the nice things said about me which have been said about you, I should simply jump out of my skin with delight. It is this bugbear about Mr Hyde that is always before Mr Woolley.

Mr Woolley: It was the peculiarity of the circumstances, that was all.

Mr Holden: What was I to do with that?

Mr Woolley: The thing was he followed me at one time; now the positions are reversed.

Holden then denied that the positions had been reversed, emphasising that in the future either man could go ahead of the other. And he continued:

But we must not have any of that spirit. You have got in the stream of a big London Bank. Just ask yourself the question how you have got into that stream? Remember, you were once a Clerk in Birmingham.

Mr Woolley: We quite realise that.

Mr Holden: Now there is another thing. I took you to task about your dress and I have improved you.

Mr Woolley: I think there was a mistake about that. I think something came to you from somewhere else.

Mr Holden: No, nothing of the kind. I saw it myself and I saw you were going in the wrong direction, and you must remember that of all the essentials of a successful man, dress is one of the most necessary, and if you neglect that, you are spoiling the whole . . .[70]

Holden would be a uniquely commanding figure in the history of the Midland Bank, but he groomed his successors with all the care of a Roman Emperor.

Typically it was Holden who adopted the bold, Lawsonian approach to one of the big questions of the day. 'I don't know if you are aware of it,' he wrote to an economist in January 1905, 'but the international finance of this country is more in the hands of the Germans . . . than in the hands of the English, and you find very few English Bankers who are acquainted with it.' By 'international finance' he meant foreign exchange. Shortly afterwards the Midland broke with British banking tradition by setting up its own foreign exchange department – a move that, the *Bankers' Magazine* recalled years later, 'met not only with criticism but with some hostility'. Headhunted to be in charge of it was Herman Van Beek, a Dutchman who had trained at the Crédit Lyonnais: noting that 'the chances of making money in Foreign Exchange, as a rule, do not wait until a committee has had time to consider the matter', and reporting directly to Holden, he ran the department with crisp authority until he was killed in a street accident in November 1907.[71]

There were other signs that some of the big joint-stock banks were gradually becoming more ambitious in this period. In the sphere of foreign and colonial government loans they began to emerge as more active participants, while the same applied to accepting. At the end of 1903 the acceptances of four banks stood at £2m or over, but the £3.5m of the leader of those four, Parr's, was less than that of four merchant banks. Ten years later five joint-stock banks had acceptances of at least £5m, whereas only four merchant banks did. These five were (in descending order) London County and Westminster, Lloyds, London City and Midland, Parr's, and Union of London and Smiths. Even so, the London County and Westminster's £7.7m was way below Kleinworts and Schröders.[72] Was such competition admissible? Morgans in London briefed New York in December 1906:

> There has been a good deal of comment on the fact that the large Joint Stock Banks here have been accepting to a large extent 60 and 90 days Bills drawn by your National City and other Banks. We consider this policy of accepting by our Banks is a wrong one, no doubt partly because they take business from Houses like ourselves, but mainly because it is against the principles of English banking. As a result of considerable pressure the Banks who have especially erred in this way have now largely reduced their acceptances and will continue to do so.[73]

The sources are silent concerning the nature of that 'considerable pressure', but it is a revealing passage about a traditional preserve under threat. The temptation is to see the joint-stock banks in this period as sleeping giants, waking up slowly and, in most cases, rather timidly. Nevertheless, they had in their midst two bankers of acknowledged stature in Schuster and Holden. The gold reserves question – which put them in direct confrontation with the Bank of England, from whose direction they continued to be excluded – would be the acid test of their ambition, resolve and unity.

*

One of those leading joint-stock men, J. Herbert Tritton of Barclays, gave a recondite paper to the Institute of Bankers in 1902 on 'The Short Loan Fund of the London Money Market'. Afterwards, Harvey of Glyn Mills looked back to the time he had come to the City in 1880 and noted the rising status of the bill broker:

> The great institutions with which we are all concerned had not then attained anything like the position which they have since ... The idea that a banker would run about after a man who had a bill, or, in the phrase of Mr Tritton, that a large body of accomplished gentlemen should run all over London to find a man who had got a bill in order to compete for the discounting of it, never entered into our heads in those charming and irrecoverable days. Now, how altered is the state of things. A man who has got a bill is like Penelope, pestered with many suitors ...

Harvey was right: bolstered by the theory of the self-liquidating bill (a theory of which the leading financial journalist Hartley Withers was the most prominent proponent), the foreign bill of exchange, payable in sterling in London, was becoming an ever more eagerly sought investment, especially as the price of Consols continued its long-term slide. By far the largest holders of these bills – bills that had been guaranteed by accepting houses and warehoused by bill brokers (also known as discount houses) – were the joint-stock banks; the following year the *Bankers' Magazine* referred to how 'much of the eager bidding for paper which takes place in the market proceeds from a nervous anxiety that a conservative policy may tend to benefit a rival institution'. Relations between discount houses and joint-stock banks were intimate and continuous, for the bill brokers not only sold large lines of bills to the banks but borrowed substantial sums of money from them on a day-to-day basis. Each needed the other, and both parties usually recognised the fact. In July 1906 the National Discount Company celebrated its fiftieth anniversary with a grand banquet at the Ritz to which all the City's eminents were invited. Natty Rothschild, unwell, was unable to propose the company's toast, and his place was taken by Alexander Wallace, the Governor of the Bank of England:

One of the most interesting parts of the conduct of the business of the Bank of England was that connected with what, for want of a better name, were in the London money market known as the bill brokers, although as a matter of fact few or none of these companies or firms so designated could rely on a simple brokerage. Their business was by no means an easy one, competition amongst themselves reduced the rate which they could charge, and raised the rate at which they must give to their principals, the joint stock and private bankers, whose money they employed. It was by reason of their existence in the complex machinery of the London money market that a holder of bills of approved credit on this country was never in any sort of doubt that he could get cash for them at a price; and it was with their help that the branches, on the other hand – the custodians of the deposits of the country – could employ for the benefit of their shareholders a large portion of cash which must otherwise remain idle. Indeed, under the present system of banking and the concentration of banking reserves in this country, it was not too much to say that the ordinary discount brokers were of the greatest assistance, if not necessity, in keeping London as practically the money exchange of the world.[74]

It was a handsome enough tribute, almost exactly forty years after the Bank had declined to come to Overend Gurney's rescue.

For an inside glimpse of this money market in action, there is no better source than the working diary kept by the bill brokers Smith St Aubyn. Most entries were very flat and factual, but the Boer War was a time of sufficient monetary strain to make the diary sometimes come to life:

> *29 December 1899.* Money very much wanted owing to the Banks being afraid of touching the Stock Exchange which is in a thoroughly rotten condition . . . Some optimists think the worst of the money squeeze is over but that is a very doubtful point on which they are more likely to be wrong than right.
> *16 March 1900.* Money worse than ever. Obliged to go to the Bank [of England] for 75ᵐ [i.e. thousand] owing to heavy calls. The biggest day we have had this year.
> *20 March 1900.* A mistake was made in the paying in today, the whole of the day's work being done on the Union Bank and the cheques received paid into Lloyds, giving them a balance of 70ᵐ and leaving Union Bank 65ᵐ overdrawn.
> *22 March 1900.* Money much wanted. Disappointed by Standard [i.e. Standard Bank of South Africa] who promised to return us £100,000 but did not.
> *26 March 1900.* Money very much wanted and we had to chance a good bit to avoid going to the Bank.

> *27 March 1900*. A very bad day. Money absolutely unobtainable. We
> were obliged to go to the Bank for £115,000. They say that they will
> charge 5% for advances as they want their loans repaid by the market, &
> they also refuse to discount short bills. This is a distinct attempt of
> Gladstone's the Governor to extort usury from the market. In conse-
> quence of this individual's action we took 15ᵐ down to S, P & S [Smith,
> Payne & Smiths] who discounted them for us at 4%. The sooner Glad-
> stone returns to his petroleum tanks the better, as this is simply another
> instance of the misuse of public money by *him*.

The Bank of England had been increasingly keen since 1890 to establish close relations with the market, signifying an end to the period of
isolation that began in 1858, and this suggests that it was succeeding,
notwithstanding certain tensions and the continuing problem of making Bank rate effective.[75]

Smith St Aubyn's diary recorded that on Friday, 30 May 1902,
'Union Discount called a meeting to discuss putting up Deposit rates,
but after rather a stormy meeting it was adjourned till Monday,
Alexanders, National Discount & Whitburn being against it.' That
weekend brought peace in South Africa, and there was apparently no
further meeting. The man taking the lead was Christopher Nugent,
manager of Union Discount and such a dominant figure there that the
company was often referred to as 'Nugent's'. As the *Bankers' Magazine* put it in 1891 without undue hyperbole, 'there is no man in the
City more keen and clear in his views, and more quick to act upon
them as soon as a decision is taken'. Union Discount and National
Discount were the big two of the discount market, and from 1894
Union's deposits were greater, making it the undisputed leader.[76] Alexanders remained third in the pecking order, transforming itself in 1911
from a private into a public company. Below these three were, at any
one time, a score of private firms of fluctuating strength and per-
manence. In addition to Smith, St Aubyn & Co, they included King &
Foà, William P. Bonbright & Co, Henry Sherwood & Co and, established in 1908, C.E. Cater (later Cater & Co).[77] There was also, until
1905 when its founder retired from business at the age of 75, M.
Corgialegno & Co. Marino Corgialegno was originally a Greek merchant based first in Odessa and then London; he suffered losses, and in
the 1860s moved to Marseilles; there he ran a flourishing grain-import-
ing business; a gigantic fraud on him led to liquidation in 1871; he
returned to London; where after spending three years as manager of
the Anglo-Foreign Banking Company, he founded his own bill-broking

firm, which prospered for the last thirty years of his working life. There was no such exotic background in 1903, when the Hon Edward Ryder left Lyon & Tucker and started his own firm, Ryder, Mills & Co, probably taking with him at that point the young Lawrence Seccombe, an important figure in the inter-war discount market. It was a small world in which much depended on establishing good relations with bankers, and an entry in Holden's diary was indicative of where the whip hand ultimately lay:

> *30 January 1905.* Saw Mr Reid of Gerrard & Reid, small Bill Brokers, at present with the London & County. They have hitherto dealt principally in Treasury Bills and Exchequer Bonds, but he has recently taken in a young fellow named Jones, who has his procuration, and he wants to go in now more for ordinary short commercial bills, and he wanted to know what discounting facilities we could offer him for first class bills. He could not tell how much he would want to go. It might be £30/40,000; it might be more. I told him we would think about it for a day or two and let him know.[78]

In the event, Reid's overture seems to have met with a negative.

We know a fair amount about two other firms. One was Allen, Harvey & Ross, its antecedents recalled by C.H. Bailey, a partner from 1910:

> The firm of Vaile & Carew was founded in 1888, Vaile being a young fellow in his twenties who had had a few years as a clerk in the discount house of M. Corgialegno & Co, and Carew was a member of a good Irish family but like other Irishmen he took more interest in horses than in business with the inevitable result. I think that it was in 1893 that Carew went out and Edward Allen came in, being the son of Joseph Allen, former head of the discount firm Harwood, Knight & Allen. Joseph Allen got cold feet in the Baring Crisis and sold his business in a hurry to the Union Discount and Edward became a clerk in the Union Discount. [In fact, when Edward left in 1893 to join Vaile, his father Joseph put money into the new firm and was promptly voted off the board of Union Discount as a result.] Vaile, Allen & Co might have prospered and at the time that I joined them in 1896 were running a book of about £700,000 – but a few years later Vaile got 'swollen head' and was convinced that he was a born financier and lost most of the firm's capital, chiefly speculating in the newly discovered West African gold mines. It then became Allen, Hellings & Co . . . Nobody ever heard of Vaile again.

In July 1905 Edward Hellings broke away to start his own firm, E. Hellings & Co. Its capital grew from an initial £15,000 to £60,000 by 1910, but a year later it failed. The name of the firm now headed by Edward Allen became Allen, Harvey & Ross, with a capital of £45,000. Ernest Harvey, in his mid-30s, was the son of a Suffolk engineer and had trained as a banker before becoming a bill broker; he had a significant future ahead of him, not only in the discount market but as a writer on finance and adviser to the Treasury. Allen, Harvey & Ross remained a private partnership until the 1930s, and Bailey recalled how 'no deed of partnership at any time existed or was called for', since 'at the commencement of each trading year each partner's share for the coming year was verbally agreed and afterwards adhered to'.[79]

The other firm was Gillett Brothers & Co, described to Rowland Hughes in 1897 as respectable but small and disinclined to talk about the size of its capital.[80] It was the question of capital that two of the partners, Ronn and George Gillett, addressed in a letter of January 1902 to the firm's senior partner, their cousin the somewhat erratic Fred Gillett. Ronn and George proposed a scheme by which the firm's capital of £50,000 would be doubled:

> We would point out to you that this scheme would meet Frank Bevan's [i.e. Francis Bevan of Barclays, the firm's principal bankers] criticism of our Balance Sheet when he said, that he considered we ought to have at least £100,000 as Capital – that the additional money would give us much greater powers in our operations on the market . . .
>
> We believe we are entering upon a period of considerable difficulty in the financial world, an opinion we share by no means alone. We therefore think that now is the opportunity & one that should be seized at once to secure the business in the best possible manner we are able. We would point out to you that the main point of our scheme is simply in accordance with the views of our Bankers, whose opinion was never asked & was therefore entirely disinterested . . .
>
> All the persuasion that is possible we would lay before you – as we are firmly convinced that to agree to Frank Bevan's advice is the only possible course now before us, if the business is to continue in the way it has been conducted before, that our good name on the market requires it & perhaps greatest of all that the safety of the business is dependent on it being carried out . . .
>
> Further we would remind you that our present Capital still remains not paid up, that Mr Grubb's health is but frail, that your Father's position in the business is one that for some considerable time you cannot hope to fill as in the first place his large experience of business & secondly his power of procuring money was a security in itself that you are far from being able to offer us at present . . .

Fred Gillett remained unmoved, which was a particular blow to Arthur Gillett, younger brother of Ronn and George. He was just down from Cambridge and spent much of the next two years working at Gilletts in the hope that an expansion of the partnership would allow him to be brought in. A couple of diary entries suggest the turbulence of being a young man of uncertain prospects lodging at 314 Camden Road:

> *30 January 1903.* I want to stay in London, well I think I do beyond that for the most part I cannot even think out my likings and dislikings . . . Commercial value from £100–£180 pa. Require £220–250 . . . Religion is whirling mass of unformed ideas or suggestions. Morality is like a string of beads, each bead a 'shall not', both ends are loose but all the beads are formed of one substance.
>
> *24 February 1903.* No change in the great problems of life except that I have decided to stay another half year if F. does not mind and nothing turns up.

That spring Arthur fell ill and he spent the early part of the summer in Italy and Austria, teaming up in Florence with his old Cambridge friend E.M. Forster. On his return to the City it became clear not only that his cousin Fred did not want him in the long term but also that the hard-drinking S.S. Grubb (a partner since 1897) was unwilling to leave, which meant there was no immediate vacancy. There was talk of trying to get into either Lloyd's or the Stock Exchange, but neither happened, and early in 1904 he went to the Oxford branch of the family bank as resident partner. Meanwhile, life at 58 Lombard Street continued its even, unambitious tenor: long sums in tiny handwriting perpetually needing to be added and checked; underpaid clerks huddling in winter round the large iron stove; and Fred Gillett relieving the monotony by telling stories of his days in Africa hunting big game. Perhaps it was not the ideal environment for someone in search of the meaning of life.[81]

*

Without the money market (using the term in its broadest sense), there would have been no recognisable Stock Exchange. William Cole, in his *JIB* article of 1899, stated the relationship succinctly: 'Nearly the whole of the "professional" speculation on the Stock Exchange is carried on with bank money, which can be borrowed on negotiable securities with ease and cheapness, and in a larger proportion to value than on any other description of security; so that a dealer can, under favourable circumstances, keep on buying and borrowing on his purchase to a remarkable extent.'[82]

Banks, and to a lesser extent insurance companies, were the main lenders to Capel Court, but they were not the only ones. 'At the heated meeting of shareholders in Stratton's Independence,' reported the *Economist* in May 1903, 'the directors were fiercely criticised for having lent the company's money to the Stock Exchange. There were cries of "The cat's out of the bag", "Those tormentors get it", and others of a similar sentiment, and the explanation of the board to the effect that the money was lent upon security fortnight by fortnight obviously failed to make itself understood.' Significantly, the paper added that 'the loan of surplus capital to the Stock Exchange for contango purposes is such an ordinary, everyday matter as to lead one to suppose its existence is universally known'. In fact the mechanism by which a Stock Exchange firm or member borrowed large sums of money in order to be able to carry over securities from one fortnightly account to the next was straightforward enough. Not only did they have to pay interest on the loan but they also had to pledge securities worth more than the amount of the loan. Usually that 'margin' was 10 per cent, but it could rise to 25 per cent or more in the case of mining securities, which not all banks would accept as collateral anyway. From the point of view of the lender, however, what mattered was less the character of the securities being pledged than the character of the borrower and the nature of his business. When in 1913, for instance, the manager of the Midland Bank's Angel Court branch interviewed a member called Arthur Bennett, the would-be borrower emphasised that he 'did purely a jobbing business and took no unnecessary risks'.[83]

For all parties to these arrangements, the proverbial crunch came with the outbreak of war in August 1914, when it transpired (though was kept highly secret) that the Stock Exchange owed to the outside world a total of almost £81m, working out at £16,634 per member. In the course of the ensuing Committee inquiry prior to deciding what should be done, Frederick Chetwynd-Stapylton of Pember & Boyle rather smugly stated 'that his firm had always used their capital for the purpose of finding the 10 per cent margin on their loans and at the same time had been careful never to have less than another 10 per cent margin in their box for the purpose of putting up fresh margin if required'. Almost certainly more typical, though, was the frank admission of Paul Nelke, of the brokers Nelke, Phillips & Co. He informed the Committee 'that he had always traded on credit and that if this were withdrawn, in five minutes he could not go on'.[84]

It was this ease of access to short-term credit that did much to make London the world's leading securities market – by 1910 about a third of the world's issued securities were quoted there. 'You must not forget that it is much easier to finance positions in London than in New York,' E. & C. Randolph of New York asserted in 1910 to Nathan & Rosselli, the London broking firm with whom it did arbitrage business. Nathan & Rosselli itself secured much of its extensive financing from the London branches of foreign banks; while the arbitrage dealings of it and other firms contributed largely to the evolution of a genuinely integrated international securities market with London as the hub.[85] Throughout the period the main centres of international arbitrage remained London and New York, and Duguid in 1904 described how, even on a dull day, the time difference ensured that business in Capel Court usually ended on an upbeat note:

> By rapid degrees the American fluctuations become generally circulated; the market seems to be full of the little pink slips that come flying in at the hands of boys and clerks stationed in a line that stretches from the offices of the cable companies outside the House to the very heart of the Yankee Market in the Stock Exchange. Again the telephone and telegraph come into requisition, and the House usually finishes up, unless there is really nothing doing, in a state of more or less mild excitement.[86]

Arbitrage was not the only part of this regular afternoon flurry, nor was it the sole reason for the London Stock Exchange's global ascendancy; but it made a far larger contribution to the House's well-being than most stolid Anglo-Saxon members remotely appreciated.

Whatever its business, by the turn of the century the Stock Exchange was a place of impressive statistics: each year, 15 million gallons of water consumed; 1 million towels used (including for cleaning patent-leather boots as well as more orthodox purposes); and 150 cubic feet of oak and teak converted by those boots into powder, swept up at regular intervals each day by specially assigned waiters. It also boasted the longest hat-rack in the world, one-eighth of a mile.[87] Membership, meanwhile, continued to increase: 3,233 in 1890, 4,315 in 1900, and reaching a peak of 5,567 in 1905. That membership was traditionally divided in roughly equal parts between brokers and jobbers, but there is some evidence in these years of a shift to a preponderance of jobbers. The membership also included some half-commission men, though the likelihood is that the great majority of this class were not members.[88] Such was the case with Helbert Wagg's three half-commission men, one of whom was Captain Osborne and who were, according to Alfred

Wagg, 'humorously known as the "gentlemen" to distinguish them both from the partners and the clerks'. The financial writer Henry Warren, in a 1905 treatise on *How to Deal with your Broker*, was disinclined to flatter: 'Though brokers are not allowed to advertise, some of them practically employ a species of tout, who is generally a positive danger to everybody who chances to come in contact with him. These men are known as "stockbrokers' terriers" or "half-commission men", and their habitat is the club or a drinking-bar, whilst during periods of excitement they emerge from these secluded spots, and, garishly attired, line the pavement on either side of Throgmorton Street.' Warren identified three types: 'the common or garden variety of tout', as described above; the 'club-tout', such as 'half-pay officers, and so on'; and 'the drawing-room tout', for example 'a younger son of a titled person'. Regrettably, the young George Studdy fell into the first category.[89] The son of an army officer, he left Dulwich College in 1896 unable following an accident to pursue a military career. Instead, after some fruitless months as an engineering apprentice, he became a half-commission man. He had little aptitude for the job, and even less relish; when orders from friends began to run out so did his prospects. After three years he turned to art, and a much more satisfying life lay ahead as the creator of Bonzo.

To become a member of the Stock Exchange, it was necessary not only to pay the relatively modest entrance and annual membership fees (though notably stiffer than they had been at the time of the Royal Commission), but also to find from amongst the existing membership two or three recommenders who would pledge up to £500 each. These recommenders appeared in person before the relevant sub-committee and had to give satisfactory replies to three questions: whether the applicant had ever been a bankrupt; whether they would take his cheque for £3,000 in the ordinary way of business; and whether they considered that he might be safely dealt with in securities for the account. It is said that on one occasion a recommender, not properly primed, replied to the second question, 'Well, I should not pick it out.' Taking the three questions together, they hardly comprised a searching examination of the candidate's likely expertise in his prospective occupation; nor was the candidate himself subjected to such an examination. It was a rare event, moreover, for a candidate to be turned down – between 1886 and 1903, for instance, 3,854 members were admitted and only thirty-nine applications for membership (excluding those of defaulters) were unsuccessful. The case against this liberal admissions policy is that it allowed in too many members of inadequate capital, untested competence and doubtful probity; the case for is that, in marked contrast to the restrictive approach of the New York Stock Exchange, it encouraged in London a membership of all the talents, drawn from abroad as well as home.[90] Few contemporaries who came into close contact with the inhabitants of Capel Court were, it has to be said, overcome with dazzled admiration.

What really counted, though, for success on the Stock Exchange were a would-be member's *informal* qualifications. For a jobber the emphasis was on establishing good relations with brokers; for a broker it was rather on establishing a profitable network of clients. In both cases, however, there was nothing quite so helpful as the family tie: throughout the period almost one-third of all firms had at least two members of the same family amongst its partners, and to be possessed of a well-known Stock Exchange name meant that, at the minimum, one would never starve.[91] Beyond family, but closely linked to it, lay the whole critical area of personal influence and connection – critical because the Stock Exchange would remain for many years yet essentially a 'people' business. 'I have known the candidate from childhood . . . He does not intend to remain as a clerk, but being backed by the members of the firm of Messrs Wedd, Jefferson & Co he will as soon as possible make terms with a suitable partner and at once, then, commence dealing.' R.H. Prance's recommendation in 1899 on behalf of his nephew George could hardly have put the matter more clearly. Even more prized was a Rothschild connection: in May 1900 the 17-year-old John Cadogan presented himself at Edinger & Asch 'with a recommendation from Mr Leopold de Rothschild' and 'was engaged after a short interview'; two years later the stockbroking firm of G.L. Jacobs & Co was established, Gordon Jacobs's all-important 'connection' being the fact that his father was a bookmaker to the Rothschild family. Personal contacts were many and various, but for most firms an intimate connection with a bank was worth its weight in gold. Take Kleinworts' rather sour historical précis of Nathan & Rosselli, written in 1913 but going back to the firm's origins in 1887:

> They started business in a small way and were principally occupied with orders which they obtained from the Crédit Lyonnais in London for whom they acted as Brokers, the Manager of the Crédit Lyonnais at that time being a brother of the original partner of the firm . . . In the meantime Mr J. Rosselli, formerly Manager of the London Agency, has been made an Administrateur of the Crédit Lyonnais in Paris, and we think that this is of considerable assistance to the stockbroking firm in London . . . They are a little 'sharp' and not overpopular in this market.

More illustrious in their connections (if not necessarily as profitable) were the increasing number of blue-blooded members: by the turn of the century these included three members of the House of Lords and almost thirty sons of peers. Almost all were brokers, the social superior of the jobber and much more intimately involved with the outside world. Someone who switched from jobbing to broking was the Hon Francis Curzon, brother of the Viceroy. 'Really Curzon,' Maynard Keynes is reputed to have remarked later in Curzon's not unsuccessful City career, 'you have all the pomposity of your brother and not a scrap of his intelligence.'[92]

There was another well-trodden route, perceptively identified by the *Rialto* in 1892:

> To become successful on the Stock Exchange it is necessary to have a reputation for something – no matter what. A well-founded reputation of being a greater fool than your neighbours has been known to serve in default of something better, but, on the whole, there is nothing much more effective than a really first-class gilt-edged fame in athletics, and we could mention one notable firm which owes much of its success to the physical prowess of its members. Hence, in great measure, the renown of the Stock Exchange for the production of first-class cricketers.

A reputation for something . . . Panmure Gordon was legendary for his expansive lifestyle; A. Tyrwhitt Drake, founder in 1893 of the broking firm that eventually became Rowe, Swann & Co, was a keen sportsman popularly known as 'Ducky' Drake; Mure Fergusson was famous for popularising golf; Percy Marsden (nicknamed 'Good Afternoon' on account of his initials) had the reputation for looking like King Edward VII, so much so that at weekends he would ride along the Brighton seafront in a landau and wave a laconic hand to the cheering crowds. A member who combined sporting prowess with top-notch personal connections was Sidney Kitcat. Educated at Marlborough College, he played cricket for Gloucestershire and hockey for England; his City apprenticeship was served with Merchants Trust, the investment trust run by Robert Benson, himself an enthusiastic sportsman; in 1896 he became a member of the Stock Exchange, looking to Benson for much of his business; about this time he was involved in setting up the Marlburian Club, an invaluable means of keeping in touch with old boys of the school; and in 1900 he went into partnership with another broker, the style of the firm in time becoming Kitcat & Aitken. Ultimately, it was the personal touch that counted – for good or ill. 'You suggested Pawle. I'm afraid he wouldn't do. You know what a bore he is . . .'[93] Such was the private, unfavourable judgement of the merchant bank Antony Gibbs, looking in 1899 for a stockbroker it could work closely with in the Westralian market. Almost certainly the rejected member was G.S. Pawle, who as a member since 1877 would have known that to be called a bore was the ultimate condemnation.

A broker (and to a lesser extent a jobber) who became a partner in an already existing firm usually had to provide a certain amount of capital as well as a connection. How much obviously varied – according to the scale of the firm's activities, according to the prospective value of the connection that the newcomer was introducing – but it was usually a four- rather than three-figure sum. This was hardly surprising, for firms were generally getting bigger in scale and needing increasingly more capital in order to be able to operate with a reasonable margin of safety. For a major broking firm, Pember & Boyle's capital of £100,000 at the turn of the century was probably typical, with Cecil Boyle's replacement as partner, George Ross Pember, bringing £4,000 capital to the partnership. Nevertheless, even by 1914, when as many as 163 firms had five or more partners, the average size of partnership was still only 3.14; many of the Stock Exchange's 910 firms (in the sense of two or more partners) jobbed along on very slender resources, concentrating on leaving the House every day with an even book. At least several hundred members ran one-man operations, supported only by book, pencil and perhaps a clerk. Borrowing facilities were highly developed and it remained true, particularly from a broking point of view, that so long as the private investor was more important than the institutional investor, then a promising personal connection was still the prime qualification. In the Stock Exchange there was an enormously wide range of ambition and approach. For all the contemporary criticisms of undercapitalised jobbers, such a range added to its strengths as a market, as well as to its charms as a club.[94]

As for actual profits, there are reliable figures for broking firms only.[95] James Capel & Co, for instance, were unable before the war to manage an annual distribution to partners as handsome as their £55,000 of the late 1880s. The Edwardian years were better than the 1890s, with a peak of £43,000 distributed in 1912–13. At J. & A. Scrimgeour, the average annual profit between 1870 and 1914 was £26,400, working out for each partner at £6,800 a year – in other words, in mid-1990s money values, up to £300,000 per partner per year in an era of light taxation. Fluctuations at Scrimgeours ranged from £2,599 profit for the firm in 1891 to £73,652 in 1913. At another, rather smaller broking firm, Oakley Norris Bros, the two partners shared £6,843 in 1905 and £6,485 the following year. Those two figures, however, were unusual in their steadiness, for traditionally it was volatility that characterised the earnings streams of Stock Exchange firms, mirroring larger market cycles of feast and famine. 'When you have a good year, spend a third, save a third, and keep a third in reserve for possible losses': this admirable advice was given to a young partner in 1909 by a broking firm's senior partner. Such circumspection was not the way of James Gingold, father of Hermione and in his way an archetypal figure of the pre-1914 Stock Exchange. 'My father was wildly extravagant; he possessed forty pairs of handmade shoes, twenty sets of monogrammed silk pyjamas, and eight Louis Vuitton trunks. In his lifetime, he went through three fortunes, only one of which he made himself.' He was also, she recalled, 'handsome, amusing, and completely unscrupulous', besides being 'always very rich or very poor'. The first ten years or so of Hermione's life saw extreme domestic oscillations: from a large house in the late 1890s in then fashionable Maida Vale to not long after 'a small attic flat in Cricklewood', as well as other equally temporary arrangements. Eventually Gingold became a Buddhist, telling his daughter that it was because they 'were kind to animals and didn't squash spiders'. The end came in the 1930s: 'He seemed as spry as ever and in the best of health when he contracted pneumonia as a result of sitting in an open-air racing car with his cousin during a rainstorm. He was convinced champagne would cure him, but he died within a matter of days.'[96]

Within the membership, and responding to the ceaseless information flow, the jobbers continued to set the daily agenda. When Harry Gibbs was investigating the British Electric Traction Co in 1900, he used in the first instance one of his brokers, who in turn reported back that he had (in Gibbs's words) 'made enquiries of two "serious" men, leading jobbers, about the companies that the BET had brought out, & how the market would take a further issue by them'. Four years later, an authoritative guide to the Stock Exchange noted how 'from sheer laziness, the great body of stockbrokers lean much too much upon the jobber'. The jobbers themselves had few illusions. George Cornwallis-West (second husband of Lady Randolph Churchill) was friendly with Graham Prentice, 'almost the biggest jobber in the Kaffir market' as well as one of the heaviest at eighteen stone; and 'he used to tell me that one of the reasons for his success as a bidder was his voice, which, when bidding for shares, would rise to almost falsetto heights easily heard above the din of the market'. Probably even more powerful in the Circus were the four brothers who comprised Hyam Bros (Higham from 1897). They had been brought up in Hoxton, where their father sold toys that had been imported from Europe; there were twelve other siblings; and Harry and Ted Hyam started the firm in the early 1880s. Ernest Hyam became a partner some ten years later, and his son recalled him as someone who rarely read a book but was 'truly fond of dogs' and 'kept his watch ten minutes fast on principle'. The firm flourished in the 1890s on the back of the Kaffir boom, Harry and Ted being particularly 'able and enterprising', but the 1900s were more difficult. By 1909, when Ernest's son went to public school, it had to be Harrow because Eton had become a little too expensive.[97]

Still, it was all relative, as Gerry Weigall would have vouched. The son of a portrait painter, educated at Wellington College and Cambridge, his main passion was cricket and in the 1890s he turned out for Kent whenever he could, an obdurate rather than stylish batsman. His personality was thoroughly extrovert and in due course he found a niche as a fairly small-time operator jobbing in the Kaffir Circus. In 1904 the *Rialto* ran a competition to find the best-dressed man on the Stock Exchange and the clear winner was Weigall, over five hundred votes ahead of Prentice (second) and more than a thousand ahead of the King Edward lookalike (fourth): the prize was 300 La Corona cigars. Only four years after this moment of City fame, Weigall's Stock Exchange career ended abruptly when he was found guilty of having transacted business for a clerk in another jobbing firm. 'Mr Johnstone held a very prominent position in the rowing world and moved in good society': Weigall's plea of ignorance that the man he dealt for was not a member failed to prevent a two-year suspension. For the rest of his life, permanently short of the ready, Weigall concentrated on his role as an ever-spruce cricket pundit, issuing a series of celebrated maxims – 'Never hook till you're 84', 'Never run to cover on a fast wicket', 'Never play back at the bottom end at Canterbury', 'Never eat pie at a cricket lunch'.[98]

The writers who accused brokers of a lazy reliance on jobbers were Godefroi D. Ingall and George Withers (a former member), and in their 1904 survey of the Stock Exchange they were rude about both classes – 'it is probable that not more than fifty members could jot down even a tolerably coherent synopsis of a Bank of England Weekly Statement' – but particularly brokers:

> We have heard the opinion quite seriously advanced by a broker with a
> very good business connection, which, it need hardly be said, was got

together by no exertions of his own, that it is rather bad form, and savouring too much of the 'bucket-shop', for a member of the Stock Exchange to possess any very intimate knowledge of the intrinsic values of securities . . . From the 'House' point of view, that broker is a demigod who can reel out the current quotations of some hundred or so active speculative stocks, and this facility is not difficult to acquire by any broker who is habitually telegraphing market fluctuations to provincial centres. Such knowledge, however, impresses a client but little. The client's idea of information lies rather in the direction of the last few dividends declared by a company, and of intimate knowledge of the individuals who compose the directorate of a concern . . .

In short, concluded Ingall and Withers with ill-disguised envy, 'the fat commissions and the good things of the Stock Exchange would appear to be bestowed upon the happy-go-lucky ignoramuses who can afford to belong to half a dozen clubs, and to ride prominently with a fashionable pack of hounds.' More or less objective assessments of stockbroking capacities did not often surface in the contemporary literature, but in 1912 the subject was touched on during a discussion at the Institute of Actuaries. After mentioning a recent paper to the Institute in which the newly created Public Trustee had 'laid great stress on the fact that he could get the opinion of a number of brokers', J.R. Hart of the Phoenix went on: 'He thought most of the members who had to do with brokers knew that their opinion from an investment point of view was not worth very much; they very seldom had the time or the organisation to analyse an investment in the way insurance companies required.' Hart's view went unchallenged; and though anyone who knew the City would have agreed that there were some individual exceptions, the general consensus remained that, in Henry Warren's words of 1905, 'the average broker . . . does not look very far ahead'.[99]

George Aylwen, a future Lord Mayor, discovered the truth of this on the ground. In 1896 he entered the office of J. & A. Scrimgeour as a clerk. Along with Mullens and Nivisons, Scrimgeours was a dominant broking force in the gilt-edged market, but Aylwen found at 18 Old Broad Street a rudimentary organisation. The only partner was Walter Scrimgeour, while among the office staff of eight was an accountant called Harold: 'Why he was labelled accountant no one ever discovered, he may have had some fleeting acquaintance with figures but they generally eluded him and the Firm, until a year or so after they were needed.' The arrival soon afterwards of John Scrimgeour made the firm rather more dynamic, but Aylwen's overall memories of the pre-1914 period remained unfavourable:

Most members were merely passers on of information and gossip, there was little or no attempt to sift information, to analyse prospects of equities, or indeed to justify the recommendation of the many and various tips toddled out by the market and the many outsiders who frequented clubs and other convivial places where people with more money than sense assemble. People looked askance at stockbrokers in those early years of a new century and, looking back, they were justified. Too many doubtful financiers were getting away with the swag owing to the fact that there were far too many so-called brokers attempting to cope with a job that called for at least a smattering of financial knowledge, and this the bulk did not possess.

Aylwen also recalled a Micawber-like character called Foskett who each day after lunch would 'make a very unsteady entrance' into the office and 'ask several damned silly questions to which he received frivolous answers', so perhaps the clients got the brokers they deserved.[100]

Arguably this mediocrity was inherent in the job itself. 'Stockbroking, the execution of clients' orders for a commission, is a non-creative, uninspiring occupation. It is a living, not a life.' Such would be the view of Helbert Wagg's Lawrence Jones, who added: 'If you live on rake-offs . . . it is the size of the heap, not your skill with the rake, that counts.' Too often it was a job of last resort. Mawdley Sambourne ('Roy' to his family) had on his mother's side a stockbroking background, and in 1898 his elder sister married Leonard Messel, son of the prominent stockbroker Ludwig Messel. He left Oxford in 1900 and spent some time working at Lewis & Peat in Mincing Lane. At this stage of his life he had little idea of what he wanted apart from achieving wealth and leisure. The Messels talked him into taking up stockbroking and in 1902 he became a member, with money put up by 'Lennie' Messel. It soon became clear that life on the Stock Exchange brought out all his manic-depressive tendencies, yet in 1910 he went into partnership with an older broker, Ernest Pohl. Capital of £5,000 was required and this time his sister found the money. He continued to grumble to her: 'Still absolutely hopeless in the City – no business and no money to be made at all – it is really worse than ever I have known it even in my short and rather unlucky experience . . .' Another ill-suited broker who succumbed to the family way was Bernard Bishop, recalled in the memoirs of his remarkable daughter, Dorothy Moriarty:

Our father was a stockbroker and, I suspect, not a very good one. William Henry Bishop, our grandfather, was a successful man with two sons who had refused to go into the family business, two daughters who were nuns, an unmarried daughter who looked after him, and Bernard who was roped into the firm with no choice of another career . . . His escape was into the world of antiques, especially clocks and watches. His greatest friend was an old watchmaker in Clerkenwell . . .

Bernard, 'a tall dapper man with a fair handlebar moustache', became a member in 1888, a year before Dorothy's birth. For another sixteen years he remained under the thumb of his autocratic father – 'a fierce little man whose red face contrasted rather harshly with his white hair and beard . . . a Santa Claus without jollity'. In 1905, following specu-lation in Rio Tintos, W.H. Bishop & Co was declared bankrupt, owing over £50,000. Bernard's father died soon afterwards, a broken man; and though Bernard eventually secured a berth with another firm, the best he had to look forward to was a life of 'genteel poverty'.[101]

The Bishops and Sambournes were not the kind that sprang to mind in 1907 when Morgans fielded an inquiry from the Paris firm, who had a client wanting to know about London brokers:

> W. Greenwell & Co, L. Messel & Co, J. Sebag & Co, are all first-rate Brokers, and you might also mention Messrs Panmure Gordon & Co, and Messrs Rowe & Pitman. Panmure Gordon are probably the most import-ant firm here and Rowe & Pitman are very conservative and active Brokers.
>
> Messrs Williams, de Broë & Co were very active in the days of the South African boom but have considerably curtailed their business since then. We understand them to be trustworthy and quite good for their engagements, but they are probably not as big or as rich as the other people we have mentioned.

Writing to Goldman Sachs a year earlier, Kleinworts provided some detail about the well thought-of Joseph Sebag & Co:

> This firm enjoys the distinction of being one of the richest and most prominent on the London Stock Exchange. The late J. Sebag Montefiore who was for some years the chief partner in the firm was a very wealthy man and at the present time the business is carried on by four of his sons. They possess a first class connection in the City and we regard them as quite undoubted for anything they may do in their line of business.

Sebags was on a rising curve, and so was Panmure Gordon, in the hands of the extremely able Willie Koch, a Belgian, following the much lamented death of the firm's founder in 1902. 'We are impressed with the way Panmure Gordon's do their business now,' commented Morgans in 1906, adding that 'they are intelligent and their methods are more sound than in the days of old P.G.' Koch himself had a high regard for the services he provided, but Émile d'Erlanger, writing his memoirs in 1931, begged to differ. Though conceding that Panmure Gordon was 'by far the leading firm of brokers for public issues before 1914', he argued that the firm's real value was the prestige attached to its name on a prospectus rather than anything more functional:

> When it came to underwriting we could give Panmure Gordon points. There was no firm better than theirs at syndicating an easy Government issue sponsored by one of the old established firms [such as Barings], but when the business was outside their usual line [such as foreign industrials] they were quite unable to underwrite. We, on the other hand, had learned the art of syndicating and placing stocks that were outside the ordinary run and unlike brokers of those early days, who constituted their underwriting syndicates with firms [mainly other broking firms] who wanted to be relieved, many of our underwriters were genuine investors making the allotment of firm stock a condition of their syndicate participation.[102]

There was probably some truth in d'Erlanger's contention, although it was a time-honoured part of City ritual that the merchant banker patronised the stockbroker.

However, if Koch and others were subjected to usually mild condescension, an exception to that rule may well have been Lancelot Grey Hugh Smith. Alfred Wagg recalled him:

> He was known to everybody as Lancie. If one talked of Lancie in City circles, or even in a great many circles outside the City, there was seldom any doubt about whom one meant. I have never met anyone who had so many friends or so many enemies. One could not be indifferent to him. The number of his enemies is perhaps not surprising, for he took no trouble whatever to win the good opinion of anybody in whom he was not interested . . .
> His faults were apparent the very first time one saw him. One resented the somewhat supercilious manner in which he took stock of one. One resented, possibly, his talk about great people he knew, and whom possibly one did not know oneself . . .

'Lancie' was born in 1870, son of the Hugh Colin Smith who ran Hay's Wharf. After Eton and Trinity College, Cambridge, which he left without taking his degree, he had spells at Hay's Wharf and Smiths Bank in Derby before going on a trip to the States in 1897. There he struck up a close friendship with Jack Morgan (son of Pierpont); in due course his eldest brother, Vivian Hugh Smith, became a partner of Morgans in London. By 1898 Lancelot had to decide where his long-term future lay, and against the wishes of his father, by now Governor of the Bank of England, he became a member of the Stock Exchange, joining the firm of Rowe & Pitman. It was a firm only recently founded, and the story goes that George Rowe and Frederick Pitman both being prominent oarsmen, they needed to recruit a dry-bob (which Lancelot was) in order to keep the office ticking over during Henley week.[103]

Lancie soon made his mark. As early as January 1899, Smith St Aubyn was doing business with Speyers 'on introduction of Lancelot H. Smith'; the following year he was sorting out Harry Gibbs's Camp Bird problem, when Arthur Wagg was so baffled. Over the next quarter of a century he was largely responsible for Rowe & Pitman's increasing stature, specialising in time in corporate finance as well as executing business for well-connected, well-heeled private clients. Alfred Wagg analysed the methods of someone who 'loved business, not merely because of the profits which it brought but because it was in his blood':

> He certainly had not got the ability of several other members of his family. He had no patience with detail, but he had great flair. He seemed to possess the gift of being able to 'smell out' that a security was attractive before it ever occurred to other people. The second reason for his success was undoubtedly the devotion of so many friends; for the third reason was that he came of a huge family, not only for brothers [others of whom were at Hambros and Hay's Wharf], but of cousins, first, second and third. He possessed a great feeling of loyalty towards all these relations, and if there was an attractive vacancy, Lancie always knew of some cousin or other who would fill it, and, what is more, I never heard of a single case where his recommendation did not turn out satisfactorily. These relations were naturally grateful to Lancie . . .

At Southsea in 1910, at a supper party after a show, he met Jean Rhys – half his age, from Dominica, and now on tour in the chorus. 'He didn't look at my breasts or my legs, as they usually do. Not that I saw. He looked straight at me and listened to everything I said with a polite and attentive expression, and then he looked away and smiled as if he had sized me up.' It was not long before she became his mistress, and for a time it was paradise: his smell of 'leather and cigars and men's clothes'; the way he looked 'just right – always'; the sheer comfort of the house at 30 Charles Street, just off Berkeley Square. He was, in her biographer's phrase, 'the love of her life', but in 1912 he went on a long visit to the States and parted from her, pensioning her off the next year.[104] For all his City reputation, for all his easy access to grand houses, for all his twenty godchildren, his claim to immortality would be as Walter Jeffries in Rhys's novel *Voyage in the Dark*, a quite fond portrait of a limited man.

*

The City may not have been short of fools, mediocrities and accomplished socialites, but nor was it short of powerful operators. Take Robert Kindersley.[105] Born in 1871, the second son of a manufacturing chemist, his schooling at Repton ended at 15 because of financial problems. He started work at the Millwall Dock Company and then went to the Thames Ironworks, where he became private secretary to the Chairman; he also, in 1896, made a good marriage, to the daughter of a major-general. In 1901 he became a member of the Stock Exchange, the following year a partner in the stockbroking firm David A. Bevan & Co, until in 1906 he was recruited by the merchant bank Lazard Bros, which had associated houses in Paris and New York but in over thirty years had not yet made a great impact in London. It was Kindersley who, through sheer ability and strength of character, turned it into a top-ranking house; and his election in 1914 as a director of the Bank of England recognised the fact.

Sir Alexander Henderson, senior partner of the stockbrokers Greenwood & Co, stayed on the Stock Exchange but still enjoyed major financial clout. He was invariably involved in anything concerning Argentine railways, while at home his chairmanship of the Great Central Railway entirely transformed that line, leading directly to his election in 1909 as Chairman of the Railway Companies Association. He is well caught by his biographer:

> Lord Faringdon [as Henderson became in 1916] was small in stature but great in personality. His handwriting was small and neat, and his notes were almost a personal shorthand as if he was determined to waste nothing: time, ink or pencil. He was practically never seen to throw away a piece of paper; he would scribble memos on the backs of envelopes, tear off the scrap and stuff it into his pockets . . . Invariably courteous to colleagues and to his staff, however junior, he was nevertheless firm in personality. He made it absolutely clear who was the chief.

He was in every sense a City man. 'A few words of advice from him', declared one of the tributes after his death, 'were worth half a dozen speeches from other people, and probably there never was anyone who could say so much in so few words.'[106]

Saemy Japhet, by contrast, was not a member of the Stock Exchange but used it on a daily basis for large-scale operations. A native of Frankfurt, he was still a boy when he started there as a banking junior in 1873. Seven years later he started his own firm, as a foreign agent and local broker, and in 1886 he paid his first visit to London. It 'made an enormous impression upon me and became henceforth the goal to which I was drawn'. In 1891 he moved to Berlin, and at last on 25 May 1896 he opened an office at 31 Throgmorton Street. Japhet's capital was only £15,000, he had few connections in the City and an imperfect grasp of English, and at first almost all his business was fed from his branches in Berlin and Frankfurt. The turning-point came in 1900 when he not only persuaded the Berlin bankers R. Warschauer & Co to inject £50,000 capital but also recruited from them a gifted arbitrageur called Gottfried Loewenstein. In his memoirs Japhet paid due tribute to Loewenstein's 'ability, knowledge, resourcefulness and straightforwardness': 'He was popular in the markets, a great thing for any trader. His "yes" was "yes" and his "no" was "no". He hated to bargain. He quoted his prices and that was "to take or to leave". And that was what people appreciated.' Soon the firm's capital was up to £200,000, necessary to finance big arbitrage positions; and by 1902, when a move was made to more commodious premises in Copthall Avenue, S. Japhet & Co was beginning to get a City reputation, at least among the more discerning:

> About this time we started a so-called Intelligence office. We kept records of almost every security which was quoted on the London Stock Exchange and special files for American Railways, as well as of every kind of International stock. With the greatest care we built up that department and brought it to such a state of efficiency that we were able to be of great service to our clients. Even in London people talked about it. We had more than 4,000 files, and our statistics and charts soon became a valuable and well-known asset.

Japhets themselves were foreign bankers and most of their client base was abroad, but by the mid-1900s the firm was starting to take on some of the functions of a merchant bank. Japhet, with justifiable pride, recalled a revealing episode:

> One evening [in 1905] at a quarter past six, a stout, rather important looking gentleman, betraying the American pure and simple, came in and,

without taking off his hat, or removing his big cigar, said: 'So, it is true!' It was Henry Goldman of Goldman, Sachs & Co and he explained what he meant: He had been enquiring all over the place, whether there was a firm where he could find a partner ready to discuss business either at 9 a.m. or after 6 p.m. He had been recommended to us and started at once to put a certain proposition before us, namely to guarantee an issue of $4,500,000 United Cigar shares on rather attractive conditions. We were expected to take one-third, i.e. $1,500,000 in the business. On Schwelm's suggestion we asked Helbert Wagg to go fifty-fifty with us and they agreed [Adolph Schwelm was a notably able recent recruit, son of a Rothschilds manager in Frankfurt]. Even a participation of $750,000 seemed a little too much for us and in carefully selected words I suggested interesting Amsterdam as well. Goldman said 'Yes', but we could not think of anyone suitable in Holland. I proposed Labouchère Oyens, who were acceptable to all, and I went to Amsterdam the same night where I arranged everything satisfactorily. On my return I found my partners nervous and inclined to withdraw from the deal; they told me a neighbour of ours had approached Hy. Goldman, stating bluntly that we, Japhets, could never carry the deal through. I calmly but firmly declared we must go on even if we should lose over the deal. Hy. Goldman behaved most loyally and we succeeded. It was a brilliant transaction, in which we were able to interest very important people . . .

Over the next few years Japhets did the European underwriting and placing for several more Goldman Sachs issues; German remained the language spoken by partners and most of the staff; and Saemy Japhet himself embodied that time-honoured pattern of the hard-working, determined outsider thrusting himself to the fore.[107]

Japhet was becoming one of the City's truly 'serious men', a class numbered in hundreds rather than thousands and often performing a multiplicity of roles. One such man, quite without frivolity, least of all in monetary matters, was Falconer Larkworthy, who joined the board of the Ionian Bank in 1898 in his mid-60s, after a notable banking career with the Oriental Bank and the Bank of New Zealand. Two years later he became Chairman, and in 1903 it was he who, against Greek opposition led by the National Bank of Greece, successfully ensured renewal of the Ionian Bank's privileges, including the right to issue notes. Larkworthy remained Chairman until 1920 and his annual speeches to the shareholders became famous for their far-reaching coverage of financial questions. Another banker just as powerful in his own predominant sphere was Frederick Goodenough. In 1896, having served directly under Schuster at the Union Bank, he became the first Secretary of Barclays following its historic amalgamation. As General Manager from 1903, and eventually Chairman, he was the crucial outsider who came to exercise an enormous influence over what could have been a *mélange* of squabbling families. It no doubt helped that he was, in his biographer's words, 'a formidable personality, a commanding figure in person and a stern disciplinarian in business'. Or, in a quite different field, that of insurance underwriting, take Edward Mountain. The turning-point of his career came in 1904 when, still in his early 30s, he became managing underwriter of the British Dominions Marine Insurance Company, starting with some £100,000 paid-up capital. 'It is a tribute to his genius,' an admiring contemporary would recall, 'that while at first brokers were rather shy of accepting the security of a new company with rather slender resources, he built up the business until his company became a power in the market.' Before the war he also became an increasingly major figure in the marine insurance market as a whole, doing much not only to standardise policy terms offered by underwriters but also to ensure that competition between Lloyd's and company underwriters was not absurdly cut-throat. A similar capacity to take the broader view characterised Cecil Budd. His business affiliation was the metal-broking firm Vivian, Younger & Bond, and in 1906 a fellow-practitioner described him to Kleinworts as 'a shrewd man' who 'does their business in the ring in a quiet & careful way'. This was the ring of the London Metal Exchange in Whittington Avenue, where under Budd's chairmanship from 1902 the number of members fell at the same time as turnover increased, reflecting a conscious policy on his part of 'closure' and stern entrance qualifications. Budd was a man of the highest standards but no sentimentalist, and his leadership consolidated the LME's position as a world player.[108]

The investment trust movement, becoming more orderly and better regulated after the spectacular boom-and-bust phase of the late 1880s and early 1890s, was a particularly fertile field for emerging City heavyweights.[109] George Touche (the 'e' was added only in 1906), for example, was an Edinburgh man who started his own accountancy firm in 1898. Physically he came to resemble a patriarchal version of George Bernard Shaw; he chaired a smooth company meeting; a particular forte was the reconstruction of companies; and, like several other leading City accountants, he was intimately involved with investment trusts. By the 1900s a handful of investment trust groups stood out, among them that controlled by John Wynford Philipps and known as the St Davids (after his elevation to the peerage in 1908) or 69 Old Broad Street group. The group was held together by an elaborate network of cross-shareholdings and interlocking directorships, with Philipps himself a master of the spider's stratagem. The doyen of the investment trust movement, however, remained Robert Fleming, who in 1900 opened a London office, a perhaps grudging recognition of the indispensable City. Six years later he was the subject of a letter of introduction written by Gaspard Farrer of Barings: 'Mr Fleming hails from Aberdeenshire and has been actively engaged in business all his life, chiefly dealing in American securities, of which I consider him to be the best judge in this country. He is now a rich man with a very large following; he is as straight as a die and in every way reliable, moreover an excellent man of business.'[110] Farrer was a demanding judge of character, as well as a specialist in American railroads, so this was a notable tribute.

Robert ('Robin' to family and friends) Benson may not have been quite in Fleming's league as a controller of investment trusts, but he was a more powerful figure in the City at large, operating discreetly behind many different scenes.[111] He was an attractive man with a keen sense of humour; a deep interest in the theory of finance ('What is money?' he would ask over the port) did not distract him from life's practicalities; he moved easily in society, enjoyed political contacts at the highest level and over the years played an important part in reorganising the British electrical industry as well as several American railroads. 'I have joined the Board of the Anglo American Telegraph Co – not that it is particularly attractive – but F. Bevan of Barclays has taken the Chair, & wanted me.'[112] So Benson wrote to the fourth Earl Grey in 1897, an eloquent reminder that for a City man like himself, who had already made the bulk of his serious money, the accumulation of directorships and other responsibilities was motivated less by mercenary considerations than those of duty and friendship. Much the same probably applied during this period to the banker Richard (Sir Richard from 1905) Biddulph Martin, MP, though since business in the City was conducted so much on a personal basis it is not in general an easy distinction to make. Take his appointments diary for a more or less typical week, in February 1895:

Monday	12	Corporation of Foreign Bondholders
Tuesday	3.30	British North Borneo Company
Wednesday	2	Charing Cross Hospital
	5	Institute of Bankers
Thursday	10.45	Martin's [Bank]
	1	Fishmongers [Company]
	2.30	Council of Foreign Bondholders
Friday	11.30	Vacuum Brake
	12.30	Anglo-American Debenture Corporation

	Foreign and Colonial Debenture Corporation
1	Assets Realisation Company
1.30	New Municipal Trust
2	Debenture Corporation

No wonder, granted these many outside distractions, that Martin's declined under his leadership; no wonder that it possessed so many connections that its decline was only gentle.[113]

In the turn-of-the-century City, however, the two *really* big operators – enormously rich, fingers in innumerable pies, their lightest word most men's command – were Cassel and Ellerman.[114] 'He is a Jew and socially a parasite. But he has the reputation of being straight in business and certainly has ability and great courage.' This view of Cassel, expressed by Dawkins to Milner in July 1901, would have been shared by most merchant bankers; but over the next few months Dawkins's admiration became less grudging, while Hamilton, having worked closely with him over Boer War finance, was by 1903 even more of a convert: 'I regard Cassel as far the ablest man in the City. He takes a broad & disinterested view: & he takes a line of his own. His has been a marvellous rise, but he has not had his head turned in the least nor at all spoilt. I like the man very much.' A plausible assessment of what made this essentially reclusive man tick comes from the memoirs of George Cornwallis-West. After noting that 'with all his cold, hard-headed, hard-hearted business nature he had many kindly feelings', he went on:

> I believe that neither money nor social position meant anything to him beyond the power they gave him. Power meant everything to him. His friendship with King Edward was, so far as he, Cassel, was concerned, founded on his love of power; it helped to that end. In his speech he was curt and to the point. I never heard him speak on any subject with which he was not thoroughly conversant, but when he did talk he was inclined to lay down the law and resent argument.

Cornwallis-West may have been a little unfair about Cassel's feelings towards Edward, but the larger point is valid. It was a power that rested partly on a marvellous array of international contacts, but above all on unrivalled judgement and decisiveness. He never quite lost the need to prove himself and until he was in his 60s worked hard and travelled widely on behalf of his multifarious global interests. Perhaps no great businessman ever does lose a certain prickliness. When an associate sent him the text of a putative reply to a shipping magnate in

May 1902, Cassel's response was – as ever – crisp, to the point and impossible to argue with: 'I am at loss to understand the scheme which you propose but since I did not intend to discuss any plan until I had an opportunity of ascertaining personally what the views of the government are it does not matter in the least.'[115]

That shipping magnate was not, as it happened, John Ellerman. One of the most remarkable men in the City, he was, like Cassel, one of the least publicised, and only the broad outlines of his career can be identified with certainty. He was born in Hull in 1862, the son of a corn merchant and shipbroker of Lutheran background who had migrated there from Hamburg twelve years earlier. He was educated at various inexpensive schools, at home and abroad, an education that ended at about the age of 16 when he became articled to a Birmingham chartered accountant. After a few years he moved to London, working for the City accountants Quilter, Ball & Co. That firm soon offered him a partnership, but he preferred in 1886 to start his own firm, J. Ellerman & Co, at 10 Moorgate. Like other accountants he appreciated early on the potential of investment trusts, and by 1891 he was in control of four trust companies. This was an impressive start to any career, but the real lift-off came in 1892 following the sudden death of the leading ship owner Frederick Leyland. Ellerman, O'Hagan and the ship owner Christopher Furness formed a syndicate that took over Leyland & Co, with Ellerman before long replacing Furness as Chairman, amidst some acrimony. O'Hagan, writing well over thirty years later, recalled the outcome:

> The company did not suffer from the change, for it got all the advantages of Ellerman's exceptional abilities; he took to shipping as a duck takes to water, threw his whole energies into the business, agreed with the view of the Liverpool management that large cargo-ships were the thing of the future, expanded his ideas, and launched out on a big shipbuilding programme . . . He quickly put the Leyland Company into the first line, and after many years, principally, although not entirely, devoted to shipping, he has become the biggest shipowner in the world and his position and influence in the shipping world have become unrivalled.[116]

By the turn of the century he was no longer an accountant at all, instead wheeling and dealing rapidly in a succession of shipping lines. During the 1900s he continued to build up his shipping interests, in 1905 he was given a baronetcy, in 1907 he was elected President of the British Chamber of Shipping. He also acquired substantial interests in breweries and collieries as well as the press. By 1910, still City-based, he was the richest man in Britain.

In his personal life, Ellerman had a daughter, born in 1894, who in time became the novelist and poet Bryher; her memoirs, *The Heart to Artemis* (1963), give a clear picture of her otherwise shadowy father. For her first four years they lived in Bayswater, until in 1898 he 'bought a small house in Worthing', in Queen's Road. 'He came down on Friday from a mysterious place where he must never be disturbed called "the office" and took the first train back on the Monday morning.' During weekends he would take his family mushroom–picking on Chanctonbury Ring; or his daughter down to the sea; or to a local football match, 'if I would promise not to cry if a ball hit me'. She adds: 'I never saw a first-class match but once. My father thought them too mechanical, he liked the small-town atmosphere of our local team, perhaps it reminded him of his own schoolboy games?' Although not a pacifist, he would not allow the Boer War to be discussed in her presence; and on a visit to the Paris Exhibition in May 1900, he hurried her out of the building containing all the Krupps guns, explaining 'that it was wrong to spend money and labour upon tools of war'. He loved travelling. 'Years later I saw his application for a passport. In answer to a question, "Do you often travel abroad?" he had replied "As much as possible, it broadens the intelligence." ' In 1903 the family moved from Worthing to 'a small house' in Eastbourne, with no thought apparently of acquiring a big country house or any of the other usual accoutrements of wealth. 'I was always more interested in money, I think, than my father. He was a mathematician and his interests were in abstractions. I have seldom known anyone more remote from the things of this world . . . He possessed the detachment that lifts finance into an art . . . I believe now that my father could have become a religious leader as easily as a financier, he had such an extraordinary inner detachment.'[117] Physically Ellerman bore (like some other City men) a certain resemblance to King Edward VII; but unlike Cassel he felt neither the need nor the wish to become that monarch's friend.

For every millionaire, celebrated or otherwise, there were many wholly anonymous functionaries – equally 'serious men' in their own right, though in a different sense. A figure memorable not only for his name is Samuel J. Pipkin, general manager of the Atlas Assurance Company for over thirty years. Reminiscing to his peers in 1916 on his life in the City, it was as if he spoke for the generation that came to the fore in the era of joint-stock organisation, a generation for whom, at last, merit rather than personal connection represented the royal road to advancement:

We are of necessity and duty restricted to the work of our Offices; consequently it is not to be expected that a body of men getting their livings out of Insurance, as paid officials of Companies, should have many opportunities of meeting the magnates of the outer world, or take part in public or national affairs . . . I do not mean by this that we are not to be, to *any* extent, occupied with other matters. But our primary duty is to mind our own business, and in doing that in these times of difficulty and pressure we shall find we have not much time for other things.

I have no doubt many of us have thought we would like to be in Parliament or occupy the Chair of London's Lord Mayor, but the official who fancies he can assume these honours and do his duty to his Company, I venture to think, makes a mistake . . .[118]

CHAPTER SIXTEEN

Something about Them

Edward came to the throne in January 1901, and Hamilton's diary recorded the social ascent of the man who had been that extravagant prince's financial adviser for five years already:

> *13 May 1901.* I quite made up my mind that, when he came to the throne, the King would have such a sense of his own dignity and be so determined to play the part of monarch that he would only dine at exceptional houses – like Devonshire House, Embassies, Lord Salisbury's &c. But after dining with Cassel [at his London home, 48 Grosvenor Square] of course he can dine anywhere. I regret it much.
>
> *18 April 1902.* Cassel appears to be quite indispensable just now. He only left the Royal Yacht a few days ago. He has now gone to Sandringham, & he has the King dining with him on Monday. It would look as if there was more than meets the eye – at least that will be the conclusion which people will come to.
>
> *8 June 1904.* The Horace Farquhars gave a ball last night in honour of the King & Queen. I went for a little time after first dining with Cassel who had a large party. He has gone up wonderfully in the social scale: so much so that tongues which were dead against him are now silenced.

It was a significant reference to the relentlessly opportunistic Farquhar, appointed Master of the Royal Household at the start of the new reign. 'An epicure, and a good man of business,' was how the King's friend Lord Esher (the former Reggie Brett) aptly described him. Esher himself had a position at the Office of Works and took responsibility for organising the King's coronation. A life change, though, was pending, charted in letters to his younger son:

> *3 December 1901.* Sir Ernest Cassel – who is one of the greatest of financial magnates – and whom I met at dinner at Frogmore, called on me today and made me much the same sort of offer that Pierpont Morgan made Dawkins. If I would leave the office and associate myself with him in great enterprises in Egypt and America – to give me a large share in his business . . . If it comes off, it will not be till June next. If I accept it will

322

be for your sake.

9 December 1901. This evening I called on Cassel as arranged. This is his offer. An arrangement for 3 years – in case we fail to get on. During that 3 years he guarantees me £5000 a year, and also 10 per cent upon any profits made in enterprises in which he is engaged. It is really a very handsome offer, as this means a large sum if things go right. His one stipulation is that the King should be got to acquiesce . . .

7 July 1902. I went on to the City, and did my first day there. It was interesting and novel.

9 July 1902. I went to the City for half an hour today – a very short spell. I think Cassel rather likes me. He is very kind and considerate at present. I don't know how long it will last.

Esher had, in *DNB*'s accurate words, 'marked ability, great social gifts, and influential connexions'; and for Cassel, at this particular stage in his career, these were qualities that seemed well worth paying for, whatever his new assistant's lack of financial training or palpable financial acumen.[1]

The moneyed circle around Edward VII was only the most prominent manifestation of what all observers saw, with varying degrees of enthusiasm, as the rapid plutocratisation of high society.[2] This process of integration, between finance and land, between the City and the British aristocracy, produced the not always industrious specimen whom modern historians[3] have dubbed as the 'gentlemanly capitalist' – like Riversdale Grenfell, son of the merchant banker Pascoe Grenfell. Born in 1880 at Hatchlands in Surrey, Rivy left Eton to become what his biographer John Buchan called 'a decorous clerk in the Bank of England'. Then, in January 1902, he was 'given a post in the office of the Charter Trust, of which his brother Arthur was a director and Lord Grey chairman'. However, Buchan went on, Rivy 'had plenty of time to spare for amusements, and his letters [to his twin brother Francis] were full of tantalising accounts of runs with the Quorn and the Belvoir and the Windsor drag, dances, week-ends at Cliveden, Ascot, and Westonbirt, parties in London, endless bachelor dinners'. The last weekend of May 1902 he spent at Terling, home of Lord Rayleigh, and among the other guests was Balfour, recipient in these final hours of war of a flurry of telegrams from Kitchener. The episode made a powerful impression on young Rivy:

After dinner on Saturday they discussed peace. Balfour said he did not like the telegram at all, but what made him hopeful was that the City was so confident. In all probability the City knew more about it than he did, as he only heard the news from Kitchener and Milner, against telegrams

323

from all over Africa. This came as rather an eye-opener to me when one considered that fellows in the City were looking to Arthur Balfour as knowing about ten thousand times more than they did . . .

Over the next few years Rivy's career in the square mile flourished in a mild sort of way, and in 1905 he managed to read Pope's translation of the *Iliad* 'largely during working hours in his City office'.[4]

It was marriage that lay at the operational heart of this fusion between the City elites and the traditional landed ruling class. 'Brien Cokayne is going to be married in October to Miss Marsham niece of Lord Romney,' reported Alban Gibbs in August 1904 of his brother-in-law, a partner in the firm and a recently elected director of the Bank of England; he added that 'all the family are much pleased'.[5] Cokayne was one of the '460', a richly suggestive sample that has recently been conducted of 460 partners or directors of the leading London-based private banks, merchant banks and joint-stock banks as well as the directors of the Bank of England, all these bankers flourishing between 1890 and 1914.[6] It reveals that almost three-quarters of them were educated at a public school and/or Oxbridge; that over a third married into the aristocracy and the gentry; that another quarter married into social groups traditionally linked with land; and that three-fifths left a fortune of over £100,000. The survey also reveals that almost half had a residence in both London and the country, that Mayfair and Belgravia were far and away the most favoured London addresses, and that the most popular club was the Carlton, followed at a respectful distance by Brooks's, the Athenaeum and the Reform. In short, to be a leading banker in the turn-of-the-century City was to be not merely within the fabled ten thousand but – in many cases at least – somewhere near the centre of that self-selecting *crème de la crème*.

Most members of the Stock Exchange were not in that ten thousand, even though the large majority had been educated at recognisable public schools. A glance at the letter 'M' in the membership book for 1896–7 confirms the broadly suburban, middle- to upper-middle-class impression: Frederick Matthews lived at 56 Marmora Road in Honor Oak; Stuart Maxwell at 19 Walm Lane in Willesden Green; Charles Mead at 31 Victoria Road in Old Charlton; Henry Medley at 11 Great Western Road in Westbourne Park; Hartwig Meyer at 53 Fitzjohn's Avenue in Hampstead; Gordon Mitchison at 35 Greyhound Lane in Streatham; Herbert Monnington at 9 Morland Road in Croydon; and Claude Muirhead at 16 Woodlands Road in Barnes. Even so, still under 'M', there are some higher-class addresses. Alexander MacRosty set out most mornings from West Bank, Esher; Walter Marshall from The Bridge, Godalming; James Martin from Woodhall, Sevenoaks; Henry Mason from The Grange, Whetstone; Surtees Monkland from Châlet, Datchet; and Lord Charles Montagu from Devonshire House, Piccadilly.[7] Montagu, a partner in Montagu, Oppenheim & Co of 22 Austin Friars, was the second son of the Duke of Manchester and, in his mid-30s, was already well embarked on his career as one of the leading 'society' stockbrokers, enjoying a rare quality of connection.[8] Another was Basil Montgomery, senior partner of Basil Montgomery & Co, one of the firms that Whitaker Wright accused of having ditched him. His town address was 5 Carlos Place, off Grosvenor Square, and by 1901 he had acquired a country property near Romsey in Hampshire. Eddy Hamilton was a typically appreciative guest over the Whit holiday: 'Basil Montgomery has made the place charming & showed much good taste. Hardwicke is here . . . B.M. has started a motor-car . . .' Hardwicke was Lord 'Tommy' Hardwicke, an impecunious young peer, an intimate of the Rothschilds, a partner in Montgomery's firm and, at least as much to the point, Under-Secretary of State for India. His appointment to the position caused a parliamentary storm in 1900, granted Salisbury's decision that he could still remain a sleeping partner; and though Carl Meyer commented privately at the time that 'everybody is sympathetic to Hardwicke and considers him straight as a die', this conjunction of interests marked in the eyes of the outside world a further stage in the Stock Exchange's chequered odyssey.[9]

Life in Capel Court could not have gone on without the existence of a substantial class of people willing to invest or speculate in stocks and shares.[10] When in March 1898 there occurred the spectacularly successful flotation of Liptons the grocery chain, with Panmure Gordon and Helbert Wagg as co-brokers, Sir Thomas Lipton took personal charge of the invidious matter of who got what. 'Dukes and Marquises were allotted in full,' according to the story passed down to Alfred Wagg; 'Earls, Viscounts and Barons received 50 per cent, Baronets and Honourables 25 per cent, and the general members of the public nil. I believe a certain number of Society beauties were considered as ranking equally with Dukes and Marquises for the purposes of allotment.' Three years later, when a National Telephone issue brought out by Morgans fared poorly, Dawkins commented to Jack Morgan that 'our underwriters have all behaved very well and are not dissatisfied, with the exception of one Peer, to whom we gave a share at the personal request of Mr Everard Hambro'.[11]

In general, though, it was not just faint hearts and coronets that comprised the British investing class – a class that, even by 1914, still probably numbered less than a million people in terms of serious shareholders. 'Ah, my good woman,' ran the caption to a celebrated *Punch* cartoon of the 1890s showing a dean being importuned for alms by a beggar, 'it is not only the poor who have their troubles; you, for instance, have probably never experienced the difficulty of finding investments combining adequate security with a remunerative rate of interest.' This anxious eminent might easily have been serviced by Foster & Braithwaite, long-established, highly respectable stock-brokers with a particular emphasis on individual client business. From the firm's voluminous copper-plate ledgers covering 1907–11, a dip into the 'B' pages shows an array of equally respectable-sounding clients.[12] The Rev J.F. Banham of St Neots, the Hon George Bruce of St James's Street, SW, the Misses Benson of Torquay, R.W. Bullard of the British Embassy in Constantinople, H.E. Blagdon-Richards of Car-marthen, T.B. Bolitho of Penzance (from the Cornish banking family), C. Bury of Wotton-under-Edge near Gloucester – all were probably, in a real or honorary sense, 'gentlemanly capitalists'. This was the age of the *rentier*, those legendary widows of Kensington and Cheltenham whose principal income derived from Stock Exchange securities, like the Schlegels' aunt, Mrs Munt, in E.M. Forster's *Howards End* (1910), living in Swanage with an irrational, unshakeable attachment to Home Rails.

*

In his old age, recalling on radio the Cookham of his childhood – how the stockbrokers used to bathe in the Thames early on summer mornings before catching their train to London, and how he would join them in order to feel that he was one of the grand people – Stanley Spencer said in a musing voice: 'They know how to live. There's something about them.' That was certainly the popular mythology, yet in practice stockbrokers, like City men as a whole, varied so greatly in their life-styles that it is hard to make sure generalisations. Living in one of the more distinctive environments was Walter de Zoete, senior partner of de Zoete & Gorton until his retirement in 1909 and owner of Layer Marney, a red-brick pile near Colchester built in 1532 to rival Hampton Court but never completed. He lived in the eight-storey tower; converted the stables into a huge pannelled room where he could display to friends his pictures and antique furniture; employed fourteen domestic staff and fifteen gardeners, and built a pavilion at the bottom of his extensive lawns, across which a butler would wheel tea on a trolley. Not so far away, in the Chelmsford area, lived another stockbroker, John Henry Vigne, whose family had been on the Stock Exchange for generations but who was still considered a poor match when he married the the daughter of a London doctor. They were not particularly rich and the youngest of their seven children, Henry, born in 1898, only went to Harrow because he won a scholarship. Even so, their rented house at Writtle Wick had eight bedrooms, giving employment to seven indoor staff and six outdoors.[13]

Alternatively, take a clutch of Stock Exchange members whose homes were all in London. Frank Gielgud, living in South Kensington and from 1912 a partner in Messels, was remembered by his son John (born in 1904):

> He was very alarming when he was angry, and very charming at other times. I owe to him such grounding as I possess in music, painting and history, and he never tried to crush my mania for the theatre, which he loved himself within more modest bounds.
>
> He deplored the extravagance which seemed to be natural to all his children . . . Father gave us all allowances and latch-keys at an early age, but frowned severely on taxis, theatre seats and expensive restaurants. He always travelled by bus himself, went to the theatre in the pit, and chose the hard seats above the organ at the Albert Hall, because you could hear there better than anywhere else.

Living nearby in Cadogan Place, but rarely travelling by bus, was Arthur Philip Cazenove, in his way a classic stockbroker of the period; genial, easy-going, and disinclined to desert a steady routine, whether mental or physical. He was a life-member of the MCC; while after leaving the City, and before returning home, he would spend most of the afternoon in his West End club. It was not for nothing that (following the Russo-Japanese war) he was known as 'Port Arthur', and in general his presence seems to have been as comforting and comfortable as the name suggests. Another, even more assiduous clubman was Edward Wagg, younger brother of Arthur. He was a bachelor who most evenings dined at the Savoy and then went on to the Garrick for a game of bridge. For weekends he had a country home near Maidenhead, and he also rented an extensive shoot at Glenlochay. His intelligence was more original than that of his brother, and during the Baring crisis of 1890 he was in Scotland when he received a telegram from his partners requiring his presence on the first floor at 18 Old

Broad Street. 'If by returning to London,' he wired back, 'I could save
Barings I would do so. If not I will remain here.' He remained at
Glenlochay.[14]

Cazenove and Wagg were both born to the stockbroking purple,
unlike Max Karo, a German born about 1876 who lived to see his
rather incoherent memoirs, *City Milestones and Memories*, published
in 1962. As a young man he left his native Breslau to join E. Spiegel &
Co, a firm of foreign bankers on the Berlin Bourse. Spiegels soon
afterwards transferred its headquarters to London, whence Karo came
at the end of 1896 as a junior clerk, running messages between the
Bishopsgate office and the Stock Exchange. Outside working hours,
this small, wiry and energetic immigrant lived in a boarding house in
St George's Square, near Regent's Park, enjoyed tea at Claridge's for
half-a-crown on Saturday afternoons, and on Sundays drove in a gig to
Richmond, with another half-crown tea there at the Star and Garter
Hotel. In the early 1900s he became an unauthorised clerk on the
Stock Exchange and moved to a boarding house in Petherton Road,
Canonbury; and in 1909 he achieved membership as well as a junior
partnership in a stockbroking firm, moving at about the same time to
'a very superior boarding-house at Lancaster Gate', where there also
lived the barrister Henry Pridham-Wippell and the Kent amateur batsman Edward Dillon. During these last years before the war, Karo also
spent as much of his summers as he could at the St Ives Hotel in
Maidenhead, being 'a nice "pension" where one could always enjoy an
easy-going and a free life'.[15]

Inevitably, there was an equal miscellany of life-styles in the commercial sector. Julius Caesar Czarnikow kept on his London home in
Eaton Square, but in the evening of his days also acquired a mansion
at Effingham Hill in Surrey. The coal merchant John Charrington III,
no longer content with the fine family house overlooking Clapton
Common, bought Shenley Grange in Hertfordshire. In 1903 a Mr
Bussweiler, late partner of the Mincing Lane merchants Alden,
Symington & Co, informed Kleinworts that he and Symington had
'always spent too much money' and that 'Symington keeps his sisters
and occupies a very nice house at Chislehurst'. A few years later the
West India merchants Henry K. Davson & Co of 79 Mark Lane were
under scrutiny:

Carey & Browne, 6 July 1906. Sir Henry Davson made money as a
Storekeeper at Berbice and put some into Sugar Estates, which are said to
be well equipped with up to date machinery. His income is believed to be

derived almost entirely from this source. He lives in a very extravagant manner especially since he was knighted, and he has extravagant sons.

C. *Czarnikow, 23 May 1907.* Very respectable people. Sir Henry Davson is vice Chairman of the West India Committee ... He rather poses as a society man since his knighthood.

These merchants were all on the free-spending side of the ledger, but there was more variety in a trio from the world of shipping. Septimus Glover of the Baltic Exchange lived in a large house in Highbury, rode every morning to Highbury Station, and always wore in his buttonhole an orchid from his hothouse. The shipbroker and chartering agent Eustace Erlebach, son of a Congregationalist minister in Wiltshire, also lived in north London, but was a life-long teetotaller, helped to found Crouch End Hockey Club, and loved nothing better than to spend musical evenings with his family. Henry Poland, son of an Oxford Street furrier and fifty-five years in 'the Room' as an underwriter at Lloyd's, moved in 1889 from Blackheath to a substantial house at Caterham in Surrey, where he waged a one-man campaign against alcoholism and formed the Caterham Village Club as an alternative social focus to the wicked hostelries.[16]

However, for that elusive 'representative figure' one turns again to a son's recollections. 'My own family,' wrote Cecil Beaton, 'was typical of the Edwardian upper-middle class, and could not have been more English.' His father was Ernest Beaton, born in 1867, son of one of the founders of Beaton Bros, a firm that specialised in importing timber, especially sleepers. Ernest continued the family business, and Cecil himself was born in 1904 'in a small, tall, red brick house of ornate, but indiscriminate Dutch style at 21 Langland Gardens in Hampstead'. The firm prospered, and soon the family moved 'nearer to Hampstead Heath into a vaguely neo-Georgian mansion named "Temple Court", also of red brick with lots of white paint, its chief assets being that it was light and spacious, that there was a billiard room, and two great oak trees with black trunks in the garden'. Ernest enjoyed billiards and rode on the Heath but his passion was cricket (he kept wicket), and it was watching him play that the young Cecil first 'knew the meaning of boredom'. His favourite book was *Vanity Fair*, which he claimed to have read thirty times; before marrying he 'had been quite a well-known amateur actor', and thereafter he 'continued to indulge his histrionic gift for mimicry'; and yet, 'my father was always so evasive of intimacy that it was often embarrassing for me to be alone in a room with him'. Each August the family rented a house in Sheringham or Cromer, in accordance with Ernest's belief that 'the rolling grey waves and the bracing winds of Norfolk would set us all up for the winter'. In sum: 'The months of the year went by with cricket, golf, tennis, billiards and croquet, and riding horseback on the heath. We enjoyed simple jokes and an occasional outing: a picnic on the river at Henley, or a very rare visit to the theatre . . . Roast beef meant Sunday lunch . . . It was a blazingly blue-eyed, happy, healthy, respectable household.'[17]

Charles Addis would have approved.[18] In January 1905, after over twenty years in the East working for the Hongkong and Shanghai Bank, he began a new phase of his career as the bank's London manager. A cultured and able man who also worked exceedingly hard, he soon emerged as a significant City figure. Addis himself (born in 1861) was the son of a Free Church minister. He married the daughter of a Scottish provost, and his diary records rather touchingly the value he placed upon family life in their home near Primrose Hill:

17 March 1905. This is a most convenient place. Five minutes to Chalk Farm where there are trains every quarter of an hour to Broad St. With my uncertain hours at night nothing could well be more convenient. On mail nights I get home about 7, other nights about 6.

30 June 1905. A heavy mail day . . . I have been working like a slave – hasty chop in office &c.

11 August 1905. What a life! Slave all day. Home at night dog-tired. Dinner, sleep of a sort, and back to work again.

27 October 1905. The last night of the Promenade Concerts at Queen's Hall. Wood's orchestra surpassed itself and Wood received a tremendous ovation at the close.

2 December 1905. Home dead tired . . . The good Eba read Ivanhoe aloud while I rested beautifully.

16 March 1906. Dined with Carl Meyer at The Carlton Hotel to meet Geo. Jamieson [a former colleague of Addis] and four others – mostly connected with the Peking Syndicate. Much talk of Chinese railways &c. It was interesting but somehow I did not much like to see my old friend mixed up with the stockbroking fraternity.

4 January 1907. Reading A.C. Pigou's Principles & Methods of Industrial Peace. I find it stiff reading. But in truth my mental powers are exhausted by night. I am being ground up in this business machine.

10 March 1907 (Sunday). Eba & I with 6 children in front seat of St Stephen's as usual. What a happy day it is! Dinner at 1. Then Eba has a quiet bible hour with the bairns while I have a quiet hour in my study. At 3 the 3 or 4 eldest set off to Hampstead Heath where the children scuttle about like rabbits – so full of glee. Tea 5. Hymns in the drawing room. Then all in study to listen to a story read aloud till bedtime. Happy happy days![19]

There are affinities between Addis and that merchant newcomer of forty years earlier, William Lidderdale, both of whom viewed City men and manners through shrewd Scottish eyes, with a healthy grasp of what mattered.

One of those City men was Panmure Gordon's Belgian dynamo. 'Koch's dinner at Belgrave Square,' noted Addis in November 1908. 'Grand affair. 12 guests and 6 serving men. Moet 93. Well done and less boring than usual.' Almost two years later Addis was in Antwerp, being collected one teatime by Koch and driven to the stockbroker's estate at Gooreynd. His descriptions to Eba over the next three days suggested a high-class holiday camp, with the occasional bout of work thrown in, although his diary for the 7th struck a rather different note: 'No time for reading here. Koch is unresting, poor man. He must keep moving.'[20]

By this time Addis was getting used to the country-house game; but a little earlier, in August 1909, his weekend visit to the country home of Carl Meyer had proved a more unsettling experience. On his return to London, he treated Eba to a detailed account of the Saturday:

> A motor was waiting at Audley End station and drove me through the beautiful wrought iron gates of Shortgrove, across the quaint old bridge with three spans under which the Cam glides sleepily below, with a vignette on one side of a curious classic temple on the bank and on the other a covey of wild duck. The drive winds up hill, through the finest timber I have ever seen anywhere, to Shortgrove itself, an old Queen Anne mansion four stories high and 13 windows wide. Two centre halls with galleries on which the bedrooms open. In the dining room a superb portrait of Mrs Meyer by Sargeant [*sic*] ... Everywhere curious furniture, old pictures, superb carpets and tapestries. Fine library but not up to the rest of the house in my idea. For many of the fine books I noticed were uncut and oh! horreur, in one corner stood a pianola.
>
> Carl Meyer met me at the door. We walked through the house and emerged on the glorious lawn backed by the most astonishing variety of trees, among them an old oak said to be over 1000 years old. The space is wonderful. Two cricket pitches, a private golf course, croquet lawn, several tennis nets and a swimming bath, not to mention the rifle range.
>
> We watched for a while the cricket match that was going on between the local cricketers and a London eleven.
>
> Tea was served in a Japanese house on the lawn from which Mrs Meyer advanced smiling to meet me.
>
> A short plump blonde, wavy grey hair, very dark eyebrows and eyelashes, beautiful white teeth which she shows a good deal, fresh complexion, earrings, different sets for morning and evening, white dress with lace about it ... She ripples along about higher education and

vocation schools and health culture and music and I don't know what all
in the best approved society style. Altogether a society beauty fashionably
interested in 'movements' and 'causes' and affairs generally, an agreeable
woman, not deep or learned but with good impulses in her fashionable
way. A Jewess but that does not strike you . . .

After tea Mrs M. took me through such lovely old gardens, roseries and
kitchen garden . . . Against the south wall was about 100 yards of tall
sweet peas of wonderful variety looking like so many butterflies. The
carnations – but I cannot go on.

We went over the stables next, old and extensive like the house, saw the
model cottages and the home farm and the pedigree herd of Jersey cows
and so to dress for dinner . . .

Excellent dinner, lobster, grouse &c . . . Coffee and cigars on verandah
in open air.

Bedroom very fine with Empire furniture. Old prints and oil paintings.
Superb views across the Cam. And there I lay, amidst all that luxury
could do to lull one pleasantly to sleep, and counted the hours as they
tolled from the stable tower until as dawn broke I fell into a short and
troubled repose.

That quizzical country-house visitor, Henry James, could hardly
have made a better job of it. He would have appreciated the
opportunity, for when the Sargent portrait of Mrs Meyer and her
two children was exhibited at the Royal Academy in 1897, a
consummation of *fin de siècle* opulence, he praised its 'wonderful
rendering of life, of manners, of aspects, of types, of textures, of
everything . . .'[21]

Almost a century later, in 1992, the Sargent painting surfaced
again, appropriately as the cover for a cut-price paperback edition
of James's *The Ambassadors*. That same year saw Anthony
Hopkins playing the embodiment of the City husband, as Henry Wilcox
in the Merchant/Ivory film adaptation of E.M. Forster's *Howards End*.
Forster's real-life Mr Wilcox was a stockbroker called Charles Poston.[22] He lived at Highfield, a mansion in Stevenage, and Forster first
met him in 1906. Poston died seven years later, and (life imitating art)
his widow Clementine moved with her two children into Rooksnest,
Forster's childhood home near Stevenage, which had served as the
model for Howards End. Poston alias Wilcox would become for
successive generations the archetype of practical, materialist man:
kindly but unimaginative; civilised but hypocritical; convinced that
everyone has his price; crucially unable to connect the prose and the
passion. He would be, among other things, the ultimate progenitor of
this book.

Certainly there was no shortage of gentlemanly capitalists in these golden years. 'We had a first rate time in Scotland,' reported Herbert Gibbs to his brother Alban in October 1902, adding that 'I got the 85th stag at 5.30 on the last day so we ran it rather fine.' The new Lord Mayor a fortnight later was Sir Marcus Samuel, whose country house (The Mote, near Maidstone) came complete with a particularly scenic cricket ground; while during the week he lived in a palatial mansion in Portland Place and travelled to and from the City 'in a victoria, with a pair of horses, and a coachman and footman on the box'. Or take Gurney Sheppard, senior partner from 1905 of the stockbrokers Sheppards, Pellys & Co: relishing a life-style that owed little to his Quaker ancestors, he lived at The Ham (near Wantage) and was especially fond of hunting, polo and steeplechasing. In the summer of 1908 the Webbs had another of their glancing encounters with the City when Sir Julius Wernher offered them the use of a small house on his Bedfordshire estate so that they could draw up in peace their report on the Poor Law, an act of generosity that Beatrice after four weeks was only semi-grateful for:

> The family spend some Sundays at Luton Hoo and a few months in the autumn, but all the rest of the 365 days the big machine goes grinding on, with its 54 gardeners, 10 electricians, 20 or 30 house servants and endless labourers for no one's benefit . . . The great mansion stood, closed and silent, in the closed and silent park – no one coming or going except the retinue of servants, the only noises the perpetual whirring and calling of the thousands of pheasants, ducks and other game that were fattening ready for the autumn slaughter. At the gates of the park, a bare half-mile distant, lay the crowded town of Luton – drunken, sensual, disorderly – crowded in mean streets, with a terrific infant mortality. The contrast was oppressively unpleasant, and haunted our thoughts as we sat under the glorious trees and roamed through wood and garden, used their carriages, enjoyed the fruit, flowers and vegetables, and lived for a brief interval in close contact with an expenditure of £30,000 a year on a country house alone.

A year and an autumn slaughter later, King Edward VII was among Sir Everard Hambro's guests for a three-day shoot at Milton Abbey in Dorset. Ten guns managed to despatch nearly three thousand pheasants, full value by even the most demanding royal standards.[23]

'Gentlemanly capitalism', nevertheless, remains a problematic, potentially reductive concept – one liable to underestimate the diversity of cultures that inhabited and shaped the City.[24] Even within the strictly limited sphere of the leading merchant banking houses, there were fundamental differences between, say, Barings and Rothschilds on the one hand, Kleinworts and Schröders on the other. 'The two brothers K work hard, are very economical & have large capital,' noted E.C. Grenfell of Morgan Grenfell in 1912. It was not that the partners in Kleinworts and Schröders did not acquire country homes, for they did; it was rather that these acquisitions tended to be of moderate size and, above all, that their single-minded attention to the counting house rarely slackened. Put another way, these two firms may have been the leading acceptors in the pre-war London market, but few in the outside world had yet heard of them.[25] Much of the City's pluralism rested on the fact that it was still an essentially 'open' place, even though there were in the Edwardian period some significant, ominous tendencies towards 'closure' – in the wool trade, on the London Metal Exchange, on Lloyd's (new members requiring deposits of at least £5,000), even from 1904 on the Stock Exchange.[26] Yet the notion of the pre-1914 City as somewhere that 'offered opportunities to all-comers and barred no-one' remains persuasive.[27] Take Lionel Robinson.[28] He was born in 1866 the son of an Australian financial journalist, as a young man bought a seat on the Melbourne Stock Exchange, and during the 1890s emerged as an authority on mining securities. In 1899 he moved to London and became a member of the Stock Exchange, followed soon afterwards by his old Australian partner Bill Clark. Specialising initially in Westralian shares, the stock-broking firm of Lionel Robinson, Clark & Co flourished in the 1900s, so much so that by 1906 Robinson was living not only in 'Kia-ora', a fine house on Fitzjohn's Avenue in Hampstead, but also at Old Buckenham Hall in Norfolk. He and Clark were also a successful team when it came to owning racehorses, and their great coup was winning the 1907 Cesarewitch, having backed Demure down from 100 – 1 to 5–2 in the ante-post betting. Do we simply place Robinson in the larger picture as yet another gentlemanly capitalist? Or rather, as an outsider who enhanced the City's pool of expertise and set an example to other colonials by doing so well for himself? The latter emphasis – on an ever-changing City of successes and failures, of exits and entrances – has the merit of making for more interesting history.

One firm heading towards the exit door was Stern Bros, in its heyday an important merchant bank but by the 1900s in a process of gentrified decline under the inadequate leadership of Sir Edward Stern. He would be remembered in his 1933 *Times* obituary 'for his connexion with the worlds of coaching, hunting, and horse breeding', as well as for being 'the last prominent City man to go daily to his office in a horse-drawn carriage', but not for his business prowess. Other gentlemanly capitalists did not even get round the course. 'Imagine last night my having to sit down and play bridge with Cassel, Carl Meyer and another man,' Esher was writing to his son by April 1903, less than a year after entering Cassel's employ. A year later he was in Paris on Sir Ernest's behalf: 'I cannot, alas, get away today. This accursed business is not finished . . . It is a nuisance, as I am bored to death here. Luckily there is something to do all day, but then it is mostly uncongenial work. Such a lot of tiresome detail.' And in July 1904: 'I had a talk with Revelstoke today about the City which I hate, and which I don't think I shall be able to stand. Still, I want to do so if possible, as I shall like you always to have as much money as possible . . . Still, it is not a nice life!' Soon afterwards Esher cracked, tendering his resignation to Cassel on the grounds that (in his son's later tactful words) 'he could not grasp the intricacies of high finance'.[29]

For a replacement, Cassel did not turn to George Cornwallis-West, who back in 1900, following his marriage to Lady Randolph Churchill and decision to leave the army, had needed to find a new profession in order to supplement only a small private income. The question came up, Cornwallis-West subsequently recalled, in the course of an after-dinner conversation with Cassel:

> It was he who broached the subject and asked me what I thought of doing with myself. I told him that the administrative side of an electrical engineering concern rather appealed to me. 'Not the City?' he asked. I replied that the prospect of going on a half-commission basis to a firm of stockbrokers and touting for orders from my friends had no allurements for me. He thought a moment and said: 'There are many young men of your class who should never go east of Temple Bar. Perhaps you are one of them.'

A classic exchange. For four years, following an introduction from Cassel, Cornwallis-West duly worked for the British Electric Traction Co. He then fell in with a clever but speculating northcountryman called Wheater, and the two started 'a sort of minor issuing house' under the style of Wheater, Cornwallis-West & Co. It survived for a few years, given some initial support by Natty Rothschild on the grounds of friendship, but in the end proved no solution to Cornwallis-West's perennial financial problems. A modicum of aptitude and application, in other words, remained indispensable, however advantageous it undoubtedly was also to be a gentleman and enjoy a high-class connection. That gentleman by nature if not by birth, Charles Addis, never doubted that the palm could not be won without the dust, whatever the personal consequences. 'I like London and I like the work, but I am not sure that I have not bitten off more than I can chew,' he wrote to a close friend in 1905. And he went on: 'I see myself neither reading nor writing nor enjoying the converse of friends but, all of me, bent to my daily task and I fear lest I should never be able to lift my head from it and death should reach me in my prison "unfreed, having seen nothing, still unblest". I look round and see no way of escape. I am afraid.'[30]

The City was not only a jealous mistress (as Dawkins had reluctantly acknowledged), but also a complex, demanding one, full of internal fractures and divisions that were part and parcel of its essential pluralism. To the outside world the Stock Exchange represented *the* daily symbol of the square mile, but to those actively engaged in *haute finance* it tended to be regarded as a regrettable necessity. 'Tell Elsie,' Meyer wrote to his wife in August 1907 referring to their daughter, 'that from lack of occupation in the Stock Exchange they have been playing diavolo there this afternoon.' Or as Revelstoke the previous year typically expressed himself to Hamilton, 'I always deprecate the suggestion that any relation of my friends should go on the Stock Exchange . . . the whole profession is so very much over-run that I consider it a dangerous and rather demoralising vocation to suggest for a young man.' How much, anyway, did individual components of the City know about other components? For all the detailed information books kept by a firm like Kleinworts, the answer is almost certainly not as much as tends to be assumed. Particularly striking is a letter written by Harry Gibbs, in his seventeenth year as a partner of Antony Gibbs, to his brother Vicary in September 1906. The occasion was a surprise visit to 15 Bishopsgate from the ageing Julius Caesar Czarnikow, anxious to press his view that the present was a highly favourable time to buy beetroot sugar for May delivery:

> He asked me to tell my 'cousin' Mr Vicary what he said about the sugar position. I replied that my brother would probably be here tomorrow & Monday next, & certainly on Tuesday. So he said his doctors would not let him come up tomorrow, but that you might send on to his firm if you wanted to do anything. For the sugar market would not wait for him, or us. However he could not think of asking one so young as myself to take any responsibility today when it really seemed as if I was alone in the office. A position which he himself would not have liked at all. So if he was alive he would call in on Tuesday & see you. I said I thought it

improbable that you alone would care to go in for a sugar spec: – but that I should be up on Tuesday also . . .

He said that I could not be more than 30 or 35 – 6 at the outside – I said that I was sorry to say that at my age of 45 I was quite pleased to be told I was so very youthful. He considers the present statistical position of sugar very favourable – and he wants us to buy or to let him buy for us, as he is in touch with the market. This no doubt he is. I asked about him at lunch – & he seems to be known as a sort of king of the sugar market. But this you doubtless knew before. He is said to be very rich, & to be the best judge of the sugar market going. I was very civil to him, & he seems to like talking to 'boys' of 45, for he stayed nearly an hour with me – during which time he reviewed the whole course of his life from the age of 21 – pointed out the destinies of France & Russia – disposed of the Gov^t of 'Mr' Campbell Bannerman – touched lightly on Bimetallism – & spoke at great length on the demerits of Free Trade. We shall have him again on Tuesday. He seems a nice old man, but I should like to limit him to one subject at a time, say sugar for choice.

Harry Gibbs rounded off his letter, a telling mix of ignorance and condescension, by noting that 'the Jews (& I suppose L^d R) have wailed in their Synagogue all the morning', adding that the talk in the office was of the need 'to get up a Pogram'.[31]

One of the major internal fault-lines was reflected by Dawkins in May 1902. 'African business,' he wrote to Milner, 'is rather looked down upon and suspected by the City aristocracy.' Sigismund Neumann was a typical object of this suspicion. Born in Bavaria in 1857, the son of a German Jew, he emigrated to South Africa in his late teens, in search of a fortune on the Kimberley diamond fields. In time he established a City base, and in 1907, towards the end of a variegated career, he set up a merchant banking house called Neumann, Luebeck & Co, his partner being the former London manager of the Dresdner Bank. Two years later, on behalf of Goldman Sachs, Kleinworts cast a distinctly jaundiced eye:

Undoubtedly Mr Neumann is a very wealthy man, but the market does not regard the acceptance of this firm favourably . . . Mr Neumann has been mixed up for many years in the South African Mining market & has acquired his wealth in this manner. Several of the enterprises which he has promoted have been questionable properties and, at the present time, a large portion of the business of the firm is in connection with the management of the various mining propositions in which they are interested . . . We think that, in our joint interests, it would be as well to refrain from buying the acceptances of this firm.

Nor did Neumann achieve ready acceptance in the wider social domain. During the late 1890s he regularly rented Invercauld, the Scottish property of Horace Farquharson; it was situated conveniently near Balmoral, and one year he persuaded the Prince of Wales to take part in a deer drive. Also amongst the rifles was Frederick Ponsonby, who tells the story of a memorable day:

> Everything went wrong. In the first place the deer refused to be driven in the proper direction; whether this was sheer bad luck or owing to the lack of skill on the part of the keepers it is difficult to say . . . Whatever the cause was, the drive that lasted two hours proved a failure and no one got a shot. The Prince of Wales, who knew the difficulties, took it with great equanimity and made light of it, but when the luncheon proved a fiasco, it was quite a different matter. Neumann, full of apologies for the failure of the drive, led us off to luncheon. He had made all the arrangements himself so that there should be no mistake. We walked down a path in single file and he assured us that it was not far. After half an hour's walk we came to a wood and Neumann explained he had chosen this sheltered spot in case it was a windy day. It seemed an ideal place but there were no signs of anything to eat. He told us to wait a moment while he looked about and, like a hound who is trying to pick up the scent, he circled round and round but with no success. The Prince of Wales, who by that time was getting very hungry, began to make very scathing remarks about rich men undertaking things they knew nothing about and ended by shouting suggestions to the wretched Neumann, who was still scouring the countryside at a trot. I then went after Neumann and asked if I could help. He produced a copy of his orders and said he had looked out the place on a map, which didn't seem to help much. While we were talking he caught sight of a shepherd and raced off after him. The shepherd explained that the place he had written down was over five miles off and that the one we had come to was differently pronounced, although spelt very similarly. The problem was how to get the luncheon and the guests together. Neumann begged me to explain the situation to the Prince of Wales and tell him that he would go as fast as he could to get a conveyance if the guests would walk as far as the road and wait there. HRH on hearing the explanation called Neumann every synonym for an idiot, but urged by hunger he agreed to walk to the road, which took us about half an hour. It was then past two and there, on a heap of stones, we sat silently waiting for a conveyance. Conversation was at first tried, but eventually we all relapsed into gloomy silence. It was past three when a wagonette arrived and we all bundled in . . .[32]

All in all it was not quite *The Shooting Party*, more Leonard Bast on a bad day.

In the end, of course, both sides of a sometimes troubled compact needed each other. 'The Duke did not seem quite to understand why he should be dragged off there,' observed Hamilton in September 1899 when the Devonshires went to spend two days with the Neumanns at Invercauld, before adding perceptively: 'The Duchess seems to delight in giving helping hands to *nouveaux riches*; partly (it may be) with a view to promoting Charlie Montagu's interests in the City.' There persisted, none the less, a strong undertow of what one might call West End resentment. In his 1904 survey of *Society in the New Reign*, Escott declared that 'Park Lane has been annexed by the South African millionaires, each newcomer more aggressively wealthy, contemptuously patronising, or insolently autocratic and absolutely uninteresting, than his predecessor.' Lady Dorothy Nevill, in her memoirs published in 1906, similarly argued that 'wealth has usurped the place formerly held by wit and learning' and as a result 'Society as it used to be – a somewhat exclusive body of people, all of them distinguished either for their rank, their intellect, or their wit – is no more.' Over and beyond such aristocratic objections there existed another critique – more classless, time-honoured and one that would continue to be voiced until being temporarily stilled by the sensational events of the 1980s. George Russell, in his *Social Silhouettes* of 1906, put it best, in words that serve to remind how the City, for all its manifest importance, would almost always remain slightly at a tangent to the rest of society:

> There is, I think, no kind of conversation known to man – not House of Commons humour, or boating-shop, or shooters' recollections – which can for a moment compete in point of dulness with the habitual discourse of the genuine City Man. True it is that there are members of the class who chatter of sport, and plays, and pictures; but they are comparatively few, and their interest in these things is superficial and their talk unreal. The genuine City Man talks of money. What is so and so worth? What did he start with? How much did he lose in Kaffirs? What did he give for that place he bought in Kent? How has he been doing at Newmarket? How long will he be able to keep it up at this rate? Did he get any money with his wife? What does he give his daughters? And so the stream flows on. It takes its rise in money; through money it runs its course; in money it ends; but only ends to begin again tomorrow.[33]

PART FOUR

1902–14

If one wanted to show a foreigner England, perhaps the wisest course
would be to take him to the final section of the Purbeck hills, and stand
him on their summit, a few miles to the east of Corfe. Then system after
system of our island would roll together under his feet. Beneath him is the
valley of the Frome, and all the wild lands that come tossing down from
Dorchester, black and gold, to mirror their gorse in the expanses of Poole.
The valley of the Stour is beyond, unaccountable stream, dirty at Bland-
ford, pure at Wimborne – the Stour, sliding out of fat fields, to marry the
Avon beneath the tower of Christchurch. The valley of the Avon –
invisible, but far to the north the trained eye may see Clearbury Ring that
guards it, and the imagination may leap beyond that onto Salisbury Plain
itself, and beyond the Plain to all the glorious downs of central England.
Nor is suburbia absent. Bournemouth's ignoble coast cowers to the right,
heralding the pine trees that mean, for all their beauty, red houses, and
the Stock Exchange, and extend to the gates of London itself. So tremendous is the City's trail!

E.M. Forster, *Howards End* (1910)

CHAPTER SEVENTEEN

Sleeping at Last

Lord Revelstoke's self-sacrificing devotion to public duty came to fruition in June 1902 when, a fortnight after the end of the Boer War, the Royal Commission into the Port of London presented its report. The case for change was obvious. London's share of the total value of foreign and colonial produce exported from the UK had dropped from 61 per cent in 1882 to 53 per cent by 1899, there was increasing competition from continental ports, and above all it was clear that the private dock companies lacked the resources and capital to expand and modernise the port in the way that was necessary. Among those who had been pushing for change was the London Chamber of Commerce. In February 1898, at the Chamber's monthly dinner at the Trocadero Restaurant, a paper by Henry Coke of David Sasson & Co emphasised 'the entire absence of any central authority for the control of the landing and shipping of goods and the provision of accommodation for ships'. The following year, at its annual meeting, Sir Albert Rollit condemned the refusal of the London and India Docks Joint Committee to interview a deputation from the Chamber, adding that 'it was not as though the trade of the Port was increasing by leaps and bounds'. The Royal Commission was appointed in 1900, Revelstoke assuming the chair the next year. Many submissions of plans were offered for the port's future, and among those giving evidence was Sir Marcus Samuel on behalf of the City Corporation. In a combative performance, his special wrath was directed towards the other LCC:

> The scheme put forward by the London County Council does not commend itself in vital respects to the Corporation nor to those who are engaged in the business of the port. In the first place, the members are indisputably elected on a political basis, and in the second place, their scheme shows a determination to subject the new authority to their control, whereas it is absolutely essential that it should be entirely independent. The Corporation cannot help feeling that they would contribute an element which could not possibly be of any service, and which might well become dangerous, since certain members of their body were respon-

sible for creating the labour difficulties under which the Port of London still suffers.

Under questioning, Samuel also asserted that 'there is a very great difference in the position of the Corporation today and what it was' and that now 'it is fairly representative of the business of London as a whole'. The Commission's eventual report, in June 1902, came out strongly for a unitary port authority to succeed the private dock companies.[1]

Few in the City disagreed, but the problem was that the Commission also recommended that London's ratepayers should guarantee the interest on the stock to be created for purchasing the docks. That autumn – following a petition whose signatories included Rothschilds, Barings and the Bank of England – the Lord Mayor, the private banker Sir Joseph Dimsdale, convened a meeting at the Mansion House of 'merchants, bankers, and traders of the City of London'. The majority came out against the notion of a rate-aided port, but it soon became clear that there was a significant element in the City, led by the London Chamber of Commerce and essentially comprising the shipping and mercantile community, for whom there was a more serious danger than being 'on the rates'. In the words of Rollit in June 1903, when the Conservative government's Port of London Bill had started its parliamentary progress: 'They hoped now to have a very deep, cheap and modern port, which was essential to the pre-eminence of the Port of London.' The crux was cheapness, the shipping and mercantile interests fearing that the price of independence would be heavy dues on goods and vessels that in turn would further affect the port's competitiveness. The following month there took place an emergency conference between the London Chamber of Commerce and representatives of such impeccably mercantile organisations as the London Sugar Refiners Association, the Home and Foreign Produce Exchange, the General Produce Brokers Association, the London Dried Fruit Association, the London Metal Exchange, and the Colonial Wool Merchants Association. The London Chamber of Commerce's Charles Charleton stated that he had convened them 'to specially consider whether action should be taken to support the Port of London Bill, in view of the hostile attitude of the Lord Mayor [now Samuel] and the Corporation of London, and a majority of the Mansion House Committee on the Port of London, towards the Bill'.[2]

Why was the Corporation, and behind it the financial and banking interest, so hostile? According to Charleton, it was not only because the City was included in the general area which the London County Council was authorised to rate for the purposes of the Bill, but also because the representation of the Corporation on the new Port Authority was to be halved. Charleton and the others present agreed that the Mansion House Committee was not representative 'of the commercial community of London' and sought to petition the Prime Minister to press on with the Bill. To no avail, because later in the summer, following intense pressure from the City Corporation – actively encouraged by the City's senior MP, Alban Gibbs – the government in effect put the Bill on ice. That November the London Chamber of Commerce's J. Innes Rogers regretfully pointed out to his mercantile friends the facts of life:

> The opposition of the Corporation of London was undoubtedly threatening to prevent the further passage of the Bill. Their opposition quite as much as the pressure of public business had prevented the Bill going through last Session. Although commercial men were quite aware that the Corporation did not in any sense voice commercial opinion yet parliamentary circles were not so well advised . . .

Such were indeed City realities, making rather academic the assertion soon afterwards of the *Chamber of Commerce Journal* that 'all delay in remedial legislation causes injury and loss to the shipping and trading interests of London'.[3]

A weak government continued to stay its hand, prompting the London County Council in April 1905 to bring forward its own Bill, proposing for itself a majority of places on the new port authority. Only twelve out of forty places were allotted to trade and shipping representatives, and not surprisingly the City was united in its opposition. The Conservative majority in the Commons ensured the Bill's defeat, and there followed a protracted debate about the port's future. Finally in 1908, the new Liberal government, with first Lloyd George and then Winston Churchill at the Board of Trade, managed to resolve the question. 'No aid will be forthcoming from the State or the municipality,' noted the *CCJ* with satisfaction in its response to the new Bill. While as for the question of the port dues to be imposed: 'Making allowance for exemptions for transhipments, etc, we apprehend that the new dues on imported goods would not exceed a range of 1d to 6d per ton.' This, it added, 'should not involve any undue pressure on trade'. A year later, on the last day of March 1909, the Port of London Authority entered into active management, with only nine of its forty representatives appointed by the London County Council. The City had triumphed – both its financial and commercial sectors – and Charleton was not exaggerating when he told delegates of the London trading and mercantile associations and exchanges that 'he believed the Port Authority was looked upon favourably among the merchants, traders and shipowners of the port'.

Built partly in the late eighteenth century, the Cutler Street warehouses now passed to new management, attracting over the years many visitors. Among them, in March 1914, was John Masefield:

> You showed me nutmegs and nutmeg husks,
> Ostrich feathers and elephant tusks,
> Hundreds of tons of costly tea,
> Packed in wood by the Cingalee,
> And a myriad drugs which disagree.
> Cinnamon, myrrh, and mace you showed,
> Golden Paradise birds that glowed,
> More cigars than a man could count,
> And a billion cloves in an odorous mount,
> And choice port wine from a bright glass fount.
> You showed, for a most delightful hour,
> The wealth of the world and London's power.[4]

*

Life returned to normal during the summer of 1902. There was even an exciting Test series between England and Australia, culminating at the Oval in August when Rhodes and Hirst got them in singles:

> 'This beats war bulletins' was the remark of a Stock Exchange man who stood watching the excited crowd gathered yesterday in the vicinity of the West Australian market, following the progress of the cricket match between England and the Australians as it was steadily clicked out on the tape. Throughout the afternoon ordinary business was almost forgotten, and the time devoted to eager discussion for and against the Mother country pulling the match out of the fire. Although the House officially closes at four o'clock, a large body of members remained till nearly half-past to wait for the result. When a waiter was espied bringing along the final news the hush resembled that which precedes a 'hammering', while the cheers that followed the announcement of England's victory must have almost reached the Oval. Of course, there was much wagering on the match; the betting started at 20–1 against England and thence gradually drew level. For once in a way even the losers were jubilant.

That same week there was an attempt by a Rand financier called Carl Hanau to kick-start a new Kaffir boom. This was the so-called

Coronation Syndicate (the delayed ceremony had just taken place), whose prospecting activities were shamelessly puffed by *The Times* as likely to lead to an extension of the Witwatersrand Main Reef. But the boom obstinately failed to materialise, as worries deepened over what was usually referred to as the 'native labour situation'. The *FT* did its best to still nerves – 'sooner or later large numbers of natives will come forward to work in the mines as they did before the war', it asserted early in October – but a month later it was compelled to report a bleak mood in the Kaffir Circus, with most dissatisfaction being vented on the mining companies: 'The market is not altogether inclined to approve the obstinate way in which the mining officials refuse to "grasp the nettle" of increased pay.' The *Statist* took the stern line that 'the future of the black race depends upon its willingness to work', but already the controversial notion of importing Chinese labour was starting to be mooted.[5]

These were not happy months for Arthur B. Franks, who since the start of 1901 had enjoyed a deeply uneasy relationship with the Stock Exchange Committee. That January he was severely censured for having failed to repay a long-standing debt to a fellow-member. Franks conceded to the Committee that 'he had had a hard struggle' in recent years; barely two months later he was again severely censured, this time for having entered into a covert partnership; and in September he was informed that his membership had ceased after he had appeared in the *London Gazette* under the heading 'Receiving Orders'. Now in August 1902, having moved from 3 Sandown Villas in Esher to a less prestigious address at Cove near Farnborough, he sought to clamber his way back. 'Gentlemen,' he wrote to the Committee on Coronation Day:

> Cannot you see your way to restore me my membership, which you deprived me of last September because a receiving order was made against me, and which order was made in spite, and behind my back, also that there was no reason whatever that the order should have been made, which was fully substantiated, not forgetting the whole thing was over a dispute for another person's liability.
>
> I have not broken any rule of the Stock Exchange, but have certainly been punished most severely for any mistake I might have made in ignorance. Gentlemen, I ask you to give my case, which is a very hard one, a little justice, and I may say a case which I doubt if any member has ever had to suffer as I have in the history of the Stock Exchange.

Only £55 was involved, but he might have spared his rhetoric, for 'no motion was made in the matter'.[6]

Franks was part of the City's flotsam and jetsam – rootless and liable to sink without trace – but Arthur Grenfell, older brother of Rivy, was a quite different matter.[7] Born in 1873, educated at Eton and given an early helping hand by Pierpont Morgan, he joined the merchant bank of which his father had been a partner. This was Morton, Rose & Co, badly hit at the time of the Baring crisis and reconstituted by the end of the 1890s as Chaplin, Milne, Grenfell & Co. 'We understand they are doing a satisfactory business,' reported Kleinworts to Goldman Sachs in August 1900, 'and we think you might take bills on them to the extent of £20,000.' Kleinworts, however, neglected the human factor. Grenfell was hard-working and resilient, possessed enormous charm and powers of persuasion, and was essentially honest – but his fatal flaw was his over-sanguine temperament. For him it was impossible that a swan could ever be a goose. Typical was the way in which, shortly before Kleinworts' verdict, he sought to interest his already considerable circle of City friends in the Mexican Mining Co, which his bank proposed to form in order to acquire mines in Mexico. 'I feel that this is a Company I can recommend with confidence to anyone prepared to lock up his money for a time with the chance of a big return.' And: 'As everyone knows, Mexico is the richest country in minerals in the world & I am confident that with good management, a big business might be built up out of small beginnings.' The following year, Chaplin Milne floated Great Coba Copper Mines, an Australian venture turned down by Morgans, and by January 1902 Kleinworts was starting to have doubts about Grenfell's firm and its bills: 'Name not particularly popular. Brokers only take small amounts.'[8]

The previous year Grenfell himself had made an excellent marriage to the daughter of Lord Grey, who in turn had a close friendship with Robert Benson, to whom he was related through his wife. These were to prove invaluable connections, above all as Grenfell came a cropper within months of the Boer War ending. Writing in late August to Hugo Baring, a trustee of Grenfell's marriage settlement, Benson tried to give a sympathetic spin to the débâcle:

> I think you have heard from others about Arthur . . .
> You know that he had made (say) £150,000 over and above the £100,000 he settled. All that is gone and his balance sheet shows a deficit of £35,000 – subject to realization.
> Many stocks are of uncertain value and difficult to realize, and meantime debts have to be paid, or he loses his partnership and has to start at the bottom with a millstone round his neck.

How to get so deep before he knew I needn't go into. He has been as much sinned against as sinning. I feel very strongly about old and experienced brokers who let young men run up big a/cs, omit to advise – or even dissuade – sales and then out the knife in at the bottom.

Arthur was 'fey', as most successful and courageous men have been once in their lives – and had temporarily lost his sense of proportion. His natural generosity also contributed.

After discussing ways and means of settling the debt, Benson went on:

There remains Arthur's partnership – but Chaplin – who has behaved like a gentleman – has agreed to discuss all that by and bye when all this has blown over and meantime Arthur's plans are unchanged viz. to go with the Greys to South Africa next month and to get back as soon as possible.

You are lucky in being away in N.Y. and out of this. The burden has fallen on Cecil Grenfell [another brother of Arthur's] of closing up everything with the brokers and he has done it I think remarkably well making each position solid in turn. It is not everybody who knows how to go ahead in such a situation. Arthur must have suffered the torments of hell. But I think he is sleeping at last again, and recovering from his madness. He knows now that we are all fools – even the youngest of us. Vera's baby was born 4 weeks ago in the middle of this anxiety and before he told anybody. But she has come through it wonderfully well and is looking very pretty!

Much depended on Hugo Baring agreeing to advance trust securities in order to get Grenfell out of his scrape. After Benson had attempted without success to persuade Revelstoke to apply pressure on Baring to this effect, Grey tried his luck, writing to Revelstoke on 4 September:

The matter is a very grave one to me and I count on your assistance. The consequence to Vera, Arthur and their child and to all concerned of allowing Arthur to go bankrupt now, lose his partnership, his Directors' fees, his reputation and position in the City is so hateful that I assure you it has made me quite ill even to contemplate its possibility – and if this terrible consequence is the result of Hugo's action it will naturally be more painful still.

Revelstoke now did the necessary and Baring in New York likewise obliged, though wrote to Revelstoke at the end of the month with heartfelt words: 'You may be sure I shall be very careful before I consent again to be trustee to any of my friends.' As for Grenfell, he wrote on the 19th to his father-in-law:

At last my affairs seem really to be on the high road to a speedy settlement. Counsel has come right round & Hugo has assented so that I am only waiting for legal documents to sign. John Revelstoke met Cecil yesterday, & was very nice about me, & said he advised Hugo to sign, he had never really understood the position. I am afraid the delay has been more than harmful, but I daresay steady hard work will get me back into my place before very long.[9]

Relief comfortably outweighed remorse, and already the sunlit uplands were starting to beckon.

There were no such post-bellum alarms for Cassel, who continued to operate with his usual virtuosity. Early in September, during his annual Swiss climbing holiday with Edouard Noetzlin of Banque de Paris et des Pays-Bas (Paribas), he arranged things at the Villa Cassel so that Revelstoke, also a guest and something of a protégé of Cassel's, was able to cement a new working alliance between Barings and Paribas. A fortnight later he was at Domodossola, writing to Esher in London: 'I walked over from Switzerland and am on my way home by way of the Italian lakes, Milan and Paris. I should not move officially in the coal matter at present but I see no harm in your discussing it quite privately with Oakley.' By the beginning of October he was back in London but laid up with a bad leg and receiving visitors, including Hamilton: 'He was much against issuing the Guaranteed Loan this autumn, which would be a very unpropitious time . . .' A fortnight later he was still laid up, still offering the weightiest voice: 'Cassel entirely approves the postponement of the Transvaal loan. Its issue now would be most inopportune and premature.' There was one more important service to perform this autumn. On 25 October the King and Queen proceeded ceremonially through the City, and Hamilton noted that 'their Majesties' reception all along the route is said to have been very enthusiastic'. However, he added: 'Some people tell me that there was an occasional cry of "Where is Alice?" She has been in retirement lately owing to the death of her mother; & is now going out to Egypt with Cassel & his party for the opening of the *barrage*.'[10] Whisking away the King's inconvenient mistress simply confirmed Cassel as the indispensable man.

It was during the first of his reclining conversations with Hamilton that Cassel complained of the timidity of Rothschilds and in particular its refusal to sponsor an issue without the guarantee of the British government behind it. The context was the imminent £5.1m Japanese issue, the first of a yen-denominated security outside Japan.[11] Rothschilds had been approached to be the lead issuer and in turn had sounded out the Foreign Office. It was intimated to New Court that Lansdowne regarded it 'as a matter of political importance that Japan should be able to raise in this Country rather than elsewhere the money which she requires, and that they hope that she will obtain a loan in London on reasonable terms'. Coming less than a year after the signing of the Anglo-Japanese Alliance it was a clear enough signal, but Natty decided that he would rather play an underwriting role in the issue than take the main responsibility. The initiative passed to Barings, which decided to bring out the issue in tandem with the Hongkong and Shanghai Bank and the Yokohama Specie Bank. On 4 October, three days before the prospectus was published, the *Statist* waxed far more lyrical than the *Investors' Review* had done a few years earlier: 'Japan is making great progress economically. Her people are highly patriotic. Her population is rapidly growing, and industries of every kind are growing still more surprisingly...' Within a week Revelstoke was reporting the glad tidings to his new, participating friends in Paris: 'We are glad to be able to inform you that we have had a most eminently satisfactory subscription from the English public. There has been a large number of applications of £500 and £1000 apiece from people who are quite unconnected with the City circles, and who seem to wish the amounts for which they apply allotted in full, with a view to keeping them for investments.' Popular enthusiasm merely echoed that of Lansdowne, who had privately assured Barings that the Japanese 'are very shrewd and they know perfectly well that it will be to their advantage to establish their credit and to get classed as something better than a semi-barbarous Power'.[12] Faced by an open goal, Rothschilds had played the square ball.

*

1902 was a fraught year for Morgans in general and Dawkins in particular. This was especially true in the case of the International Mercantile Marine (IMM), a giant transatlantic shipping combine brought about by Pierpont Morgan, involving the absorption of two large British shipping companies (Leyland and White Star), and capitalised at $170m.[13] 'Are you not sometimes afraid at the very large figures in which modern finance works?' Everard Hambro, from the old school of merchant banking, asked Morgan. More relevantly in the short term, the American financier's plans led to vehement British press criticism and significant political opposition, leaving an exposed Dawkins in the firing line. The strain, as he reported to a New York partner in June, was considerable:

350

We have had a good deal of trouble and friction with the Government here over all this shipping business, or rather I may say with one particular member of the Government, Mr Chamberlain, who has, unfortunately, been put at the head of a Committee of the Cabinet appointed to deal with this matter. Most of the other Ministers are reasonable and the public excitement is quietening down but both J.P.M. and I have argued and discussed with Chamberlain till our tongues were tired, without making any impression.

By late summer the Cabinet agreed, under certain conditions, to accept the shipping combine, and Dawkins wrote ruefully to the more amenable Gerald Balfour, President of the Board of Trade, that 'I am afraid that private speculation has been mixed up with patriotic suggestion by certain advisers of the Govt all through this shipping business to a very unpleasant and discreditable extent.' For Morgans in London there was a price to pay not only in terms of unpopularity, as another partner recalled:

> In Dec 1902, large cash paymts of over 5 millions Stg were due here to pay for purchases of White Star & other shipping shares & throughout the previous 2 months, a dead set was made in the daily papers against the credit of JSM & Co. The arrangem^{ts} w^h had to be made for this payment, involved consid difficulty . . . The full remittances were duly made with great ability by JPM & Co without the movement of any specie & after the Decr payments, the newspapers ceased their attacks & little more attention was paid to the matter.

Still, as late as August the following year, Dawkins was complaining to Jack Morgan that 'we have about £500,000 or a quarter of our capital locked up in shipping', the Englishman adding laconically: 'Not a nice prospect.'[14] The episode had also been a salutary reminder that, in the new century, national considerations and international finance would not always sit easily.

Dawkins's other main headache concerned 'tubes'. Following the successful start of the London Central Railway in 1900, a plethora of schemes were floated to modernise and greatly extend London's underground system.[15] By 1902 two main groups held the initiative: one fronted by the rascally American financier Charles Yerkes, strongly backed by Edgar Speyer, and the other under the sway of Morgans. Briefing New York in July, Dawkins was confident of success:

> We are emerging with flying colours from a tremendous battle for a Parliamentary bill – you would call franchise – for the construction of a

great through route of electric tube through London linking on with the new tramway systems NE & SW. Every kind of prejudice & trick was invoked against us, but after an unusual full dress discussion we got a majority of 181 in the H. of Commons for our scheme.

The so-called 'Morgan tube' seemed set fair to happen – an ambitious route from Hammersmith Broadway to Southgate via Piccadilly and the City – but Dawkins reckoned without the street-fighting qualities of Speyer. The turning point came in October when, to general astonishment, London United Tramways, chaired by George White and supposedly in alliance with the Morgan group, sold out to Yerkes for a higher price. Dawkins called it an act of the 'most unexampled treachery', White defended himself on the grounds of 'the lamentable want of knowledge on all practical questions' displayed by the Morgan group, and there ensued a public spat in the columns of *The Times*. 'The acquisition by Messrs Speyer Bros of the London United Tramways shares in the interests of the District group,' Dawkins responded to Speyers' self-exoneration, 'was very far from having "really no influence on the destiny of the Piccadilly & City Bill of this session". On the contrary, it had a decisive influence . . .' Dawkins also made much of how that acquisition had been kept secret until the last moment, but in his heart he knew that the horse had bolted. It was thin comfort that Pierpont Morgan himself, an acknowledged master in these matters, sympathetically condemned it as the 'greatest rascality and conspiracy I ever heard of'.[16]

Over the next few years the nucleus of London's modern underground system (the Northern, Bakerloo and Piccadilly lines) took shape. Underground Electric Railways of London was the company responsible, and by 1905 it was Speyer who called all the shots, overseeing the running of the tube system as well as being responsible for raising its capital. It was in many ways a thankless task, granted the severe financial problems involved, and Speyer certainly did not receive the thanks of the City establishment. He was a cultured man, much involved in the Promenade concerts at the Queen's Hall, but there was something about him that rubbed up people (not just the partners at Morgans) the wrong way: perhaps his competitive instincts, perhaps his Liberal sympathies in politics, perhaps a certain arrogance. One of London's benefactors, he deserves to be remembered more fondly than he is.

CHAPTER EIGHTEEN

Worth Twopence

Monday, 10 November 1902 was the day of the Lord Mayor's Procession. This year's elevated alderman, only the third Jew to hold the supreme civic office, was Sir Marcus Samuel:

> I passed a sleepless night. I had to be dressed & to leave for the Mansion House by 10 a.m. My wife & daughter accompanied me & the Viscountess Hayashi wife of the Jap Minister with sons, her little granddaughter followed. We started from the Mansion House in the State Coach at 10.45. I found it unexpectedly comfortable to ride in. After breakfasting at Guildhall, I started from there at 11.40. From the very first I had a splendid reception from the Populace, culminating in a great ovation through my own Ward. At Aldgate Church I received an Album from those who had subscribed £500 for decorations, & this diary from Children of the Gravel Lane schools to whom I expressed my thanks. At the offices of my firm I received an address from my employees in a handsome silver case & also thanked them. Reached the Law Courts at 1.45 & was received by Lord Alverstone at 2 p.m. He delivered a most kind address expatiating upon the early age at which I attained the Mayoralty. (I was 49 on the 5th Inst.) On leaving the Court, I had an opportunity of seeing the Show & I felt glad that my own idea of the Naval Cars & the Jap car had worked out satisfactorily. The kind reception I had received in the City was fully maintained in the West End & we returned to the Guildhall at 4 p.m. after passing through enormous & enthusiastic crowds. I retired to my private room to try to rest but was continually disturbed through the arrival of innumerable telegrams of which hundreds reached us during the day. At 6 o'clock I met the Lady Mayoress & we proceeded to the Dais to receive & had a constant stream of visitors to greet until the arrival of the premier Mr Balfour who conducted the Lady Mayoress to the Hall, I taking Lady Evelyn Gifford. The evening passed off most successfully & my speeches numerous as they were, caused me no trouble or anxiety. I had the satisfaction of announcing the intention of the King & Queen to open the London Hospital & learnt from Mr Balfour that he & Mr Chamberlain had seen & enjoyed the Show. We left the Banqueting Hall for the Library soon after ten seeing the dancing & left for Portland Place at 11.30 deeply grateful that everything had been so wonderfully successful & that we had been

blessed by one of the finest days by way of weather ever known at this time of year.

Getting into the diary habit, the new Lord Mayor continued the next day: 'I took the Bench at the Mansion House at 11 . . . My first case was one of murder, a rare thing fortunately in the City.'[1]

Rare indeed, but the murder had happened while the procession was still in progress, presumably unbeknown to Samuel. Over the next few weeks London's more lurid papers, notably the *Illustrated Police News* and *Lloyd's Weekly Newspaper*, had a field day. The basic facts were clear enough:

> A well-dressed young woman called at the Lombard Street Post Office, and was soon afterwards joined by a man several years her senior, to whom she had sent a note by express messenger. They had no sooner met than a quarrel began between them, and it was continued as they left the building. Arrived in the street the young woman produced from her muff a clasp knife, and, attacking her companion with it, inflicted three wounds, one just above the temple on the left side of the face, another on the left breast, near, but not over the heart, and a third behind, near the left shoulder. The victim of the assault fell to the ground bleeding profusely, and the woman was at once seized, still grasping the knife in her hand. To the police, who were on the scene in a few seconds, she gave the name of Kitty Byron. She was taken to Cloak Lane Police Station, while the man was conveyed with all speed to St Bartholomew's Hospital, where he was pronounced to be dead. His assailant was then charged with wilful murder.
>
> The murdered man was Arthur Reginald Baker, on the Stock Exchange, of 19 Duke Street, Great Portland Street. Deceased was married at Torquay about four years ago, great local interest being evinced in the wedding. His wife was the daughter of Alderman Harrison, of the Queen's Hotel, who was Mayor of Torquay at the time. The deceased, it is stated, lost money on the Stock Exchange, and, consequently, had to give up his flat in London. Mrs Baker then returned to Torquay, bringing her little daughter with her. She has since assisted her father in the conduct of the hotel. She was greatly distressed when the police brought her the terrible news on Monday evening. She had instituted proceedings for divorce against the deceased.

Reggie Baker had been a jobber in the Westralian market, Kitty Byron was a 23-year-old milliner's assistant, and on Tuesday morning she found herself in front of the new Lord Mayor:

> The prisoner is a well-dressed young woman, slightly built and of medium height, with dark hair. She was accommodated with a seat in the

dock, and exercised perfect composure throughout the hearing of the case. The court was crowded. The only witness called was Inspector Fox, of the City Police. He deposed that he was station inspector at Cloak Lane Police Station. When the prisoner was brought in, and he gave her the usual warning, she said, 'I killed him willingly, and he deserved it, and the sooner I am killed the better.' She was charged and placed in a cell. Witness subsequently visited her in the cell at twenty minutes to six p.m., when she voluntarily said, 'Inspector, I wish to say something to you. I bought the knife to hit him, but I did not know I was killing him.'

Kitty Byron was remanded for a week, and on the Friday the inquest began on Baker, two days after what would have been his 45th birthday:

William Coleman, telegraph messenger at Lombard Street Post Office, said he was given an express letter to take to the deceased. The coroner read the letter, which was as follows: 'Dear Reg. – Want you a moment importantly. – Kitty.' Witness, continuing, said after one unsuccessful effort he found Mr Baker, who gave a verbal answer that he would come. He entered into conversation with Miss Byron, and they walked into the street together, the lady talking very rapidly. Suddenly he saw a knife flash in the lady's hand. He ran out, and found Mr Baker lying on the ground.

John Finn, clerk at Lombard Street Post Office, saw Miss Byron, whom he had seen on several occasions, come to the post office about five minutes to two on Monday afternoon. She asked, 'When will that boy be back?' The boy came in almost immediately, and said he had not been able to deliver the message. Miss Byron was greatly put out, and ordered the boy to take the letter back and tell Mr Baker he was to come at once. Baker returned with the boy, and had a conversation with another clerk, in which he refused to pay a charge of twopence imposed because the messenger had waited longer than the authorised time to deliver the letter on the first occasion. He then left, and almost immediately Miss Byron re-entered and remarked to a clerk, 'All right, old boy; I am worth twopence.' Mr Baker then entered again, and spoke to the accused, who said to him, 'You must pay the twopence.' He replied, 'I shall not.' She said, 'You must pay it; pay it with this,' at the same time producing a florin. She endeavoured to force this coin into the waistcoat pocket of the deceased, but failed, as he backed away, and gradually got to the door. Having passed the door, Mr Baker paused for a moment, and then turned to the right. The accused had followed him quickly, and witness saw her spring from the top step in the direction Mr Baker had gone. In reply to a question witness said he thought the accused had taken some alcoholic stimulant before seeing the deceased, although her speech was clear and her gait steady.

Later the Coroner produced the knife – 'a very formidable weapon, with a blade fully four inches long'.

The inquiry was then adjourned until Monday, when an array of witnesses gave further evidence. Arthur Chivers, clerk in the Post Office where Kitty Byron waited for the messenger to return, recalled her appearing 'worried' and 'brooding over some trouble'. William Lockie, a labourer who had been passing through Post Office Court, saw her strike two savage blows with a knife. He ran up and seized her by the shoulders; she struggled to get away, shouting, 'Reggie, dear Reggie'; he gave her into custody, saying to her, 'You've done enough now.' Edward Russell, another Post Office clerk, found a man on the ground and a woman being held by Lockie. As he lifted Baker up, a florin fell from his clothes. 'Let me go to him, let me kiss my Reggie,' she cried out. James Moore, cutler of Oxford Street, was in his shop at 12.30 on the day in question when a young woman asked to see a selection of knives. She wanted a 'strong, single-bladed knife'. He showed her a sailor's knife. 'Oh, yes,' she said, 'it is nice and sharp.'

The inquest ended later in the week, and on the final day there were two key female witnesses. The first was Mrs Afflick, night matron at Cloak Lane police station and on duty from nine o'clock on the night of the 10th, as Kitty Byron lay in bed:

> After about half-an-hour the prisoner turned from the left to the right side and felt down by her side under the clothes. Witness asked if she wanted a handkerchief and she said, 'No, dear.' She brought up in her right hand a long, black hat-pin. She said, 'I have no right with this, have I?' Witness said, 'Oh, no,' and made a grab at it, and asked how she came by it. She replied, 'Oh, I smuggled that all right, and did intend killing myself if I could, and would have done so somehow if I had been badly treated in here, for I am very unhappy. I did intend killing myself with the knife had I not been prevented by the outsiders. I only wish I had done it in the morning.' She went on to say, 'Oh, my poor Reggie. When he gave me a cup of tea in bed this morning before he went to business I got up and put a piece of pink lint on a bad toe that he had, and then I kissed it, little thinking it would be the last time I should kiss him again.' She said he went to business about 9.30, and after he had gone a young woman in the house (meaning the servant) had told her that Baker meant to discard her after the divorce proceedings. She (the prisoner) said she thought she went mad, for she said, 'Will he? I'll kill him before the day is out.' With that, she continued, she dressed herself, and went out to buy some brandy. Going along she bought the knife, and then went and had some more brandy. She then went to the Post Office, and asked for him. At first they could not find him, and while waiting she had another three of brandy and sent in again . . .

The other testimony came from Madame Adrienne Liard, landlady at 19 Duke Street:

> Witness said on 8 November she gave them notice because Baker kicked up such a row. He owed rent, and on one occasion when they made a noise the witness went in to see what was the matter and asked for her rent. The counterpane was on the floor, and Miss Byron's hat was broken. The witness asked what was the matter, and Miss Byron replied, 'Oh, nothing; we have been playing millinery.' Baker was always drunk, but Miss Byron was perfectly sober. On the Saturday witness gave Baker notice he accused the prisoner of being drunk and said, 'Well, she is not my wife; she is no class. She will go tomorrow, and can I stop another week?' Witness thinking he could not fight with the chairs – (*laughter*) – told him he could. Miss Byron came up to apologise for the noise that had been made, and witness mentioned that she was going. She told witness that in a week there would be something in the papers as to a lawsuit about Baker, and asked witness not to say anything to him because he would 'knock' her so. She mentioned about not being Baker's wife, and witness said, 'If you are not his wife, why do you stop with him?' She said, 'I love him so, and another thing, I cannot get a character for another place.'

The coroner then summed up and the jury retired, returning after twenty-two minutes to record a verdict of 'manslaughter'. In the dialogue that ensued there was little meeting of minds:

> *Coroner*: Do you mean unlawful killing without malice?
> *Foreman*: Yes, on the impulse of the moment. She did not go there with the intention of killing him.
> *Coroner*: Do I understand there was no malice?
> *Foreman*: Exactly. She did not go there with the intention of killing.
> *Coroner*: Well, gentlemen, it's your verdict, I have pointed out to you what manslaughter is.
> *Foreman*: We are unanimous.

Quiet satisfaction was felt in the Stock Exchange at the jury's verdict. 'There was a profound hope that the crime of murder would not be laid to the charge of the hapless creature who committed the terrible deed,' reported the *Economist*. But the Lord Mayor begged to differ. 'At 11 took Bench,' wrote Samuel in his diary for the 25th, '& commenced at 11.30 trial of Emma Byron for murder, sitting until 4.30 committing her on the Capital charge, although the Coroner's jury had returned a verdict of man slaughter, a conclusion on the evidence, impossible to understand.'

At the Old Bailey on 17 December, with the court 'crowded to inconvenience', the jury found Emma Byron guilty of wilful murder, but made 'the strongest possible recommendation to mercy'. Mr Justice Darling sentenced her to death, and the press piled on the emotional pressure: 'Her entire aspect was pitiful, for her figure was so slight and frail that she seemed little more than a child. Her dark blue dress was quite plain, she wore a neat white linen collar, her dark hair was drawn back simply and knotted behind, and she looked exactly what the evidence had shown her to be – a little milliner's assistant who had been dragged down by association with a man of loose habits.' Over the next few days, numerously signed petitions were got up – by Stock Exchange members, by Stock Exchange clerks, by girls in the millinery trade in London – all calling for reprieve. On Christmas Eve it became known that the Home Secretary had advised his Majesty to commute the sentence of death into one of penal servitude for life; and on 29 December Emma (Kitty) Byron was removed from Holloway Jail to Aylesbury to undergo the first six months of her imprisonment. It was a just end to the City's 'Fatal Stabbing Affray'.[2]

*

The death that really saddened fellow-members in the closing weeks of 1902 was not that of Reggie Baker but Henry Heppel. Also 44 and married, he had been a member since 1885 and jobbed chiefly in East Rands and Randfonteins. 'Our Kaffir share list tonight tells a tale of devastation,' declared the *FT*'s Mining market report on the evening of 18 November; the fortnightly settlement was imminent; and just before four o'clock the following afternoon Heppel went down to the lavatory in the Stock Exchange's basement, thronged with members washing their hands before leaving for the day, locked himself in and blew his brains out with an army revolver. The bullet passed through a partition and wounded another member in the arm. The inquest heard evidence from Heppel's brother:

> Witness acted to him in the capacity of clerk. The deceased was a particularly abstemious man, and was of a distinctly religious turn of mind. Recently he had been worried by financial embarrassments, but witness had never heard him threaten his life. Witness saw deceased in the Stock Exchange at about ten o'clock. He looked very worried and excited, and witness said to him, 'Won't you come into the office at four o'clock and look things over, and see exactly what the position is?' The deceased replied, 'That is no good. I have it all in my books. I must make

a clean breast of it tonight.' Witness left him, but saw him again at twelve o'clock, when, however, nothing of importance passed between them. Witness did not see his brother again alive.

It emerged that Heppel had bought his gun shortly after noon at the Civil Service Stores in Queen Victoria Street, claiming that he wished to purchase a revolver for a young man who was going out to South Africa; and on his body the police found a note which read, 'I have speculated madly this Account, and am ruined.' A City doctor stated that Heppel had placed the muzzle of the revolver in his mouth, while the family doctor deposed that he had 'for some time suffered from an affection of the membranes of the brain, which produced sleeplessness and extreme depression', and that he 'had left his West-End residence at Notting Hill, and had been living at Southend'. The *Economist*, meanwhile, sought to draw out 'The Lesson of the Stock Exchange Tragedy':

> Although to all appearance he was perfectly sane when he stood chatting in the market on the very afternoon of the fatal day, members of the House have no hesitation in declaring that his mind must have been unhinged at the idea of being hammered. After all, it was so small a matter which to his unhappy mind formed the bridge between life and death – death by his own hand. Some £5,000 is nothing so very serious to the Kaffir Circus, and it needed but the opening of his mind to a few friends for something to be done by way of assistance. But the fatal shot was fired, and all the might-have-beens are useless regrets. Again, however, has the question of gambling by members of the House forced itself into the front rank of problems connected with the Stock Exchange. Despite a very general impression to the contrary, there is nothing whatever to prevent a member from speculating to the top of his bent if he can find people to deal with him, and that is perfectly easy . . . How legislation is to be framed which shall grapple with this obvious evil, and yet maintain that perfect freedom of dealing which is a vital essence to the greatest stock and share market in the world, it is very difficult to discover . . .

Suicide was in the air. Less than a fortnight later, on 3 December, a 51-year-old member called George Bennett killed himself at his home in Richmond, having told his wife the previous evening that he 'had sustained some financial loss'. Among those giving evidence to the inquest was a neighbour who revealed that Bennett had told him 'that he did not believe in the future state, and that he worshipped money'.[3] How many members did believe in the future state? Perhaps not all that many, but despite Heppel, despite Bennett, few voluntarily tested that unbelief.

A. Stanley Rowe successfully bottled it all up that Christmas.[4] He was, like Herbert Hoover, a junior partner in the City-based firm of mining engineers, Bewick Moreing. In his mid-30s, he lived at 22 Hyde Park Square, had five children under the age of 7, and on Boxing Day he and his wife accompanied the Hoovers to dinner followed by a show. At one point during the performance he asked the future president whether Mrs Hoover would look after his children in the event of any misfortune befalling him – a question that the Hoovers attributed to a liverish depression. Boxing Day was a Friday and, after a quiet Saturday, Rowe spent much of Sunday writing a lengthy letter to Hoover (partner in charge in Moreing's absence in China), before he shaved off his moustache, explained to his wife that he was a ruined man, said farewell to her and the children, and left home without saying where he was going. Hoover got the letter the next day. It explained that over the last nine months Rowe had been speculating heavily in Great Fingall shares and that, as secretary to that West Australian mine managed by Bewick Moreing, he had been forging quantities of Great Fingall share certificates in order to finance borrowings of up to £70,000 from four different firms of stockbrokers. One of those firms was Lionel Robinson's. By Christmas he had not only smelt a rat but had interrogated Rowe and not been satisfied by his explanations. 'Knowing the real value of the mine all the time,' Rowe wrote to Hoover, 'you will not wonder so much as outsiders might, at my confidence in being able to repay as the shares regained their true value in the market. I had seen the shares at nearly $9\frac{1}{2}$ and when they fell to $5\frac{1}{2}$ I had lost £70,000 to £80,000 . . . I clung on to the whole of my Great Fingalls in the fervent belief that they could not fall below 7 or thereabouts – and they went to $5\frac{1}{2}$!' Then came the inevitable, self-pitying appeal to Hoover's emotions:

I have endured such fearful torments since I first erred that I can no longer keep up & I have gone far away, after arranging with my family & my wife's to look after her & the children. It has torn my heart to part from them but I have been going mad & could not stay . . .

I have led an honest & a moral life, & have a good record behind me. If I can escape the worst consequences of my mad acts I shall endeavour to redeem the faults committed. If that cannot be, I am prepared to take a longer journey than the one I shall have entered upon before you receive this letter. I have done good many times when I could. It has been done to the poor and weak and not to the rich & powerful, but some of the

former will think on my name with gratitude, and with regret if I have to
suffer public shame. The latter I shall never endure & I have a sovereign
remedy against it.

It is a cruel thing for you and Wellsted [another partner] & my heart
aches when I think of your kindness to me and of your horrible perplexity
over this affair. May your counsels be guided aright! I shall never cease
to dwell with kind but pained feelings upon my association with you
both, and by one of those dreadful ironies of life, I never felt so much
drawn to you both & so much to appreciate your splendid qualities –
each in his own sphere – as I have done since the shadow of this trouble
has hung over me.

I wanted to spend a last Christmas with my children & dear wife, & so
deceived you a little by not telling you fully before this. When you came
to see us you must have seen, exercise what self-command I could, – that
I was suffering mentally. Dear Hoover, forgive me. I meant well.

It was a considerable mess that Rowe left behind him, more complex
and more serious than his letter had intimated, a mess that Hoover
began to clear up in 1903, adding to his City reputation. Rowe himself
was tracked down in Canada in September, on the verge of becoming
a partner in a Toronto stockbroking firm, and at his Old Bailey trial
three months later was sentenced to ten years' imprisonment. It did not
help his cause when it emerged during the trial that he had already, as
a young man, spent nine months in prison for embezzlement. His sister
heroically brought up the children, his wife eventually divorced him,
and he was released in 1911 after serving eight years. Appeals followed
for help in putting him back on his feet and Hoover responded not
ungenerously – especially considering that, as he bluntly told Rowe,
'when all is said and done, your actions caused me five years of
absolutely fruitless work in the best portion of my life'.[5]

The Rowe defalcations caused ripples but were not a first-class City
scandal, unlike the *cause célèbre* that afflicted Lloyd's in 1903.[6] The
Economist put it in salutary context:

> The Committee of Lloyd's, unlike the Stock Exchange Committee, has
> little or no disciplinary powers, and has no official cognisance of what
> goes on in the underwriting rooms. It is simply a body which directs the
> collection of shipping news, appoints agents through a sub-committee,
> and looks after the general interest of members. The Committee fixes the
> amount of deposit – not less than £5,000 – which underwriting members
> must lay down before they are admitted, and elects new members.
> Comparatively few of the underwriting members themselves actually
> work the insurance business, the real operations being in the hands of a
> few members, each of whom has behind him a sort of syndicate of

'names' of other members, for whom he writes risks. An underwriting member may also be a broker, and often is. He may, and often does, receive instructions as broker, and executes them himself as underwriter. There is no pay-day which is generally observed, and business is often conducted with a want of system which brings with it serious evils. Quite recently a case occurred in which an underwriter's official india-rubber stamp, impressed with his string of 'names', was improperly used by a broker without his authority, and this was only discovered by an accident.

It speaks well for the high standard of integrity which generally prevails among members and subscribers of Lloyd's that this body of private underwriters, who publish no accounts, and are subject to practically no disciplinary rules, holds its own against the competition of powerful companies and maintains its credit.[7]

For those in the know, the scandal at Lloyd's broke early in April, when Percy Burnand, from a historic Lloyd's family and a member since 1885, failed. He had been deeply interested in Gaze & Sons, a struggling travel agency which never recovered from the postponement of King Edward's coronation in June 1902, having rashly bought up seats overlooking the route. In effect Gaze's was kept going by Burnand's underwriting syndicate, the members of which were wholly unaware of what he was doing.

At the ensuing court case in June, after Brown Shipley had joined with Hambros in an attempt to recover from the underwriters the amount of their acceptances which Gaze's had failed to pay, one of those underwriters, Colonel G.A. Draffen, was questioned by H.H. Asquith, appearing for the prosecution:

> He was 45 years of age. In 1885 he became a sleeping partner with Burnand in his brokerage business. He went to Lloyd's occasionally, and was from time to time out of England on military duties. He first ascertained in January 1903 that he was being made the guarantor of the solvency of others . . . He never went into the books with Burnand. He trusted Burnand to adjust them for him. He never inquired what losses he was paying. Burnand paid both his (witness's) subscription at Lloyd's and the price of his seat there. He had full confidence in Burnand. He had not examined the inside of a day-book for years.

Another of the defendants was Burnand's father-in-law, and Mr Justice Bigham ruled that the members of the syndicate were not liable, on the grounds that Burnand had been acting solely for himself. The *Economist* agreed, but as usual looked for the wider lesson:

It has been known at Lloyd's for two years at least that Mr Burnand was doing an exceptional kind of business. That he should have been allowed to go on unchecked, and should even during the period have been able to add a 'name' to his list, shows how complete a lack of control over individual members exists at Lloyd's, and how necessary it is that the members, as a body, should take steps to arm the Committee – or some special disciplinary committee – with powers which will protect the public in its dealings with Lloyd's underwriters.[8]

The reverberations of the Burnand affair were profound, but it would take one more campaign – led by Cuthbert Heath, perhaps inevitably – before fundamental reform was achieved at Lloyd's.

*

Intensifying a trend that had been apparent from the 1880s, finance and diplomacy would become ever more enmeshed during the Edwardian period, throwing into confusion traditional assumptions about separate spheres. When in December 1902 Britain and Germany took strong action against debt-defaulting Venezuela – seizing gunboats, sinking two of them and imposing a blockade until Venezuela gave way by the end of the month – this was seen by many as having wider import. 'The market welcomes the strong policy adopted by this country and Germany towards Venezuela,' reported the *FT*, 'as there are hopes that this action may stir up other defaulting South American Republics to a keener sense of their financial obligations.' In line with convention, the Under-Secretary for Foreign Affairs, Lord Cranborne, insisted to the Commons on the 15th 'that it is not the claims of the bond-holders that bulk largest in the estimation of the Government', stating that the government would not have acted as it did 'if it had not been for the attacks by Venezuela on the lives, the liberty, and the property of British subjects'. He added, however, that whereas the Liberal opposition 'seemed to think the bond-holder a sort of *hostis humani generis*, who might be attacked and spoiled at pleasure, and was not entitled to consideration', his view was that 'the bond-holders have conferred very great benefits on these South American Republics, and are entitled to protection from their own country'. The authoritative government view came from Balfour as Prime Minister:

I do not deny, in fact, I freely admit, that bond-holders may occupy an international position which may require international action; but I look upon such international action with the gravest doubt and suspicion, and

I doubt whether we have in the past ever gone to war for the bond-holders, for those of our countrymen who have lent money to a foreign
Government; and I confess I should be very sorry to see that made a
practice in this country.

The *FT* two days later, in its usual measured way, probably expressed
mainstream City opinion in its response to this studied disavowal of
the notion of going to war on behalf of bondholders:

> No one has suggested such a thing. If it were made a practice, however,
> we should have a good 'casus belli' against five-eighths of South and
> Central America, and some European States to boot. But there is no
> reason why the bondholders' claims should always be ignored or ex-
> cluded when others are arranged for, or why they should not on occasion
> be afforded diplomatic support. War is the ultimate, but by no means the
> only, method by which redress may be sought for flagrant breaches of
> faith, and on more than one occasion the moral support only of the
> Government would have been invaluable in negotiating arrangements
> with defaulting States. Providentially our diplomacy, which has been
> forced to recognise commerce, is now beginning to take note of finance,
> and our little adventure with Germany promises not to be without
> usefulness in this respect.

A close examination of the evidence shows that the bondholders
played little or no part in determining the government's policy towards
Venezuela in 1902; while as for the consequent settlement, the government did relatively little for the bondholders, who complained loudly.[9]
Nevertheless, as the *FT*'s last sentence suggested, the sands were shifting.

Nothing illustrated better the treacherous nature of these sands than
the City's fraught involvement in the question of the Baghdad Railway.[10] Germany's plan to build a line from Berlin to Baghdad, with a
proposed extension to the Persian Gulf, seemed to many in Britain a
clear threat to British interests not only in the Persian Gulf but in India
beyond. Strategic and commercial considerations mixed uneasily.
From the City's point of view the story began in February 1901, in the
context of a new German scheme for an extension of the Anatolian
Railway to Baghdad. Babington Smith, now based in Constantinople
on behalf of the Ottoman Public Debt, asked Dawkins to form an
English group to complement the Deutsche Bank and the French
group. Dawkins was doubtful – 'there appears great distrust of Turkish
enterprise in any form here, and a disposition to leave Turkey to the
Continent' – but agreed to talk with Arthur von Gwinner of the

Deutsche. He reported back in late June. Gwinner's proposal was that an English group should take a 20 per cent interest in the business, leaving 60 per cent for Germany and France together and 10 per cent each for Russia and Austria. Dawkins had then approached Cassel with a view to jointly forming and managing a London syndicate. The great man, Dawkins related, was 'willing to join with us, but makes a stipulation in which I thoroughly agree with him – that the English participation shall be at least equal to that of any other country'. Cassel's reason was not only the general British position in the Near East, but also that, as Dawkins put it, 'it would be easier to handle the business in London if we stood as well in it as any other Power'. And Dawkins added for himself: 'The whole business is, I do not disguise from myself, very problematical. There is not much profit in it, and I doubt whether our national policy would derive benefit from it.' Much would turn, as all parties knew, on the attitude of the British government. The following spring Dawkins reported on his recent conversation with Lansdowne: 'He is not desirous (nor are any of us) to have the railway built, but realises that it would be inexpedient for the Government to attempt to stop it, and that all that can be done is to help to secure London an equal participation.' For the moment they were singing from the same hymn sheet. 'I remember you expressed satisfaction,' Dawkins in September 1902 reminded Lansdowne of their initial conversation on the subject, 'that for once "politics and finance could go hand in hand".'[11]

After further lengthy conversations with Gwinner in the course of the winter, Dawkins in February 1903 spelled out to Babington Smith the delicacy of the larger situation:

> The fact is that the whole financial character of the operation has changed owing to the great improvement in Turkish credit and the appetite for Turkish Bonds in France and also in Germany. We are perfectly well aware that the financial assistance of the London market would be practically useless and Mr Gwinner is under no illusion on this point. What he wants of course from the English group in return for the participation given them is, to put it briefly, political co-operation.

In the light of this, Cassel and he had, Dawkins went on, gone to see Lansdowne – who, 'rather to our surprise, stated that the Government was favourable to the project'. So favourable that, later in the month, Lansdowne persuaded Revelstoke to allow Barings to assume management of British participation in the scheme. By mid-March a London Committee had been formed, comprising Revelstoke, Cassel and Dawkins; and by the end of the month, following discussions in Paris with Gwinner and the French, a full-blown international consortium was in place with Germany, Britain and France each taking 25 per cent, minor groups (Swiss, Austria and so on) 15 per cent, and the Anatolian Railway Company 10 per cent.[12]

It all fell apart in April. A minor blow was the decision of Rothschilds not to get involved. 'He declares they could not touch the business,' Hamilton noted Leo as saying, 'as there was too much "plunder" in it. I doubt myself whether there was much plunder to be made. What I believe determined the Rothschilds was timidity.' The major blow, in retrospect perhaps equally predictable, was a fierce press campaign against the hitherto secret scheme, a campaign led by *The Spectator* and fuelled by anti-German sentiment. 'There is a hitch,' Dawkins wrote to Babington Smith on the 15th, relating how Lansdowne had sent for Revelstoke and 'told him in confidence that he had never taken the sense of the Cabinet on the question, that he had never dreamed that the Cabinet would not have accepted the FO view, but that as a matter of fact there was a considerable divergence of opinion.' The dissenters were led by Chamberlain, always a powerful opponent. Dawkins also clarified the position of the London group: 'None of us, as you will readily understand, wish to be associated with the affair against the wishes of the Govt. Nor will we be connected with it if the Govt attempts to be neutral & says "do as you like". This would not be fair to the Germans . . .' Soon afterwards the British government announced that it could not pledge itself to any official countenance of the Baghdad scheme. 'The fact is,' Dawkins wrote regretfully to Gwinner, 'that the business has become involved in politics here, and has been sacrificed to the very violent and bitter feeling against Germany exhibited by the majority of our newspapers, and shared in by a large number of people.'[13]

There remained only the mutual recriminations. Dining at the Horace Farquhars on the 21st, Hamilton met Revelstoke, who complained that he had been 'made to "look small" ' and that 'it is one thing to embark on such an enterprise at the request & with the backing of the Government, but quite another thing to proceed with it when the Government take a different line'. Hamilton added that 'Cassel has already withdrawn & I can see that Revelstoke intends to follow suit'. Dawkins also pulled out, and on the 27th wrote sardonically to Babington Smith: 'Notes were exchanged between Ministers, and the question was discussed and studied during the Easter Holidays – in the intervals of golf.' Lansdowne for his part had the gall to accuse the financiers of having done a 'scuttle', arguing that if they had not done so he would have been able to face down the Chamberlain faction. It was an absurd claim, and the virulently anti-German *National Review* hit the nail on the head in its May issue: 'We have been careful to avoid making any reflection in these pages on the British group of financiers who became involved in the concern owing to Lord Lansdowne's encouragement. They have probably realised by now that he is not an ideal man to go tiger-hunting with . . .'[14] The Turkish problem, unfortunately for relations between City and Foreign Office, was not a tiger that would readily go away.

Concurrently with the Baghdad fiasco, the postponed Transvaal loan was once again back on the table. Hamilton took his usual, rather sceptical soundings:

> *17 March.* Natty Rothschild came. He goes in a for a $2\frac{3}{4}$% loan. It is difficult to justify a higher rate; but the City is 'breast high' for a 3 per cent loan. He had evidently mentioned the matter to many others, whereas we only want from him what New Court thinks.
>
> *19 March.* I sounded Granville Farquhar today about the Transvaal Loan . . . He, like Daniell, is hot & strong for a 3 per cent Loan which alone can be a success. He never remembered a time in which the scarcity of money was so great. There was not enough to go round. There were many competitors in the field for borrowing – India, London County Council & Colonies.
>
> *30 April.* The question of the Transvaal Loan is reaching an acute stage . . . We had a talk this evening with Schuster, whom Ritchie [Chancellor of the Exchequer] thinks so highly of. Schuster is strongly in favour of a 3 per cent loan as against a $2\frac{3}{4}$ per cent loan.

Hamilton was unconvinced, especially with Consols now a $2\frac{1}{2}$ per cent stock; but when the next day he saw the Bank directors as well as Daniell the Government broker, they were all adamant that 3 per cent was necessary to ensure success. Natty Rothschild and Cassel reluctantly agreed, telling Hamilton on 4 May that 'they still thought a $2\frac{3}{4}$ per cent loan most suitable for the government, but were prepared to come with the majority in making it a 3 per cent loan', Cassel conceding 'that a loan of this denomination would be absorbed much more quickly'. Three per cent it was, and on the morning of the 7th, large dealings having already taken place in the new stock at $1\frac{1}{4}$ premium, the *FT* looked forward to the formal prospectus that day:

> A great popular success for the new loan would indeed go some way –
> very possibly a long way – to lift markets from their present depression.

That, at any rate, is the opinion of the Stock Exchange, and more or less of Lombard Street also. No stone will accordingly be left unturned in the City to make the issue go off with éclat . . .[15]

The £30m loan was to be floated on the London market only – important symbolically after the New York dimension to Boer War finance – so it was always likely to be priced attractively.

The prospectus was issued by the Bank of England at two o'clock, with queues for it stretching four-deep from the Threadneedle Street doorway to the entrance in Bartholomew Lane; by the evening the issue was said to be already subscribed eight times over. The next day, the 8th, Hamilton was at the Bank to discuss allotment, and it was decided that the recently introduced system of preference to small investors had been abused and that it should no longer be continued. 'So,' he noted, 'the List will be closed at 11 a.m. tomorrow and the small "stags" will be *sold*.' Applicants for £2,000 or less were to receive nothing. The storm was predictably intense. Alfred Rothschild was 'very angry', telling Hamilton that 'it is most un-English to cut out the small applicants', while a flurry of cross letters appeared in the press, including one from 'A City Clerk' that added inside information to bitterness:

> It is not only on small lines that stagging has been done. I can inform you of a dozen foreign and City firms and individuals who applied for an average of half a million each for stagging purposes alone. The small or £100 applications, we are told, numbered 20,000. Even so. What about the foreign capitalists who helped to swell the other 95,000 applicants? Perhaps the small investor, who is now made to suffer for the benefit of a few millionaire stags, will be wanted later on to help subscribe to a loan when the now favoured capitalists do not see quite such an attractive chance, and when the country is in need of help, and perhaps the small investor will then stop to think before he goes to the trouble of withdrawing his small savings from the Savings Bank.

The *Economist* agreed, arguing that the small investor, so important in the Boer War loans, had been badly let down. The official justification was that the market had run out of all control and there was no alternative.[16] But it was not a happy episode in the history of popular capitalism.

The Transvaal Loan was a temporary diversion from the great European diplomatic game, a game where spheres of influence seemed to count for everything. One of those spheres was Morocco, and towards the end of April, just as the Baghdad Railway scheme was collapsing, Cassel found himself in unwilling conflict with the British government.

Lansdowne wanted him to advance £300,000 to what Hamilton called 'the Moorish Government', but Cassel was unwilling to do so unless the British government abandoned its position of expressly disclaiming any pecuniary liability. Hamilton sympathised with the financier: 'There is no use "beating about the bush". A man like Cassel is asked to do the Government a favour by making an advance . . . He is not very keen about locking up several hundred thousands in Morocco; but of course he is glad to oblige the Government at home . . .' Cassel was, as Hamilton acknowledged later in the year, 'the only man to carry a thing through of that kind', and it seems the loan went ahead. Morocco itself was one of the spheres of influence that would form the basis for the historic Anglo-French entente of 1904. Despite the assiduous efforts of Alfred Rothschild in recent years to foster a more pro-German line on the part of the Foreign Office, it was an entente fully in accord with City sympathies. A Thursday afternoon in July 1903 demonstrated as much:

> The French Deputies 'did the City' in excellent style, and after their reception at the Mansion House they proceeded in a body to the Stock Exchange, looking in at the Guildhall on their way. The Stock Exchange reception was undoubtedly the most cordial, and, perhaps, the most boisterous of all the greetings that met them in the City . . . Members cheered to the echo – cheered, in fact, everyone who came in at the Capel Court door just ahead of the visitors, and burst into a still mightier shout when the guests themselves appeared, the two first stealing in with a kind of shy embarrassment at the vociferous cries raised in honour of themselves, President Loubet, and their fair country. Strains of 'La Marseillaise' broke out every now and then, and the Deputies, catching the infection of enthusiasm, brandished their opera-hats on their walking-sticks in reply to the deafening salutations on both sides of them. The procession occupied less than five minutes, but it probably left effects that will be felt directly and indirectly for at least as many years to come.[17]

The *Economist* was only half right, for though the entente cordiale was signed the following year, it was another ten before Britain went to war to defend the French.

*

Traditionally there existed a symbiotic relationship between brokers and jobbers, each capacity needing the other; but by the early 1900s, in the context of increased numbers of members and generally slack business, it was becoming seriously frayed at the edges. Towards the end of November 1902 twenty-two jobbing firms, many of them leading ones, called on the Committee to prevent brokers from transacting business outside the market. Herbert C. Blyth, claiming that over 800 members supported him, personally described how 'during the last few years certain large and wealthy outside firms have established themselves as dealers in various securities in competition with inside dealers', with the result that 'it has become a rapidly increasing custom for brokers to accept from these firms a commission for executing their clients' orders with them'. Blyth gained the day: in February 1903 the Committee ruled that a broker receiving a double commission would have to state the fact on the contract note; but immediately afterwards came the counter-attack of the brokers, the Committee receiving later that month a memorial from Whiteheads & Coles and 1,096 others, wanting it to forbid jobbers from transacting business directly with, or sharing profits with, non-members. In March the annual election to the Committee turned on the question of capacity, leading to a clear vote in favour of a more rigid distinction between broker and jobber. The protagonists again assembled. The most cogent advocate was Herbert Leon, the leading Yankee jobber with arbitrage a speciality: 'The House was now too big to be divided into two classes only: there were at least seven classes, the old-fashioned jobber, the speculator, the bona fide broker, the option dealer, the money-lender, the arbitrageur, and the shunter.' And: 'Why should the brokers wish to tie their own hands? In cases of double orders brokers were often in a position to make a price without infringing the functions of a jobber: this was all the more so, now that many brokers were themselves speculators or option dealers.' And: 'He objected to the proposed licence to the foreign arbitrageur as though he were a hawker or publican.' Early that summer the Committee decided, by fourteen votes to nine, to make no change in the rules.[18] It was not, however, an ephemeral issue, and battle lines had started to be drawn between the great mass of small firms, whether brokers or jobbers, and the numerically fewer large firms – firms that included that unpopular, usually foreign species dealing in unintelligible business, the arbitrageur.

On May Day, a Stock Exchange holiday and the Friday before the Transvaal loan, eighty-seven members set out to walk from London to Brighton. The event had originated from wagers made in the Kaffir Circus and had generated enormous publicity. 'The heaviest member of the party,' noted the *FT* in its preview, 'is Mr G.S. Pawle, who is 48 years of age, stands 6 feet 3 inches in his stockings and weighs about

14 stone. There are many who fancy Mr Pawle's chances on the handicap, especially as his weight and age will entitle him to a liberal time allowance.' This was the same Pawle who had been dismissed by Gibbs as such a bore. On the sartorial front, most of the walkers were 'expected to don a light flannel or woollen under-vest, a sweater or "blazer", and the orthodox "shorts" ', though 'some, possibly from motives of strict propriety, may prefer thin cricketing trousers'. As it turned out, anyone in longjohns would have been grateful:

> As early as 4.30 on a cold and dismal May morning a string of pedestrians and cyclists found their way towards Westminster bent on at least seeing the start of the Throgmorton Street athletes. Gradually the crowd thickened until by six o'clock it numbered several thousands, and the police had some difficulty in keeping open the roadway in front of the Houses of Parliament. From Palace Yard to Westminster Bridge the people lined the roads some ten deep; a crowd, too, composed of all classes, and many of whom must have risen hours earlier than usual in order to be present.
>
> At 6.27 a cheer greeted the arrival of the two Oxo motor-cars, and a few minutes later the competitors, who had mustered at the Westminster Baths, appeared in sight, escorted by a body of mounted police and followed by a long line of motor-cars.
>
> The start, which was superintended by Mr Jack Angle, the well-known boxing amateur, took place at 6.33 exactly and a big roar, 'They're off,' greeted the commencement of the contest. A section of the crowd at once moved off to accompany the racers on the first stage of their long tramp, and the walkers being hindered by the pressure, they had little difficulty in keeping up. All through Kennington and Brixton spectators continued to overflow the pavements into the roadway, and the walkers were encouraged by much good-humoured chaff. 'What are they here for, Bill?' inquired one working man. 'Because they're fools, like us,' was the cynical answer; and a gust of wind and thin driving rain emphasised the speaker's point.

Soon the rain was heavy as the walkers pressed on towards Streatham Hill and Croydon, scene of Packy's finishing line twelve years earlier. By Horley, almost the halfway point, Pawle lay sixteenth and, 'with set jaw and regular swing, bore himself bravely, his herculean proportions rendering him a particularly conspicuous figure'. After Horley the weather improved, though remaining very gusty:

> The procession now covered some eight miles. Along this long line there was a constant procession of motor cars, cyclists and horsed vehicles of all kinds, and every inn was fully occupied in attending to the needs of the

pedestrians and their friends. Admiring comments on the stamina and endurance displayed were heard everywhere . . .

The last mile of the way was lined on either side with a cheering crowd, which towards the finishing post thickened to ten deep, and a heterogeneous collection of cabs, 'flies' and private vehicles, including motors galore, formed a solid phalanx in the great open space fronting the Aquarium.

The first indication of the approach of the leaders was a frantic rush on the part of the crowd, which for a time baffled the attempts of the strong force of mounted police to secure a lane for the victors. The first man home narrowly escaped being trampled upon by one of the horses, although in the end he managed to fight his way through. To Mr E.F. Broad fell the honour of first place. He breasted the tape at three minutes past four, having thus covered the $52\frac{1}{4}$ miles in $9\frac{1}{2}$ hours. He is about 22 years of age and is a clerk with Percy Marsden & Co, the well-known brokers. He had been at Margate for the past two weeks with two professional trainers, and those who were in the secret had pinned strong hopes upon him all along . . .

Pawle took the veterans' award and was warmly congratulated in the House the following day. 'The Stock Exchange Walking Match A Brilliant Success' was the *FT*'s headline, and reputedly this was the event that set all England walking.[19]

The Kaffir Circus needed a few side-wagers to relieve its gloom, for 1903 was a pedestrian year in every sense. Alfred Beit had a paralytic stroke in January and thereafter rarely left his country house in Hertfordshire. 'For some years past business has been diminishing, until now it has shrunk to quite meagre dimensions,' noted the *Statist* in July; while in the context of many mines still not working to full capacity, the *Citizen* in its weekly column on the Kaffir market tackled the dominant labour theme:

Many of the best-informed South Africans have never favoured the importation of Indian coolies, but lean entirely to Chinese labour. The arrival of our Indian fellow-subjects in South Africa in any great numbers might easily lead to serious political troubles, as it would be impossible to refuse them the same political rights as are obtained by every Briton throughout the world, irrespective of colour. The class of labour wanted for the Rand is Chinese. The Chinaman can be brought over with a return ticket on his back, and sent home when no longer required. Moreover, he does not ask for political rights, and is both cheaper and better than the Indian coolie. All these circumstances tend to make the importation of Chinese labour inevitable, and when this actually comes about it will doubtless synchronise with the long-deferred improvement, for which holders of Kaffir shares are so patiently waiting.

Patience was the key word, as the report of the Native Labour Commission sitting in Johannesburg was persistently delayed through the autumn. Inevitably gloom pervaded the Circus. On 6 October: 'Whether the worst has even now been experienced remains to be seen...' Two days later: 'A sagging tendency was soon developed... The leading houses, it is said, are not disposed to come in and support the market...' And on the 9th: 'Kaffirs sank into still deeper depression than formerly.' By 7 November the mood conveyed by the weekly circular of Lockwood & Co, big outside brokers of 3 Throgmorton Avenue, was one of ill-concealed exasperation:

> Perhaps the best that can be said of the Circus is that the leading Kaffirs are fairly holding their ground under a heavy cross-fire of adverse circumstances... The continued delay in the publication of the Labour Commission report is producing some unsettlement, suspicion being aroused that the Commissioners do not show that unanimity in favour of the importation of coolies which we were led to expect.[20]

Short of profits and hot for certainties, an overmanned market now believed as an article of faith that if only the Transvaal would legislate for the importation of Chinese indentured labourers then happy days would be back again.

*

Samuel's year was drawing to a close:

> 21 *September*. The Lady Mayoress accompanied me to the Bench for the first time to hear a case of wholesale robbery. I sat from 11 to 12. At one o'clock entertained 30 to lunch & afterwards went in State to Christs Church Newgate St to service at which the Blue Coat School Boys were present. They subsequently came to the Mansion House where I distributed about £60 in money among them, giving them also each a meat pie & a piece of cake for consumption on the premises & two buns each to take away.
> 7 *October*. Rode in the morning & afterwards presided on Bench from 11 to 12 & heard a case of stealing & receiving furs. I made some strong remarks about Street betting having to send a young man to prison for three months who had been ruined by the practice.
> 22 *October*. Rode in the morning but on reaching St James Park were caught in heavy rain & returned drenched... Left with Sheriffs at 11.40 to go to Colchester oyster feast... We were met at Colchester by the deputy Mayor & taken to the Town Hall whence we walked to the Corn

Exchange where the feast was held. I ate no oysters but had cold chicken & tongue.

The end came as a relief, even though, unlike most Lord Mayors, Samuel would not return to aldermanic anonymity:

> *9 November*. At 11 went in State to Guildhall & breakfasted there & at 12 proceeded to Courts of Justice. The procession was a poor one with no cars & the populace was singularly undemonstrative.
> *10 November*. We return to Portland Place today, having thoroughly enjoyed our year of office, but being heartily thankful it is well over. I may truly say that I resign office without a sigh . . .[21]

CHAPTER NINETEEN

A Little too Hot

'Chamberlain has been presented this afternoon with the freedom of the City, & got a great reception. He is the idol of the City.' Hamilton's diary entry of 13 February 1902 was confirmed by the *FT*'s report. As Chamberlain rose to speak at a packed Guildhall, having received a congratulatory address, he was 'greeted with round after round of ringing cheers by the upstanding audience' of some 2,000. Thirteen months later, with the war won, the Secretary of State for the Colonies returned from South Africa to receive another congratulatory address at the Guildhall. All of the Cabinet was present, and Chamberlain was 'received with prolonged cheering', but the *FT* kept its feet sufficiently on the ground to discern 'a special significance attaching to the occasion':

> If we ask ourselves the questions – Why are markets stagnant? Why is money dear? Why are Consols within a shade of 91? Why is every department of enterprise more or less depressed? – there is but one reply – that the explanations are to be found in the South African war and the conditions to which it has given rise. Apart from the battlefield, the struggle has adversely affected the City more than any other interest, and in spite of all this, the statesman whose name will always be associated with the conflict (which, as he again tells us, could have been averted only by an ignominious surrender) finds his most cordial greeting in the very centre of financial disturbance.[1]

Irrational perhaps, but more than any other politician before or since, Joe was the City's man.

On 15 May 1903 – against the long-run background of perceived British economic decline since the late nineteenth century, a decline made painfully obvious by the military humiliations of the Boer War – Chamberlain made his historic speech at Birmingham in which he proposed the abandonment of free trade and its replacement by a system of tariffs loaded in favour of colonial imports.[2] Early reactions from the financial press were mixed: the *Economist* passionately against any form of protectionism, the *FN* under Harry Marks even more vehemently for, and the *FT* sitting on the fence. The aged Lord Goschen got the even more aged Lord Avebury to sound out City opinion for him; and, that favour accomplished, he reported privately to the editor of *The Spectator* on 18 June that 'what I found out is not that Chamberlain will win on the food tax part of his projects, but that "retaliation" will find much support in the City . . .' Also sounding out opinion, and as staunch a free-trader as Goschen or Avebury, was Eddy Hamilton. On 3 July he dined with Natty Rothschild: 'He is evidently rather taken by Chamberlain's plan. So I fancy is the majority of City folk. But City folk have done badly of late . . .' Two days later Hamilton was staying with Cassel at Moulton Paddocks: 'He is decidedly protectionist but fair-minded. His main arguments are (1) that he does not like the country should be so dependent on other countries, and (2) too much thought here is given to the consumer.' What Cassel did not tell Hamilton, nor anyone else for that matter, was that he had recently sent Chamberlain a cheque for £5,000 to help him launch his campaign. 'I have felt for some considerable time,' Cassel's accompanying letter ran, 'that the present commercial situation differs widely from what it was in Cobden's time and may call for different treatment on our part. I greatly admire your action in bringing this matter up for discussion . . .' On 16 July his helpmate Esher wrote to his son from the City that 'here the only topic is the Chamberlain Campaign', and on the 29th there took place the first set-piece City response in the form of Schuster's address to the annual general meeting of the Union of London and Smiths Bank at the Cannon Street Hotel:

> No issue of such gravity and of such importance in its consequences had been placed before the nation for several generations . . . The prosperity of banking must depend on the prosperity of the nation at large, but as bankers, perhaps, they might approach the subject from a different, possibly a wider, point of view, for they were not engaged in any particular trade – all trades, all interests, coming under their survey.

There followed the key passage in Schuster's speech, the classic defence from a City point of view of unfettered economic liberalism:

> London was admittedly the banking and financial centre; go where they would, a bill of exchange on London was the one medium of exchange which always had a ready market. Continental and American bankers held their reserves in bills on London. Many of the larger foreign banking

institutions had found it necessary to establish their own agencies in London in order to deal with the business which inevitably flowed there. Why was this? . . . The principal reason was that a bill on London was created in every part of the globe. There was always a seller because goods were shipped here, there was always a buyer because goods were obtained from here, because our ports were free, because our doors were open to the trade of the whole world. It was through being the centre of the world's commerce that we had become the world's clearing house . . .

Schuster knew his own mind and was not afraid to express it, which could hardly be said for the collective wisdom of the London Chamber of Commerce, already starting to be embarrassingly divided on the issue. 'The feeling amongst commercial men is certainly in favour of a searching inquiry being made into the whole question of our trade relations,' declared the August issue of its *Journal*, using that bland formula over the coming winter to disguise its inability to make a firm pronouncement either way.[3]

Chamberlain's resignation from the Cabinet on 17 September, in order to pursue his campaign unhindered by the constraints of office, did not unduly perturb the City:

> A member of one well-known firm said that the House regarded the position with equanimity. There was no big account open, and consequently the announcement fell flat on the market. If there were the question of the Government being turned out and of the Liberals being put into power it would have been another matter. But no election is expected immediately, 'and', added the member, 'when it does take place I do not anticipate that the Conservatives will be beaten'.
>
> Another broker expressed the view that the effect of the resignations would be beneficial, as it would be apt to induce the Government to pull out of the rut in which it had so long been wallowing. 'In any event business on the Stock Exchange,' he said, 'could not be injured by it, as it could not be worse than it had been for some time past'.

The *FT* – probably the surest guide to mainstream, middlebrow City opinion – continued to back the Prime Minister as he sought to hold together a badly divided party, though without writing off the hero of the City:

> Let us divest our minds of cant, political and otherwise. It may be that Mr Chamberlain's policy is a little in advance of public opinion and Imperial necessity, but it might also be as well to learn precisely what the policy is before we finally make up our minds on the subject. On the other hand, the economic position taken up by Mr Balfour is clear enough. He

simply desires that we should regain that power of negotiating for concessions from foreign countries which we have voluntarily abandoned. We
have reason to believe, moreover, that the balance of commercial opinion
in this country is beginning to turn decidedly in this direction.

Chamberlain began his countrywide campaign with a major speech at
Glasgow on 6 October. His faithful ally Henry Chaplin reported the
next day from the Carlton Club:

A well-known City member told me, taking me on one side, that your
speech had had a remarkable effect in the City – This was confirmed at
dinner when I met 3 City men, Alfred Rothschild among them. I asked in
an innocent way what they thought of the Glasgow Speech in the City and
they all burst out at once. Only one opinion!!!!! Some well-known and
prominent Free Traders and others who had always been opposed – come
round entirely, general satisfaction, followed by a boom – Consols going
up 1 or $\frac{3}{4}$ – the precise details in City matters I never can remember and it
doesn't matter. Alfred R, whom I asked afterwards privately, more than
confirmed all this. He has been in the City today, and entirely agreed that
there is no doubt as to the impression you have made in those circles, and
after all, the City is very important.

Rothschild, however, seriously overestimated the City's enthusiasm.
The *FT* on the 9th complained that the pace Chamberlain was setting
was, 'to use a sporting phrase, "a little too hot" for those who wish to
thoroughly examine the various sides of this most complex problem
before they definitely range themselves for or against so momentous a
change'; and a few weeks later, as Chamberlain continued his relentless stump, he was subjected to a strong if little-publicised attack from
J. Herbert Tritton of Barclays, in his inaugural address as President of
the Institute of Bankers:

Over foreign politics we have little or no control, but what shall be said
of the man or men who, however great their political ideals, when all the
commercial and financial signs in this country pointed to its need of a
period of quiet, of caution, of relief from harassing and unsettling anticipations, so that the natural recuperative forces might have undisturbed
play after the strain of a great war, ignored all but politics, precipitated a
Cabinet crisis of the first order, and drove Consols, low enough before,
to below 87? The effects of the war are bad enough, but the effects of such
ill-timed action may be worse. Whether the proposals now before the
country are good or bad, acceptable or not, the common sense of the
country after hearing both sides will determine at the hustings. We may
not be agreed as to the issue to be desired, but I do not think there can be

much difference of opinion among City men as to the inopportuneness of the proposals.

In short, 'the City is sick and tired, and wants repose'.[4] From a community of men never much drawn at the best of times to larger questions of political economy, it was a damning assertion.

Nevertheless, many prominent City figures did take a view one way or the other. Those in the free-trade camp included Avebury, Schuster, Holden of the London City and Midland, the Governor of the Bank of England (Samuel Morley), Sir Edward Sassoon and Sir Edgar Vincent. Tariff reformers included, in addition to Cassel and the Rothschilds as private sympathisers, such well-known names as Beit, Dawkins, Sir Vincent Caillard, Sir Alexander Henderson (Treasurer of the Tariff Reform League), and Vicary Gibbs and his brothers. Caillard, Henderson and Gibbs were all members of Chamberlain's specially appointed Tariff Commission, but no City bankers as such sat on it, a shortfall that Chamberlain admitted in his revealing letter of invitation to Gibbs early in 1904: 'We are weak in the representation of Finance but that is not our fault, but is due to the difficulty of finding representative men & partly to their timidity where they are connected with Joint Stock Banks & have co-Directors to consult.' Chamberlain was writing shortly after perusing a memorandum dated December 1903 from the right-wing journalist H.A. Gwynne, comprising the fullest contemporary assessment of the City's response to his fiscal proposals. Gwynne usefully divided the City into four main sectors. The first was its financial (as opposed to commercial) interests:

The majority of Bankers and large money dealers are against . . . On the other hand the stock brokers are almost to a man in favour. It is especially in Banking circles that the opposition shows itself very strongly. The City seems to pay enormous respect to reputation and the names of Lord Goschen, Mr Schuster, Mr Giffen [the economist], Mr Harvey of Barclays [in fact Glyn Mills] and Mr Tritton have great weight. Indeed it may be taken for granted that these bankers or members of large financial houses who, either from indolence or lack of time have not been able to examine the merits of the question personally are willing to follow almost without questions the lead given by these authorities. On the other hand I am told that several Governors [i.e. directors] of the Bank of England, Messrs Hambro, Gibbs and several colonial bankers are all in favour . . . But speaking quite impartially and after a thorough inquiry, I should say that the bulk of interests represented, the best reputed financial abilities and most of the great financial authorities are opposed.

By contrast, Gwynne found the shipping interest 'decidedly more in favour of the new proposals', though Lloyd's was 'much divided'. As for 'the middlemen or large export and import merchants, I find there is much opposition'. More specifically, 'all those who deal with foreign markets such as Germany, America, France, Austria are against Mr Chamberlain while those who deal in raw material, colonial goods generally and with neutral markets such as Japan and China are divided, the majority perhaps being in favour'. Gwynne's fourth group was the colonial houses, which he found to be broadly supportive of Chamberlain's proposed policy. Finally, Gwynne returned to the key group, the financial interest, and argued that it had two main objections. The first was its assumption, almost impossible to shift, 'that the position of London as the money centre of the world is entirely due to Free Trade'. The other was the belief that what the protectionists' lobby was seeking to do was 'to foster and increase the home trade at the expense of the foreigner', the immediate result of which 'would be an obvious shrinkage in foreign money and the City would suffer considerably'. This latter objection, Gwynne added, was also felt strongly by commercial interests, which feared a reduction in imports.[5] Overall, Gwynne's memorandum brings out the sectional, fragmented character of the City: each grouping defending its own local corner, with little or no regard to the greater good. It is an unflattering picture that makes nonsense of such grandiose notions as 'the mind of the City', but at least it has the merit of realism.

On 16 December, at about the time Gwynne was composing his memorandum, Schuster gave a lengthy paper to the Institute entitled 'Foreign Trade and the Money Market' and essentially about the fiscal question. He began with a *cri de coeur* to his fellow-bankers:

> In all the arguments that have been used on both sides, the interests of this great City of London have hardly been touched upon; yet it can rightly claim that the services it renders to the nation, both as regards its contribution to the general prosperity and the employment it finds for millions of workers, are equal, if not superior to those of any other centre of industry, and these surely ought to be taken into consideration in a general enquiry. We are, it is admitted, the financial centre of the world; this is more than a phrase, it is a fact. Our position has indeed been assailed, but so far without effect. I wonder how many politicians realise what it means; I wonder whether even we, here in the City of London, fully realise it.

Schuster then launched into the unique importance of the bill of exchange on London – 'the coffee that is shipped from Brazil into

France or Italy, the cotton from New Orleans to Poland, sulphur from Sicily to the United States, and agricultural machinery from the United States to the River Plate, all these trades find their Clearing House in Lombard Street'. He emphasised that the continuing existence of this clearing house was not just in the City's interest, for 'it is not beyond the mark to say that on the greatness of our banking resources, the greatness and development of our industries must depend'. There followed a detailed exposition of the free-trade position supported by a mass of figures, before Schuster in conclusion called for caution: 'Let us safeguard what we hold; let us know where we are going; let us not take a leap in the dark . . .' The bulk of those present made it clear they supported Schuster, though in the discussion Richard Biddulph Martin was bold enough to declare that the employment question demanded tariff reform and that such reform was perfectly compatible with the continuing primacy of the City of London. More typical were the sentiments of Harvey of Glyns, backing Schuster's call for an expert inquiry into the condition of British trade. 'It has seemed to me,' noted Harvey, 'an appalling thing that the complex fabric of the trade of this country should be submitted to the electorate.' On which democratic note the discussion was adjourned to 13 January.[6]

At this next meeting Luke Hansard of Martins Bank took up the cudgels on behalf of his chief and explicitly admonished Schuster:

> Any action dealing with the future must necessarily be a leap in the dark. But why should we discountenance any efforts to adjust the fiscal conditions of our free imports or avoid trying to remove the prohibitions on our foreign trade? For myself, I cannot see why we should have this craven fear. Where is the old spirit of enterprise by which the British merchant and banker made this great City of London pre-eminent for commerce and finance?

Most of the discussion, though, went along predictably free-trading lines; and in reply, Schuster attempted to turn the 'enterprise' tables on the man from Martins: 'I appeal with Mr Hansard to that old spirit of enterprise which has made British commerce great, to that spirit of energy, perseverance, and resource on which to this day unassisted it has prospered, rather than to State aid, which is after all what protection amounts to.' Again he stressed his conviction that 'our pre-eminence in the money market is due to our enormous trade' and that 'it is trade that makes the bill and nothing else'. And finally: 'This is not a matter for the electorate . . . I say men of business ought to make it their business to see that it be taken away from the electorate until after there has been a serious impartial inquiry into this question from every point of view. That is the crux of my paper.'[7]

Six days later Chamberlain wound up his national campaign by coming to the City itself. Before making his speech he lunched in St Swithin's Lane with Sir Joseph Dimsdale, the former private banker and Lord Mayor, while outside there gathered an expectant crowd seemingly oblivious of the filthy weather:

> The Stock Exchange was well to the front, not only in the procession, but at the entrance to the City Carlton Club; and, although not in quite such strong force as had been anticipated, its representatives more than made up in enthusiasm what was lacking in numbers. While waiting for Mr Chamberlain's appearance they beguiled the time by singing in front of the club, and on his entering the carriage they headed the procession in files of six abreast, and, to the invigorating strains of 'Poor Old Joe', literally sang the right hon gentlemen into the Guildhall. With admirable foresight, itinerant vendors were on the spot with a full supply of 'Joey's Eyeglass', which met with a rapid sale at a penny . . .

From the City's point of view, the crux of his speech to a packed meeting came fairly early on:

> It was said London was the centre of the world's finance, and, provided she remained the clearing house of the world, any other nation might be its workshop. Now, that view was putting patriotism altogether on one side. Granted they were the clearing house of the world, were they entirely without anxiety as to the permanence of their great position? Were they as certain as a generation ago that their command of the financial world was as unassailable as it was then?
>
> He pointed out, as a sign which gave rise to grave reflections, that within the last six years the rate of money had been higher in the City of London than in Berlin and Paris. (*A Voice: 'The war.'*) Yes; he did not lay stress upon the fact, but it had never been produced in the course of any other war. He also pointed to the large increase in the number of foreign banks and foreign financial and commercial agencies as another significant indication of the growth of competition. Then, turning to the broader issues, he asked whether anyone who knew about trade or commerce and the position of the City, would seriously maintain that it was independent of influences which affected the rest of the country? If the character of the population changed, and those who were formerly producers found other employment, the greatness of the Empire would be serious interfered with, and London would be affected, because the secret of London's financial greatness was the productive energy and capacity which had been creating new wealth. At least, they could recognise that the prosperity of London was intimately connected with the prosperity

and greatness of the Empire of which it was the centre. Mr Schuster, a London banker, whom he was afraid he could not claim as a supporter, in a recently published article, pointed out that banking followed trade, and not trade banking. From that it followed that banking was not the creator of our prosperity, but its creation. It was not the cause of our wealth, but the consequence of our wealth. (*Cheers.*) If the industrial energy and development which had been going on for so many years in this country were to be hindered or relaxed, then finance and all that finance meant would follow the trade of the countries that were more successful than ourselves. That was not a prediction based on theory – that was a lesson of history.

Having thus rejected the notion of the City as somehow an autonomous offshore island, independent of the fortunes of the rest of the country, Chamberlain made his familiar case for the economics of tariff reform. Finally, in a typically stirring peroration, he played the imperial card as hard as he could:

> He asked from them no cruel sacrifice. He asked them to be worthy of their past, and to remember that the future of this country and of the British race lay in our colonies and possessions. They were the natural buttresses of our Imperial State. It behoved us to think of them as they were now in their youth and promise, and to think of them as they would be a century hence, when grown to manhood and developed beyond anything we could hope. Let us share and sympathise with their aspirations after a closer union, do nothing to discourage them, but show willingness to co-operate with them in every effort they made or proposed. So should we maintain the traditions of the past, the renown of this Imperial City and the permanence of that potent agency for peace and civilisation that we called the British Empire. (*Loud cheers.*)

Was his audience – that wider City audience beyond those cramped into the Guildhall – convinced? Dawkins, writing on the 22nd to Milner, was doubtful: 'Joe has been down among us & has unfurled his flag . . . It seems to be generally admitted that his incursion was rather a failure. Banking opinion is on the whole against him & he did not deal with the arguments that have been put forward, tho' they were by no means impossible to deal with.'[8]

The rest of 1904 was a rather dull anti-climax in terms of the City and the tariff reform controversy. On 8 February the Duke of Devonshire addressed a free-trade meeting at the Guildhall, with the vote of thanks proposed by Avebury. Significantly, among those on the platform was Natty Rothschild: perhaps by this stage he had reverted to his usual cautious self. In March the annual meeting of the Association of Chambers of Commerce of the United Kingdom carried by fifty-eight chambers to forty-five a distinctly mudge-and-fudge resolution put forward by the London Chamber of Commerce that Britain had 'just cause of complaint of certain restrictions and unfair arrangements directed against the commerce of the Empire', that the Chambers would support the government 'in measures of negotiation', and that the time had come for a Royal Commission 'to investigate and report upon the whole Fiscal Policy of the nation'. By early summer the debate was virtually dead, and in the July issue of the *Bankers' Magazine* W.R. Lawson, himself a tariff reformer, was distinctly critical about the response to the whole question:

> In the City it has been paralysed by what proved to be an absurdly superfluous cry of alarm against 'rushing' the country. We may well ask now who has been 'rushed' or who seems to be in any danger of being 'rushed'? Certainly not the Institute of Bankers, who joined so vigorously in the false alarm. In the course of a long winter session it has had the fiscal question before it twice – only twice.[9]

It was as if the City, with its overwhelmingly Conservative loyalties, was waiting for the power battle to be resolved in that party before raising its head above the parapet.

Albeit passively, then, the City retained its predominantly free-trading allegiance – an allegiance that arguably owed as much as anything to its innate preference for the status quo. It was a deep-rooted conservatism cogently summed up by the *Bankers' Magazine* in January 1904:

> We have frankly acknowledged that Mr Chamberlain was perfectly correct in insisting that free trade should not be regarded as some cardinal doctrine, never to be departed from by a hairsbreadth under any conceivable circumstances; but it may be well, on the other hand, to bear in mind that, although the adoption of free trade principles for over fifty years does not necessarily constitute a reason why it should never be abandoned, it *does* constitute a very valid reason why it should not be given up without a most careful consideration of the net results which it has achieved, and the probable far-reaching effects of any new system to be introduced. For if there is one thing true in a commercial as in a monetary system, it is that sudden and frequent changes are detrimental to the activity and stability of commerce.

Inasmuch as tariff reformers in the City looked beyond their own immediate situation, it was almost certainly the imperial dimension to

Chamberlain's programme that appealed to them, rather than the opportunity to modernise British manufacturing industry. Chamberlain himself, who had been brought up in the City and never lost a certain emotional allegiance to it, seldom appeared to threaten the free flow of capital, as opposed to goods. Nevertheless, as the various exchanges during the winter of 1903/4 showed, there was an implicit and fundamental conflict involved: did the prosperity of finance depend upon industry's well-being, or was it the other way round? Schuster himself would remain sensitive to the charge of selfishness on the part of bankers, emphasising to the Institute in November 1904 that 'the banker can only be prosperous if the country, if trade generally, is prosperous'. All the same, the underlying logic of his position was that London's continuing dominance as the world's clearing house was necessarily part of the larger national good. It was a position that Lawson, writing in the *Bankers' Magazine* in March 1904, explicitly challenged: 'Activity in bill business and in foreign exchange may not always coincide with public prosperity ... Bill discounters may be making money when the creators of the bills are losing it. In no case can banking operations by themselves be accepted as conclusive signs of general well-being.'[10]

Coming from inside the citadel, its whole rationale scarcely challenged for over half a century, this was a startling admission. The battle lines were emerging, in rhetoric at least, between the national interest on the one hand, cosmopolitan finance on the other.[11] For the young Winston Churchill, that dogmatic free-trader, the choice was simple. Beatrice Webb, who had sat next to him at dinner the previous summer, recorded his views then: 'Looks to *haute finance* to keep the peace – for that reason objects to a self-contained Empire as he thinks it would destroy this cosmopolitan capitalism – the cosmopolitan financier being the professional peacemaker of the modern world, and to his mind the acme of civilization.' But the Birmingham economist W.J. Ashley, whose incisive book on *The Tariff Problem* was published in the autumn of 1903, saw things differently. His fourth chapter dealt with 'The Outlook under the Present Policy', concluding with a less than enchanted vision of a post-industrial future:

> More and more of our capital will probably be invested in the establishment of manufactures abroad. And while London and a few other great towns will become even larger agglomerations of labouring population, the rest of England will remain an agreeable place of residence for *rentiers*, big and little, and will flourish on the 'tourist industry'. And – though with some new features – the history of Holland will have been repeated.[12]

CHAPTER TWENTY

Chrysanthemums

On 24 November 1903 – a Tuesday, just over a year after the murder of Reggie Baker, and the very day that Stanley Rowe, charged with forgery and embezzlement, was being placed in the dock at Guildhall Police Court – the usual placid rhythm at the Bank of England was rudely disturbed:

A respectably dressed man of medium height and ordinary appearance, apparently some thirty years of age, who subsequently gave the name of George Frederick Robinson, entered the Bank and made his way to the Discount office, where he asked to see Sir Augustus Prevost, the ex-Governor. The man was shown into the Library, where the Secretary, Mr Grahame, inquired as to his business.

Robinson tendered what appeared to be a scroll containing a petition, and asked Mr Grahame to read it, but the latter replied that he had not time. Robinson remarked, 'Oh, then, you will not read my petition!', pulled out a revolver and fired three shots at Mr Grahame, dancing about and attitudinising wildly as he did so. Luckily the Secretary was near the door, and was able to escape, locking the door behind him, leaving his assailant a prisoner.

The police were summoned, and there was something of a dilemma as to the best method of securing so dangerous an intruder, but the ingenious suggestion of one of the clerks to turn the fire hose on him was promptly adopted. On the door being cautiously opened to admit the hose, Robinson fired a fourth shot, again, fortunately, without hitting anybody. A well-directed stream of water, under high pressure, instantly knocked him over, and he was quickly secured and handcuffed, though in the struggle damage was done to the room. The revolver was thrown through a bookcase, and a chair was also smashed in the *mêlée*. The prisoner probably suffered more damage than anybody else, and it was found necessary to remove him to the Mansion House on a stretcher, where his injuries were first attended to. It was decided not to bring him up before the magistrate then, and he was accordingly replaced on the stretcher and removed to Cloak-lane Police Station . . .

Mr Grahame, we are glad to say, suffered no injury at all. He is absolutely at a loss to account for the attack, and it is believed that

Robinson was in a demented state and quite unaccountable for his actions, though there is some suggestion that he expressed Anarchist ideas.[1]

'As safe as the Bank of England,' the phrase went, but Kenneth Grahame was not alone in raising a quizzical eyebrow.

*

In the same month that hardy perennial the gold reserves question, in temporary abeyance since 1900, returned to the agenda – though, in comparison with the tariff reform controversy, at a distinctly rarified level. Tritton, in his presidential inaugural to the Institute, called on his fellow-bankers no longer to look to either government or the Bank of England, but instead to take the matter into their own hands. His plan was that they should increase their capital by one-fifth through an issue of 3 per cent preference stock, thereby raising £15m in cash. This they should devote to the accumulation of gold into a special fund to be known as the 'bankers' reserve of gold', to be physically deposited at the Bank of England but not merged in the figures of that institution. 'The boldness of the suggestion is apparent to all,' the *Bankers' Magazine* noted, before going on to doubt its feasibility:

> The whole cost of the reform would fall upon the banking community, and, taking all things into account, the cost would not be light. If Mr Tritton's own bank [Barclays] is taken as an example, it would mean that the net profits would be drawn upon to the extent of about £16,600 per annum in order to pay the dividend upon the preference capital, the raising of which would fall to its share . . . We are afraid that there would be great difficulty in persuading the general body of bank shareholders to recognise the virtue of the step.

The *BM* was also doubtful whether the Bank of England would agree to manage the new fund, presumably involving some cost to itself; wondered how easy it would be to accumulate £15m in gold; and predicted that the Bank's existing reserves would inevitably suffer. The debate broadened in January 1904 when, at the half-yearly general meeting of the Union of London, Schuster told his shareholders 'that it was not on the shoulders of bankers alone that the responsibility should fall, although they should do their utmost to co-operate with the Bank of England in the attainment of the object in view and to impress on the Chancellor of the Exchequer that he also was conducting a banking business much larger than any of them'.² Almost certainly this was what his anxious shareholders wanted to hear.

Three weeks later, on 17 February, the Institute heard a paper from Alfred Clayton Cole called 'Notes on the London Money Market'. Cole was a merchant (the family firm was W.H. Cole & Co of 85 Gracechurch Street), a director and future Governor of the Bank of England, and would be remembered in his obituary as 'a man of great ability, of strong convictions, with fearless courage in expressing them'. Even though W.R. Lawson would later claim that he had watered down his remarks under pressure from the Institute's 'editorial committee', there was nothing timorous about Cole's tone to the assembled bankers:

> As regards the proposal to increase the capital of the banks, my reply is that the floating of a loan in this market of £15,000,000, or of £100,000,000, will not add one single golden sovereign to the bankers' cash reserves. We can only increase our stock of gold in this country by getting it from abroad. To do that we must offer to holders of gold abroad something that they will take in exchange for their gold. A loan in this market to increase the capital of the banks, to be subscribed for by the public who have deposits with them, is merely transferring a liability now existing on the part of the bankers to the public from their depositors to their shareholders. The only way the bankers can increase their cash in hand, or balances at the Bank of England, is by following the method now pursued, namely, calling in their short loans so that the market has to borrow at the Bank of England. To put their position permanently on a sounder basis they must agree that, instead of calling in their loans temporarily, they must all keep permanently larger balances at the Bank of England. Then the gold reserves of the country will be increased . . .

It was an old Bank song, most eloquently sung in the old days by Lidderdale, but the question remained as to who would most immediately benefit from these 'permanently larger balances'. In the discussion, not long after Schuster had made his usual point that the main beneficiary would be the Bank, there occurred a testy exchange:

> *Cole*: Mr Tritton hit the nail plump on the head. He said, We want fifteen millions more, and if we have to have this amount, the banks will have to pay the cost. Mr Schuster, who is an eminent Free Trader in most things, wants to throw this duty on the State. I, as a tax-payer, say, why should the State bear this burden? We are told by the bankers themselves that it is desirable in their interests (and this has nothing to do with the Bank of England) that they should increase their cash by fifteen millions.

Mr Schuster says, 'I am willing the banks should bear part of the cost, but the rest of the cost should be borne by the State.' He did not state so tonight, but it was implied in what he did say, and I am –

Schuster: I have never mentioned the State in this matter, and I further say we do not advocate having this fifteen millions for the benefit of the bankers, but for the benefit of the community at large.

Cole: If the bankers are not going to pay for it, who is? Mr Schuster says it is not the duty of the bankers to bear the heavy burden, but I ask whose it is? If it is not the bankers, whose is it? It must be the State or the Bank of England. I have here a report of an interview with Mr Felix Schuster, published quite recently, which says it is essentially a matter for the State.

Schuster: I am really sorry to interrupt, but I must say that I cannot be held answerable for statements attributed to me in an alleged interview, which was published entirely without my authority, and which I deny ever having made.

Cole: Then I will say no more on that, but I would like Mr Schuster to answer who is to bear the rest of the burden?

Schuster: I say that the Bank of England and the bankers together should consider who is to bear the burden.

Cole: Now we have got at it . . .

No wonder that the *Bankers' Magazine* commented wearily in its report of the meeting that 'it seems hopeless to expect a satisfactory solution of the reserves question'.[3]

The question was not one that would go away, especially as the gold reserve averaged only £33m between 1903 and 1906 – hardly reassuring, granted that the well-being not only of the British banking system but also of the international gold standard in effect rested on the Bank's stewardship.[4] Resources and responsibilities were clearly out of kilter, far more worryingly so than they had been at the time of Goschen's ill-fated currency proposals. In practice the Bank could accumulate gold only if it was able to make Bank rate effective in the money market; this in turn meant that it depended, in order to stiffen the market at such times, on borrowing funds from the big joint-stock banks that would otherwise have been lent there; the uncomfortable long-term implication of this dependence was power-sharing between the Bank and the banks.[5] At the Bank, proud of its traditions but embarrassingly naked at the putative conference table, the inevitable suspicion grew that the large banks were using the whole gold reserves question as a convenient handle to advance their own power and influence. Thus Schuster's plea in November 1904 for more dialogue ('I think a great deal more could be done if we were in closer touch with one another. We all mean the same thing, but we have not the opportunities of really understanding one another. We are not in close touch . . .') must have seemed to the Bank the thin end of the wedge. Yet for the big joint-stock bankers, thoroughly conscious of themselves as the *nouveaux riches* of the City, resentment was equally sharp. The oft-repeated complaint that the Bank was using bankers' balances to compete commercially against them was arguably as much symbol as substance.[6] Two cultures were in conflict, and during the decade before the Great War the conflict intensified, especially once Edward Holden decided to enter the fray.

*

By the autumn of 1903 war between Russia and Japan was almost inevitable, and Samuel during his last days as Lord Mayor unsuccessfully tried to persuade the British government to guarantee its new ally a £10m loan. Further pressure from Japan to obtain direct financial assistance from the British government proved unavailing, and by January 1904 they had no alternative but to turn to private financiers in London.[7] Paris was out of the question because of the French alliance with Russia, while New York was not yet fully developed as an international capital market. Over the next few weeks, with actual war breaking out in early February, some complicated manoeuvrings took place. In theory this was another wonderful opportunity for Rothschilds – intensely hostile to the anti-Semitic policies of the Russian government – but the usual New Court caution prevailed. Barings, which had acted for Japan barely a year earlier, had no such hang-ups about the plight of Russian Jews, but did have its traditionally close ties with the Russian government to consider. Although coming under considerable pressure from the Hongkong and Shanghai Bank to participate, Revelstoke on 8 March informed Hugo Baring in New York that 'we have decided, after mature deliberation, not to take part in a public issue at the present moment'. He explained that if the war went against the Japanese, 'they might have to come again for a still further issue' and 'you will understand how averse we should be to making an issue which might go to a discount'. He went on:

> We have explained our attitude fully to the Hongkong & Shanghai Bank, who are on the most friendly terms with us, and who quite recognise the wisdom and soundness of our views. They are evidently in a different position from ourselves: they have a large business with the East, and are above all things anxious that no competitor should wrest any good business from them.[8]

It was not just, in other words, that Revelstoke feared to jeopardise his firm's Russian connection, but he also had little confidence that a sizeable Japanese loan would 'go' in London.

By late March, having set out from Tokyo on 19 February, Korekiyo Takahashi had arrived in London, staying at De Keyser's Royal Hotel by Blackfriars Bridge. He was now Vice-Governor of the Bank of Japan and was empowered to negotiate a £10m loan. He encountered several early rebuffs, against a background of Japanese bonds faring appreciably worse on the Stock Exchange than their Russian counterparts; and it was soon clear that the only banks that would agree even potentially to take on the business of issuing a major Japanese loan were Parr's (the old Shand connection still in place), the Hongkong and Shanghai, and the Japanese government's almost tame bank, the Yokohama Specie. But from mid-April things improved: the military tide began to turn Japan's way, Japanese government bonds rose appreciably in price, and by the 24th the three banks had agreed to issue half of Takahashi's required £10m. What about the other half? The key figure was Cassel, who brought together his good friend Jacob Schiff, of the New York investment bank Kuhn Loeb and currently in London, with Revelstoke, who despite Barings' official stance of neutrality was still looking to advance the Japanese cause and earn something in the process. In early May, Schiff agreed to place the outstanding £5m in the New York market, with Barings receiving a half per cent commission (£25,000) for the introduction. The firm's name would not appear on the prospectus, the Russian government would be none the wiser, and Revelstoke in his ascent up the ladder of international finance again owed much to Cassel's helping hand.[9]

By 4 May rumours had leaked to the London market of the imminent loan. The timing could not have been more favourable, with news arriving of the Russian defeat on the Yalu as well as the reported Japanese capture of Niu-chang. By Friday the 6th the bonds were trading at a premium of $1\frac{7}{8}$, even though the price of the loan was not yet known. The widespread expectation was $93\frac{1}{2}$, and the *FT*'s market report that evening was sanguine that it would not be raised at the last minute, arguing that 'a widespread financial success at this stage would do much to help the Japanese cause, while, in addition, the Mikado's advisers will doubtless bear in mind the probability of having to make further visits to the Money Market'. The next morning an *FT* leader on 'The Coming Japanese Loan' referred warmly to 'the plucky little nation' and, though distinctly sceptical about the claim that no other loan would be needed during the duration of the war, anticipated 'a decided popular success'. By Monday the premium was touching 3 and on the afternoon of Wednesday the 11th, after some delay, the prospectus was published, formally announcing an issue price of 93½. 'There is no question,' that evening's market report noted, 'that the loan will be an enormous success, for already it has created quite a furore in the City, the various banks of issue being besieged today by intending subscribers.' Inside the Stock Exchange, two of the managers had that day personally escorted Takahashi through the House, where he 'naturally received a hearty welcome', the new bonds by now having been dubbed as 'Chrysanthemums'. The market report gave three reasons for the flotation's enthusiastic reception. Firstly, 'the new bonds look decidedly cheap'. Secondly, 'the amount asked for is comparatively small, and the plucky fight made so far by the Japanese, coupled with the fact that they are our allies, has aroused a widespread feeling of sentimental sympathy here towards them'. Thirdly, 'the new scrip already commands a substantial premium of 3½ in the market, a fact which will necessarily lead to an enormous amount of stagging'.[10] Sentiment and self-interest, in short, made its usual seductive combination.

The issue, which took place simultaneously on either side of the Atlantic, was almost thirty times oversubscribed in London and some five times in New York. Tokyo was grateful to get the money, but complained that the issue price was too low and the rate of interest (6 per cent) too high. Undoubtedly the terms were unfavourable to the borrower, but the fact was that Takahashi during most of the negotiations had had a weak hand to play. On the face of it, it was a triumph for the London capital market – but only on the face of it. The real significance of the loan, in terms of financial history, was that it served as an important landmark in the development and stature of New York as an international capital market. Revelstoke in March had thought the very most that New York could absorb of the new bonds was £2m, one of his reasons not to put forward Barings as an issuing bank. In so judging he had only shared the conventional wisdom, and that was now proved conclusively wrong. Or as Gaspard Farrer, more percipient than most, remarked at the end of the year: 'It cannot be very long before New York becomes the financial centre of the world . . . I fear for our sakes it is coming too quickly.'[11]

The war dragged on. Takahashi stayed in London, and in November 1904 a £12m Japanese loan was floated, split equally between London and New York. The issuing banks were the same as in the first loan, the terms almost the same, the grumbles from Tokyo somewhat louder. Cassel again played an important part quietly co-ordinating the various interests, while Speyers tried to muscle in as one of the issuing banks, but had to make do with underwriting £½m. The issue was more than thirteen times oversubscribed in London, one-and-a-half times in New York. Japan returned to the international capital market in March 1905, this time for a £30m loan, and Speyers was again not allowed into the London issuing consortium. The prospectus was published late on the afternoon of Tuesday the 28th:

> Long before four o'clock the offices of the three banks concerned in the issue were besieged by would-be applicants or their emissaries, and some wild scenes were enacted when the distribution of prospectuses began. At the Hongkong and Shanghai Bank a solitary commissionaire was posted at the entrance for the purpose of regulating the ingress of applicants. So great was the rush, however, that the swing doors of the bank were quickly forced, and a junction effected between the inside and outside mobs, in the midst of which the commissionaire became lost to view. At the Yokohama Specie Bank the pressure for a time was terrific. At the first onslaught the crowd swept everything before it, including a huge mat placed at the entrance to the building. The mat caused the vanguard to stumble, and for a short time the spectacle was witnessed of a mass of people all struggling together on the ground. The distribution of prospectuses at first involved a free fight, in which fists were freely used and hats and clothing badly treated. The scene at Parr's Bank was more orderly, but there was, none the less, a keen struggle for the precious documents, and after surmounting the problem of getting into the bank it was necessary to begin the conflict anew in order to get out.

Applications were received the next day, leading to more hectic scenes at the Hongkong and Shanghai, as Eba Addis confirmed in the connubial diary: 'Six stalwart policemen at the Bank door carried away by the crowd. Football team of the Bank rushed in to the rescue.' But there was a gratifying pay-off, as Eba wrote two days later: 'Charlie got £400 for underwriting the Japanese loan. Since the loan is such a success it is almost like a gift. "In the time of our wealth" – he quotes to me.'[12]

By the end of May, following the Battle of Tsushima, it was clear that Japan had won the war. There was time, however, for a further Japanese loan before peace was signed on 5 September. This took place in July and was again for £30m: it was oversubscribed ten times in London and four-and-a-half times in New York, and Farrer wrote complacently to a colleague at Barings that 'we have managed to secure our little share of profit as usual'. But fourth time around there was a new twist, in the shape of a substantial part of the loan being formally issued in Germany, through German banks linked with Kuhn Loeb. This was against the opposition of Panmure Gordon's Willie Koch, who in all the loans had been much involved in the underwriting process. But his wishes were overridden and the loan was as oversubscribed in Germany as in London. The wearying process almost over, Addis jotted down a characteristic diary entry on 4 August: 'Dinner at Savoy Hotel given by Parr's Bank to meet Takahashi. This is the 5th dinner I have attended in honour of the Japs. It is a satisfaction to know it is the last. They are a sinful waste of money.'[13]

As Addis well knew, in his capacity as a director from 1905 of the British and Chinese Corporation, the London market's enthusiasm for Japan was in marked contrast to its lukewarm attitude towards Chinese railways.[14] Carl Meyer was on the London committee of the Hongkong Bank as well as being Chairman of the Pekin Syndicate, which by the early 1900s was working increasingly in tandem with the British and Chinese Corporation in order to exploit Chinese railway concessions; and he put the matter plainly in an April 1904 memorandum to the Foreign Office. Against the long-term background of investor nervousness following the Boxer Rebellion of 1900, he explained, the question of indigenous management was a crucial stumbling block: 'Unless one is able to make out that the security is undoubted and is under European control, it would be useless to appeal to the public at all.' He argued that this reluctance was compounded by the traditional *laissez-faire* assumptions of the British government, assumptions that offered minimal protection to nervous investors. Continental syndicates, he went on, were to be condemned for their frequent resort to bribery, but nevertheless were in an enviable position:

> There is no doubt that the methods employed by our foreign competitors are not such as would in all cases commend themselves to our idea of promoting railway and other industrial schemes, but all the same they receive strong support from their respective governments. It is unfortunately true that British syndicates are a good deal handicapped in their endeavours to compete with the foreigner and that their efforts to create an interest in the circles of English capitalists proportionately to the preponderating influence which English trade in China enjoys over that of other nations have hitherto not been very successful.

In fact, by this stage it was the City that was holding back, the British government that was pushing. 'The Corporation has been dilatory and slack,' a Foreign Office minute noted shortly before Meyer's self-justi-fication, 'but they are substantial people whom it is proposed to support and who else is there?' Much hinged on the £2.25m issue made in July 1904 by the Hongkong Bank, acting as agents for the British and Chinese Corporation, to build the line from Shanghai to Nanking. The *Statist* anticipated success – 'Bearing in mind the fact of a Five per Cent bond at the issue price of $97\frac{1}{2}$, having a mortgage on the railway and the security of the Chinese Government guarantee, plus a partici-pating profit certificate, and bearing in mind, further, that the country now to be served is densely populated and has a large export trade, the loan will doubtless be readily taken up' – but the issue flopped. A Foreign Office official put it graphically that September:

> We have given strenuous backing, spent thousands of pounds of public money on telegrams, have bullied the Chinese to a considerable extent even, and when at last the result of all this we have secured concessions, the great British public won't put a shilling into it. What could be more disheartening than the fiasco of the Shanghai-Nanking loan . . . ?

The only solution, reached the following year and probably prompted as much by Meyer and Addis as by the Foreign Office, was to establish formal Anglo-French co-operation over Chinese railway business north of the Yangtse. Mirroring the larger diplomatic reality, the agreement pointed the way ahead to a financial world of international groups and consortia – a world in which 'finance' and 'diplomacy' were thoroughly enmeshed. Being more articulate and philosophical than most, Addis as usual had the last word, reflecting that 'an imperial policy is essentially a commercial policy and to resent the intrusion of politics into business is to do injury to both'.[15]

One of the British representatives sitting on the reconstituted board of Chinese Central Railways, following the Anglo-French agreement, was Edmund Davis, an epitome of the cosmopolitan financier.[16] A Jew of French extraction, he was born in Australia in 1862, educated in England and Paris, and by the 1890s was based at 27 Old Jewry in partnership with a German called Wertheimer, the firm's name being Jacob Picard & Co, foreign agents. He operated in several fields, but his particular forte was mining, in which he went well beyond the usual emphasis on gold and diamonds. He had, in the words of his biographer, 'a gift for organising cartels or cornering key supplies', a gift that later would earn him the sobriquet 'the Chrome King', reflect-ing his virtual control of the world's chrome output. In 1901 he became the first Chairman of the Chinese Engineering & Mining

Company, whose main assets were the immensely valuable Kaiping collieries in China. These collieries had been in Chinese ownership, until in the immediate aftermath of the Boxer Rebellion the firm of Bewick Moreing, with Hoover intimately involved, had compelled a Chinese Mandarin called Chang Yen-Mao to transfer ownership to the CEM. By the terms of the memorandum of agreement, a source of intense subsequent controversy, the Chinese shareholders were short-changed by some £375,000, receiving as ludicrous compensation bearer warrants that exercised no control in the company's affairs. Davis eventually ceded control to a Belgian directorate, but in Chinese eyes the damage had been done. Chang Yen-Mao came to London and in January 1905, amidst considerable publicity, began his lawsuit against Bewick Moreing. The case was immensely complicated, but on 1 March Mr Justice Joyce essentially found for Chang. The tone of the London press the next day was less abashed than might have been expected. 'The difficulties of doing business with the Chinese are well exemplified in this case,' commented the *FT*; while according to *The Times*, the lesson of the case was that Chang's 'countrymen who are suspicious of Western finance will know that redress can be had if they are wronged'. Almost certainly, though, the affair had a quite opposite effect, acting for up to a decade as a significant drag on British commercial interests in China. Davis escaped judicial opprobrium, leaving him free to pursue his career as an art collector (specialising in Rodin statuary) and bon viveur as well as financier. Dr G.E. Morrison, the celebrated Peking-based foreign correspondent, had no doubt either where the prime guilt lay or what the wider consequences had been, writing trenchantly to Chirol of *The Times* in 1906:

> We are paying dearly for our connection with this swindle. At present it is chiefly Belgium but with the protection of the Union Jack. We do the dirty work and the Belgians reap the reward. The Chairman of the Company is a jackal of the disreputable King of the Belgians Colonel Thys but the previous Chairman is the notorious Edmund Davis – a Jew who would cheat his blind grandmother at cards . . .[17]

*

For all the occasional flurries of excitement over the latest news from the Far East, the issue that continued during much of 1904 to preoccupy the collective mind of Capel Court – and not just Capel Court – was the contentious one of the Chinaman on the Rand. The City, Dawkins assured Milner on 22 January, 'will be solid for Asiatic labour or for anything that promises more gold & dividends on all the capital locked up in mines'. The next day the weekly circular of the outside brokers Lockwood & Co accurately reflected the prevailing, rather desperate sentiment:

> The Labour Importation Ordinance is being hurried on [in Pretoria] with the utmost dispatch, and is expected to pass its second reading this week. Such rapid progress shows that the Government is fully aware of the urgency of the matter. It is reported that the blacks show a better disposition now that the money they earned in war time has been dissipated, and as they find themselves seriously threatened by the competition of 'yellow boys' from across the sea. As to the market, we find little change in prices, gains of $\frac{1}{16}$ and $\frac{1}{8}$ one day being wiped out on the morrow. The truth is that business has reached a low ebb, and dealers make prices at will, with practically no shares changing hands.

In February the House of Commons debated the Chinese Labour issue. Lord Alwyne Compton, a Panmure Gordon partner as well as Conservative MP for Biggleswade, declared that 'the question before the House was perhaps of the very greatest importance that had ever been brought before it in this generation' and went on to defend strongly the conditions that the Chinese would work in in the Transvaal. Others were less complimentary. 'Speaking for himself,' said William McArthur the Liberal MP for St Austell, 'he would as soon be responsible for introducing the plague into the City of London as have any part or lot in assenting to the introduction of what would be a moral plague-spot into the community of South Africa.' Charles Fenwick, one of the Lib-Lab mining MPs from the north-east, asserted bitterly that 'it was for this that we had spent millions of treasure and sacrificed thousands of lives, that wives had been made widows, and children left fatherless – that we might further increase the huge dividends of the men of Park Lane who held this Government in the hollow of their hand'; while the Irish Nationalist member Swift MacNeill referred contemptuously to 'Messrs Beit and Eckstein and Swindleheim and Co'. Predictably some of the most impassioned rhetoric came from John Burns, who with Keir Hardie had led the labour movement's opposition to the Boer War. After calling it 'the most momentous debate he had ever heard' in thirteen years in Parliament, and describing the Ordinance as 'another milestone on the Jingo rake's progress', he went for the throats of the Randlords and their friends:

He had no prejudice against the Chinaman. His virtues, not his vices, were to be exploited to his own detriment and to the white man's undoing, by men who were not as virtuous as the Chinaman they sought to use. As to the Chinaman's morality, it was comparable to the drunken morality of drunken Rhodesians from Throgmorton Street, who, on Friday night at the Covent Garden ball, in the presence of Inspector French, disclosed more disgusting immorality than he himself had ever seen in Chinatown, San Francisco. He did not protest against the China-man as a Chinaman, but he protested against 10,000 men of any nation-ality being violently dumped down in the heart of any community at the instance of Sir George Farrar, Mr Phillips, Mr Beit, and other patriots who sung 'God save the King' in broken English, and wanted an inter-preter for the top notes.

The government, in short, had become 'the instrument of German Jews'. All strong stuff, and the issue served as a wonderful means of uniting Liberal and Labour opposition to Balfour's faltering Conserva-tive administration, but the Commons by a majority of fifty-one sup-ported Milner's policy of introducing Chinese labour into the South African gold mines. 'A vast deal of sentimental nonsense is being written and spoken by well-meaning but ignorant persons,' noted the next issue of Lockwoods' circular, 'but we are confident that the good sense of the nation will prevail, and that the rather far-fetched agita-tion against the Asiatic will now be allowed to die down.'[18]

Johnny Chinaman, however, was not yet in the bag. Early in May, at the Royal Academy dinner, Dawkins bumped into 'old Wernher', who was 'much perturbed' about the prospects for Chinese labour; soon afterwards, having been 'dining with Revelstoke, "Haute Finance" Cassel, Hambro, Rothschild &c & Balfour & Lansdowne', Dawkins noted that 'Natty took upon himself to ask Balfour why this delay about the Chinese labour'. Later that month the Colonial Office at last agreed to the new Labour Ordinance and in June the first batch of indentured labourers arrived on the Rand. A Reuters wire – dated Johannesburg, 2 July – broadly reassured the outside world: 'All the Chinese are now working underground, and are giving great satisfac-tion. They are working amicably with the Kaffirs. There have been 42 cases of beri-beri up to date.'[19] Put another way, the fundamentals were in place for a revival of financial confidence.

All in the City agreed that, after five years of almost unrelieved gloom, such a revival was badly needed. By early in 1904 things were so dismal, Rivy Grenfell reported to his twin brother Francis, that stockbrokers were beginning to pick up cigarette ends in the street.

That spring, in their full-length survey of the Stock Exchange, Godefroi Ingall and George Withers pointed out that the earnings of both brokers and jobbers had been much reduced in recent years. About the same time a Kaffir jobber was quoted in the *Financial News* lamenting the squeeze on what slender trading there was: 'A great fuss is made about the bubonic plague in Johannesburg, but nobody takes any notice of the Teutonic plague in London . . . Business nowadays is cut so fine by the German sweater that it is next to impossible to get a turn out of a deal anywhere.' And at the end of June, the *Daily Mail* ran an invidious piece about a member called Kenyon Mason, who lived at Maidenhead, was being sued by several local tradesmen for having failed to pay his bills, and claimed to have earned less than £20 over the past three months. The new South African dispensation, however, made little immediate difference. 'Could you not prolong your stay a bit abroad?' Gaspard Farrer wrote on 17 August to Revelstoke, enjoying his annual holiday at Aix-les-Bains. 'There is really nothing doing here to bring you back; we rarely see a stockbroker, and are told the Stock Exchange is nearly empty.' Revelstoke took his partner's advice and later in the month put in some days at Villa Cassel, where those present included not only Cassel and himself, but also Hamilton, Winston Churchill and Schuster, the latter according to the indefatigable diarist having 'walked over from a neighbouring hotel – he is a great Alpine climber'.[20]

Most of Capel Court's inhabitants stuck to the foothills during 1904. Early in the year 'Midas', the *FN*'s well-informed House columnist, put matters plainly:

> The truth is that there are too many men trying to make a living out of the Stock Exchange. In normal times, taking the good with the bad, there is not enough in the business to go round . . . It is clear that, in some way, the membership must be restricted. One may admire the tenacity and pluck of small men without capital, who plod on with big hopes and small bank accounts; but it certainly does not tend to the dignity of the Stock Exchange as an institution that it should number among its members a large body who are perpetually on the raw edge of circumstance.

By early March, following extensively signed petitions to the Committee, it was clear that at least half the members were in favour of membership restrictions. Much was made of the shortage of the space in the House, but the *Economist* was wholly on the money when it argued that 'the kernel of the demand for limitation . . . is the advantage of a pecuniary nature that would accrue to members'. The campaign for a ceiling on numbers was led by the stockbroker Ferdinand Faithfull Begg. Scottish, a former Conservative Unionist MP and an active supporter of Chamberlain's tariff campaign, he was renowned for his loquacity and was one of life's inveterate letter-writers to the press. According to one rather hostile profile, 'he regards himself as a public man, and affects the exclusive, though nobody is anxious to hear his opinions a second time'. Begg now assured his critics that there was 'no proposal to limit the membership for all time', and later in March his party triumphed at the annual Committee election. The *Economist*, hostile to restriction, claimed 'a mass of authoritative opinion inside the Stock Exchange remains strongly opposed to limitation of membership'; but popular opinion among the small brokers and, above all, the small jobbers was running the other way.[21]

The newly elected Committee, moving slowly, had its detailed proposals ready by the autumn. In essence, a new member would have to find the money not only to pay for three shares in the Stock Exchange itself but also to acquire the nomination of a retiring or deceased member. 'Nearly everyone in the House maintains, and with surprise at the bare suggestion,' the *Economist* noted, 'that the public have no interest in the matter, and that it is a purely domestic affair, affecting the Stock Exchange alone.' The new rules were confirmed by the Committee on 14 November, and during a hectic fortnight before these rules were actually implemented some 664 clerks of almost certainly very mixed resources took advantage of the breathing space to become members under the old, less expensive dispensation. One member of the Committee, the leading Westralian jobber Edward Ridsdale, resigned in order to test the wider waters, but in the subsequent by-election was roundly defeated (2,107 to 925) by a pro-restriction candidate. It was a result that had the effect of, in the words of the *FN*, 'proclaiming with no uncertain voice the determination of members of the "House" not to have their reform scheme interfered with'.[22]

It took some time for the legislation to work through, and membership hit an all-time high of 5,567 in 1905 before declining to 5,078 by 1908 and 4,855 on the eve of the war. The actual expense of the new mandatory qualifications fluctuated according to the fortunes of the Stock Exchange as a whole: the price of a single Stock Exchange share during the ten years from 1904 tended to be between £150 and £250, while the going rate for a nomination varied from as high as £170 in March 1910 (and at other times perhaps higher) to as low as £15 in June 1907 and even reputedly, on the outbreak of the war, a packet of Players. In 1910 a member computed that the total cost of entrance amounted to about £1,315.[23] The contrast with the comparable 1870 figure of £60 was certainly quite stark – though at no point, in comparison with, say, Lloyd's or the New York Stock Exchange, could the required sum be termed gargantuan. Nevertheless, an ostensibly open market had given way to the closed shop.

Many jobbers, especially in the Kaffir Circus, were also pushing the door shut when it came to the day-to-day dealings of perfidious brokers. Predictably, their main man was Blyth, who in the mid-1900s continued his campaign against 'double commissions'. 'Brokers would deal with outsiders in preference to inside jobbers,' he told the Committee in July 1904, adding that 'many brokers had private telephones to these outside houses'. These outside houses were mainly a mixture of foreign banks (such as Crédit Lyonnais, Deutsche Bank, Dresdner Bank and Disconto-Gesellschaft) and mining houses (such as Wernher Beit and Consolidated Gold Fields), and the obvious attraction for the broker was that he could receive the commission not only from his purchasing client but also from the outside house selling the securities, in other words a double commission. The Committee election of March 1905 turned on the issue, with members using the financial press in the days immediately before voting to indulge in some fierce public debate. 'I suggest that the jobbers who complain of lack of business today may attribute it to: – 1. Want of capital. 2. Want of brains. 3. Want of public. The first two propositions will hardly be contested by any member familiar with the personnel of the Kaffir Circus.' That was the trenchant view of one broker, while according to another, who claimed to be of twenty years' standing, 'the whole business is a howl on the part of some out-of-work jobbers in the Kaffir market'.[24]

The election produced a 'Crushing Defeat of the "Anti-Double Commissioners" ', a result that the *Economist* attributed in part to the way in which 'the manner of introducing proposals for a change was wanting in tact, and opposed to the best interests of the House, inasmuch as it tended to give the public a bad impression of business methods of the Stock Exchange', above all by publicising the very term 'double commission'. In the immediate aftermath of defeat a Kaffir jobber wrote to the *FN* in gloomy terms: 'The public will not purchase mining shares unless it is assured that when it wants to sell, a price will always be made by dealers. This used to be the great strength of the Kaffir Circus; but things have gone from bad to worse, until now bargains which would at one time have readily been entered into by any jobber have become a matter of negotiation.' This jobber blamed the outside mining houses, also known as the 'shops': 'Prudent jobbers simply refuse to take the risk, having little relish for becoming the dumping ground for shares when public dealings are all one way.'[25] Yet this jobber and the other followers of Blyth, not only in the Kaffir Circus, failed to admit the possibility that the markets as a whole had become over-jobbed; too many newly admitted jobbers were operating on too little capital; and problems of marketability inside Capel Court may have helped cause the growth of the outside houses as well as the other way round. The small Kaffir jobber eking out a living in the Edwardian Stock Exchange had become a superfluous man.

The same year, 1905, also saw a wrangle over the 'constitutional' implications of the new membership qualifications. The managers had sanctioned with the utmost reluctance the rule that new members were henceforth to be shareholders in the Stock Exchange; they now sought to safeguard the power of the biggest shareholders, proposing that the voting system be changed to one vote for each share up to fifty shares. Their argument was the essentially self-interested one that if the present system remained in force, in other words one vote per shareholder, a future plethora of shareholders might well decide to make substantial reductions in the annual subscriptions, since they stood to lose relatively little by a cut in income and therefore dividends. Under Begg's leadership, championing the small man, considerable opposition built up against this proposal, and eventually the managers with fairly poor grace gave way.[26] The writing was on the wall – in the long if not the short term – for the system of dual control that had governed the affairs of the Stock Exchange for over a century.

In 1904 only a quarter of members were also shareholders in the Stock Exchange, a proportion that rose to about half by the eve of the war. It was an aggravating situation, granted that the managers were supposed to provide a service to the membership as a whole, and yet were answerable only to their shareholders. Few believed it was a satisfactory service. 'Had not the question of paying huge dividends to the proprietors of the Stock Exchange shares been a pressing consideration, the London Stock Exchange would before now have been in possession of a building equipped with every imaginable facility for the expeditious transaction of business, and worthy to house the largest, wealthiest, and most important Stock Exchange in the world.' That was the view of the *Economist* in November 1904, and it returned to the attack the following May, accusing the managers of having 'in some measure departed from the original objects of its founders'. In July 1905 a member, almost certainly a broker, added flesh to the critique in a powerful letter to the *FN*:

Our members have every right to expect facilities such as do exist on other Exchanges. Every frequenter of the Exchange is aware of the quantity of outside institutions which have sprung up, and which, by the aid of private telephone boxes outside the Exchange, are doing a large and increasing business, serving their customers in the provinces, on the Continent, or in America, either as outside brokers or arbitrage dealers, on terms more advantageous than the 'House' man can offer. Look round Shorter's-court, under the new building, which the managers of the Exchange might have been wise enough to acquire, with great benefit to themselves and for the advantage of our members. Go upstairs, down the basement, right under the asphalt of the court, and you will see innumerable telephone boxes and a small army of alert boys handing slips to the busy telephone manipulators. You have in this court two cable companies, who, unable to gain access to a corner of the 'House', again swell the messenger boys' brigade.

Why should the members of the 'House' not be able to install their direct telephonic connections inside the building? Why, again, should the cable companies not be permitted to have their room within the building, thus giving our paying members a slight start in receiving and sending their messages?

At Lloyd's, the Baltic, and elsewhere, the Exchanges provide a most exhaustive supply of telegraphic communications, which are posted up as soon as received. Barring a very scanty supply of news sent over the Exchange (tape) machine, we are left to our own resources. Why?[27]

It seems to have been a wholly justified broadside.[28] In 1904 ten firms doing large-scale arbitrage business in the American market had vainly asked the managers for pneumatic tubes to be provided from the offices of the Anglo-American Telegraph and Commercial Cable Companies into the Stock Exchange: in 1907 the managers gave their usual niggardly response when the Exchange Telegraph Company sought improved facilities in order to speed up the process of transferring price changes to the tape, which, the company stated, compared unfavourably with the swiftness of the 'ticker' service on the New York Stock Exchange; over the next two years the managers agreed with only the greatest reluctance to erect more telephone boxes; and in 1911 a member made a vain complaint to the powerless Committee about the poor telegraphic facilities between the Stock Exchange and the Continental bourses, stating that he had been 'informed by the late Secretary of the Post Office that if the Managers could give them more room they could greatly increase the number of operators'. Against the background of an increasingly integrated global market for securities, nine stubborn old men continued to be more preoccupied by the conspicuous consumption of blotting pads and other stationery –

'the waste in slips, particularly squares which are used for cuff paper, is enormous', one report gravely noted – than London's place as an international financial centre.[29]

Yet on a day-to-day basis, it was prices, not facilities that caused brows to furrow. 'City firm, always except South Africans which are as dead as mutton,' wrote Carl Meyer to his wife on 20 February 1905. The Kaffir Circus continued to be overshadowed by political controversy concerning Chinese labour, strongly though Lord Harris, prominent cricket administrator and Chairman of Consolidated Gold Fields of South Africa, insisted that the Chinese had 'undertaken migration to South Africa very readily' and were 'showing themselves admirable workmen'. The situation had changed little by April, as the indomitable Arthur Grenfell, shrugging off earlier personal disappointments, reported to his father-in-law Lord Grey:

> We have made quite a lot of money in underwriting in issues such as Pennsylvania, Canada Northerns, *Daily Mail* shares, Japanese loans etc. It looks as if we should make more money out of these good things than out of Africans. The big houses have been trying to attract the public to the African market but without success. There are too many shares about & they are too high. The public find they make money quicker out of good things. The Goldfields have floated a Trust, Neumanns the same & now Beits are to increase the Venture Syndicate into a big 6 million Trust, but these Trusts represent the same article under a new name & look like relief Cos. At any rate the City man sees through it & won't be tempted.

It was a perceptive assessment on Grenfell's part. Of these new trusts formed by the big mining houses, the most important was the Central Mining and Investment Corporation, an ambitious reconstruction by Wernher Beit and an attempt to instil confidence into the battered market. It failed to do the trick, as Wernher tacitly conceded in July when he presided over Central Mining's statutory meeting held at its resplendent offices in London Wall Buildings:

> For some time a feeling of distrust and uncertainty in South African ventures had prevailed, but it was difficult to find an explanation for this lack of confidence. The holders of shares did not seem to lose confidence during the long period of war and disorganisation, when their properties were really partly in the hands of the enemy; in fact, they held on then with remarkable tenacity, whereas in the last few months there had been an inclination to sell. As he had said, it was very difficult to find an explanation for this . . .

Confidence, so readily given in the mid-1890s and briefly when the war ended, where had it gone? The word was on everyone's lips, and later in 1905 Grenfell wrote to Grey of how 'the public seem to have lost confidence in the "Rand Lords", and though the output is very satisfactory and constantly on the increase, so far (in spite of what is said to the public) they have found the Chinaman extremely expensive'.[30] And in Capel Court, though its most extrovert market would remain an important element for many years to come, the heyday of the Kaffir Circus was over, never to return.

*

'The Cassell [sic] dinner was very amusing . . . I sat between Cole-brooke and John [Revelstoke], the latter overwhelmed me with comps, gown, figure, face and prettiness. I was quite embarrassed! He really was quite crude!' So wrote Lady Elcho to Balfour on 19 January 1904, but within a few weeks Revelstoke's mood was not so much steamy as steaming. Dawkins on 16 February told Jack Morgan the story:

> The other day Revelstoke came in, labouring under some excitement. We had been the victim of Speyers. Now he wished to tell us how they had treated him.
> When R was last in the US, so he went on, Stillman [President of the National City Bank in New York] told him there was some possible business with Cuba & he Stillman was in a good position with the US Govt, but the market for Cuban bonds would probably be in London & the Continent like all Spanish-American things.
> R consented to take up the business provided the US Govt would assure benevolent consideration & provided Cuba would pass a law in a form known to European investors, deposit of customs duties &c. Stillman got the assurance. R then with much study & pains elaborated a law for Cuba to pass & after much negotiation Cuba passed it in a satisfactory form.
> Thereupon R suddenly received a visit from Speyers and a demand that he would go in half & half with them. He naturally refused: they had done nothing towards the business: but he (weakly as I think) offered to give them a large share on the *ground floor*. This was not enough for them, & negotiations broke off.
> R continued & began to prepare for his Syndicate, getting the Rothschilds & the Paris people to begin with. But he had made his contract 'subject to the maintenance of peace'. War broke out: the Paris people became nervous: Rothschild, the embodiment of timidity, talked of 'liabilities in troublous times &c'.
> R drew back & tried to postpone the business 'till better times &c'. Speyer at once jumped in: offered to take it & took it, without any

condition as to war & all R's large labours in drafting laws for Cuba & educating Cuba up to them – all lost.

Speyers, I understand, took the contract at $89\frac{1}{2}$ & syndicated it at 91. The underwriting, I believe, has been eagerly taken up here & on the Continent . . . R talks of getting all the big houses here to boycott Speyers, which is easier said than done. Still this incident will greatly increase the feeling against them & Hill ['Consols' Hill, the former Panmure Gordon partner] goes about hanging his head like a dog.

Revelstoke's own correspondence earlier in February confirms that Dawkins did not exaggerate the anger felt at 8 Bishopsgate. 'His attitude savours only of blackmail,' he wrote to Noetzlin in Paris of Speyer's behaviour; to Stillman he accused Speyers of 'presenting a pistol at our heads'; and to Cassel he lamented the great man's temporary absence from London, which meant that Speyer 'made his demonstration when I was deprived of the advantage of your heavy artillery'.[31]

Unabashed, Speyers continued to set a cracking pace. 'Our friends in Lothbury will surely get themselves into trouble before long,' Farrer wrote in August to Revelstoke, ensconced as usual at the Hotel Bernascon. 'I cannot yet get over the way in which they were prepared to bid for those £27,000,000 Water Stock without having even formed a syndicate to protect themselves. They are concerned with the Banque de Paris and the Disconto in a Venezuelan Loan, and we hear this week they are interesting themselves in a prior lien note of the Manila Railway; they appear to have a catholic taste.' It was the same story the following spring, as Revelstoke himself reported to Cassel, staying at the Savoy Hotel in Cairo: 'The activity of our friends in Lothbury knows no abatement. The Hongkong and Shanghai people were round here yesterday and told us that they were at bitter enmity with Messrs S., in consequence of their having competed with them with reference to the recent Chinese Rail Road issue.' And: 'Natty Rothschild, who was dining with me last night, was also up in arms for other reasons, one of them being that S. had become alive to the fact that there was such things as the Pekin Syndicate, and was trying to get hold of it.' In fact, 'altogether there is a good deal of feeling, as you may imagine, in a good many quarters'. But in the end, for all their hostility, Revelstoke and Farrer had no alternative but to cut a deal with Edgar Speyer. Its basis was that Speyers kept its nose out of Argentine business, while Barings left Cuba and Mexico strictly alone. 'Dirty little beast!' was Hugo Baring's verdict on Speyer, but such patrician rhetoric failed to mask his arrival in the premiership.[32]

Edgar Speyer had the robustness to stay there – for some years anyway – but Clinton Dawkins possessed neither the physical endurance nor the business capacity. By early 1904 at the latest, and probably much earlier, old Pierpont Morgan was convinced that he had made a profound mistake in appointing him as resident senior in London. That April, visiting London, he revived the old dream of the Morgans–Barings alliance, essentially one in which Barings would act for Morgans in London and Morgans for Barings in New York.[33] Granted the fundamental affinities between the houses – old-fashioned, Protestant, wholly untainted by Speyerism – it was a notion that on the face of it made much sense. Ultimately, though, it was a non-runner. Revelstoke, though much attracted by the thought of simultaneously knocking out a London rival and solving the problem of what to do about Baring Magouns' mediocre performance in New York, dreaded the loss of independence which he believed was implied in Morgan's approach. Morgan for his part, as his father's loyal son, retained a deep emotional allegiance to the London house and could not bring himself to see it dissolved.

For a year negotiations chuntered on spasmodically. In April 1905, as Farrer reported on the 14th to an American correspondent, events took a seemingly significant turn:

> We have had much confirming testimony as to the state of poor Dawkins' health – bad heart attacks; and his intimate friends greatly fear he will never again be fit for any hard work. If this turns out to be true, it looks as if our arrangements with the old man would be likely to materialise, but I wish the cause for determining the arrangements had been any other than what it is.

The reports were true, as Dawkins himself wrote to Milner two days later from his London home at Queen Anne's Gate:

> I am in fact in a generally penitent and ashamed condition, for I have been making an ass of myself, and my troublesome heart has got into a condition which threatens to make me a useless crock and loafer for the rest of my days, if indeed I could stand existence at all on those terms.
> But I am going to have one more try to get it into moderate working order, and we are off to the Italian Lakes on Tuesday . . .[34]

Despite Dawkins' self-sacrificing disappearance – he never returned to 22 Old Broad Street – the alliance failed to come to fruition. In the course of the summer it emerged plainly that a significant obstacle was

Pierpont's son Jack, who enjoyed spending half the year in London and was not prepared to see his business base there disappear. Bestirring himself, he recruited a new London partner. This was Vivian Hugh Smith, brother of Lancelot, and the announcement effectively signalled the end of the possibility of the grand alliance, just as the appointment of Dawkins six years earlier had done. It would have required two more accommodating characters than Pierpont Morgan and Revelstoke for it ever to have become a reality.

Smith was in his late 30s and, coming from one of the City's leading dynasties, possessed credentials that more than made up for his hitherto limited business experience. 'A charming man, straight as a die, & from a social point of view everything that one wd desire in a partner': Farrer's favourable assessment, despite his thwarted wishes for an alliance, fairly hit the mark. Unaided, though, these were not qualities that would have sustained a major London house – accomplished a business-getter as Smith turned out to be. Fortunately for Morgans, there was already *in situ* a partner who was starting to emerge as a genuine City heavyweight. This was Smith's cousin, E.C. ('Teddy') Grenfell, son of the bimetallist Bank of England director H.R. Grenfell. He was three years younger than Smith and had had early experience with Brown Shipley and the Smith, Ellison & Co bank at Lincoln before coming to Morgans in 1900 as a junior partner. He cut a classically tall and elegant figure, had a quick mind, a sardonic turn of phrase, and was not afraid of hard work. By 1905 he was manifestly a coming man, signalled by his election that year as a Bank of England director. And at the end of that year, on the death of Dawkins on 2 December at the age of 46, he formally became resident senior in London.[35] All who knew the former civil servant regretted his passing, and the *FT* published a snapshot taken that summer at a Varenna hotel on Lake Como, showing Dawkins with a panama hat standing next to his wife, Lord Milner and Lady Victoria de Trafford. Five years in the City had done for him, giving a retrospective poignancy to a letter that Milner sent his faithful protégé from Johannesburg in the spring of 1904:

> I am anxious about your health . . . I do not want you to be *too long* chained to money-making. As I told you when in England, I think it was, and is worth while, to give up even ten years of life (from the beginning) in acquiring so much money that one *has never to think of it again.* But that is long enough . . .[36]

CHAPTER TWENTY-ONE

Across the Herring Pond

By the summer of 1905 it was clear not only that the Russo-Japanese war would end shortly but that Russia, in the midst of severe internal convulsions since the start of the year, would need funds sooner rather than later. Revelstoke sounded out his good friend Lord Lansdowne, the Foreign Secretary, first in June and then, with peace signed, on 11 September: 'I should be infinitely obliged if you could see your way to send me one word by telegraph. "Revelstoke – London" will always find me.' Lansdowne's telegram was satisfactory – 'I have not in any way modified my view' – as the British government, starting to look to a diplomatic alliance with Russia, lined up behind the international loan. It was never going to be the most popular of causes, with 'Bloody Sunday' in St Petersburg still a vivid memory, and Revelstoke concentrated on squaring the press. 'You will be interested to know,' he wrote to the British ambassador in St Petersburg on 5 October, 'that I went to see the "Times" people about three weeks ago, and told them in confidence of the various possibilities which seem to be on the horizon; they expressed themselves most amiably, and I think you will agree that the result since has been satisfactory. It is such as I think should give pleasure to the authorities in St Petersburg.' Willie Koch as ever busied himself, writing almost every day to Revelstoke, including on 9 October from his home in Belgium:

> Should it be any 'comfort' to you to syndicate say 5,000,000 before you go to Petersburg, I think that could be done quietly, and privately so to speak, without much fear of indiscretion.
> Forgive my bothering you so much. The interest I take in this loan, even apart from business considerations, must be my excuse.

First, though, Revelstoke travelled to Paris, where there took place on the 10th and 11th major international conferences on the prospective loan – a reminder that, when it came to Russian finance, London's relationship with Paris remained strictly subordinate.

For one of nature's autocrats it was not an ideal scenario. Farrer on the 14th reported to Hugo Baring in New York:

> The whole of the Paris backers assembled and representatives from Hopes [of Amsterdam] and Mendelssohn [of Berlin]. I gather that the state of jealousy and hatred between the various French credit institutions is indescribable, and you probably know better than I what these French-men are when they get together on any subject – talk, talk, talk and nothing accomplished. John got sick of it at the end of two days and returned Wednesday night, and has this morning left for Petersburg with Everard.

Everard was one of Revelstoke's younger brothers, and the two men had entrained on the Nord-Express, going via Ostend. They arrived in St Petersburg on Monday the 16th and put up at the British Embassy. By the time the French representatives arrived, which they eventually did on the 19th, Revelstoke had probably received Farrer's dispatch of the 17th, giving him the latest City reaction to the prospective loan:

> Kiddie [i.e. A.W. Kiddy, City editor of the *Standard*] told me yesterday that he found comment outside universally in opposition to a Russian Loan being issued here, but he thought this opposition as much the result of people being full of other things and not wishing for further loans at the moment as any special bias against Russian securities.
>
> E.C. is at Newmarket; Davidson [Cassel's assistant], who I saw this morning, was triumphantly pessimistic on any chance of success here . . . I told Speyer that there was a possibility of the amount being reduced; he asked immediately whether his proportion would be reduced *pro rata*, and expressed disappointment when I said 'yes probably'; but I doubt whether he was in his heart as sorry as he pretended to be; he certainly approved of the total being less . . . Granny [i.e. Granville] Farquhar has this moment been to say that he had been asking Horace as to his views; his reply was: he should go 'for a cold bath only'. We must endeavour to contrive that he does not get even that. I suppose Horace's nose is fairly sensitive and accurate in gauging public opinion here.

On a more titillating note, Farrer added a scribbled postscript: 'Fleischman [sic] is absent pursuing a petticoat. It is to be hoped the lady will find him a good husband. I don't suppose he will be any more use as a broker.' Louis Fleischmann was a partner of Messels and notoriously unpopular in Capel Court. His nickname was 'Louis XIV' – so called because reputedly the only time he was ever asked to a dinner party was if someone dropped out at the last moment and he was roped in by a desperate hostess.[1]

Revelstoke, keeping Farrer posted on the 22nd, was in no mood for Stock Exchange humour:

> I write these few lines after days of the hardest and most complicated work I've ever experienced . . .
>
> I can assure you that the work, bother, and responsibility is out of all proportion to the profit we may make in this affair, and that I only continue here from a sense that the presence of England in the matter is felt to be so vitally important by all concerned that the whole affair would at once break up should we refuse to lend our co-operation. You see the French and Germans are as ever at each other's throats . . .

By Wednesday the 25th, with no trains leaving for the frontier and talk of a general strike, Revelstoke's discontent had switched to the locals:

> It is evident that if things get worse we shall have something uncommonly like a revolution, in which case it will obviously not be the moment to embark on a public issue . . . M. Witte is named Prime Minister, as he probably will be, and if he grants at once a constitution, things may improve. But at the moment there is no real Government, and I fancy these people are often apt to do things 48 hours too late.

There ensued a flurry of urgent wires:

> *26 October, Barings to Revelstoke, despatched 10.35 a.m.* It cannot be right for us to appeal to public for money while strikes prevail throughout the country verging on revolution – no dispassionate onlooker could approve our action and nothing could justify us if accident occurred.
>
> *26 October, Barings to Revelstoke, later in day.* We confirm previous message – Even W. Koch says it would be a perfect farce issue now – you must put your foot down.
>
> *26 October, Revelstoke to Barings, despatched 8.22 p.m., received 27 October.* Of course you are right, you need not fear any precipitate action, never any idea of it.
>
> *27 October, Barings to Revelstoke.* Sir E. Cassel [in Paris] in full accord with us and says same feeling prevails in Paris – we hope any action taken will be united – Lord Lansdowne would regret to see our place filled by Germany.
>
> *28 October, Revelstoke to Barings, despatched 5.48 p.m.* Entire Syndicate expressed Russian Minister of Finance this morning loyal unanimous desire rally round him recognising supreme importance maintaining complete cohesion with view unhesitating action when moment favourable. Russian Minister of Finance expressed full appreciation our good will and strong sense undesirable annul international arrangement to which Government attaches special value. He suggested we now draft project

contract in which we can agree with him all detail omitting only price and date issue with view signature contract later when possible. Shall do this and leave soon as circumstances permit.

30 October, Barings to Revelstoke, despatched 11.55 a.m. We recognise value of complete cohesion and congratulate you on your success in maintaining it, but think that project contract should not bind us positively to issue in London even if Paris wish to issue unless we feel sure of success with our general public.

30 October, Hugo Baring to Barings. What is the news Lord Revelstoke?

30 October, Barings to Baring Magoun & Co. Lord Revelstoke still Russia – We have no anxiety – All quiet this morning.

31 October, Revelstoke to Barings. Sailing today German steamer 'Trave' for Lubeck.

The senior partner of Barings had made his getaway, paying the captain £100 for the exclusive use of his cabin. 'John and Everard got home Sunday evening,' Farrer reported to Hugo Baring on 7 November, adding that 'John in good spirits and health, but poor Everard seems to have had a baddish time on the Baltic, four days without a meal'.[2]

The postponement of the Russian loan to 1906 opened the way to yet one more international loan on behalf of the Japanese government.[3] With French investors at last able to enjoy a slice of the Japanese action denied them during the war, it was not surprising that Paris offered the most attractive terms and took the lion's share – £12m of the £25m loan, leaving £6½m for London and £3¼m each for Berlin and New York. Business on the Stock Exchange was slack towards the end of November, but when the prospectus of the new loan was published on the afternoon of the 27th 'there was the usual large crowds of applicants for the precious documents outside the premises of the various banks of issue', the *FT* adding that 'no doubt is entertained about the success of the loan'. Any doubts would have been foolish, for London's tranche was oversubscribed by almost thirty times. The novelty of this loan was not just the leading role for Paris but the fact that the usual London issuing group of Parr's, Yokohama Specie and Hongkong and Shanghai was now supplemented by Rothschilds, in turn a reflection of the part played in Paris by Rothschild Frères. Poor Addis, who could have been at home having *Ivanhoe* read aloud to him while he rested, had to attend one final banquet, given to Takahashi by the three regular members of the consortium. 'Lord Rothschild made an excellent speech . . . Fine dinner. Superb claret.'[4] Perhaps it was not such a hardship after all.

An important by-product of this series of Japanese loans were the huge Japanese balances that accordingly accumulated in London – balances that were liable to be removed at any time in the shape of gold. 1905 was generally a nervy year in the continuing gold reserves saga, and undoubtedly the existence of these balances played its part. Shortly before Christmas a short, sharp squall in the money market served to point out the underlying tensions, though on this occasion the joint-stock banks acted as poachers turned gamekeepers. The episode began on 7 December when £14m of Treasury bonds were paid off, thereby releasing £4½m to £5m of cash on the market, prompting bill brokers sharply to reduce prevailing discount rates. This had the effect of making the French exchange immediately fall, leading to a direct danger of substantial withdrawals of gold from London, where the Bank's reserve, of less than £23m, was much lower than it should have been at that time of the year. Over the following week the reserve fell by £972,000, of which £610,000 was in exported gold, mainly to South America. At this point the Bank decided to adopt a new tactic, and Holden's diary entry for the 13th is suggestive: 'Had an interview with Mr Schuster of the Union Bank, who called in a representative position with reference to financial arrangements between the leading Joint Stock Banks, and the Bank of England.' What were those arrangements? Briefly, that the leading clearers should agree to take the surplus money off the market and place it on deposit with the Bank at a low rate of interest. One of those clearers was J. Spencer Phillips of Lloyds, who subsequently described the outcome of the manoeuvre: 'The Bank then charged 5 per cent on their advances, and the effect was electrical. No bills were discounted under 4 per cent, the French exchange accordingly rose, and the danger of the withdrawal of gold ceased.' Whether this successful request presaged a period of long-term co-operation between Bank and bankers remained to be seen. The discount houses were thoroughly disgusted. Smith St Aubyn's record of business on the 13th said it all:

A very sudden change has come over the market owing to the underground machinations of the Bank of England who appeared to have borrowed all available supplies. The Consol Market have borrowed a million & a half at 5% which is the rate the Bank are charging in revenge for not having been able to get the market for some time. Owing to this organised blackmail the discount rate has gone up.

It was, of course, only a temporary abatement of the larger gold reserves question. Soon afterwards Hamilton was anxious that the new

Chancellor of the Exchequer, Asquith, should consult with City eminents on the question and gave him a short list of 'wise men'. Asquith
thanked him on the 27th: 'Do you include Schuster in this same
category? He came to see me today, and offered to be useful at any
time.'⁵

Asquith had become Chancellor following the fall of Balfour's ministry earlier in the month. The City was at first surprisingly calm about
the change of government, the *FT* arguing that the Liberals would be
'pledged to economy' and that 'the lightening of the burden of taxation
cannot but produce an excellent effect upon the prosperity of the
country'. As for the prospect of an imminent general election, widely
foreseen for at least six months, that was 'no more excuse for being
down in the mouth than is our defeat by the New Zealand footballers'.
The mood of calm did not last long, as during the election campaign
the Liberals systematically exploited the emotional undertones of the
Chinese labour issue. The financier Sir Vincent Caillard, fighting a
Bradford seat, manfully argued that the plight of the Chinese coolie
was no worse than that of the Eton schoolboy – 'confined to bounds',
yes, but hardly 'a slaveboy'; while according to the *Economist* on 13
January, 'so much is the coolie question promenaded in front of all else
that from a study of the political pictures and literature to be found in
the Stock Exchange, one might almost fancy that no other important
problem is before the electorate'. That same day news came through of
the first round of crushing defeats for the Tories. Balfour had gone
down in Manchester, Caillard and Vicary Gibbs in Bradford, the Hon.
S.F. Ormsby-Gore (a member of the Stock Exchange) in Bury: a Liberal
landslide was inevitable. Over the next week markets more or less kept
their nerve – a Conservative victory had hardly been expected – but the
election of twenty-nine Labour MPs soon emerged as a new bogey.
Heseltine Powell's recently instituted weekly circular to clients referred
darkly to 'the triumph of Labour and Socialism', but the more philosophical Addis poured scorn on the City's hysteria: 'Security, Property,
&c., are in danger. The country is to be pillaged. I do not share those
fears.'⁶ Labour and the City: a tragi-comedy in innumerable acts was
beginning.

In the twin-member City of London seat itself, there were four
candidates in January 1906. Alban Gibbs and Sir Edward Clarke (a
former solicitor-general) for the Conservatives; Felix Schuster and Sir
Joseph West Ridgeway (a director of the British North Borneo Company) for the Liberals. A key moment occurred on the 5th when
F. Huth Jackson, senior partner of the merchant bank Huths, wrote an

open letter to Schuster calling on all Unionist Free Traders in the City –
like himself – to support Schuster and Ridgeway, Jackson's argument
being that 'the official Unionist candidates for the City of London have
stated in their addresses that they are in favour of Tariff Reform in one
form or another'. The fiscal issue was, in other words, an explicit fault
line. On the afternoon of Monday the 15th, the eve of polling day,
Gibbs and Clarke paid a visit to Lloyd's and, according to *The Times*,
were 'accorded a hearty welcome by the hundreds of business men
present'. Just as they were leaving, each having made a short speech,
Schuster arrived on the first floor of the Royal Exchange, and 'the large
room was again crowded within a few minutes'. Whereupon, 'although
subjected to considerable interruptions, Mr Schuster was accorded a
fairly good hearing, and he dealt in his remarks especially with the
way in which our shipping industry would be prejudiced by protection'. That evening, at a meeting at Houndsditch presided over by Sir
Marcus Samuel, Clarke stressed that 'a change was desirable with
regard to the country's fiscal relations'. Late on Tuesday night the
City's result was declared: Clarke 16,019, Gibbs 15,619, Schuster
5,313, Ridgeway 5,064.[7]

There was no doubt that it was a crushing Conservative victory –
but, from what after all was a tiny electorate, did it represent the City's
considered verdict upon fiscal reform? Joseph Lawrence, Chairman of
the City Conservative Association and reputedly the man who coined
the term 'tariff reform' in the spring of 1903, had no doubt in public
that it did, stressing in a letter to *The Times* that Clarke and Gibbs had
been billed in their election posters as 'Tariff reformers and Anti-Home
Rulers'. *The Times* itself seems to have agreed with Lawrence's interpretation, but Natty Rothschild did not. 'I am perfectly certain,' he
wrote to Balfour later in the month, 'that the large majority by which
Clarke & Gibbs were returned, in no way represented either a feeling
for Tariff Reform, & certainly not for Chamberlainism.' Natty was
surely right. The City over the past twenty years had become so
gut-loyal to the Conservatives that it would have needed an issue of far
greater moment than tariff reform to persuade it to jettison that
allegiance. Significantly, in an open letter published during the campaign, Schuster noted that he had 'been somewhat surprised to find
that, as far as I am aware, the members of the Stock Exchange have
taken so little interest in the proposed changes in our fiscal system'.
For members of the City Conservative Association the tariff issue may
have been a life and death question; to the great majority in the City it
was not. And as Natty had added in his letter to Balfour, accurately

assessing tribal loyalties: 'After your defeat at Manchester, the citizens of London made up their minds that they would give you a safe seat, & in order to do so, returned Gibbs & Clarke by such an enormous majority, that all opposition to you would be futile & not thought of for an instant.'[8] Put another way, Chamberlain himself may have been a popular hero in the City, but in the end it was the party that mattered.

And the leader of that party needed a seat. Alban Gibbs, knowing that his father would probably die soon and that he would thus have a seat in the Lords, was within the week writing to Balfour to signify his willingness to step down. By the end of February, following a whirlwind adoption and campaign, Balfour had become one of the City's MPs. The highlight of the campaign had been a visit to the Stock Exchange, where according to Natty Rothschild's source he had been 'loudly and enthusiastically cheered'. How had Balfour penetrated the hallowed precincts? The answer was that incorrigible arch-Tory Charlie Clarke, who introduced his leader into the House and subsequently had to appear before the Committee, where he was 'cautioned against doing such a thing again'.[9] The jobber's namesake was, in his way, equally incorrigible. Sir Edward Clarke had long been antagonistic towards Chamberlain and it is likely that during the election campaign he had only accepted the tariff reform precepts under duress from Lawrence. In March, in the context of Balfour having been compelled to come somewhat off the fence and shift the position of the party as a whole towards the tariff reforming wing, he made a speech disavowing his leader. Lawrence and the other tariff reformers in the City Conservative Association thereupon mounted a campaign to drive out Clarke. By a decisive majority it expressed its lack of confidence in him, he was compelled to resign at the end of May, and within a few weeks Balfour's fellow-member for the City was Sir Frederick Banbury.[10] The former stockbroker and Stock Exchange manager was a tariff reformer, but first and foremost he was a reactionary – a man deeply inimical to even the faintest whiff of radicalism or social reform. The City had got the right man to fight the good fight over the next eight turbulent years.

*

'On the whole,' Natty Rothschild wrote at the start of 1906 to his cousins at Rothschild Frères in Paris, 'I think it is the heaviest 1ˢᵗ of January I ever recollect, & we never had such a mass of letters, drafts, cheques & remittances to deal with.' Natty's City memories went back to the mid-1860s, those of Edwin Waterhouse stretched even further. On 2 January the grand old man of City accountancy – senior partner of Price Waterhouse – announced his retirement, along with the admission of his son Nicholas into the partnership. Waterhouse had no illusions. 'My dear boy,' he advised, 'though you are pretty hopeless in your work, for goodness sake be one of the first in the queue every morning so at least my partners will think you are trying.' Young Waterhouse could not be faulted for gentlemanly charm, but his promotion to the partnership, three years after he had only just scraped through his accountancy exams, was a classic case of nepotism. Meanwhile, waiting in the ranks – for another seven years – was Gilbert Garnsey, who as a newly qualified accountant had been recruited by Price Waterhouse in 1905. Garnsey, the fifth son of a Somerset butcher, had been articled to a firm in Walsall, where in his time he had played soccer for Aston Villa reserves. From Walsall he had written to Price Waterhouse asking for a position, and on arriving there soon made his mark through discovering irregularities in a business that was about to be floated. Enormously diligent, and possessed of an acute intelligence, he was a born accountant. 'To me,' he once remarked, 'figures have always possessed individuality. I can remember a figure connected with an individual long after I may have forgotten his features and his form.'[11] Garnsey and Waterhouse: together they represented the City's chequered twentieth-century progress towards meritocracy.

In the square mile at large, the tone early in 1906 was generally muted, affected not only by the adverse election result but also by the protracted diplomatic conference at Algeciras over the Moroccan question. Gaspard Farrer, hoping to persuade Gwinner of the Deutsche Bank in Berlin to visit him in London, took the usual *haute finance* line: 'If you can come, you will find Englishmen who can still sleep soundly in their beds without fear of waking to the boom of German guns and the news of German warships in the Thames. Can anything be more ridiculous than the fuss our newspapers have been making?' With markets 'Morocco-bound', as the slang went, it was the Kaffir Circus that as usual attracted the most attention. 'Just inside the main entrance to the Stock Exchange, and where the Kaffir Circus drags out its dismal days,' noted the *Economist* towards the end of January, 'there is stretched a substantial expanse of canvas, designed to exclude the draught. The canvas is thickly studded with little paper darts, which stand out like so many quills upon the fretful porcupine.' By mid-February, with government intentions on the Chinese coolie issue still uncertain, boredom was starting to give way to consternation, culminating on Wednesday the 21st, a day of outright panic. The *Economist*, often in this period unfriendly to Capel Court, found something admirable in 'The Philosophy of the Stock Exchange':

> Well-known names inside and outside were mentioned as being in distress, the owners, whispered rumour, flinging over every share they possessed, the gold industry described as ruined, while the market fell prostrate under incessant sales. The flatness filtered through to other markets; all the talk ran upon possible failures at the settlement, and a broker dealing in the American market probably voiced the opinion of a good many when he described the Kaffir slump as child's play in comparison with what would be seen when the real fall in Yankees commenced. Yet through it all the Stock Exchange retained a good humour and cheeriness in vivid contrast to the state of prices . . . The sweepstakes on the Waterloo Cup were organised, the practical joking continued, the wrangling of the politicians, fed by a huge sheet of statistics concerning the trade of the United States before and after the introduction of the McKinley tariff, went on as though no cause for anxiety existed. Even at one or two of the private meetings, unhappily rendered necessary by the fall in prices, there were quips and jests – the risks run in helping a fellow member over his troublesome settlement treated as a joke . . .

The situation was grim enough as Wernher remarked to a colleague on the 24th: 'Losses are terrible. I know a jobber who sold for £21,000 what cost him £82,000; even big and hitherto quite undoubted firms are in a sore plight.'[12] And when a few days later a prominent Kaffir speculator called Whamond killed himself in a West End hotel and had his accounts closed, gloom was further compounded. The *Investors' Review*, now edited by A.J. Wilson and Son, took a grim satisfaction at the turn of events. It argued that the unfortunate man had been 'lured into the purchase of Kaffir shares' and was merely 'one of the multitude which was beguiled about the time of the close of the Boer War by the calculating share peddler and by his tipster press into a belief that peace was to bring a "boom" '. The lesson was clear: 'There is but one way to peace of mind . . . the way of complete abstention from any speculative dealing on the Stock Exchange in these mine shares.' A diatribe followed against Kaffir shares, culminating almost biblically: 'It has been an abomination from first to last, this African market, and for all that has been suffered and lost retribution has yet to come.'[13]

These were sentiments with which Natty Rothschild would, in a more understated way, have essentially agreed. In the face of increasing rivalry, from abroad as well as home, for the lucrative privilege of issuing sovereign loans, his approach to business was becoming ever more conservative. Letters to the cousins in Paris that spring summarised a telling episode:

> *16 March*. We are in negotiations with the Chilian Finance Minister for a Loan of about £4,000,000 & at the end of this week have to telegraph out the prices & conditions at which we are prepared to tender. Although one has long been accustomed to, & prepared for competition, still it is unpleasant to find oneself obliged to make propositions in company with other banks & financial institutions, but one must accept the situation as it presents itself, & be prepared either for public competition, or retire from the contest; &, as the latter would certainly have a negative result, the former is perhaps preferable or rather inevitable.
>
> *28 March*. We understand that the Deutsche Bank, Speyer, the Banque de Paris & others obtained the Chilian Loan, they paid a high price for it, & in view of the large number of new operations ready to be launched they are not likely to find a very easy market for it.
>
> *29 March*. The group who took the Chilian Loan . . . paid a big price for it, after adding on various commissions to the price, syndicating & sub-syndicating it, and the bringing it out almost higher, in fact higher, than the present quotations. It is not a proceeding which we should have cared to adopt, & if one only has patience, there is business for everyone.

The final letter in the sequence came from Natty's brother Alfred:

> *30 March*. I have never or seldom known the Stock Exchange so grumpy as today, & especially about the Chilian Loan, as they think it unpardonable policy to bring out £4,000,000 of stock at a higher quotation than the existing prices. Speyer Brothers here say that they have nothing to say to it, & are only acting under instructions from the Deutsche Bank . . .

It was another black mark for Edgar Speyer, who a week later dined with the Webbs and was described by Beatrice as 'a shrewd little Jew – taciturn and almost gloomy, but lighting up at the end of the evening when he thought he had impressed Sidney'.[14] Speyer had been given a baronetcy by a grateful government, presumably for his financial contributions to the Liberal party, and his popularity in the City further waned.

In April 1906, with revolution having being forcibly suppressed, Russia returned as supplicant to the international capital market. Negotiations as usual took place in Paris, Germany dropped out because of local reasons, and it was eventually agreed to make an

£89m issue, with London's share under the leadership of Barings amounting to a little over £13m.[15] Rothschilds never even contemplated getting involved in the loan, but other Jewish houses in the City faced an acute moral dilemma. Alfred Mildmay of Barings, writing on the 19th to Windham Baring in Buenos Aires, summed up the state of play: 'The demand for underwriting was enormous, and it has been very difficult to avoid offending people . . . Some of the Jews, including Sterns, have refused underwriting participations from conscientious scruples, others of the same persuasion have taken the line that the more money they could mulct the Government of the better pleased they would be.' By this time news had come through of the catastrophic earthquake in San Francisco, but even so the loan managed to stand at 1 premium on the 20th. The prospectus was published on Monday the 23rd – 'not a very skilful document & very awkwardly drawn up', Natty Rothschild commented – and by Thursday the subscription list was at last filled. How had Barings managed it? 'We are told,' Natty informed Paris on the 30th, 'that it hung in the balance for a considerable time, & very large purchases were made here & all over the world in the first two days when the Loan was brought out here.' Teddy Grenfell, writing the next day to Jack Morgan, concurred that it had been a close-run thing and expressed the belief that 'the bulk of the applications came from France and Germany'. For the City's underwriters, in gratifying receipt of 2 per cent of £13m, it mattered little where the applications had come from so long as they came. 'At the moment of writing we are popular in this market, having made money for everyone in the Russian loan,' Farrer informed Windham Baring on the 11th, and it did not need a cynic to discern that that was the surest way to popularity.[16]

Perhaps inevitably, the City was less concerned about the iniquities of the Tsar and Count Witte than with those of the unwelcome Liberal ministry at home. 'The result of 3 months of C.B. government,' Arthur Grenfell wrote on 13 May to his father-in-law, 'has developed a state of nervousness in financial circles which though in my opinion exaggerated shows no signs of improving.' That government's finance minister was equally unimpressed, Asquith writing to Hamilton twelve days later in the context of his early attempts to wrestle with the intractable reserves question:

> It is quite true I have spoken to 2 or 3 City men about the gold inquiry, always however with the double reservation, that I had come to no decision in the matter, and that what I said must be treated as strictly confidential.

> In what other way one is to get any independent opinion of any value,
> I fail to see. The truth is all these people, & not least the Bank directors,
> are as jealous of one another as a set of old maids in a Cathedral town.

At this stage Asquith was apparently thinking of setting up a Royal
Commission 'about various matters connected with finance', as Natty
Rothschild put it in a letter of 6 June to the cousins in Paris. But, as
Natty went on: 'I learn at the Bank of England they have told the
Chancellor of the Exchequer that this Commission would be ridiculous
& might be mischievous.' Asquith's thoughts then turned to more
specific reform. Hamilton on his behalf sounded out the Bank; and on
18 June the Governor, Alexander Wallace, replied to Hamilton that,
having consulted his fellow-directors, there was general agreement
that 'if the Banks were compelled to publish their cash balances
weekly, it would go a long way towards creating a sounder position',
in other words eventually leading to 'an increase in the stocks of
gold'.[17]

Two days later the Lord Mayor gave his annual dinner to the
Chancellor of the Exchequer and the Governor of the Bank of England.
In the Mansion House's Egyptian Hall 'a large and representative
gathering of bankers and merchants assembled', and Asquith began his
speech with a little judicious flattery:

> It was one of the happiest features of our commercial and financial
> position in London – grounded, as it was, upon ancient and unassailable
> foundations, efficiently buttressed, as it was, by the fresh and constantly
> renewed skill and experience of generation after generation – that while
> the best Chancellor of the Exchequer could do the City very little good,
> the worst Chancellor of the Exchequer could do the City very little harm.

All ears, however, were on the gold reserves question, on which 'he
was not ashamed to confess that in this matter his mind had not as yet
got beyond the receptive and the reflective stage'. Here Asquith argued
that it would help the debate, in terms of assessing the cash balances
on which the banks were working, if the banks were to publish their
accounts even more frequently than they had started to do following
Goschen's promptings of fifteen years earlier:

> The question which he wished to put to the distinguished and eminent
> gentlemen whom he saw around him was this, had not the time come for
> them to take the public a little more into their confidence and to publish
> their returns, particularly their cash balances, at still shorter intervals?

The Bank of England was obliged by statute, and conformed to that obligation, to publish returns every week. Why should not the joint-stock banks do the same? Dead silence seems for the moment to have followed that suggestion. To use a slang term which sometimes appeared in the vocabulary of the City, 'window-dressing' as he understood it, was an easy thing to practise at the end of every six months; it was conceivable that it might be practised at the end of every month; but he thought that window-dressing would be difficult to a point of impossibility to the joint-stock and private banks if they published their returns every week.

Wallace in his speech was thoroughly conciliatory. 'There could,' he said, 'be no question of the Bank of England's competing with the other banks'; and he described the Bank as 'the one institution in the country whose main aims were anything but that of serving its own interest', granted that 'the interests of the proprietors or shareholders had invariably to give way when national or more important issues were at stake'.[18] Between them it was a strong *démarche* on the part of Chancellor and Governor, but the 'dead silence' was ominous.

Over the next week or two, as the City pondered or ignored Asquith's remarks, the London City and Midland's Edward Holden found himself under considerable pressure. 'I have had a very rough time of it here in the City since we shipped the Gold for you,' he wrote on 9 July to his correspondent at the National City Bank in New York. 'A certain class of our competitors have been crying out all over the City that I was an unpatriotic Englishman, and that I ought to be, not an Englishman, but an American.' Significantly, Holden added that 'they have wanted to get at other arguments, and they have been hammering here at the Finance Bill'. Holden, like Speyer, was well-known for his Liberal views and he had won a seat at the recent general election, though he tended to say little in the Commons for fear of antagonising customers and shareholders. This wave of unpopularity would not have upset Barings' Gaspard Farrer, who in 1904 had described him as 'an ambitious energetic banker of very second or third rate character, unscrupulous, and distrusted by his fellow-bankers'.[19]

Neither man, as it happened, was present on the 11th at the Ritz for the National Discount's Jubilee dinner, when the guests included Asquith, Hicks Beach (now Lord St Aldwyn), Cassel, Wernher, Montagu, Schröder, Alban Gibbs, d'Erlanger, Benson, Schuster and Speyer. Lord Goschen proposed the toast of 'Prosperity to Trade and Finance', and for him, forty-five years after the publication of *The Theory of Foreign Exchanges* had won his reputation as 'the fortunate youth', the occasion marked a City swansong. Inevitably the gold reserves question loomed large in his speech:

Men write upon the subject; but the ordinary London business man – I hope I am not going to be offensive – does not love the man who writes upon finance. (*Laughter.*) I do not think they are sufficiently appreciated when they evolve the whole of the position and place before the practical man, as he is called, the theoretical difficulties of the situation. But these difficulties exist and I believe most of you who are present recognise them – not all, because there are optimists in every assembly, and after dinner especially, and there are many who say 'Well, there is no reason – we have gone on very comfortably with the reserves which we have – the gold reserves as they stand. Why disturb us?' Well, we have gone on very comfortably indeed since the year 1890, but there have been times when that comfort has been rudely disturbed by crises and catastrophes. Do not let it be thought, although at present all is smooth, although at present the great current of trade and finance is going on upon a sound basis, that those times may not recur . . .

As to remedies, Goschen stressed the cost factor, arguing that 'if a certain amount of cash is to be kept unemployed for emergencies, somebody must lose the interest upon that cash'. He asked: 'Who is to lose it? That is the great question.' And he then posited some alternatives:

The bankers ought to hold more reserves themselves. The Bank of England ought to hold more gold. (*Hear, hear.*) I see the majority are in favour of making the shareholders of the Bank of England responsible for the increased cost. Well, that is the question. I am not controversial; after dinner I will never be controversial; but I am putting the various alternatives. There is the Bank of England or there are the bankers. Then there is the Government. Perhaps there will be greater unanimity there, because now the representatives of the Bank can join with the representatives of the bankers in saying it is the Government who ought to bear the increased cost. Well, gentlemen, those are difficult questions, but I do think it would be worthy of the City of London – that it would be worthy of this great community who are responsible for the finance of the country – if they could agree to go upon some plan by which, perhaps by mutual sacrifice, by mutual compromise, by wise counsels, they might discover some method by which the present position might be remedied. I do not think it ought to be beyond the resources of banking statesmanship.

The *FN* in its report of Goschen's speech rightly stressed his emphasis on the cost factor. 'It was significant,' the paper noted, 'that there was dead silence, in an audience largely composed of bankers, when he spoke of the possible duty of the joint-stock banks in this connection, loud applause when he suggested the Bank of England as an alternative sufferer, and vehement cheers when the Government was mentioned as a last resort.'[20] Would the state bail out the joint-stock bankers? As the Bank of England's Cole had robustly charged Schuster, that was now the not-so-hidden agenda of the debate.

Almost immediately, as it turned out, the City big-wigs had much else on their minds. Late on the afternoon of 13 July, a Friday, Morgans in London received a telegram from Jack Morgan in New York. 'Speyer & Co NY have heard important Banking house is in trouble in London. Do you hear any rumours if so what. Cable as soon as possible.' Within the hour Grenfell had wired back:

> A few brokers are in trouble and the losses of South African houses have been very large. The idleness of markets and depression in prices gilt-edged has given rise to the wildest rumours of difficulties affecting even Baring Bros & Co on account of fall in Russians & Speyer Bros on a/c of undergrounds. From Bank of England & from other sources I believe no important house in difficulties.

The Russian loan had come back to haunt Barings, as the situation in Russia once again deteriorated, the price of the loan stock went to a discount, and 8 Bishopsgate was believed to be a large holder. At the start of the following week Charles Goschen was sent by Wallace to New Court to reassure Rothschilds that none of the rumours about City houses had any foundation; while Grenfell the next day wrote along similar lines to Jack Morgan about the absurd rumours which, according to him, had touched on every major City house with the exception of Rothschilds. On that Tuesday evening, as fate transpired, Revelstoke found himself giving a banquet to General Julio Roca and other prominent Argentine personages. Mildmay, writing to Windham Baring, described a memorable occasion.

> I think Roca and all the Argentines were very pleased. As you may imagine the function was rather a ghastly entertainment but it went off very well. The food and drink were not at all bad . . . The feature of the evening was John's Spanish speech which excited the greatest admiration: he really did it very well. The only contretemps were that the toastmaster insisted on calling the guest of the evening General Roco, and when all stood up in solemn silence to hear the Argentine National Anthem the band played some tune which the Argentines present informed us had nothing at all to do with their country. When John sent to expostulate with the bandmaster the bandmaster was so angry that he made all his men pack up their instruments and walked straight out of the hall. They were, however, brought back and made to play a waltz as a

punishment, but we never succeeded in hearing the Argentine National Anthem.

Banquets buttering no parsnips, the rumours continued to swell. 'Something serious must be happening,' noted Smith St Aubyn's somewhat baffled diarist on Thursday the 19th. 'Forced sales of gilt edged stocks continue, & all sorts of names are mentioned as being in trouble. Barings, Speyers, even Morgans & more especially Erlangers. Nobody seems to be able to trace where the selling is coming from . . .' The next afternoon, under renewed interrogation from New York, Morgans sent back a further reassuring cable: 'We consider there is no foundation for the rumor whatever. Barings still talked about and on very best authority know them exceptionally strong. Speyer Bros have withdrawn their new scheme for financing underground which created comment.'[21] Two days later the Duma was dissolved, the Russian loan slumped to as low as 11 discount, and all the fine spring words about the loan paving the way to a more democratic future seemed at best fatuous.

The rumours about other houses gradually died down, but it was now that Revelstoke underwent what must have been a somewhat humiliating experience, described by Farrer in a letter to New York early in August:

> John went round to the Bk of England with our figures & by good fortune found the head of the discount department with the Governors [i.e. the deputy-governor was also present]. One Search by name, a real croaker but far the ablest of the Bank's permanent officials. The Governor commented that there cannot be another house in London in so liquid a position: & Search added 'no nor any other two put together Mr Governors' and his interview ended.

In another letter Farrer added the detail that when Revelstoke had arrived in the Governors' room he had asked for Search to remain – a wise tactic. Mildmay, in his regular despatch to Buenos Aires, offered a perceptive overview on the whole unpleasant episode:

> I am not altogether surprised that rumours regarding our affairs reached Buenos Aires. We heard here that our name was 'mentioned', principally, I think, in the west end of the town; I suppose people thought that the Russian loan had not really been taken up by investors and that we had been left with more of it than we could afford to pay for. We think, or rather we hope, that the better informed people realise that in the issue of loans our position is that of intermediaries between the public

and the borrower. Our resources are not nearly large enough to enable us to retain any considerable portion of any loan we may happen to bring out, and we should much prefer making the underwriters take up a proportion of their liability, disagreeable though that would be, to hampering our own position in any way. The Russians we hold, taking into account our profit on the issue, stand us in at next to nothing.[22]

Sancho Panza rather than Don Quixote, perhaps, but even if the City remained its usual credulous, rumour-ridden self, there was no doubting that the lessons of 1890 had been fully learned and digested at 8 Bishopsgate.

*

I have decided to turn myself into a Company . . . This will of course be a private C° & I shall own all the stock. But I think it preferable to eliminate myself personally & try & build up a big business *im*personally. It is much easier to do so under an organised & established C° than to conduct such business under one's own name, as if things go well I receive all the profits, on the other hand if things go wrong – the failure will not be associated with my name . . .

Arthur Grenfell was writing in August 1906 to his father-in-law Lord Grey, now Governor-General of Canada, and the name of the new concern was to be the Canadian Agency. The enthusiast, still a partner at Chaplin, Milne, Grenfell & Co, went on:

If I am successful it will mean that the best of Canadian business is introduced into England through me, & though that means great responsibility & much work, it will interest me & pay me. No one else seems keen to assume the load, so why should not I have a go! . . . You may wonder from all this whether I am inclined to drift from Chaplins! I suppose I am doing so, but very little. Chaplin & the other partners are away most of the time & don't care about taking on the new & untried, so I let them jog along slowly & hope gradually to steer them into the position of a banking house pure & simple. This would be much more in line with Chaplin's ideas – he simply wants to draw his £10 or 12,000 a year & enjoy his holidays . . .

Grenfell added that he was recruiting his brother-in-law Guy St Aubyn, ex-army, to help run the Canadian Agency. And, in a rare flash of self-revelation: 'He is extremely good at detail, rather precise, & easily frightened & as I am entirely lacking in these qualities (so necessary for a business man) I think he will be most useful to me.'[23]

'City other than the American market is not very good,' Grenfell in the same letter observed of the current mood. 'We are afraid of dear money & other bogies.' During September these fears intensified, against a background of feverish speculation in New York and an increasingly worrying drain of gold from London across the Atlantic. 'Why Does New York Need So Much Gold?' asked W.R. Lawson in the *Bankers' Magazine*. The answer, he had no doubt, was the relatively new phenomenon of finance bills – as opposed to commercial bills – and the existence of 'an ever-obliging milch cow like Lombard Street to draw upon'.[24] The City's more conservative accepting houses resisted these new-fangled bills. 'You know that the class of draft we prefer to accept is that which bears on the face of it some indication of having been drawn against a particular lot of merchandise,' Mildmay wrote to Windham Baring in June 1906. 'Drafts expressed in round amounts and perhaps drawn at periods when movements of merchandise would not naturally be expected are always open to criticism on the score that they are Finance Bills.' Farrer reiterated the point soon afterwards, asserting to an American correspondent that 'generations of experience have shown us that credits issued for strictly mercantile purposes are a safe business'. By September there were probably about $400m worth of finance bills drawn from the USA on London and (to a lesser extent) Paris, and Lawson prepared to sound a full-scale alarm:

> The money raised in Lombard Street by means of finance bills can be made to perform a variety of clever tricks on the other side of the Atlantic. If taken away in gold, as it often is, every sovereign may become the basis for bank loans to four times its own value. It is with bank loans that most of the conjuring in Wall Street is done. They are the essential part of the hocus-pocus by which stocks are rigged and bogus markets are made. Indirectly the big railroad and industrial corporations depend also on the banks for the engineering of their new capital issues.[25]

The finance bill, however, had come to stay – even though the Bank of England now started actively to discriminate against such bills. It has been calculated that in 1913, of the £350m in prime bills that was outstanding, some £210m represented finance bills. Or in the words of Hartley Withers, writing in about 1910: 'Out of bills of exchange, originally drawn against merchandise actually shipped, grew the finance bill drawn sometimes in anticipation of produce or merchandise to be shipped, sometimes against securities, and sometimes against the credit of the parties to it.'[26] It all added to the liquidity of the London money market, and in turn the London Stock Exchange, but during these

Edwardian years also imposed formidable strains on the custodians of the national gold reserve.

Thursday was traditionally the day on which directors of the Bank of England met to decide any change to Bank rate, and on 4 October 1906, with the rate standing at an acceptable 4 per cent, a large crowd of Stock Exchange members gathered in the Consol market, where there was 'a shout of welcome as the board went up which marks No Change'. But by Wednesday the 10th, with gold withdrawals mounting and the reserve dipping, there was even money in the House on the rate rising on the morrow. 'The City has been haunted for so long by a vision of a higher official minimum,' asserted the *FT*'s man in the markets, 'that a 5 per cent rate would by many people be welcomed as putting an end to a period of suspense.' Bank rate duly went up to 5 per cent and 'London accepted the decision with resignation'. The following Thursday the rate remained unchanged but gloomy talk persisted of a further rise – 'Threadneedle Street has, of course, arrived at the season when the demands upon it from abroad are usually keenest, and naturally a Reserve of under 19 millions makes the market sensitive to every rumour of possible further withdrawals.' The next day, Friday the 19th, paid for all:

> Business in the Stock Exchange during the first hour was of the ordinary humdrum character, and prices moved narrowly. Consols showed a tendency to dribble away, but that is too characteristic of Consols nowadays to excite general remark. At half-past twelve the Government broker, unobserved except by a small knot of bystanders, entered the Consol market and announced that the Bank Rate had been raised to 6 per cent. Instantly there was a rush on the part of the few early informed ones to other parts of the House, more especially to the Yankee section, with selling orders. It was, of course, not many minutes before the news became generally known, although it was at first hard to make some members really credit the fact.[27]

Bank rate had not been at 6 per cent since the closing days of 1899, and this time there was no patriotic cause to dull the shock.

The following morning, shortly before noon, the still-traumatised City heard that the firm of P. Macfadyen & Co had closed its doors, having been compelled to suspend payments. Merchant bankers of the second rather than the first order, doing a substantial Indian banking business principally with Madras, Macfadyens was rumoured to have engaged in disastrous operations 'bearing' copper. That afternoon the firm's senior partner, Patrick Macfadyen, walked from the firm's Old

Broad Street offices to the Old Street terminal of the City and South
London Railway, went down to the platform, stepped on to the line
and started walking. He kept walking for thirty or forty yards and then
lay down in front of an oncoming train, the driver of which subsequently reported that he had run over an obstruction. The body was
so badly mutilated that it could not be identified until Monday. At the
inquest the main evidence was given by Ernest Wallace, the firm's
manager: 'During the week he had said to Mr Macfadyen, "You won't
desert us, will you? Do your best, and we will work with you, but don't
desert us." He replied, "We will see." '[28]

With Bank rate at 6 per cent it was scarcely more fun being a bill
broker. 'Money very much wanted,' noted Smith St Aubyn on Monday
the 22nd. And on Tuesday the 23rd: 'Money worse than ever.' And
Wednesday the 24th: 'Money in a frightful condition.' Over the next
few weeks a more or less similar tone prevailed in these daily diary
entries, and on 13 November no one queried the title when the Chartered Institute of Secretaries gathered that evening to hear a lecture by
Lawson on 'The Abnormal State of the Money Market'. He began in
his usual arresting style:

> London might still claim to be the monetary centre of the world – there
> was no harm in clinging to family traditions – but the monetary world
> grew bigger every day, and it was doubtful if the centre was keeping pace
> with it. The heart might be no longer strong enough for the body. Where
> Lombard Street formerly ruled supreme it was now only one in a
> multitude of competitive centres, all pulling against each other.

Temperamentally prone to the apocalyptic, Lawson was more sure
than ever that these were momentous times:

> The latest 'creations of credit', which were now exercising the astute
> minds of Lombard Street, had certain peculiarities that challenged more
> than usual vigilance. In the first place, they appeared to be upon a wholly
> unprecedented scale. Secondly, their foreign origin admitted of less con-
> trol over them than domestic creations of credit would be subject to.
> Thirdly, they were enveloped in a quite impenetrable mystery. Their
> amount and their distribution could only be guessed. No bank would
> admit having any considerable quantity of such paper, though all of them
> were quite candid as to there being a lot of it somewhere. Fourthly, the
> principal creators of those credits were notorious speculators in New
> York and elsewhere. Those speculators had used the paper capital raised
> on them in practically cornering all the principal markets in their own
> country. Land, house property, staple commodities and stocks had been

run up to giddy heights, and, on the security of those dangerous prices, loans and discounts were being freely granted in London. The London Money Market, in short, was holding the candle to a vast army of foreign speculators, not American only, but Argentine, Brazilian, Mexican and Egyptian . . .

The unknown and undiscernible mass of that foreign credit paper hung like a pall over Lombard Street. It perplexed and tantalised the official heads of the Money Market in Threadneedle Street. Rather late in the day they had begun to take special precautions against it, but so far without obvious success. It had so greatly aggravated their chronic difficulties in maintaining an effective Bank Rate, that the attempt might by-and-bye have to be abandoned. The Bank Rate itself represents one of the abnormal conditions of the Money Market. Next to surreptitious foreign credits, that was the most sinister anomaly of the day . . .

Lawson's language was overheated but symptomatic, and he was right to stress that it was not only American influences to which the London money market had become so dangerously susceptible. The final factor precipitating the rise in Bank rate to 6 per cent had in fact been a heavy demand for gold from Egypt, where a bumper cotton crop inevitably attracted much speculative attention.[29]

Eventually, as Mildmay updated Windham Baring on 29 November, the tone improved:

Conditions are much the same as they have been for the past fortnight except that a bullish feeling is gaining ground. Markets are very firm all round and the publication of a better Bank return today has had an excellent effect, the reserve being nearly equal to what it was a year ago. Gold has been coming to this country and the movement in our favour is expected to continue, although we quite realise that there are limits to the supply available from France. We are ourselves shipping £150,000 to Brazil by tomorrow's boat, and Rothschilds are shipping a larger quantity, making it is said £600,000 in all.

The reference to France was significant, for the Bank of France, apparently on its own initiative, sent £2½m of gold to London, largely because it had no wish to see Bank rate go up to 7 per cent. Even so, as Mildmay's letter had indicated, the rest of the world did not cease demanding London's gold, and there was an ominous note to E.C. Grenfell's telegram on 8 December to Morgans in New York:

Strictly confidential & for your own use only. In view of large demand for gold threatened by USA, Brazil, Egypt, Argentine Confederation Bank rate advance not improbable unless Bank of England secure some incom-

ing gold before 1st January. In any case Bank rate will advance instantly
if any gold is taken from it.

In the event Bank rate remained at 6 per cent for the rest of the year,
business on the Stock Exchange almost ground to a halt, and nomina-
tions for new membership were down to a pitiful £30 or so. 'Thus ends
this most unprofitable of years, with money dearer than it has been for
40 years': Smith St Aubyn's diary entry for New Year's Eve betrayed
the sometimes formidable cost to the natives of running an international gold standard.[30]

By contrast, Arthur Grenfell was in predictably bullish mood as 1906
drew to a close. Writing to his father-in-law while at sea, and giving
his address as '3 days off Havana', he announced that he had decided
to increase the capital of the Canadian Agency to £150,000 and for
that purpose was seeking to bring in some friends. 'I approached
Morgans first & offered them 5,000 shares. Vivian Smith listened to
my story & then told me he would think it over.' In fact, Grenfell went
on, Smith and his partners wanted to take 55,000 out of the 100,000
ordinary shares, provided Pierpont Morgan agreed. 'I need hardly say
I was very much touched at the confidence which they apparently feel
in me . . . If Morgan agrees I feel I have really got my foot on the ladder
& provided I keep my head my Canadian Agency's future should be
assured . . .'[31]

*

For those in the City who enjoyed such things – always a minority –
two 'questions' dominated the winter of 1906/7. The first, inevitably,
was gold reserves. On 30 October, against a background of the severe
drain on gold and ensuing mini-crisis, Hamilton sought on Asquith's
behalf to press the Governor of the Bank, Alexander Wallace: 'Would
you . . . kindly tell me whether of the many proposals laid before you
for increasing the metallic reserve of this Country, an Act requiring the
Joint Stock Banks to state every week what is the amount of gold they
have at the Bank is not the best, all things considered?' In reply,
Wallace accepted that such a measure would certainly increase the
reserve, but wondered 'whether this is altogether a happy moment to
introduce any such Act'. For, 'if the Banks have to keep a larger
metallic reserve, they necessarily must reduce their holdings of
Securities, and in the present position of matters I think the Chancellor
would consider it rather unsatisfactory in many ways that Consols,

which would represent mainly what could be sold, should have another depressing influence brought to bear upon them'. Hamilton in turn bowed to this logic and said that Asquith was instead 'rather minded at present to try Mr Goschen's plan by the issue of small notes'. Wallace countered on 2 November:

> Your letter . . . starts another hare and a very big one. The question was very seriously considered here and ruminated on fifteen years ago and I think the balance of opinion, and the best opinion, was against Lord Goschen's suggestion for the issue of £1 Notes. Any action interfering with the status quo may carry with it such serious consequences that I cannot too strongly urge that nothing should be done without the most serious and exhaustive enquiry . . .

So much for that hare, stopped in its tracks almost as soon as it had been released. Over the next few weeks Asquith seems to have come to the conclusion that to attempt to introduce legislation, of whatever sort, would be counterproductive. In effect he returned the ball firmly back into the court of the bankers.[32]

No joint-stock banker was more intimately identified with the debate than Schuster, and on 19 December he gave a paper to the Institute on 'Our Gold Reserves'. He insisted that if he and his colleagues were to increase their balances at the Bank of England, such balances would have to be strictly ring-fenced – for 'merely to add them to the ordinary funds of the Bank of England, would only add to the profits of that institution at the expense of the other banks'. Instead, this distinct second reserve, amounting to about £8m, would be managed by 'a small permanent committee, to be formed of representatives of the bankers, to act with the Bank of England'; and 'such a committee would form a nucleus of a general consultative committee with the Bank of England, the want of which has been long felt'. As for the remit of this 'general consultative committee', Schuster was the model of tact: 'With the management of the affairs of the Bank of England itself such committee would have no concern whatever; it would only meet for purposes of consultation and co-operation on questions of general interest.' Yet undeniably it was a potential foot in the door for the joint-stock men, and there was a thoroughly sour note to Leo Rothschild's letter to his cousins in Paris: 'Sir Frederick [sic] Schuster, Chairman of the Union Bank, who is supposed to be a great luminary & authority, read a long paper . . . two evenings ago, but I cannot say that I was much struck by his propositions, nor have they met with much favour in the mercantile community in general.'[33]

Discussion was adjourned to 15 January, when before 'an exceptionally brilliant audience' Holden 'first criticised Sir Felix's suggestion, and then branched off into what was practically the proposal of a new scheme'. So he did, arguing that, in his own words, 'to take the reserves of the joint-stock bankers and place them in the Bank of England as a secondary reserve is unsound according to banking principles ... I cannot conceive any body of directors, or of shareholders, of any bank ever agreeing to such a proposition.' As for his alternative to such an illiquid, publicly exposed reserve:

> Assuming that we agree to find 1 per cent of our liabilities in gold, I maintain that that gold would be in the best position in the vaults of the banks themselves. There it would be unseen; it would not be in view of the whole world; and in case any individual banker holding a reserve in that form should desire, under the press of the circumstances, to use his gold, there it is to be used.

It was a suggestion that not only challenged Schuster's intellectual leadership but also raised the stakes of the whole debate. Significantly, Holden did not quarrel with Schuster's suggestion of forming a general consultative committee to liaise with the Bank of England. In reply to Holden and other critics, Schuster stuck to his guns, insisting that the second reserve should be in the Bank of England rather than the vaults of the individual banks. His final words, however, were loaded: 'The position has changed to such an extent through the enormous growth of the joint-stock banks, that the Bank of England is no longer in a position to command the situation without the co-operation of the joint-stock banks. If that co-operation is brought about, then the difficulty will be solved.'[34]

Still, it was all very well to speak the language of the heavy, but it behoved the joint-stock banks also to speak with a united voice. The manager of the London Joint Stock Bank, Charles Gow, in a memorandum written that February apparently for Bank of England consumption, expressed general satisfaction with the status quo: 'The Bank of England is by our system the holder of the only gold reserve in the Country which is of practical use, that is to say, which can be drawn upon in need, and which can be replenished by the action of the exchanges influenced by the Bank rate.' The following month the Committee of London Clearing Bankers did agree to form a special sub-committee to consider 'the best means of increasing the gold reserves of the country', but few in the City held their breath. 'He was more confident than ever that a proper solution would be arrived at before long,' Schuster by late summer was telling his shareholders.[35] If he really was so confident, he reckoned without the inherent conservatism of most bankers and the vaulting ambitions of the man at the Midland.

The other 'question' during the winter of 1906/7 concerned the conduct of business on the Stock Exchange. In September the Committee read a memorial from Blyth and others demanding an inquiry into the questions of double commissions, minimum commission, shunting (i.e. direct dealings between jobbers in London and members of provincial stock exchanges) and dealer/non-member relations as a whole. Blyth the following month made his case in person:

> There had been an increase of membership of 800 in two years, and by means of telephones, country brokers could deal with London jobbers as well or better than the London brokers . . . Business was driven away from the House by foreign bankers and by provincial brokers dealing direct with the jobbers, to the serious injury of both jobbers and brokers in the Stock Exchange. Liverpool, Paris and Manchester were prosperous, while the business in the House was most unsatisfactory. These people dealt at 3d prices. He would be willing to deal at 1d prices if he knew which way his broker was.[36]

Eventually the Committee agreed to an inquiry, and between November and February evidence was heard from fifty-three members. Inevitably, as with the earlier Blyth-initiated agitation, the underlying issue was whether the capacity distinction between broker and jobber was to be hardened or further loosened.

The veteran jobber Alfred Baker described the condition of the younger members as 'deplorable' and 'believed these 30 foreign houses who had come into existence of late years were the cause' – indeed, 'he heard that one outside firm had 200 telephones'. Leonard Higgins, author of a learned treatise on *The Put and Call*, 'said the South African market had been extinguished, and thought it was largely because of the business done by the outside houses: it was not so much a depression in South Africa'; though in all honesty he admitted that 'he could not say that the public were pressing for a reform in this matter, though he had seen certain articles in the Press from time to time'. Harry Higham 'could not produce any evidence of outside houses spoiling the market of a broker who had opened his book', but 'he knew it was the case from things he had heard'. Levy Schaap, of the brokers Schaap & Co, affirmed that 'the tendency was for the big firms to get all the business, the small ones none'; and 'he thought a fixed commission would remedy this'. In contrast, Henry Pulley, of the brokers Laurie, Milbank & Co, 'considered that the freedom allowed the jobbers to deal direct with provincial exchanges was of great advantage to brokers, who thus dealt with men in close touch with the real market and to the clients who employed them'. Willie Koch was likewise robust, arguing that the prohibition of double commissions 'would not prevent business being taken outside, because brokers would deal with outside houses with an eye to "favours to come" '. Overall, more brokers than jobbers gave evidence, and the only point of unanimity was that there was not enough business to go round.[37]

Eventually, in February, the Committee voted against making any change to the rules. Over the next few weeks a so-called reform party sought to gather support for a reversal of this policy, but at the annual Committee election in March achieved a net gain of only one. Among the unsuccessful candidates was Harry Paxton, who came next to last in the poll. His glory days as a jobber had long gone, as he migrated from market to market (latterly the Russian Mining market) without any great success. Over the next few years he would find himself being predeceased by his wife, his only daughter (Dollie), and his son-in-law A.C. Graham who had become a member and joined his firm in 1905. 'Packy' himself, the man who walked to Croydon but wisely went no further, died on 23 December 1916: intending to spend Christmas in Brighton, he was taken ill in the train, assisted out, and died on Victoria Station.[38]

*

The itinerant jobber's sudden interest in Russian mines was largely explained by the minor boom that took place during 1906 in Siberian undertakings. 'Absence of information as to detail of purchase consideration, &c, is noticeable in recent formations,' noted the *Statist* on 12 January 1907, adding that 'before even any development has been done to prove the value of ground acquired the process of pushing up the shares to a considerable premium is merrily pursued'. In short, the usual mining promotional scenario was being played out. The *Statist* was especially critical of the Siberian Proprietary group, well known in the market for having offloaded its Troitzk Goldfields shares upon the public at exorbitant prices. On the last day of the month the board of Siberian Proprietary Mines issued a circular denying that and other invidious rumours, but on the floor of the Stock Exchange 'it was remarked that the circular was not very convincing'. The *Economist* on 2 February referred darkly to how 'the full story of the marketing of the shares of these companies remains to be told', but Lord Carrington in his diary the next day was less inhibited:

> A Siberian gold-mining company has been formed by some Jew speculators. Francis Knollys, Lord Stanley, Lord Howe, Sir West Ridgeway and others accepted directorships, and the shares were rushed up to £16. They have gone down with a rattle, and Horace Farquhar is said to have netted £70,000. He is supposed to have secured all those names, and the papers are open-mouthed at this scandal. It is deplorable that the King's private secretary and the Queen's Lord Chamberlain should have been 'let in' and mixed up in an affair like this.

Deplorable perhaps, but with Kaffirs and Westralians singularly failing to recapture their old lustre, there was by the mid-1900s a strong appetite in the City for mining ventures in places previously regarded as outlandish. The Caucasus Copper Company, for example, saw Grenfell and Smith at Morgans acting on their own account in an essentially speculative venture, masterminded by F.W. Baker of Strattons Independence fame, to exploit mining possibilities in the Morgol Valley – an involvement in which they were joined, sometimes fractiously, by Revelstoke and Everard and Eric Hambro. 'This mine has had even more than the ordinary vicissitudes,' Grenfell would eventually write, 'and we all wish we had never heard of it.'[39]

The flow of the yellow metal around the world continued to determine Bank rate and thus the mood of the City. On 16 January 1907, a Wednesday, Natty Rothschild informed Paris that 'there is some idea that the rate of Discount may be lowered tomorrow, but of course it will all depend how the Bank's accounts read at the last moment, but we should not be at all astonished if some reduction were made'. And, with the suggestion of being on the inside track, he added that 'anyhow we know that some of the Directors will advocate a movement in this direction'. As usual a large crowd of members gathered in the Consol market, and this time the Government broker obliged:

> After these protracted weeks of waiting for a reduction – weeks that have seen contangoes of 6 per cent paid on Consols, 10 per cent on Home Rails, 13 per cent on Americans, and still more on certain Industrials – the relief at the actual receipt of the 5 per cent declaration was profound. It found vent in cheers, which are usual, and in the clapping of hands,

which is so uncommon as to deserve comment . . . But the thankfulness met with a cold check. There was much shouting; there were no shouts to buy. Exuberance confined itself to noise that carried no practical consolation to the holders of stock. Knots of brokers waited about in the Consol market on the look-out for such bidding for Goschens as would encourage the remainder of the markets and lead an all-round revival. Only disappointment came. Nobody appeared eager to buy, or even eager to deal. The price of Consols was quoted $\frac{1}{16}$ better, that is, the turn of the market, and even this improvement did not last long. Members looked at one another with half-quizzical expressions: 'It's the same old story,' said one man, 'Discounted again.'

Five per cent, in other words, was hardly a comfortable rate, and on the last day of the month the Smith St Aubyn diary noted that it had been 'a horrible day – money was tighter than ever – the whole market was short and the Bank did a big business'.[40]

The situation did not improve in February, and on the 19th, with a prospective Japanese loan in the offing, Natty Rothschild gave his cousins an earful:

> To talk and to write about new issues at present seems almost an absurdity as never have I known such a heavy pall as has fallen over the City and the Stock Exchange during the last two days. The depression, and it is general, is probably without a previous example and no doubt it is owing to one fact and to one fact alone, the small bona-fide holders of English Securities, be they Government Stock or Bonds of Municipal Undertakings or Railway Stock or shares in industrial enterprises, are in a morbid and nervous state of mind. No doubt many of them helped to put a radical Government in power and now that they have got that radical Government they cry out timorously, you were put in power on the free trade plank and you are ruining us by your political and socialistic programme. Sooner or later these symptoms are bound to have a great effect . . .

Natty's mood, however, gradually improved. 'When I came into the City this morning there was a dense fog and prices were generally lower all round,' he wrote on the 28th, 'but the depression did not last very long and all the markets have sensibly improved and leave off very firm.' And the next day, as negotiations for the loan reached their conclusion, he referred to how 'Mr Takahashi as usual behaved admirably.'[41] The new Japanese loan was for £23m at 5 per cent, shared equally between London and Paris; in London the usual triumvirate of issuing banks was joined by Rothschilds; and all involved were uncomfortably aware that, in difficult market conditions, there no longer obtained that enthusiasm of two or three years earlier for all things Japanese.[42]

'Arrange underwriting for new Jap loan. Always a trying experience. Townsend's relations & Cameron's relations & friends multiplied ad nauseam. It is all wrong.' So wrote Addis in his diary on Tuesday, 5 March, referring with some bitterness to two of his bank's senior figures. The Rothschilds likewise kept the underwriting as close as they could, with a distinct preference for friendly mining houses and wealthy individuals rather than rival merchant banks. The next day a potentially nasty squall was avoided over another foreign issue – the Argentine Government 5 per cent Internal Gold Loan for £7m, to be issued in Paris and Berlin as well as London. 'The arrangement was concluded in order to prevent outside houses getting into the Argentine business, which you and we considered our own, and it was advisable for us to avoid any competition between ourselves,' Grenfell at Morgans reminded Revelstoke, recalling an agreement between the two houses reached in December 1904. He added: 'I am at your disposal any time during the day.' Revelstoke duly called in at 22 Old Broad Street and agreed to allow the Morgan name to appear as joint issuer of the London portion of the loan, with Morgans for their part agreeing not to send a representative to Buenos Aires to compete against Barings for other government business. He behaved, Grenfell with satisfaction reported to Jack Morgan, 'according to the best traditions of Christian houses'. Meanwhile, with the underwriting safely completed, the prospectus for the Japanese loan was published on Friday. 'Rather a poor opening,' noted Addis the next day, 'but we hope for a change on Monday.'[43]

It proved a close-run thing, as over the first three days of the following week a marked reaction set in, itself a response to the way in which prolonged over-trading and over-speculation in the United States was beginning to lead to palpable signs of weakness. Consols were at their lowest since the Overend Gurney crisis in 1866, and this despite renewed buying by the Government broker amidst rumours of 'a leading Anglo-American house' in difficulties. On Thursday, following a big overnight fall on Wall Street, Consols were down to $84\frac{5}{8}$, the lowest point since the Chartist year of 1848. Natty Rothschild was duly grateful that the Japanese loan had been just about fully subscribed, but complained to Paris on the 15th that 'our telegrams from America do not tell us much more than is in the papers and even the best informed like Sir Edgar Speyer can only conjecture . . .' Had the Japanese loan not gone as well as it did, Grenfell wrote to Jack Morgan

CITY MEN

International Financier and Private Banker: 8 ABOVE *Sir Ernest Cassel;* 9 LEFT *Bertram Currie.*

Rogues' Gallery: 10 LEFT *Whitaker Wright*;
11 BELOW *Barney Barnato*; 12 OPPOSITE ABOVE
Horatio Bottomley; 13 OPPOSITE BELOW *Ernest
Terah Hooley*.

14 *Watching the Gold: the Court of Directors of the Bank of England, 2 July 1903.*

J.S. Gilliat   J.P. Currie   *Sir M.W. Collet*   *H.C. Smith*   *Sir A. Prevost*
                              A.G. Sandeman   *S.S. Gladstone*   *C.H. Goschen*

A.F. Wallace   *S.H. Morley*
Deputy Governor   Governor

G.W. Henderson   Lord Revelstoke   W.D. Hoare   R.L. Newman   W. Cunliffe   A.C. Cole

                   C.G. Arbuthnot   F.H. Jackson   R.E. Johnston

                                 W.M. Campbell   E. Lubbock   Hon. E. Hubbard

H. Brooks   E.A. Hambro   H.C.O. Bonsor

The Old Firm: Rothschilds and Barings: 15 ABOVE Lord ('Natty') Rothschild, with his brother Leo to his left; 16 RIGHT Lord Revelstoke.

Joint-Stock Giants: 17 RIGHT *Sir Felix Schuster;* 18 BELOW *Sir Edward Holden.*

The City's Pleasures and Pains:
19 ABOVE *Sir Charles Addis*; 20
RIGHT *Arthur Grenfell.*

the next day, 'we should have found it impossible to place [i.e. under-write] our Argentine business; even as it is now the German group are very anxious to postpone the Argentine'. The German bankers were denied their wish, and the next week the Argentine loan came out amidst gloomy news from Paris, the expectation of a higher Bank rate in London, and a host of unwelcome rumours from elsewhere. Sub-scriptions closed on Friday the 22nd, and Vivian Smith's tone to Jack Morgan the next day was predictably downbeat: 'It could not have come out at a worse time, and we and Barings received between us applications for about 25%, which is not very satisfactory, but we could hardly look for success in anything just now.'[44]

Markets failed to improve during the week before Easter, and by Wednesday the 27th the air was poisonous with the darkest whispers and allegations. Farrer gave a full account to Mildmay, in Buenos Aires visiting Windham Baring:

> Since writing to you last week we have had quite exciting times here and in New York, New York prices all making new low records and markets both there, here and in Berlin on the verge of panic. Needless to say that with it came all the usual crop of rumours, from which happily we were exempt, Lothbury [i.e. Speyers] and Old Broad Street [i.e. Morgans] coming in for their full share – absolutely without foundation so far as both are concerned to the best of our belief, though the faces and manner of the partners at the latter place were enough to shake anyone's faith . . . There have been a few minor failures on the Stock Exchange and I believe our old friends named on the enclosed slip [viz the brokers Brunton, Bourke & Co] have actually failed though not officially.
>
> On the worst day of the crisis our New York, New Haven & Hartford prospectus was due to come out so as to be contemporaneous with the Paris issue . . . We managed to conceal the notice of the issue on the outside sheet of the 'Times' with half a dozen lines saying particulars might be obtained at our office; I do not think anyone seems to have discovered it . . .
>
> In these gloomy days of the Stock Exchange crisis one nice tale has been told us: a broker telephoned to a noble lord at the other end of town asking him for funds to settle his differences, the reply being 'no funds available', and the stockbroker's comment was that 'dealing for him was a distinction without a difference'.

Natty Rothschild, in his dispatch that day to Paris, confirmed that Brunton Bourke had been running its own book disastrously and was now being privately bailed out by various City connections, almost certainly including Rothschilds. And he went on: 'These are not pleasant occurrences, but in times like these if you can prevent a grain of sand or two from interfering between the axle and the wheel, you may succeed in removing all danger of greater disturbances.' What about the agitated partners at 22 Old Broad Street? Morgans, in its five o'clock telegram that Wednesday afternoon to Jack Morgan, preferred to shift the focus elsewhere:

> London City & Midland Bank has been much talked about lately. Have made inquiries and believe there is no foundation in the rumours – they have undoubtedly withdrawn large amount from Stock Exchange and Lombard St to protect their Branches owing to rumours. Are informed that London City & Midland Bank much annoyed at persistency rumours.

Farrer, writing again to Mildmay shortly after the Easter break, elaborated:

> Since the holidays there has been a better feeling on the Stock Exchange, though all is not yet well, partly I think because the mystery of the selling just before Easter is still as great as ever. The Joint Stock Bank (our aggressive friend in Threadneedle Street) which was accused of being the heavy seller, liquidating the collateral put up for advances, has been extraordinarily foolish in its conduct, its manager having gone round to other Joint Stock Banks to deny the one hundred and one rumours floating about and to impart reassuring statements.[45]

Holden and his bank had risen so far, so fast that there were many people not sorry to see them embarrassed.

For someone more used to embarrassment, and altogether more of a City insider, it had been an unhappy winter seriously affecting his judgement by the spring. Arthur Grenfell, in company with his wife Vera and brother Rivy, had travelled via Cuba to Mexico before going on to Canada, where the party stayed with the Greys at Government House, Ottawa. Vera died there in February. A few weeks later he was back in England and no longer content with Morgans' demand, in return for putting £50,000 into the Canadian Agency, of a veto over any new operations it did not approve of. 'You told us that,' Smith wrote to him on 19 April following a recent conversation, 'you would prefer to have a freer hand,' and that therefore Morgans now agreed 'to cancel all the arrangements, as we should be the last to wish to start an alliance which would not be as satisfactory to you as it would to us.' Soon afterwards Teddy Grenfell told the story to Jack Morgan, relating how his cousin Arthur had, on his return to England, proposed modifying the agreement, 'as he felt the restrictions we had imposed would tend to destroy his prestige and power in dealing quickly in large matters with Canadians'. Teddy added, perhaps with some relief: 'I admire his go and his energy but he is a most dangerous partner unless strictly under control.'[46]

Bank rate stayed at 4 for most of the summer and by 12 June Farrer was able to report to Windham Baring that 'we have had distinctly more cheerful markets' since he had last written. 'Not that there is any business to speak of,' he added, 'but every broker who comes into the room is not now prophesying the end of the world.' Ten days later, amid some pomp, Speyer's latest tube line (the Charing Cross, Euston and Hampstead) was opened. 'As you know,' Mildmay wrote to Baring, 'the whole of Speyer's underground railway undertaking has been a gigantic failure, but this undertaking and some of its competitors have agreed to put up their fares so that they are likely to do a little less badly in the future than they have in the past.' Another undertaking spurned by some of the leading houses, and given a lukewarm press, was a Manchurian railway loan guaranteed by the Japanese government and issued by the Hongkong and Shanghai Bank in mid-July. Addis, typically, drew the wider lesson: 'Manchurian loan decried by papers but in reality a financial feat. Paris wouldn't look at it, or Berlin, or New York. London is a great place.'[47]

Nevertheless, it was a great place under a cloud. America, as was becoming dismayingly familiar, was the problem. There was trouble on the New York Stock Exchange, Yankees in London tumbled, and again there was the looming worry of autumnal gold flows across the Atlantic.[48] 'Bills of all dates are very firm – the market is not at all keen and holding back through funk of the approaching autumn.' That was Smith St Aubyn's view on 6 August, and the following week the London banks panicked and temporarily stopped taking in new bills at all. 'I feel far from cheerful myself, owing to the terrible state of things in the City,' wrote Meyer to his wife on the 8th; and a week later Bank rate went up from 4 to $4\frac{1}{2}$, essentially a pre-emptive action. The dispatch that Kleinworts sent on the 19th to New York could hardly have been more heartfelt:

> The discount market has apparently lost its head ... Rates have jumped up, there is much wild talk about what is going to happen in America and we believe quite a number of our banks and discount houses decline to take any American-drawn bills no matter on whom they are

drawn! We have rarely seen our market in such a foolish and hysterical condition. From what I can hear it would appear that our good friends Schröder and ourselves are the houses that come in for the greatest talk . . . Whatever may be heard on senseless or ignorant fronts and jealous competitors our business is in perfect shape and does not give us a moment's pre-occupation but I confess that it makes me clench my teeth to hear it said that this or that bank is full on KS & Co.

Over the next few weeks the situation somewhat eased, and on 4 September Natty Rothschild was able to write in cousinly fashion that, 'I am going North tomorrow & hope to see you at Doncaster, my dear Jimmy, & trust that we shall see some of the horses we are both interested in, successful on the Town Moor next week.' A further bull point later in the month was the announcement of the Anglo-Russian Entente. It wholly lacked the popular appeal of the understanding reached with France three years earlier, and at New Court was greeted with outright hostility, but as the *FT* pragmatically put it, 'an element of danger has been at least temporarily removed from the political arena'.[49]

The respite was only temporary. 'I am afraid we are in for a severe storm in the City,' Arthur Grenfell wrote to Grey on Saturday, 12 October after a week in which gold drained steadily from the Bank. 'We have had more anxious times than any since the Baring crisis. The American crisis was probably bound to come but Roosevelt has started the machine downhill before anyone had time to adjust the brake.' Grenfell, with his quick intelligence, was ahead of the game, for when on Monday morning 'all the great financiers', including Natty Rothschild and Cassel, began their working week by attending a meeting of the finance committee of the King's Hospital fund, Natty reported to Paris that, 'although they all acknowledge that prices are decidedly low and disgusting just now, they evidently appear to think well of the future, although it may take some time for everything to recover'. News from New York continued ominous during the week – especially with the dramatic failure on Wednesday of a stockbroking firm that had speculated heavily in the copper market – but the City as a whole continued to put on a brave public face. None more cheery than the brokers (and American specialists) Heseltine Powell in its weekly circular to clients issued on Saturday the 19th:

There is very little change to record this week in the Stock Exchange position. Renewed liquidation of speculative positions has caused a further fall in speculative stocks; the buying power of would-be supporters of the markets becomes further restricted with each successive slump in prices; the bears continue to take full advantage of the general weakness, while the public holds aloof. It may be that a further fall has yet to be faced, that some financial disaster is impending which may precipitate panic, but the prices of speculative stocks are low and the yields to be obtained are such that should appeal to the greediest investor . . .

We shall be happy to particularise further and make suggestions, not recommendations, to any of our friends to whom this present situation appeals.[50]

*

The present situation appealed to few from Tuesday, 22 October 1907, the start of the City's first full-scale crisis of the new century. 'When I read the newspapers early this morning,' Natty Rothschild related later that day, 'I was filled with bright hopes as I saw the prices at New York were considerably higher even than the unofficial quotations in London. But the moment I arrived in the City I was welcomed by an avalanche of brokers who all had selling orders in connection with the Knickerbocker Trust Co . . .' The news that an important American trust company had failed sent markets in London plunging, and according to Natty as many as 100,000 shares were sold between half-past ten and half-past twelve. 'Almost a panic in Yankee market,' noted Smith St Aubyn, while in after-hours dealings in Shorter's Court the *FT* reported that 'the market became very wild' on conflicting reports from New York. Years later Saemy Japhet recalled how many of the cables coming across that evening strongly urged European buying, on the grounds that there would shortly be a sharp rally, but his top arbitrageur Gottfried Loewenstein had disagreed, cabling back: 'Abstain from any transactions, keep books absolutely closed today.' Events fully vindicated Loewenstein's judgement, as over the next day or two the transatlantic atmosphere worsened. 'I confess I am quite unable to describe that crisis accurately,' Natty Rothschild wrote to Paris on Wednesday about what was taking place on Wall Street, 'to account positively of what has taken place and still less in any way to forecast the future.'[51]

Compounding the City's anxiety was the near-certainty that there was about to be a severe drain of gold from London to the States. That drain began on Monday the 28th, when 'as expected', the *FT*'s Money market report noted, 'New York was a keen bidder for the bar gold offering in the open market today, and by paying 78s per ounce (or $1\frac{1}{4}$d per ounce above last week's quotation) secured £1,000,000, or practically the total available.' Natty Rothschild by Tuesday believed that the directors would be 'wise' on Thursday to raise Bank rate from $4\frac{1}{2}$ to 6, with gold withdrawals from the Bank that day totalling over £1.6m, of which all but £40,000 was on American account. Wednesday was pay day on the Stock Exchange and, although no firms were hammered, there was an abundance of rumours, so much so that according to the *FT* 'names of firms alleged to be in trouble were bandied about with such freedom as to provoke the remark from one leading member that "not to be talked about is proof that you are a Stock Exchange nonentity" '. Bank rate went up on Thursday, but only to $5\frac{1}{2}$. Few in the money market, however, believed they had seen the last rise, 'having regard to the energy with which New York is still striving to get further facilities for importing gold'. Friday, 1 November was a Stock Exchange holiday, and Natty Rothschild took advantage of the lull to explain his position to Rothschild Frères. After referring to the successful gold-procuring operation of a year earlier, he went on:

> Now on this occasion we have not been approached by the Governor of the Bank of England nor have we been summoned to the Bank parlour and unless we are directly invited I see no peculiar reason why we should put ourselves forward on this occasion. Incidentally we know and we think it quite natural, there is a strong feeling in the Bank parlour that the foreign Bankers and Institutions who wish to send Gold to America . . . should not rely on the Bank of England only to find the precious metal but should obtain some and a considerable quantity in their own Country and from their own Banks. If the Governor of the Bank was to send for us, we should not hesitate one instant to do our duty and to help to the best of our ability.[52]

Yet as Natty well knew, London was the world's only free gold market, and to have expected 'foreign Bankers and Institutions' to act otherwise was mere wishful thinking.

The Governor, William Campbell, walked into the Bank on Monday the 4th, looked at the figures and did two important things. The first, wholly off his own bat, was to raise Bank rate from $5\frac{1}{2}$ to 6 – a decisive 'Governor's rise' that much impressed the newest director, Montagu Norman. The money market 'expressed no surprise' and partly interpreted the action as 'a hint to houses here to guard against further facilitating the flight of eagles by extending loans to New York'. On the Stock Exchange, by contrast, the news caused 'a rude upset', as 'a rush of selling ensued which carried prices down all round'. Campbell's other action that morning was to send for Natty Rothschild and ask him to arrange with the Paris house to secure a major tranche of gold from the Bank of France – a request made plausible by the new, more attractive rate. With the reserve rapidly approaching the previous year's low point of just over £18.1m, the news on Tuesday late afternoon that the Bank of France had agreed to supply £3m of gold was warmly greeted in the City, and the thoroughly unwelcome prospect of a rise to 7 per cent began to be discounted, at least on the Stock Exchange, always the most volatile of weather bells. By Wednesday evening even the money market was relatively sanguine – 'the market apparently regards the coming shipments of gold from France as doing away with the necessity of a higher official minimum' – but not so Natty Rothschild. Not only was he disturbed by the prospect of continuing large withdrawals of gold by New York, but he continued to be exasperated by the failure on the other side of the pond to take decisive action about resolving the American crisis. Shortly after seven o'clock, Morgans in London sent this message from Natty and his partners to Morgans in New York:

> They feel very strongly indeed that the time has come for the Executive with you to think seriously what relief can be given . . . They do feel & very strongly that you must not look for nor expect much more relief from this side and the fact that the Bank rate will probably be raised to 7% tomorrow is the best proof that the Directors Bank of England are determined protect their stock of gold which is already more than sufficiently diminished. N.M. Rothschild & Sons hope you will use your great influence.

To which Morgans added, in words almost certainly written by Teddy Grenfell, who had no exaggerated respect for the sagacity of New Court: 'Foregoing is their message which we send you at their urgent desire and therefore cannot refuse, though seems to us to throw no new light on situation.'[53]

Grenfell's cousin, writing the next day to Lord Grey in Ottawa, was for once on the side of the pessimists:

> We have had a very nasty week here & I am afraid have worse ones before us. The banks here have rather got the funks & have been calling in loans right & left, so that one has had a difficult job financing. Provided we don't have a really bad crisis, I am in a pretty good position but I can't help being anxious. Though I saw the Americans were drifting into troubled waters, it was impossible to foresee such an utter collapse of credit & it has been impossible to withdraw altogether from markets. The position here is sound & except for America we should have had fair markets. The American position has however plunged us into the worst

crisis since the Overend Gurney smash in 1866. It is absolutely impossible
to sell anything or even borrow from one's bank. Such a state of affairs
has not been seen by many people . . .

That same day, Thursday the 7th, Bank rate rose from 6 to 7 – its
highest level since 1873. On the Stock Exchange the announcement
was a 'decided blow', causing 'a general reaction in prices'. Any sense
of surprise, however, wore off in the afternoon when the Bank return
was issued, showing that the reserve had fallen to the perilously low
figure of £17,695,000. Natty Rothschild expressed full agreement with
the Bank's step: 'They had no choice and were bound to act in that
way, the accounts were low and it was absolutely necessary to give
those on the other side of the Atlantic a serious warning.' And the next
morning, in a leader headed 'Soaring Bank Rates', the *FT* conceded
that 'for the moment all is gloom', but reiterated its usual stern line at
such moments that 'so long as London remains a free market for gold,
and so long as the exigencies of affairs in the States causes importers
there to override ordinary exchange considerations by paying a premium upon gold, just so long will the flight of eagles across the herring
pond continue'.[54] There was, in short, no alternative; and few ruled out
the possibility of the rate going above 7.

Over the following week, with money exceptionally tight, the City
became increasingly critical of the American failure to take effective
action about what was after all a home-grown crisis. The Rothschilds,
Vivian Smith reported to Jack Morgan on Wednesday the 13th, were
voicing 'a pretty general sentiment here by saying they could not
understand why the American Government should be absolutely
powerless or unwilling to do anything to relieve the crisis except to say
"thank you" for the assistance they receive from other Governments'.
The Stock Exchange two days later was racked by rumours that, in the
context of continuing gold outflows, the Bank's directors were thinking of going to 8 per cent; while on Saturday the 16th, according to
Arthur Grenfell, there were fears of an imminent rise to 9 per cent,
even of the Bank Charter Act being suspended for the first time since
1866. 'Bankers have been pressing for loans,' he added on the Monday, '& as it was impossible to realise securities, the position has been
much worse than it has appeared on the surface.' However, even as
Grenfell wrote, news came through that, in Smith St Aubyn's words,
'the United States Government has at last moved to help the situation',
this action taking the form of the issuing of Treasury securities. 'The
Yankee Relief' was the expressive title of the *FT*'s leader the next

morning, and the worst of the crisis was over, especially as gold flowed into London over the next few weeks, attracted by the 7 per cent rate.[55]

Many had been scarred by the experience, among them Arthur Grenfell. 'I have not had an easy time in the City,' he wrote to Grey on the 25th, '& like nearly everyone else I have had to face big losses. I saw the crisis coming on from the first & had pretty well cleared my decks last year . . .' But Grenfell's boldness had been thwarted, and he went on to lament how, since his wife's death, 'I have found it so difficult to pull myself together that matters have drifted'. Then came the breast-beating, the blaming of others, and the final late flurry of self-confidence:

> However it is my fault. I deserve all I get. I have had to get a loan from my bankers & in normal times this would be considered quite right. But times are not normal & one never knows whether one's banker won't get frightened & call it in. Otherwise I am in a fairly strong position – & as soon as the American position rights itself, we may look for a good recovery here.[56]

*

During the autumn of 1907, in an exeat from Eton, the young Osbert Sitwell spent an evening on the town. He saw little evidence of financial crisis:

> In the world outside, the era of the Stock Exchange was in full swing. The institution now set every standard. Musical Comedy filled the theatres devoted to it, and this was its peak, the Age of *The Merry Widow*. This play, first produced at Daly's on 8th June 1907, ran for over two years, during which time its music, by Franz Lehar, served as background to every meal in a restaurant, every dance and every garden-party that was given . . . We sat in the stage-box, and so I was able to watch the expressions of the members of the audience, reproducing in their own fashion the sentiment and humour that came to them from the stage.
>
> > I am going to Maxim's
> > Where fun and frolic gleams;
> > The girls all laugh and greet me;
> > They will not trick or cheat me
>
> reflected the current ennui with the responsibilities of life to perfection; how marvellous, many of those seated in the theatre felt, to be able to say that and to cast away your cares in this manner. And as, later, the banal, but in a way charming, waltz sounded out, and Miss Lily Elsie came

down the stairs to her prince, and as the glare from the stage fell on those in the front row of the stalls, on the stiff white shirts, flashing studs, white waistcoats and self-indulgent faces, brown or white, on the noses, hooked or snub, and gleaming, pouchy eyes, of these members of the Cosmopolitan Bourgeoisie, I can recall contemplating them and wondering whether it were possible that in the future such entertainments or such an audience would – or could – be considered as being typical of their epoch, or providing a clue to it, in the same way that we looked back, past our fathers, to *La Vie Parisienne* or *Die Fledermaus*. I decided, then, that to adopt such a view would be to overrate both entertainment and spectators – but I was wrong. It held a suitably designed mirror to the age, to the preference for restaurant to palace, for comfort to beauty, and to the idealisation of Mammon. Mammon underlay the smudgy softness and superficial prettiness of the whole performance, as the skull supports the lineaments of even the youngest and freshest face.[57]

CHAPTER TWENTY-TWO

Hardly Our Business

'Prosperity to Trade and Finance' was the toast that Goschen proposed at the National Discount's jamboree at the Ritz in July 1906:

> . . . I denounce any theory which would dissociate the prosperity of finance from the prosperity of trade. (*Cheers.*) I denounce any theory which would say that in the City of London they may be driving a fine business, the profits of the bankers may be great, they may be raking in the means for increased dividends, and at the same time over the great area of the country there is depression. No, gentlemen, I hold in the strongest degree – I hold still more the theory, since the system of limited liability has developed, that there is a community of interests – an inalienable community of interests – between the finance of the City of London and of the great towns and the prosperity of the country at large. If there is prosperity in the country there will be prosperity in the City of London.

After a lengthy disquisition on the gold reserves question, Goschen returned to his main theme in a pointed peroration:

> You have no doubt a sense of the great responsibility which rests upon you. Let it not be thought that the City is composed simply of a group of rich and grasping men who are endeavouring to accumulate those vast fortunes which figure in the annals of some other countries. You are doing your best in order to promote the prosperity of trade and finance in the country at large. By your wisdom as you are wise, by your prudence as you are prudent, by your capacity as you have that capacity, you will help to mould to a great extent the course of business in the country at large and to maintain, by sound and orthodox and unfantastic methods, that great structure of British trade and finance to the prosperity of which I now ask you to drink. (*Loud cheers.*)[1]

The complacency was striking, but so also was the need to justify the City's activities to the nation at large. A debate was beginning that henceforth, sometimes to the City's ill-disguised exasperation, would never quite go away.[2]

Crucial to the shaping of this debate in the mid-1900s were the two years – 1906 and 1907 – of extraordinarily high Bank rate. 'Under the present circumstances of home trade a 5 per cent Bank Rate was, to use plain language, a scandal, and a 6 per cent rate was a war measure in time of peace. If it were to be long maintained it would provoke a revolt among commercial borrowers.' Such was W.R. Lawson's typically trenchant view in his November 1906 lecture to the Chartered Institute of Secretaries, and he added: 'The foreigner carefully husbanded his domestic resources, while we invite all the world to come in and exploit ours. Millions a year were being lost by the British manufacturer in having to pay famine rates for his working capital.' The following March, at the annual meeting of the Association of Chambers of Commerce, Arthur Lee of Bristol moved 'that the constant and violent fluctuations in the Bank of England rate of discount are injurious to trade and commerce'. After referring to the twenty-eight Bank rate changes of the past seven years, ranging between $2\frac{1}{2}$ and 6 per cent, he went on:

> It was easy enough to see that these great fluctuations were injurious to trade and commerce, but he did not believe that the great majority of business men had any conception of how much their interests were mercilessly sacrificed, or the price they had to pay in one way or another for these fluctuations . . . Our system paralysed the action of our bankers, discouraged trade and made us the easy prey for foreign speculators, and it was one which he asked them to say they were determined to reform.

The motion was seconded by Hull's Victor Dumoulin, who argued that the Bank Charter Act had become 'entirely inadequate to our increasing trade' and regretted that 'the Bank of England was not a State bank' – that, in other words, 'the State had no voice in its management, notwithstanding that the Bank enjoyed extensive and inclusive privileges'. Schuster counterattacked – 'he did not think it could be denied that the banking system as carried on here was of immense importance to traders . . . they must not forget that bankers' interests and traders' interests were absolutely identical' – but Lee's motion was accepted, once he had agreed to replace the phrase 'constant and violent' with the more moderate 'frequent'.[3]

Soon afterwards, in April 1907 at its annual dinner at the Trocadero, the London Chamber of Commerce was treated to some reassuring bromides by the President of the Institute of Bankers, J. Spencer Phillips of Lloyds:

Banking was the handmaid of commerce; their interests were identical
and interwoven with each other. The commercial supremacy enjoyed by
this country in the past, and which he hoped it would continue to enjoy,
although, of course, they had great rivals – (*hear, hear*) – was due in the
first instance to the energy and enterprise of the race, coupled with certain
natural resources of the country. He thought, also, that the development
and extension of the banking system, by which means the savings and the
loose money of the country were gathered together by the bankers, and
by them employed to assist and further the trade of the country, had been
of considerable value in promoting that supremacy. (*Hear, hear.*) He
thought there was no sound undertaking which had ever been crippled in
this country for want of capital.

Dudley Docker, Chairman of the Midlands-based Metropolitan Amalgamated Carriage and Wagon Company (a recent merger of five
rolling-stock companies), disagreed. His speech at the AGM in Birmingham at the end of May was an explicit rebuke to such institutional
inertia:

> We find the great assistance given by foreign Governments, foreign
> business, and foreign commercial houses to the industrial enterprises of
> their respective countries has been a very potent factor indeed in this
> matter of securing business, and some of us are beginning to ask whether
> there is no prospect of our ever getting such assistance, and whether the
> day will ever come when gentlemen who come to London for money will
> find that one of the conditions of the loans will be that at least a portion
> of the money shall be spent in this country. I can assure you, ladies and
> gentlemen, that this matter is becoming year by a year a more important
> one. Our splendid isolation and superb cosmopolitanism is no doubt very
> pretty indeed, and very flattering to our vanity, but it is playing the very
> deuce with our business. The time is coming, and is coming very rapidly,
> when this aspect of the case will call for the very serious attention of the
> manufacturers of this country, as well as of the great financial houses,
> including, of course, the bankers of the country. I should like to see our
> great commercial concerns drawing more closely to one another for the
> common benefit in this matter. The game is in our own hands, and if we
> care to assert ourselves, and if the existing financial institutions are not
> able to cope with the matter, there ought to be no great difficulty
> establishing others which would meet the serious situation which is
> rapidly being created.

Tied loans would become one of Docker's hobby-horses, but it was the
latter part of his comments that the *Bankers' Magazine*, mustering all
its usual affronted dignity, preferred to address:

Bankers would be only too glad to be shown the way to earn larger profits with safety, but the last two words weigh heavily with them, and they will certainly require to be convinced that extended accommodation to traders can be granted without in any way interfering with their responsibilities to their depositors and other creditors . . . We are told that in Germany this kind of banking business is done. We point, in reply, to the banking and industrial crisis of a few years ago which arose out of it.[4]

For the time being Docker kept his powder dry – unlike Arthur Lee. In September 1907, at the autumnal meeting held in Liverpool of the Association of Chambers of Commerce, the Bristol agitator proposed that the state be adequately represented on the Bank of England, though with the Bank staying independent: 'He contended that some independent authority was wanted standing between the Bank as a State institution charged with the care of high national interests, and the Bank as a private company charged with the immediate pecuniary interests of its proprietors.' And, according to Lee, the leading mid-Victorian banker George Carr Glyn had advocated this halfway house many years earlier. His motion was again seconded by a Hull man, T.H. Sissons, who in his speech emphasised not only Bank rate considerations: 'Another great point concerned the competition between the great banking corporations and the Bank of England itself. A few years ago friction arose because the funds provided to a large extent by other banks were employed in such a way that serious exception was taken. That kind of thing seemed to point to the necessity of some State interference.' The next three speakers – from Aberdeen, Edinburgh and Sheffield – all opposed the resolution, praising the Bank of England's directors and fearing that body's politicisation. The final speech of the debate was made by Sir Albert Rollit, a former President of the London Chamber of Commerce and himself a Bank of England shareholder. He came down in support of Lee:

> It was not a question of the individual characters of the directors of the corporation of the Bank of England. Those, no doubt, were of as fair average quality as those of the financial community in the City of London (*Laughter*.) . . . The directors were really co-opted. Those who held power today determined who should hold power tomorrow; so that they had a body which was not only privileged, but was reproductive of itself, and which was under no control of shareholders, or Government, or of the community . . .

Rollit wanted about three representatives of the state to be directors:

Such representatives would be gentlemen who would realize their duty not merely to the corporation, but to the country, and who would take care, whenever any financial action was taken, that the general public was at least made aware of the course which had been adopted, of the reasons upon which it was founded, and be given the opportunity of judging whether it was conducive to the welfare of the country and the advantage of trade and business. (*Applause.*)

The applause was significant, for Lee's resolution was adopted.[5]

Within a few weeks, in response to the American crisis and the drain of gold, Bank rate was up to 7 per cent. It was probably at this time that the tag was coined in the London money market that '7 per cent brings gold from the moon'. Nevertheless, even within the City cracks now started to appear. In his inaugural at the Institute of Bankers later in November, Schuster drew a clear lesson from the recent crisis – namely, that 'we ought to be able, if necessary, to spare £5,000,000 or £10,000,000 without having resort to a 7 per cent Bank-rate and fears of even higher rates'. In his vote of thanks, Frederick Huth Jackson (a director of the Bank of England as well as a partner of Huths) implicitly addressed the 7 per cent context: 'As long as we retain the position of the free gold market of Europe, so long, I think, our Money Market should respond to demands made upon it for gold, and I am sure you will all agree with me that it is of the utmost importance to this country that its position as the free gold market should under all circumstances be maintained.' But Schuster in reply to Huth Jackson was notably unrepentant:

> I want the freedom of our gold market to be maintained. That is the very object I have had in view for many years since I have tried to learn something about the subject: but I would only ask Mr Jackson whether that market is quite so free as we should like to see it, considering that for two years running, at a time of stress, we had to go across the Channel to borrow a few millions, because, after all, that is what the transaction came to, and in order to export – after all, not very large sums of gold – 5 or 6 millions is not a large amount when you come to think of the whole volume of our trade, which is something like 1,000 millions – I think that might have been attained without hoisting that danger signal, that invitation or notice that we are ready to borrow which he alludes to at so high a rate as 7 per cent. I think 4 per cent or 5 per cent should have been sufficient.[6]

In the City/industry debate now underway, the big joint-stock banks – London-based, but with their roots largely in the provinces – would come to occupy an often awkward position.

Importantly, whatever his criticisms of the Bank of England, Schuster had few if any doubts about the validity and effectiveness of the unique, highly specialised English model of banking. 'Bankers are the servants of industry,' he told his Institute in November 1908; and looking back on the recent period of high rates, he claimed that there had been 'no inconvenience to trade through the withdrawal of credit', that indeed 'in somewhat troubled times no accommodation has been denied to those who were entitled to it'. A passionate defender of the joint-stock revolution in banking, and the ensuing amalgamation movement, he was asked at about the same time by an American inquiry into the English financial system whether he believed that 'the banking situation is stronger and better and the country is better served through the system of branches than through the independent banks'. Schuster's reply claimed the moral high ground: 'I am quite convinced of that, if only for one reason, that I do believe the indiscriminate granting of credits to the individual is injurious to himself, the private bankers being too much in the habit of regarding old family associations and not so careful as the joint-stock company would be.' His views echoed those of Francis Steele of Parr's, who in a debate at the Institute in December 1907 took it as a positive compliment that 'one of the commonest forms of complaint against joint-stock banks is that they are not inclined to look at most loans from the personal point of view, but to look at them in a strict business light'.[7]

So, no artificial bolstering the plausible chancer – and this self-image of objectivity and professionalism is supported by the generally favourable picture drawn in the most recent survey of bank lending practices in this period.[8] Methods of assessing and monitoring loans were surprisingly modern, including the use of outside advisers; banks systematically preferred short-term accommodation, though cumulatively this could become long-term; in practice they were generally adaptable and supportive, in the context of a reasonably competitive banking market; and there was no discernible bias against the newer, more unproven industries. An old-established semi-private bank that made a speciality of industrial finance was Glyn Mills, and an examination of its lending between 1890 and 1914 brings out its almost invariable willingness to go the extra mile, not least in its relationship with Vickers during the pre-war armaments boom. Or take that giant of joint-stock banking, the London City and Midland, which made a point of drawing its directors from people closely connected with industry. Holden, as one would expect, was never short of advice for industrialists prepared to listen. 'Saw Dudley Docker & had a talk with him about the Metropolitan Amalgamated,' he noted in January 1905. 'I suggested to him that it would be a good thing if he would appoint one of his best men to be an Inspector to go thro' all the Works, & to make him a report of what he considered to be wrong in the management. He said he would adopt the suggestion.' There were plenty of other examples, with grateful clients including Harland & Wolff, Guest Keen & Nettlefold, and the Bradford Dyers' Association.[9] However, although this was all well and good, ultimately what distinguished the British system of deposit banking was its stability – a stability which meant that there was no major bank failure after the City of Glasgow smash of 1878. It was stability that Schuster emphasised whenever he spoke on the subject, and it was stability that the *Bankers' Magazine* threw back in the impudent Docker's face in 1907. *Could* there be too high a price to pay for banking stability? Many – understandably, after the recurrent financial crises of the nineteenth century – thought not.

Nevertheless, this obeisance to the god of liquidity rendered the banks vulnerable to five main criticisms in the sphere of industrial finance.[10] The first concerned the effects of the amalgamation movement, which led to a lending policy that was not only more rigid, bureaucratic and London-based, but also biased towards big companies and thus against forces of innovation. Secondly, there was the unwillingness to provide long-term credit – an unwillingness freely admitted by such as Schuster. 'The bank ought never to supply the trader with working capital,' he told the American inquiry. 'I think it is bad for the trader. I think the banker ought to give temporary accommodation to tide the trader over the time when he is short until the time the money comes in again – for temporary purposes only. If a trader is not sufficiently provided with working capital and depends on the bank, there is sure to be trouble at some time.'[11] Thirdly, the unwillingness of banks to hold industrials in their portfolios – on the grounds of poor marketability and high risk – inevitably helped create a vicious circle as far as that type of share was concerned. Fourthly, related to this refusal to become long-term stakeholders, there was the absence of any significant managerial role in individual companies, again quite unlike German banks. And finally, there was the failure to get actively involved in the domestic capital market and thus the structure of British industry as a whole. In sum, there was at work a deep-rooted conservatism.

As for the City's merchant banks, who might have been expected to assume a leading role in the flotation of domestic industrial concerns, there existed a gut prejudice against such issuing and intimate involvement – partly rational on the grounds of low profitability in comparison with generally larger-size foreign issues (especially sovereign loans), partly irrational. 'I confess that personally I have a horror of all industrial companies,' Revelstoke wrote in 1911, 'and that I should not think of placing my hard-earned gains into such a venture.' Nevertheless, there were exceptions on the part of the City's elite financiers. Barings itself pushed the boat out early in 1905 when it made an issue for the Mersey Docks and Harbour Board, described by Farrer as 'the biggest job we have had single-handed since the inauguration of the new firm'. Important support came from Cassel, who was in Cairo when Revelstoke sent him a cheque for £2,500 in connection with the underwriting: 'I am glad to be able to say that the issue has been a great success. We got but little assistance from the Stock Exchange, as the stock did not seem to recommend itself to the stagging element . . .' Similarly against the larger trend, Morgans over the years took a close interest in the fluctuating fortunes of United Collieries, a grouping of Scottish coal mines. In 1902 it led an underwriting group that sold on to the public a large block of the company's debentures: during difficult years in the mid-1900s it kept the company afloat by lending upwards of £125,000; and first through Walter Burns junior and then Vivian Smith, it exercised a direct and fruitful management supervision on the company's board, on the lines of American-style investment banking. Or again, as another jolt to easy stereotypes, take the case of Immingham Dock, built on the Humber entirely under the financial auspices of Sir Alexander Henderson and opened by King George V in 1912. Even that battle-scarred concern Associated Portland Cement benefited from a high-level City involvement, when in 1910 it was rescued by a syndicate led by the leading investment trust figure Lord St Davids, the former John Wynford Philipps. 'They have come into the speculation because they have heard of your devotion to the company, of all you have done for it, of your efforts to amalgamate the trade, and your belief that if you have sufficient capital at your disposal you can bring about a complete combination of the cement makers, which should make their shares worth ten pounds or more,' O'Hagan's solicitor told the veteran company promoter. Even so, Morgans (offered 10,000 shares out of the 100,000 to be bought by the syndicate) preferred to look the other way. 'As the liability might be about £3 or £4 a share,' Grenfell wrote to Vivian Smith, 'I think probably you will not care about it. I myself am rather averse to it.'[12]

A crucial – and increasingly invidious – vacuum remained to be filled. In 1904 Cornelis Rozenraad, in his annual paper to the Institute of Bankers on 'The International Money Market', regretted the way in which the public had 'suffered so much by the action of unscrupulous company promoters' and called for a new, soundly run institution to be established in London to compete for the business done so unsatisfactorily by the promoters. Five years later an article in *The Times* on 'Bankers and Industry' complained bitterly how 'in Great Britain money for industrial purposes has to be raised through the independent financier, who looks upon the "industrial" as a means of making promotion money or profit on the Stock Exchange, rather than a steady income, and to him a successful flotation is of more importance than a sound venture'. Ultimately, it was a lack of quality control that beset the domestic capital market centred in London. In 1916 a Board of Trade committee, chaired by Lord Faringdon (the former Sir Alexander Henderson), considered the question of trade relations after the war. Much of the committee's work, essentially based on the pre-war situation, focused on the question of tied loans; but there occurred a particularly pregnant exchange between Frank Tiarks of Schröders, giving evidence, and Gaspard Farrer of Barings, sitting on the committee:

> *Tiarks*: I believe that what we really want to do in London is to care for business that is not being cared for, that is business which the issue houses and the banks . . . do not do. We will say it is a question of raising money for helping industrial businesses which are going to be started abroad or at home. I think Mr Farrer can bear me out that the issuing houses have many businesses brought before them which may be excellent businesses but which require expert examination and all sorts of technical knowledge, about which, though perfectly good, we simply say, We are not going to be bothered with it. Am I right?
>
> *Farrer*: Yes; it is hardly our business perhaps.
>
> *Tiarks*: It is hardly our business. We might consider that it is very likely good business, but it is not our business and we are not adapted for making the necessary expert examinations. I believe that there should be an institution in which all the joint-stock banks had a limited interest, but quite a large limited interest, which was formed for the purpose of studying questions such as I have spoken of which are brought to many of us . . .

Later in his evidence Tiarks amplified on the value of such an institution and the thorough investigation it would provide of propositions made to it:

That would at once do away with the fate of all these sorts of concerns that get turned down because of the difficulties of examination, which are then brought out speculatively by people who know absolutely nothing about what they are dealing with. Syndicates are formed on the waves of good times and people are most frightfully let in. I think such an institution would do away with a great amount of that sort of evil in the issuing business.

In addition to Faringdon and Farrer, the committee's members included Docker, Huth Jackson, Richard Vassar-Smith of Lloyds, and Walter Leaf, the former textile merchant who had become Deputy-Chairman of the London County and Westminster Bank. In its report it asserted that 'there is ample room for an Institution which, while not interfering unduly with the ordinary business done by the British Joint Stock Banks, by Colonial Banks, and by British-Foreign Banks and Banking Houses, would be able to assist British interests in a manner that is not possible under existing conditions'. All signed the report – except the man from the City's oldest and arguably still most highly respected merchant bank.[13]

The absence of quality control on the part of those sponsoring home industrial issues was, unfortunately, exacerbated by continuing serious regulatory deficiencies.[14] 'Is the New Companies Act a Failure?' asked the *Bankers' Magazine* in 1903, three years after it was passed: 'It has not shown itself to possess that protective value which was claimed for it, while it has served as a restraint on the expansion of legitimate joint-stock enterprise, and by its presence on the Statute Book has stimulated the shady promoter, against whom it is aimed, to additional zeal in the discovery of fresh subterfuges.' In particular, the 1900 Act's 'stringent provisions' had directly led to 'the reprehensible, but rapidly growing, practice of introducing shares to public notice without any prospectus at all', in other words, 'the very worse form of all of company promotion'. For a time, early in 1907, it seemed that members of the Stock Exchange were about to revolt against this non-prospectus method of introducing shares, a method in which jobbers played a key role; but in the end no movement developed aimed at ending the Committee's practice of granting special settlements to prospectus-less companies. After all, as the *Economist* commented, 'it is natural enough that there should be a general dislike on the part of members to come forward, and, as it were, to bell the cat'. That same year a new Companies Act laid down that it required that a 'Statement in lieu of a Prospectus' be compulsorily lodged at Somerset House. But the non-prospectus method of introducing shares remained common in the Stock Exchange's more speculative markets, including the Miscellaneous. Nor, generally, was investor protection significantly enhanced by the 1900 and 1907 Acts, the requirement in the latter that a balance sheet be submitted to the Registrar of Companies being seriously flawed, not only by the failure to insist that it be a current balance sheet but also by the exemption of profit and loss figures from disclosure. The 1900 legislation did tighten up on allotment procedures, and legalised the use of under-writing in equity issues, but that was about all. Put another way, market-making was still the norm, *caveat emptor* the order of the day.[15]

Yet arguably the investing and speculating classes got the capital market they deserved. 'Britons as a rule are careless investors,' contended Henry Lowenfeld in an investment treatise published in 1909, 'who never take the trouble to ascertain the real character and sound-ness of any investment, with the result that they permit themselves to drift in a happy-go-lucky fashion . . .'; and although welcoming recent parliamentary attempts to curb the machinations of the company promoter, by means of tightening up on prospectuses, he insisted that these 'failed to grasp the fact that the credulity of the investor was the source of the evil'.[16] Perhaps. But if over the past quarter of a century the financial press had markedly improved its contribution to the larger evaluative process, the same could not be said for the City as a whole, where the ease of helping oneself to market-making and stagging spoils naturally encouraged adherence to the traditional philosophy of self-help.

High cost and poor marketability were two further elements adver-sely affecting the flotation of home industrials on the London capital market. There were, according to Lowenfeld, 'some firms of brokers and solicitors who consider themselves but poorly remunerated by a fee of 1,000 guineas for merely giving the promoters the right to print their name on a prospectus, their work and out-of-pocket expenses being paid extra'; while it was 'quite easy to spend £5,000 on advertis-ing a prospectus'. He might also have mentioned the cost of sweetening the press, as Hooley had found – as well as the often generous slice taken by such as Hooley. In all, issuing costs (including underwriting) could run to as high as £25,000 out of a total issue of only £50–100,000. This was, obviously, a distinct disincentive for those thinking of coming to London for long-term funds. As for marketability, Ingall and Withers in their 1904 guide to the Stock Exchange offered a useful background passage:

Of recent years the Miscellaneous market has grown enormously, for it is in this market that the various industrial stocks are dealt in and the tendency to convert home industries into joint-stock companies has received a tremendous impetus during the last ten or fifteen years. Here is to be found the market in brewery companies, in cycle companies, in cold storage and meat-supply concerns, in catering companies, in manufacturing concerns of all kinds, in drapery businesses, in electric supply companies, in telephone and telegraph companies, in amusement ventures, in armament and shipbuilding companies, in iron, steel, and colliery companies. Neither does the Miscellaneous market by any means confine its attention to home 'industrials', for in this market we find the Indian tea-plantations shares, together with the timber companies of the east and Hudson's Bays. It takes much close observation to know which particular firm of dealers to approach in each individual one of this curious medley of securities, and moreover in many of the stocks dealt in in this market there is a better and a freer market in the provinces.

In a general piece that year on marketability, the *Economist* concurred:

It is when the industrial market comes under review that the non-negotiability of certain stocks and shares is most fully apparent. For a jobber to undo at once a transaction he has made with a broker is a matter of rarity, except in the cases of the few issues in which there still remain liquid dealings . . . The dealers in the Miscellaneous market have to run big books if they would do a large business, and 300 different stocks and shares are mentioned as one example of what a firm of jobbers have accumulated on their book in the process of making prices. It may be the very vastness of the field covered by industrial investments which makes, or helps to make, for narrowness of market in so many.

There survives a sheet of Stock Exchange closing prices for 18 December 1906 issued by the brokers James Shepherd & Co of 9 Old Broad Street: out of the more than 200 securities listed, only five came in the home industrial category – namely Aerated Bread, J. & P. Coats, Lyons (J.) & Co, Nelson (James) & Son, and Vickers, Sons, & Maxim. In other words, although the Miscellaneous market had undoubtedly grown – so that by the mid-1900s there were ten times as many securities officially quoted for companies engaged in domestic manufacturing and distribution as there had been twenty years earlier – it still remained a junior market, which many of its jobbers had entered on the back of the wave of domestic promotions that had characterised the second half of the 1890s.[17] Some notable jobbing names were poised to emerge from the ruck – Bone, Oldham & Mordaunt, F. & N.

Durlacher and Edward Bisgood & Co all catch the eye in Edwardian membership books – but so long as the Stock Exchange's orientation remained essentially international, and so long as most home industrial issues were of generally small size, then the Miscellaneous would remain subservient to the great markets of Capel Court.

*

Britain may have led the world in the first Industrial Revolution, but the second was a quite different story. 'I challenge anyone to point out a single industry in this country which has taken root, and has grown and flourished during the past 20 years,' wrote Gustav Byng, chairman of GEC, in 1901. And he went on: 'I do not dispute that we make a few motor cars, that we have produced a limited number of dynamos, and electric motors. We are responsible for electric telephones, and I have heard that there is such a thing as an English-made typewriter . . . Such attempts cannot be called industries. Compared to the achievements of other countries, our establishments are as backyard workshops to colossal factories.'[18] Contemporaries were especially conscious of deficiencies in Byng's own sector, one of crucial importance to Britain's future competitiveness.[19] 'Hitherto we have been backward in electrical matters,' noted the *Statist* in 1903. 'In the case of electrical traction, we have made very great progress during the past few years, but in electrical enterprise generally we are behind the US, Germany, and France . . .' Ten years later, British electrical output – products and equipment – was lagging at under half that of Germany.[20] Less inglorious, but nevertheless distinctly chequered, was the progress in the Edwardian period of British motor-vehicle manufacturing, another key 'new' industry.[21] By the eve of war the gap between French and British levels of output was being steadily narrowed, but the comparison with American production had become painful in the extreme. The *Economist* in January 1914 struck a gloomy note: 'The American car is a factor which the British small car trade has got to face if it is to exist . . . The British manufacturer has been content to sell his moderate output at a good profit, and meanwhile the Americans have got a footing.' Significantly, the *Economist* added that 'to embark upon any scheme of big-scale production by automatic machinery would, of course, require additional capital'. Taking the two sectors together, electrical and automobile, what blame for this unsatisfactory state of affairs attached to London's financial institutions and intermediaries? Keynes would write that 'the social object of skilled investment should be to defeat the dark forces of time and ignorance which envelop our future'.[22] How did the City score in that Manichean struggle?

For the best part of three decades the memory of the ill-fated Brush boom of the early 1880s cast a long, long shadow on almost all things electrical. In 1894 the Chairman of Cromptons, one of the most go-ahead electrical engineering firms, complained bitterly that 'the want of ready money cripples us in dealing with such matters as we have to deal with in a business of this kind'. In October 1902 the journal *Electrical Investments* asserted that 'capital must come with a certain freedom if a young industry is to expand freely', but was compelled to add that 'during the last year capital has been either non-existent or held with an exceedingly miserly grip'. And in 1911 that experienced observer Sir Carl Meyer conceded in a letter to *The Times*, 'that it is difficult to find money for electrical and similar undertakings in England is a well-known fact'. There is little doubt that many companies involved in the industry, including Brush itself, suffered badly in this period from liquidity problems – problems caused not least by an excessive reliance on burdensome fixed-interest securities, in the context of deep market suspicion of industrial equities. Lack of investor confidence led directly to lack of marketability, which in turn accentuated lack of investor confidence. Electrical manufacturing securities remained particularly out of favour for a long time, and phrases like 'changes in price are few and slender' continued to characterise market reports. In December 1903 the *Economist* reported an optimistic member of the Stock Exchange trying to sell Brush Electric Second Debenture stock, which nominally – but only nominally – stood at 84 to 89: 'The various dealers he applied to said they had no buyers, and did not want the stock themselves. Eventually, however, he was offered 65, and, his client agreeing to accept that price, the bargain was done.'[23] One company significantly hindered in its pre-1914 growth by an understandable mistrust of the London capital market was GEC, which only twice took the risk.[24] On the second occasion, in 1912, 15,000 cumulative preferred shares were offered at the relatively high coupon of 6 per cent, a rate decided on after the company's broker, Faithfull Begg, had expressed the presumably correct opinion that $5\frac{1}{2}$ per cent would not be enough. It was, in short, a thoroughly difficult market for the electrical industry to satisfy. Given all of which, it was hardly surprising that in 1909 the Chairman of Cromptons lamented 'a lack of financial support in London' and called for 'the establishment of a strong industrial bank, with able men at the head doing business on the lines of the Deutsche Bank in Germany'.[25]

In fact, while not denying the existence of excessive market pessimism towards the industry, there is a respectable case to be made in the City's defence.[26] The argument is partly negative – based on non-financial reasons for the industry's problems and the often dismayingly low profitability that inevitably discouraged investors – but there is also an important positive aspect. Take the leading stockbroker Joseph Braithwaite, whose application in 1893 to become a member of the Institution of Electrical Engineers was a model of finance and industry in harness. Stating that he had 'always been exceedingly fond of engineering', he went on:

> In 1882 I became the chairman of the Great Western Electric Light & Power Co, and during the two or three years that I held that position I devoted much time to the development of the early electric lighting stations at Bristol and Cardiff. On the amalgamation of this company with the Brush Electrical Engineering Co I became a director of the latter company, a position which I have held ever since . . .
>
> You are aware also that my firm were largely instrumental in obtaining the capital for the City of London Electric Lighting Co, and I have taken an active interest in endeavouring to promote a more efficient telephone service in the City. As a director of the Electric & General Investment Trust, which was formed in the interests of the electrical engineering industry generally, I have been able to render valuable financial assistance . . .

Less emotionally committed, but in his way an equally valuable contributor to a somewhat beleaguered industry, was the tough-minded accountant Andrew Tait. In 1905, following the insolvency and then reconstruction of Ferranti, he became the company's new Chairman and, in the words of his biographer, his 'expertise was valuable in reviving the business on a profitable basis'. Nor, despite not being the Deutsche, can all the banks be charged with indifference. Glyns, for example, consistently stepped into the breach with short-term loans during British Westinghouse's difficult first decade and a half after its establishment in 1899. Above all, perhaps even more than the merchant banker Robert Benson, there was the indefatigable Holden. In 1903 he was letting it be known that he favoured having 'sounder business men' on the board of one of the emerging electrical manufacturers. Two years later he was agreeing to find £25,000 for Brush to help tide it over one of its liquidity crises. But it was towards GEC that he was a particularly pivotal figure, striking up a close working relationship with Hugo Hirst. At the start of that relationship, in 1903,

Holden typically insisted on the Midland having all of GEC's business, even though Gustav Byng's account was with Barclays; but in return the company received overdraft facilities of up to £50,000. Increasingly Holden assumed an advisory function almost akin to that of a merchant banker. In 1913, for instance, he recorded Hirst reporting his profits for the past year: 'He was very desirous of increasing the ordinary dividend from $7\frac{1}{2}$ to 10%, and I agreed that it would be quite right for him to do so.' Later that year he had long discussions with Hirst over the financing of GEC's new headquarters in Kingsway, eventually agreeing to lend the company £100,000; while in January 1914, when Hirst wanted to issue £400,000 of new capital, Holden consented 'to take the whole of the issue and put it out quietly'. On the eve of the war, in an Electrical Press publication, two specialist journalists made the 'perfectly safe claim' that 'for the most part British traders do not understand finance' and that 'British financiers do not understand trade'.[27] Overall this was a justified assertion – but clearly there were in the City some notable exceptions.

A similarly mixed picture emerges in terms of the City and the British motor industry. *Motor Finance* at the start of 1908 reviewed that industry's history, going back to 1896 and the Lawson era:

> The vicissitudes of the pioneer companies are now a matter of history, and it is not beyond the truth to say that practically all the capital provided in the early days has been utterly lost in reconstructions and in buying the experience necessary for inaugurating a new industry, such as the making of motor-cars.
> The years 1905 and 1906 may be correctly regarded as the high watermark of the industry. For the first time several companies were able to produce balance sheets and declare dividends . . . The inevitable result followed. Shares which had been gladly exchanged at wallpaper prices, took to themselves wings and soared to extraordinarily high figures. Investors lost their heads, and assumed that the motor industry was going to continue to provide handsome dividends . . .

Then came 1907 and the reckoning, as a trade depression set in and 'the dire effects of gross overcapitalisation and mismanagement' began to be felt. In the event it would take several years to recover, significant capital not starting to flow into the industry again until 1911. By then, in one historian's words, 'Henry Ford had settled in to dominate the lower end of the market with Model-Ts gushing from his Trafford Park plant'.[28]

There was no shortage of poor management – on occasion notoriously prodigal, as in the case of Argyll, more often neurotically unwilling to cede control, a factor that constrained the growth of both Singer and Hillman. It is arguable, indeed, that if a company at this stage of the industry's evolution acquired capital *too* easily, this was a positive disadvantage to the company's chances of survival.[29] Even so, that was hardly the perception at the sharp end. Holden at the Midland did much to keep things ticking over for Daimler and Austin, while Barclays did the same for Standard, but companies that struggled during the 1900s to obtain adequate working capital included Lanchester, Maudslay and even Rolls-Royce, the latter embarrassed by its public issue flopping in December 1906 and having to be rescued by a well-disposed woollen manufacturer. 'For the most part of 10 years,' *Motor Trader* asserted shortly before the Rolls-Royce issue, 'the British motor industry has been swinging on an ebb tide. It is generally agreed that one of the chief factors in prolonging the period of suspense and trial has been the disinclination of the British capitalist or investor to put money into the British motor industry.' *Motor*, in May 1907, expanded on this theme:

> The British investor stands out as being singularly sceptical of motor industrial stock compared with the capitalists of other countries, for, whereas American, French, and German firms can secure all the money they want, even the most firmly-established concern on this side is received with indifference . . . That there is a scarcity of money we cannot believe, for any foreign loan or well-known industrial issue is always over-subscribed. The prosperity of the country is unquestionable.

There was nothing academic about such complaints. Contributing to the *Chamber of Commerce Journal*'s regional trade review of 1907, 'Our Special Correspondent' in Birmingham had this to say about that city's nascent motor industry:

> Generally speaking, the profit stage has not yet been reached in the Birmingham industry, owing to the large expense on plant and experiments. Some firms who extended their business in this direction have given up the new departments owing to lack of capital and inability to compete. It is believed this trade will be, in the not distant future, one of Birmingham's great industries.

So eventually it would be; but with Herbert Austin continuing to play a waiting game until eventually going public in 1914, a year after he had complained to Krupps that his company was 'rather cramped for want of capital', it was little thanks to London's not entirely appetising financial institutions.[30]

That in a sense is the real case against the City: qualitative as much as quantitative. During the post-Lawson dog days there was too little disinterested appreciation of the motor industry's long-term potential; during the boom between 1905 and 1907 the usual promotional malpractices flourished; and throughout there was a harmful mixture of poor marketability in the secondary market and high issuing costs in the primary.[31] 'Properly conducted motor-manufacturing concerns offer, on the whole, as good investments as can be found throughout the industrial market,' observed *Motor Finance* in March 1907, 'but it often happens that by the time they have passed through the mysterious operations of promoters their value decreases almost to vanishing point, and the public find themselves saddled with a well-squeezed orange.' Just over a year later, *Motor Finance* in its 'Answers to Correspondents' conveyed a distinctly murky, morning-after flavour:

ARGYLL MOTORS (Claygate). – You should have taken our advice, and cleared out of your ordinary shares when we advised.

DAIMLERS (Clapton). – If you paid £7 for these, they are not worth buying even at the present price for averaging. You should keep your *Humbers* for the present. You might have realised both shares had you followed our advice. There is every probability of *Humbers* going better, but you must not anticipate dividends as hitherto . . . *Humbers* balance sheet was referred to in our issue of 20th February, 1907. The shares were then 47s 9d, due to a rig by the jobbers, and they have fallen gradually ever since.

BEAUFORT MOTOR CO. – You have evidently forgotten what 'Non-skid' said in the issue of February, 1907, or you would not be holding these shares. A most reprehensible promotion.

GEARLESS MOTOR 'BUS CO. (Twickenham). – The meeting and accounts are long overdue; the shareholders have the remedy in their own hands.[32]

The reference to anticipating dividends is significant. Analysis suggests that the market continued to support the motor industry only so long as companies continued to pay high dividends, an attitude distinctly unhelpful to longer-term growth prospects.[33]

Among many candidates, three villains or semi-villains of the piece stand out. S.F. Edge was an Australian and a one-time racing cyclist who had cut his commercial teeth as Lawson's sidekick. He developed an unwavering belief in the future of the motor car, but unfortunately selling, rather than either engineering or financial probity, was his forte. In March 1907 he was responsible for the public flotation of the British arm of the De Dion Bouton, a manoeuvre justly headlined by

Motor Finance as 'Mr S.F. Edge's Benefit: A Lawsonian Prospectus'. Most of the nominal capital went on flotation expenses and to the owners of the so-called patent rights, chiefly Edge himself; and the profits of the new company never matched those that had been obtained by the old, private one before 1907. *Motor Finance* itself may have been, as someone who knew Edge recalled many years later, 'a blackmailing rag of a newspaper'. But it also had a serious purpose, as it made clear in its explicit justification of the 'Lawsonian' charge: 'We regret to say there is very direct evidence to confirm this; we do not want history repeating itself – no more mushroom companies, such as Horseless Carriage, etc., etc., formed solely to enrich the promoter at the expense of the public.'[34]

The other two were both members of the Stock Exchange with an eye for the main chance. Charles Birch Crisp was the son of a Bristol law clerk and worked for newspapers before migrating to Capel Court in 1898. A broker, he was soon engaging in industrial issues, to the discomfort of his partners before he left to start his own firm, C. Birch Crisp & Co. The *FN* editor Ellis Powell would later recall 'the absolute inability of Crisp's brain to rest' and his 'eagerness to be moving, to be doing something'. Politically that restlessness took the form of two unsuccessful attempts (1900 and 1906) to be returned to Parliament as a self-styled 'Tory Democrat'; financially it focused on company promotion. Crisp's main vehicle at this stage was New Industrial Issues Ltd, in which he was the largest shareholder and which in June 1906 was responsible for the much-criticised flotation of Delahaye & Co, motor manufacturers operating in France. The promoters took no less than £13,000 out of the £60,000 capital; an additional expense was the £2,000 charged by Crisp's firm to act as broker to the company. The issue flopped, but for Crisp it was all part of a learning curve on his way to greater things.[35]

The other member-cum-promoter, enjoying close links with Crisp, was a jobber called Arthur Salisbury-Jones, to the fore in the ill-fated London motor-bus boom of 1905–6. His methods were highly dubious, and much criticised by the *Economist* in particular, involving as they did considerable watering of capital and a grave shortage of working capital – with the eventual result that in 1908 his Vanguard group of bus companies was taken over by the London General Omnibus Company. Salisbury-Jones himself seems to have jumped off in time to have made a handsome profit, and by 1907 was devoting most of his energies to promoting Coalite Ltd, a grossly overcapitalised concern pushing a new type of smokeless fuel. By mid-June 1910 he found himself at the wrong end of an uncomfortable interview with Holden at the Midland, during which he managed to blurt out his belief that the British Coalite Company (as it was now called) 'was a business with an enormous future'; but he received little sympathy from Holden, who insisted that the £94,000 he owed must first be paid off. Holden added that he wanted the account cleared out of his books, advising him to take it to the Union of London and Smiths Bank. Soon afterwards, Salisbury-Jones seems to have retreated from company promoting and concentrated on his jobbing instead, mainly in the Kaffir and rubber markets. He would eventually die in the Sevenoaks railway smash of August 1927, returning to his home in Deal after a day in the City. 'Nearly all the dead,' *The Times* noted, 'came from the Pullman car.'[36] It was an apposite end for a member of the generation that had never really grown out of the assumptions of the railway age.

*

No significant unsatisfied demand for capital, the London capital market's relative unimportance, the continuing primacy of local finance as well as self-finance – several modern historians have accepted this comforting line of argument, despite the disconcerting evidence not only of the new, struggling industries, but also the larger backdrop of the British economy moving into more-or-less permanent industrial decline in comparison to international competitors.[37] Between 1899 and 1913, years of a rapidly developing global economy, the domestic economy grew at little more than 1 per cent pa, aptly described as 'the poorest sustained peacetime performance in Britain's history as an industrial nation'.[38] Perhaps it did not matter, as some have argued, granted that Britain's long-term future lay increasingly in services, not manufacturing.[39] Certainly the Edwardian City, flourishing as never before, was doing its share for the invisibles: in 1907, for example, its provision of financial, commercial and shipping services yielded the British economy a net gain of £107m, a figure put into perspective by the US equivalent of only £12m.[40] Yet at the time, few if any believed that British manufacturing industry could be fatalistically consigned to the rubbish-heap of history – and nor should they have. In a very real sense, across a whole range of industries, Britain remained the workshop of the world.[41] The question was how long that would continue to be the case.

A significant component of the contemporary debate focused on the harmfulness or otherwise of capital exports. In January 1906 – just as there gathered force a new, astonishingly powerful wave of such exports that would last more or less up to the war – the *Statist* offered a broad defence:

> This country has to draw from abroad a large part of its food and of the raw materials of its industries. A revenue from investments abroad affords a very convenient means of paying for such imports. Again, the countries which need foreign capital for their development usually pay a higher rate for that capital than is paid at home. Consequently, foreign investment is generally more profitable than home investment. Moreover, foreign investment is generally made in the form of commodities, and therefore gives immediate employment to British capital and British labour. And if the investment is judiciously made, it increases the purchasing power of the country where it takes place, and thus helps to increase the world's trade.

These were sober if debatable claims, but writing later in the year in the *Financial Review of Reviews* that he edited, Lowenfeld was positively poetic about the phenomenon:

> It is a truism that capital knows no patriotism. Like water it spreads itself over the earth's surface, only instead of seeking the lowest level it finds the highest. There was a time when artificial restraints left it within well defined boundaries marked out by national or dynastic considerations. But with the growth of the means of communication, the wide diffusion of commerce and the spread of intercourse between nations, capital has declined to be hemmed in by arbitrary boundaries, and more and more it has become cosmopolitan in its manifestations.

There is little doubt that contemporaries saw the question as a conscious choice, a choice pointed up by the perceived existence of an investor-unfriendly Liberal government. Robert Benson, in his annual address to the Merchants Trust, demonstrated in February 1907 that American railways and the Argentine were where the Trust invested most heavily, before (for all his personal friendliness towards the British electrical industry) going on:

> All the board's experience was in favour of sending capital abroad; they had positively found it safer as well as more remunerative to do so. Under present conditions Great Britain was not the field for them, and it would not become so until John Bull learned the lesson of how to let capital make money, instead of maintaining antiquated conditions, or prescribing new ones in the imaginary interest of the community, whereby producers, capitalists and labourers together, got an inadequate return for their risk, and less than in other countries.

That would remain the conventional wisdom, but eventually some dissenting voices started to be heard from the mainstream. After giving figures, based on 119 companies, showing a return for the year so far of 5.8 per cent on money invested in industrial ordinary shares, the *Economist* in October 1909 went on to regret the fact that 'for three or four years politicians and journalists have, in season and out of season, been preaching the insecurity of British investments and the wisdom of placing money abroad', that 'the great craze of investors has been for foreign Government securities yielding between $4\frac{1}{4}$ and 5 per cent'. As a result, 'the industrial market has been rather foolishly neglected'. The *Statist* in June 1912, with the Liberals still in office, argued similarly:

> The eyes of a fool are said to be in the ends of the earth. During recent years there have been many home investments yielding high returns and attaining an improved position every year which have been sadly neglected, because it was foolishly supposed that Great Britain was a played-out country and on the down-grade. The Preference and Ordinary shares of conservatively managed industrial companies operating at home give very handsome returns, and are meantime little appreciated. Most investors are so lazy that they will not trouble to examine things for themselves.[42]

The ends of the earth indeed. Whereas sterling securities issued for overseas borrowers totalled £819m between 1893 and 1904, over the ensuing ten years 1905 to 1914 the total was £1,642m (over £70bn in modern values), and few parts of the world failed to benefit.[43]

Was the City, whether as a capital market or a secondary market, *irrationally* biased in favour of foreign securities? Inevitably there has been a ferocious debate on the subject, involving sophisticated analysis of relative rates of return, but arguably more heat than light has been engendered.[44] Where there is perhaps a degree of consensus is over the view that Edwardian investors naturally favoured securities that (a) were reasonably safe, and (b) were reasonably good payers – and that, as it happened, most of the available securities that fell into these two desirable categories were foreign non-industrial rather than domestic industrial. In the eyes of most investors, the term 'industrial' was associated with the attractive possibility of high returns, the less attractive possibility of capital loss. It was a skewering – away from coolly appraised risk and the terrors of Lloyd George, towards rentierdom and the reassurance of geographical spread – that had profound consequences. Cain and Hopkins put it best:

If bursts of foreign investment had short-run beneficial effects on exports, they may have retarded the development of export industries in the longer term by cushioning them against the need for technical and organizational change. If, for whatever reason, there had been less foreign investment, then staple export industries might have been forced to adapt themselves more quickly and investors would have had a greater interest in other domestic opportunities – with radical effects on the structure of capital markets and financial institutions. Foreign investment, like formal empire, proved to be a considerable force in favour of conservatism in industry, not only by keeping up overseas sales of traditional manufactures from a number of export-producing regions but also by offering easy alternatives to new and risky domestic ventures.[45]

When Chamberlain, in the course of the 1906 election, apparently suggested that the holding of large foreign investments was not necessarily helpful to British trade, he was jumped upon by Schuster, who insisted that 'the placing of our capital in foreign countries leads to the export to such countries of ships, railways material, and innumerable other articles, and thus creates employment for our working population'.[46] Schuster's arguments were far from unanswerable – but, as yet, only a muffled challenge was heard to these nineteenth-century tenets.

One could hardly have expected otherwise. Despite some fluctuations, the Edwardian City was doing extremely well out of its predominantly international orientation; most leading members of the Stock Exchange were far more at home in Monte Carlo than Manchester; the merchant banks for the most part held aloof from domestic industry, the clearers on the whole stuck to their unambitious remit; liquidity and profit-taking were the name of the game, rumour and clubbiness the language of the market. As to how that market made up its collective mind about the merits or otherwise of new issues, some passing remarks by the *Investor's Monthly Manual* in 1910 conveyed a wealth of meaning:

> Much of the present-day underwriting is done on the Stock Exchange, and a member will approach another with sometimes little more than a slip of paper, upon which are jotted brief particulars of the people connected with the matter, the proposed capital, profit estimates, etc. The names on the paper are what really count, and if first-class people are connected with any concern, underwriting will present no difficulties.[47]

The Victorian precept may have been that 'servants talk about people, gentlefolk discuss things', but in Capel Court the residents clung steadily to the socially inferior, conceptually less demanding way of interpreting the world. The future was tomorrow, the next account a remote contingency, and the long-term potential of new technologies rather less relevant than a Wellsian fantasy. 'Beating the gun', the Americans called it, and it was nice work if you could get it.

CHAPTER TWENTY-THREE
A Parish Vestry

> Cassel told me this morning that the crisis in the US is the most interesting financial situation within his experience. He has no belief in an immediate revival. It will, he thinks, take two years for confidence and trade to revive.
>
> He does not now propose to go to America, but he goes to Egypt for two months, and then to Sweden. He said he had a million and a half in Sweden, and he feels obliged to look personally after his interests.

So wrote Esher – no longer in the City, but still on good terms with his chief – in his diary at the start of December 1907. In fact general confidence was restored surprisingly quickly, as Bank rate came down steadily during the early months of 1908, reaching 3 by mid-March and $2\frac{1}{2}$ by the end of May, at which level it stayed for the rest of the year. The rising tide of activity on the London capital market was concisely if a little grudgingly caught by Natty Rothschild on 12 March, writing to Paris:

> Messrs Baring Brothers are bringing out a loan for the City of Moscow, they ask for 2 millions of money & I believe the Loan has been underwritten. The London & Brazilian Bank have had a loan of £500,000 underwritten for the City of San Paulo. New South Wales is borrowing £3,000,000, presumably, in part to pay off existing liabilities, & part for Railway purposes. The Grand Trunk Pacific (through Speyer) are issuing some Mortgage Bonds guaranteed by sections of the line; & various electric power companies are also in the market.
>
> There is always a great demand for participation in underwriting syndicates, but to what extent the public will come forward it is very difficult to say.

Natty's doubts were fully justified about the Grand Trunk Pacific issue, which flopped to such an extent that the underwriters were landed with 90 per cent. Vivian Hugh Smith, writing to Jack Morgan on the 21st, wept few tears:

473

There was 2% underwriting on it. Speyers gave the underwriting to a good many of their Underground friends, telling them they looked on it as a small dividend for them, so that altogether there has been a certain amount of feeling about. Arthur Grenfell told me he went to a business dinner the other night at which Edgar Speyer was present. He had never seen Speyer and he asked someone who he was. This gentleman replied that he was not sure but he rather thought from his appearance he must be the Cuban Consul. (I think this will amuse you.)

Ten days later Smith wrote to Morgan again:

Hambros brought us in a very nice bit of business the other day, to grant a Credit to Denmark for £1,100,000, half of which is guaranteed by the Danish Government and half by a Syndicate of the principal Banks ... Hambros took £400,000, we took £350,000, Raphaels £200,000, Schroeders £150,000, and I hear from Hambros today that the bills are very much liked in the market.[1]

The City's inner circle was a wonderful club to belong to, but Edgar Speyer's admission remained at best occasional and only on sufferance.

There was certainly no room for him in the following month's highly successful Pennsylvania Railroad £5m issue. Alfred Mildmay of Barings, writing to Windham Baring on 25 April, described the profitable carve-up:

Jacob Schiff of Kuhn Loeb & Co was over here and offered us the business and John got Rothschild to join in. Cassel took a large interest and we placed a third of the English half of the loan in firm participations at the issue price before the loan was made. We were therefore able to do without underwriting and I think that the business will turn out to be even more profitable than the Moscow Loan. The loan is already enormously over-applied for, of course, largely by stags; but there is no doubt that a 4% bond secured by a mortgage on the main line of the first railway in the world appeals to investors.

Teddy Grenfell was less enamoured, writing to Jack Morgan the next day that 'John Baring has been very cock-a-hoop over the Pennsylvania issue which I presume was hatched by Cassel and Schiff when they were in Egypt together'. And he added that 'since their return they and John Baring have been inseparable'. Over the next few weeks foreign issues continued to flood the market, leaving Natty Rothschild to wonder aloud to his cousins in Paris where it would all end:

Circumstances have completely changed from what they were formerly when first of all the number of issuing houses with good credit was comparatively very small and the new financial operations, issued or to be issued, were few and far between. Now there are a large number of issuing houses, endless new operations and great opportunities for capital seeking investment, and if a large number of these operations was not successful trade, commerce and manufacturers would come to a standstill. In olden days an issuing house always kept a large amount of stock; the majority, if not all of the new institutions are more than satisfied if they can place the Bonds or shares which are entrusted to them . . .[2]

Autre jours, autre moeurs. Effective international distribution was ever more the key to this lucrative if risky aspect of merchant banking, and over the years Rothschilds had failed to cultivate a web of connections comparable to that now enjoyed by both Barings and Morgans.

The recently established Canadian Agency had, through Arthur Grenfell, some good connections – but at this stage, neither the reputation nor the resources to enable it to absorb early blows painlessly. Guy St Aubyn wrote at the start of July to Lord Grey about that peer's incorrigible former son-in-law:

You will remember that when I came to stay with you in Ottawa last February you asked me how his finances were.

I told you that, having missed the opportunity of getting his affairs in order after the successful promotion of his two land companies, & of doing a deal in Messina shares when copper was at a record price in 1906, he had gone off to Mexico leaving a large 'bull' account open, & with liabilities far too heavy for his resources.

As a result, when the slump came, his unrealized profits were swept away, & a big loss followed in his speculative account. Further heavy shrinkage in values during 1907 naturally worsened the situation: but by February of this year it looked as if the low water mark in the price of securities had been reached, &, when I left for Canada his position had been temporarily patched up.

A relief policy had been defined, & on this he promised to work.

Naturally, in execution, it called for stringent economy, & much humdrum, persistent effort. This proved distasteful & boring to him, & he plunged once more into heavy speculation in stocks – as a short cut to the rehabilitation of his finances.

The market went against him at first, &, in order to avoid a catastrophe, he borrowed money which should not have been utilised to finance private speculations.

An inkling of what was going on reached me in Canada, & brought me home early in April when I should have otherwise gone West.

Since then security prices have shewn some appreciation; but Arthur

will never take a profit when he has one. That is, he will not sell out, &
realize, although he treats differences in his favour as profits earned, &
allocates them to other purposes. As a consequence, if the market goes
against him, he has nothing to fall back on wherewith to meet his
obligations.

As a result, Grenfell's presence in the country had become indispensable, for 'no one but he can successfully juggle with these loans, &
figures, which may require to be shifted, & switched any day'. Counselling therefore against Grenfell going ahead with his proposed
autumnal tour with Grey, St Aubyn went on:

> This then is the situation in plain English, & it is the very one which,
> for his own sake, one was most anxious to avoid; from the business
> standpoint because this craze for speculation unbalances his judgment;
> from the personal aspect, for the reason that the effect on his health is
> deplorable.
> Almost the last time I saw Vera she said 'It is stocks, not work, which
> make Arthur look ill & increases his deafness'. Moreover, far more
> serious than this, the desperate gambler has recourse, under pressure of
> necessity, to expedients which otherwise he would never dream of adopt-
> ing. This blunts the moral sense, one of the consequences of which is that
> misunderstandings arise in business relations with others, which the latter
> set down as breaches of faith. Hence you will never get Rivy to join
> Arthur in business, however close they may be outside. For the same
> reasons (A's financial position, the difficulty he has in hearing, & his
> tendency to excessive commitments) it will be extremely difficult for me
> to leave him, & come to Montreal . . .
> My responsibility in the matter is considerable, because my friends, &
> relations, have at my instance put up a substantial amount of hard cash
> for the Canadian Agency, & I do not mean it to be lost, if I can help it,
> by reckless finance, and improper loans to individuals.
> The fact, I fear, is that A. suffers from a sort of financial megalomania.
> Figures, facts, transactions, & ideas appeal to him because they are big
> rather than because they are sound. Consequently facts are often con-
> founded with fiction – with disastrous results.

Grenfell spent the latter part of the summer on a three-week musketry
course at Hythe in Kent, while his younger brother Rivy continued to
keep his distance, instead hobnobbing with the new Prime Minister,
Asquith. 'He told me,' Rivy wrote to his twin brother Francis, 'that in
talking with financiers and asking their opinion he always found that
they based their argument on no foundation – in fact, had no logic. I
think this is very true. There is a famous Jew who, when asked about

his partner's capacity for making money, said he had a wonderful *nose* for it. I think that is the only way to put it.'[3]

*

1908 marked a turning point in the history of two of the City's great markets: Lloyd's on the first floor of the Royal Exchange; and the Stock Exchange in Capel Court.[4] The consequences proved beneficial in the case of the former, pernicious in the case of the latter. The contrast is both instructive and piquant.

Calls for internal reform at Lloyd's had been heard since the Burnand scandal of 1902, but the institution had chuntered on more or less untroubled, fortified in its self-regard by its strong, stoical response to the heavy losses incurred by the San Francisco earthquake of 1906. Matters, however, started to come to a head in the summer of 1908, against a background of generally lean business and several members of a large syndicate finding themselves in financial trouble. On 17 July the Financial and Commercial Supplement of *The Times* published a main leader on 'Troubles in the Marine Insurance Market' that was designed to cause a stir and did so. The anonymous author was a journalist called Harcourt Kitchin who specialised in insurance matters. Having stressed the lack of centralised control exercised by Lloyd's over its members' operations, he argued that the existing system of deposits of £5,000 payable by each underwriting member of marine risks had become badly outdated:

> The bulk of the business at Lloyd's is now done by large syndicates of underwriters, and these syndicates of 'names' – managed and controlled by a 'leading underwriter' – do as much business as even large marine insurance companies. The largest syndicates have a premium income of from half a million even up to a million pounds a year, and although the 'names' no doubt receive accounts from their leading underwriter, yet no policy-holder has any knowledge at all as to how this large premium income is used . . . As compared with the large sums which should be readily available to meet liabilities of large syndicates for unexpired risks, it must be owned that the amount of the official deposits is insignificant.

Then came the posited remedy:

> What really is needed is not so much an increase in the amount of deposit, but a system of audit of underwriters' accounts . . . We believe that the public would be satisfied if the underwriting syndicates had properly audited balance-sheets prepared every year, and submitted them

privately to the Committee of Lloyd's. The mere fact that such a balance-sheet had to be submitted would automatically compel underwriters to make sure that all their liabilities for unexpired risks were provided for and their funds properly invested . . .

We believe that the credit of underwriting members would again become practically invulnerable, if they took the necessary steps to secure a semi-private audit.[5]

Almost certainly Kitchin was writing at the instigation of Sidney Boulton, a reform-minded member of the Committee; and only a week after the article appeared, a meeting of underwriters approved the establishment of a special joint committee to put forward an audit scheme.

Cuthbert Heath, who for the last two years had demanded an auditor's certificate before guaranteeing any of his fellow-members, predictably dominated the committee's proceedings. He also, shortly before the meeting of underwriters early in November to consider the committee's proposals, played a tactical masterstroke. In the context of quite a strong tide of opinion swelling against what were seen as inquisitorial, continental-style innovations, he persuaded over forty underwriters – more or less the leading men of Lloyd's – to declare themselves to the Committee as willing to submit to an audit. In the event the well-attended meeting on the 3rd agreed not only to the introduction of the audit, but also to the principle of 'premiums in trust', in other words the device for not allowing a future Burnand to use underwriting money for outside purposes. 'In thus keeping pace with the times Lloyd's underwriters have achieved for themselves probably the greatest reform on record,' declared the *FT* with perhaps a touch of hyperbole, while *The Times* added to its enthusiasm about 'The Strengthening of Lloyd's' some perceptive analysis: 'The acceptance of this plan by every member is voluntary, but as the names of all those who comply with its requirements will be marked on a board, members who do not see their way to agree to the audit will, no doubt, soon find themselves left out in the cold.'[6] Lloyd's remained very much a club, but the rules of the club were changing for the public good as well as its own.

The ultimate club, though, was still Capel Court: governed by the creed of private faces in private places and lacking a commanding figure like Heath. The question of capacity – enmeshed with brokers taking double commissions and jobbers shunting with provincial stock exchanges – came to the surface again in 1908, this time decisively so. During January and February the Stock Exchange Committee was once again treated to a series of submissions and counter-submissions. Samuel Gardner, a well-known broker, 'said that our fathers had built up a sound system by which the broker as an agent kept the dealer who made prices at arm's length'. The inveterate Blyth declared that 'members of the public living near provincial exchanges were dealing year by year more with the provincial and less with the London brokers, because the former boasted that they could do as well or better for their clients', in other words by dealing with London jobbers. And the Westralian jobber Bernard Moore got close to the heart of the aggrieved feelings about shunters when he declared that the existing single-capacity rule 'was loyally kept by 90% of the members', but that a privileged minority 'had obtained private telephones, which their fellow-members were unable to obtain'.

The more compelling if less popular arguments ran all the other way. Claiming to have shunted with country exchanges for over thirty years, the jobbers G.H. & A.M. Jay took the line that they had 'expended an immense amount of time, money and thought in developing this class of business', that 'it has taken us years to secure advantageous positions for the telephones and telephone boxes, and to do this we have had to enter into contracts in some cases for five or even seven years'. So too the experienced shunter Gerald E. Phipps, who stated that 'arbitrage between dealers and the provincial exchanges has been vigorously carried on ever since the Shilling Telegraph Law was passed some 40 years ago' and 'contended that his business was an advantage to all the larger dealers as well as the brokers, though possibly the smaller jobbers might have suffered'. Particularly cogent was Cecil Braithwaite, emerging as a leader of the lobby to abolish the distinction between brokers and jobbers. His letter to the Committee, backed by 903 signatures, stressed the economic logic of the situation:

> Brokers have no doubt lost some of their business owing to shunting, but, on the other hand, a very large number of members have gained a considerable amount by the present facilities in the way of being able to deal in such shares as cotton descriptions, cycle and motor shares, at close prices, where a few years ago the provincial exchanges were the only market . . . The shunter has made it possible to deal in anything in which there is a market anywhere, often at a moment's notice and within a very short space of time . . .
>
> The market in all securities will follow the money and those who control the stock, and it is impossible for any rule to make it otherwise . . . The whole tendency of all classes of business is to go to the men who can serve you best, i.e. the shop, and, what is more, the public demand it.

If you deal with a man who makes his price outside the shop quotation you soon hear about it.

In person he 'drew attention to the fact that although his petition had been signed by a minority of the members, it had received the support of the great majority of the biggest firms'; and he even pointed out that his own firm, Foster & Braithwaite, 'had suffered from the "shunting" business, because these firms had had the pluck to acquire the facilities at great cost which his firm might have had'.[7] It was a remarkably objective way of looking at the situation, but in the numbers game small was beautiful.

The issue of capacity and related working practices was effectively settled in March by the annual Committee election.[8] The organisation that mobilised opinion to defeat Braithwaite and his followers was the Stock Exchange Members' Association, in which Blyth was a predictably prominent figure. Significantly, whereas the twenty-five successful (and all SEMA-backed) candidates in that election who were still in active business belonged to firms that had an average of 3.5 partners, the nine unsuccessful candidates (including Henry Vigne and Willie Koch as well as Braithwaite) still in active business came from firms with an average of almost five partners. Blyth, the day after the election, 'received quite an ovation in the Kaffir Circus' – justifying Braithwaite's subsequent observation that 'the question of double commission was originally raised by certain members of the South African market' and that indeed 'the whole agitation emanates from inside the House'. Following the election, the new Committee enacted in July 1908 what was in effect a trade-off to come into force from the following February. On the one hand brokers were specifically forbidden from making prices or taking a second commission, on the other hand jobbers were equally specifically forbidden from dealing directly with non-members. An exception to this latter restriction was made in the case of arbitrageurs dealing with members of foreign stock exchanges. A House correspondent of the *FT* convincingly explained the inconsistency:

> Logically, nothing can be said in favour of allowing arbitrage dealings with foreign bourses and tabooing the 'shunting' between London and the provinces. But from the average English broker's point of view, and that of most jobbers too, there is a very great difference. The fact of the matter is that most of them neither know nor care to know anything about the mysteries and movements of exchange, hence arbitrage dealings are outside their ambitions, as well as beyond their scope. But however

insular alike in his language and his knowledge of foreign moneys, the
House broker can see quickly enough that if, say, a Glasgow broker buys
10,000 'Caleys' through a jobber in London, there is no commission for
the London broker thereon.

It was not only in Capel Court that this nimble ninepence business
across the international securities markets remained largely a mystery.
'Nothing in the world would induce me to undertake an arbitrage
business,' Gaspard Farrer at Barings wrote a few years previously to
Hugo Baring. 'It requires a very special training and mind to do it
successfully – John thinks someone born in the Ghetto at Frankfort.'[9]
For the moment they were allowed to continue their incomprehensible
activities in peace.

The new rules received a predictably poor press, typified by the
Investors' Review accusing the Committee of 'behaving like a parish
vestry, whose members are anxious that none of the "perks", sacred
through old usage, shall go past them'. The hardening of capacity
certainly did nothing for the Stock Exchange's marketability. According to Lowenfeld in 1909, there was at any one time a genuinely free
market in only about 400 out of the 5,000 or so officially quoted
securities, less than half of the proportion estimated by the stockbroker
Charles Branch in 1877 as fully marketable. Among those minority
members of the Committee who resigned in March 1909 in protest
against the new rules which had just come into force was the stockbroker Gerald Williams. His letter of resignation included this alternative vision of the market's future:

> To make it worthwhile for men possessing capital, brains and enterprise
> to be dealers on the Stock Exchange, and to make it possible for brokers
> to deal for a living wage without undercutting one another to a ruinous
> extent, I am therefore desirous of inducing brokers to deal on the floor of
> the House, if by so doing they do not prejudice the interests of their
> clients, and I am equally desirous that the only competition which bro-
> kers shall be allowed to use is that consisting of energy, honesty, and
> intelligence. There is no need to say a word in favour of wealth, which has
> always and will always command special advantages.[10]

The give-away, as far as his opponents were concerned, was the final
sentence. Certainly, the theme of a sacred barrier between jobber as
principal and broker as agent, a barrier acting in some time-honoured
way as a safeguard to the investing public, was at best only marginal
in a campaign conducted for quite other reasons to harden the distinc-

tion between the two capacities. As numerous as they were undercapitalised, the small brokers and the small jobbers had combined forces to
lock the Stock Exchange into an ossifying, thoroughly short-sighted
institutional structure that would survive for another three-quarters of
a century.

*

None of which – at this stage at least – significantly affected London's
standing as the world's greatest capital market. Charles Addis, in his
darker moments, might have wished it otherwise. 'I have been for over
a month immersed in exciting loan negotiations,' he wrote on 1 October 1908 to his old friend Colonel Dudley Mills. And he went on:
'The absorption of business is progressive as well as inevitable, dynamic and not static in a way I had not quite realized. It is not pleasant
to think I may be in a few years what the French call "gaga". My
doctor gives me five years. Well, one must face that or break off
altogether. There is no middle course in finance.' The negotiations
concerned a £5m issue to enable the construction of a new line from
Peking to Hankow and, in the arcane and diplomatically sensitive
world of Chinese railway finance, involved almost daily visits on
Addis's part to the Foreign Office. Addis's diary recorded a nerve-racking, ultimately gratifying outcome:

6 October (Tuesday). Great excitement. Bulgaria has declared her
independence and Austria has annexed Boznia and Herzogovina in defiance of the Treaty of Berlin. Called at FO. Sir Edward Grey takes a
hopeful view of situation which he thinks may be arranged without
provoking a European war.
8 October. Loan agreement signed at Peking today. It is most unfortunate this action of Austria in the Near East at such a juncture. Were not
able to underwrite today. Hope it may be possible tomorrow. A trying
and anxious time.
9 October. A busy day . . . I went alone to the Queen's Hall concert and
refreshed myself with music.
12 October. After much discussion and amid many croakings I got my
way. We issue the loan tomorrow. I rushed off in taxicab to Chinese
Minister; got his letter; then to FO and so back to office to hurry up the
printers. Prospectuses all posted by 8 or 9 p.m.
13 October. Loan made a good start this morning.
14 October. Loan closed at 3 p.m. Amply covered. What a relief!
15 October. City very loud in praise of H&SBC and its handling of loans.
Many personal compliments to myself from Koch and others.

There is no doubt that the market environment in the early days of this sequence could hardly have been worse. The Stock Exchange took the news from the Balkans extremely seriously, culminating on Friday the 9th – in the *FT*'s words, 'a decidedly uncomfortable day' when 'the violence of the selling and the inroads made upon prices constituted it the worst since the present political scare began'. However, things steadied on Saturday, while on Monday markets 'displayed quite a buoyant tone', helped by a reassuring statement in the morning from the Foreign Office.[11] Perhaps Addis, then, was not taking such a risk when he defied the croakers and insisted on pressing the button. Even so, it was a well-earned triumph for a man whose City career was in fact, despite the prognostication of his doctor, only just entering its prime.

The reputation of Baron Bruno Schröder and his house was also on a rising curve. Coffee, the state of San Paulo and Brazilian federal government finance make for a complicated story, but the fundamental background was the glut in the coffee market by the mid-1900s putting particular strain on the producers in Brazil, the source for most of the world's coffee.[12] In 1905 a delegation from San Paulo sought Roth-schild backing for a so-called 'valorisation' scheme that would stabilise prices through large-scale purchases of coffee that would then be withheld temporarily from the market. Not only did Rothschilds flatly turn down the scheme as costly and unworkable, but as traditional king-pins of Brazilian finance it brought pressure to bear on the Brazilian federal government early in 1906 to prevent the issuing of a loan whose proceeds would be used to underwrite the enormous purchases. Soon afterwards Schröders got involved, Baron Bruno agreeing to assemble an international syndicate of eleven firms (including Schröders and Kleinworts in London) that would advance funds for valorisation purposes. By early in 1907 a stockpile of 3 million bags had been purchased on behalf of San Paulo – just as it was becoming apparent that the size of the San Paulo crop of 1906 was 4 million bags more than had been anticipated, thereby throwing into jeopardy the whole scheme. Confidence may well have wavered in Leadenhall Street. Natty Rothschild early in April noted a visit from Sir Walpole Greenwell, Schröders' stockbroker, 'with a message from the great firm ... that they did not believe in the valorisation of Coffee', together with 'some obscure hints about Schroeder being obliged to issue a certain amount of Treasury Bills'. Nevertheless, Baron Bruno and his syndicate pressed on, accumulating yet more millions of bags of unwanted coffee. It cannot have been an easy experience during the generally testing circumstances of 1907. 'A good deal of the Coffee was carried last year by Finance bills drawn from your side on Kleinworts and Schroeders,' Teddy Grenfell wrote to Jack Morgan in 1908. 'You may also remember that in November 1907 there was considerable talk here about the paper of both these Houses; in fact some of the discount people refused to take the paper. This was largely due to the distrust caused by drawings to a very large extent on these Houses to carry Coffee.'[13] By the spring of 1908 there existed a spectacular accumulation of 8 million bags.

From the point of view of Schröders, with almost a sixth of its capital exposed in advances to San Paulo, much hinged on the successful floating of a loan to enable that state to pay off its borrowings. International negotiations started in the summer of 1908 for an enormous £15m loan, to be secured upon the vast stockpile of coffee built up by the now defunct valorisation scheme. Granted the uncertainties attached to that commodity, even though the 1907 crop was blessedly smaller, it was crucial to investor attitudes that the Brazilian federal government guarantee the payment of the 5 per cent coupon, a guarantee that in turn was only possible with the blessing of Rothschilds. 'Certainly not for that damned swindle' was Natty's initial response when Frank Tiarks called on him and his brothers. However, on the grounds partly of the wider repercussions if the loan did not go ahead, and partly of a profitable £500,000 participation 'practically on bedrock terms' of the £5m of bonds offered for sale in London, Natty changed his mind. 'If it had not been for New Court,' he wrote to Paris in November, 'we are quite convinced that it never could have been carried through, and no doubt Messrs Schroeder fully realise this.' The actual loan was issued in December and proved a great success, being subscribed in London four times over. 'Messrs Schröder are perfectly jubilant,' noted Natty, and for that house the episode was a major feather in its cap, a satisfactory end to three highly stressful years.[14]

'It might be civil to ask Schroeder whether he'd like some Russian if it comes along next week?' Revelstoke suggested to Farrer on 7 January 1909, just before he set out to Paris for final negotiations over an imminent Russian loan. The total amount was for a little over £55m, with London's share rather meagre at less than £6m. Despite the signing of the Anglo-Russian entente in 1907, there remained a considerable undertow of hostility towards the Russian government's persecution of the Jews – a hostility naturally encouraged in the City by Rothschilds but opposed by Cassel, who argued that Russian policy could best be influenced through co-operation rather than a boycott. 'It amuses me to see how the Jews, though hating the Russian Government, are always ready to give them money if they themselves can "make a bit"!' was the less than fair interpretation of Cassel's motives offered by Sir Charles Hardinge of the Foreign Office; while Farrer on the 8th took particular pleasure in reporting to Revelstoke that 'we have had a number of applications for underwriting this morning, chiefly from the German Jew contingent'. By the 14th, surrounded by renegades, Natty Rothschild found little to cheer:

> We are assured by Mr Koch, to whose firm, namely Messrs Panmure Gordon & Co, Lord Revelstoke entrusted more than £3,000,000 of stock, that the underwriting on that amount went most smoothly & easily, & it now remains to be seen whether the public in general will respond equally favourably; it is however nowadays futile to prophesy because 9 times out of 10 the contrary happens to what is expected & what is predicted.

Four days later the loan was brought out and fully subscribed, leaving Natty to scratch his head in puzzlement:

> Messrs Baring sent out their allotment letters last night and the applicants received just under 50% which I fancy was more than a good many expected. The theories of modern finance are peculiar, there is always a tremendous rush for underwriting and a very large proportion of stags, these are things which cannot be helped. Moreover so far as new issues are concerned one must always remember that there are ever so many new things always coming out that it is extraordinary that so many of them should have been placed.

The City's other leading peer had, for all his patrician arrogance, a far surer grasp of latter-day finance. Revelstoke wrote to the Ministry of Finance in St Petersburg on 1 February:

> I am not in the least surprised at your criticism of our action in cutting down the small applicant for under £1,000. To anyone not familiar with the conditions here such a procedure would, indeed, seem inexplicable and would give the idea that our wish is to discourage the small investor. As a matter of fact, such a wish is very far from our thoughts; but our experience here in London during the last five or six years is that the art of 'stagging', as it is called here, or applying so as to sell instantly at a premium, has been carried to such perfection by the small applicant, that even people who are well off send in countless applications for £100

apiece without any sense of shame, in the hope of securing a larger proportionate allotment.[15]

The stag would never go away as a feature of City life, nor an instinctively higher regard for premiums in the pocket than principles in the sky.

Still, as principles went, there were few higher ones than the territorial imperative. Morgans since 1890 had been muscling in on the Argentine; Barings had tried not unsuccessfully to fight back; and during the winter of 1908/9 a culminating battle was waged.[16] The story is best told through the out-letters from 22 Old Broad Street:

16 September, Smith to Grenfell. Here everything is very dead but there are rumours of a new Argentine loan. I saw John Revelstoke yesterday, who was extremely amiable, and he said nothing about it.

26 October, J.S. Morgan & Co to Morgan, Harjes & Co, Paris. For your private information we may say that although we have worked jointly with Barings in other Argentine issues we have latterly not found that arrangement to work very easily, and on this occasion we have thought it well to work independently in New York and London, while Messrs Baring take their own course.

8 December, Grenfell to Harjes. I cannot find out anything here with regard to Barings having signed for the new Loan. You will understand it is extremely difficult to do so without showing one's hand . . .

9 December, Grenfell to Jack Morgan. When he is obliged to do so John Baring [i.e. Revelstoke] professes he is most anxious to work with us on joint account, but unless it is definitely so laid down in New York by you he will not put our name on Prospectuses, or on Coupons, or divide the money deposited; in fact he will be a thoroughly selfish bed-fellow. Naturally I should prefer to have the London end done solely by us or jointly with Barings with ourselves first.

8 January, Grenfell to Jack Morgan. Revelstoke has been in to embrace Vivian and myself . . . As neither of us has missed anything yet we are still in the dark as to what the peer may want. He begged us, as a special favor, to accept £100,000 of the Russian Loan.

15 January, Grenfell to Harjes. It would appear that the French group tied up to Barings includes practically every Bank except the Comptoir; in fact the group is so large and strong that there will be very little plunder to go round at all. The German group includes the Deutsche, Disconto and Dresdner. I have received no answer from the Dresdner and though we could detach them from Barings I doubt if it would be much good.

I have therefore made it pretty clear to Jack that the only free European market would be London, and for London – with active opposition from Barings and the rest – I admit 5 millions is a big lump . . .

Both houses, for whatever motives, now called a truce: the underlying reality was that Morgans had the financial firepower in the States, Barings in Europe; while in London itself, the outright antagonism of one could make life very uncomfortable for the other. Barings and Morgans therefore agreed to share the honours over the imminent £10m Argentine loan. It eventually took place towards the end of February and, writing to Jack Morgan in New York, Grenfell was his usual attractively sharp-tongued self:

> Servia on this side and cuts in steel prices on yours have made a sad difference to the financial outlook and we were not very sanguine about our Argentine issue this morning. The subscriptions, however, were pretty good . . .
> The effect of working with Barings amicably ??? has been that Vivian and I have developed the tempers of archangels, as while pretending to be friendly they have kept everything back till the last moment, and without giving actual cause for quarrel have been as offensive as possible.

Revelstoke may have been getting 'much too big for his boots', as Grenfell had written to Morgan a few weeks earlier, but it is possible that the faults did not lie solely on one side.[17]

Arthur Grenfell remained, perhaps to Guy St Aubyn's surprise, still in business by the spring of 1909, though St Aubyn himself left his employ to become a member of the Stock Exchange. Grenfell was poised to take advantage of what would be a major shift of capital into new Canadian concerns. 'I have been working so hard during the last 2 years that we have worked the Agency into rather a big position – bigger than our organisation & the result is we have to work double shifts,' he informed Grey towards the end of March. And, in entirely characteristic vein:

> We have not appeared publicly as doing the Lake Superior. I have taken your tip & am letting others appear; as there is a certain amount of jealousy about our success. I have got rather locked up myself as I have had to put up more money for settlements & have turned all my energies into the Canadian Agency. So that at the moment I am rather worried but provided we don't have a European war & politics quiet down all will be well.[18]

*

Few could guess how soon the world would change utterly. Winston Churchill, defending (as the new President of the Board of Trade) the

Manchester seat that he had held since the 1906 election, expounded to his constituents in April 1908 what most people would have unquestioningly accepted as the immutable verities of the gold standard:

> In the transactions of States scarcely any money passes. The goods which are bought and sold between great Powers are not paid for in money. They are exchanged one with the other. And if England buys from America or Germany more than she has intended to buy, having regard to our own productions, instantly there is a cause for the shipments of bullion, and bullion is shipped to supply the deficiency. Then the Bank rate is put up in order to prevent the movements of bullion, and the rise of the Bank rate immediately corrects and arrests the very trade which has given rise to the disparity. (*Hear, Hear.*)
>
> That is the known established theory of international trade, and everyone knows, every single business man knows, it works delicately, automatically, universally, and instantaneously. It is the same now as in January 1906, and it will be the same as it is in 1908 when the year 2000 has dawned upon the world. As long as men trade from one nation to another and are grouped in national communities you will find the differences of free trading are adjusted almost instantaneously by shipments of bullion corrected by an alteration in the Bank rate.[19]

Such confidence, and in 1908 apparently such justified confidence. In the event, his relationship with the yellow metal was to blight this ambitious politician's career.

Churchill was speaking in the aftermath of the successful resolution, from the English point of view, of the 1907 American crisis. And when, at about the same time or soon after, the National Monetary Commission (appointed by the US Senate to inquire into the lessons to be learned from the different banking and currency systems operating in Europe) came to London, almost inevitably its first interview was with William Campbell, who had been at the Bank of England's helm during the crisis. His answers gave every impression of a well-rehearsed routine, as he explained the gold-related circumstances in which Bank rate was changed, but things then got a little more tricky:

> Is London the only free market for gold in Europe? – In practise; yes.
>
> Do the joint stock and other banks rely upon the reserves of the banking department of the Bank of England as their ultimate resource in case of trouble? – Yes.
>
> Do you favor an increase in the fiduciary note circulation? – No.
>
> Do you favor the issue of £1 notes? – No.
>
> If not, what is the reason for your objection? – Our objection is based principally on the opinion that if there were £1 notes in circulation they

would take the place of gold in the pockets of the people and thus tend indirectly to drive gold from the country.

Does the proposition for a secondary gold reserve meet with approval? – The question of a secondary gold reserve is one upon which no definite agreement has so far been reached.

Is it desirable that bank reserves generally should be strengthened? – Probably.

Most of the Commission's interviews were less than revealing, not helped by the failure to ask Holden to give evidence, but that with Schuster included an important sequence:

Would you say the Bank of England is in any way a competitor of the other banks in England? – Yes. That is a source of very grave complaint by the other banks.

The Bank of England do not pay interest on any accounts? – No; but in some cases they act as intermediaries for lending money. It is a very subtle distinction. It will probably be denied by the representatives of the Bank of England that they are competitors; it is a constant source of disagreement between us. There is absolutely no doubt that they are. To start with, they have our balances, which they use in the market, or 40 per cent of which they use in the market. That in itself is competition. If we held our balances ourselves (this bank's balance alone is £3,400,000; they use probably £2,000,000 of that) – if we held it here, they could not; but in other directions also they compete.

Do you care to state in what direction? – It is very difficult to . . . say where they compete with us. They might say the joint stock banks compete with them. The fact is the course of business is altered. The Bank of England despised business at one time which at the present time they would be glad to do. They allowed the other banks to grow up round them and get very strong and powerful, and, having perceived that, they rather tried to retrace their steps and get a little of that business themselves. It is an anomalous position.[20]

In fact, the Bank's recent 'competitive' phase had lasted only from the early 1890s to at the latest the mid-1900s; but even the intelligent joint-stock bankers were still making what was essentially a knee-jerk reaction.

Would Schuster and his fellow-clearers at last reach agreement? J. Spencer Phillips of Lloyds told his shareholders in January 1908 that as a result of the previous autumn's crisis 'the open market in gold has been brilliantly vindicated'; but as far as the clearing bankers' committee set up to consider the general question of gold reserves was concerned, he was unable to 'give much hope of any conclusion being voluntarily arrived at, or anything being done in this matter beyond what each individual bank sees fit in its own eyes'. Soon afterwards, responding to wider concerns about high levels of Bank rate, the London Chamber of Commerce set up its own Gold Reserves Committee, and the deliberations of the other seem to have been suspended. Schuster, Holden and Tritton all sat on the new committee, while the Governor of the Bank of England declined to serve or to nominate any of his colleagues. Proceedings were rather sporadic, but the nub began to be reached in the winter of 1908/9 when Tritton formally proposed the establishment of a secondary reserve, 'to be held by the Bank of England not as bankers but as warehousemen'. Schuster was broadly supportive but not so Holden, who insisted that 'he had not met one Bank Manager who would consent to have his reserves taken from him and kept in another place'. Tritton tartly responded that it would have been better if Holden 'had done me the honour of reading my remarks a little more carefully'. The eventual outcome was that the report, presented to the Chamber in July 1909, included as possible solutions *both* the approaches – Tritton's proposed visible secondary reserve physically based at the Bank, Holden's preference for a detailed public statement by each bank of its gold holding. With more hope than conviction, the report described the two schemes as 'not being altogether incompatible'.[21] What would be the next step? Asquith had already made it pretty clear that government was not prepared to intervene in order to bang heads together; while the Bank had offered precious little leadership in the matter since the end of Lidderdale's governorship seventeen years earlier. The new Governor was the coffee merchant Reginald Johnston and there was little hope of a radical new initiative from that quarter.

Accordingly the question remained in a state of more or less animated suspension. The policy of the Bank seems to have been little more than hoping that somehow the whole matter would miraculously go away of its own accord; while the bankers did not yet have either the cohesion or self-confidence to alter the power relationship. In November 1909, as the new President of the Institute of Bankers, 'Fritz' Huth Jackson gave his inaugural address and called for unanimity from the clearers over the question. Jackson, as a merchant banker, was also a director of the Bank; and in his vote of thanks, Walter Leaf of the London County and Westminster (the merger had taken place earlier in the year) was tact itself – some might have thought servility – as he dwelt on the 'peculiar relation in which Joint Stock Banks stand to the Bank of England':

It is very largely a sentimental relation, and one is continually learning how large a part sentiment plays even in the dryest financial business of the City of London. In some respects it might be called a filial relation; in some respects it reminds us of the relations of the Colonies to the Mother Country. But in any case I am sure that the attitude of the banks of England to the Bank of England is one of the highest respect and extreme admiration for the manner in which they have dealt with the difficult task which has been laid upon them.

The keeping of a gold reserve is, as we all know, a very expensive, and in some ways an uneconomical process. It is one which we are very glad to have done for us by the Bank of England, and it is only the pressure of public opinion which would drive the large proportion of the Joint Stock Banks into using their own strong rooms for the purpose . . .

The Old Lady's representative was suitably self-deprecating in reply. 'As Dr Leaf says, the Bank of England holds a peculiar position in the banking world, and whether the directors of the Bank of England would be competent to conduct the affairs of the other banks in the country I do not pretend to say.'[22]

*

I am sure the people of this Country, be they Liberals or be they Conservatives, will applaud you if you will follow up without hesitation public opinion which says 'give us eight Dreadnoughts or even more'. There is one fact, however, which you ought to put before your Chancellor and your Prime Minister, and that is, while practically every Country has a War Chest, we have nothing. We ought to set about at once to accumulate gold.

Holden's letter of March 1909 to the Liberal minister Reginald McKenna was a pointer to the urgency the gold reserves debate was starting to assume against the larger international backdrop. It also reflected the sharpening anti-German mood in the City – a mood that had become notably apparent during the German loan episode a year earlier, in April 1908. In fact the loan comprised two issues in one: a Prussian loan of £20m, proceeds to be devoted to improving Prussia's railway system, and an imperial loan of £12½m, for what the *Statist* bluntly described as 'warlike purposes only'. Both issues had a 4 per cent coupon and neither was to be redeemable or convertible until 1918. The Stock Exchange nicknamed it the 'Dreadnought loan' (treated as one because the issues were not brought out separately) and the City as a whole blew a less than cordial raspberry. H.A. Gwynne, editor of the *Morning Post*, writing soon afterwards to the Canadian Prime Minister, described the outcome:

> The recent German loan that was launched at a very low price and a high rate of interest, was regarded by the City as a war loan, and word was given by all the big houses that on no account was money to be invested . . . So high was this feeling that . . . a single individual . . . who sold £50,000 of consols to invest in the German loan . . . was forced by City opinion to withdraw his application for money, it being put pretty plainly to him that he might be boycotted in consequence . . . A few insurance companies did give a little money, but they, too, under the same pressure have . . . sold out.

The *Economist*, most peace-minded of organs, sought to argue that pragmatism had also played a part ('with the prospect of more borrowing in the autumn, German credit will suffer still further depreciation'), but was unable to deny that 'people here naturally do not care to invest their money, even at a high rate of interest, in German battleships', or in short that the mighty operative force of 'sentiment' had been at work.[23]

As Germany pushed on with its shipbuilding programme, naval matters increasingly preoccupied the City – by March 1909, with the Germans believed to be secretly speeding up their programme and the jingoistic rallying cry 'we want eight, and we won't wait' passing into the English language, in a state of extreme agitation. 'In the City today,' Natty Rothschild wrote to Paris on the 17th, 'the Public was much more interested in the Debate which took place yesterday on the Naval Estimates, & general dissatisfaction was expressed at the Government proposals which only deal with 4 Dreadnoughts at present.' A fortnight later the Guildhall was the scene for another display of City ritualism, as the ancient building was packed out for a meeting – summoned by the Lord Mayor but initiated by the Naval and Military Defence Standing Committee of the London Chamber of Commerce – 'to consider the state of the Navy'. *The Times* wrote glowingly how 'men stood in serried ranks around and beyond the seats, surging about the statues of Nelson and Wellington and Pitt, filling the distant corners and recesses, and even content with precarious foothold upon a staircase'. The Lord Mayor, flanked by Balfour and Natty Rothschild, noted in his opening remarks how 'numerously and influentially signed' had been 'the requisitions from the banking interests, the Stock Exchange, the Baltic, the Commercial Sale Rooms, the Mincing-lane houses, the metal and timber trades, the London Chamber of Commerce, and merchants and traders generally'. There followed a long, rapturously received speech by Balfour, before Banbury successfully moved that four further Dreadnoughts be built. Natty Rothschild then equally successfully moved that all necessary support be given to attain that end:

> He felt convinced that all of those present, in advocating a very strong Navy, had no intention of urging an aggressive policy. (*Hear, hear.*) To them it mattered not whether foreign Powers built up navies; all they wanted was that the British Navy should be predominant and strong . . . Looking round that great hall and seeing the memorials the citizens had put up to great men, he could only trust that the feeling which had inspired the citizens of London to erect them would continue. He was sure he was only voicing the feelings of the citizens of London when he said that they called upon the present Government or their successors to keep the Navy of this country as strong in the future as it had been in the past. (*Loud cheers.*)[24]

Natty lacked the demotic touch, and his house may have been slipping in the ratings, but he remained the City's spokesman.

Cassel was almost certainly not present that boisterous afternoon at the Guildhall. Since 1908 he had been actively mediating between the two countries, doing his best to ease Anglo-German tensions. Inevitably he left himself open to criticism. 'Of course he takes the German and Semitic point of view of it all,' Esher privately reflected. 'That is only natural. After all, *we* are fighting for our lives, for our Imperial and possibly National existence, which will be at stake ere long. The Cassels are at home in all lands – equally rich, equally composed.' Yet the truth of the matter was that Cassel, with his essentially cosmopolitan outlook, had a far more acute understanding of where the City's fundamental long-term interests lay than had the serried ranks who wanted eight and would not wait. And, of course, he was not alone. When, a few days before the Guildhall meeting, Teddy Grenfell wrote to Jack Morgan about the current Balkan crisis that 'I still cannot believe that the five Great Powers will be at each other's throats for such a rotten little country as Servia', he was expressing the same deep-rooted commercial conviction that, as Gladstone said on another occasion, 'the resources of civilisation are not exhausted'.[25] This tension between on the one hand an almost crude patriotism, and on the other an earnest desire not to destroy the wonderful global money-making machinery built up over the previous century, remained the City's most profound paradox, rarely explored by contemporaries at a conscious level. In 1899 there had been a certain economic logic to buttress gut instincts; this time round that logic was much more tenuous.

CHAPTER TWENTY-FOUR

Slightly Disturbed Financiers

Lloyd George, in a nicely judged presidential speech in 1896 to the annual music festival of Welsh nonconformist choirs, described the English as 'a nation of footballers, stock exchangers, public-house and music-hall frequenters'. In the City, if not necessarily on the terraces, the disapproval was mutual. Lloyd George's first Budget was the subject of a host of rumours during the months before he delivered it, Natty Rothschild reporting to Paris in January 1909 that the government's financial intentions 'are said to be predatory, certainly spiteful and very revengeful'. The following month J. Spencer Phillips, addressing the shareholders of Lloyds, attempted to get his retaliation in first:

> I am told every day by leading brokers in the City that there is quite a respectable amount of money coming forward for investment, but the invariable instructions are, you must invest it either in foreign stocks or foreign railways. (*Hear, hear.*) Rightly or wrongly, the trend of home politics, the uneasiness with regard to future legislation, and the fear of what this year's Budget may produce, is driving our capital every day more and more to other climes. (*Hear, hear.*) Please don't misunderstand me – I am only stating bare facts; I am no political partisan; I have never touched politics in any way; and in a bank board room politics are never discussed, except only so far as the political horizon may affect the money market. (*Hear, hear.*)

'Everybody is on tiptoe of expectation with regard to Thursday's budget,' Carl Meyer wrote to his wife from the City on 27 April; two days later the anxious wait was at last over.[1]

The 'People's Budget', as it soon became known, involved increased licence and death duties, super-tax on large incomes, tax on unearned increment – and, generally aimed at the landed rather than manufacturing interest, was never likely to appeal to many gentlemanly capitalists. 'A patent and deliberate determination to use the machinery of finance to establish schemes and systems which, for want of a more specific term, may be called Socialistic' was the immediate appraisal offered by the *FN*, and Natty Rothschild on 3 May fully concurred, describing the Budget to his cousins as 'a vindictive one', with its most malevolent feature being 'the proposed taxation in connection with land' and in general its proposals 'most socialistic and remarkably unfair'. Two days later that austere financier Arthur Grenfell remarked to Grey that the Budget was 'very dangerous' and that 'the general result seems to be to discourage thrift'; while by the 10th the City was preparing to make its grand remonstrance. 'A petition is being drawn up which will require a good deal of skill and attention, a petition which will be largely signed and then presented to Parliament,' Natty informed his cousins, adding that he did not anticipate the petition having much effect in the Commons but surmising that 'it may have a great effect in the country'. On the 14th he formally presented to Asquith a memorial from 'Bankers, Merchants and others largely interested in the trade and commerce of London and of the Country':

> We realise that the increased and increasing expenditure of the country necessitates additional taxation, and of this we are prepared to bear our full share; but we view with alarm the increasing disproportion of the burden which is being placed on a numerically small class of the community.
>
> The great increase and graduation of the Death Duties – already materially raised but two years ago – and of the Income Tax coupled with the Super-Tax, will, we are confident, prove seriously injurious to the commerce and industries of the Country . . .
>
> We feel that the prosperity of all classes has been greatly due to the fact that this country has afforded indisputable safety for Capital, and we should deeply regret if this conviction were in any way weakened.
>
> In conclusion we would point out that though the taxes to which we have taken exception will in the first instance fall with excessive severity on Capital, they will also in our opinion tend to discourage private enterprise and thrift, thus in the long run diminishing employment and reducing wages.

Signatories included Rothschilds, Barings, Gibbs, Huths, Hambros, Brown Shipley, Morgans, Alexanders, Knowles & Foster, Raphaels, Smith St Aubyn; and, as individuals, Avebury, Phillips of Lloyds, F.A. Bevan of Barclays, and Schuster, the latter despite his Liberal credentials being privately described later in the month as 'violently opposed' to the Budget. One of the many firms to sign was Chaplin, Milne, Grenfell & Co, but Arthur Grenfell's younger brother Rivy took a more iconoclastic line about the City's unprecedentedly outspoken reaction to Lloyd George's proposals: 'They have hit the rich from every corner, and so everyone is crying out. Personally I think there is a great deal to be said in favour of these socialistic Budgets. Old Rothschild will not eat any less *foie gras* because he has to pay a little more for his motor cars.'[2]

Lloyd George declined to withdraw his proposals, so on 23 June, in the crowded great hall of the Cannon Street Hotel, there took place a big City protest meeting. Natty was in the chair, and those present included the usual range of suspects – Lords Avebury, Goschen, Milner and Revelstoke; Sir Alexander Henderson, Sir Joseph Dimsdale and Sir Everard Hambro; Herbert Gibbs, Leopold de Rothschild, F. Faithfull Begg, H. Cosmo Bonsor, A.G. Sandeman, Carl Meyer, Robert Benson and W. Capel Slaughter; Stanley Machin (Chairman of the London Chamber of Commerce), Major Bridges Webb (Chairman of the Baltic) and Sir John Luscombe (Chairman of Lloyd's). The speakers duly went through their paces. Natty Rothschild: 'To his mind the whole principle was vicious. (*Loud cheers.*) The Government wished to establish the principle of Socialism and collectivism – (*applause*) – and if they succeeded in land there was no reason why they should not succeed in every other kind of property. (*Hear, hear.*)' Avebury: 'This was not a political meeting. It was a financial and an economic meeting. (*Hear, hear.*) They were not there to attack the motives of the Government, but because they were perfectly convinced that the Government policy would be ruinous and injurious to the interests of the country. (*Applause.*)' Schuster: 'Let the commercial classes make a stand together and try to point out to the Government how injurious their proposals would be, and he believed they would be listened to. (*Applause.*)' Whereupon a resolution condemning the Budget was 'enthusiastically received and adopted'.[3]

The next day Lloyd George spoke at a lunch at the Holborn Restaurant. He poured scorn on the City's best efforts:

> Here was a meeting purely non-party – with no party motive at all – a meeting of business men, of great financiers, who are very much disturbed by the financial effects of the Budget upon the country. You might have expected in a meeting of that sort to have sound financial criticism .and at any rate some sound financial suggestions. I look in vain through the reports to find one such suggestion. You have simply the same old drivel about Socialism, and, of course, 'the thin end of the wedge' – which is becoming very thin by constant use – which you can find any morning in the columns of the 'Daily Mail' . . .

Lloyd George referred to the big City meeting earlier in the year at which Natty Rothschild had successfully moved the resolution about the need for increased naval expenditure; delivered the shrewd thrust that he had based his Budget upon the revenue-raising implications of that meeting; and then proceeded to get personal:

> Really, in all these things we are having too much Lord Rothschild. We are not to have temperance reform in this country. Why? Because Lord Rothschild has sent a circular to the Peers to say so. We must have more 'Dreadnoughts'. Why? Because Lord Rothschild has told us so at a meeting in the City. We must not pay for them when we have got them. Why? Because Lord Rothschild has told us so. You must not have an estate duty and a super tax. Why? Because Lord Rothschild has sent a protest on behalf of the bankers to say he won't stand it. You must not have a tax on reversions. Why? Because Lord Rothschild, as Chairman of an insurance company, said he wouldn't stand it. You must not have a tax on undeveloped land. Why? Because Lord Rothschild is Chairman of an Industrial Housing Company. You ought not to have Old Age Pensions. Why? Because Lord Rothschild was a member of a committee that said it could not be done. Well, I should like to know, is Lord Rothschild the dictator of this country? Are we really to have all ways of social and financial reform blocked? 'No thoroughfare, by order – Nathaniel Rothschild'? Now, there are countries where they have made it perfectly clear that they are not going to have their policy dictated merely by great financiers. And if this goes on this country will join the rest of them. (*Loud cheers.*)

Natty Rothschild could afford to smile. 'I have been very much amused today,' he wrote to Paris after reading the papers. 'Mr Lloyd George did not appreciate the meeting in the City and he indulged in a violent diatribe against myself.'[4]

In fact the government was not without friends in the City as the crisis consequent upon Lloyd George's Budget gradually unfolded. Lord Swaythling (the former Samuel Montagu) assiduously warned his fellow-peers of the financial chaos that would ensue if they chose to reject the Finance Bill. Holden, from 1908 the Chairman of the London City and Midland and newly made a baronet, was a willing provider of financial advice. Speyer, another recent baronet, continued to dig deep into his pockets for the sake of the Liberal coffers and was rewarded in 1909 with a privy councillorship. One of the leading figures in the investment trust world, John Wynford Philipps, was another generous benefactor and had already become Lord St Davids. And towards the end of the year Alexander Kleinwort was made a baronet soon after writing out a cheque for £20,000. There was also the support of Cassel, who in November stressed to his son-in-law his 'absolute loyalty to whatever government I happen to be serving, and if whoever happened to be in power could not be certain of that he would not give me, and I certainly would not wish, his confidence'. Even among unswerving Conservatives there were some, like Teddy Grenfell, who felt that the City's sustained outrage was overdone. 'In my opinion the Budget is an ill-considered measure but it does not justify the excitement and bad feeling which has been exhibited during the past 6 months,' he asserted to the senior partner of Bleichroders on 30 November 1909, as there drew to an end what was, from a City point of view, one of the more remarkable parliamentary debates.[5]

It began on Monday the 22nd, as the Lords debated the Finance Bill, and in the course of that first evening Revelstoke made his maiden speech. The City, he explained, 'daily – I may say hourly – in various ways, and mainly through its quotations of public securities, focuses the judgement of experts, which usually become finally the judgement of the entire people, concerning the welfare of the country'. That striking claim made, the senior partner of Barings then asserted that 'as one in daily touch with these financial quarters, I have tonight to affirm that much – not all – of the unparalleled depreciation in British credit and British stocks is but the result expressed by the financial barometer of the unsettlement occasioned by a growing lack of confidence as to property of all kinds held in this country'. Capital was being driven abroad to an unnatural extent by this loss of confidence; and he produced figures showing that over the past three years Consols had depreciated by over 6 per cent and English railways by over 10 per cent. 'This is a steady and hopeless depreciation of the securities in which the most conservative of us have been brought up to pin our faith.' And Revelstoke blamed not just the Budget but the fact that 'we have had speech after speech from our legislators of which the purpose has been to set class against class and to represent the interests of capital as antagonistic to the welfare of the people' – a novel doctrine, he concluded, that 'ignores the extent to which the prosperity of this nation has been due to its great capital resources, its heritage of financial supremacy, its unshaken credit'.

The following evening, Earl Russell specifically addressed himself to Revelstoke's speech:

> He gave us a picture from the City point of view which was perfectly clear and perfectly intelligible. He told us how capital was doing this and that, how people who had money to invest were asking this and that, how

capital was leaving the country, and how there was a feeling of insecurity. The noble Lord showed us all the columns of the Temple of Mammon – *totus teres atque rotundus* – with its swept courts, its strong walls and protecting fences, and asked whether it was right that anything should be done to disturb the security of this temple. Are you justified, he asked, in doing this by your Budget? That explained to me more fully than I have ever understood before why it is that the City as a whole is always found in the rear of social progress and advance, because although the view was clear cut, it was a view which was obviously a narrow and a limited one. It was cut off at one point. It by no means embraced the country or the inhabitants of this country as a whole.

To some of us, hypocrites though the noble Lord may think us, there also arose a vision, not only of these slightly-disturbed financiers, of these unfortunate people who make a quarter per cent less on their money, and whose securities have fallen by so much per cent, but of those people who are to be seen homeless every night on the Embankment, of those who are unemployed up and down the country, of those who are starving, of those who are being sweated and are unable to compete on fair terms for a livelihood in the labour market of the world; and some of us felt that a slight disturbance in the temples of high finance is worth while if something is done to alleviate the lot of those unfortunate people, and to bring stability and enjoyment of life to a larger portion of the population of this country. The noble Lord ventured to doubt whether the Chancellor of the Exchequer understood the meaning of the word credit. May I venture to doubt whether the spirit of the City which was there expounded quite understands what some of us mean by social service and social improvement? There is as much to be learned on one side as on the other.

Over the next few days much of the debate turned, albeit in a rather generalised way, on the question of whether the domestic economy was being harmed by excessive exporting of capital – a debate in which no one broadly denied the beneficial consequences to British trade and commerce of the raising of foreign loans; but it was Russell's *tour de force* that had got under the City skin, as was clear on the 29th when Natty Rothschild made his long-awaited, typically brief contribution. 'When I talk of the City,' he emphasised, 'I do not mean only the members of the Stock Exchange and those who noble Lords opposite seem to think frequent Capel Court and Shorter's Court, but I am talking of men who are associated with the trade and commerce of this great country, without which trade and commerce England could not exist.' So too the second Viscount Goschen (Chairman of the London County and Westminster Bank), in words his father would have approved:

The City is not only composed of a number of financiers who are thinking of their own profit. It is the financial nerve-centre of this country, to which flow the savings and earnings of all classes of the community . . . And surely, if not from the highest motives, at least from their business instincts, those who are responsible for the use and custody of this money might be credited with a recognition of the fact that it is upon the mutual dependence of their own interests upon those of their customers and of their clients that the stability of credit rests. It is upon the character of their policy that really depends the credit of this country.[6]

It was not a particularly able defence of enlightened self-interest, but that defence was one that the City was not yet practised in expounding.

The Lords rejected the Budget by 350 votes to 75 and Natty the next day informed Paris that 'the majority has been welcomed in the City by very firm markets', adding that 'Consols have improved as the Stock Exchange are in hopes of a Unionist majority'. The inevitable general election followed in January 1910, earning headlines in the *FN* like 'Lloyd George Finance; or the Gentle Art of Robbing Hen-Roosts'. The Unionists indeed scored some early successes – 'The Nation Wins the First Round of the Fight against Dictatorship, Bureaucracy, and Reaction, Arrayed in Giant Phalanx to Destroy its Liberties' ran the *FN*'s understated headline – and Arthur Grenfell, neglecting work for the stump, was in bullish mood. 'I have always gone for L.G.'s meanness in appealing to their worst passions,' he wrote to Grey on the 22nd, '& told them how capital & labour must pull at the same end of the rope & co-operation should be seriously taken up by the Unionist party, now before it is too late, if we are to destroy these unhealthy symptoms of a fevered socialism.' But in the end the election produced, from a Conservative standpoint, nothing more satisfactory than a loss to the Liberals of their overall majority. Even while his excitable cousin was lecturing the populace, Teddy Grenfell noted to a correspondent in India that the political situation was 'more muddled than at any time in our History'. And he went on: 'At present, people think Redmond [the Irish Nationalist] will call the tune for about two months, and that there will then be another Dissolution. I must say, this seems a singularly Chinese way of governing.'[7] It was an understandable frustration with the political process, but the City over the past year had done much to raise the stakes.

The City itself was a contested constituency during the election, after the prominent Middlesbrough iron master and colliery owner Sir Hugh Bell had made a late entry into the lists on behalf of the Liberals. Balfour and Banbury, the sitting MPs, stood for the Conservatives, and in one busy day Banbury canvassed in Billingsgate Market (where he 'conversed with a large number of stall-holders'), the Coal Exchange and Lloyd's (the visit to the latter resulting in 'one of the most enthusiastic meetings ever held there'). Balfour and Banbury won comfortably, receiving over 17,000 votes each, while Bell got less than 5,000. Significantly, Bell had fought his campaign on an explicitly free-trading ticket, and after the count the defeated candidate said that 'he was sanguine enough to hope to see the time when the City would return to its old traditions and be in the proud position it was when the merchants in 1820 penned that magnificent appeal'. To which Sir Joseph Dimsdale, one of the most prominent City Conservatives, responded that if Bell 'went still further back into history he would find that the City of London was not created, made, or developed upon Free Trade', but that 'she was made, created, and developed when the trade of this country was absolutely Protectionist'.[8] Undoubtedly the City by now had moved firmly into the protectionist camp, further testified to by the failure of a Conservative free-trade association to develop in the City in any meaningful way.[9] Why had the City made this shift?[10] Mainly out of instinctive allegiance to the now protectionist Conservative party; partly as an intellectual response to the problem of how to pay for increased expenditure – above all increased naval expenditure – granted that dramatically raising direct taxation was wholly unacceptable; and very little out of convinced adherence to Chamberlainite precepts of industrial regeneration. Or put another way, a liberal economic world order remained the City's ideal, the free flow of goods and capital continued unfettered until 1914, and the City prospered as never before or since.

Lloyd George's Budget had become history by the time the constitutional question led to a second general election in 1910, held at the end of the year. In November the Stock Exchange Committee considered a letter from that veteran walker G.S. Pawle:

> In view of new Rule No 17, the Committee may censure or *suspend* any member who in his conduct may act in a manner detrimental to the interests of the Stock Exchange.
>
> Seeing that at least five-sixths of the members regard His Majesty's present Government and administration as 'detrimental to the interests of the Stock Exchange' I shall be obliged by a formal letter from the Committee giving or withholding their consent to my accepting an invitation to contest the Eastern Division of Hertfordshire as a supporter of the present ministry.

Pawle's letter, which may or may not have provoked a smile, was 'allowed to lie on the table'. To the City's disappointment the second election barely altered the political landscape, and in the course of 1911 the constitutional crisis, turning on much-truncated powers for the House of Lords, slowly moved to a resolution. Ultimately the City seems to have lined up with the 'hedgers' rather than the 'ditchers'. Natty Rothschild was certainly in the former camp, while the Stock Exchange greeted the passing of the Parliament Bill with palpable relief. Better a Conservative-dominated upper chamber, even without any authority over money bills, than 500 new Liberal peers seems to have been the general feeling. The putative 500 included Thomas Hardy as well as Edgar Speyer, Bertrand Russell as well as Edward Holden, and for Revelstoke at least it would have been a mind-broadening experience.[11]

*

Capital flight was a handy stick with which to beat a Liberal government but a shade hypocritical granted the City's fundamentally global orientation. Undoubtedly, though, the City between 1909 and 1911 enjoyed an almost unprecedented boom in the sphere of foreign issues. Inevitably there was much jockeying for position and, equally inevitably, much ill-feeling.

On the ever-vexing Argentine front, an uneasy truce held between Barings and Morgans. When in May 1910 a Grand Banquet was arranged at the Hotel Cecil to celebrate the centenary of the Argentine Republic's independence, Revelstoke presided and the partners of Morgans were first left out of the preparations and then invited only in the most infuriatingly casual way. Just over a year later the question arose of a major new Argentine government loan, but Buenos Aires insisted on such a high price, with little opportunity for profit in London, that Barings and Morgans agreed to let the business go. Instead it went to a consortium of French and Belgian bankers, with Schröders handling the relatively minor London tranche. Revelstoke, quite without justification, was livid with Schröders. 'If they were a little bigger people,' he wrote to Farrer in June 1911, 'they might have told Bemberg [the associate who had offered the participation to Schröders] to go to blazes and come round here to say they had done so, but the semitic blood which runs so freely through their veins does not seem to permit them to take the course which would have been obvious to a good Englishman.' Neither Baron Bruno nor Tiarks was Jewish, and it was Revelstoke at his very worst. A little of the venom may be attributed to his realisation that Schröders, for so long a major accepting force, was now moving quickly up the issuing league table, in the wake of the San Paulo Coffee Valorisation triumph of 1908. The following year Schröders felt strong enough to decline to participate in a long-term Russian syndicate being organised by Barings, on the grounds that, in Baron Bruno's words, 'we could not associate ourselves with any group in London in which our firm played a secondary rôle'; and in February 1910 Schröders successfully lead-managed a £3.9m loan for the Royal Bulgarian government – its first European sovereign client.[12]

Still, at least Schröders was a merchant bank and thus traditionally entitled to undertake issuing activities. Lloyds Bank was an altogether different matter. 'The long-talked-of Budapest loan makes its appearance today,' the *FT* noted on 1 February 1910 (just a week before the Bulgarian loan), as Lloyds in conjunction with Neumann, Luebeck & Co – the enterprise started three years earlier by that eternal outsider Sigismund Neumann – undertook a £2m bond issue at 4 per cent for that municipality. After two days the loan was at $1\frac{1}{2}$ discount, after three days at 2 discount, and in the end only a nominal sum was subscribed by the public. 'It is generally considered that the flotation of the Budapest loan was not very well managed,' the *FT* commented, adding that 'it appears not unlikely that the tendency for loans of this class to be placed in the hands of joint-stock banks has received a check'. Nevertheless, Lloyds and the other leading joint-stock banks by now enjoyed formidable financial resources denied to private banks (whether clearing or merchant); and it was indicative that in 1909, when Revelstoke created his syndicate in a conscious attempt 'to centralize Russian government business in London', he brought into it both Lloyds and the London City and Midland, partly with a view to being able to tap the customers of those banks. Lloyds did not last long, as Revelstoke towards the end of 1911 retrospectively complained to his French ally Noetzlin:

> Lloyds Bank made an issue of Russian Railway bonds in September 1910, and we then told them that we considered their action as being in distinct contradiction to our agreement. They behaved very badly, and were conscious they had done so. It was a satisfaction to us to notice during the ensuing months that they had prominently figured on almost every unsuccessful and second-rate issue which made its appearance between last year and now. Their placing power is absolutely nil, and their want of brains and management is so deplorable as to have become a by-word in the City of London. It is Crisp who has inveigled them into the sponsorship of the group of which he forms an important part, and

Crisp, as you know, seems to be on intimate and confidential terms with our friend Mr Davydoff.

Davydoff was at the Russian Ministry of Finance, and Revelstoke assured Noetzlin that the Anglo-Russian Trust, formed in 1909 by Charles Birch Crisp 'and his friends', was only 'a small matter, and enjoys no sort of consideration here in the City, or indeed anywhere else, except perhaps with Mr Davydoff'. Like others, however, Revelstoke rather underestimated the ambitious stockbroker, who at this time, in conjunction with Lloyds, showed a greater appreciation of Russian industrial potential than some of the City's staider figures.[13]

Emulating French and German practice, one of Crisp's professed aims was to encourage capital to go to Russia in order in turn to stimulate Russian industrial orders to come to Britain; but in general, as Docker and some other critics lamented, the profitable world of foreign issuing existed in the City in a complete vacuum from British industrial concerns. A fascinating exception to this rule occurred at the very end of 1910, when Holden published in the *Manchester Guardian* a letter that caused a profound stir. In the context of an imminent flotation on the London market of a £6m Japanese loan – for the South Manchurian Railway and to be issued by the usual Japanese consortium, led by the Hongkong and Shanghai – he argued that British banks and industry should not support the loan unless Japan was willing to modify her new tariff:

> This is not a political question – it is a question of loyalty to our industries by our investors. If our industries suffer the whole country suffers, and our investors themselves suffer . . .
>
> Let our investors be loyal to our industries, let our banks be loyal to the commerce and industries out of which they make their profits, and show Japan that if they want our assistance they must be just to our manufacturers and traders or our pockets will be closed against them.
>
> My justification for writing this letter is that, as a banker, I am largely interested in the industries of Lancashire and Yorkshire which will be affected so severely by this tariff.

That same day, New Year's Eve, Japanese were reported 'easier' in the stock market, 'on the approach of the new South Manchurian issue, and the talk of a possible boycott'. On Monday, 2 January, with the loan due to come out on Wednesday, an anxious Addis stayed late in the City discussing with Koch the issue's prospects. On Wednesday itself the loan went to a rather nominal premium of $\frac{1}{4}$, but Addis was not grumbling, granted the 'dead set' that had been made against it by Holden 'and others': 'It just managed with a good deal of buying to scrape through. For this relief much thanks!' Teddy Grenfell, writing to Jack Morgan, offered an afterword: 'I can assure you we were not instrumental in getting the Manchurian Loan crabbed by Holden. He did do some good incidentally by enabling the financiers here to put pressure on Japan to go easy in the matter of new Loans.'[14] Holden had in effect invited the public to boycott an issue made by other banks, and his invitation had probably had some effect; but it did not herald any underlying change of priorities on the City's part.

*

'Here Canada is attracting the attention of everyone,' Natty Rothschild told Paris in February 1911, adding that 'Canadian securities are all the rage here today.' It was a rage that Rothschilds never contemplated joining in, unlike Morgans, who indulged in a brief flirtation. Teddy Grenfell wrote to Jack Morgan that May:

> We have been considering with Lazards, several schemes for an Industrial and Timber Undertaking in Canada, especially one with regard to the biggest Lumber and Saw Mills property in Ottawa. This was introduced to us by your Mr Porter and we thought favourably of it. In the last two months however, so many Canadian issues have been made, many of them of the 'wild cat' description, and both Lazards and I are of opinion that we must call a halt, or there may be trouble as well as scandal here.

Gaspard Farrer would have entirely endorsed these remarks. 'We have had a deluge of issues here,' he wrote to a New York correspondent later in 1911, 'Canada as usual being the most importunate of beggars: £7,000,000 one day for the Canadian Northern, £5,000,000 the next for the Canadian Pacific, besides innumerable other issues of similar dimensions. It will be a miracle if there is not trouble there before long.'[15]

Canada, preferring its policy parameters to be governed by the City of London rather than its southern neighbour, imported £500m of capital between 1900 and 1914, almost three-quarters coming from Britain.[16] This outflow of capital to Canada peaked between 1909 and 1912, years of an intensive wave of large-scale Canadian industrial mergers. The City's leading merchant banks may have eschewed this risky if potentially highly profitable boom, but there were plenty of other houses and financiers eager to fill the vacuum.[17] Ion Hamilton

Benn, for example, was a one-time timber merchant in the City, with the firm of Price & Pierce, thereby acquiring a familiarity with Canada that stood him in good stead when he formed the Western Canada Trust, soon a very active issuing house. He worked closely with Max Aitken (the future Lord Beaverbrook), who between August 1909 and June 1910, while still based in Canada, used the London capital market to promote three large-scale mergers in Canadian manufacturing industry. Aitken himself settled in England later in 1910, but other Canadian financiers had already made that migration, notably Mackay Edgar and James Dunn.[18] Edgar had been a Montreal-based stockbroker and company promoter before coming to England in 1906, two years later accepting a partnership in the broking firm Sperling & Co. Sperlings under his influence moved increasingly into issuing, above all of Canadian industrials, and prospered despite enjoying a rather dim reputation elsewhere in the City. 'Very second rate' was Teddy Grenfell's typical verdict. As for Dunn, he was the son of a Canadian boat-builder, a childhood friend of Aitken, and having bought a seat on the Montreal Stock Exchange in 1902 he specialised in arbitrage and company promotion before coming to London in 1905. There he went into partnership with a Swiss Jew, Charles Louis Fischer, and over the next nine years Dunn, Fischer & Co undertook a wide range of arbitrage and issuing business, but with Canadian utilities and industrials a particular speciality. The firm's driving force was Dunn, a fact made clear in 1913 when Fischer, owing to personal financial troubles, abruptly left London and retired from the partnership. 'Mr Dunn stated to Sir Felix Schuster,' the Union Bank's information book noted in September, 'that there was absolutely liquid capital in the firm in good marketable securities amounting to £400,000 to £500,000, after disposing of all Fischer's liabilities.'[19] Jimmy Dunn himself was a shrewd operator, with an ability to manipulate men as well as markets. He did well for himself in his London, Surrey and Côte d'Azur homes; took a close interest in wine, women and fast motor cars; and was a valuable patron to the young Augustus John. He was, in short, an attractive, not untalented rascal – and that alone almost guaranteed him a long-term future in the City, though never quite at top table.

There was one other leading figure in the Canadian boom, definitely a native not an immigrant. 'Business has been good during last year. Canadian Agency did a record for 1909–1910, so we can't expect to do so well the year 1910–11. But still I have got our credit better established – & we think we see big things ahead!' That was on Boxing Day 1910, and a few weeks later Arthur Grenfell wrote again to Grey

in Ottawa: 'I have sold your Laurentide shares at 206. I have done this
as I can put you into Lake Superior Paper Co on Syndicate terms; the
success of the issue is practically assured as big market people here
have already taken $2,500,000 of bonds and are asking for more.' But
only a month later, at the start of March 1911, Grenfell had found
something even better:

> Since writing to you . . . we have concluded the arrangements for the
> purchase of certain lands next to our Southern Alberta, to which we have
> added lands purchased recently from the Hudson Bay Company, so that
> we are in course of forming a new Land Company which will have about
> 95,000 acres of land, at an average price of, approximately, $9 per acre.
> We have formed a Syndicate of £200,000 to pay for these lands and as
> the business should show us a very large profit, I have invested £5,000
> which I have to your credit here . . .
> We think we shall be able to sell these lands for at least five times the
> price we gave for them, which should show you very much bigger profits
> than the Paper Company so that at the moment I have not put through
> your subscription for the paper.

Over the next few weeks the prices of Canadian land shares rose
sharply, but Grenfell remained convinced, as he wrote to Grey towards
the end of April, that 'there is a good deal of room for further
appreciation before one gets on a speculative basis'. He therefore
planned to press ahead with his Alberta Land Co, informing a perhaps
unconvinced Governor-General: 'You will remember that I have invested £5,000 of your money in a Syndicate formed to purchase the
land. We hope to form a Canadian Company and to be able to sell the
bonds so as to give us back our money, leaving us with a good bonus
in shares for nothing. These will one day be very valuable – & we shall
be able I hope to keep your money turning over.'[20]
   The last phrase had an ominous ring, and it would have confirmed
the judgement of Kleinworts earlier that month as it recommended
Goldman Sachs to continue to steer clear of the acceptances of
Chaplin, Milne, Grenfell & Co: 'The methods of Mr G. appear to give
rise to criticism – whether rightly or wrongly we cannot say – and we
believe that this is one of the main if not the main reason why the firm
does not enjoy the standing it perhaps otherwise would.' To which
Grenfell might have countered that he now enjoyed the visible proof of
success. That August, recently remarried and on his way by boat to
South Africa, he wrote to Grey in what even by his standards was an
upbeat mood:

I believe my boldness & Hilda's taste has resulted in our making Roehampton [i.e. Roehampton House] one of the nicest & most beautiful places near London. We have made mistakes, some of which will cost money to rectify, but considering the rush, it really is extraordinary how nicely it has worked out. We had 220 men on day & night during the early part of May – otherwise we should not be in today. The new rooms we built on have been a great success & the pictures look splendid. We contemplate further improvements to the ball room & the garden.

Was it really such paradise? Raymond Asquith, writing to Lady Diana Manners (later Cooper) from France in July 1916 following an impromptu ball before the resumption of trench warfare, seems to have thought not: 'Except for the banal booming and flashing of the guns one might be at one of those old-fashioned balls in Arthur Grenfell's garden at Roehampton – the same tiresome noise of electricity being generated in the too-near foreground, the same scraggy oaks, the same scramble for sandwiches, the same crowd, the same band playing the same tunes, the same moon in the same sky.'[21]

*

It was no doubt handy for Grenfell to have a former father-in-law resident at Government House in Ottawa, but in Britain's 'informal empire' the interface between finance on the one hand and politics and diplomacy on the other operated in a far more subtle – and vexed – way. Three areas of the world stood out: China, Persia and Turkey.[22] Each by the early twentieth century was in the throes of internal crisis; each had a long-standing British commercial presence; and each was the object of increasingly acrimonious rivalry between the great powers. Much was going on in all three areas between 1909 and 1911, and if there was a common thread, it was that life was never simple for the financier.

Following his Peking–Hankow triumph of 1908, Addis was even more than before the Foreign Office's main man. By early in 1909 he was able to convince the diplomats that the best way ahead lay in forming an Anglo-Franco-German banking consortium to deal with future Chinese railway business – above all the financing of the Hukuang Railways, comprising the lines from Canton to Hankow and Hankow to Szechuan. After several stressful months shuttling between London, Paris and Berlin, tripartite negotiations were successfully concluded in May. Then came the American *démarche*. The Taft administration insisted on a US involvement in Chinese railway finance; and with Morgans in New York appointed to represent the American group, Teddy Grenfell in London inevitably found himself in close dialogue with Addis. 'A particularly nice young fellow,' was Addis's view of Grenfell, though harmony was soon strained over the question of what the American portion of the loan should be. The Taft administration put political pressure on Grey, who in turn tried to get the non-Americans to yield, which with less than total grace they did. 'For future peace,' Grenfell wrote to Jack Morgan in August, 'it is wiser for the Americans as last comers to deal gently with the Old Group.' Further negotiations over the next nine months proved intensely trying. 'It is a pretty difficult job to get the Anglo French and German Banks to agree to anything,' Grenfell wrote in November 1909 to a partner at Morgans in New York. 'The European Groups will each trust the Chinaman, but will not trust each other at all.' Addis for his part was more inclined to blame the newcomers, though not Grenfell personally. 'It is a weary job,' he reflected in May 1910, 'and of all the negotiators with whom I have had to deal the Americans are the worst.' Eventually, in November 1910, an agreement between the four banking groups was signed. Addis's diary entry was relatively mild but entirely heartfelt: 'And so closes the longest most arduous negotiations in which I have ever taken part'. China itself signed the Hukuang Railways agreement in May 1911, and for a month or two the only significant area of contention seemed to be whether £4,000 was adequate remuneration to Morgan Grenfell for negotiating with the European groups. Vivian Smith thought not, writing with some heat to Jack Morgan in July: 'Teddy has been so busy at times with this thing for days together, that it has been impossible to attend to other business, very often impossible even to see people . . .'[23]

In fact, while these negotiations had been going on, there had been other heartburnings in the City. Against the background of the London capital market being potentially far more receptive to Chinese loans than ever before, Erlangers in the summer of 1909 made a strong pitch for the business, only to be told by the Foreign Office that it declined to support another City firm in preference to the Hongkong and Shanghai. Then, in the autumn of 1910, there was an attempt by Dunn Fischer & Co, in alliance with the London City and Midland Bank and on behalf of a Belgian-led syndicate, to float on the London market a Peking–Hankow railway loan for £450,000. A frustrated Fischer called on Holden shortly after Christmas:

He said he had furnished a great deal of information to the Stock Exchange Committee, but that Mr Koch of Panmure Gordon & Co,

brokers for the Hong Kong and Shanghai Bank, who was on the Committee, had strenuously opposed a quotation and a settlement at every
sitting the Committee had had during the past three weeks, and now the
Committee were not satisfied as to the responsibility of the Chinese
Imperial Government. Mr Fischer said he was not disturbed about it; he
felt we could keep the market and he had got a quotation in the 'Financial
Times'. I agreed that we could create a market for the sale of the stock,
but I told Fischer that when Koch saw me he had come in a very different
way, and had not told me he was opposing it . . . I told him I intended to
approach each individual member of the Stock Exchange Committee and
that I would expose Mr Koch's action.[24]

A typically aggressive response by Holden, but there is no evidence
that he followed through, for at that point the matter seems to have
been dropped. It was a moot point, however, how much longer the
Foreign Office would feel able to give most-favoured treatment to
Addis and his bank.

If the Hongkong and Shanghai was the FO's chosen vehicle in
Chinese finance, its counterpart in Persia was undoubtedly the
Imperial Bank of Persia. This bank had been established in 1889 with
backing from Schröders and David Sassoon & Co, but City antipathy
to Persian economic and political prospects was such that during its
first twenty years it floated only one loan in London for the Persian
government, an issue in 1892 that flopped. Nevertheless, 'sterling
diplomacy', as it has been called, remained central to the FO's thinking. 'The broad principle upon which we must necessarily proceed,'
Grey argued in 1906, 'is to obtain leverage over the Persian government by assisting them in a financial sense.' By 1910, following
Persia's successful constitutional revolution and amidst general
enthusiasm for foreign loans, the City for once was disposed to invest
in that country. Seligman Bros – a second-rank merchant bank but
perfectly respectable, with one of its partners a director of National
Discount – approached Grey in May with a view to making a loan to
the Persian government. During the summer the FO sent out mixed
signals and Seligmans pursued the possibility of a £2m loan, the
amount apparently wanted by Persia. In September, however, the firm
made a significant tactical error, asking if the FO minded Seligmans
looking to 'the co-operation of our correspondents in Holland, France,
Germany and Switzerland'. On which Grey commented: 'If this were
done, would it not give the other Powers a footing in the Gulf?'
Matters came to a head in the second half of October. 'It is not at all
desirable that the Seligman Loan should succeed . . .' Mallet of the FO

argued on the 18th. 'Its success would mean the substitution of this mongrel institution in Persia, for the Imperial Bank which has acted always most loyally with the Foreign Office & which is a thoroughly straightforward British concern.' Accordingly, 'the question is what is the best way of choking Seligman off', Mallet referring for good measure to that firm as 'a German Jew Branch of an American Bank & British in name only'. The FO now made it unambiguously clear that it was backing the Imperial Bank, and on the 25th an aggrieved Seligmans complained that:

> We shall be compelled to explain the position of the matter to our friends, and we fear it may leak into the financial press . . . In the future, should the Persian Government ever require a fresh loan, no respectable firm would negotiate, knowing that at the eleventh hour the great might of the Foreign Office is liable to be used in support of a competing house . . .

The following summer the Imperial Bank successfully issued a loan for £1.25m. Seligmans for its part, having let off steam, quietly dropped the alternative issue, and the firm was even praised by the FO for having 'behaved quite decently'.[25]

The FO also failed to give universal satisfaction in the case of the Ottoman Empire. 'We shall make no progress till British capital of a high class takes an energetic interest in Turkey,' was Grey's view in September 1908, as he prepared to give a degree of official backing to Cassel's plan to establish there an equivalent to his National Bank of Egypt.[26] Such an institution in Constantinople would, Grey believed, counter the German threat in that part of the world not only through the inflow of British capital but also by putting Anglo-French financial co-operation on a more equal footing, granted the long-standing ineffectiveness of the London committee of the essentially French-run Imperial Ottoman Bank. Over the next few months Cassel consulted with Revelstoke and Sir Alexander Henderson, who agreed to come in with him, and by 1909 the National Bank of Turkey was a reality. Sir Henry Babington Smith was recruited to head it up, and he was soon the recipient of a steady flow of instructions, guidance and questions from Cassel, who rarely stayed long in one place.

Relations with the FO deteriorated sharply in 1910. Towards the end of May, with Babington Smith paying a visit to London, Cassel wrote from his son-in-law's home, Broadlands in Hampshire:

> My coming to Town tomorrow will depend upon my daughter's condi-
> tion in the morning, and I will telegraph to the City as soon as I know. In

case I cannot come, I hope you will speak to Sir Edward Grey in the sense
we have discussed on several occasions. Perhaps it will be best not to
hand him the written statement. When unpleasant things have to be made
clear, it is so much easier to do it in conversation, and they do not appear
to be so harsh as when put on paper.

The next day, Cassel stayed by his daughter's side and Babington
Smith followed his master's advice. The written statement, however,
survives, accusing the British government of having, in connection
with the Baghdad Railway, 'formulated demands which, from the
financial point of view, must be regarded as unreasonable'. And:
'The question therefore arises whether there is any useful scope for the
activities of the Bank, and whether it will not be better to withdraw
from an untenable position, and discontinue expenditure which is
necessarily upon a large scale.' Nevertheless, as a letter to Babington
Smith a few months later made clear, following negotiations with the
Turkish finance minister, it was not just the British government with
which Cassel had to contend:

> The position is really, in a nutshell. Under normal conditions as regards
> price we cannot compete with the French, because, their market being
> practically closed to industrial undertakings, they are able to pay for State
> loans a price higher than we can give. When other conditions are put
> forward such as those now claimed by the French, we have got a chance
> of competing. If then, for political reasons, we are also to be debarred
> from doing business, we had better put our shutters down. It might just
> as well be known generally that our good feeling towards France goes to
> the extent of withdrawing from competition in financial matters . . .[27]

That indeed *was* the position in a nutshell: the National Bank was
operating under an almost crippling double disadvantage of the London market being largely unreceptive to Turkish securities (a long-
running problem going back to the 1876 default) and the FO's anxiety
about offending its French ally.

The 1910 Turkish loan proved, even by Byzantine standards, a
thoroughly tortuous affair, but the upshot was that the National Bank
did not participate. At the end of September a fairly stormy meeting
took place at the FO between Cassel and Grey. Cassel 'pointed out
that, in consequence of untrue reports in the French press, violent
personal attacks had been directed against him in the papers, and that
so far as his own personal position was concerned, he had every reason
for withdrawing from his connection with Turkey which exposed him
to this annoyance'. Grey expressing the hope that the French might

become more co-operative, Cassel snapped back 'that the French were not in the least likely to accept co-operation on a basis which could be regarded as satisfactory' and that 'they had hitherto entirely refused to consider co-operation on terms of equality'. Against this background, one of the National Bank facing persistent opposition from the strongly Paris-backed Ottoman Bank, the British ambassador in Constantinople had a point when he observed a few days later that 'our position is somewhat ridiculous if we urge Cassel at great expense to establish a bank here and when he wants to do business we oppose him'.[28]

Babington Smith wrote to Grey early in October in the strongest terms, calling on the British government actively to support the aim of 'a footing of equality' with the Ottoman Bank. This Grey was willing to do. 'We support the fusion of the National and Ottoman Banks for political reasons of great importance,' he minuted on the 17th – but over the next fortnight the Ottoman Bank (represented in London by the second Viscount Goschen) refused to budge, rejecting all proposals of a merger between equals. By the end of the year Revelstoke was all for winding up business, on the grounds that the chances of satisfactory profits were slight, while Cassel himself announced his retirement from active business in the City. Teddy Grenfell, writing to Jack Morgan early in 1911, offered a shrewd analysis:

> He has been having a pretty bad year as his daughter, after picking up a little after Egypt, has had two relapses and it does not look as if she would live much longer. As she is his only child the loss would be irretrievable coming on the top of that of the King, to whom he was quite a friend.
>
> Cassel also started a new Bank in Turkey, with which to compete against the Germans and the Imperial Ottoman. He has not been able to do any good with it, and he feels very bitterly that the English Government has not supported him in any way for doing what was a patriotic act. In some ways he was the biggest financial power in London, and though not a pleasant man yet he is a loss to the financial world.

Cassel's disenchantment would have been complete if he had been able to read the despatch sent soon afterwards by Sir Arthur Nicolson at the FO to the British ambassador in Constantinople:

> We cannot rely with certainty on any of these financiers being animated by disinterested and patriotic motives. They look solely and simply at the profits which they may derive from their enterprises and leave entirely on one side the political character of the questions with which they have to deal. It is a matter of perfect indifference to them . . . whether the ends

which they pursue are or are not in harmony with the interests of this country.[29]

Or, as Nicolson's son Harold might have put it: some people . . .

Grenfell's valedictory tone was a little premature, for despite his daughter's death Cassel remained actively involved in the National Bank's affairs through the continuing frustrations of 1911. Partly they concerned a new agreement over the Baghdad Railway, partly difficult negotiations over a prospective issue of Turkish Treasury bills. Writing to Babington Smith in June – from his new office just round the corner from his London home in Grosvenor Square – he noted, 'I have not been near the Foreign Office since you were here, as I am afraid I have come to look upon the time spent there, under existing circumstances, as wasted.' In July, writing from his Villa Cassel in Switzerland, he simply observed in relation to Nicolson: 'To what a sad state our diplomacy has come!' In fact the Turkish bills were successfully placed in the London market, but the wearisome subject soon returned, so that by early 1912 Cassel was sounding off to Babington Smith in a thoroughly jaundiced state of mind, clearly suspecting his man in Constantinople of having gone native:

> I am by no means willing to admit that in the circumstances in which Turkey finds herself now a rate of 8 to 9% is excessive. Assuming that Turkey had a state Bank with an official rate of discount, I am strongly of opinion that the rate would not be very different from that which I have indicated. I am afraid I do not attach any value to the sense of obligation under which a Government may find itself. Such experience as I have had has not led me to expect much.[30]

The sad story was drawing to an end. In 1913 Babington Smith fired a last broadside at Grey – 'the impression has been produced in the minds of our competitors and of the Ottoman Government, that we are not trusted by the British Government or regarded as the appropriate agency for taking the lead in British enterprises' – and by the outbreak of war the National Bank was barely functional. Subsequently it was taken over by the British Trade Corporation, before eventually giving up the ghost altogether in 1931. 'So far as Turkish business is concerned, I must confess that I am stupid enough not to understand this great desire to issue a Turkish loan and to run the risk of all the events, which are occurring or may occur very shortly in the Ottoman Empire . . . Turkish Finance is not our business.'[31] Natty Rothschild, writing here in 1911, may have been too cautious for the long-term good of his family bank, but in this instance he surely had the right of it.

*

There was, to the well-ordered mercantile mind, nothing more irritating than false information. Some merchants gathered in November 1909 to discuss the problem, among them a former Governor of the Bank of England:

> Mr Sandeman said there were many things which were represented as being what they were not, especially Port Wine. He took exception to the prevailing description of many kinds of Port, which did not come from Oporto; which were allowed to be sold with a prefix such as 'Australian' Port, 'Hamburg' Port. He contended that this ought not to be allowed . . .

J. Collie Foster, a textile merchant, was sympathetic:

> Poor people were often recommended to take Port. They went to Grocers' shops in the district and very probably the so-called 'Port' obtained did more harm than good, they having no technical knowledge of the matter. In his own trade, the Textile trade, a similar state of things existed. Take the well-known article 'Flannelette'. He considered that many persons were under the impression that that was a kind of flannel. The experts in the trade know that it is entirely composed of cotton . . .[32]

So was founded the London Chamber of Commerce's Trade Misrepresentation Committee, a valuable forum for those who enjoyed letting off steam.

Signs of commercial organisation were everywhere. Almost a century after Dicky Thornton's infamous tallow corner, the London Oil and Tallow Trades Association was formed at a meeting held in February 1910 in the Baltic Exchange. By the time of the first ordinary general meeting, held in July at the Baltic Sale Room at 24 St Mary Axe, the Association had a hundred members, but its chairman, J.W. Hope of John Knight Ltd, was still a little disappointed:

> I regret that our efforts so far have been unsuccessful in securing the co-operation of some houses in the tallow trade, and it is a matter of regret to know that the only reason put forward by these houses against joining the association is that of 'Let well alone'. Now, gentlemen, have you ever heard of any progress being made under a motto of that nature?

... What are our competitors for the trade of London doing? Are they letting 'Well alone'? How is it we have to go to such ports as Liverpool for supplies of certain classes of Tallow and Oils? Is it not because they have been more far-seeing than some of us in London, and have put their house in order to attract shippers and buyers alike? ...

By January 1912 firms represented on the Association included J. H. Vavasseur & Co, Blythe, Greene, Jourdain & Co, and M. Samuel & Co; while the thirty-one contracts issued by the Association included No 1 for Coconut Oil, No 2 for European Rapeseed Oil, No 5 for Oriental Soya Bean Oil, No 19 for American Spirits of Turpentine (c.i.f. terms) and No 28 for Oriental Fish Oil.[33]

The world of shipbroking was less exotic, but writing in *Fairplay* in September 1910 a veteran member of the Baltic called David Pinkney deplored 'the gradual decadence of the professional shipbroker' and 'the lack of any attempt at combination amongst shipbrokers themselves for their protection'. Pinkney defined a professional shipbroker as someone 'whose success depends solely on his ability to get the utmost farthing of freight for his client against the competition of his fellow-brokers'; and this ability in turn depended on 'knowledge of merchants and shipowners, their history, their standing, and even their fads; knowledge of ship construction, stowage, insurance, port charges, the world's crops, times and seasons, and a thousand other things before one can appraise the value of a freight; and, if necessary, the ability to make up a detailed voyage account and show the shipowner that you know every point of the game'. Accordingly, Pinkney called on shipbrokers to form a professional institute and thereby 'give its members an official standing and a dignity to which they are clearly entitled'. Percy Harley, another shipbroker, wrote the next week heartily concurring ('what fine attributes are necessary to make a broker'), and later that autumn a meeting was held that led to the formation of the Shipbrokers' Institute. T. L. Devitt of F. Green & Co took the chair and, no doubt to the considerable comfort of those present, 'it was stated that Sir John Ellerman was in complete accord with the movement'.[34]

Glimpses into the ever stressful life of commerce come from the correspondence of Archibald Williamson (Sir Archibald from July 1909), senior partner of Balfour, Williamson & Co, Liverpool grain merchants who by this time had moved their head office to 2 Great St Helen's in the City and were becoming a fully fledged 'investment group' with a wide variety of interests in different parts of the world. 'We certainly have scope for a good man in Chile,' he wrote in May

1909 to his aged uncle in Liverpool. 'I must say that both Mathieson [i.e. his partner Kenneth Mathieson] and I, who are getting older every year, have suffered heavy losses and have to bear much more anxiety than we ought to be called upon to bear, through having incapable men at the other end . . . We would welcome relief from the strain . . .' The firm's profits had averaged over £72,000 for the past three years, so the losses had been local, but the worry was undoubtedly real. Williamson was also a Liberal MP, involved in many late-night sessions during this period of sustained political crisis. 'It is pretty hard work to get through one's labour in the City by three or four o'clock in the afternoon and then commence again at the House of Commons and remain there till two or three, and sometimes even six, in the morning,' he wrote on one occasion to his man in Lima. His reward, however, came not only with his 'K', but when in September 1910 he was able to entertain no fewer than five members of the government, including Churchill, at his hunting lodge in Inverness-shire. 'They all made themselves agreeable and got some sport,' he reported to his brother Harry in Chile, almost with the suggestion that it was businessmen rather than career politicians who instinctively possessed the gentlemanly virtues.[35]

One of Balfour Williamson's interests was in the Peru-based Lobitos Oilfields, and in October 1909 Williamson reported to Lima that 'there has been quite a boom in Lobitos Shares during the past fortnight'. He went on:

> A Jew clique on the Stock Exchange have been booming them in the papers and otherwise, and got the price up from 25/6 to 30/6. We told those who asked us, however, that we thought the latter price unduly high on the immediate prospects . . . It is a curious thing the information about Well No. 118 seemed to have reached the Stock Exchange a day or two before the cable came to the Company.

Oil shares were indeed starting to boom and some significant City fortunes were made as a result, including by the jobbers Cull & Co. Sir Marcus Samuel remained a vigorous propagandist of the industry's glittering long-term prospects, but the older-established houses tended not to take a punt. 'We unfortunately have never had a very great interest in them,' Natty Rothschild observed to Paris in April 1910 apropos oil shares, 'and I am very much afraid that it is too late to venture very largely.' So too the tea merchants turned investment group Harrisons & Crosfield, who might more plausibly have been expected to get involved. 'I am afraid I am of no use to you at all in regard to Oil,' a director replied in 1911 to an American inquiry. And he continued:

> I do not understand it . . . I have no doubt Oil is a very good thing, but like everything else if you want to succeed you must make a study of it, otherwise, no doubt – however good it may be – one only runs the risk of burning one's fingers. The reason I cannot take up anything fresh is that the administration of our own affairs is quite enough to give me all the work I want, and I have made up my mind that I will not, under any circumstances, interest myself in any other direction.[36]

*

The partner eschewing oil was Arthur Lampard, then in his late 40s. His father had been a tea merchant in the City, and so it was natural that as a young man he first spent a year with the tea brokers William Sentance & Co before moving to Harrisons & Crosfield in 1881, becoming a partner in 1894. Lampard was largely responsible for transforming Harrisons & Crosfield, in the words of its historians, from 'a small, family-run partnership into a dynamic world-wide plantations and trading company'. In 1895 he made his first trip to the East, where he established houses in Ceylon and subsequently in India, the Federated Malay States, Sumatra and Java; from his experience there, he came to believe that rubber could be cultivated in the East, and produced far more cheaply than by cultivation from wild rubber trees scattered through the forests of Brazil and elsewhere. It was, in the dawning of the automobile age, a crucial perception. There were, of course, other pioneers, but Lampard could fairly claim to be one of the first men to tap a rubber tree in the East. Above all he had the enterprise and management skills to enable him to transform his faith in rubber into practical results. Rubber concerns with which Lampard was intimately connected included Pataling, Anglo Malay, Golden Hope, Tandjong, Sialang, London Asiatic, and Sungkai-Chumor; he became Chairman of the Rubber Plantations Investment Trust; and Harrisons & Crosfield, a public company from 1908, acted as managers and secretaries of the largest group of rubber companies in Britain.[37]

From a wider City point of view, rubber matters started to hot up in the late 1900s.[38] 'Having of late frequently been asked by clients who either already possess an interest in Rubber planting ventures, or contemplate acquiring such an interest, for particulars of the various companies engaged in the industry, we have compiled this little manual as a ready and convenient means of providing the sort of information required.' So Fritz Zorn in January 1907 introduced the first edition of *A Manual of Rubber Planting Companies*, compiled by his stockbroking firm Zorn & Leigh-Hunt. Two years later he introduced the third edition: 'Statements appear from time to time in certain sections of the press, to the effect that rubber shares cannot be dealt in upon the Stock Exchange, and that the only market for them is in Mincing Lane. This is quite a mistaken idea. There is a considerable market in Mincing Lane and a considerable market in the Stock Exchange.' The price of rubber was also on the move. From 5s 3d per pound early in 1907, it was down to 2s 9d at the end of the year because of the American financial crisis, but then rose – despite many fluctuations – through 1908 and 1909, reaching 9s 2$\frac{1}{4}$d by November 1909.[39]

It was a market that needed a lot of watching, not least on the part of an accepting house like Kleinworts. In June 1908 an investigation was mounted into Hecht, Levis & Kahn, Fenchurch Street merchants and the family firm of Carl Meyer's wife. Lewis & Peat, best known as spice brokers but now themselves moving largely into the rubber business, were reassuring: 'We have done business with them for 25/30 years. Are highly respectable, wealthy, absolutely 1st class & quite good for anything they do.' So too the credit ratings agency Seyds: 'We have a very favourable opinion of them and estimate their capital at round about £150,000. We think that they have held their own during the fall in prices.' But not so the senior partner of the merchants Wm Symington & Co:

> We want to find out something about these people ourselves: they are 'very dark horses' and it is extremely difficult to get anything definite. Our *impression* is that the last year has made a considerable hole in their capital through the drop in prices: they have too many branches, keeping large stocks in Hamburg, Antwerp, Bordeaux & London, and we know that in the first named place they have a lot of old & unsaleable Rubber. We would like to find out whether any of Mr Hecht's money (if so, how much) is still in the concern, but cannot; neither can we find anyone to verify (or contradict) our above impressions.

Heilbut, Symons & Co, themselves leading rubber merchants, confirmed this unfavourable impression:

> We do not consider this concern well-managed. Everyone is surprised at the great quantities of medium quality Rubber they are buying – they already have huge stocks, yet yesterday they bought about £80,000 worth

in Antwerp sales. Have gone in far too deep. They don't do a 'clean' business; they take Rubber that we cannot & would not tender to Clients, sell it as good, & then argue & compromise with Buyers. Undoubtedly they have lost a lot of money the last 2 years. There is none of Max Hecht's or Albert Kahn's money in the business – it is all Paris money and *was* we would say ab^t £150/200,000 – but we don't know what it is now.

Kleinworts continued to give acceptance credits, but with an uneasy mind; and, almost two years later, the Union Bank of London noted:

> Mr Berg [of Hecht, Levis & Kahn] called in to say that he understood rumours were circulating abroad, as to the firm's position, it being reported that they had been heavily caught short of rubber. Mr Berg assured me this is absolutely untrue and produced his rubber book to shew that their position was quite a level one. He also stated that the firm's profits, for the last two years, were very large & estimated their present capital at about £400,000.

That was on 11 March 1910. The price of rubber was well over 10s per pound, by late April it would be almost 13s, the share prices of rubber companies were moving rapidly upwards, new companies were being floated at a hectic pace (the public subscribing for more than £16m of rubber shares in the first five months of the year), and altogether the City was in the midst of rubber fever.[40]

In Capel Court the scenes were even more frantic than those experienced during the Kaffir boom fifteen years earlier. One morning, the story goes, a member fainted in the middle of the Rubber market, but no one knew anything about it until after four o'clock in the afternoon, when the crowd which had been supporting him all day dispersed and he fell to the ground. Companies with unpronounceable names were daily being placed on the market, and on one occasion a broker, struggling through the crowd, asked, 'What's the feature?' and the jobber replied, 'An eighth to a quarter, I believe, but I'll just check the market.' Most rubber shares were in two shilling denominations – a far cry from the £5 shares familiar thirty or forty years earlier – and accordingly a new type of speculator was attracted, so much so that one highly respectable firm of stockbrokers reported a charwoman calling at its office one day and asking to have ten shillings invested in rubber shares.[41]

This broadening social base gave one financial paper its chance. Whereas the *FT* tended to adopt a faintly negative tone towards the whole phenomenon ('We are afraid that when the boom is over many rash investors who have been tempted into Rubber will be left contemplating bundles of doubtful scrip,' it sniffed, admittedly with some justification, on 8 April), the *FN*'s gifted if ultimately unbalanced editor Ellis Powell grasped from the first the social significance of what was afoot. His devices to attract new readers and advertising were many, including extremely full reports of the rubber share markets in both the Stock Exchange and Mincing Lane; but his master-stroke was the 'Voice of the Rubber Public' column, subtitled 'Further opinions, gleaned from a wide area, with regard to the absolute and comparative merits of rubber securities now before the investor'. On 22 April, for example, an array of rubber-fanciers added their opinions to the debate on which shares to choose, including 'Bon Accord' of Canonbury, North London, on the prospects for Chersonese and Malang: 'I beg to second your correspondent "Suburbanite's" opinion with regard to these two sound companies, whose shares, as a lock-up, have a very promising outlook and may go to 25s or 35s in the not very distant future, while Anglo-Johores, comparatively speaking, should be £3 instead of 25s premium.' 'Japhet' of West Norwood put in his twopenn'orth: 'May I endorse the views of your correspondents, "G.C.", "Para", and "Albert Leonard", as to Diamantino Rubbers? I look upon them as the pick of the bunch at present. The company has already got some rubber here, and I understand regular shipments will be coming along very soon.' And from Holmlands Park in Sunderland, 'Northerner' wanted to know why the Telogoredjos Company had been overlooked in previous columns of the 'Voice': 'Situated in the fertile Malang district of Java, it should this year produce enough to pay 10 per cent, and steadily rising as the 7,000 acres are planted out with rubber. There are already 160,000 trees planted, many being nine years old, and these are being rapidly added to.'[42] In short, popular capitalism – and, arguably, never again so popular during the twentieth century.

Lampard himself, following a trip to the East, was back in the City on 23 May. His correspondence over the next few weeks showed him in buoyant, confident action:

> *25 May. To Mrs Clifford, Empress Club, Dover St, W.* If you are not engaged, and it is a fine day, I will endeavour to call for you on Sunday next, and take you and your daughter out for a run, when we can discuss the question of your investments.
>
> *25 May. To E. Murray, 5 Copthall Buildings, EC.* The first things that I am going to bring out will be Djasinga to be followed by Bajoe Kidoel, both very safe and very good.

25 May. To W.T. Littlejohns, 42 Coleherne Court, SW. In any investments in Rubber you should be very careful. All those Companies which are honestly floated and honestly managed have, in my opinion, a very brilliant future before them, but to my great regret there are a great number that have been formed, particularly recently, which are nothing more than absolute swindles, and these have been floated by men who had no experience of the East at all, and the management and control of tropical agriculture is a business of itself, which requires practical experience and expert knowledge, and if this is not present it can only end in disaster to the Shareholders.

26 May. To H.S.E. Bowle Evans, Dieppe. You are in a country now where you can easily satisfy yourself as to the probable demand for Motor Cars during this and the coming years. As a matter of fact, for tyres alone, the world this and next year will require at least 35,000 tons of Rubber per year which is practically half the world's supply. How in the name of goodness are the other claims upon Rubber to be met?

In June he was still optimistic. 'I am perfectly certain no one need have the slightest anxiety in holding Rubber shares in sound genuine properly managed undertakings,' he assured Sir Henry McCallum, British Governor in Colombo, Ceylon. 'This is not an industry with a short life. It is the inauguration of a permanent Industry of vastly greater possibilities and importance than the Tea Industry.' But by 8 July, writing to Harrisons & Crosfield's own man in Colombo, he was sounding a more cautious note:

In view of the increasing demand the policy which I am adopting on behalf of the Companies which we represent is to sell on arrival, but not to contract forward. We must bear in mind, however, that the present price of Rubber is, as compared to past years, abnormally high, and that in view of this it is not a wise thing for us to carry large stocks costing us anything about present rates. The possible margin of profit is not commensurate with the possible loss which might be incurred if, by a combination, it were possible for the manufacturers to break the market. I do not think it *is* possible for this to happen mind, but at present levels I do not think it is a time for us to get committed to large stocks of unsold Rubber.

Soon the inevitable aftermath of any boom was fully underway, and Lampard on the 27th wrote tough-mindedly to a Scottish correspondent:

The set back in Rubber I think is only due to a sympathetic fall in connection with everything else. I quite expect to see a different complexion placed on things in general when people have recovered from their present state of panic.

Everyone seems to be anticipating all sorts of evils, and my experience proves that in such cases all such possibilities are discounted, and the evils looked for do not occur. What everyone thinks, as a rule, does not happen.[43]

Lampard over the past few years had been working phenomenally hard, since devoting himself fully to rubber from about 1907, and that autumn he was seriously unwell. He was away from work for over three months and did not return to the City until early in 1911.

Back in harness, he wrote almost at once to the Harrisons & Crosfield manager in Nedan, counselling safety first: 'The natural tendency of men in the East is to anticipate a quick turn from depression to sanguineness and returned prosperity, but there has been such an enormous number of flotations of a doubtful description and the shares of these concerns are held throughout the country and are unmarketable, that it precludes, in my judgment, any improvement for a very long time to come.' Over the next few years his unflinching long-term optimism, allied to short-term pragmatism, did much to carry the rubber industry through a difficult phase. In 1915 one of his sons was killed in action and the following March he more or less retired from business, removing to Holme Park in Rotherfield, Sussex. There, on 21 September 1916, he shot himself in the head. A few weeks later, at the annual general meeting of Harrisons & Crosfield, held in the Council Room of the Rubber Growers' Association at 38 Eastcheap, the company's Chairman, C. Heath Clark, who had worked with Lampard for some thirty-five years, paid due tribute: 'A man of highly strung nervous temperament, he never spared himself or thought of rest when there was work to be done that might advance the interests that absorbed his life . . .'[44] One of the City's few great pioneers in relation to the wider world, he had deserved a happier end.

*

The rubber boom was even more stressful because of the unavailability, in theory at least, of the noxious weed to calm Stock Exchange nerves. In January 1910, after Arthur Oldham of the jobbers Bone, Oldham & Mordaunt had complained of 'the daily disregard of the regulation as to smoking before 4 o'clock', claiming that 'members with delicate throats' were obliged to leave the House early, the

Committee banned smoking altogether. According to the *Economist*, however, there was a hidden agenda:

> Underneath the Stock Exchange are strong-rooms that contain millions of pounds' worth of securities during the year, the amount varying very considerably from time to time. Many thousands of pounds have been spent – much to some of the shareholders' disgust – in the fortifying and enlargement of the strong-rooms, which are let to members for rents that bring in a substantial amount annually. The risk of fire while smoking was allowed is manifest. As may well be understood, the floor of the Stock Exchange at the end of the day is covered with circulars, envelopes, papers of every description, and a carelessly-dropped match or cigarette end might lead to a vast amount of damage, even if the strong-rooms escaped unscathed.

Many members were less than gruntled by the ban, signing a mass petition presented to the Committee by Charlie Clarke and others. 'It was true the Committee had appealed to the good sense of members without success, but members generally did not read notices,' one of the protesters remarked. As for the conductor, he simply asked 'how the Committee proposed to stop it, if members persisted in smoking'. The Committee, typically, offered no answer.[45]

Clarke's periodic scrapes did nothing to diminish his popularity, but the same was probably not true of Paul Schweder, the broker accused by a fellow-member in 1897 of being 'a dirty Polish Jew'. Three years later the Kaffir jobber Herbert Blyth claimed that there was 'no firm in the market that stuck to their prices less than P.E. Schweder & Co', a remark that he reluctantly agreed to withdraw under the Committee's guidance. Schweder ran an ambitious money-making outfit, appraised in March 1908 by S. Japhet & Co on behalf of Kleinworts: 'Firm generally considered to be very good – doing an extensive business, principally in the American market. In some quarters their business is considered too large.' Two years later the King's Bench Division heard the case of Schweder & Co versus Walton & Hemingway, stock-brokers based in Halifax acting on behalf of about fifteen clients:

> In June 1909 the plaintiffs [i.e. Schweders] had purchased for the defendants 4,890 shares in the British South Africa Co, to be taken up or carried over by the defendants. It was alleged that on 3 June Walter Ware, a partner in the plaintiffs' firm, telephoned that Schweder had received confidential information, the source of which was not disclosed, that a heavy fall in the price of the shares was likely to take place during the day, and they insisted that the defendants should sell all the shares they had

bought through them without delay, as the adverse news might be published at any moment. The defendants thereupon agreed to the sale [without consulting their clients], and the plaintiffs sold the shares for £6,400 1s 3d. It transpired subsequently that the information was based upon a letter to Schweder's mother-in-law, from her son, a farmer in Rhodesia, stating that rinderpest had broken out near Salisbury and that he feared that he would be seriously affected by the outbreak. It was asserted that no such outbreak was taking place at the time, and that the plaintiffs could readily have ascertained the truth, and owed a duty to the defendants to do so. The shares did not fall in price, but rose rapidly, and between 3 June and 7 June, when they should have been taken up or carried over, reached a value, it was alleged, of £7,290 1s 3d . . .

The unlucky if over-trusting Halifax firm claimed that the case was 'one of breach of a duty to investigate the accuracy of the information imparted', but Counsel on behalf of Schweders contended that a stockbroker 'was employed for reward to execute orders given him' and that 'any advice he volunteered was quite gratuitously given, and his only duty was to give it *bonâ fide* if he gave it at all'. Mr Justice Ridley came down on the side of Schweders, with the defendants therefore paying the balance. But if justice failed to be achieved in a court of law, it was soon afterwards. In 1913 another Kleinworts report on Schweders noted that 'this firm of Stockbrokers used to do an extensive and important business, but some twelve months ago they were reported to have made very heavy losses, and we believe that they lost most of their capital'.[46]

How much did it cost to be put on the outside track in the esoteric world of rinderpest? In late 1908 the Stock Exchange Members' Association, not content with having pushed through the new rules over shunting and double commissions that cemented the distinction between brokers and jobbers, persuaded the Committee to set up a sub-committee to consider the question of an authorised scale of brokers' commissions. It took soundings between December 1908 and February 1909. Edward Herbert of the brokers G.S. Herbert & Sons, specialising in highly respectable private clients, justly attributed the agitation to 'the ridiculously cut rates charged to certain large financial institutions'; while according to Charles Bowerman, 'in many cases some brokers were now practically the salaried clerks of the banks, who were in reality acting as stockbrokers'. Arthur Tritton of the old-fashioned brokers Ellis & Co took the old-fashioned line. He 'objected to any interference between brokers and their clients. If his clients suggested his dealing at rates which he considered unfair, he let them go. He was against the cutting of commissions, but these were days of competition.' The majority feeling, however, was on the other side. 'Small businesses are being cut to ribbons by the low commissions charged,' was the view of John Farrar, and Edwin Dawes, a member for almost forty years, complained bitterly about the banks:

> They look upon their brokers, in many instances, almost, if not literally, as their paid servants, and they impose terms on them which are more than unfair to brokers generally. The worst offenders are probably foreign banks, large and small, and certain financial institutions, which have grown up of late years and which, through advertising and other means, exist, and do well, on business which properly belongs to members of the Stock Exchange, the cruellest part of the situation being, that they all have their agents within the walls of that institution.

Walter Busby of Govett, Sons & Co added a further twist to the argument when he 'said that commissions were now so low that they had become an indirect incitement to dishonesty', adding that his firm 'had heard that the malpractice of brokers taking a turn in addition to their commission was increasing'. Eventually, the sub-committee narrowly voted to recommend no change, which the Committee accepted by eleven votes to eight.[47]

Few of the brokers in their submissions stressed the intrinsic value of the services they provided, but F. Granville Johnson was an exception. After referring to 'the expert knowledge of the members of the Stock Exchange', he suggested that the charges made by stockbrokers should be determined through comparison 'with other technical businesses or professions for the employment of capital, such as architecture, surveying, engineering, or auctioneering'. Perhaps so, but Montague Newton's critique of over forty years earlier to the Royal Commission on the Stock Exchange, stressing the lack of apprenticeship served by stockbrokers and describing the majority of them as 'decidedly an ignorant class who know very little more beyond 8ths, 16ths and 32nds', remained essentially unanswered.[48]

The Committee election in March 1909 produced a pro-SEMA majority and within weeks a new sub-committee was considering the question of a fixed scale of brokers' charges. Only months after the new rules designed to harden capacity had come into effect, there seemed an irresistible head of steam behind the introduction of a fixed scale. The *Economist*'s analysis was surely correct:

> The innovation is mainly devised with the object of rendering the previous reforms fully operative, and the results it is to achieve are

detailed as follows: to form a standard of fair and reasonable commission; to do away with undercutting both inside and outside the Stock
Exchange; to restrain dealers from dealing (in a veiled way) with a
non-member (the function of brokers); to frustrate evasion of the laws of
shunting and double commission. Reduced brokerage is the chief medium
employed for rendering the rules a dead letter. It is introduced as a mere
film between the dealer and the non-member, and combined with the use
of a jobber's book it is a transparent device for defeating the rule against
double commission.

Behind these rational if not necessarily justifiable objectives lay a mass
of human frustrations. Henry Evers, a member since 1893 and writing
to the new sub-committee from the National Liberal Club, was particularly eloquent:

> Even in the case of wealthy, long-established, well-connected firms, the
> ordinary commission business barely covers current expenses. Why? Not
> because the aggregate volume of business is less than it used to be in
> normal times. I maintain it is greater than it was fifteen years ago, say in
> 1894. But two things have happened. On the one hand the number of
> members has enormously increased, and on the other the commissions
> commonly paid are half, or less than half, of what they used to be. The
> only word to describe the present state of commission rates is 'chaos'.
> One never knows what to charge . . .
> And then there is that unholy sharing of commissions with Dick, Tom,
> and Harry. I am sure there is not in the whole world a more god-forsaken
> crowd of cosmopolitan, wolfish adventurers than can be seen hanging
> round the doors of the London Stock Exchange; rendering Throgmorton
> Street hideous. These people are subject to no control. They insinuate
> themselves with monumental coolness upon any one they may spy out as
> having any money, and when they have collared him take his business to
> some broker at coolie rates . . . The whole thing has become so contemp-
> tible that any bone is thought good enough to throw to a broker. I have
> had what is called 'good business' offered me if I would return 75% of
> the commission. 'Would I do a certain firm's business for so much a year
> all told?' I understand there is a good deal of the latter kind of dealing
> now in the House, the broker in such a case being a mere hired hack,
> working for a salary.

In September 1909, after hearing much inevitably contradictory evidence, the sub-committee made up its mind to back a scheme for a
formal scale of charges. Among those dissenting was its chairman, and
also chairman of the main Committee, Robert Inglis: 'Owing to the
present freedom from restraint as to commission charges, the London
Stock Exchange is *the* market of the world. Begin to tamper with that

freedom and I do not hesitate to express my firm belief (and I have been over 50 years in business) that the Stock Exchange will receive a check from which its members may never recover.'[49]

Over the next few months the main Committee worked its way through the proposed scale, before passing a revised version on 3 February 1910, subject to confirmation a month later. During the intervening weeks the Committee was the object of a flurry of memorials and counter-memorials, as well as individual submissions. The most candid point was made by the brokers Rubens & Reichenbach: 'The primary object of making rules as to the fixing of commissions is to protect broker against broker, and not the public against the Stock Exchange generally.' On 2 March, with the annual election imminent, the Committee sensibly voted to postpone its decision. The result, however, was a profound anti-climax, as the *Economist* indicated on the 12th:

> It is no exaggeration to say that the mid-March nineteen-day account, which ends for practical purposes with today, has proved a record settlement for the Stock Exchange generally. There has not been so much speculation in the City for 15 years. In one department only – that for Consols and other gilt-edged securities – there has been literally nothing doing, in consequence, of course, of the political situation . . . The coming Committee election, described by some as the most important ever fought, arouses only the most languid interest amongst members who, to use the colloquialism, are up to their eyes in work, and who take their places at the clerks' desks in the evening in order to render every possible assistance to their overworked staffs.

The rubber boom, in fine, created such a heap that it swept away all worries about the size of individual rake-offs. On 3 May the Committee voted by seventeen to four against proceeding with the further consideration of a fixed scale, and for the moment the question was dead, if unlikely to be buried.[50]

Indeed, as soon as the following March, a blow was struck for the House's small men when by eleven votes to eight the Committee voted that permission not be granted, except under special circumstances, for a member to carry on arbitrage business with more than one correspondent in the same city. Inevitably the big men grumbled. 'His firm had two correspondents in New York,' stated Campbell Holberton of Chinnery Bros, 'one of whom was a specialist in bonds, the other in certain classes of shares in which there was not a free market here. It was only by going to the right person in New York and being kept posted by that correspondent that they were enabled to run a book on this side and make reasonably close prices.' George Beeman of Vivian, Gray & Co agreed and, probably with some justice, 'said that the Committee did not appear to have decided what arbitrage was and urged that a more precise definition should be framed'. In practice the new rule was interpreted quite flexibly, but it played its part in the cumulative Edwardian trend towards a Stock Exchange riddled with restrictive practices.[51]

Among those affected were the brokers Nathan & Rosselli, starting by this time to build up an arbitrage business with the New York stockbrokers E. & C. Randolph. 'You must not forget that it is much easier to finance positions in London than in New York,' Paul Stamm of that firm wrote to 7 Adam's Court in June 1911, and over the next few weeks relations between the two ends of the business became increasingly prickly, culminating in a vexing foul-up in August. 'Of course we both had the wrong tendency,' Stamm wrote to Louis Sanders at Nathan & Rosselli, 'but the main thing in arbitrage is, surely, not to let your opinion influence you.' The New Yorker then took the moral high ground:

> What I miss in our relations is the mutual feeling & understanding, which I had with former friends, where I could have been sure for instance today on getting a lot of stock sold before our opening upon receipt of my estimates. But it is this understanding I miss all day. I may quote my head off, there is no response on your part, where formerly I could tell myself such & such a thing was sure to be done in London. I could act accordingly often without waiting advices from the other side. It is this mutual understanding we got to learn more than anything else. You would be surprised how little business others have been doing & how little they cabled. With exception of Marks & Biedermans firms, who are not on my side of the rail, we cabled more today than anybody else. Even Hoffman did next to nothing today. They all have lost money in these erratic markets & often were whipsawed. Leon, Huggins & Co, Japhet, Dresdner Bk, Heseltine, Schweder are almost out of the race . . .[52]

Sanders's reply is not recorded, but he may have reflected as he returned home that evening to 24 De Vere Gardens, W8, that arbitrage, almost half a century after the cable was laid under the Atlantic, remained a thoroughly tricky kind of business.

*

Gold reserves spluttered only fitfully as an issue during much of 1909 and 1910. It took George Eliot's husband, the retired merchant banker

Johnny Cross, to revive it. In a pungent article on 'Finance and Defence', published in *Nineteenth Century and After* in March 1911, he brought together the twin themes of inadequate gold reserves and threatening international context, arguing that 'we are now content to jog along, much pleased with the record figures of our imports and exports, taking no thought for the morrow, while all the time it is to be feared that there is real danger of our financial power being gradually sapped and weakened'. Currently standing at £37¼m, the reserves were 'certainly . . . too little today merely in view of the enormous increase in the deposit liabilities', with Cross emphasising the growth of foreign banks' deposits in London and the fact that, though providing the world's only free gold market, the City was peculiarly vulnerable:

> For instance, if any foreign banking institution should want a million in gold some morning, it can call up its loans to that extent from Lombard Street, draw a cheque on its London bankers, and demand to payment Bank of England notes which the Bank of England is obliged to pay in gold without any questions asked, and this gold can be carted away from the Bank and shipped to Paris, Berlin, New York, Brazil, or Buenos Ayres the same afternoon. Such sudden procedure cannot be effected in Paris, Berlin, New York, or any other market in the world. We have always to bear in mind this uniquely vulnerable position of the London Money Market, especially in view of what has been so much remarked in the last few years, viz. the extraordinary increase in our loans to foreign countries . . .

That same month, meeting in London, the Associated Chambers of Commerce endorsed the London Chamber of Commerce's remedy that all banks should increase their stock of gold according to their liabilities. That obdurate stockbroker F. Faithfull Begg, a senior figure at the LCC and who may well have been the driving force behind the proposal, called for sacrifices all round including from the banks, 'who carried on a lucrative business, and who, he thought, could afford a little slice out of those dividends for the benefit of the commercial community'. Schuster, adamantly opposed to this approach, stressed that the Bank of England had not been adequately consulted and called for a royal commission. It was a turn of events that alarmed the *Bankers' Magazine*, which in its April editorial regretted the initiative 'passing from the hands of the banking to the commercial community' and, hostile to legislation, much preferred the Bank of England and the banks finally to sort the matter out between themselves.[53]

During the summer of 1911 there were two key issues. First, would the banks come clean and, as even the *Bankers' Magazine* recommended, give in their balance-sheets actual figures concerning the amount of gold held in their vaults? Second, would the Bank and the banks stop scoring points off each other and begin to act in unison? The answer to the first was that the bankers were not yet ready for transparency, and the potential lack of banking elasticity implied, preferring instead to make blandly reassuring statements. The answer to the second question was a little more promising, with even Schuster conceding that the joint-stock banks now had less to resent in the way of unduly commercial behaviour on the Bank's part. The new Governor was Alfred Cole, and on 21 July he made, to the bankers and merchants assembled at their annual Mansion House banquet, an important announcement:

> I am one of those who have always refused to believe that the interests of the bankers are opposed to those of the Bank of England . . . There is no conflict of interest between the banks and the central institution, and I have hailed with the utmost satisfaction a proposal that has been made unanimously by the representatives of the London Clearing Bankers that will bring the Governor of the Bank into more direct personal relations with the Clearing Banks. The resolution is that there should be quarterly meetings of the representatives of the London Clearing Banks at the Bank of England . . . While it will probably only be on rare occasions that important matters will come up for discussion, still I believe the proposed meetings will prove beneficial to the banking interest.[54]

Faced by the disturbing possibility of legislation, Cole had preferred as the lesser evil to let the bankers get, if not a foot, at least a toe in the door.

The 21st was a Friday, with weather 'so hot', Natty Rothschild reported to Paris, 'that it is said to beat all records'. He added that 'there has been no disposition in the Stock Exchange to do any business at all' – which was perhaps a relief to G.S. Pawle, who spent much of the day at the Guildhall prosecuting one of his firm's ledger clerks, a 50-year-old called Septimus Hallifax who lived in Catford, for stealing a cheque for £1,700 as well as falsifying ledgers. Meanwhile, at a more elevated level, not only was the constitutional crisis approaching its dramatic conclusion, but since the start of July the German gunboat *Panther* had been anchored in the Moroccan harbour of Agadir. Preceding Cole at the Mansion House dinner was the City's favourite, Lloyd George. He raised an early laugh: 'There are only two parties in this country. One is the party of expenditure and the other is the party of economy. There are only two members of the party of economy – Sir Frederick Banbury and myself.' The serious bit came later:

> I would make great sacrifices to preserve peace. I conceive that nothing would justify a disturbance of international goodwill except questions of the gravest national moment. But if a situation were to be forced upon us in which peace could only be preserved by the surrender of the great and beneficent position Britain has won by centuries of heroism and achieve-ment, by allowing Britain to be treated where her interests were vitally affected as if she were of no account in the Cabinet of nations, then I say emphatically that peace at that price would be a humiliation intolerable for a great country like ours to endure. (*Cheers*.)

Coming from someone with such unjingoistic credentials, it was a critical moment in what became known as the Second Moroccan Crisis. Churchill would later claim that Lloyd George's 'City audience, whose minds were obsessed with the iniquities of the Lloyd George Budget and the fearful hardship it had inflicted on property and wealth – little did they dream of the future – did not comprehend in any way the significance or the importance of what they heard'. Possibly, though it seems unlikely; while as for the Stock Exchange the following morning, the *FN*'s report made its reaction perfectly clear:

> Mr Lloyd George, for once in his career, succeeded in pleasing the market in his speech at the Mansion House. His references to the outlook for British trade and to the necessity for national economy were especially liked; but the possible effect of these remarks was entirely overshadowed by Mr Lloyd George's pointed allusions to Germany in connection with international politics, it being surmised that the Government now regard the situation in a serious light. Consols were heavy at the opening . . .

Or in the words of a headline, 'The Heat And Morocco Combine To Shrivel Up Business In Mines'.[55] The City's mood may have swung congenitally from wild optimism to wild pessimism and back again, often with little rational foundation; but the possibility of war, and all that might ensue, was never entirely absent from its collective uncon-scious.

CHAPTER TWENTY-FIVE

Personal Interviews Necessary

The Yorkshire Penny Bank, established in Halifax in the 1850s 'to encourage thrift among the working classes of Yorkshire', was in deep trouble by the summer of 1911, running a deficiency of over £½m in its reserve account. There ensued a dramatic if low-profile rescue.[1] When the crisis was safely over, the directors of the Bank of England heard part of the story – but only part – from their Governor, Alfred Cole:

> On Saturday, the 22nd July, I received a telegram in the country [Cole's out-of-town home was West Woodhay House near Newbury] from the Chief Cashier stating that Sir Edward Holden had sent over to the Bank as he wished to see me on important business. When he heard I was absent he proposed to motor down to call on me. I replied by telegram that I could see him at any time on the following day, Sunday, the 23rd, but my telegram was not in time to reach him on the Saturday. I arranged to see him at the Bank on Monday morning. He then informed me that, in his opinion, the condition of the affairs of the Yorkshire Penny Bank was serious . . . Sir Edward Holden informed me that he had communicated with the Chairman of the Union of London and Smiths Bank and the National Provincial Bank; also that he had prepared a scheme by which the business of the Yorkshire Penny Bank should be taken over by a group of Bankers, if those Bankers would agree to raise a capital of £2,000,000 sterling so as to ensure the safety of the Yorkshire Penny Bank on a reconstituted basis. He asked me as Governor of the Bank to assist him in raising the Capital.[2]

For Holden, this was a golden opportunity, twenty-one years after the Baring crisis, in which the clearing bankers had been treated as second-class citizens by those responsible for saving the day, to show that the Midland and its joint-stock peers were capable of overcoming any difficulty that might occur in the national banking system. Even so, he recognised that this could not be done entirely without the assistance of the Bank of England, and thus Cole's rather harassed weekend.

Cole himself, on the Monday, saw the Penny Bank's general manager, who confirmed Holden's information, and that afternoon, at a meeting at the Bank attended by Cole, Holden, Schuster and the chairmen of Lloyds and Barclays, 'it was decided to proceed on the lines of Sir Edward Holden's scheme'. Would it work? Holden himself clearly had doubts, for twice during the week he tried to get Lloyd George to pledge government backing:

> *27 July*. The Governor of the Bank of England and I have been working day and night for a week trying to prevent the most awful catastrophe of the institution I discussed with you coming down. Up to last night we had hopes, but this morning I despair. I think that you and Mr A[squith] should know exactly what the position is as some help from you may enable us to pull through.
>
> *29 July*. I know you are very much engaged with policy affairs, but I should like to point out to you that the matter I wrote to you about is equally important. If this debacle comes it will lay in ashes the whole of Yorkshire and a great deal of Lancashire. I cannot help but think it would do a great deal of damage to the Government in these districts.

Lloyd George declined to get involved – justifiably, for over the next few days the Penny Bank's rescue was successfully effected. The rescue took two main forms: the injection of £2m of working capital, with the list of subscribers headed by the London City and Midland ($£\frac{1}{2}$m), followed by the London Joint Stock Bank, Barclays, Lloyds, and the Union of London and Smiths Bank ($£\frac{1}{4}$m each); and a guarantee fund of £1m, headed by the Bank of England and the London County and Westminster ($£\frac{1}{4}$m each) and Parr's, the Capital and Counties, Glyn Mills, and the United Counties Bank (£100,000 each).[3]

Significantly, during the composition of the guarantee fund, Rothschilds 'volunteered to come in for £100,000 if private firms were to be asked to contribute'; but, apparently, they were not. That was no skin off Barings' nose. 'Mercifully we have not been asked to guarantee,' Farrer wrote to Revelstoke (taking his usual August holiday in Aix) on 2 August. 'I have seen no official lists but gather most of the Banks are in except National Provincial who have from the first sturdily scouted the idea.' And two days later: 'The National Provincial are to be congratulated on having kept out of it. Apparently Selwyn Prior went over to interview Cole, and we are told the meeting was most amusing; and I can well imagine it, for Prior is quite as rude as Cole and quite as tactless.' But for Holden, making the running throughout, the episode had been an unarguable triumph. Whether it enhanced his patchy popularity in the City was perhaps another matter. Towards the end of the month Farrer informed Revelstoke, by now staying at Villa Cassel, that 'Schuster is far from well and is in Switzerland at the present moment'. And he added: 'Holden seems to be having all the luck.'[4]

In 1911 the dog days of August were more publicly dominated by the heat (excessive), the constitutional crisis (at last resolved), the Moroccan crisis (not yet resolved) and a generally nervy, jumpy atmosphere in the markets. 'Very uneasy feeling on Stock Exchange & Yankees come over weak,' noted the bill brokers Smith St Aubyn on Wednesday the 16th. That same afternoon there occurred what the *Economist* called 'a unique incident in the House', as one of the day's defaulters in the Stock Exchange met his fate:

> Upon the fall of the hammer a great hush ordinarily comes over the whole House when the waiters rise in their stands to perform the unpleasant duty of hammering a member. But the American market happened to be singing a lusty chorus to a well-known man, and did not notice the signal for default. Consequently the hammering was carried out to the accompaniment of song by the unconscious Yankee market, which did not realise that anything untoward was about until it was practically over. It was tragedy and comedy brought more closely together than most members can recollect in the course of their City life.

The young John Braithwaite, son of Joseph and a partner in Foster & Braithwaite only since 1908, was not among those in singalong mood. Just over a fortnight later, on holiday with his wife and baby son, he wrote to his father:

> I think we have made a great mistake in regarding the bringing out of companies as a definite branch of our business . . . We have suffered great financial loss and still worse we have ruined our reputation with those who followed us into Oil. We know nothing about [it] yet we presumed to pose as competent advisers. What induced us to do it? . . . I could kick myself when I think of how we sat in our office last year and were fooled by the specious show of one promoter after another into putting our names to enterprises of questionable integrity – which in the event have brought profit only to their promoters and vendors . . .

Braithwaite then dwelt on the likelihood of one of those oil companies going into receivership, with the possibility that that might lead to the smash of Foster & Braithwaite itself:

> You may perhaps be surprised that I have spoken of the possibility of failure. It is because it has been before my mind like a nightmare day and night more or less continuously for the last month and more – I have

suffered it all mentally over and over again – when the hammer has gone in the House it has sounded like a knell in my ears – I have thought of the long list of our names and the awful staggering hush afterwards – in a sense the bitterness of it seems past having realized it so – [illegible], and anything would be a relief.[5]

In fact the firm survived, and Braithwaite would remain a partner for another sixty years. Most City men know fear at one time or another in their careers, but hardly anyone has expressed it so vividly.

Montagu Norman of Brown Shipley was undergoing a rather different sort of personal crisis, one that the firm described on 4 October to Brown Brothers in New York:

> Mr Norman, as you know, has had a good deal of business to attend to lately, and apparently has not been in very strong health for some months past: of this, however, his Partners had little suspicion, as, on any enquiry being made, he himself was so sensitive that it was impossible to insist on it.
>
> About ten days ago, however, things came to a climax, and he felt compelled to leave the office under the impression that he had contracted a severe chill. Fortunately he went down to his Father's (Moor Place), and after arriving there (from all we understand) he had a serious collapse, and for 3 or 4 days was quite incapacitated with acute pains in his head and a high temperature. The family Doctor was called in, and at once pronounced it a case of nervous breakdown.

The City in late September was expressing its profound relief over the settlement of the Moroccan question, but of this, and almost everything else, Norman was oblivious. The illness continued, and in November he was seen by a London specialist. 'He says M. is like a sick animal who has gone away into a corner alone,' a relative reported, 'and he doesn't want us to poke him into activity of mind or body.' What had happened? It is clear that Norman by 1911 was increasingly at odds with at least one of his partners over Brown Shipley's recent emphasis on issuing securities and underwriting other issues, often of a speculative nature (several of them Canadian land issues), a trend that he saw as alien to the traditional and much sounder virtues of accepting; but in such a complex, elusive character it is unlikely to have been business alone that caused the breakdown. Norman himself professed bewilderment. Having been advised to take a long voyage to recruit his health, he wrote on Christmas Eve to an American partner:

I remember, tho' not very clearly, that I had a letter from you on the very day that my machine stopped working. That letter has vanished, and I don't know what it said, and from that time until now I have neither read nor written a letter. Indeed I have been a close prisoner and to me it seems that the Prison was constructed on the lines of Hell! . . . Anyhow I want no better imitation![6]

*

In the winter of 1911/12 the Committee of Imperial Defence conducted, in the wake of the Second Moroccan Crisis, an inquiry into the financial and commercial implications should war break out between Britain and Germany.[7] Chaired by the Earl of Desart, a sub-committee quizzed various City eminents, including Huth Jackson. He argued that the creation of an earmarked war reserve of gold would work only if it was a secret one; insisted that, in the event of war, 'to suspend the export of gold even for twenty-four hours might be to jeopardise our position as the principal bankers of the world'; and generally took the line that if London could get through the first few days of war then all would be fine, because by lifting the Bank rate it would be able to call in gold from all quarters of the globe. Huth Jackson was an accomplished witness, rather more at his ease than the senior partner of Barings:

> *Revelstoke.* I should imagine that a declaration of war between England and Germany would create such chaos as would result in the ruin of most, if not of all, accepting houses.
> *Desart.* Would that not include nearly all the big joint-stock banks?
> *Revelstoke.* I regret to say that such has been the trend of the activities taken by the London Joint Stock Banks during the last twenty years that they would be seriously prejudiced as to their acceptances.
> *Sir Robert Chalmers (of the Treasury).* Can you see any way of getting over that?
> *Revelstoke.* These are questions which it is easy to put, but to which it is difficult to formulate a reply without consideration.
> *Desart.* I do not think that is our idea. We want to formulate what is in our minds, and we want to see what occurs to you upon those points.
> *Revelstoke.* The only way to remedy such a state of affairs would be a moratorium.
> *Chalmers.* And a moratorium not in the realm of the Bank of England, but between private individuals and banks in this country; that is the sort of moratorium you mean, is it not?
> *Revelstoke.* No moratorium could affect the Bank of England, of course. The Bank of England really is the source of the whole credit of the British Empire.

A little later, Revelstoke let himself go:

> I do trust you will do what you can to arrange for measures being taken
> in advance now by a competent body towards minimising the ill-effects
> of the catastrophe – which would be dreadful – of a declaration of war. I
> can only tell you that my conviction is . . . that, should a European war
> take place, the chaos in the commercial and industrial world would be
> stupendous, and would result in the ruin of most people engaged in
> business. It certainly would lead to a disastrous run and to the shutting of
> the doors of most of the joint-stock banks.

Governor Cole also gave evidence and, like Huth Jackson, strongly
deprecated any notion of a wartime embargo on the export of
gold. Inevitably he trotted out the familiar argument that it was
the 'free market for gold' that more than anything had made London 'the international banking centre of the world'. Anyway, he
went on, in the event of war 'probably failure would be confined to
one or two accepting houses, and the City as a whole would escape
any great financial disaster'. And in terms of defending the gold
reserve, he concluded not unportentously, 'the adjustment of the discount rate to meet the ever-varying circumstances of each moment'
was an instrument that 'had never failed us in the past' and 'might be
relied on in almost any conceivable eventuality, so long as we retained
command of the sea'. Schuster, equally inevitably, was unconvinced
and continued to plug his idea of a special war reserve of actual
gold. 'The Bank of England is so circumscribed,' he told the sub-
committee. 'In ordinary times the system works admirably; but directly
there is abnormal pressure, such as is bound to arise on a great war,
the Bank of England cannot meet all the commercial needs. There is
no doubt about that in my opinion.' In short, the experts could not
agree.

Other figures from other parts of the City also gave evidence. The
most striking testimony was provided by Robert Ogilvie, a leading
underwriter at Lloyd's. He confirmed that there was a large amount of
German marine insurance placed in London; and related how in 1905,
after German propaganda to the contrary, Lloyd's had emphasised
that all claims would be met, even in wartime. There ensued an
exchange of views that encapsulated the gulf between economic nationalism and economic liberalism:

> *Desart.* I want to put to you the particular case of a German ship which
> has been insured in England, captured by a British cruiser and either

destroyed or condemned; do you consider your honourable obligation
extends as far as paying in that case?

Ogilvie. If we had insured her before the outbreak of war I think so,
certainly.

Desart. Just consider the meaning of that.

Ogilvie. Of course bargains are very often unpleasant, or fulfilling them
may mean something very unpleasant.

Desart. We are at war with Germany; the navy of your country is
endeavouring to put pressure on the Germans by destroying their trade,
and in pursuance of that has captured a ship and destroyed it or condemned it, whichever it may be; do you not see that you destroy the whole
effect of that act of war by compensating the German owner for the loss
he has experienced?

Ogilvie. I quite see that point, and I saw it all through; but that is rather
governed, from our point of view, by the honourable carrying out of our
bargain . . .[8]

Elsewhere in its investigations, the sub-committee found that much of
Germany's flourishing foreign trade relied on the financial mechanism
provided by the City of London; and the same fundamental dichotomy
presented itself. Ultimately, British strategic considerations were incompatible with London's continuing role as the world's great financial and commercial clearing house. Not surprisingly then, despite
Revelstoke's urgent plea, remarkably few preparations were made over
the next two and a half years over what to do with that fine-tuned
machinery if war broke out.

Instead, for all their lurking fears, City men preferred to believe
that, in the last resort, the worst would not happen. It was a belief
that drew much comfort from Norman Angell's highly influential treatise *The Great Illusion*. On 17 January 1912, not long after
it had gone into its sixth edition and a few weeks before
Ogilvie's evidence, the author delivered a paper to the Institute of
Bankers on 'The Influence of Banking on International Relations'.
Angell 'drew a crowded audience' and 'his arguments were followed
with marked attention and evident sympathy'. At the core of those
arguments was the thesis that the world's finance and commerce were
now so inextricably entwined, crossing all national boundaries, that
the price of war between nation states must be so high as to make the
prospect inconceivable. Angell concluded by seeking to refute the
often-made charge 'that it is sordid that the conduct of men and
nations should be guided by what they are pleased to call money
considerations':

I know that you would not want me to indulge in high falutin in this matter. But this condition of commercial interdependence, which is the special mark of banking as it is the mark of no other profession or trade in quite the same degree – the fact that the interest and the solvency of one is bound up with the interest and solvency of many; that there must be confidence in the due fulfilment of mutual obligation, or whole sections of the edifice crumble, is surely doing a great deal to demonstrate that morality after all is not founded upon self-sacrifice, but upon enlightened self-interest, a clearer and more complete understanding of all the ties which bind us the one to the other. And such clearer understanding is bound to improve, not merely the relationship of one group to another, but the relationship of all men to all other men, to create a consciousness which must make for more efficient human co-operation, a better human society.

In discussion the only sustained challenge to Angell's paper came from the independent-minded Cornelis Rozenraad. 'You cannot separate, gentlemen, politics and finance,' he insisted. 'Both go hand in hand, but the political relations influence the banking and financial operations, and not these operations the political relations.' Francis Steele of Parr's complained about the vulgarisation of Angell's theories and expressed his gratitude to their influence: 'I believe that there is really now getting into the minds of men the thought that peace is perhaps the greatest material interest that they have.' W.R. Lawson observed that 'it is very evident that Mr Norman Angell has carried this meeting almost entirely with him', but Huth Jackson at the very end sounded a note of caution: 'It is all very well to get the bankers on your side, but that is not sufficient. What you have to do is to get the whole body of all the peoples in the world on your side.' And he concluded: 'But, gentlemen, bear in mind one thing, and that is that until you get that thing done, there is, I am afraid, little prospect of any change in the international position – that is to say, war will still remain a possibility.'[9] The Institute's President was only a moderately successful senior partner of Huths, but more than most of his fellows he had a grasp of the big picture.

*

Over two years after Lloyd George's infamous Budget, Consols continued in a depressingly southerly direction.[10] 'Sales to pay death duties are practically forced sales,' Cole argued at the historic Mansion House banquet in July 1911, 'and the amount that has to be found now is some £26,000,000 per annum . . . Here you have a definite

cause for the depression of what are known as gilt-edged securities.'
Four months later, addressing the Institute of Bankers, Huth Jackson
reviewed the recent sorry history of Consols – down from a 1903
average of 90¾ to a 1911 average (to the end of September) of 79⅞ – and
went on: 'Consols have, in fact, lost their negotiability, which was in
the past one of their greatest attractions . . . This is not a question of
party politics, but a matter of national concern; and I believe that if the
best brains in the City were asked to suggest a solution of the difficulty, a satisfactory one could be found.' Few of the jobbers in the
gilt-edged market would have denied the impeachment, business in
Consols having by this time almost ceased to be done in 32nds of a
point, whereas in olden days that fraction had been quite usual. Early
in 1912, during the round of AGMs, the leading joint-stock bankers
addressed the question of what to do about Consols – among them
Holden, who on 26 January put forward the suggestion that income
tax on Consols be remitted. That same day he sent Lloyd George a
copy of his speech: 'I want you to read it very carefully & not throw it
into the waste-paper basket until you have done so.' The Welsh wizard
presumably glanced at it, and just over a week later, on 3 February, he
told a packed meeting at the City Liberal Club that any suggestions
that he might receive on how the position of Consols be improved
would receive 'careful and impartial consideration'.[11]

Letters did not exactly flood the Treasury over the next few weeks,
and those that were written came mostly from outside the City. However, some based in the City did respond. Saemy Japhet, who had been
present at the meeting, suggested that government departments receive
deposits in the form of Consols rather than cash. James A. Malcolm of
58 Lombard Street wanted a quarter of the unearned Increment Tax to
be devoted to reducing the National Debt, a move that he believed
would 'give an impetus – a spice – to the Consols Market of which it
has long been in need'. James H. Loewe of 33 Old Broad Street was
sure he had the answer: 'To make a success you must go with public
opinion and the views of leading Bankers. The only point on which
absolute unanimity is reached is that some redeemable stock is
wanted.' And W.H. Collins of the stockbrokers Galloway & Pearson
enclosed a scheme by which holders of existing 2½ per cent stock would
be able to exchange into new 2¾ per cent stock. One thing all these
proposals had in common was that, ultimately, it was the taxpayer
who would shoulder the cost of restoring the value of Consols. The
point was not lost on Sir Alexander Kleinwort, who wrote to Lloyd
George on 15 February: 'In my judgment, the Government would

make a very serious mistake were they to allow themselves to be inveigled into any scheme having for its object the artificial raising of the market price of Consols. The present price of Consols is due to natural economic causes . . .' After explaining that the main cause was the current plethora of attractive foreign investments, Kleinwort went on:

> There is in the City a very widespread and very natural desire to see Consols go up. All Bankers, Banks and Financial Houses hold them in more or less large quantities and would, of course, be glad to recoup the heavy losses shown by the present price. Many would, therefore, welcome some sort of action on the part of the Government to help them to realize their wishes.

But, the Liberal-sympathising baronet insisted in best Gladstonian fashion, 'any Government legislation can only give a fictitious value and fictitious values are never sound'.[12] In the end, as Lloyd George probably intended, nothing significant emerged from the exercise.

Far better, in most City eyes, to have a change of government altogether. In October 1911 Herbert Gibbs informed Natty Rothschild that the Conservative Party Chairman, Sir Arthur Steel-Maitland, was about 'to make a systematic appeal in the City for funds for the Central Office'. Gibbs had typically strong views on the subject:

> If the Rich men in the City and elsewhere are going to find money for the Unionist Party surely we might ask that the Party should be pledged if not to reduce the Death Duties, at least to devise a check on all excess taxation. If the Party are so pledged it would be good business to support them, but if they will not pledge themselves it seems to me bad business to support them, because all they would do, at the best, would be to mark time while the Socialists regained strength for a fresh assault.
>
> If you subscribe to this new appeal without any conditions no doubt a great many will follow you and the appeal will be more or less successful: but I am sure that it would be much more successful if you obtained the pledge which I suggest; and the appeal will be a failure if you refuse to subscribe.

The next day Gibbs instructed Steel-Maitland himself how the Conservatives should set about getting money from the City. He suggested that, before launching a private appeal, Steel-Maitland should 'personally, accompanied by a man like Mr Walter Long [a leading Tory], call on about 10 of the principal people in the City and get (what you must have here) a good heading to the List'. Such a heading would presumably include Natty Rothschild. Then, Gibbs went on, Steel-Maitland 'should see personally two or three people out of each commercial centre, i.e. the Stock Exchange, Baltic, Lloyds &c and invite them to see personally the Conservative members of their own trade'. And in general: 'You must have the most popular men in their own profession to see members of that profession. You cannot get money by circulars or even letters to any extent. Personal interviews are necessary.'[13] Steel-Maitland presumably got the message, but it was arguably a sign of changing times – with a less easy overlap between a more professional City and a more professional political class – that it had to be spelt out.

In the event Natty declined to reply and the immediate possibility of an appeal lapsed; but Gibbs and other like-minded City men, including Kindersley, Eric Hambro (son of Everard) and Dimsdale, continued to press the Tory leadership to pledge itself to policies that would explicitly aim to roll back the fiscal tide. Unless this was done, argued a memorandum to Bonar Law (who had succeeded Balfour), 'there is little reason to expect either economy among the governing masses, or confidence among the small and numerically powerless class'. In March 1912 an unabashed Gibbs wrote again to Natty, asking him to endorse and involve himself in an invitation to Bonar Law to come to the City and explain his financial policy, as a prelude to an appeal to the City to reach into its pockets. This time Natty responded, in person rather than by letter. He argued that it would be a mistake to invite Bonar Law to come to the City and said that he saw no reason to depart from Disraeli's practice of declining to make any detailed statement of policy before taking office.[14] What ultimately happened about the appeal is uncertain – but what is clear is that, so long as Natty retained his moral ascendancy, the 'ultras' would not, despite the rising temper of the times, capture the City.

*

My Lefevre firm are writing to you today on the subject of your investments. I could almost wish you did not carry your sporting propensities into the regions of finance, but, if you must have 5% and the countries you name, it is easier got in sound enterprises in Argentina than in Canada.

Buenos Aires Great Southern is one of the principal Railways there, under capable English management and with a magnificent past record as a dividend payer. It is a big stock with a fairly free market . . .

The writer was Gaspard Farrer and the recipient of his advice, given in November 1911, the Earl of Cavan, of Wheathampstead House, Wheathampstead. Over the next few weeks it emerged that Cavan, a military man, had been approached by his brother-in-law, a member at Lloyd's, to participate in an underwriting syndicate. Farrer was unimpressed: 'I do beg that before you risk your securities or your credit you will take a sound and independent judgment on the question. It so rarely happens that people outside the City can take up City business without repenting it.' But Cavan was adamant, and Farrer, admitting he was 'an old woman in the matter', replied on 6 December:

> I presume you will be allowing your friends at Lloyds to use your name for underwriting, that is to underwrite in your name. If that is the case, how can you limit your liability? ... You must by the necessity of the case be in the hands of those who decide what risks are to be taken. It is notorious that underwriters at Lloyds have made little or no money of recent years, and in a case which has recently come before me apparently on the same lines as that which you now propose, it was simply disastrous.

The next morning the brother-in-law called on Farrer, who was relieved to learn not only that Cavan's interest would not constitute him a partner but also that business was to be done through Messrs Heath – 'I believe the firm to have an excellent reputation,' he assured Cavan. Even so, 'I confess I wish for your sake that you had never heard of the business.'[15] There the correspondence ends, with the sporting propensities still all on one side.

Farrer was also a sceptical observer of the flurry of foreign issues that characterised the winter of 1911/12. One week's correspondence (mainly to Revelstoke, in Paris on Argentine business, but the last letter to Sterling in New York) was typical:

> 24 *November*. Schröder's Peru loan is $5\frac{1}{2}$% at $98\frac{1}{2}$. Peruvian Corporation Sixes redeemable at 105 are now $105\frac{1}{2}$ cum 3% interest, so that the new issue will not look particularly cheap. Henderson has a Lima loan, Koch thinks 5% at 94, but this seems hardly likely. Koch tells me that New Court have done nothing in the way of supporting the Chilian market, at least so far as he can see. Under the circumstances it is really rather extraordinary that the price has kept so good. Everyone seems to believe that 'stagging' has taken place on a large scale, but if so I am puzzled to think who the buyers at the premium can be ... Crisp's lists [for an Anglo-Russian Trust issue] close tonight. The market believe underwriters will get 90% of the Preferred shares that were underwritten

and do not believe that any of the Ordinary shares were subscribed for by the public. They think, however, the latter will be put away under one or other of Crisp's thimbles . . .

27 November. Fleischman [sic] has been in hungry for the balance of the Oregon Bonds and suggests an immediate issue, thinking the present a more favourable time than the last days of December . . .

28 November. Koch tells me in strict confidence that Crisp is again negotiating with New Court for the issue of his Brazilian Railway Bonds, that so far they are not in agreement but that C. is persistent. Looking to the past I should think he would win hands down . . .

1 December. Nothing very fresh here in the way of business, but there seem to be endless projects on foot for the near future, not many coming our way, or rather not many that we should care to undertake. The rage is all for high interest and nobody seems to pay any attention to security, so we are standing aside.

However, as the flood of issues continued unabated, an increasing proportion failed to be fully subscribed, leading to grumbles by under-writers on the Stock Exchange compelled to take up large amounts of stock. In turn this meant that the issuing houses had gradually to buy back the stock from the market – an expensive process, but such were the customary dictates. 'We have been asked if there is any remedy,' Natty Rothschild wrote to Paris on 28 February, 'and at present the only thing that suggests itself to our mind is that most of the loans brought out have not been of the highest quality and the price of issue has been too high.' None of these costly flops, he insisted, had been sponsored by N.M. Rothschild & Sons.[16]

Less than a week later, on 5 March, business took second place in Natty's despatch:

We had the pleasure of telegraphing to you last night that our dear brother Leopold had had a most miraculous escape. A miscreant who I am sorry to say is of our own persuasion fired at him five times with a revolver when he was driving out of the court yard in his motor. All the windows were broken and the car was riddled with bullets. Unfortunately the Policeman on guard at the door was badly wounded. No one knows exactly what object the miscreant had in view . . .

An assassination attempt in New Court was quite an event, and a flood of sympathetic telegrams, cards and letters poured in to the shaken but fortunately uninjured Leo. From Churchill at the Admiralty: 'Earnest congratulations on your providential escape from murderous attack.' From Cassel in Tunis: 'Too sorry to hear of the dastardly attempt. My most sincere congratulations on your providential escape.' From Alfred Wagg at 37 Threadneedle Street: 'I have never forgotten your great kindness to me when first I came into the City – and I am heartily glad you escaped from your great danger.' From Asquith at 10 Downing Street: 'I can only imagine the man to be a maniac to wish to hurt the best & kindest of men.' From Vicary Gibbs at 22 Bishopsgate: 'Felicitations chaleureuses on your truly marvellous escape scot-free from that maniacal assault.' But for all the outrage, attention soon moved elsewhere. 'It is rumoured this afternoon in the Stock Exchange,' Natty relayed to Paris on the 7th, 'that Captain Scott has reached the South Pole and has secured the triumph for England . . .'[17]

But the Stock Exchange's main preoccupation during the winter of 1911/12 was the question of a minimum scale for brokers' commissions, which this time returned to the agenda decisively. 'Shunting and the "Dummy" Broker' was the title of an *Economist* article in September 1911 explaining how, following the 1909 legislation designed to harden the divide between brokers and jobbers, there had emerged, albeit evasively, 'a new semi-class amongst the members of the House':

> The firms doing a broking-jobbing business – that is, most of the previous shunters – found that under the new rules they were compelled to give up one side of the business or the other, and to declare themselves either brokers or jobbers, and, with their usual good sense, Stock Exchange members, though many grumbled, adapted themselves as quickly as possible to the new regulations. It was perfectly obvious that a broking-jobbing firm, with a good connection on both sides, would split up into two different parts under separate names, one conducting the business of a broker, and the other that of a jobber. The jobbing firms who had been dealing directly with members of country exchanges discovered that they could obey the letter of the law while evading the spirit, by putting transactions through the books of the broking firm which had nominally split off from them. To such an extent has this practice grown of late, that a strong demand has arisen in the Stock Exchange for some further extension of the rules, so that this system of 'dummy' brokers shall be declared irregular.

The method hit on was a minimum scale, which of course would also tackle the problem of 'coolie' commissions paid by some of the big outside houses and banks. Debate raged through the winter, as the Committee drew up a detailed new scale before eventually, in late February, deciding to postpone confirmation of the new rules until a ballot of members had been held.[18]

The Stock Exchange Members' Association at once issued a pamphlet. It stressed that 'the proposed New Rules do not stand alone but follow of necessity from the determination emphatically asserted a few years ago by the general body of Members that the Rule forbidding Members to act in the double capacity of Broker and Jobber should be enforced and strengthened'. It argued that a minimum scale would curb outside brokers: 'They have found the Stock Exchange a milch cow, and have milked it vigorously. They have found it possible to obtain the services of Members of the Stock Exchange to transact their business for them on any terms that they may be pleased to offer, and they have taken full advantage of this privilege.' It called on jobbers to remember that the 1909 rules could not be 'maintained and the Jobbers' position preserved, unless the Jobbers in their turn are willing to assist Brokers to protect their business'. And it concluded by taking the high ground: 'It has been shown [i.e. by the proposals] that the Stock Exchange is a most highly organised body of men; that it is the home of the most scientific market in public securities, and that it affords complete guarantees for the punctual and honest execution of all the obligations its Members undertake.' The ballot produced only a narrow 'yes' vote (1,670 to 1,551) and, though the Committee on 4 March confirmed the new rules by seventeen votes to eleven, to come into force on 1 June, it was clear that much would hinge on the annual Committee election later in March. On its eve a hundred of the Stock Exchange's leading firms made a strong public appeal against the fixed scale. They tended to be the larger firms, with five or more partners – such as James Capel & Co, Cazenove & Akroyds, Heseltine Powell & Co, Laing & Cruickshank, Rowe & Pitman, Sheppards, Pelly, Price & Pott, and H. Vigne & Sons among brokers, Barron Bros, F. & N. Durlacher, S. Kennedy & Co, George Kitchin & Co, and Wedd Jefferson & Co among jobbers – but as in the crucial 1908 vote it was the little men who won, with a 72 per cent turn-out returning the SEMA-endorsed candidates. The minimum scale was duly introduced, with relatively little fuss; and the mass of members had succeeded, taking the 1912 rules in conjunction with those of 1908/9, in more or less ring-fencing the Stock Exchange.[19] It was, in short, a thoroughly comfortable, club-like dispensation.

Yet if public interest was well down the list of priorities, at least that investing public now knew where it stood. The following winter *The Stock Exchange Christmas Annual* published some apposite lines:

Still do I mourn my broker and my friend.
  I loved his florid cheeks and portly size;
I loved the slow, wise smile that lit his face
  When asked if this would fall or that would rise,
His pros and cons, his ready flow of speech
  Would leave you quite convinced he really knew;
Yet never once did he commit himself –
  He merely took commission out of you.

A helping hand he gave to all who asked,
  While asking naught but friends he might regale;
But he would charge his clients what he wished
  Till came the day of that accurs'd fixed scale.
It killed him; and this epitaph was writ
  Upon the victim of the base assault: –
'Sins of omission never once were his;
  Sins of commission formed his only fault.'[20]

The author of 'A Broker's Epitaph' was a member called Norman Stickland, and the 'florid cheeks and portly size' might have been based on any number of real-life candidates.

*

Alan ('Tommy') Lascelles was a nephew of the fifth Earl of Harewood and, after coming down from Trinity College, Oxford, tried and failed for the diplomatic service. In September 1911 he had a long talk with Patrick Shaw-Stewart 'on careers, so far as I remember, and the effect of the City on the Soul'. Shaw-Stewart himself, after a glittering undergraduate career at Oxford, had recently migrated to Barings. Two months later a rather doom-laden diarist heard the bell tolling:

> I went early to see Ronnie Norman, who had to tell me of a job which he thought might suit me. It proved to be City, as I expected. Gerry Bevan, a partner in Ellis's, wants men to go into the office on half-commission. I went round to see him at 1 Cornhill, and liked him, and he said I could think about it to the end of the year. Which I shall do. I have always told myself I would never go into the City. But it might be a good thing, temporarily at any rate. Bevan did not disguise the fact that the first eighteen months are hell.

Over the winter Lascelles half-heartedly tried to get a job on *The Times*, but by January realised that journalism was not for him. And at the end of February 1912, admitting defeat, he 'went down to

Ellis's, where Bevan introduced me to one of his partners, Tritton, a rather repellent young man, but said to be very successful'. Still, he had made a sound choice. Ellis & Co was, the company promoter O'Hagan would recall in his memoirs, 'one of the leading firms of London stock-brokers, old-established and prosperous'. Indeed, 'so old-fashioned was the firm's reputation that I never attempted to secure them for my underwriting list; new undertakings were the last thing I should have expected them to interest themselves in'. The firm enjoyed an excellent connection, with Tritton and Bevan both coming out of the Barclays family stable. Gerard Bevan also had talent on his side. 'Rarely, if ever, have I known a man able to explain a business in a clearer and more concise form than he did,' Émile d'Erlanger would recall, adding that 'his command of figures and memory were exceptional'.[21]

Lascelles began at 1 Cornhill on 1 April, not long before his 25th birthday: 'My first day in the City. I was bored and bewildered, understanding little of what I saw and nothing of what I heard.' The next day, 'Tritton started me off in the Transfer Department, the lowest rung in the ladder. I want to go through the office thoroughly and comprehensively.' Two days later Lascelles was smitten by the romance of finance: 'My fellow-clerks are perfectly charming to me, and love me. They spare no pains to explain everything, and in return I think I am beginning to make myself quite useful. It excites me very much. Both sides of this elementary office work appeal to me – the dashing-about with stock to deliver against time, and the book-keeping . . .' That was on Thursday the 4th. A week and a half later, on Monday the 15th, stock-delivering and book-keeping suddenly seemed unimportant:

> About noon the streets were full of posters announcing that the *Titanic* had struck an iceberg, half-way across the Atlantic on her maiden voyage. She got into touch with the mainland by means of her wireless installation, and hour by hour we were kept informed of her movements. There was something extraordinarily dramatic in the thought of this great overgrown monster wallowing about in mid-ocean, while we in Cornhill could almost watch her flounderings. Then suddenly the messages became blurred and ceased altogether; it was put about – no one yet knows by whom – that all the passengers were saved and that the ship was being towed into Halifax by one of the rescuing liners, and we all went to bed regarding it as a good joke.

Press reports endorsed Lascelles's account. 'Business on the Stock Exchange was again very brisk yesterday, and few departments were without a share in it,' began the *FN*'s market résumé compiled on Monday evening. And: 'Consols were made a little easier by way of precaution induced by the alarming reports concerning the "Titanic"; but second thoughts dispelled this anxiety, and the apparition of the Government broker in the market sufficed to harden the quotations . . .'[22]

By Tuesday morning the awful truth was known and, again in the *FN*'s words, 'members came to the City with the one thought uppermost in their minds, and some time elapsed before transactions actually commenced upon anything like a normal scale'. Over the next few days rumours and counter-rumours swelled about the fates of individual City men. Among those who had booked berths but in the end did not undertake the voyage were Vivian Hugh Smith and Robert Benson's son Guy ('very well groomed, quite the young man in the City' was one verdict as he began his career). At least two members of the Stock Exchange drowned. One was Austin Partner: he had become a member on 1 April and joined the broking firm of Meyers & Robertson two days later; the managers were informed that 'he left a widow and children poorly provided for, and it was unanimously resolved under the very exceptional circumstances to return the entrance fee'. The other was J.H. Loring, a partner in the brokers Rose, van Cutsem & Co. Refusing to jump after the boats had gone, 'he was brave to the end, and his farewell words were an expression of love and devotion to his wife and two children'. The Lord Mayor at once set up a *Titanic* relief fund and early donors included the King (500 guineas), the Queen (250 guineas), Speyers (a showy £1,050), Rothschilds (£525), Barings (£500) and the Bank of England (a sober £262 10s). Lloyd's inevitably bore the business brunt, and it was said that the only prominent underwriter that had declined to accept the *Titanic* was Edward Mountain, justly renowned for his intuition. It was an event that acquired, in the City as elsewhere, an instant momentousness. To Natty Rothschild it was 'one more proof, if it was wanted, how natural forces baffle human ingenuity'; while to Lascelles it was 'Nature's most effective *tour de force* since Sodom and Gomorrah', the ill-fated boat having been 'the last word in ostentatious luxury, and the very embodiment of our insolent claims to have conquered the elements'.[23]

Life, however, went on, and later that month the apprentice broker moved from Bedford Court Mansions to Egerton Gardens in South Kensington. May brought an invitation – hardly to be refused – to dine with Bevan at his home in Upper Grosvenor Street:

His walls are hung with Corots, Raeburns, Hoppners, his wife with strings of pearls – everywhere evidence of excessive wealth. She is a gaunt, slouching woman whom I didn't take to, and who began by asking me if I had found my way all right – as if I had walked from Balham. It was a Dinner-Party of the sort I rarely see, but which I suppose I shall know only too well in middle age. I took a plump, mature sister of Nigel Playfair, the actor, in to dinner . . .

Later that week Lascelles allowed himself 'a day's respite' from what he now called 'Nibelheim': the short-lived romance was over.[24]

CHAPTER TWENTY-SIX

All In

The British government and the Marconi Company began negotiations in 1910 over the construction of a chain of long-distance wireless stations round the Empire. They were difficult negotiations, conducted on the company's behalf by Godfrey Isaacs, Managing Director of the English Marconi Company and brother of Sir Rufus Isaacs, the Attorney-General. At last, on 7 March 1912, the Post Office signified its acceptance of the general terms of Marconi's tender. As the negotiations went on, theoretically in secret, so the shares of English Marconi boomed, from around $\frac{3}{4}$ at the beginning of 1911 to $9\frac{7}{8}$ by 19 April 1912. On that latter date, on which much would turn, dealings were formally begun in London in the shares of the American Marconi Company, seeking to raise its capital from $1\frac{1}{2}$m to $10m. The natural place to float the issue was indeed London, where in the spring of 1912 Marconis of all descriptions, shares in the Spanish and Canadian companies as well as the English, were booming wildly – especially after details of the *Titanic* disaster and ensuing rescue of survivors began to come through, giving striking proof of the value of wireless telegraphy. In these auspicious circumstances American Marconis were introduced on the London Stock Exchange on 19 April at a considerable premium.[1]

The Marconi boom proved short-lived, and within weeks rumours were rife in the City that Liberal ministers, including the Attorney-General, had made use of privileged information to get in on ground-floor terms, sell at the top and thereby make a handsome killing for themselves. On 20 July, in a weekly called the *Outlook*, the intrepid W.R. Lawson came out: 'The Marconi Company has from its birth been a child of darkness. Its finance has been of a most chequered and erratic sort. Its relations with certain Ministers have not always been purely official or political.' Referring to Godfrey Isaacs by name, Lawson went on:

> All the world knows that a similar surname exists among the members
> of the Asquith Cabinet . . . It is also a matter of common knowledge that

the Postmaster-General for the time being bears the honoured name of Samuel. Here we have two financiers of the same nationality pitted against each other, with a third in the background acting perhaps as mutual friend. If expedition and equity could be looked for anywhere, it was surely in such a combination of business and political talent . . .

During the rest of the summer the investigative and rhetorical running, of an increasingly explicit anti-Semitic character, was made by another weekly, the *Eye-Witness*. Its founder and until recently editor was Hilaire Belloc, whose family history had been moulded by ill-advised stockmarket speculation back in the 1870s and who dreamed of an England not only returned to the old faith but expunged of Jewish cosmopolitan finance.[2] By August the phrase 'The Marconi Scandal' was starting to stick, and in October the Commons voted to appoint a select committee of inquiry, which began sitting later that month. Its first few months were concerned mainly with technical matters concerning the contract between government and Marconi, and it was not until early 1913 that the affair returned to the boil.

In the meantime, attention focused on another City-related scandal.[3] In January 1912, Ernest Franklin of Samuel Montagu & Co had suggested to Schuster, one of whose roles was chairing the Financial Committee of the India Office, that this year the Indian government could obtain its silver bullion more cheaply if it did so secretly through them rather than through its usual bullion brokers. In effect this meant bypassing the Bank of England, which usually mediated between the India Office and the brokers; accordingly, between March and September 1912, Samuel Montagu bought £5m of silver secretly for the Indian government and despatched it to India. Montagu's rivals soon discovered what was happening, and in November a Conservative MP drew public attention to the striking fact that the Under-Secretary at the India Office, Edwin Montagu, had no fewer than two brothers, a brother-in-law and a cousin all in the family firm of Samuel Montagu. Montagu defended himself reasonably adequately, while the City's leaders attempted to close ranks. 'Revelstoke called me up on the telephone last night to say that he thought the subject had been pushed far enough, and asked me to check its further development,' the Conservative Chief Whip noted later that month; while soon afterwards Natty Rothschild wrote to Paris that, in the context of 'somewhat strained' relations between the India Council and the Bank, 'I have done my best with Crewe [Secretary of State for India] to bring about a change in this very ridiculous policy', in that, 'great as may be the financial and parliamentary ability of the various members of the House of Samuel Montagu and Company, their intrigue against and their jealousy of the other bullion brokers have not been conducive of much good to anyone but themselves'.[4] Schuster's position was not without its invidiousness, granted that the Union of London was banker to Samuel Montagu & Co, but the person in the harshest spotlight was Sir Stuart Samuel – a partner in Samuel Montagu, Liberal MP for Whitechapel and elder brother of the Postmaster-General. Eventually, in the course of 1913, he was compelled to resign his seat and fight a by-election, which he managed to win with a sharply reduced majority. He also, through the invocation of arcane legislation, had to pay a fine of £25,000. Samuel's cause had not been helped by his firm's founding father, Samuel Montagu himself, who in 1907, four years before his death, had received a peerage from the Liberal government, becoming Lord Swaythling. He marked the historic event by commissioning an enormous painting by Solomon J. Solomon, to be hung on the grand staircase leading from the main lobby of the House of Commons. Entitled 'The Commons petitioning Queen Elizabeth to marry', it depicted (though in Elizabethan dress) various current members of both Houses – among them, with almost laughable prominence, Swaythling himself. It was a remarkable, culminating piece of self-advertisement on the part of the boy from Liverpool who had made his fortune through unremitting attention to 'the quarter pfennig and the half centime' – but, inevitably, was one more piece of provocation to the anti-Semitic 'Radical Right'.

Isaacs, however, remained the number one target, and on 25 March 1913 the Attorney-General gave evidence to the select committee. He admitted that he had bought American Marconis for himself and other members of the government. 'There was absolutely nothing wrong in the transaction,' Natty Rothschild remarked to his cousins that evening, 'but it was a very stupid thing to do.' That in general, though it is hard to be sure, seems to have been the attitude of the City. A few weeks later the *Economist* described the mood in the Stock Exchange:

> It goes without saying that the House bears little love to the Government. Those, however, who blame some ministers complain not that they had a deal in American Marconis, but that they did not admit it in the House of Commons long ago. Rightly or not, the Stock Exchange appears to see little harm in the fact of ministers having a flutter, like the rest of the world, in American Marconis; and there is a feeling that had they frankly said so when the question first arose nobody would have thought a penny the worse of them after the inevitable newspaper storm had

blown itself out. The Stock Exchange critic objects to even a similitude of evasion, and the almost pathetic earnestness with which American Marconis were defended as an 'investment' has enabled the jesters to use that word 'in its Cabinet sense'.[5]

It no doubt helped Stock Exchange spirits that, though Isaacs had shown some business sense, the same could not be said of Lloyd George. From his evidence it was clear that, after an initial profitable deal, he had bought too late, sold too soon, and altogether shown little grasp of how to play the market – even allowing that it was permissible for him to have attempted to do so in the first place. His fumblings were in painful contrast to the cool mastery displayed by Percy Heybourn, the jobber at the centre of the American Marconi market operation. He gave evidence on 9 and 10 April 1913, almost exactly a year after that operation, and proved at least a match for his inquisitors.

He began by describing, albeit with minimal circumstantial detail, how in March 1912 he went over to America with Godfrey Isaacs and agreed to take from him 250,000 American Marconis at $1\frac{1}{4}$, in other words just over par. Then, on 18 April, as it was clear that there was a boom on his hands, he took from Isaacs first another 50,000 shares at $2\frac{1}{8}$ followed later in the day by a further 50,000 at $2\frac{7}{16}$. He then circulated, for the start of business the next morning, a market slip introducing the shares at $3\frac{1}{4}$. At which point in the narrative Leo Amery, a Tory member of the select committee, asked Heybourn how many of the 250,000 shares he had placed among his friends at $1\frac{1}{2}$ before the 19th – that is, *before* the shares were generally available. 'That is a question I am afraid I cannot answer,' replied the jobber. 'That is entirely my own firm's business. It is not anything material to this enquiry.' A long discussion ensued between the select committee and Heybourn's legal representative, the leading Stock Exchange barrister Walter Schwabe, at the end of which the witness agreed to hand in the following day, for private consideration only, a list of persons with whom he had placed shares. Schwabe explained why Heybourn felt himself unable to go any further:

> The reason is this: I understand my client did place a considerable number of shares with members of the Stock Exchange who are in the habit of following him; that is to say if he has some shares of some company to place they have confidence in him and they take some, some take so many and some so many others. In this particular instance one knows that the price was about $1\frac{1}{2}$ when a large number of those shares were placed. If it is stated in public by the witness how many he placed

on that date, he will be conveying to every single one of the persons with whom he dealt what proportion they got of the whole that he had to dispose of, and that he objects very strongly to giving.

Lord Robert Cecil, another Tory hot for certainties, took up the attack:

> (*Cecil*.) You object to the members of the Committee knowing what profits you made? – Yes, I do.
> (*James Falconer, Liberal*.) Before the 19th all the shares which you placed were placed at $1\frac{1}{2}$ or less? – Yes, before the 19th – up to the 18th.
> (*George Faber, a Tory banker*.) Do you mean all the 350,000? – That is the part I object to answer.
> (*Falconer*.) All the shares you placed before the 19th were placed at $1\frac{1}{2}$? – Yes.
> I quite realise that after the 19th there were an enormous number of transactions which it might be exceedingly difficult for anyone to trace, as we have been told over and over again. Are you willing to give us all the assistance you can to enable us to trace the shares which you either placed or sold? – I will give you the names of the people whom I placed them with.
> (*Cecil*.) That is all you will do? – I cannot disclose my clients' business; they might object. If they like to disclose to you they can.
> (*Sir Frederick Banbury, arch-Tory*.) This is a Court of Law; you do not seem to understand that? – I did not know it.
> It is the High Court of Parliament.

The final words were presumably uttered with some majesty, coming as they did from a former stockbroker who probably took a dim view of jobbers anyway.

The next day Amery took up the questioning and Heybourn again gave as good as he got:

> When you came back from America on April the 9th did you then provisionally settle a coming-out price? – No, I did not settle the price until the evening of the 18th.
> When you arranged with your friends that they should have the shares at 30s, did you then give them to understand what the introduction price would be? Did you mention an introduction price or a probable introduction price? – When I arranged to give them what?
> The shares at 30s? – I might have discussed it as somewhere about $1\frac{1}{4}$ to $1\frac{1}{2}$ like that. I did not give any definite price.
> Premium? – No, not premium. All in.
> Then what advantage would it be to them to take shares at $1\frac{1}{2}$ if they were only to go on to the market at $1\frac{1}{2}$? – I am sure I do not know, except

if I introduce shares into the market they always go straightaway.

If you place shares among your friends at a certain price and discuss the price of introduction . . .? – I did not discuss the price of introduction with them.

You did not? – No.

You asked them to take these shares at a certain price and gave them no indication as to what they would fetch in the market? – No, they were quite satisfied to take them.

Heybourn now handed in a list of the people with whom he had placed shares at $1\frac{1}{2}$ up to the 19th. There soon followed some fairly friendly questioning from a Liberal MP, Handel Booth, in which Heybourn was asked whether he could defend all that he had done before the Stock Exchange Committee. 'Yes, I was most careful,' was the jobber's reply. Heybourn also explained to Booth that the Marconi boom of the previous spring had not been an artificial one but had sprung out of technical and business developments in wireless, allied to the impact of the *Titanic* disaster:

It was like a snowball; as the shares rose so it went all over the country. My business was in thousands of small bargains. I should call it a public boom.

And you being a stock-jobber, if you had kept outside it would have meant that you were neglecting your business? – I was not keeping outside. I had been waiting 14 years for it.

You were there to do all the business that was going? – Yes.

That was a rare autobiographical glimpse; Heybourn's working practices were further fleshed out in a sequence of questions from Falconer:

All the shares prior to the 19th which you did distribute were distributed at $1\frac{1}{2}$? – They were put down on the 19th, because that was the first day, but verbal arrangements were made subject to the thing going through. Certain brokers who assist me in my flotations were to have some shares at what I called a low price, for the consideration of supporting my market in the various things. They always follow me.

That is how you do your business? – Yes.

Your business is to have a certain number of brokers all over the country who support you? – Exactly.

In anything which you take up? – Yes.

And, of course, your practice is, when you have anything to deal with, good or bad, to give them a share of it, and they take a share? – Yes.

The amount you can give to them is dependent entirely upon the amount of the demand that your various clients, if I may put it in that way, make upon you? – That is so.

Heybourn by now was playing for stumps, but at the last had to surmount a Tory attempt to provoke him into disclosing whether he had had an understanding with Godfrey Isaacs over the marketing of the 150,000 shares that Isaacs retained out of his original 500,000, the provocation being that it would have been a dangerous tactic on Heybourn's part not to have had such an understanding. 'That is entirely my affair, I think,' Heybourn replied. Cecil tried again:

> But did you, in fact, regard it as a risky transaction? – I am not inclined to say whether it was a risky transaction, or safe, or anything else.
> Surely we are entitled to ask you whether it was a risky transaction? – Not at all.
> You decline to answer that? – Yes.
> You regard that as affecting your private affairs? – I do not think you should ask me that kind of thing.
> May I ask on what ground? – It is waste of time.
> That is rather an impertinent observation.
> (*Banbury.*) I must draw the attention of the Committee to the way the witness is behaving.
> (*The Chairman, Sir Albert Spicer, a Liberal.*) We cannot look at things just as you may look at them, Mr Heybourn.
> (*Cecil.*) It has nothing to do with that. It is not for the witness to tell the Committee it is waste of time.
> (*Heybourn.*) I withdraw that.
> (*J.G. Butcher, a Tory.*) If that is not your ground, what ground have you? – It is my own private affair.
> Do I understand you regard it as a matter of your private affairs, and it would be injurious to you to answer the question I put? – I do not say injurious to me, but I do not wish to.
> (*Amery.*) Does that come within your ruling, Mr Chairman?
> (*Chairman.*) Yes, I think I must rule that does come in.
> (*Amery.*) That any question he does not wish to answer, he need not?
> (*Booth.*) No, that is not the point.
> (*Chairman.*) To disclose any further private details.[6]

The Liberal chairman of the Liberal-dominated committee had got the jobber off the hook, though he probably could have taken care of himself.

'The Marconi inquiry drags on,' Natty Rothschild wrote to Paris after Heybourn had finished his evidence, 'but it has become very tedious and several members of the Committee know nothing about

business and those who do go on asking endless questions which lead
to no result.'[7] In fact, the scandal had a further twist left in it, when at
the end of April a stockbroker called Charles Fenner was hammered in
his absence and a few days later his firm, Montmorency & Co, was
declared bankrupt. From an examination of his books it transpired
that the Master of Elibank, until recently the government Chief Whip,
had in the spring of 1912 purchased 3,000 American Marconis for his
party. In June the select committee published its reports: a majority
one signed by all its Liberal members whitewashing the government;
and a minority one, written by Cecil, damning the actions of the
ministers. Neither Isaacs nor Lloyd George went to the back benches,
as would surely have happened in a later political era; and that
autumn Isaacs became Lord Chief Justice, prompting (at first for private circulation only) Kipling's infamous, fiercely anti-Semitic poem
Gehazi.

Percy Heybourn's personal reckoning was to come. Along with his
partners Alexander Croft and William Bagster Jnr, he was summoned
before the Stock Exchange Committee and, though acquitted of having
made a false market in American Marconis, then accused of a breach
of trust towards the brokers who had sent orders to his firm before the
fateful 19th. Heybourn strongly denied that, in the context of a sharply
rising market by the 19th, he had retained an undue proportion of
shares for himself and failed to supply the brokers with as many as he
had pledged. 'He did not consider that he was in a fiduciary position
with regard to the orders he had received. When he bought the two lots
of 50,000 he did not know what firm orders he had received, and these
orders did not influence him to buy the further amount. At about eight
o'clock on the evening of the 18th they started making out a list of
orders and were surprised at the number received.' And: 'There
appears to be some misapprehension in the minds of the Committee as
to orders. We in no instance asked brokers to apply to us for shares but
in response to brokers who made enquiries of us all we said was "If
you like to send in we will see what we can do".' And again: 'The
position in which we were placed was one of extreme difficulty. It was
not easy to determine what was the best thing to do in all the circumstances. We gave it very careful consideration and decided upon the
course which in our judgement was the right one. I would ask you,
gentlemen, what course we should have adopted than this and what
you would have done under similar circumstances.' And finally: 'We
had every reason to believe that the brokers appreciated and accepted
the course we adopted.'

The Committee voted by nineteen to three against accepting Heybourn's explanation and then eighteen to three that Heybourn, Croft and Bagster, trading as Heybourn & Croft, had brought themselves under rule 16. There followed the inevitable letter from Heybourn with the inevitable phrases – 'profoundest astonishment . . . deepest regret . . . honourable association with the Stock Exchange and the members thereof for the past 18 years . . . never a single word or complaint regarding my honesty, integrity, and fair dealings . . .' – but the resolution was confirmed by fifteen votes to four. Punishment awaited, but first the Committee got Heybourn & Croft to hand in a list of the forty-seven broking firms – including five in which members of the Committee were partners – to whom it had sold American Marconis at $1\frac{1}{2}$. On 10 November 1913 the Committee formally announced that Heybourn, Croft and Bagster had each been suspended for five years, the maximum sentence less than expulsion; but that the brokers who had bought shares at such a spectacularly lower price than that available to the public when dealings formally began on the 19th would not be punished, on the tenuous grounds that the shares offered to them personally were for delivery, while those for their clients were for special settlement and they had no authority to buy for their clients for delivery, especially as those clients could have repudiated the bargains. 'The question immediately arises,' the *Economist* observed in a justifiably sardonic tone, 'whether, had the clients been given the option of buying at $1\frac{1}{2}$ for delivery, or at $3\frac{1}{4}$ for special settlement, they would have been likely to have hesitated a minute in their choice . . .'[8] As for Heybourn, he had brought off his long-nurtured market coup but lost his livelihood: yet another occasion when a Stock Exchange man cursed the existence of politicians.

*

The Marconi Scandal was *the* City story of 1912–13, but life in Capel Court continued to follow its predictably unpredictable rhythm. 'Stock Exchange's First Derby Throws Business In The Shade' was the *FN*'s headline on 6 June 1912, after Walter Raphael's Tagalie had come home by several lengths, heavily backed by the owner's fellow-members. Four months later the House's predictive powers were put to a more significant test. Natty Rothschild on 2 October referred to 'the numerous on dits and canards which have been circulated in the Stock Exchange all day', on the 3rd to how 'in the Stock Exchange as usual endless rumours have been in circulation'. The cause was yet another

Balkan crisis. According to the *Economist*, on Saturday the 5th, members had shown commendable calmness and done much to steady public nerves:

> The House declined to be ruffled. Prices went flat, and the markets, instead of giving way to fear, remained quite cheerful. The papers spoke of panic on the Bourses; the Stock Exchange went in its scores to see an impromptu fountain in Broad street . . . Somebody in the House started the grave report that Servia had ordered 2,000 lbs of powder, but this was not taken seriously. The Stock Exchange never does believe in war until war breaks out, but it takes time by the forelock in a liberal lowering of prices in advance . . . Doubtless the House has earned a sort of surprised respect for refusing to lose its head, and if part of the credit for this comes as the natural result of incurable, traditional optimism, by far the greater share is due to sober common-sense of members as a whole . . .

But the members got it wrong, and within days Turkey was at war with Montenegro, Bulgaria, Greece and Serbia. Prices crashed, though to general surprise there were only three failures. By February 1913 there was still a Balkan cloud hanging over the markets, as business one day ground almost to a halt. 'The brokers moving round the House merely stopped to chat with the jobbers standing idly from 11 o'clock to 4 o'clock,' noted the *Economist*. 'That they "have never seen anything like it before" is the old cry of Stock Exchange men; that they "don't know what things are coming to" is its necessary corollary.' A fastidious jobber called Duncan Scott had weightier matters on his mind. 'I shall be much obliged if you can see your way,' he wrote to the managers the following month, 'to point out officially to Mr Norman Herbert that the towels placed in the members' lavatory are not intended to be used as handkerchiefs. It is with great regret that I should have to bring this disgusting practice to your notice, but do so in the interests of fellow members who use the washing room.' Herbert had been a member since 1879 (twenty-two years before Scott's admission) and the Committee, to whom the letter was passed on, declined to take action. Peace eventually broke out in the Balkans, but 1913 as a whole was not a good year for Stock Exchange business. Even the annual pre-Christmas japes had something forced about them, 'like drinking a sparkling wine without the sparkle' thought the *Economist*. However, 'huge hilarity was caused by a quite novel game introduced into the markets through the agency of the balloons such as are loved by even smaller children. Water was artfully poured into some of these toys, which were then thrown into one of the popular markets always ready for a game. When the inevitable burst came those underneath received unexpected showers, and this sort of thing went on for quite a long time.'[9]

As ever, individual markets went up and down, but in the Kaffir Circus there seems to have been an increasing realisation that the salad days would never return. Few of those jobbers, though, could have put it as cogently as Louis Reyersbach, of Central Mining, did in a letter in May 1912:

> Today you have huge speculation going on in oil; English and Russian industrials; Home Rails, to a smaller extent in Rubber. Canada has come along and is absorbing immense amounts of money; Japan takes all the world will give it; South America is by no means to be considered as out of the running; and even from the United States of America a large number of propositions are constantly put forward, as with all their wealth, the Americans find difficulty in financing themselves. In addition to this you have gilt edged securities yielding fully $\frac{3}{4}$% to 1% more than they did ten or twelve years ago. You have Sweden, Bavaria and other States borrowing at 4%; and the City of Paris issuing a loan at 3% below par, which carries a lottery chance which is always attractive.

There were, in short, a host of competing attractions – a fact that, with physical congestion still often the case as the membership reforms of 1904 only slowly took effect, inevitably led to moments of tension. Shortly after Reyersbach's letter it was suggested to a sub-committee that the Brighton market, one of the less flourishing parts of Home Rails, might move to a more out-of-the-way position. A bunch of leading railway jobbers attended en masse to object: 'If any market moved, it should be the Oil market, which was a very new creation and might not last very long.'[10]

Few would have dared trying to shift the Foreign market, even if it had not been booming; and it was probably to that market that an increasingly disenchanted Tommy Lascelles migrated in the spring of 1913. Early in March he walked home from the City with his cousin Reggie, a partner in Miller & Lascelles, who advised him to leave Ellis & Co and become a jobber. Five days later, though without a firm offer from his cousin, he did so: 'I shook the dust of Ellis's from my feet, with very considerable relief. Bevan is in bed with the flu, which simplified my leave-taking.' Lascelles subsequently added that, 'apart from general dissatisfaction with a broker's life, the immediate cause of my leaving was that Bevan, having encouraged me to put my few clients into Sopa diamonds at about £3$\frac{1}{8}$, sold his own holding at £3$\frac{1}{4}$

and never warned me that they would shortly be worthless'. The next day, to his relief, he did secure a berth at Miller & Lascelles – £100 per annum and the prospect of a partnership – and on 2 April spent his first day on the floor of the Stock Exchange: 'A bewildering place of many noises. The members are incredibly light-hearted and affectionate one towards another. I hope I shall acquire the right manner.' It helped when in October his uncle's horse won the Cambridgeshire at 33–1: '£50 to me, and the devil of a good advertisement among the blades of the Stock Exchange'. Lascelles was lucky to have a like-minded, ironic friend in Conrad Russell, a member since 1911. He enjoyed pointing out Stock Exchange celebrities to the more recent recruit, including Fleischmann shortly before Christmas. Russell duly told the Louis XIV story, and Lascelles added: 'It is his partner, by the way, the melancholy Messel, who has never been known to smile except once when he had the luck to see a child run over by a motor-bus in Threadneedle Street.'[11] A few months later the young jobber went off to South America, in theory to study railways, and never returned to the City.

The Stock Exchange, approaching the end of an era, was still fundamentally overmanned. Norman F. Wells, in a *cri de coeur* of April 1913 to the leading banker Sir Richard Biddulph Martin, encapsulated a wider plight:

> When I called upon you in Hill Street about 18 months ago you said 'Get something to do, and then ask your friends to help you.' I have now been on the Stock Exchange for one year and I have called practically every day at Martins Bank in the hope of getting an order, so far without success. Could you not see your way to give me an order now and then, it would make all the difference to me. I know, of course, that you have any number of brokers, but I should be so grateful if you could possibly give me some business.

Wells's position is unlikely to have improved by October, when Teddy Grenfell of Morgans observed to a New York partner that 'most of the smaller Brokers find it hard to get a square meal and are in a very sad way'.[12]

Still, at least the partners of Helbert Wagg had done their bit for their fellow-brokers – by deciding to leave the Stock Exchange altogether. Their reason was threefold. The firm since the turn of the century had increasingly lost out to Panmure Gordon as 'pet brokers' to Rothschilds, especially in the lucrative area of placing underwriting; its gifted recent recruit from Japhets, Adolph Schwelm, was pushing hard for the firm's business to assume a larger, more financial character; and thirdly, perhaps the decisive factor, the firm had been in the vanguard of unsuccessfully opposing the introduction of a fixed scale of commissions, culminating in March 1912 when Arthur Wagg, a member of the Stock Exchange Committee for some forty years, was unceremoniously turfed out. 'Great City Sensation' announced the *Globe* on 6 December 1912, as the firm's decision became known. A day or two earlier Alfred Wagg had paid a courtesy visit to Rothschilds to tell them what was afoot. The grace note was conspicuous by its absence:

> On arriving at New Court, I asked to see Lord Rothschild privately and he came to see me in a little room at the back of the building. I gave him the letter, the terms of which couldn't have been nicer. He sat down and read it attentively. He then got up saying 'Well, you know your own business best', and walked out of the room. Not one word of good wishes or of regret that the hundred year old intimate connection between the two firms was to cease.[13]

*

For one stockbroker, 1912 was the year of a public prominence that few if any of his peers obtained. A complex background may be baldly summarised.[14] Following the Chinese Revolution of October 1911 – in part a reaction against foreign financial interference and spoliation – Addis of the Hongkong and Shanghai Bank deemed it wise early in 1912 to bring Russia and Japan into the international consortium dealing with Chinese finance, so that the old Four-Power group became the Six-Power group. He also managed to ensure, though with some difficulty, that the Hongkong Bank continued to enjoy the Foreign Office's exclusive support. On 12 March all the members of the international consortium met for dinner at what Addis in his diary called 'Mr Koch's magnificent house' in Belgrave Square, where they were served by 'footmen in kneebreeches & black satin'. Complications inevitably ensued. 'The Chinese loan negotiations are dragging out their weary length,' noted Addis on 21 May. And a fortnight later: 'I late home after an interview at FO. Politics & business are sadly mixed up nowadays.' Eventually, though, it became clear that the Chinese government, under nationalist pressure, would not accept the consortium's undeniably severe terms for a proposed big Reorganisation Loan. This gave Charles Birch Crisp, hitherto mainly involved in Russian and Brazilian finance as well as the motor industry nearer home, his window of opportunity. Willard Straight of Morgans in New York would call him 'a clever little fellow, sharp and weasel-like', but the self-publicising broker and financier was about to become a hero of the Stock Exchange.[15]

On 23 August he called at the FO, announced that he was negotiating a Chinese loan wholly independently of the consortium, mentioned that City institutions supporting him included the London County and Westminster Bank, and was firmly told that he would not receive the support of the British government. Unabashed, Crisp a week later signed terms with the Chinese government to issue a £10m loan. A key figure hovering in the background was Dr Morrison, formerly *The Times*'s celebrated correspondent in Peking, now political adviser to the President of the Republic. Partly motivated by dislike of Sir Carl Meyer, prominent on the London Committee of the Hongkong Bank and in Morrison's considered opinion 'a Hamburg Israelite who bought his baronetcy, and a man to whom no such words as integrity or high standing could be applied', he justified his policy on 8 September to Gwynne of the *Morning Post*:

> The British Government gives exclusive support, to the exclusion of all other banking corporations, to the Hongkong & Shanghai Bank. Naturally the Bank takes every advantage of this privileged position. Resentment is felt by purely British bankers at this monopoly granted to a bank in which German influence is very marked . . .

Two days later Crisp called again at the FO, where he admitted that he was acting in defiance of declared government policy but asserted 'that he knew the public was prepared to take up the loan, and that he did not see how his Majesty's Government could prevent the transaction being carried through'. Addis by the 23rd was in his somewhat belated cups: 'The Blow has fallen . . . Chinese have settled a loan of £10m with Birch Crisp . . . And so the patient work of all these weary months is dashed at a stroke to the ground.'[16]

The next morning, Tuesday the 24th, with the first half (£5m) of the loan about to be issued, a leader in the *FT* anticipated 'a pronounced success' and sympathised with the Chinese government in not accepting the Six-Power terms, which would have led to a dangerous outburst of anti-foreigner feeling in China. The paper also praised Crisp for 'the courage and skill shown in the negotiations'; referred admiringly to him living in a big country house ten miles from Ascot and being 'a good tennis player, sportsman and agriculturalist'; and reckoned that, following his earlier forays into Russian finance and his subsequent 'incursion into the guarded realm of Brazilian "haute finance" ', this 'new and brilliant venture' would 'make another big step forward' for his firm, C.Birch Crisp & Co. That day the great financier successfully completed the underwriting, despite Reuter's reporting the lodging of an informal protest by the British government against the loan, and Addis noted gloomily that evening that 'the papers are full of the Birch Crisp loan and the defeat of the Six Powers consortium'. Dealings began on the Wednesday at a satisfactory $\frac{3}{8}$ premium, but Thursday proved altogether more testing, following the release to the press of telegrams to the effect that the salt tax (on which the loan was secured) was regarded by the British government as already pledged elsewhere. That evening Natty Rothschild, no friend to the stockbroker after his Brazilian incursion, related the outcome:

> Some of the underwriters of the loan after reading the newspapers did not quite like the idea of having been misled by Mr Crisp's plausible language and some of them even went so far as to say they wanted to withdraw, but the astute broker was equal to the occasion and was quite prepared to cancel the underwriting and even went so far as to offer a small premium. Naturally the discontented people then stuck to their bargain. The prospectus is out this evening and subscriptions are to be received by several prominent banks. The general impression is that the public will not write for any very large amount.

The banks backing Crisp did *not* include the London County and Westminster, but he still had behind him Lloyds, the Capital and Counties, and the London and South-Western, as well as the Chartered Bank of India, Australia and China. He also, the *FT* noted on the 27th, was 'supported by nearly every influential newspaper in Great Britain, the Radical organs not excepted'. The *Economist* the next morning, with the lists still open, declared that 'in recent years there has not been a more interesting financial drama than the story of this issue', that 'in any other country but Great Britain (and possibly the United States) such action would have been impossible', and that 'whatever the ultimate result, it stands at present as a unique victory for English finance and the London Stock Exchange'. Advocating free trade in all things, the journal was sure that the firmness of the underwriters on Thursday had been due, at least in part, to the Stock Exchange's 'strong and healthy objection to permanent officials who tell it where and how it must invest its capital'. Crisp would never again know an hour of such glory; and even though it emerged on Monday the 30th that the underwriters had been left with over half the loan, Teddy Grenfell of Morgans was almost certainly right when he informed New York the following week that the episode had made both the FO and the Six-Power consortium look 'foolish', that the loan had confounded all the City's 'wiseacres', and that Crisp had enjoyed much support from the Stock Exchange's smaller firms, which considered that he 'had done a plucky thing in standing up to the big fellows'.[17]

During October the two sides slugged it out. Crisp orchestrated a campaign against the Hongkong Bank, on the grounds of it having four German directors and therefore being pro-German; while Addis took comfort from FO's continuing loyalty in the face of hostile questions in Parliament. 'Charlie has almost "paid blood",' his wife Eba noted on the 18th, while Addis himself wrote five days later to his friend Colonel Mills:

> The press is against us, financial, tory, radical; the last worst of all. We are peppered in the House . . .
> Grey is between the devil and the deep sea or rather he was. His party clamour against the monopoly and wish him to withdraw. If he does, down goes the 6 Power consortium and China is thrown to the Powers to scramble for. Accordingly he has taken his courage in both hands and plumps, along with the other 5 Powers, for the maintenance of the Consortium.

Or in Grey's unsentimental words soon afterwards, to an FO official, 'the Charybdis of indiscriminate borrowing is worse than the Scylla of the groups'.[18] On the 29th the FO published a White Paper of papers and correspondence showing, among other things, that Crisp had misled it over the London County and Westminster's participation in his syndicate; and over the next day or two it became clear that the price of the FO's continuing support for Addis was that he must broaden the British group, so that it was not the preserve solely of the Hongkong Bank, and thus allay criticism from both the City and the wider public.

The emotional temperature rose sharply. On Wednesday the 30th Eba recorded Addis having 'an important interview with Lord Revelstoke', who 'said many kind things'. And on Thursday 31st, 'an awful day of telegrams, meetings, interviews', he saw Koch, who 'had heard of the interview with Lord R. last night and accused Charlie of wanting confidence in his old friend, etc, etc, nearly weeping!' Presumably

Koch took it so amiss because he felt that it should have been *he* who was responsible for the initial approaches. Also on the 31st, Addis wrote formally to Revelstoke suggesting that a revamped British group should comprise the Hongkong and Shanghai (30 per cent), Barings (25 per cent), Rothschilds (25 per cent), the London County and Westminster (10 per cent) and Parr's (10 per cent).[19] The percentages referred to carve-up of the putative business and the emphasis was firmly on old money rather than new.

Crisp's position weakened perceptibly early in November as it became known that he had told the Chinese that, owing to the Balkan crisis, he was unable to find more money – an attempt, in other words, to cancel the second part of the loan. In the other camp Addis was as busy as ever, calling in at the FO on the 4th to say that both Revelstoke and Rothschild agreed in principle to participate in the group, though the latter wanted an explicit assurance about the monopolistic nature of government support for that group. Four days later Crisp played his populist card, a letter from him appearing in *The Times* attacking the alternative of 'a cosmopolitan group, in which Great Britain is in a hopeless minority', and defending himself:

> In acting as I did I sought to show that the London money market is not the extinct volcano that some of our friends abroad try to make out. I have endeavoured to keep the door open in China to British capital and British enterprise. True, I have sorely displeased the Secretary of State for Foreign Affairs, but the verdict is with my fellow-countrymen, on whose judgment I am content to rely.

By this stage, though, his real aim was to inveigle himself into the London group. It was a prospect that appalled the FO, which told Addis on the 13th that it would 'never countenance' Crisp's admission and that he 'must submit the names of any financial houses he intended to admit' – 'to which of course he agreed', the memo added. With Grey trying to stay aloof of what was liable to become a contentious question, another FO memo, a week later, took the reassuring line that 'it is natural that both Rothschilds and Barings should make it a sine quâ non of their participation, as they owe Mr Crisp a standing grudge for having cut into their business in Brazil and Russia respectively', and that 'their opposition is probably the best safeguard against his admission to the group'. As it happened, Addis went to see Alfred Rothschild at New Court on the 18th and discovered that Rothschilds had decided against participating in the group. He then consulted with Revelstoke and Koch, and between them they decided that the natural replacement was Schröders. Revelstoke meanwhile insisted that the condition of Barings' participation was the exclusion of Crisp. What could a poor man do? First, Crisp tried to secure an interview with Grey, who declined. An FO memo of about the 21st had a pleasing tartness:

> Neither the Chinese nor Mr Crisp would take our advice. The Chinese now want more money and Mr Crisp cannot find it. It is for them not for us to find a way out of the difficulty but Mr Addis has indicated in conversation that the proper course for the Chinese to take would be to buy out Mr Crisp. That is probably a sound opinion from the point of view of the financier.

That indeed is what Morrison in Peking now tried to arrange. But before that could be resolved, Crisp had one other card to play. Addis's diary entry for 26 November was to the point: 'The notorious Crisp called on me. Wants his group to be incorporated in British group. Listened & told him I would give him an answer after seeing my friends.' The main friend was Revelstoke, currently staying in Cassel's flat in Paris, and that evening Farrer wrote to him with characteristic incisiveness:

> Crisp has seen Addis who unfortunately parleyed with him and eventually sent him away saying he would reply definitely in a few days! Koch assures me Addis's reply will be a definite and absolute refusal. Meantime Crisp's story was, not that he had made an offer to China which had been accepted, but that China had made him a proposal which he was considering and which he, Crisp, would accept when he had obtained the money; that unless Addis took him and his Banks in he, Crisp, should proceed to get together people here and on the continent for the £5,000,000 loan and, when his money was assured, accept the Chinese proposal ... These repeated overtures of Crisp's must mean that he does not see his way very clearly to find £5,000,000 before the end of the year; I certainly cannot imagine he would find any money on the continent ...

That too, after clearly some serious thought, was the view of Addis, who the next day told Crisp's secretary that he declined to entertain Crisp's proposal for incorporation into the London group.[20]

Someone else was hoping for a party invitation. Holden on the 28th saw Koch and, as he put it in his working diary, 'expressed my mind about the Hongkong & Shanghai Bank', adding that 'they had no right to take up the position of monopolists'. The next day Samuel Murray, one of Holden's joint general managers, called on J.D. Gregory at the

Foreign Office. Gregory's subsequent memo paraphrased Murray's exposition of his Chief's views:

> Sir Edward Holden thoroughly appreciated the policy of HMG in regard to the loan question and their action with regard to the Crisp transaction. He had held aloof from it and was anxious not to come in any way into collision with the Foreign Office. He now however wished it to be known that he felt *most strongly* that the Hongkong & Shanghai Bank should invite the London City and Midland Bank to form part of the British group. The London City and Midland Bank was after Lloyds probably the most extensive and important Bank in this country . . . He said that he could not lay enough stress on the urgent desire of his Bank to be taken in. He also said that the Bank had been approached with a view to independent business with China, but that Sir Edward Holden was determined to act only in accordance with the wishes of the Foreign Office. At the same time if the Hongkong & Shanghai Bank had made up its mind not to approach him, he would feel that he was not being treated fairly . . .

Accordingly, Murray asked Gregory to secure the Midland's place in the British group; he promised to consult Grey; but the Foreign Secretary predictably stuck to the economical-with-the-truth line that the decision whom to include and whom to exclude rested solely with the Hongkong Bank. Holden tried one final gambit. On 7 December, Lord Rotherham, a director of the Midland, wrote to Grey to press the bank's case; Grey allowed himself five days to reply and then played an aggravatingly dead bat, advising the Midland to apply direct to the Hongkong Bank.[21] Plainly, there were limits to what even a gentlemanly capitalist could achieve.

By the 11th – perhaps explaining Grey's delay – the British line-up was complete: Hongkong and Shanghai (33 per cent), Barings (25 per cent), London County and Westminster (14 per cent), Parr's (14 per cent) and Schröders (14 per cent). The next day Revelstoke wrote to Cassel ceding him a 20 per cent proportion of Barings' interest, which in effect meant that Cassel had a 5 per cent participation in the British group as a whole. Crisp and Holden were definitively excluded, but for the former there was the consolation two days before Christmas of the second half of his loan being cancelled and the Chinese government agreeing to buy him out for £150,000 – from his point of view, a tolerable end to the story. The early months of 1913 were dominated, from Addis's vantage point, by interminable, multilateral negotiations over the proposed £25m Reorganisation Loan to China. 'French make some objecting, Loan abandoned in the meantime!' Eba noted early in

February. 'It is only Charlie's great Faith and Courage that keep him from breaking down under the continuous long & hard work, and nervous strain. I marvel at him.' There was an awkward moment in March when the American group pulled out, as a result of moral scruples on the part of the newly elected Woodrow Wilson; but it did not prove a fatal blow, invidious though it was for Morgan Grenfell in London. Koch as ever busied himself and in his way was as indispensable as Addis. His was the key influence, against the background of changing political and monetary conditions, in reducing the coupon from $5\frac{1}{2}$ per cent to 5 per cent. Almost a third of the loan was to be issued in London, and on 15 May, with D-Day imminent, Addis, Revelstoke, Farrer, Goschen (of the London County and Westminster), Whalley (Parr's), Baron Schröder, Tiarks and Koch met at the Hongkong Bank and agreed that participations be offered to Morgan Grenfell, the Union of London and Smiths Bank, and the London City and Midland. Holden remained unmollified, for later that day Koch 'called and offered us £500,000 of the Chinese Loan, which however I refused'. On the 20th Addis was a happy man: 'A long queue stretching down Lombard St waiting for prospectuses of the new Chinese reorganization loan. It will be a huge success.' And Eba too the next day: 'Loan a huge success; applied for about 7 times over. Charlie receives congratulations . . .'[22]

Even so, the events of the past year had made it as clear to Addis as to the Foreign Office that the days of preferential support on the part of the British government were numbered. An exchange of correspondence to that effect took place between Grey and Addis later in 1913, ending with Grey's expression of appreciation for 'the good-will and the public spirit that made you respond so promptly to my appeal'. That was on 2 October, and less than three weeks later Addis received a note from Asquith offering him a knighthood. 'A tardy recognition of his great services for China and British interests there during the last few years' was the view of Meyer. The Hongkong and Shanghai had had a wonderful run for its money – some seventeen years – as the British government's chosen arm in Chinese finance, leaving Addis with an undimmed belief in the moral as well as economic efficacy of 'responsible lending'.[23]

*

The flood of foreign issues continued unabated during 1912 and 1913. 'There are continually new issues in our market,' Natty Rothschild told his Paris cousins in May 1912. 'Today Hambro bring out a 4%

Danish Loan which @ 97 will no doubt be fully subscribed as there is a curious belief in Scandinavian stocks which perhaps after all their wealth does not justify.' Similarly in December 1913: 'Here our Colonies are insatiable, one prospectus is followed by another, they all want money and are anxious to borrow and these continual borrowings are not good for Stock Exchange prices.' No wonder that autumn that Lord Milner, by now a director of the London Joint Stock Bank and becoming something of a City figure, delivered a solemn lecture on 'A Scramble for Capital'. Sterling issues in these years were running at about £200m a year (the equivalent of about £9bn today), and despite periodic signs of market indigestion there were handsome profits for London's issuers and underwriters.[24]

Natty Rothschild had no doubt who was responsible for the continuing bias abroad. 'The Chancellor of the Exchequer may argue as he likes,' he told his cousins in July 1912, 'but the fact remains, the investor in English securities is frightened and there is every reason that he should be so . . .' Natty had in mind the increasingly high-profile land question, and when a few days later, at the annual banquet to bankers and merchants, Governor Cole uttered what Natty called some 'home truths' that very much represented the City's attitude, Lloyd George apparently left in 'a violent rage'. On the 18th, Lloyd George tried to justify himself in the Commons, but according to Natty this only led to the Government broker being 'busy all day buying Consols for the Sinking Fund and trying to steady the market'. And, with Consols just over 74: 'Mr Lloyd George always accuses the City of trying to lower the credit of the country for party purposes. He quite forgets that if they did this they would be cutting their noses to spite their faces and he cannot or will not realize that they are only too anxious for better prices, less legislation and greater security.' In a word, declared the City's acknowledged leader for the past quarter of a century and more, 'he is no Financier, has no sound financial advisers & is not fitted for the high office he holds'.[25]

The most important foreign issue that Rothschilds itself did in these years was an £11m 5 per cent loan for Brazil in 1913. By mid-April the issue was firmly on the cards, and New Court soon received the usual supplicant letters for underwriting – among them, on the 25th, a rapidly scribbled note to 'Dear Mr Leopold' from 'Charlie C. Clarke', writing from the Stock Exchange. It read *in toto*: 'Will you please if you can let me underwrite 25,000 Brazil. I went over to see you but unfortunately you were away but Lord Rothschild kindly put me on a list. I am only writing this as a reminder don't trouble to answer. I am sorry Lorenzo did not go, it looks as if he ought to have won.' Monday the 28th was underwriting day, a task that Natty told his cousins was executed 'not without considerable efforts'. Half the underwriting (£5.4m) went to Panmure Gordon, who in turn would have distributed it widely, while £800,000 went to Sebags, £600,000 to Greenwells, £400,000 to Pember & Boyle, £100,000 to Cazenove & Akroyds and £100,000 also to Helbert Wagg, even though that firm was no longer on the Stock Exchange. Clarke got only £10,000.[26] If the underwriting really was done with some difficulty, why did he receive significantly less than he had asked for? Presumably the answer is that *not* to have given less would have looked like a sign of weakness, leading to possible market rumours and so on. Rothschilds had, after all, been in the game a long time.

After almost a week of Balkan-induced delay, the prospectus was published on the afternoon of Monday the 5th, with terms more or less as expected. That evening's market report prepared for the *FT* made interesting reading:

> There were some dealings in the loan today, presumably by underwriters, and the scrip was finally called 1 discount. Such development before the lists are open is very unusual. No doubt, recent experiences of new issues have made some underwriters ultra-cautious and determined to assure themselves of a portion of their commission by advance selling. While it is necessary to place these dealings on record, it should be added that they were not extensive in relation to the size of the loan, and need not be taken as necessarily indicating the response that will be made by the public . . .

According to Natty however, writing at about the same time to his cousins, the selling had been led by a clutch of what he called 'foreign brokers', in other words brokers dealing largely with other financial centres and who 'have been large bear sellers for Foreign Account'. 'I need hardly tell you,' he went on, 'that they have not underwritten the loan, but they evidently think that by offering the loan they will prevent the public from subscribing and that ultimately they may be able to buy some cheap stock from the underwriters. I hope that they will be disappointed in their speculation.' But by Wednesday, with the lists closing at four o'clock, the price was at a new low of $1\frac{3}{8}$ discount and the expectation in the market was that about 95 per cent would go to the underwriters.[27]

On Thursday morning the *FT* devoted a leader to the subject:

Naturally this ante-allotment discount has been the subject of much comment in market circles. While no doubt the size of the loan made underwriting a necessity, this has been a case where underwriting instead of being a supporting influence, has militated against the success of the issue from the point of view of its absorption by the general public. In some quarters the view was expressed that the results attending the issue of this loan will kill underwriting of the general character that has been practised in the City of late.

The issue had indeed flopped, it emerging during the day that 94 per cent had been left with the underwriters. Natty, writing to Paris that evening, took a very different view from the *FT*:

Underwriting certainly has its disadvantages but on this occasion it proved very advantageous. We placed the whole Loan in a few hours and although the public abstained from writing as the Loan was quoted at a discount, during the last 3 days they have been purchasing for investment in large amounts and in small amounts. The jobbers say that from $2\frac{1}{2}$ to 3 Millions £ Stock have changed hands and one of the jobbers sent word to us that during the last hour of the day he had bought £250/M [i.e. £250,000] and sold it all in small amounts . . .[28]

In the past Natty's argument had always been that the underwriting system artificially propped up weak houses with inadequate resources. Now, he saw the matter rather differently.

Brazil was a familiar borrower on the London capital market, Rumania almost unknown. Later in 1913, on 28 August from his Belgian estate, Koch wrote to Revelstoke that, when at Carlsbad recently, he had run into an old friend of his, now finance minister in Rumania. 'He is a "gentleman",' Koch vouched, 'and is absolutely truthful and "dependable".' The broker scented possibilities:

Roumania will want a loan, mainly for railway construction purposes, and I told him that I thought that now, and if he will make his first appeal to the British public on liberal terms, there was a good chance of opening up the London market to Roumanian bonds. The King, it appears, is very wishful of this. I wonder if it would suit you that I should endeavour to follow this up, and try to direct this business towards your house. Roumanian finances have been well managed, and their budgets have been showing good surpluses. My opinion, for whatever it may be worth, is that there would be a good public in England for Roumanian bonds, whereas I think there will be practically none for Bulgarian, Servian, Greek or even Turkish securities, for a long time. I make bold to say that my idea would be a 5% issued to the public at a maximum of 98.

Revelstoke was away in Paris (staying at the Hôtel Bristol), but Farrer enclosed Koch's letter and remarked, 'I am quite ignorant as to the finances of Roumania, and do not even know whether they have any considerable amount of external debt quoted on our market.' Koch, who had the instincts of a terrier, wrote again on the evening of Saturday the 30th, this time direct to Farrer: 'Why I ask you to let me know your opinion soon is that the Minister will be finishing his cure soon: he will then go to Paris, and I would like to get, if possible, at closer quarters with him about this Loan before he gets to Paris.' Revelstoke returned to London that weekend and at once wrote a typically stuffy letter to Koch:

> We are grateful, as always, for the thoughtfulness for which you so constantly bring interesting business to our notice, but I think that, on the whole, we should hardly be inclined to take upon ourselves the responsibility for the issue of loans in this connection. It is difficult of course to speak with any certainty of our willingness or the reverse to take an active part in the finances of a country with the budgets and credits of which I am but little familiar, but as you ask for an immediate reply, I feel bound to say that our present attitude is that we have so much business in prospect that we should hardly like you to rely upon us as far as any London issue in this connection is concerned.

Koch in turn replied on the evening of the 2nd, asking Revelstoke to give the matter a little more thought, hoping that his 'insistence' would be excused, and declaring that 'what there is left of "flair" in me tells me that it is a business worth trying for'. It was not to be, at least not at 8 Bishopsgate. By early October, arrangements for a Rumanian loan were being made by Disconto Gesellschaft, which sought a London end to the deal. The Germans had both Barings and Schröders in mind, but though a brother of Baron Bruno was a director of the Disconto they gave first option to the senior house. Revelstoke, however, reiterated to the Disconto's London representative that Barings 'felt little disposed to assume any such fresh responsibilities in connection with a London issue for one of the Balkan States'; and as a result, it was Schröders who in November brought out the London end of a £2m Rumanian loan.[29] Barings in the Edwardian period resisted ossifying tendencies far more effectively than Rothschilds, but it was yet one more sign that the old duopoly belonged to the past.

*

Little of all this engaged the thoughts of Montagu Norman.[30] 'We much regret,' Brown Shipley wrote just before Christmas 1912 to

Brown Brothers in New York, 'to have to inform you that Mr Norman's health has lately been giving us considerable anxiety. He has worked at the Office consistently and steadily since his return last April . . . The last few days he has been suffering a great deal, and it has now been decided that he must take a trip of some weeks' duration in order to give his health a chance of recovery.' It had been decided therefore to send Norman, with another partner as a companion for him, on a swing through Trinidad and the West Indies, thence up to the West Coast of the USA, and eventually reaching Vancouver in March, 'when we think it is quite possible that some important business with regard to a new loan for the City will have to be decided'. It was only because there was this eventual working purpose involved, the letter added, that 'we were able to persuade Mr Norman to take such a long absence from this Office'. February found Norman in Panama, where he met a sympathetic bank manager who recommended the treatment of certain Swiss physicians, among them Carl Jung. With this hope in mind, Norman soon afterwards came straight back home from Costa Rica, not continuing with the proposed trip to Vancouver. His firm remained admirably sympathetic. 'Mr Norman, we much regret to say, is still very poorly,' it wrote to New York on 4 April, 'and is shortly leaving for Switzerland to see if he cannot obtain some opinion which will at any rate get at the bottom of the trouble from which he is suffering, and put him in the right line to recovery.' Norman had three sessions with Jung (two on the 15th, one on the 21st), but they failed to do the trick, and by May he was in Lausanne seeing a new doctor. This was a specialist in nervous diseases and he was sufficiently effective that Norman was back – if not necessarily back in harness – at Founders' Court by September. A snatch of Brown Shipley correspondence two months later catches him negotiating with the general manager of the Stockholm Handelsbank a possible loan for the City of Stockholm that in the event went to Hambros. What, though, had really happened in April between him and Jung, an encounter of two twentieth-century icons? It seems that Jung tested Norman's blood and spinal fluid and, though the results were negative, reckoned that Norman's general condition was such that he was unlikely to survive the summer. Norman had, Jung believed, the symptoms of syphilis, causing general paralysis of the insane. If so, it was not a judgement he openly shared with his patient. Norman himself at the time paraphrased Jung's stated opinion:

Perfectly sound throughout, including blood serum etc., but head entirely exhausted and therefore unresponsive. Consequently unable to undergo his or any other cure. After a complete rest, lasting a 'lot of months', may come back to him and if sufficiently recovered, shall go thro' his treatment . . . Meanwhile lead quiet, easy, selfish life: no work at all: plenty of rest and amusement: travelling (and tropics): bed: massage and medicine useless: grub and air good . . . Cannot predict time needed for recovery nor ultimate result.

'That verdict was the finishing touch,' he wrote later, 'having been going slowly downhill ever since January; I collapsed and nursed a raging head . . .' And that is all we know – apart from some lines of doggerel written, when exactly is not clear, in Norman's diary for 1913. They suggest that even in his depths he kept the sense of humour that over the years would be a saving grace, the humour of a man never known to laugh aloud:

The Züricher get-behind-the-other-fellow-before-you-push System

So here, at last, is Küsnacht, hidden beside the lake
Here dwells the farfamed conjurer. Here gladly for his sake
I've come from Panama & brought my head, my back & ache
    all the way.

x x x

Now freundlich Dr Brunner, [illegible]
Then put a spigot in his spine & test his blood & head.
But don't suppose that I believe the half of what he said.
    No, not much.

x x x

Indeed I grieve Herr Norman that you have here a pain.
But someday, when its quite gone by, come back to see me again
And then I'll try & set you up, with all our might and praise [?]
    Not till then!

x x x

Meanwhile, Herr Norman, hurry home & stay there till you're well.
Just live some other fellow's Life. Enjoy the warmth of hell
Try dull teetotal-gluttony. And there perhaps you'll quell
    All your pains![31]

*

Norman retained his position as a director of the Bank of England, but had nothing to do with the gold reserves question that so dominated pre-war banking debate. In February 1913, at the by now well-established quarterly meeting between the Bank and the leading joint-stock bankers, Governor Cole took the chair for the last time and decided to move the thorny issue into a new phase. He pointed out that whereas at the end of 1892 the total liabilities (in deposit and current accounts) of the clearers was £256m to the Bank's £42m, twenty years later it was £616m to £67m. He argued that the government had done its bit: 'It has of recent years increased its balances at the Bank of England and thereby does assist in maintaining Gold against those deposits.' He also argued that the Bank itself was in the clear: 'You will find by its published figures that its average proportion [i.e. of cash to liabilities] which in 1892 was 44.2 per cent increased in 1902 to 46.4 per cent and in 1912 to 47.8 per cent. The Bank of England has to earn a dividend for its shareholders like any other bank, and if it keeps a proportion of cash approximately towards 50 per cent I, personally, do not think it can be asked to do more.' Cole then looked the joint-stock men straight in the eye: 'The question I want to put to the Clearing Bankers is – Has their reserve of cash to liabilities increased during late years in the same ratio as the figures I have given you for the Bank of England?'[32] The implication was clearly – and correctly – that they had not. Faced by this challenge, the decision was taken soon afterwards to set up a new Clearing Bankers' Gold Reserves Committee, this time to be chaired by Lord St Aldwyn, the former Hicks Beach. Its formation was publicly revealed early in April, just before the end of Cole's governorship, and the first meeting set for 7 May.

Holden, to general surprise, spoke first. 'Bankers should not allow themselves to be subject to the criticism, from practically all over the world, that they did not assist the Bank of England in holding a sufficient amount of gold. He thought they held a large amount, but the public did not know it.' He therefore put forward his familiar suggestion involving compulsory publication of balance sheets showing the amount of gold held. J. Herbert Tritton of Barclays was unwilling to go so far. Rather, 'the first step was to ascertain as far as possible the amount of gold held by the bankers'; and he reckoned that, since 1900, the banks had increased their gold holdings from £25m to £50m. Tritton's resolution, that confidential returns be requested for concerning gold holdings on 28 May next, was unanimously adopted. Having lost the first battle but by no means the war, Holden continued to make the running in the City at large. Referring to him as 'undoubtedly a pushing ambitious man, also very clever', and to 'the City and Midland Bank' as 'a powerful and well organised business', Natty Rothschild went on in his letter to his cousins on 27 May:

He is a strong Radical and avowed open enemy both of the Bank of England and of the India Council. At the present moment he declines to take any bills in the London market . . . Sir Edward Holden is a man of considerable influence, and if he does not always believe what he says himself, he has the power to make others believe, and during the last few days he has been continually telling stock brokers and bill brokers alike that he views the money situation in the near future with considerable alarm. He thinks the gold reserve at the Bank of England too small . . .[33]

The next day the secret census was taken, and on 11 June the CBGRC was informed that the quantity of gold held in British banks was just under £45m, compared with just under £38m at the Bank of England. St Aldwyn asked if £45m was a satisfactory figure, to which both Schuster and Holden 'dissented'. Holden still wanted compulsory publication and Schuster as usual disagreed. St Aldwyn for his part wanted the recently compiled figures communicated to the Bank, to see whether it 'had any observations to make concerning them'. Tritton demurred, saying that they should first report to the clearing banks themselves the result of the inquiry – for 'he had found a good deal of suspicion in the minds of the banking fraternity that something might be sprung upon them'. The discussion was adjourned for a week, whereupon Holden said that although he himself still wanted legislation to ensure compulsory publication, he accepted that most round the table did not; and so he called on his fellow-bankers to decide upon a policy and adopt it voluntarily. It was eventually decided to send a deputation, including Schuster and Holden, to discuss the return with the Bank's new Governor, Walter Cunliffe.[34]

There was, meanwhile, another aspect to the whole question. Holden's animosity towards the India Office, referred to by Natty Rothschild, derived in part from his recent campaign to establish a gold currency in India, thereby he believed reducing the drain of gold from London. Holden's intervention was part of a complex background, also involving the Montagu silver scandal, that led to the establishment in 1913 of a royal commission, chaired by Austen Chamberlain, on Indian finance and currency.[35] Alfred Cole, explicitly representing the Bank, gave evidence on 27 June, and Chamberlain asked him whether he regarded the existing system – highly developed since the turn of the century, by which the India Office lent out India's substantial balances to the London money market – as 'open to objection in principle'. Cole replied in the affirmative, stating that it weakened the Bank's control over the money market. 'That control is the only buttress for the gold reserve of England?' Chamberlain asked. 'Quite correct,' the former Governor confirmed. Nevertheless, as Cole conceded later in his evidence, the lending out of India's balances was, *in a sense*, of benefit to the London market, in that it lowered the rates of discount – even if it did not help the Bank of England in terms of maintaining the gold reserve.

It was a tension that the young, super-confident John Maynard Keynes, a member of the Commission and author of *Indian Currency and Finance* (published a fortnight earlier), explored:

> When you expressed the rather paradoxical opinion that the Indian cash balances in London were disadvantageous, were you speaking narrowly from the point of view of the Bank of England, or from the point of view of the whole of the London market? – I was speaking from the point of view of the Bank of England, and I hope I made that clear . . .
>
> I can understand that if London were to cease to be an international money market the life of the directors of the Bank of England would be a less anxious one; and you are merely stating this as a particular application of that? – I am asked here to give the view of the Bank of England, and I am giving you the view of the Bank of England.
>
> And the view of the Bank of England is that any increase in the extent to which London is an international money market makes their time a more anxious one? – Any increase in the volume of transactions which pass through London for which the London money market is responsible, makes the maintenance of an adequate gold reserve here all the more important.
>
> But you would not deprecate the extension of England's liabilities in that way, would you? You would not wish London to be less an international money market, would you? – No; I want to see England maintained as the international money market, and that it should have the position it holds today.
>
> Then you would be sorry rather than glad if India was to give up holding its balances here? – From the point of view of the Bank of England I would rather they were what I call kept within more moderate limits; that is all.
>
> From the point of view of the position of the money market, you would be sorry? – I should not be sorry; it is merely a question of size.[36]

It was the first of Keynes's run-ins against the Old Lady, though on the larger question they were agreed, as against Holden, that India should retain a gold-exchange rather than a gold standard as such.

It was also Cole who, at Cunliffe's request, spoke for the Bank when they met the CBGRC deputation. Having been given the figures, he observed that 'he was disappointed at the return of gold, which he expected would have been larger'. Otherwise, the meeting seems to have been pretty inconclusive. The CBGRC itself met again on 30 July, with Tritton in decidedly gloomy mood:

> The question had been before them for years, it had been debated at the Chamber of Commerce, at the Institute of Bankers, by the whole banking community; it was in the hands of the Press, and the Press were waiting to see what the Committee were going to do. The Committee were in this position, they had asked for a return of the gold held, which they had received; it was a profound secret at present, but how long it would continue a secret none could say . . .

Further discussion did not get very far, and finally it was agreed to communicate the results only to the clearing banks, not to the wider world. It was with some justice that the *Bankers' Magazine*, in its September editorial, took the line that the whole question was being shrouded in needless secrecy and that 'the public may perhaps be fairly excused in imagining either that the problem of higher gold reserves is incapable of solution or that action is chronically crippled by disagreement among the eminent banking experts'.[37]

Apparently unmoved, the Committee did not meet again until 12 November. Schuster now made his old suggestion of an independent secondary reserve, but kept physically at the Bank of England. In response Holden laid into Schuster before deliberately upping the ante:

> Sir Felix Schuster had not told the Committee if the total of gold, under his scheme, would be published, and the conditions under which each banker could withdraw it . . . Further, Sir Felix had not told the Committee what would be the effect of any withdrawal of such gold, and how it would reflect on the whole and not any particular bank . . . If the Committee could not come to any agreement in the matter, he personally would most strongly recommend his directors to publish their gold: he felt that if one bank published its gold, that bank would have a tremendous advantage over the others.

Having fired his big gun, Holden stayed silent for the rest of the meeting. St Aldwyn tried to mediate. 'It would be a pity,' he observed, 'if, the meeting having expressed its opinion, there was any independent action such as Sir Edward had outlined'; and 'he could not see why some arrangement should not be made whereby the banks would keep a certain amount of gold ready to assist the Bank of England if required'. It was then unanimously passed that the Committee should be supplied twice a year with a return of gold coin and bullion held by the joint-stock banks. Just before the meeting broke up, Tritton (a supporter of Schuster) 'insisted' that 'the City of London must be spared the ignominy of going to the Bank of France for gold', a lame end to another largely fruitless session.[38]

The situation was not helped by the fact that the Governor at this time was Cunliffe, one of the City's more rebarbative figures.[39] 'A little of Mr Cunliffe's society fills me up for the year,' Teddy Grenfell had remarked to Jack Morgan a few years earlier, and the opinion seems to have been general. Even so, that rude and arrogant, not unaccomplished operator was only part – however vivid, even extreme a part – of a larger duality already located at the heart of the City for arguably a quarter of a century or more. In a crucial if ill-documented area, key testimony comes from a former Governor, W.M. Campbell, discussing privately in 1917 whether the Bank should at last allow professional, joint-stock bankers to become Bank directors:

> My experience & knowledge of the Bankers generally is, that their views are extremely narrow, & each considers only their immediate needs of their own Bank as measured by their Profit & Loss Account.
>
> The training of the Directors of the Bank of England leads them to take a more comprehensive view, & the needs of Commerce in General, rather than the paying of Dividends, is the dominating Factor in their Policy.
>
> On the other hand I am strongly convinced that it would be of great value if some scheme could be devised, whereby the responsibility of national Banking could be shared with the Directors of our great Joint Stock Banks.
>
> This was aimed at some years ago, in Cole's Governorship, & meetings took place – & they were I know appreciated – but unfortunately they have been wrecked by the present Governor [Cunliffe] – and the bitter feeling which now exists, not with all but with most, will prevent any foregathering for some time.
>
> There is some how an innate antagonism against the Bank of England, very largely due to the 'Superior' manners of some past Governors.[40]

Campbell's account applied partly to events after the outbreak of war, but by no means wholly. On the eve of 1914 itself, Tritton and Schuster were genuinely seeking to bridge the gap, but found themselves outflanked by Holden on the one hand, Cunliffe on the other. It was not a happy prospect.

*

1913 had one final monetary twist to offer. 'The great silver speculation has failed and the Indian Specie Bank is bankrupt. What a tragedy!' So wrote the newly knighted Addis in his diary on Friday, 29 November. He also recorded the outcome, of which to a gratifying extent he was at the centre:

1 December. Great excitement over Specie Bank failure. Sharpe & Wilkins [a firm of bullion brokers] called on me & detailed their affairs. It appears they are carrying £3,000,000 silver at 27^d. Failure would spread disaster in India & China. Wired to HO proposing form syndicate take over the silver.

2 December. Bullion Brokers & Fraser & Whitehead of Chartered met in my office. We agreed to form syndicate of 6 to purchase all the silver at 26$\frac{1}{2}$. Lord Rothschild, whom I saw, declined to join. So far we are 5 and Sir Edward Holden of City & Midland Bank is suggested as a 6th.

3 December. Saw the Governor of Bank of England, Cunliffe, and expound our plan. He was sympathetic . . . Later saw Holden who wished to make his being appointed one of the managers a condition of joining. We can't have that.

4 December. Silver syndicate again met my office . . . The situation is saved.

Relief all round – and, shortly before Christmas, John R. Villiers, a partner in the bullion brokers Mocatta & Goldsmid and resident of 49 Hans Place, SW, wrote in suitable terms to his senior partner, on holiday in Pau. After thanking Edgar Mocatta and his wife for the 'charming presents' they had given Villiers's boys, and giving his seasonal good wishes, he went on:

> The recent crisis . . . in the Bullion Market, though a terrible time to have gone through, has left us with much to be thankful for and I look forward with great confidence to an ever increasing business to M & G. Never did any market so stand shoulder to shoulder, as we all did through that anxious week, and the unity in which we all worked for the one object was very uplifting and helped one to lose sight of one's individual anxiety.
>
> As it is, I think we shall have had a decidedly good year; and with your generous extra division of the profits, we ought all to be able to furnish our drawing-rooms!! in spite of having two motor cars!!!

If the bullion market had survived, courtesy of the eastern banks and the Bank of England, so too had family capitalism. Looking ahead to the new year and beyond, Villiers went on to evoke a world – cosy, yet not wholly bereft of competitive edge – that would remain familiar in the City for almost the rest of the century:

> I feel I cannot close this letter without alluding to and once more thanking you for allowing Arthur to come in as a clerk . . . It naturally will be an anxious time to me as it must be to any Father who has his son working under him, but I think you know me well enough to know that

I would not have suggested such a step if I thought he was likely to be a failure, and if he is a failure I should be the last person to wish to keep him there. I have the interests of the firm and the work in the office far too much at heart for that. On the other hand I know he will be given a fair chance and altho it must *entirely* depend on his own capabilities, there might be an opening for him and I am grateful to you for giving him the *chance* of proving himself worthy of it.[41]

CHAPTER TWENTY-SEVEN

Random Harvest

The jostling, the looking over the shoulder at the pecking order remained as obsessive as ever. 'Kleinworts seem to have taken the bonds & issued them at very little profit to themselves in order to appear as an issuing house, and no doubt they have repented at leisure,' Teddy Grenfell responded on New Year's Day 1914 to an American inquiry about Cuban Ports. These bonds, he also mentioned, 'were offered to us some years ago, and, though the concession seemed quite good, we knew that there had been considerable graft over the getting of it, and we, therefore, turned the business down even though it was brought to us seemingly complete'. Natty Rothschild, as usual, was worrying about Brazil, a country in increasing political and economic turmoil since the large loan of the previous spring. 'A good deal remains to be done in order to place Brazilian credit on that very firm footing, which alone will allow the country to be prosperous and to improve,' he wrote to Paris on 7 January, against the long-term background of difficult preliminary negotiations for a large new federal loan. 'There are great economies to be made and probably great changes of administration to be carried through.' At a less rarified level the stock market trod water, Williamson reporting it to Lima on the 17th as being 'in a deplorable condition', adding that 'the last good issue that was made of gilt-edged security was left on the hands of the underwriters almost entirely, and is now being offered by them at a discount'. Patrick Shaw-Stewart, the golden boy of Barings since his arrival there from Oxford, was probably glad to get away. Gaspard Farrer explained on the 21st to an American correspondent why the young man was being sent for six months to New York and Boston:

We have found him not only exceedingly intelligent, as you may suppose, but very modest. He is a charming companion out of office, indeed one of the reasons we are sending him away – but this entirely between ourselves – is in the hopes of distracting him from the social and fashionable life here where he has become extraordinarily popular. He has in consequence been sitting up night after night till four o'clock in the morning dancing and otherwise amusing himself, which is not a good beginning for a day's work at No. 8.

Shaw-Stewart was presumably bright enough to guess the reason, though a year earlier, on being made a director of Barings, he had missed a trick by not taking a partner's advice and using the name 'P. Stewart' to sign documents, a tactical error he appreciated after the first 500 dividend warrants.[1]

On Friday the 23rd, as usual at the Cannon Street Hotel, Sir Edward Holden addressed his shareholders. Referring to the increasing size of the German war chest in the Julius Tower at Spandau, stressing London's 'great liabilities' and the Bank of England's 'small gold reserves', arguing that the 'Central Bank system' that had come into operation in 1844 was ripe for overhaul, regretting that English banks did not publish gold holdings – it was all familiar, until he dropped his public bombshell:

> As far as their own bank was concerned, he was authorized by the directors to say that they regarded this subject as of such great importance that unless some such arrangement were concluded during the next 12 months, they would publish in the balance-sheet for December next the amount of gold held by their bank.
> If ever a Royal Commission were needed, it was needed today for the purpose of thoroughly investigating the gold question in this country.

Holden had taken his campaign to its logical conclusion. Why? 'It is by no means clear,' *The Times* commented in a leader on his speech, 'precisely what is to be gained from increasing the holdings of gold in the vaults of the joint-stock banks, independently of the Bank of England, unless it is simply to assert their independence.' Few in the City's inner circle would have disagreed with that analysis. Natty Rothschild, only indirectly threatened, referred to Holden's 'very ridiculous ideas'; while Walter Cunliffe, as Governor of the Bank, at once wrote to Lloyd George asking if he could 'spare me a few minutes' to discuss Holden's pronouncements, which he reported as 'creating a good deal of discussion in the City'.[2] Mainly no doubt in order to take advice, but perhaps partly due to his good relations with the Midland's Chairman, for the time being Lloyd George put him off.

Over the next fortnight, as markets suddenly and unexpectedly improved, the old order complacently divided up the spoils. Vivian Smith's letter of 2 February to Teddy Grenfell (staying at the Palace

Hotel, St Moritz) encapsulated much. Of a Buenos Aires loan that Barings was negotiating for: 'I told them that we would, of course, do exactly what they liked regarding the matter. Gaspard was extremely nice about it . . . They would be quite willing, in view of the attitude we had taken up, to treat it as if it were Government business and give us a quarter and issue with them.' Of a prospective Budapest loan: 'I am going to see Koch about it tomorrow. It looks, at first blush, as if there might be something in it for us.' And of a Montreal loan shortly to be issued by Lazards: 'There should be a nice turn on this.' There was still no assured place at the table for Arthur Grenfell. Three days later he wrote to Grey from the *Lusitania*, on his way to New York:

> I seem to have been looking through the wrong end of the telescope. The part that has worried me most has been the anxieties I have caused to all those most precious to me. If only the anxiety had been put on those who have made so much out of me. I shouldn't mind but they have been more or less free of anxiety thinking I should wriggle out somehow, whereas my friends & you more than anyone have I know had sleepless nights in consequence of my rash folly. I *do* wish money had no value. Life would be so much more interesting – when you have it, you don't know it, & when you haven't you do. But I must try & build up a bank account for my family & come a bit more out of dreamland.

Grenfell was in a bad way. After a serious riding accident in 1912 he had been away from the office for a long time, and on his return those close to him were aware that his judgement, never his strongest suit, had been impaired. It was a particularly uncomfortable feeling for his younger brother Rivy, who for the past few years had been working for Arthur but never seems to have had a clear grasp of the Canadian Agency's tangled activities. How happy by comparison was Sir Charles Addis. While Arthur Grenfell scribbled on deck, Eba noted in their shared diary: 'Tom reading "Pendennis" to Father of an evening. He does not tire, and it is very fascinating. Charlie hears it with fresh delight and it rests him. For he is much over-tired.'[3]

Addis was not present – but Banbury, Holden, Cole and Crisp were – at a big City meeting on Monday the 9th 'to assure the Government of the support of the commercial community in any measure that might be necessary to give effect to the recommendations of the Admiralty for ensuring the supremacy of the Navy and the protection of the mercantile marine on the high seas'. A wordy motion, but the main purpose of the meeting was completed in twenty-two minutes. 'As practical business men,' *The Times* reported, 'those present had met together for a settled purpose, and were prepared to carry it through in a businesslike way. There was no need for oratory and persuasive arguments.' They knew it made sense, and were willing to give up a little of their valuable time to demonstrate so, even if there were a few vacant places owing to settling day on the Stock Exchange.[4]

The next three weeks were dominated by gold reserves. On 10 February, in explicit response to Holden's most recent pronouncement, Schuster circulated a memorandum to the Clearing Bankers' Gold Reserves Committee. At last the time was ripe, he claimed, to implement the Goschen proposals of 1891 and strengthen the central reserve. He therefore formally proposed the establishment of a secondary gold reserve at the Bank of England, comprising an amount equivalent to 2 per cent of each bank's liabilities on current and deposit accounts. This reserve would total about £16m 'and would only be used in consultation with the Gold Committee of Bankers'. Stressing the urgency of the situation – 'in case of an outbreak of war foreign nations would have the power, and would use it ruthlessly, of inflicting serious financial disturbance by demanding gold for the sterling assets with which they are provided' – he insisted that this back-up reserve should be in the physical custody of the Old Lady, not the individual banks. For if 'we each of us say we will maintain su.ficient gold reserves of our own, then we assume a responsibility to the community which is not properly ours, and we relieve the Bank of England from the responsibility which is theirs.'[5]

St Aldwyn's committee of quarrelsome bankers would eventually consider Schuster's proposal along with the others, but in the meantime Lloyd George had to prepare himself for Cunliffe's impending visit. At the end of the month Sir John Bradbury sent him the Treasury view. It argued that for a reserve to be useful 'above all it should be subject to a single control' and expressed hostility to Holden's proposal for a royal commission on the subject. Bradbury listed three main objections:

(1) The abstruse character of the problem and the fact that it has long been the playground of every species of faddist and crank.
(2) The danger of such a Commission becoming a mere cockpit for the jealousy between the Bank of England and the Joint Stock Banks which is really at the bottom of the whole agitation.
(3) The fact that the Commission would have to be very largely composed of representatives of the Banking Community who would no doubt set

themselves to transfer as large a part as possible of the working expenses of their business to the Exchequer.

Cunliffe at last saw Lloyd George on 3 March and likewise deprecated such a commission.[6] The sources do not tell us what Holden's friend said in reply, but he would have known that the Bank and the Treasury made a formidable coalition.

In the City at large the euphoria of early February did not last long. 'We scarcely expect the public to make any large application,' Brown Shipley forewarned its American partners on 9 March about the firm's imminent issue of City of Vancouver Local Improvement Bonds. 'The Markets are at the present moment very depressed in every direction, mainly in consequence of the International financial position (Brazil, Mexico and Paris) and to the uneasy feeling in connection with the Home Rule question.' Ireland now dominated politics and would continue to do so until July; predictably, the City adopted a strident pose as honorary Ulsterman. But at least there was no need to worry about Germany. Having recently been entertaining that country's ambassador at Tring, Natty Rothschild reported to Paris on the 16th that 'he said most decidedly that as far as he could see and as far as he knew there was no reason for fear of war and no complications ahead . . .'[7]

That comfort notwithstanding, the general tone was still poor – 'jobbers and brokers alike stand in the Stock Exchange pondering over the result of the boat-race and discussing the political situation,' Natty told his cousins at the end of March – when on 2 April the Clearing Bankers' Gold Reserves Committee met for the first time since November. St Aldwyn began by announcing Holden's resignation from the Committee consequent upon his decision to give the gold figure in his balance sheet in January 1915. It was unanimously resolved that Holden be requested to withdraw his resignation and St Aldwyn undertook to see him. That trial of strength won, Holden gained another victory as Tritton detached himself from Schuster's proposals: 'He did not believe any banker would give up, in the slightest respect, control over his own gold. For that reason, they were driven to the multiple reserves of the individual banks . . . He regretted having to differ from Sir Felix . . .' The rest of the discussion turned on the attitude of the Bank of England, and St Aldwyn agreed to communicate the general wish 'that the Court might be represented at a meeting of the Committee' called to consider the rival proposals.[8] The Bank, in other words, was being given the chance to shape the debate, perhaps decisively.

'We opened the subscription list jointly with Messrs Schröder today for the Austrian loan with a much greater success than I had expected,' Natty Rothschild told Paris on 6 April. The £16.5m Treasury note issue for the imperial Austrian government was the last major sovereign loan of the year and marked the conclusive arrival of Baron Bruno's firm in *haute finance*. Brazil was less satisfactory. Natty had been trying since March to avoid issuing a new Brazilian loan – 'as the last loan was a considerable discount', he explained, probably needlessly, to his cousins – while at the same time attempting unsuccessfully to impose, in concert with Paris banks, a fairly drastic economy plan on the Brazilian government. 'We believe our friends to be still floundering,' Farrer at the end of April surmised to Shaw-Stewart, 'and quite unable or unwilling to face the position and deal with it.' Natty soon had another source of anxiety, being told 'in more or less strict confidence' on arrival in the City on 11 May that Arthur Grenfell had 'an enormous account' open in various Canadian and American securities. 'I was much astonished,' he went on. 'Mr Arthur Grenfell has failed before, but that brokers should have been found to buy three millions sterling Transatlantic securities for this young and speculative gentleman beats my comprehension.'[9]

Grenfell's fraught affairs remained hush-hush for the time being, as did the bankers' deliberations on gold reserves. Meeting again on the 14th, with Holden back in the fold, St Aldwyn reported that Cunliffe had declined their request that a Bank representative attend the Committee's meetings. Significantly, 'he understood that the Governor was personally not unfavourable to the request' – and perhaps, as a forceful character with a penchant for strong-arm tactics, Cunliffe relished a scrap with Holden. Either way, it seems he could not carry enough of his directors with him: the merchants, with their innate conservatism, preferred to wait on events. St Aldwyn having made his report, the discussion moved decisively in Holden's favour – that is, towards an agreement that bankers should keep an agreed proportion of their liabilities in gold. Holden wanted 6 per cent, but the Committee as a whole preferred 5 per cent. The meeting ended with Holden agreeing 'to formulate a scheme in detail, in collaboration with Mr Tritton and Sir Felix Schuster'.[10]

Arthur Grenfell's open account had been settled on 12 May, several major City houses intervening privately so as to avoid a drastic, unregulated liquidation that would have severely shaken Stock Exchange confidence, and it was also announced that Grenfell was no longer a partner of Chaplin, Milne, Grenfell & Co.[11] The private

agony was intense, the odd flashes of optimism endearingly characteristic if one was not a creditor. On the 30th he wrote to Grey from
Roehampton House:

> I have refrained from meeting you at the ship for several reasons which
> I am sure you will appreciate . . . I have made a real mess of things & am
> in a bad hole. I don't know how angry you will be with me, & how much
> I shall have disappointed you, but in either case I feel that I must have a
> long talk with you, as I have had no one with whom I could really discuss
> the whole situation. Very exaggerated accounts of my dealings have been
> going round but times have been so bad & so many accounts have had to
> be liquidated that it is small wonder that they should all have been put
> down to me & that I should be made a general scapegoat . . . I have had
> to cut a big loss in Trunks & let go all my Lake Superiors & face a big
> loss there too, thº both concerns are doing better than any one expected
> considering the times. With these big losses we have found it impossible
> to meet the repayment of the deposits. The case against us therefore looks
> very bad. You will hear stories about my having gambled wildly but I
> think you know these are not true . . .

Grenfell then further justified himself: why for the best of reasons he
had got too deep into Lake Superiors, the shares of the Lake Superior
Corporation, a large metallurgical and chemical concern that he had
helped to reconstruct after a financial crisis in 1910; and why, against
Grey's advice, he had got involved in the affairs of the Grand Trunk
Railway, not 'as a Stock Exchange speculation' but 'from a wish to
build up the railway & help to develop a Canadian sentiment in its
favor'. He went on:

> The great mistake I made has been having two such big things in hand
> at the same time & I am the first to admit a great error of judgement but
> I do feel hurt at the way some even of my closest friends have misunder-
> stood my motives. I was & am a fool, I could easily have retired in
> comfort & luxury, but some fatal impulse has driven me on & on – & I
> stuck too long to my guns, in the vain hope that we should have been able
> to float off the oil Cº & that I should have been able to regain my
> position. At this moment I have practically lost everything. I should look
> forward with confidence even now, if I didn't feel so frightfully respons-
> ible for the losses I have inflicted on others & the trials & anxieties I have
> heaped upon those I love best. But desperate as my position may appear,
> every sort of mistake & muddle has been made in my office & I have been
> working till late hours getting things straightened out. Ponsonby &
> Samborne have retired so Rivy & I have had to work double shifts, but I
> think I see my way clear now to a reorganisation of Canadian Agency,

Golden Years

which would mean that in time all our deposits & loans should be repaid in full, if I can raise about £200,000. Of this I have I think promises of nearly £100,000 – but the City is dead against me. I am told behind it all has been the Morgan Vivian Eddy Grenfell influence. Vivian has I believe never forgiven me for not buying his piece of land & I think there has been jealousy at my short lived success. I don't know anything for certain but I have very good reasons for my suspicions . . . Except for Hilda's pluck & the kindness I have received from certain friends I should I think have thrown up the sponge but I am determined now to see it out & given time & a little assistance I may get on my feet again . . . I failed lamentably to surround myself with the right men . . .

I believe you will get me through. I have been counting the minutes till your arrival. We managed to let our London house & so are living here, but as we have had to give notice to all the servants I don't quite know what we are to do later on.[12]

Grenfell was not the only one looking for a helping hand. Holden's diary for 4 June contains a short, meaningful entry: '*Chaplin, Milne, Grenfell & Co.* I saw Lord Nunburnholme, Mr Ernest Chaplin and Mr Robertson Lawson with regard to a loan of £300,000 to the above firm. I wrote them a letter after my Board the next day, regretting that we could not see our way to grant the advance.' On Saturday the 6th the stoppage was announced of Chaplin Milne, followed later by the Canadian Agency. 'For a long time their paper has been hardly saleable,' commented Smith St Aubyn's working diary, '& must have been considerably reduced during the last six months. It was not now unexpected and the market is not greatly troubled.' So too in Capel Court, where Natty noted on the Monday that 'although the newspapers indulge in considerable lamentations . . . the Stock Exchange considers that so far as they are concerned it is a matter of past history'. Arthur Grenfell himself had unwisely given an unconvincingly self-justifying interview to *The Times*. It 'may be inaccurate', his cousin Teddy wrote to Grey also on the Monday, 'but I cannot tell you what a bad effect it has had on people's minds in the best City quarters & it is destroying all the sympathy left for poor Arthur . . .'[13]

Holden on the 4th had conducted another interview:

Mr Manville and Mr Walker called to see me with reference to the supply of manser rifles to Servia and Turkey. They were very anxious to get into this market, and Servia were now prepared to place an order with their BSA Company for £350,000 worth of rifles, delivery to extend over a period of 4 years . . . The rifles were to be delivered by instalments of £50,000 and I was of opinion they were justified in taking the order . . .

592

Later in June, on the 22nd, the London Chamber of Commerce hosted a visit from a party of 120 members of the Association of Merchants and Manufacturers in Berlin. A morning session discussing Anglo-German litigation and direct telephonic communication with Germany was followed by lunch at the Cannon Street Hotel, with Schuster and Holden among the notables present. Expressions of goodwill abounded in the inevitable speeches and Sir Algernon Firth, President of the Association of Chambers of Commerce, 'urged that the question of Anglo-German relations was not one for politicians but for the commercial men of the two countries'.[14]

Neither Serbia nor Germany was on Vivian Smith's mind the following Monday, the 29th. 'My dear Charley,' he wrote to the Hon Charles Hanbury-Tracy at Woodcote House, Woodcote:

> I think you cannot do better than buy some Interborough Rapid Transit Co First Mortgage 5% Bonds. I think they are about 99 New York. They will pay you 5% & might easily have a fair rise, as they are a first mortgage on practically all the underground railways in New York.
>
> Many thanks for the offer about Le Touquet, but don't do anything until you hear from me again. I enjoyed my Ascot with you immensely & so did the rest of my family. Please give my love to Celandine & tell her how much I enjoyed myself.

Natty Rothschild had more on his mind that Monday. Earlier in the month he had finally reached an agreement with the French and German groups over the terms for an unavoidable £20m Brazilian loan. According to Teddy Grenfell, who had attended some of the meetings, Natty had 'made strenuous efforts to get better terms for Brazil than were acceptable to other Bankers'. Now, however, the Brazilian government was unable to make up its mind whether to accept the terms, including as they did the hypothecation of the customs duties for the service of all the country's loans, as well as weekly remittances to London; and Natty informed his cousins that the issue of a loan would have to be deferred until the autumn at the earliest. He added, almost as an after-thought:

> Unfortunately we can never be without appalling news and yesterday was no exception: the fate of the late Archduke Franz Ferdinand and of his wife is an awful tragedy. It is a sad example both of Servian brutality, the hatred of the Greek church for those of the Catholic Faith and last but not least of the morals and doctrines of the anarchical party.

Morals were one thing, markets another, and the *FT* breathed reassurance. 'The tragic death of the heir to the Austrian throne and his wife was taken calmly by the Foreign market,' it noted before moving on to other matters.[15]

In early July Natty continued to mull fruitlessly over the Brazilian situation ('they are children in the matter of finance and have an exaggerated view of their own credit'), to castigate Lloyd George ('an utterly reckless demagogue'), and to hope that a civil war could be avoided in Ireland without the betrayal of Ulster. 'It is useless to conceal from oneself that the times are anxious,' an anxiety that on the 6th included the possible consequences of Sarajevo: 'Will the Austrian Monarchy and people remain quiet? or may a war be precipitated, the consequences of which no one can foresee?' At least, he reflected, markets were good, better than they had been for most of the year, and 'all the new issues which were at a discount are now at a premium'. The City as whole went about its normal business. 'Canadian Loans in New York' and 'Railway Interim Dividends' on Monday the 6th, 'North Borneo Progress' and 'BET Capital Reduction' on Tuesday the 7th, 'The Half-Year's Foreign Trade' and 'English Cotton and American Thread' on Wednesday the 8th – the *FT*'s leader columns accurately reflected the prevailing blinkers. For those paid to peek their heads over the parapet, Natty's view on the 14th that 'there is a considerable amount of anxiety in some circles about Austro-Servian relations, but . . . the chief source of anxiety here is always Ulster', would have found general consent. Lockwood's London Letter on Saturday the 18th, headed 'Foreign Liquidation and Politics Check Markets Temporarily', was as cheery as ever: 'There has certainly been no definite happening in the week which gives ground for alarm. The friction between Austria and Servia is of long-standing, and there is no more reason to suppose that peace is threatened more seriously at this time than at any other . . .'[16]

That afternoon the City was at play. The Surrey Walking Club's Brighton-and-back race was won, predictably, by E.F. Broad. In cricket the London County and Westminster dismissed Private Banks for 96 and then knocked up 213 for 9, Bank of England II went down to Dulwich by 3 wickets and 23 runs, and Lloyd's Register II scored 222 for 7 against Canadian Pacific's abject 49. In golf the Shirley Park Links in East Croydon were opened by the Lord Mayor, Sir Vansittart Bowater, who drove the first ball, before C.B. Macfarlane, a well-known City man, created an amateur record with a round of 76. And in athletics, the staffs of the London Joint Stock Bank, National

Provincial Bank and Union of London and Smiths held their annual meeting at the Three Banks sports ground at Beckenham. The National Provincial's athletes fared best, including providing the winning pair for 'Tilting at the bucket', but W. Paulton of the Union won the costume race. Schuster was supposed to present the prizes, but was unable to attend because of illness. Several hundred spectators were present and 'after the presentation of prizes a concert was given on the lawn'.[17]

The mood on Monday morning was altogether darker. 'Everything seems to be going wrong everywhere at present, but I hope the sun will shine again one day,' Teddy Grenfell wrote to New York; and in the Foreign market 'a heavy tone' prevailed, the *FT* reported, 'owing to the weakness of the Continental Bourses, where fears were entertained regarding Austrian-Servian relations'. The next day it was still unclear how Vienna would respond to the assassination, let alone what would be the outcome of the Buckingham Palace conference that was beginning on Ulster, and markets continued 'in a nervous and depressed condition'. Farrer was just back from a long stay in America, and he wrote to Kidder Peabody in Boston: 'I find everyone here in very good spirits and many of them soon to disperse for their holidays. Business unfortunately at a low ebb and political affairs both at home and in the Near East in too disturbed a state to make anyone even wish for greater activity.' There was no change on Wednesday the 22nd, 'A Dismal Tone' being the *FT*'s markets headline. Natty Rothschild, however, was inclined to a cautious optimism: 'Nothing definite is known about an Austrian Ultimatum, but I rather fancy the well founded belief in influential quarters that unless Russia backed up Servia the latter will eat humble pie and that the inclination in Russia is to remain quiet, circumstances there not favouring a forward movement.'[18] Even the man of all City men supposed to be on the inside track could only whistle in the wind.

Wednesday the 22nd also saw the usual round of company meetings. Southern Alberta Land Co shareholders were addressed by Arthur Grenfell, who had been striving in vain to reconstruct the Canadian Agency. On this testing occasion he showed, according to Grey's account, 'nerve and ability'; and having come to the meeting 'prepared to stamp on him,' they ended 'by voting unanimously that he should be re-elected President of the Company'. Schuster, at the Union of London meeting, was under less pressure and struck a bullish note on the diplomatic outlook: 'In the south-east of Europe the great Powers seem as determined as ever that peace between them shall be preserved, and we may trust that such troubles as still disturb those unhappy regions will soon be equitably adjusted.' Back in harness, Schuster faced a busy day, going at two o'clock to the Bankers' Clearing House for a Gold Reserves Committee meeting. With St Aldwyn and six others present, he, Holden and Tritton laid their joint scheme on the table. The banks were to hold 5 per cent of their liabilities in gold; aggregate gold returns were to be publicly communicated twice a year; any bank wishing to publish its holding of gold in its balance sheet was to be at liberty to do so; and the Bank Charter Act of 1844 was to be amended to give greater flexibility to the Bank of England in terms of the emergency issuing of notes. After Holden had explained and justified the scheme – essentially his – in detail, Schuster observed that there had been sacrifices all round in order to achieve unanimity. Tritton then made a short speech that said much: 'He had had a strong aversion to any legislative requirements being mooted; but after the action of the Bank of England in refusing to participate in the discussion and formulation of a scheme, he had concluded that the line of least resistance was to . . . leave nothing to the discretion or goodwill of the Bank of England . . .' The Committee was given a week to consider the scheme.[19] The joint-stock bankers were at last – too late – getting it together.

*

The machine whirred on. 'At certain points where the mass of humanity is more than usually congested – for example, at Liverpool Street Station between 8.30 a.m. and 10 a.m. or on London Bridge about 6 a.m. – the spectacle is really startling, alike in the magnitude of the aggregate, and in the hurried, serious, preoccupied aspect of the human units who compose it.' So Ellis Powell in 1910 introduced his readers to *The Mechanism of the City*, a Darwinist treatise in which the author claimed that 'the life of the City generates in those who live it an intellectual alertness, a rapidity of apprehension, an up-to-dateness which is quite a unique psychological phenomenon'. The census taken in 1911 showed that on one day in April between seven in the morning and seven in the evening, just over a million people and almost 100,000 vehicles (the majority horse-drawn) entered the City; while in terms of those who worked full-time, the 1911 total was 364,000 (compared with 301,000 twenty years earlier), of whom only 20,000 were residents. One of those hurried and preoccupied commuting souls was Ronald Colman. The son of a not particularly well-off silk importer, he became in his teens a clerk for the British Steamship Company, working his way up to book-keeper and then junior accountant, earning 57s a week by the summer of 1914.[20] Quite as much as Arthur Grenfell that July, he needed something to happen.

The forces of conservatism remained formidable. The tone was set at the top. 'In the past the choice of new Directors has been very narrow,' W. Duoro Hoare, a Bank of England director since 1898, would note in 1917. 'We all come more or less from one clique in the City: our Fathers and Grandfathers have probably been connected in the past.' In 1914 itself the Deputy-Governor was R.L. Newman, known in the Bank as 'the port-wine man', a reference to his firm's merchanting speciality. Underneath Hoare, Newman and the rest of the Court was a stultifying, deliberately overmanned world. The *Financier* in 1910 described the Stock Transfer Office:

> In each 'pulpit' sit two stern-looking gentlemen, looking uncommonly like schoolmasters watching over a large class. And, in point of fact, that is exactly what they are, for their only business seems to be that the staff are not playing cards, or 'noughts and crosses', or 'blind man's buff', instead of checking and entering the transfers in the books. Time must hang very heavily on their hands during the long hours between ten and four! But at 3.55 principals and clerks are alike very busy, for then begin hasty preparations for departure. Here is the program: 3.55, Coat-brushing; 3.57, hat-brushing; 3.59, putting on gloves; 4, hats on, and – exeunt omnes.

Lloyd's too was still struggling to move into the new century. By 1913 the method of signing policies had become scandalously inefficient and haphazard; but when the sensible suggestion was made that the Captains' Room be changed from a restaurant to a bespoke space for policy-signing, a populist campaign led by John Povah, a sea captain who had turned himself into a leading figure in the overdue market, compelled the Committee to back down in June 1914. A similarly retrogressive spirit affected the Stock Exchange. In July 1914 the leading Westralian jobber Herbert S. Stoneham issued a circular to fellow-members forcefully criticising the institution for its anachronistic methods. 'It disregards the fact,' he wrote in relation to the ban on advertising, 'that the mass of the population has not the honour of any broker's acquaintance, that the total number of shareholders in the country does not exceed 500,000, and that the permanent welfare of the Stock Exchange must depend upon a constant increase of this number.' And: 'This is the only country in the world where the Stock

Exchange clings to the antiquated system of registered shares, and by its neglect of bearer shares for home securities, capable of being bought in small units for cash, refuses to the mass of the population the facility to offer its support to investment in Imperial or joint-stock enterprises.'[21]

Yet neither on Lloyd's nor the Stock Exchange, nor indeed the City as a whole, was there likely to be the infusion of a more dynamic approach as long as the dominant unit remained the small or smallish family-run firm. Costs were low, business usually adequately plentiful, the way of life pleasant and generally undemanding – what incentive was there to turn a club into a meritocracy?

The City was, in short, still a very personal world full of 'people' businesses. Connection remained paramount. 'With regard to your son,' Andrew Devitt, senior partner of the leading commodity brokers Lewis and Peat, wrote in 1914 to the father of a recent recruit, 'I think most people in Mincing Lane would heartily congratulate your good fortune in getting him such a chance of training as he is getting in our business. It is only the lucky ones who are able without special interest to get such an opening . . .' It was not an approach that commended itself to Addis, who in 1909 decided the time had come to launch a systematic campaign to recruit university graduates. His bank's annual dinner provided a platform:

> I confess, for my part, I have no patience with those laudators of times past, of the so-called *practical system* of mercantile education, which consists in snatching a lad from school at a tender age, and plunging him during the most impressionable years of his life – between 15 and 20 – in the mechanized routine of an office. Can you imagine anything more deadening to the mind and spirit of a future captain of industry? I say these old rule-of-thumb methods will no longer suffice. Men will be compelled to recognise that commerce is becoming, has become, a science in which none can hope to excel but he who has mastered its laws.

Despite the Hongkong and Shanghai being a joint-stock bank, not a private, family-owned concern, Addis's campaign failed. There was no dispelling the anti-graduate prejudice of London managers and heads of department, who failed to grasp the connection between reading Greats and operating in foreign exchange. Similar assumptions obtained at the Bank of England, which before 1914 moved tentatively and ineffectually towards the recruitment of university graduates. Elsewhere, the experience of Sir Archibald Williamson was illuminating. 'I am now in communication with the Appointments Boards of both Oxford and Cambridge,' he wrote in May 1912 to his brother in Valparaiso. 'We propose to take one young man from each . . . We will try to select men who have good appearance and good address in addition to the other necessary qualifications. It is of course difficult to foresee whether such men will become good business men . . .' In the event he gave lunch, separately, to two candidates from Oxford only, and wrote at the start of July to that university's Appointments Committee: 'I have decided to give the preference to Mr Covington in connection with our South American business. I think that Mr Humphrey has equal, if not greater, ability, but perhaps Mr Covington's manner is the better of the two.'[22] The unsuccessful candidate came from All Souls, where learning went to a higher premium than in the City of London.

Crucially, however, the lifeblood of foreign talent – the tradition of Rothschild and Hambro, of Peabody and Kleinwort, of Cassel and Japhet – showed no sign of drying up. Chester Beatty, for example, was the son of a New York banker, made his initial fortune in North American mining (including an involvement in the Venture Corporation's notorious acquisition of Stratton's Independence), and in 1911 set up in the City at No. 1 London Wall Buildings, on the floor above Herbert Hoover's suite. A year later Ernst Friedlander, who came from a German banking family and was the first Chairman of the Johannesburg Stock Exchange, migrated from South Africa to England and joined Julius Singer's recently established stockbroking firm. Max Bonn's family background was German-Jewish banking, and in 1906 he was described by Farrer as 'the live man in the business' at Stern Bros. Soon afterwards, with a cousin, he established his own firm of Bonn & Co, based at $62\frac{1}{2}$ Old Broad Street. It did a high-quality, very international banking business, and members of Bonn's carefully selected team included Rudolf Hohenemser, a German, and Robert Bonzon, a Frenchman. Bonn himself, who had become a naturalised Englishman, would be remembered by a partner for 'his subtlety, his imagination, his resource, his astonishing memory', as well as his 'sad, brown, monkey's face and a toothbrush moustache'.[23]

How did the City, grown increasingly jingoistic, even xenophobic over the past quarter of a century, view the continuing stream of newcomers from abroad? ' "Another half-commissioned officer in the 64th Highlanders," said a grim old member of the Committee, when an evidently Semitic applicant for membership presented himself with a name that had been distinguished in the charge of the clansmen at Prestonpans.' Hartley Withers, in his 1910 guide to the Stock

Golden Years

Exchange, then explained the allusion: 'This jibe riddled in one sentence the readiness of a certain class of foreign immigrant to deal for half the usual commissions, their introduction of the sixty-fourth of a pound as a fraction in Stock Exchange business, whereas the thirty-second had hitherto been the smallest division known, and their passion for disguising their origin.' Withers, sanest of City commentators and the nearest to Bagehot's heir, went on: 'English members sometimes growl at the manner in which their brethren of alien extraction cut the terms on which business is done, but it is probable that the Stock Exchange, like many other English industries, has learnt a great deal from foreign influence, and has been saved by it from the "take it or leave it" attitude which is one of the vices of our national character, except when we are spurred by the example of a keener and more hardworking race.' One of those alien brethren was a jobber called George Merzbach, a member of the House since 1904. In the words of his partner Conrad Russell, son of Lord Arthur Russell: 'His person is not handsome, his birthplace Frankfort a/m. His religion unreformed Jew. He is the best and kindest man in the world.'[24] Not all the locals, aristocrats by neither birth nor nature, were as liberal-minded.

Despite New York, despite Paris, despite Berlin – each of them on the rise – London in 1914 was still the leading international financial and commercial centre.[25] As the world's only free gold market, it offered a unique attraction to overseas depositors; it was the centre of international banking; bills of exchange drawn on London financed most of the world's trade; its capital market raised almost half the world's total exported capital; it remained the main market for insurance, many commodities, and such specialist activities as the chartering of ships. The City was, in short, as much as ever the indispensable place. Only one thing could spoil the party.

*

Thursday, 23 July was reasonably steady in the markets, but the next day the City was hit by a double blow: the failure of the Buckingham Palace conference and the news that Austria had presented an ultimatum.[26] 'It is to be hoped that Servia will give every satisfaction,' Natty Rothschild wrote to Paris. Teddy Grenfell described this Friday as 'one of the most depressing days in the Markets here, Berlin and Paris that I can remember'; the Smith St Aubyn journal noted 'pessimism everywhere', with 'Stock Exchange very flat' and 'Bourses very nearly in panic'. Amazingly, one intrepid financier was still willing to press

600

ahead with a putative £10m loan to China. 'If Crisp is willing to tie himself up in engagements of such a character at a time like this he is welcome to the business so far as we are concerned,' Farrer wrote to Cecil Baring. Lockwoods on Saturday morning did its usual uplift job – 'it is probable that the difficulties between Austria and Servia have been exaggerated' – but the Stock Exchange proceeded to have its worst day of price falls since 1870 and the discount market, according to Smith St Aubyn, 'stopped working'. Farrer by chance was in the City, unusually for him on a Saturday, and (he would recall) 'learned that some of the foreign bill brokers were offering large lines of the finest bank acceptances at $3\frac{1}{8}$ without finding buyers; obviously some one had taken alarm'. Sunday was spent thinking about Monday. 'I have an appointment in the City at 12 o'c I cannot miss,' the stock-broker Ranald Laurie wrote to his client Francis Whitmore, 'and tomorrow is Settling day, and a beastly anxious one at that! with all these wars & rumours of wars about, & there is a lot of financial trouble all over the City.'[27]

'The Slump in Missouris' was the *FT*'s main leader on Monday the 27th, but the breaks were now everywhere. 'The end-July Settlement commenced under disastrous conditions,' the paper's market report written that evening began. 'The gravity of the war menace in Eastern Europe was such as to dwarf all other considerations . . .' Predictably, the underwriters of Canadian Northern Railway, issued by Lazards, were expected to be left with over 80 per cent, with the lists having been shut during the morning 'in order, it was said, to stop the withdrawal of applications'. With 'conditions in discount market chaotic', Smith St Aubyn drew some temporary comfort from the fact that 'on the whole the Joint Stock Banks behaved well' and did not call in too many loans. Serbia by now had rejected the Austrian ultimatum; and Brien Cokayne, a Bank of England director and partner in Antony Gibbs, informed a correspondent that 'the general feeling seems to be that there will not be war on the Continent, but it is by no means certain'.[28]

The next day, Tuesday, the discount market started to come under pressure from the joint-stock banks, which (following the example of foreign banks based in London) were also calling in loans from Stock Exchange firms, as well as starting to withdraw gold in significant quantities from the Bank of England itself. 'A Day of Forced Sales' was the *FT*'s market headline: 'From start to finish, with scarcely one rallying interlude, the Stock Exchange today has been plunged in gloom . . . While on Saturday and yesterday much of the selling came from holders who were scared into throwing stocks overboard, the heaviest liquidation of stock today consisted of stock that simply had to be sold, because the facilities for carrying it had been summarily removed.' Foreign bonds fell particularly sharply – 'hardly surprising', the *FT* commented, 'having regard to the way in which the Bourses have allowed London to be the dumping-ground for Europe', a reference to the main continental stock exchanges being more or less closed by this stage in the crisis. In which light, 'London has risen to the occasion as the world's financial centre.'[29] Shortly after the House closed, news came through that Austria had formally declared war.

'No company was ever issued with a more timely title than this morning's "J.M." Shock Absorbers,' the *FN* mordantly noted on the morning of Wednesday the 29th. They were intended to alleviate the joltings endured by a motor car and, according to the *FN*, 'the market ought to have a large supply'. It proved a predictably dreadful day, prompting the *FT* to open its market report that evening with the bald sentence: 'This has been one of the worst days in the history of the Stock Exchange.' Seven firms were hammered, jobbers practically refused to make prices, and 'a further severe fall' took place in all markets, Consols at one point reaching $69\frac{1}{2}$. 'Stock Exchange is more or less demoralised,' the British Bank of South America cabled its Rio de Janeiro branch, while Brown Shipley explained to its New York partners that 'the moment dealers attempt to make prices they are flooded with offers of Stock from the Continent', adding that 'the oldest Members of the Stock Exchange do not remember any time when London has been so near a panic'. As for the money market, where business continued very restricted, Smith St Aubyn recorded that 'the Joint Stock Banks began calling today in earnest and a very bad feeling was evident'.[30]

Natty Rothschild, meanwhile, gave an interview to the *Pall Mall Gazette* in which he claimed that 'there is more chance of the war being localised'; but Revelstoke, after much indecision, decided this day not to travel to Aix-les-Bains for his usual summer holiday. There were also two significant meetings. Bradbury of the Treasury paid a visit to the City, where Cunliffe, Cole, Revelstoke and Hambro all assured him that the Bank of England had the situation well under control; and at four thirty, St Aldwyn and the bankers convened at the Bankers' Clearing House. There the Gold Reserves Committee basically agreed the scheme that had been put to them a week earlier. It would now go before the Clearing House Committee and then, apparently, to the Bank of England. 'Before rising, Sir Felix Schuster expressed the thanks of the Committee to the Chairman for his conduct in the Chair and referred to the fact that this was the first Committee he had known which had reached the present stage.' The next meeting was arranged for Thursday, 13 August – but would never be held.[31]

'Prices Again Heavily Down' was the familiar story in Capel Court on Thursday the 30th. There were few dealings, 'the virtual cessation of the usual practice of price-making', and 'prices fell in very limp fashion, closing at the bottom'. The day's failures included Derenburg & Co, brokers doing a large business with Germany. By this stage the atmosphere inside the House was reasonably calm, and it seems that many members drifted outside, with the City's bars and restaurants doing a roaring trade. 'Cheerful Stoicism' the *FT* called it:

> In face of the declaration and practice of war between Austria and Servia, with all its possibilities of a general European conflagration, Throgmorton Street indulges in high spirits. Edition after edition of the evening papers comes out, with staring announcements of panic. It is doubtful if their sensations sell a copy. The Prince of Wales' Stakes [at Goodwood] have a keener interest. Your City man likes something that is moving. The Stock Exchange is not moving. It hasn't been moving for a long time. During the last few days there have been slumps in Canadian Pacifics, Rio Tintos and the rest, but these have scarcely affected the average member. They have been academical. Most of the money that has been lost has been lost on paper only. It will come back with the return of normal times. A horse-race is an event with immediate possibilities of gain or loss. You know the best or you know the worst . . .

'They talk in rather a loose way of closing the House,' Natty Rothschild mentioned to Paris; and indeed Koch that day proposed to the Stock Exchange Committee that it be closed on the morrow 'in view of the exceptional circumstances existing', but it was agreed to delay the decision until Friday morning itself. The real alarm on Thursday, however, resided more in the parlours of the accepting houses, becoming increasingly aware that remittances due to London from the continent were drying up, and in the money market. 'A very bad day,' Smith St Aubyn recorded. 'People are getting really alarmed and are flocking to the Bank of England to change notes for gold. Discount business has practically ceased.' Bank rate that day went up from 3 to 4 – modest enough, granted that the Bank had shelled out £14m to the discount market in the past three days and almost as much again to the banking system. In Lombard Street only Ronny Gillett seemed unconcerned, still planning (in Fred's dismissive words) 'to take his departure, to assist at some bun handing function, at which everybody sings "for *I'm* a jolly good fellow" '.[32]

Ronny changed his mind on Friday and decided to stay as, in Fred's words, 'things began to move'. The Stock Exchange Committee closed the House until further notice; Bank rate was doubled; and Gilletts itself was able to discount £150,000 of bills at the Bank only after going back three times. Smith St Aubyn's diary entry was all the more expressive for its brevity: 'A bad day. Looks like panic. All business ceased.' With the clearing banks now starting to refuse or semi-refuse to pay out sovereigns, a queue formed outside the Bank of England, people going there to exchange notes for gold. On the steps of the Royal Exchange a crowd gathered to watch, no doubt including some homeless members of the Stock Exchange, others of whom found relief playing dominoes in the long room at Lyons. At one point a red-cloaked Bank of England official shouted ironically to the queue, 'Silver! Anybody want silver? Plenty of silver going cheap.' But he was greeted only with silent, sardonic smiles.[33]

In the distant, unimaginable world outside, Austria was mobilising against Russia. 'The situation looks very black,' Cokayne wrote to his correspondent. 'Credit has already virtually broken down & the Bank Act will be suspended shortly.' Hope had not yet gone of the European conflict being localised – 'there are persistent rumours in the City,' Natty told Paris, 'that the German Emperor is using all his influence at both St Petersburg & Vienna to find a solution which would not be distasteful either to Austria or to Russia' – but the main focus was the financial crisis itself. In particular, as Natty also related, there was that day 'a great deal of talk among a great many of the large Houses in favour of a "Moratorium" ', talk that was particularly urgent on the part of houses like Kleinworts and Schröders who did a large German and Central European acceptance business. 'There is a great deal to be said for & against this policy,' Natty thought, 'but on the whole after very mature consideration, under the circumstances, it would be more than justified.'[34]

Saturday, 1 August opened with the money market on the rack. 'Our profit for the half-year had vanished into smoke,' Fred Gillett would recall:

> At 9 a.m. the Discount Houses met to discuss matters, Mr F. [identity unclear] was so excited that he rubbed his silk hat round & round the wrong way & kept rising to his feet to gasp out that 'all he wanted to do was to pay his way even down to his last shilling', till at last Mr Nugent

[of Union Discount and still the market's acknowledged leader] had to ask him to keep his seat as he had spoken quite enough. The only result of the Meeting was that most houses declared they would not pay out a single cheque until they were certain of having the money to do so. Our Firm paid away altogether about £100,000 . . .

That was emotion recollected in relative tranquillity, but the Smith St Aubyn diary was written in white heat: 'The Joint Stock banks panicked and it was only at $\frac{1}{4}$ to 1 that we were able to get anything. A truly fearful Saturday. Clearing kept open till 2 o'clock & we just managed to get home [i.e. in the sense of getting enough money] in time to pay our clearing. The worst day we have ever had since the business began.' The discount market was further handicapped by the Bank of England's reflex action, one that in the particular situation was wholly counter-productive, of raising Bank rate by a further two points, so that it attained the traditional 'crisis rate' of 10 per cent. With the clearing banks still more or less refusing to pay out sovereigns, an even longer queue than the previous day's straggled from inside the Bank into its courtyard; though as *The Times* patriotically reported, 'everything went off quietly' and 'everyone got his notes promptly exchanged'.[35] With the necessity looming of a large-scale issue of notes in order to protect the remaining gold reserves, Cunliffe managed by the end of the morning to obtain that familiar prop of any full-blown financial crisis since 1847 – namely, a 'chancellor's letter' permitting suspension, if need be, of the Bank Charter Act.

No one this Saturday imagined that would be enough. 'The joint stock banks have made absolute fools of themselves and behaved very badly': so Basil Blackett at the Treasury wrote to Keynes in Cambridge, imploring him to come to London as soon as possible. Or as Shaw-Stewart, back in England, correctly appraised the bigger picture, if perhaps overestimating the City's sang-froid: 'The simple fact is that, while there is no panic in London and no one is "talked about" or in a weak position, yet the entire existing machinery of credit is unequal to the international situation, and something new has got to be devised to carry us along.'[36]

On Sunday the 2nd, war was formally declared between Russia and Germany, a divided Cabinet discussed British policy long and fruitlessly, and the City's leading figures began to spend much of their time at the Treasury engaged in high-level consultations. By the end of the day it was clear that a month-long moratorium would, against Cunliffe's wishes, be granted for bills of exchange, thereby saving the skins of several accepting houses. Meanwhile, the leading joint-stock bankers, joined for the purpose by the managers of Union Discount and National Discount, devoted most of the afternoon and evening to lengthy meetings that eventually produced a coherent plan of action on the non-accepting side of the crisis. Writing to Lloyd George at 2 a.m. that night from his home at 20 Elvaston Place, SW, Robert Martin-Holland (Hon Secretary of the Clearing Bankers) outlined its main points: a subvention by the bankers to the Bank of up to £15m in gold; the issue as soon as possible of up to £45m of notes; suspension of the Bank Charter Act, including suspension of cash (i.e. gold) payments as soon as £1 notes were issued; and the application of a general moratorium. Such a package would, Martin-Holland asserted on behalf of Holden and the rest, 'allow of the business of this country being carried on under the present financial conditions which seem likely to become more onerous at every moment'.[37]

Monday, fortunately, was a Bank Holiday anyway. At a meeting that Cunliffe convened at the Bank that morning, all the leading bankers and others insisted that three more days of holiday were needed if adequate measures were to be taken. Cunliffe passed the request on to Lloyd George, who readily agreed. 'Saved for the time being' was Smith St Aubyn's graphic diary entry. Lloyd George himself was by this time shifting decisively towards the interventionist camp; and on Monday afternoon, against a background of the German ultimatum to Belgium and its rejection, Grey made his historic statement in the Commons that in effect committed Britain to military action. 'War seems to be an absolute certainty,' Teddy Grenfell wrote to a former Morgans partner.[38]

Keynes by now was ensconced at the Treasury – having ridden down from Cambridge in the sidecar of his brother-in-law's motor cycle – and in the course of Monday the 3rd he wrote for Lloyd George a memorandum that, in the words of an appended note, argued 'if the foreign drain is not likely to be very large [which all the indications so far were that it would not be], and the internal drain can be obviated by other means [he had in mind mainly the issue of notes], it is difficult to see how such an extreme and disastrous measure as the suspension of cash payments can be justified'. Suspension, Keynes insisted, would 'damage our prestige as a free gold market'. And, in the memorandum itself, he took the forceful line that, 'if we suspend now, a marked tendency will set in for the secondary countries to keep a far larger proportion of their free resources in gold at home'. Nor was that all:

Other important classes of business, as is well known, depend also, though much more indirectly, upon a continuance of this confidence. The existence of this confidence in the past has been one of the most import-ant *differentiations* between London and Paris or Berlin. It ought not to be endangered except for the very gravest cause.[39]

Still a full believer in economic liberalism – the creed of free-trading internationalism with the City of London and all-powerful gold stand-ard at the very centre – Keynes saw no reason why the golden age should end simply because of the panic-struck reaction of a bunch of joint-stock bankers seemingly incapable of distinguishing the suspen-sion of specie payments from the suspension of the Bank Charter Act.

'More meetings at the Union Disc. Much talk & little done.' Smith St Aubyn's experience was no doubt mirrored elsewhere in the City on Tuesday the 4th, a day of shut banks, closed markets and little visible excitement. The leading accepting houses each received an invitation from Huth Jackson to gather at Huths at noon the following day to discuss the position. There was still a lot of talking to be done – above all at the House of Commons, where in late afternoon there began what would turn into a three-day conference between Lloyd George, various other politicians, and what the minutes described as 'repres-entative bankers and traders'. After Yorkshire industrialists had stressed the need to be able to pay wages to their workforces on Friday, Holden endorsed their remarks from a banking point of view. The 'traders' then withdrew, while the bankers stayed behind. After some sparring about how many notes would be ready by Friday morning, Lloyd George – who had almost certainly read Keynes's memorandum earlier in the day – asserted that 'we are not ready for a suspension of specie', a policy that hitherto it had been assumed that he endorsed. To which Holden, still seeing the suspension of gold as inextricably linked to the emergency issuing of notes, replied: 'We are all against it, but it is a matter of life and death to us.' A little later, with the traders back in the room, there occurred a charged exchange between an unnamed colleague of Holden's and Cunliffe:

> *A Banker*: I understand one of the difficulties today is that the Bank of England cannot help us because they are afraid of a run on the gold supply. It is really a question for the Governor of the Bank of England whether he wants people to come and ask for specie and not get it.
> *The Governor of the Bank of England*: It is not true that if the Bank is open today I could not pay my way in gold.
> *A Banker*: I am very glad to hear it.

> *The Governor of the Bank of England*: And if you could see the
> accounts of the Bank, which the Chancellor of the Exchequer has seen,
> you would be surprised that there is so much fuss.[40]

The question of abandoning the gold standard had become the new
symbol of an old power struggle; and fortified by the support of Lloyd
George and the Treasury, Cunliffe was not the man to underplay his
hand. At about eight o'clock the conference broke up. Three hours
later the British ultimatum to Germany expired.

*

Later in 1914, no longer at the centre of events, Keynes recalled the
crisis. 'Schuster and Holden were the spokesmen of the bankers . . .
The one was cowardly and the other selfish. They unquestionably
behaved badly . . . By no means all of the other bankers trusted Schuster or Holden or agreed with their immediate proposals; but they were
timid, voiceless and leaderless and in the hurry of the times did not
make themselves heard.' Specifically, he levelled four charges against
the bankers: that they had failed to stand by the Stock Exchange and
thus prevent its closure; that by precipitately calling in loans from the
discount houses, and thereby forcing those houses to borrow at punit-
ive rates from the Bank, they had brought the money market 'near to
demoralisation'; that the internal drain of gold had been caused 'not
by the public running on the banks, but by the banks running on the
Bank of England'; and that they had been needlessly ready 'to force
suspension of specie payment on the Bank of England, while its resources were still intact, without one blow struck for the honour of our old
traditions or future good name'.[41] Historians since have sought to
defend or at least to explain the bankers' actions – on the grounds of
most of their assets having become illiquid (as Holden stressed several
times on the 4th), of their fear of gold hoarding by the public, of their
wish for self-aggrandising reasons to maximise their own contributions to the emergency pool of gold once the government had accepted
their gold-for-notes plan – but whatever the validity of these interpre-
tations, Keynes's larger claim is surely justified: this was not the
joint-stock men's finest hour.[42]

Was it anyone's? 'In these troublesome times everyone is very selfish
and has no brain either and only thinks of strengthening his own
position,' Natty Rothschild wrote to his cousins on 30 July. Just over
a week later Teddy Grenfell looked back, giving his account a particu-

lar spin for Jack Morgan's benefit: 'People have all worked very hard but from your knowledge of 1907 you will be aware that Bankers and Trust Companies develop all sorts of jealousies and it is very hard to make them work for the common good . . . I can only say that I realise to the full what the world has lost when your father left it. We did want a strong man to knock everybody's heads together and make all pull together for the common weal.' Lloyd George, in his first close experience of financial men, was fascinated by the sight of the City in action. His somewhat egocentric account of 'How We Saved the City' in his *War Memoirs* includes a tactful but telling passage: 'Many of its leaders were too overwhelmed by the great dangers to which they saw themselves exposed to be able to think with their accustomed composure and to preserve unshaken their wonted touch. Financiers in a fright do not make an heroic picture. One must make allowances, however, for men who were millionaires with an assured credit which seemed as firm as the globe it girdled, and who suddenly found their fortunes scattered by a bomb hurled at random from a reckless hand.' Significantly, though, he added that 'the strongest and sturdiest figure amongst them was Sir Edward Holden, with the brogue and stout heart of Lancashire in all his utterances', a man who 'stood out amongst all these money barons'.[43]

Whatever the rights and wrongs of the financial crisis itself, the larger question remains: why did the City offer such negligible resistance to British intervention in a conflict so profoundly damaging to the City's interests? 'Whatever otherwise may be thought of the Government of Great Britain,' the *FT* wrote with misplaced confidence on Wednesday the 29th, 'it may at least be trusted to keep this country out of the area of conflict unless forced by some extreme and improbable contingency.' Two days later *The Times*'s day editor reported to his colleagues that the Rothschilds, convinced that the paper's leading articles were 'hounding the country into war', had urged him to do what he could to reverse the aggressive tone. 'We dare not stand aside,' *The Times* declared on Saturday, its forceful response to New Court. On that Saturday, Lloyd George received a visit from Cunliffe, 'to inform me on behalf of the City that the financial and trading interests in the City of London were totally opposed to our intervening in the War'. It was an opposition wholly endorsed by the *Economist*, which in its issue that day enjoined 'strict neutrality' and argued that the 'quarrel' on the continent was 'no more our concern than would be a quarrel between Argentina and Brazil or between China and Japan'.[44]

Over the next forty-eight hours the picture fundamentally altered. In Lloyd George's own words: 'By Monday there was a complete change. The threatened invasion of Belgium had set the nation on fire from sea to sea.' There is no record of any attempt by the City, between the 2nd and 4th, to prevent British intervention. When on the 4th the *FT* reappeared after its three-day break, it made no mention – no mention at all – of whether Britain should go to war. Natty Rothschild himself, however, wrote to Paris later that Tuesday that 'there is no doubt that the Germans have invaded Belgian territory, and as that is an act which England could never tolerate the English Government will no doubt inform the German Government to that effect either tonight or tomorrow'.[45] Most City men over the long weekend seem to have fallen into patriotic line with little or no questioning. Such was patriotism's emotional charge in the late-Victorian and Edwardian City, who would have expected otherwise?

'The war came like a bolt from the blue and no one was prepared,' Farrer admitted frankly on 7 August. Withers agreed. 'It came upon us like a thunderbolt from a clear sky,' he began *War and Lombard Street*, written that autumn. Even Cassel, most astute of financiers, was caught somewhat humiliatingly on the hop: as late as Saturday the 1st he was still at the Villa Cassel in Switzerland and only with the greatest difficulty managed to struggle back to London. Another financier who knew all the angles, Émile d'Erlanger, would recall being 'incredulous that such an incredible thing as a European War should be allowed to break out'. 1914 showed with a cruel clarity that the City had no special purchase on events – vaguely fearing them, yes, but neither shaping nor understanding them. The guns of August were a particularly bitter blow to one man. Ellis Powell, editor of the *Financial News* and propagandist of an ever more elaborate and perfect financial machinery, had expressed two years earlier his most profound belief:

We have, up to now, been accustomed to think that the destinies of the world were, in the main, entrusted to the hands of politicians ... But within the last few years it has dawned upon the most competent observers that this progress and contentment depend very much more upon financial than upon political factors ... The financial and economic forces have become the predominant factors in our twentieth-century life, while the political elements have receded into the second place ... This is a distinct gain for humanity as a whole, since political forces are capable of being distorted, minimised, and outwitted, while economic power is the absolute and inexorable auxiliary of every effort to advance the prosperity of the world.[46]

Surrounded by frightened monarchies and restless masses, *that* was the great illusion of the age on the part of the commercial middle classes, an illusion shared by merchants in Lübeck and stock jobbers in Capel Court as well as humble scribes in Queen Victoria Street.

Notes

ABBREVIATIONS

Addis   Papers of Sir Charles Addis (School of Oriental and African Studies Library)
B of E   Bank of England Archives
BB   Baring Brothers & Co Archives
BM   *Bankers' Magazine*
BS   Records of Brown, Shipley & Co (Guildhall Library)
BSP   Papers of Sir Henry Babington Smith (Trinity College, Cambridge)
BW   Records of Balfour, Williamson & Co (University College London)
CCJ   *Chamber of Commerce Journal*
CP   *City Press*
DBB   David J. Jeremy (ed), *Dictionary of Business Biography* (1984-6)
FN   *Financial News*
FT   *Financial Times*
Gibbs   Records of Antony Gibbs & Sons (Guildhall Library)
Grey   Grey Papers (University of Durham Library)
Hamilton   Papers of Sir Edward Hamilton (British Library)
Harcourt   Harcourt Papers (Bodleian Library)
IR   *Investors' Review*
JIB   *Journal of the Institute of Bankers*
Kleinwort   Records of Kleinwort, Sons & Co (Guildhall Library)
LCC   Records of London Chamber of Commerce (Guildhall Library)
MF   *Motor Finance*
MG   Records of Morgan, Grenfell & Co (at Morgan Grenfell)
Meyer   Letters of Sir Carl Meyer (c/o Sir Anthony Meyer)
Midland   Midland Bank Archives
Milner   Papers of 1st Viscount Milner (Bodleian Library)
Morgan   Records of J. S. Morgan & Co (Guildhall Library)
ND   Records of National Discount Company (Guildhall Library)
NW   National Westminster Bank Archives
PRO   Public Record Office
RAL   N. M. Rothschild & Sons Archives
RBS   The Royal Bank of Scotland Archive (London)
SE   Records of the London Stock Exchange (Guildhall Library)
SSA   Records of Smith, St Aubyn & Co (Guildhall Library)

CHAPTER ONE

1. SE, Ms 14,600, vol 60, 4 Aug 1892; *FT*, 8 Dec 1890.
2. Gibbs, Ms 11,040, vol 1, 10 Dec 1890; H. Osborne O'Hagan, *Leaves from my Life* (1929), vol I, p 368.
3. SE, Mss 19,297, vol 12, 11 Dec 1890, 14,600, vol 58, 15 Dec 1890, 29 Dec 1890.

4. *Rialto*, 20 Dec 1890; *FT*, 19 Dec 1890; Printz P. Holman, *The Amazing Electric Tube: A History of the City and South London Railway* (1990), W. J. Passingham, *Romance of London's Underground* (1932), p 52.

CHAPTER TWO

1. *JIB*, April 1907, p 206; Francis W. Hirst, *The Stock Exchange* (1911), pp 80–1.
2. Ranald C. Michie, *The City of London: Continuity and Change, 1850–1990* (1992), p 21.
3. Most of this paragraph is derived from R. S. Sayers, *The Bank of England, 1891–1944* (Cambridge, 1976), vol 1, p 8, Ranald C. Michie, 'The Myth of the Gold Standard: an Historian's Approach' in *Revue Internationale d'Histoire de la Banque* (1986), pp 177–9, and Tessa Ogden, 'An analysis of Bank of England discount and advance behaviour, 1870–1914' in James Foreman-Peck (ed), *New perspectives on the late Victorian economy: Essays in Quantitative Economic History, 1860–1914* (Cambridge, 1990), p 333. Hamilton, Add Ms 48,654, 8 Jan 1891.
4. Institute of Bankers in Scotland, *Lectures to Local Centres, 1949–50* (Edinburgh, 1950), p 62; Michie, 'Myth', p 173.
5. *Economist*, 8 Aug 1891, 12 Sept 1891.
6. W. T. C. King, *History of the London Discount Market* (1936), pp 261–2.
7. Richard Roberts, 'What's in a Name? Merchants, Merchant Bankers, Accepting Houses, Issuing Houses, Industrial Bankers and Investment Bankers' in *Business History* (1993), pp 28–9.
8. BS, Ms 20,111, vol 3, 4 March 1891; Richard Roberts, *Schroders: Merchants & Bankers* (1992), p 99.
9. Roberts, *Schroders*, pp 94–100 is the source of this analysis.
10. Youssef Cassis, *City Bankers, 1890–1914* (Cambridge, 1994), pp 5–6.
11. The 1890 figure is from D. T. A. Kynaston, 'The London Stock Exchange, 1870–1914: An Institutional History' (London PhD, 1983), p 6. The other major (and technically more ambitious) survey of the Stock Exchange in this period is R. C. Michie, *The London and New York Stock Exchanges, 1850–1914* (1987).
12. All the quotations in this paragraph are taken from the three-volume edition of Anon, *Modern London: The World's Metropolis* (c.1890) at the Guildhall Library.
13. James Salmon, *Ten Years' Growth of the City of London* (1891), pp 101–29.
14. Michie, *City*, pp 16–17.
15. *Economist*, 20 Dec 1890; C. M. Woodhouse, *The Woodhouses, Drakes and Careys of Mincing Lane* (1977), p 30.
16. *Modern London* (volume starting with London and Lancashire Life Assurance on p 81), p 111; Allen, Harvey & Ross scrapbook (Cater Allen records). On Samuel in general, see: Robert Henriques, *Marcus Samuel, First Viscount Bearsted and founder of The 'Shell' Transport and Trading Company* (1960); DBB, Geoffrey Jones, 'Marcus Samuel, 1st Viscount Bearsted', vol 5, pp 43–6.
17. Stanley Chapman, *Merchant Enterprise in Britain: From the Industrial Revolution to World War I* (Cambridge, 1992), pp 202–3, 186; Michie, *City of London*, p 42.
18. Michie, *City*, p 33.
19. LCC, Ms 16,719, vol 1, 5 Aug 1885; *Economist*, 7 June 1890.
20. Michie, *City*, p 34.
21. Ibid, p 39.
22. Graham L. Rees, *Britain's Commodity Markets* (1972), p 325.
23. Robert Gibson-Jarvie, *The London Metal Exchange* (Cambridge, 2nd edn, 1983), pp 11–42; Rees, p 348.
24. Anon, *The London Commodity Exchange* (1967), pp 14, 11; Hugh Barty-King, *Food for Man and Beast* (1978); Hugh Barty-King, *The Baltic Exchange* (1977), p 229; Percy Harley, *My Life in Shipping, 1881–1938* (c.1938), p 142.

25. Michie, *City*, pp 52–4.
26. *Economist*, 11 Feb 1888; London Produce Clearing House, Ltd records (Guildhall Library), Ms 3,641, vol 1, 28 March 1888; *Statist*, 28 April 1888; *Independent*, 22 Feb 1988; Rees, p 175; *Contemporary Review*, June 1894, p 791.
27. NW, 5,995, Frederick Burt & Co, status reports on firms, 1887–1902.
28. John Galsworthy, *The Forsyte Saga* (1922), p 176; Salmon, p 101; Edgar Jones, *Accountancy and the British Economy, 1840–1980* (1981), p 43.
29. Laurie Dennett, *Slaughter and May: A Century in the City* (Cambridge, 1989), pp 1–37, 56–70, 86.
30. D. E. W. Gibb, *Lloyd's of London: A Study in Individualism* (1957), pp 152, 157.
31. Andrew Brown, *Cuthbert Heath* (Newton Abbot, 1980), pp 61–2.
32. Brown, *op cit*; *DBB*, Oliver M. Westall, 'Cuthbert Eden Heath', vol 3, pp 136–41; S. D. Chapman, 'A history of insurance broking' in Roderick Clews (ed), *A Textbook of Insurance Broking* (2nd edn, 1987), p 8.
33. *FT*, 19 Dec 1890.
34. *Public Ledger*, 18 Dec 1890.
35. *Public Ledger*, 19 Dec 1890; *FT*, 19 Dec 1890; *George Dornbusch's Floating Cargoes Evening List*, 18 Dec 1890.
36. *FT*, 19 Dec 1890, *Statist*, 13 Dec 1890.
37. *Quarterly Review*, July 1912, p 94.

CHAPTER THREE

1. P. Villars, *London and its Environs: A Picturesque Survey of the Metropolis and the Suburbs* (1888), pp 49–50; H. G. de Fraine, *Servant of this House* (1960), pp 128–9; de Fraine, p 129 (kerb space), Villars, p 7 (traffic), *Rialto*, 10 Sept 1892 (cuffs); Villars, p 7; Hurford Janes, *de Zoete & Gorton: A History* (?1963), pp 39, 47.
2. *Building News*, 6 Sept 1889; *Statist*, 18 Feb 1888; Harold P. Clunn, *The Face of London: The Record of a Century's Changes and Development* (1932), p 37; George and Pamela Cleaver, *The Union Discount: A Centenary Album* (1985), p 30; W. J. Loftie, *London City* (1891), pp 279–80.
3. de Fraine, p 9; Alfred Wells, 'Fifty Years in a Lawyer's Office' (unpublished, c/o Freshfields), p 13; Villars, pp 7–8; Wells, p 12; Sir Francis Oppenheimer, *Stranger Within* (1960), p 64.
4. George J. Emanuel, *Memories of Lloyd's, 1890 to 1937* (1937), pp 47–52; SE, Mss 14,609, vol 2, 11 May 1904, 19,297, vol 11, 10 Nov 1887.
5. Janet E. Courtney, *Recollected in Tranquillity* (1926), pp 155, 164–5.
6. Anon (Wilfred Maude), *Antony Gibbs & Sons Limited: Merchants and Bankers, 1808–1958* (1958), p 60; Richard Roberts, *Schroders: Merchants & Bankers* (1992), p 122; P. G. Warren, *One Hundred Years of Stockbroking, 1851–1951* (1951), p 20; *Evening News*, 23 April 1934.
7. Ranald Michie, 'Dunn, Fischer & Co in the City of London, 1906–14' in *Business History* (1988), p 195.
8. Frank H. H. King, *The History of the Hongkong and Shanghai Banking Corporation* (vol II, Cambridge, 1988), p 175; N. B. Harte, 'The Growth and Decay of a Hosiery Firm in the Nineteenth Century' in *Textile History* (1977), p 48.
9. George Grossmith and Weedon Grossmith, *The Diary of a Nobody* (1945 Penguin edn), p 17; *Nineteenth Century*, Oct 1897, pp 594–6.
10. Barry Supple, *The Royal Exchange Assurance* (Cambridge, 1970), pp 378–88.
11. *CCJ*, 5 Aug 1887.
12. *Times*, 13 July 1887; Roberts, p 122; Hurford Janes and H. J. Sayers, *The Story of Czarnikow* (1963), p 34; G. L. Anderson, 'The Social Economy of Late-Victorian Clerks' in Geoffrey Crossick (ed), *The Lower Middle Class in Britain, 1870–1914* (1977), p 133; *Nineteenth Century*, May 1887, p 734.

13. Stanley Jackson, *The Sassoons* (1968), p 84; diary of Edward Clodd (c/o Alan Clodd), 1 July 1890.
14. Ranald C. Michie, *The City of London: Continuity and Change, 1850–1990* (1992), p 14; de Fraine, p 130.

CHAPTER FOUR

1. ND, Ms 18,130, vol 1, 14 Jan 1891.
2. Sir Albert Feavearyear, *The Pound Sterling: A History of English Money* (Oxford, 1963 edn), p 328.
3. *DBB*, P. E. Smart, 'Joseph Herbert Tritton', vol 5, pp 558–9; Roger Fulford, *Glyn's: 1753–1953* (1953), p 224; R. S. Sayers, 'Twentieth Century English Banking' in *Transactions of the Manchester Statistical Society* (1953–4), p 2; A. R. Holmes and Edwin Green, *Midland: 150 years of banking business* (1986), pp 84–5.
4. *Bullionist*, 28 Feb 1891; *Economist*, 20 June 1891.
5. Youssef Cassis, *La City de Londres, 1870–1914* (Paris, 1987), p 23.
6. K. F. Dixon, *Alexanders Discount Company Limited, 1810–1960* (1960), p 6.
7. The best discussion of this subject remains L. S. Pressnell, 'Gold Reserves, Banking Reserves, and the Baring Crisis of 1890' in C. R. Whittlesey and J. S. G. Wilson (eds), *Essays in Money and Banking in honour of R. S. Sayers* (Oxford, 1968).
8. Hamilton, Add Ms 48,654, 8 Jan 1891; B of E, G23/85.
9. *Times*, 29 Jan 1891.
10. *Times*, 30 Jan 1891; Hamilton, Add Ms 48,655, 30 Jan 1891; B of E, G23/85; Hamilton, Add Ms 48,655, 5 Feb 1891.
11. *BM*, June 1891, pp 1007–10; Fulford, pp 214–17.
12. Hamilton, Add Ms 48,655, 24 May 1891.
13. *Rialto*, 10 Jan 1891; SE, Ms 14,600, vol 65, 15 Feb 1897; A. C. Pointon, *Wallace Brothers* (Oxford, 1974), p 64.
14. Gibbs, Ms 11,040, vol 1, 19–21 January 1891.
15. *Financial Critic*, 24 Jan 1891; *Rialto*, 31 Jan 1891; *Economist*, 21 Feb 1891; *Rialto*, 28 Feb 1891; Elizabeth Hennessy, *Stockbrokers for 150 Years: A History of Sheppards and Chase, 1827–1977* (1978), p 27.
16. *Rialto*, 21 March 1891, 28 March 1891; Guy Nickalls, *Life's a Pudding* (1939), p 79.
17. *Economist*, 23 May 1891, 30 May 1891; B of E, G15/182. On Nivison, see: R. S. Gilbert, 'London Financial Intermediaries and Australian Overseas Borrowing, 1900–29' in *Australian Economic History Review* (1971); R. P. T. Davenport-Hines, 'Lord Glendyne' in R. T. Appleyard and C. B. Schedvin (eds), *Australian Financiers: Biographical Essays* (Melbourne, 1988).
18. Norman Mackenzie (ed), *The Letters of Sidney and Beatrice Webb: Volume 1, Apprenticeships, 1873–1892* (Cambridge, 1978), p 282; *Rialto*, 15 Oct 1892.
19. *Stock Exchange Journal*, June 1963, pp 14–15.
20. SE, Ms 14,600, vol 59, 22 Oct 1891; R. C. Michie, *The London and New York Stock Exchanges, 1850–1914* (1987), p 84.
21. SE, Ms 19,297, vol 13, 12 May – 4 Nov 1891.
22. Hamilton, Add Ms 48,656, 19 Nov 1891; Welby Collection on Banking and Currency (London School of Economics), vol VII, fos 374–97; Pressnell, p 213.
23. JIB, Dec 1891, p 620; Hamilton, Add Ms 48,655, 30 Jan 1891; Bertram Wodehouse Currie, *Recollections, Letters and Journals* (Roehampton, 1901), vol II, p 212.
24. *JIB*, Dec 1891, pp 622–39; Hamilton, Add Ms 48,656, 2 Dec 1891; *FT*, 3 Dec 1891; Welby Collection, vol VII, fo 419; Hamilton, Add Ms 48,656, 4 Dec 1891, 7 Dec 1891.
25. Hamilton, Add Mss 48,656, 18 Dec 1891, 48,657, 19 Dec 1891; Currie, vol II, p 216; Hamilton, Add Mss 48,615 A, 21 Dec 1891, 48,616, 27 Dec 1891.

26. *BM*, Jan 1892, p 8, Feb 1892, pp 243–5; *JIB*, March 1892, pp 150–2; Hamilton, Add Ms 48,657, 24 Jan 1892; RBS, A4/4/18.

27. Pressnell, p 219; Holmes and Green, p 99; Feavearyear, pp 330–1.

28. *BM*, March 1892, p 378; RBS, GM/7.

29. Marcello de Cecco, *Money and Empire: The International Gold Standard, 1890–1914* (Oxford, 1974), p 95. My emphasis on this rivalry owes much to de Cecco's pioneering analysis.

30. *JIB*, May 1892, p 345.

CHAPTER FIVE

1. *BM*, Jan 1892, pp 44–5; Hamilton, Add Ms 48,655, 22 Jan 1891.

2. Kathleen Burk, *Morgan Grenfell, 1838–1988: The Biography of a Merchant Bank* (Oxford, 1989), p 55; Stanley Chapman, *The Rise of Merchant Banking* (1984), p 160.

3. SE, Ms 14,600, vol 60, 3 March 1892.

4. *FT*, 12 May 1892; D. T. A. Kynaston, 'The London Stock Exchange, 1870–1914: An Institutional History' (London PhD, 1983), p 267.

5. PRO, B 9/397.

6. *FT*, 31 May 1892, 1 June 1892; *BM*, April 1887, pp 341–6.

7. Hambros records (Guildhall Library), Ms 19,063, bundle 32, 23 April 1892; *FT*, 5 July 1892.

8. Robert Vicat Turrell, ' "Finance . . . The Governor of the Imperial Engine": Hobson and the Case of Rothschild and Rhodes' in Rob Turrell (ed), *The City and the Empire, Volume 2* (Collected Seminar Papers no 36, Institute of Commonwealth Studies, University of London, 1986), p 89; RAL, XI/153/0, 13 July 1892; S. D. Chapman, 'Rhodes and the City of London: Another View of Imperialism' in *Historical Journal* (1985), p 659.

9. *Rialto*, 20 Aug – 1 Oct 1892.

10. *Rialto*, 3 Sept 1892.

11. *DBB*, Esmond J. Cleary, 'Jabez Spencer Balfour', vol 1, pp 129–34.

12. *Economist*, 30 Nov 1895; H. Osborne O'Hagan, *Leaves from my Life* (1929), vol 1, p 145; George Robb, *White-collar Crime in modern England: financial fraud and business morality, 1845–1929* (Cambridge 1992), p 185.

13. *CP*, 1 Oct 1892; *FN*, 30 Sept 1892; *Times*, 4 May 1909 (I owe this reference to Dilwyn Porter).

14. Laurie Dennett, *Slaughter and May: A Century in the City* (Cambridge, 1989), pp 99–105.

15. *Economist*, 6 Aug 1892; SE, Ms 14,600, vol 60, 2 Aug – 10 Oct 1892.

CHAPTER SIX

1. Norman Mackenzie (ed), *The Letters of Sidney and Beatrice Webb: Volume I, Apprenticeships, 1873–1892* (Cambridge, 1978), p 396.

2. For the fullest discussion of the controversy, see: E. H. H. Green, 'Rentiers versus Producers? The Political Economy of the Bimetallic Controversy, c1880–1898' in *English Historical Review* (July 1988); A. C. Howe, 'Bimetallism, c1880–1898, a controversy re-opened?' in *English Historical Review* (April 1990); E. H. H. Green, 'The Bimetallic Controversy: empiricism belimed or the case for the issues' in *English Historical Review* (July 1990). See also P. J. Cain and A. G. Hopkins, *British Imperialism: Innovation and Expansion, 1688–1914* (1993), pp 151–3; Youssef Cassis, *City Bankers, 1890–1914* (Cambridge, 1994), pp 299–301.

3. Hamilton, Add Ms 48,657, 12 May 1892; *BM*, June 1892, p 889; Harcourt, Dep 166, fo 43; Hamilton, Add Ms 48,658, 20 Aug 1892; Harcourt, Dep 166, fo 46.

4. Harcourt, Dep 166, fos 50–1; Hamilton, Add Ms 48,658, 31 Aug 1892; Welby Collection on Banking and Currency (London School of Economics), vol V, fo 18; Harcourt, Dep 166, fos 59, 61–2, 66, 68, 77, 87.

5. Gibbs, Ms 11,021, vol 25, 7 Oct 1892; Harcourt, Deps 221, fo 62 and 163, fos 40–2, 45–6.

6. Harcourt, Dep 387, fos 86–7, 93.

7. Harcourt, Dep 388, fos 27–8; Meyer, 27 Nov 1892; *BM*, Jan 1893, pp 38–40; Bertram Wodehouse Currie, *Recollections, Letters and Journals* (Roehampton, 1901), vol II, p 239; BSP, HBC 15, 1 Dec 1892.

8. Harcourt, Deps 167, fos 5–6, 11–14, 26 and 388, fo 57.

9. Welby Collection, vol V, fos 73–4; Harcourt, Dep 389, fo 23.

10. Richard Roberts, *Schroders: Merchants & Bankers* (1992), pp 117, 119.

11. Welby Collection, vol VII, fo 419; David Kynaston, *The Financial Times: A Centenary History* (1988), pp 37–8.

12. *FN*, 11 Feb 1893; SE, Ms 14,600, vol 60, 30 Jan 1893; Gibbs, Ms 11,040, vol 2, 21 Feb 1893.

13. *FT*, 9 March 1893, *Times*, 10 March 1893; *Times*, 1–20 Nov 1899; *FT*, 20 Nov 1899. See also H. Montgomery Hyde, *The Life of Rufus Isaacs, First Marquess of Reading* (1967), pp 34–5.

14. *FN*, 15 April 1893, 4 May 1893; *Rialto*, 6 May 1893; *Times*, 30 Jan 1931, *FT*, 30 Jan 1931; *FN*, 3 June 1893.

15. *Economist*, 20 May 1911.

16. On the City and the Ottoman Empire, see: R. P. T. Davenport-Hines, 'The Ottoman Empire in Decline: The Business Imperialism of Sir Vincent Caillard, 1883–98' in R. V. Turrell and J. J. Van-Helten (eds), *The City and the Empire* (Collected Seminar Papers no 35, Institute of Commonwealth Studies, University of London, 1985); Cain and Hopkins, pp 402–7.

17. *Economist*, 12 Nov 1892; *Rialto*, 15 April 1893.

18. *Statist*, 21 Jan 1893; Hamilton, Add Ms 48,660, 15–16 March 1893.

19. Harcourt, Dep 389, fos 81–2.

20. Cain and Hopkins, pp 375–7, with an array of references.

21. RAL, T43/35, 26 March 1892; Robert Vicat Turrell with Jean-Jacques van Helten, 'The Rothschilds, the Exploration Company and Mining Finance' in *Business History* (1986); *Times*, 17 Jan 1893.

22. *DBB*, Jean Jacques Van-Helten, 'Alfred Beit', vol 1, pp 253–5, 'Sir Julius Carl Wernher', vol 5, pp 736–41.

23. Frank Harris, *My Life and Loves* (1966 Corgi edn), pp 823–5; Jamie Camplin, *The Rise of the Plutocrats: Wealth and Power in Edwardian England* (1978), p 46.

24. The best guide to Beit and deep-level mining is Robert V. Kubicek, *Economic Imperialism in Theory and Practice: The Case of South African Gold Mining Finance, 1886–1914* (Durham, NC, 1979), pp 61–6.

25. *FN*, 8 April 1893.

26. On the City and Australia, see Cain and Hopkins, pp 243–54.

27. *CCJ*, 10 May 1893.

28. On the City and the Argentine, see: Carlos Marichal, *A Century of Debt Crises in Latin America* (New Jersey, 1989), pp 159–70; Cain and Hopkins, pp 293–8.

29. *Economist*, 11 Feb 1893; *Statist*, 17 June 1893, 24 June 1893, 30 Dec 1893; *FT*, 20 June 1893.

30. S. R. B. Smith, 'British Nationalism, Imperialism and the City of London, 1880–1900' (London PhD, 1985), p 326; *FT*, 13 Dec 1893.

31. *Rialto*, 24 June 1893, 19 Aug 1893.

32. Hamilton, Add Ms 48,660, 8 June 1893; *FN*, 15 July 1893; Jardine Matheson records (Cambridge University Library), sect IV, B31/5; *Rialto*, 29 July 1893.

33. BS, Ms 20,111, vol 3, 23 Aug 1893; Morgan, Ms 21,760, HC3.1.1. (118), 20 Sept 1893.
34. *Economist*, 16 Sept 1893.
35. *IR*, vol I, no I, 1892, p 87; *Statist*, 29 Sept 1894; *F & B News* (1975).
36. *Rialto*, 25 Nov 1893; Harcourt, Dep 397, fos 19–20; *Rialto*, 23 Dec 1893; *FN*, 23 Dec 1893, 30 Dec 1893.
37. D. T. A. Kynaston, 'The London Stock Exchange, 1870–1914: An Institutional History' (London PhD, 1983), p 100; BB, Dep 33.2, 29 Dec 1894.
38. *Times*, 31 Aug 1923; H. Montgomery Hyde, *The Other Love: An Historical and Contemporary Survey of Homosexuality in Britain* (1972 Mayflower edn), pp 178–9.
39. *BM*, Nov 1883, p 1158; Hamilton, Add Ms 48,661, 5 Sept 1893, 12 Sept 1893; Turrell, 'Exploration Company', pp 201–2; *Statist*, 3 March 1894.
40. *FT*, 1 March 1894; *Times*, 21 March 1894.
41. R. S. Sayers, *The Bank of England, 1891–1944* (Cambridge, 1976), vol 1, p 17.
42. Hamilton, Add Mss 48,661, 11 Aug 1893, 48,615 B, 19 Sept 1893, 23 Sept 1893.
43. B of E, G4/116; Janet E. Courtney, *Recollected in Tranquillity* (1926), p 153; Elizabeth Hennessy, *A Domestic History of the Bank of England, 1930–1960* (Cambridge, 1992), p 224; *BM*, Dec 1889, pp 1490–1, Dec 1893, p 807.
44. B of E, G8/47; Harcourt, Dep 180, fo 50; Hamilton, Add Ms 48,661, 12 Nov 1893.
45. Harcourt, Deps 396, fos 76–8 and 170, fo 55.
46. *FT*, 3 Jan 1894; *IR*, Jan 1894, p 4; *Times*, 6 Jan 1894; Harcourt, Dep 170, fo 78.
47. In general, see: Anthony Howe, 'From "Old Corruption" to "New Probity": the Bank of England and its directors in the Age of Reform' in *Financial History Review* (1994); Elizabeth Hennessy, 'The Governors, Directors and Management of the Bank of England' in Richard Roberts and David Kynaston (eds), *The Bank of England: Money, Power and Influence, 1694–1994* (Oxford, 1995).
48. Hamilton, Add Ms 48,654, 8 Jan 1891; Currie, vol II, p 278; Harcourt, Dep 170, fos 62–3; Bo Bramsen and Kathleen Wain, *The Hambros* (1979), pp 332–6; Hamilton, Add Ms 48,662, 25 Jan 1894.
49. B of E, G15/139; Bramsen and Wain, p 335.
50. *BM*, Feb 1894, pp 185–92, March 1894, p 374.
51. *Times*, 16 March 1894; Harcourt, Dep 416, fos 85–6.
52. *FN*, 6 Oct 1893.

CHAPTER SEVEN

1. *Rialto*, 3 Feb 1894; Harcourt, Dep 401, fos 35–6; *FT*, 5 March 1894.
2. SE, Ms 14,608, vol 1, 31 Oct – 1 Dec 1893; *Rialto*, 25 Nov 1893.
3. SE, Ms 14,608, vol 1, 4 April 1894; *FN*, 7 April 1894; SE, Ms 14,608, vol 2, 10 Oct 1894.
4. SE, Ms 14,600, vol 62, 18 June – 2 July 1894.
5. *Rialto*, 9 June 1894, 7 July 1894; *FN*, 3 Nov 1894, *Rialto*, 10 Nov 1894; Stephen Koss, *The Rise and Fall of the Political Press in Britain, Volume One: The Nineteenth Century* (1981), p 404.
6. *FN*, 10 Nov 1894; *Economist*, 22 Sept 1894; *The Autobiography of John Hays Hammond* (New York, 1935), vol 1, p 298.
7. David Kynaston, *The Financial Times: A Centenary History* (1988), pp 39–40.
8. On Vincent generally, see Richard Davenport-Hines and Jean-Jacques Van Helten, 'Edgar Vincent, Viscount D'Abernon, and the Eastern Investment Company in London, Constantinople and Johannesburg' in *Business History* (1986).
9. Imperial Ottoman Bank records (Guildhall Library), Ms 23,993, vol 4, 6–9 Nov 1894.
10. *FN*, 17 Nov 1894; *Economist*, 24 Nov 1894; *FN*, 21 July 1894.
11. *FN*, 1 Dec 1894; *Rialto*, 1 Dec 1894; *FN*, 1 Dec 1894.

CHAPTER EIGHT

1. *Quarterly Review*, July 1912, p 98. The sources for most of this paragraph are: Jean-Jacques van Helten, 'Mining, share manias and speculation: British investment in overseas mining, 1880–1913' in J. J. van Helten and Y. Cassis (eds), *Capitalism in a Mature Economy: Financial Institutions, Capital Exports and British Industry, 1870–1939* (Aldershot, 1990), especially pp 167–73; Robert Vicat Turrell with Jean-Jacques Van Helten, 'The Rothschilds, the Exploration Company and Mining Finance' in *Business History* (1986), especially pp 186–96; Richard Davenport-Hines and Jean-Jacques van Helten, 'Edgar Vincent, Viscount D'Abernon, and the Eastern Investment Company in London, Constantinople and Johannesburg' in *Business History* (1986), especially pp 44–6; Charles Harvey and Jon Press, 'The City and International Mining, 1870–1914' in *Business History* (1990); Jean-Jacques van Helten, 'Empire and High Finance: South Africa and the International Gold Standard, 1890–1914' in *Journal of African History* (1982), especially pp 538–40. The gold production figures are from R. R. Mabson, *The Statist's Mines of the Transvaal* (3rd edn, 1904), p 8. In addition, Russell Ally, *Gold and Empire: The Bank of England and South Africa's Gold Producers, 1886–1926* (Witwatersrand, 1993) offers important insights.

2. J. W. McCarty, 'British Investment in Overseas Mining, 1880–1914' (Cambridge PhD, 1961), p 89; *Nineteenth Century*, Oct 1895, p 538; W. J. Reader, *A House in the City: A Study of the City and of the Stock Exchange based on the Records of Foster & Braithwaite, 1825–1975* (1979), p 114; Hubert A. Meredith, *The Drama of Money Making: Tragedy and Comedy of the London Stock Exchange* (?1931), p 245; *City Times*, 9 Feb 1895; *Evening News*, 19 March 1895; MG, private letter books, no 5, 3 June 1911; Anon (Richard Roberts), *Henry Ansbacher: The First Hundred Years* (1994).

3. *Investors' Chronicle*, 12 March 1949, Max Karo, *City Milestones and Memories* (1962), p 4; FN, 3 Feb 1920; Alan Jenkins, *The Stock Exchange Story* (1973), p 104; Robert V. Kubicek, 'The Randlords in 1895: A Reassessment' in *Journal of British Studies* (1972), p 99. Geoffrey Wheatcroft, *The Randlords* (1985) gives a convincing portrait of Barnato.

4. FN, 8 Dec 1894, 22 Dec 1894; *Economist*, 29 Dec 1894; FN, 29 Dec 1894.

5. FN, 12 Jan 1895; *Statist*, 19 Jan 1895, 26 Jan 1895; FN, 2 Feb 1895.

6. *Citizen*, 16 March 1895.

7. *Evening News*, 20 March 1895; FN, 21–23 March 1895; SE, Ms 14,600, vol 63, 21–22 March 1895; Gibbs, Ms 11,040, vol 2, 22 March 1895; Charles Duguid, *The Story of the Stock Exchange* (1901), p 336.

8. *JIB*, June 1894, p 374; LCC, Ms 16,532, 4 June 1894, 5 July 1894; *JIB*, Dec 1894, p 550.

9. Thomas J. Spinner, Jr, *George Joachim Goschen: The Transformation of a Victorian Liberal* (Cambridge, 1973), pp 182–3; Hamilton, Add Ms 48,666, 14 Feb 1895; *City Times*, 16 Feb 1895; *Oscar Wilde's Plays, Prose Writings, and Poems* (1930 Everyman edn), p 369.

10. FT, 4 April 1895; RBS, A9/3/3.

11. RBS, A9/3/3.

12. RBS, A9/3/3; Bertram Wodehouse Currie, *Recollections, Letters and Journals* (Roehampton, 1901), vol I, pp 104–8; RBS, A9/3/3.

13. Harcourt, Dep 163, fos 79–83.

14. Harcourt, Dep 163, fos 84–98; RBS, A9/3/3.

15. *JIB*, Dec 1895, p 552; RBS, GM/180/24/13, GM/180/24/1.

16. J. W. McCarty, 'British Investment in Western Australian Gold Mining, 1894–1914' in *University Studies in History* (1961–2) is probably the best guide to Westralians.

17. David Cannadine, *The Decline and Fall of the British Aristocracy* (1990), pp 412–13.

18. *FT*, 2–6 April 1895, *Economist*, 6 April 1895.

19. *FT*, 23 April 1895; Harcourt, Dep 418, fo 12.

20. *FN*, 4 May 1895; *Citizen*, 11 May 1895, *FN*, 11 May 1895.

21. Harcourt, Deps 418, fos 12, 22–3, 50–1 and 419, fo 8.

22. Robert V. Kubicek, *Economic Imperialism in Theory and Practice: The Case of South African Gold Mining Finance, 1886–1914* (Durham, NC, 1979), p 67; SE, Ms 14,600, vol 63, 8 July 1895; *South Africa*, 13 July 1895; A. G. Gardiner, *The Life of Sir William Harcourt* (1923), vol II, p 367.

23. In general re this loan, see: David McLean, 'The Foreign Office and the First Chinese Indemnity Loan, 1895' in *Historical Journal* (1973); Frank H. H. King, *The History of the Hongkong and Shanghai Banking Corporation* (vol II, Cambridge, 1988), pp 264–72.

24. PRO, FO 17/1253.

25. *FT*, 8–9 July 1895; Roberta Allbert Dayer, *Finance and Empire: Sir Charles Addis, 1861–1945* (1988), p 36.

26. Pat Thane, 'Financiers and the British State: The Case of Sir Ernest Cassel' in *Business History* (1986), pp 83–5.

27. *FT*, 3 July 1895; Thane, 'Financiers', p 97.

28. The two best biographical accounts are: Kurt Grunwald, ' "Windsor-Cassel" – The Last Court Jew' in *Leo Baeck Institute, Year Book* (1969); *DBB*, P. Thane, 'Sir Ernest Joseph Cassel', vol 1, pp 604–14.

29. Anthony Allfrey, *Edward VII and his Jewish Court* (1991), p 137; S. Japhet, *Recollections from my Business Life* (1931), p 130.

30. *Economist*, 17 Aug 1895; Laurie Dennett, *Slaughter and May: A Century in the City* (Cambridge, 1989), p 88.

31. McCarty, 'Overseas Mining', p 87; Kubicek, *Economic Imperialism*, pp 121–2.

32. *FT*, 28 Aug 1895; *City Recorder*, 31 Aug 1895.

33. *FT*, 3 Sept 1895; Kubicek, *Economic Imperialism*, p 122.

34. *Economist*, 14 Sept 1895; Hamilton, Add Ms 48,667, 1 Oct 1895; *FT*, 4 Oct 1895; *Statist*, 12 Oct 1895; Kubicek, *Economic Imperialism*, p 68; *FT*, 19 Oct 1895; *Economist*, 26 Oct 1895.

35. Hamilton, Add Ms 48,668, 7 Nov 1895; *Times*, 8 Nov 1895.

36. Richard Meinertzhagen, *Diary of a Black Sheep* (1964), pp 217–19.

CHAPTER NINE

1. *Mammon*, 22 Nov 1895; *FN*, 23 Nov 1895.

2. *FN*, 2 Jan 1896; *Citizen*, 18 Jan 1896.

3. *FT*, 15 Jan 1896; Robert V. Kubicek, *Economic Imperialism in Theory and Practice: The Case of South African Gold Mining Finance, 1886–1914* (Durham, NC, 1979), p 122, and 'The Randlords in 1895: A Reassessment' in *Journal of British Studies* (1972), pp 99–100; *FN*, 1 Aug 1896; *Citizen*, 22 Feb 1896.

4. Jamie Camplin, *The Rise of the Plutocrats: Wealth and Power in Edwardian England* (1978), p 46; Kubicek, *Economic Imperialism*, pp 71–2, 68; SE, Ms 14,600, vol 73, 7 Jan 1903; Jean-Jacques van Helten, 'Mining, share manias and speculation: British investment in overseas mining, 1880–1913' in J. J. van Helten and Y. Cassis (eds), *Capitalism in a Mature Economy: Financial Institutions, Capital Exports and British Industry, 1870–1939* (Aldershot, 1990), p 174.

5. SE, Ms 14,600, vol 64, 24 Feb – 9 March 1896; *FN*, 29 Feb 1896.

6. Hamilton, Add Ms 48,669, 7 May 1896; R. R. Mabson, *The Statist's Mines of the Transvaal* (3rd edn, 1904), p 11; *FN*, 17 Oct 1896; *Citizen*, 3 Oct 1896 (Nickalls), 20 March 1897.

7. J. W. McCarty, 'British Investment in Western Australian Gold Mining, 1894–1914' in *University Studies in History* (1961–2) tells the story.

8. SE, Ms 19,515, app 132; *Statist*, 4 April 1896; *Economist*, 28 March 1896; *FT*, 20 May 1896.

9. On Bottomley, see *DBB*, Christine Shaw, 'Horatio William Bottomley', vol 1, pp 391–6. On Wright, see *DBB*, R. P. T. Davenport-Hines, 'Whitaker Wright', vol 5, pp 901–4. On both, see R. T. Appleyard and Mel Davies, 'Financiers of Western Australia's Goldfields' in R. T. Appleyard and C. B. Schedvin (eds), *Australian Financiers: Biographical Essays* (Melbourne, 1988).

10. H. Osborne O'Hagan, *Leaves from my Life* (1929), vol I, p 268; Appleyard and Davies, p 166, Robert Vicat Turrell with Jean-Jacques van Helten, 'The Rothschilds, the Exploration Company and Mining Finance' in *Business History* (1986), p 200; Frank Harris, *My Life and Loves* (1966 Corgi edn), pp 174, 464–6.

11. *FN*, 1 Feb 1896; *Citizen*, 23 May 1896.

12. Gibbs, Ms 11,040, vol 2, 15 May – 31 July 1896.

13. *Statist*, 28 Nov 1896; *FT*, 10 Feb 1897.

14. *Statist*, 1 May 1897; O'Hagan, vol I, p 278; *FT*, 27 April 1897; *FN*, 22 May 1897.

15. Harcourt, Dep 419, fos 34–5, 41–2; *FN*, 15 April 1896. In general on the cycle boom, see: P. L. Cottrell, *Industrial Finance, 1830–1914: The finance and organization of English manufacturing industry* (1980), pp 173–5; A. E. Harrison, 'Joint-Stock Company Flotation in the Cycle, Motor-Vehicle and Related Industries, 1882–1914' in *Business History* (1981).

16. *FN*, 13 May 1896.

17. Harris, pp 826–7. On Hooley in general, see *DBB*, Kenneth and Margaret Richardson, 'Ernest Terah Hooley', vol 3, pp 329–32.

18. H. F. M. Weston-Webb, *The Autobiography of a British Yarn Merchant* (1929), pp 162–4; Ernest Terah Hooley, *Hooley's Confessions* (1924), pp 140–1.

19. *Citizen*, 16 May 1896, 30 May 1896; SE, Ms 14,600, vol 65, 3 Nov – 7 Dec 1896.

20. *FN*, 24 Oct 1896, 20 Nov 1896; John Armstrong, 'Hooley and the Bovril Company' in *Business History* (1986) is the standard account; Douglas A. Simmons, *Schweppes: The First 200 Years* (1983), pp 52–3; Hooley, p 12.

21. *DBB*, Richard Storey, 'Henry John Lawson', vol 3, pp 685–7.

22. The best account of the industry's early history is probably Kenneth Richardson, *The British Motor Industry, 1896–1939* (1977).

23. Simms Papers (University of London Library), folder 15 (Daimler), 1 Feb 1896; *Statist*, 15 Feb 1896; *FN*, 11 May 1896; *Statist*, 23 May 1896.

24. *Economist*, 14 Nov 1896; *FN*, 16 Nov 1896; *Citizen*, 21 Nov 1896.

25. *FT*, 30 Nov 1896; *Economist*, 28 Nov 1896; *FT*, 30 Nov 1896; *Citizen*, 19 Dec 1896; *Economist*, 22 May 1897, 2 Oct 1897.

26. Richardson's account stresses the capital aspect, especially pp 29–30, 39, 54–5, 60. See also: William P. Kennedy, *Industrial structure, capital markets and the origins of British economic decline* (Cambridge, 1987), pp 139–40; John Armstrong, 'The rise and fall of the company promoter and the financing of British industry' in van Helten and Cassis.

27. *JIB*, March 1896, p 160; W. J. Reader, *A House in the City: A Study of the City and of the Stock Exchange based on the Records of Foster & Braithwaite, 1825–1975* (1979), pp 98–9.

28. *FT*, 15 Nov 1895; SSA, Ms 14,894, vol 5, 14–16 Nov 1895; BS, Ms 20,111, vol 3, 24 Jan 1896; *BM*, May 1895, pp 713–15.

29. B of E, G15/39. On the 'competitive' theme, see R. S. Sayers, *The Bank of England, 1891–1944* (Cambridge, 1976), vol 1, pp 17–22.

30. Esther Madeleine Ogden, 'The Development of the Role of the Bank of England as a Lender of Last Resort, 1870–1914' (London PhD, 1988), pp 376, 378; Midland, M 153/45.

31. Midland, M 153/44.

32. *FT*, 10 June 1896; P. W. Matthews and A. W. Tuke, *History of Barclays Bank Limited* (1926), pp 8–9, *DBB*, P. E. Smart, 'Frederick Crauford Goodenough', vol 2, pp 603–6.

33. *BM*, June 1896, p 819; *JIB*, March 1897, p 135.
34. Midland, M 153/47/4.
35. Ogden, pp 380–1; Midland, M 153/47/2.
36. Sayers, vol 1, p 18; B of E, G15/39; Sayers, vol 1, p 61.
37. Richard Meinertzhagen, *Diary of a Black Sheep* (1964), pp 311, 285, 287, 314.
38. *Statist*, 15 Aug 1896, 5 Sept 1896, 12 Sept 1896; L. E. Jones, *Georgian Afternoon* (1958), p 133.
39. SE, Mss 14,609, vol 1, 3–7 Dec 1896, 14,600, vol 66, 10 March 1898.
40. SE, Ms 14,600, vol 65, 15 Feb 1897; *Citizen*, 20 Feb 1897.
41. Meinertzhagen, pp 328, 336–40.
42. C. L. Currie, *Bertram Wodehouse Currie: A Memorial* (1897), pp 8–9; Bertram Wodehouse Currie, *Recollections, Letters and Journals* (Roehampton, 1901), vol II, p 357; Hamilton, Add Ms 48,670, 30 Dec 1896; Roger Fulford, *Glyn's: 1753–1953* (1953), p 218.
43. George Gissing, *Born in Exile* (1978 Harvester edn), pp 264–5; George Gissing, *The Whirlpool* (1984 Hogarth Press edn), pp 45, 48.
44. Arthur C. Young (ed), *The Letters of George Gissing to Eduard Bertz* (1961), p 213; D'Abernon Papers (British Library), Add Ms 48,929, fo 229; Geoffrey Wheatcroft, *The Randlords* (1985), pp 192–5; *Citizen*, 19 June 1897; *FN*, 21 June 1897; Meyer, 16 June 1897.
45. *FN*, 21 June 1897, 23 June 1897, *FT*, 23 June 1897; George Robb, *White-collar Crime in modern England: financial fraud and business morality, 1845–1929* (Cambridge, 1992), p 115; Jacob Korg (ed), *George Gissing's Commonplace Book* (New York, 1962), p 45; *Times*, 23 June 1897.

CHAPTER TEN

1. Hamilton, Add Ms 48,671, 31 July 1897; *JIB*, Oct 1897, pp 436–7. For a close analysis of this episode, see Youssef Cassis, *City Bankers, 1890–1914* (Cambridge, 1994), pp 291–3.
2. Hamilton, Add Ms 48,672, 16 Sept 1897; *FT*, 20 Sept 1897; NW, 11,416, Parr's Bank board minutes, 23 Sept 1897.
3. RBS, GM/180/22; *BM*, Oct 1897, pp 430–1.
4. *JIB*, Nov 1897, pp 492–7; Hamilton, Add Ms 48,672, 17 Oct 1897; Balfour Papers (British Library), Add Ms 49,852, fos 228–9.
5. *JIB*, Jan 1898, pp 10–12, 14.
6. Arnold P. Kaminsky, ' "Lombard Street" and India: Currency Problems in the Late Nineteenth Century' in *Indian Economic and Social History Review* (1980); A. C. Howe, 'Bimetallism, *c.*1880–1898, a controversy re-opened?' in *English Historical Review* (1990), pp 385–7; P. J. Cain and A. G. Hopkins, *British Imperialism: Innovation and Expansion, 1688–1914* (1993), pp 344–6.
7. Kaminsky, p 323; B of E, G20/4/8; Farrer Papers (London School of Economics), vol 3, 13 May 1898.
8. Farrer Papers, vol 3, 13 May 1898, 16 May 1898.
9. *BM*, June 1895, p 828; Gibbs, Ms 11,042, vol 1, 25 March 1897.
10. *Citizen*, 9 Oct 1897, 16 Oct 1897, 31 July 1897, 30 Oct 1897, 12 Feb 1898.
11. *Times*, 17 Sept 1897; Charles Duguid, *The Story of the Stock Exchange* (1901), p 374; SE, Ms 19,297, vol 14, 1 Sept 1897.
12. Richard Trench, *London before the Blitz* (1989), p 117; *CP*, 20 Nov 1897 – 15 Jan 1898.
13. BS, Ms 20,111, vol 3, 15 Nov 1897; Kathleen Burk, *Morgan Grenfell, 1838–1988: The Biography of a Merchant Bank* (Oxford, 1989), p 57; Hamilton, Add Ms 48,672, 12 Dec 1897.

14. The Marquess of Winchester, *Statesmen, Financiers and Felons* (1934), p 235; Pat Thane, 'Financiers and the British State: The Case of Sir Ernest Cassel' in *Business History* (1986), p 86.

15. Frank H. H. King, *The History of the Hongkong and Shanghai Banking Corporation* (vol II, Cambridge, 1988), pp 275–91 covers the second and third indemnity loans; Hamilton, Add Mss 48,672, 11 Jan 1898, 22 Jan 1898, 48,673, 11 March 1898.

16. Richard Davenport-Hines and Jean-Jacques Van Helten, 'Edgar Vincent, Viscount D'Abernon, and the Eastern Investment Company in London, Constantinople and Johannesburg' in *Business History* (1986), p 52; Winston Fritsch, *External Constraints on Economic Policy in Brazil, 1889–1930* (1988), p 7, Cain and Hopkins, pp 304–5; Roberta Allbert Dayer, *Finance and Empire: Sir Charles Addis, 1861–1945* (1988), p 44.

17. Barings, Dep 33.3, 11 Dec 1897.

18. J. W. McCarty, 'British Investment in Western Australian Gold Mining, 1894–1914' in *University Studies in History* (1961–2), pp 19–20; *DBB*, R. P. T. Davenport-Hines, 'Whitaker Wright', vol 5, p 902; R. T. Appleyard and Mel Davies, 'Financiers of Western Australia's Goldfields' in R. T. Appleyard and C. B. Schedvin, *Australian Financiers: Biographical Essays* (Melbourne, 1988), pp 169–70; George Robb, *White-collar Crime in modern England: financial fraud and business morality, 1845–1929* (Cambridge, 1992), p 108.

19. *CP*, 12 Jan 1898; *Economist*, 15 Jan 1898, Ruth Dudley Edwards, *The Pursuit of Reason: The Economist, 1843–1993* (1993), pp 442–3; G. M. Young, *Portrait of an Age* (1960 Oxford pbk edn), p 146.

20. *Economist*, 31 July 1897; *CP*, 11 Dec 1897; McCarty, pp 17–18.

21. *DBB*, Edwin Green, 'Sir Edward Hopkinson Holden', vol 3, pp 290–8.

22. Cassis, *City Bankers*, pp 51–2; *FN*, 23 July 1901; A. R. Holmes and Edwin Green, *Midland: 150 years of banking business* (1986), p 97; Cassis, p 51.

23. *National Review*, March 1898, pp 75–86.

24. *IR*, 24 June 1898.

25. Dudley Edwards, pp 403–4.

26. See Dilwyn Porter, ' "A Trusted Guide of the Investing Public": Harry Marks and the Financial News, 1884–1916' in *Business History* (1986).

27. *Nineteenth Century*, May 1898, p 742; *Contemporary Review*, Aug 1898, p 201.

28. Jamie Camplin, *The Rise of the Plutocrats: Wealth and Power in Edwardian England* (1978), p 65; *Times*, 28 July 1898.

29. *Times*, 18 Aug 1898; David Kynaston, *The Financial Times: A Centenary History* (1988), p 26; *National Review*, Sept 1898, p 115.

30. *Times*, 8 Nov 1898, 3 Nov 1898, 15 Nov 1898.

31. Hamilton, Add Ms 48,673, 18 Nov 1898; *National Review*, Dec 1898, pp 574–84.

CHAPTER ELEVEN

1. Hugh Barty-King, *The Baltic Exchange* (1977), pp 251, 243–6.

2. *FT*, 25 Jan 1899; Alan Hyman, *The Rise and Fall of Horatio Bottomley: the biography of a swindler* (1972), pp 275–9; A. J. P. Taylor, *English History, 1914–1945* (1970 Pelican edn), p 243; Ernest Terah Hooley, *Hooley's Confessions* (1924), p 294.

3. *Investors' Chronicle*, 26 March 1949; Gibbs, Ms 11,040, vol 3, 1 June 1899; J. W. McCarty, 'British Investment in Western Australian Gold Mining, 1894–1914' in *University Studies in History* (1961–2), p 20; *FT*, 7–8 Sept 1899.

4. J. W. McCarty, 'British Investment in Overseas Mining, 1880–1914' (Cambridge PhD, 1961), pp 173–9.

5. *The Autobiography of John Hays Hammond* (New York, 1935), vol 2, pp 491–2; *FT*, 13 May 1899; T. A. Rickard, *Retrospect: An Autobiography* (1937), p 76.

6. NW, 205, Parr's Bank records; Toshio Suzuki, *Japanese Government Loan Issues on the London Capital Market, 1870–1913* (1994), pp 69–70; Frank H. H. King, *The*

History of the Hongkong and Shanghai Banking Corporation (vol II, Cambridge, 1988), p 146.

7. *IR*, 3 June 1899; Suzuki, pp 73–4; Morgan, Ms 21,760, HC.5.2.17, 4 Sept 1900.

8. Morgan, Ms 21,799, fo 112.

9. Hamilton, Add Ms 48,673, 7 Oct 1898; Milner, Dep 207, fos 20–1; Hamilton, Add Ms 48,675, 5 July 1899; Spring Rice Papers (Churchill College, Cambridge), 1/32, 9 July 1899, 18 Sept 1899.

10. Vincent P. Carosso, *The Morgans: Private International Bankers, 1854–1913* (Cambridge, Mass, 1987), p 445; J. Leighton-Boyce, *Smiths the Bankers, 1658–1958* (1958), pp 289–97; Midland, M 153/62.

11. Midland, M 153/62; NW, 11,417, Parr's Bank board minutes, 22 June 1899, C. A. E. Goodhart, *The Business of Banking, 1891–1914* (1972), p 102.

12. *BM*, Aug 1899, pp 148–51, 232.

13. Maryna Fraser and Alan Jeeves (eds), *All that Glittered: Selected Correspondence of Lionel Phillips, 1890–1924* (Cape Town, 1977), p 107; *Citizen*, 11 March 1899; *FN*, 24 June 1899.

14. Meyer, 6 Feb 1899, 25 Aug 1899, 28 Aug 1899; *FT*, 6 Sept 1899; Gibbs, Ms 11,040, vol 3, 26 Sept 1899.

15. Charles Duguid, *The Story of the Stock Exchange* (1901), pp 383–4; *Citizen*, 14 Oct 1899.

16. G. K. Chesterton, *Autobiography* (1936), p 113; J. A. Hobson, *Imperialism: A Study* (1902), p 359.

17. P. J. Cain and A. G. Hopkins, *British Imperialism: Innovation and Expansion, 1688–1914* (1993), pp 373–4.

18. McCarty, 'Overseas Mining', p 92.

19. *DBB*, Jean-Jacques van Helten, 'Sir Julius Carl Wernher', vol 5, p 739; Meyer, 28 Aug 1899.

20. A helpful overview is Robert Vicat Turrell, ' "Finance . . . The Governor of the Imperial Engine": Hobson and the Case of Rothschild and Rhodes' in Rob Turrell (ed), *The City and the Empire, Volume 2* (Collected Seminar Papers no 36, Institute of Commonwealth Studies, University of London, 1986), pp 85–6, part of a paper subsequently published in *Journal of Southern African Studies* (1987).

21. Both the quotations and the argument derive from Andrew Porter, 'The South African War (1899–1902): Context and Motive Reconsidered' in *Journal of African History* (1990).

22. Gibbs, Ms 11,040, vol 3, 8 Sept 1899; Richard Davis, *The English Rothschilds* (1983), pp 217–19.

23. *Times*, 17 Oct 1899.

CHAPTER TWELVE

1. *JIB*, Dec 1899, pp 533–4, 538–9.

2. *BM*, Feb 1900, p 313; *JIB*, May 1900, pp 255, 258–9.

3. Maryna Fraser and Alan Jeeves, *All that Glittered: Selected Correspondence of Lionel Phillips, 1890–1924* (Cape Town, 1977), p 112; Jardine Matheson records (Cambridge University Library), sect IV, B31/5; *FT*, 12–20 Dec 1899; BB, Dep 33.4, 22 Dec 1899.

4. Charles Duguid, *The Story of the Stock Exchange* (1901), pp 384–95; *Daily Mail*, 15 Jan 1900; Max Karo, *City Milestones and Memories* (1962), p 22; SE, Ms 14,600, vol 69, 17 Jan 1900, 22 Jan 1900; Duguid, pp 402–3.

5. Guy Nickalls, 'Skulling' in W. A. Morgan (ed), *The "House" On Sport* (1898), p 348; SE, Ms 14,600, vol 69, 26 Feb – 12 March 1900; *Economist*, 17 March 1900; Guy Nickalls, *Life's a Pudding* (1939).

6. Midland, M 153/67/2; PRO, T 168/87; Hamilton, Add Ms 48,676, 26 Feb 1900.

7. Duguid, pp 395–7; Norman Mackenzie (ed), *The Letters of Sidney and Beatrice Webb: Volume II, Partnership, 1892–1912* (Cambridge, 1978), p 125.

8. PRO, T 168/87.

9. PRO, T 168/87; R. S. Sayers, *The Bank of England, 1891–1944* (Cambridge, 1976), vol 1, p 16; Hamilton, Add Ms 48,676, 16 March 1900, 28 April 1900.

10. SE, Ms 19,297, vol 15, 22 Nov 1899; Duguid, p 404; Mark Girouard, *The Return to Camelot* (1981), p 173; *FN*, 14 Nov 1902; *Rialto*, 14 April 1900.

11. Heather Gilbert, *The End of the Road: The Life of Lord Mount Stephen, volume 2, 1891–1921* (Aberdeen, 1977), p 181; *FT*, 21 May 1900.

12. Hamilton, Add Ms 48,676, 19–20 July 1900; B of E, G23/88; Hamilton, Add Ms 48,676, 24 July 1900.

13. Kathleen Burk, *Morgan Grenfell, 1838–1988: The Biography of a Merchant Bank* (Oxford, 1989), pp 115–18.

14. Hamilton, Add Ms 48,676, 31 July – 2 Aug 1900.

15. *Statist*, 11 Aug 1900; PRO, T 168/89; Meyer, 7 Aug 1900; *FT*, 8 Aug 1900; Hamilton, Add Ms 48,676, 8 Aug 1900.

16. Milner, Dep 177, fos 155–6.

17. *Economist*, 14 July 1900; *FT*, 16 July 1900, 14 July 1900; *Times*, 16 July 1900; H. Osborne O'Hagan, *Leaves from my Life* (1929), vol II, p 52; *FT*, 17 July 1900; Meyer, 18 July 1900; *FT*, 19–25 July 1900; O'Hagan, vol II, p 53.

18. *FT*, 19 July 1900; SE, Mss 19,515, app 185 and 14,600, vol 70, 7 Aug 1900; Alfred Wagg, 'Autobiography' (unpublished typescript, *c.* 1958, held by Schroders), p 16.

19. Gibbs, Ms 11,040, vol 4, 31 Aug 1900, 14 Sept 1900.

20. Gibbs, Ms 11,040, vol 4, 5 Sept 1900; Milner, Dep 213, fo 161; J. W. McCarty, 'British Investment in Overseas Mining, 1880–1914' (Cambridge PhD, 1961), pp 176–7; J. H. Curle, *The Gold Mines of the World* (2nd edn, 1902), p 281.

21. Richard Price, *An Imperial War and the British Working Class* (1972), p 199; *FT*, 30 Oct 1900.

22. *Investors' Chronicle*, 26 March 1949; *DBB*, R. P. T. Davenport-Hines, 'Whitaker Wright', vol 5, p 902.

23. *FT*, 11 Dec 1900, 18–19 Dec 1900.

24. *FT*, 29 Dec 1900, 31 Dec 1900; Duguid, p 431; *FT*, 2 Jan 1901; Hubert A. Meredith, *The Drama of Money Making: Tragedy and Comedy of the London Stock Exchange* (?1931), p 197.

25. This paragraph is based on Meredith, pp 197–205.

CHAPTER THIRTEEN

1. Hamilton, Add Ms 48,677, 1 Jan 1901; *Citizen*, 26 Jan 1901; Charles Duguid, *The Story of the Stock Exchange* (1901), pp 417–18; *FT*, 5 Feb 1901.

2. Anon, *Irons in the Fire: A Record of the Matthews Wrightson Group of Companies, 1901–1951* (1952), pp 23–7.

3. In general for the two 1901 war loans, see Kathleen Burk, *Morgan Grenfell, 1838–1988: The Biography of a Merchant Bank* (Oxford, 1989), pp 118–21.

4. BB, 200241, 23 Jan 1901; Milner, Dep 214, fo 40; PRO, T 168/89; Burk, p 119; Hamilton, Add Mss 48,677, 6 Feb 1901, 48,614, 6 Feb 1901.

5. Hamilton, Add Ms 48,677, 8 Feb 1901, 11 Feb 1901; *FT*, 13 Feb 1901.

6. Hamilton, Add Ms 48,678, 28 March – 19 April 1901; PRO, T 168/89; B of E, G23/88; Midland, M 153/67/2.

7. *FT*, 23 April 1901; PRO, T 168/89; *FT*, 24–5 April 1901; PRO, T 168/89.

8. Meyer, 5–6 May 1901; *FN*, 7 May 1901; Morgan, Ms 21,802, vol 9, 6 May 1901.

9. Vincent P. Carosso, *Investment Banking in America: A History* (Cambridge, Mass, 1970), pp 110–11; Meyer, 8 May 1901.

10. *FT*, 10 May 1901, *FN*, 10 May 1901.

11. Morgan, Ms 21,802, vol 9, 11 May 1901; *Economist*, 18 May 1901; SE, Ms 14,600, vol 71, 13 May 1901; *FN*, 14 May 1901; *Economist*, 18 May 1901.

12. *BM*, June 1901, p 897; BB, Dep 33.5, 24 May 1901; SE, Ms 14,600, vol 71, 23 May 1901; Kleinwort, Ms 22,033, vol 1, fo 90.

13. Vivian Nickalls, *Oars, Wars, and Horses* (1932), pp 81–3.

14. SE, Mss 14,609, vol 2, 18 Nov 1901, 14,600, vol 72, 9–18 Dec 1901.

15. J. W. McCarty, 'British Investment in Overseas Mining, 1880–1914' (Cambridge PhD, 1961), pp 171–3.

16. *Engineering and Mining Journal*, 21 April 1900; *FN*, 12 July 1901; *Engineering and Mining Journal*, 3 Aug 1901.

17. Robert Vicat Turrell with Jean-Jacques van Helten, 'The Rothschilds, the Exploration Company and Mining Finance' in *Business History* (1986), p 196 discuss the change. J. W. McCarty, 'British Investment in Western Australian Gold Mining, 1894–1914' in *University Studies in History* (1961–2) illuminates the Westralian aspect.

18. George H. Nash, *The Life of Herbert Hoover: The Engineer, 1874–1914* (1983), pp 226–30.

19. Peter Richardson, 'Collins House Financiers' in R. T. Appleyard and C. B. Schedvin (eds), *Australian Financiers: Biographical Essays* (Melbourne, 1988), p 237; *Times*, 28 Oct 1926; *The Memoirs of Herbert Hoover: Years of Adventure, 1874–1920* (New York, 1952), p 79.

20. *Citizen*, 23 Nov 1901; *Westminster Gazette*, 12 Feb 1902; SE, Mss 14,609, vol 2, 11 May 1904 (square footage figs), 14,600, vol 72, 2 April 1902, 14,609, vol 2, 15 May 1902, 6 June 1902; D. T. A. Kynaston, 'The London Stock Exchange, 1870–1914: An Institutional History' (London PhD, 1983), p 72.

21. Burk, pp 121–2 covers the loan.

22. Hamilton, Add Ms 48,679, 7 Feb 1902; Milner, Dep 215, fo 40; Hamilton, Add Ms 48,679, 18 March – 17 April 1902; Morgan, Ms 21,800, vol 1, 15 April 1902; B of E, G23/88; Morgan, Ms 21,800, vol 1, 16 April 1902.

23. *FN*, 29 May 1902; *FT*, 30 May 1902; *FN*, 1–6 Oct 1902; *Economist*, 11 Oct 1902, 18 Oct 1902; *FN*, 31 May 1902, 2 June 1902; Anthony Allfrey, *Edward VII and his Jewish Court* (1991), p 195.

CHAPTER FOURTEEN

1. George R. Sims (ed), *Edwardian London* (1990 Village Press reprint of *Living London*), vol 1, pp 199–202, 126.

2. Ranald C. Michie, *The City of London: Continuity and Change, 1850–1990* (1992), p 14; *Stock Exchange Journal*, Sept 1969, p 14; Donald J. Olsen, *The Growth of Victorian London* (1979 Peregrine edn), p 320; Meyer, 8 Aug 1900.

3. Anon, *Two Centuries of Lewis & Peat, 1775–1975* (1975), p 20; R. D. Blumenfeld, *In the Days of Bicycles and Bustles* (? New York, 1930), p 124; *DBB*, G. Tonge and David J. Jeremy, 'Austin Leonard Reed', vol 4, pp 873–6, Berry Ritchie, *A Touch of Class: The Story of Austin Reed* (1990), pp 9, 19; Charles Duguid, *The Story of the Stock Exchange* (1901), p 318; Blumenfeld, pp 217–18; F. H. Cripps, *Life's a Gamble* (1957), pp 54–5.

4. Hugh Barty-King, *The Baltic Exchange* (1977), p 289; Richard Trench, *London before the Blitz* (1989), p 136; *Statist*, 13 Oct 1900, Blumenfeld, p 81; *Independent*, 11 July 1988; Thomas Burke, *London in My Time* (1934), pp 178–9; *BM*, March 1902, p 455; P. G. Wodehouse, *Psmith in the City* (1993 *The World of Psmith* Penguin omnibus), p 30.

5. C. H. Holden and W. G. Holford, *The City of London: A Record of Destruction and Survival* (1951), p 173.

6. Harold P. Clunn, *The Face of London: The Record of a Century's Changes and Development* (1932), pp 87, 34, 21; *FN*, 30 March 1905; Richard Roberts, *Schroders: Merchants & Bankers* (1992), p 122.

7. Leon Edel and Lyall H. Powers (eds), *The Complete Notebooks of Henry James* (New York, 1987), pp 274–7, 280.

8. Burke, pp 231–2.

9. Ranald Michie, 'Dunn, Fischer & Co in the City of London, 1906–14' in *Business History* (1988), pp 195–6.

10. David Kynaston, *Cazenove & Co: A History* (1991), p 82.

11. S. J. Diaper, 'The History of Kleinwort, Sons & Co in Merchant Banking, 1855–1961' (Nottingham PhD, 1983), p 368; Heseltine, Moss & Co records (consulted at 3 Trump Street *c.*1980); Diaper, p 356.

12. *Quarterly Review*, July 1912, p 94; Elizabeth Hennessy, *A Domestic History of the Bank of England, 1930–1960* (Cambridge, 1992), pp 48–52 on the timeless pattern; Frank H. H. King, *The History of the Hongkong and Shanghai Banking Corporation* (vol II, Cambridge, 1988), p 176; Hurford Janes and H. J. Sayers, *The Story of Czarnikow* (1963), pp 34–5, 43; Captain Cyril F. Bird, *I Remember* (1955), pp 38, 41–2.

13. R. S. Sayers, *Lloyds Bank in the History of English Banking* (Oxford, 1957), p 55; Wallis Hunt, *Heirs of Great Adventure: The History of Balfour, Williamson and Company Limited, 1901–1951* (1960), pp 11–12; Diaper, p 349; Meyer, 13 Feb 1905; BB, 200406; George and Pamela Cleaver, *The Union Discount: A Centenary Album* (1985), pp 42–3; *BM*, March 1902, pp 432–3; C. H. Woodhouse, *The Woodhouses, Drakes and Careys of Mincing Lane* (1977), p 30.

14. *Independent*, 11 July 1988; Sims, vol 4, pp 3–4.

15. David Wainwright, *Government Broker: the story of an office and of Mullens & Co* (1990), p 54; R. S. Sayers, *Gilletts in the London Money Market* (Oxford, 1968), p 35; Sir John Clapham, *The Bank of England: A History* (Cambridge, 1944), vol II, p 396; *Lewis & Peat*, p 21; R. S. Sayers, *The Bank of England, 1891–1944* (Cambridge, 1976), vol I, p 14; Judy Slinn, *Linklaters & Paines: The First One Hundred and Fifty Years* (1987), p 93; Roberts, p 122; *The Westminster*, March 1938, p 72.

16. Anon, *And At Lloyd's: The Story of Price, Forbes and Company Limited* (1954), pp 46–8; Wainwright, p 54; King, p 587; Roberts, p 122; Diaper, p 356.

17. Tierl Thompson (ed), *Dear Girl* (1987), pp 39, 102–3.

18. Theresa Whistler, *Imagination of the Heart: The Life of Walter de la Mare* (1993), p 140.

19. *The Private Diaries of Sydney Moseley* (1960), pp xi–xiii, 4–51.

CHAPTER FIFTEEN

1. George R. Sims (ed), *Edwardian London* (1990 Village Press reprint of *Living London*), vol 4, pp 198–9; C. H. Woodhouse, *The Woodhouses, Drakes and Careys of Mincing Lane* (1977), pp 28–9.

2. Gordon D. Hodge, *56 Years in the London Sugar Market* (1960), pp 17–18; Ranald C. Michie, *The City of London: Continuity and Change, 1850–1990* (1992), p 64.

3. Sims, vol 4, pp 199–201; Anon, *Cook's of St Paul's* (1957), p 9; Frederick Thomas, *I. and R. Morley* (1900), pp 76–99. On the textile sector in general, see: Stanley Chapman, *Merchant Enterprise in Britain: From the Industrial Revolution to World War I* (Cambridge, 1992), pp 167–90.

4. Graham L. Rees, *Britain's Commodity Markets* (1972), p 171.

5. Rees, pp 325, 327; W. Eden Hooper, *The London Coal Exchange* (1907), pp 21–2; Michie, *City*, p 39, part of a pioneering exposition of 'office trade'; Rees, pp 144–5, re LCTA; Michie, *City*, pp 62, 64, Hodge, p 13.

6. Michie, *City*, p 38; *Statist*, 8 Aug 1903.

7. The whole theme of the communications revolution and merchants' responses is explored by Chapman, *Merchant Enterprise*, part III.

8. Robert Greenhill, 'Investment Group, Multinational or Free-standing Company: Brazilian Warrant, 1909–1952' in *Business History* (1995); Michie, *City*, p 42.

9. Chapman, *Merchant Enterprise*, p 233. Investment groups have been the subject of controversy in *Economic History Review*. See: S. D. Chapman, 'British-Based Investment Groups Before 1914' (1985); Robert Vicat Turrell and Jean-Jacques van Helten, 'The investment group: the missing link in British overseas expansion before 1914?' (1987); S. D. Chapman, 'Investment groups in India and South Africa' (1987).

10. Chapman, *Merchant Enterprise*, p 5; N. B. Harte, 'The Growth and Decay of a Hosiery Firm in the Nineteenth Century' in *Textile History* (1977), pp 46–8; Charles A. Jones, *International Business in the Nineteenth Century: The Rise and Fall of a Cosmopolitan Bourgeoisie* (Brighton, 1987), p 185; Chapman, *Merchant Enterprise*, p 211; *JIB*, March 1900, p 133.

11. Chapman, *Merchant Enterprise*, pp 280–1.

12. Kleinwort, Mss 22,033, vol 1, fos 65, 110, 22,030, vol 2, fo 85.

13. Kleinwort, Ms 22,030, vol 2, fo 176.

14. Kleinwort, Mss 22,030, vol 1, fos 124, 130, 169, vol 2, fos 158, 96.

15. Stanley Jackson, *The Sassoons* (1968), including p59 re the 'nerve-centre'; Kleinwort, Ms 22,030, vol 3, fos 130–28, 131.

16. Youssef Cassis, 'The banking community of London, 1890–1914: a survey' in *Journal of Imperial and Commonwealth History* (1985), pp 112–13; Sir Henry Clay, *Lord Norman* (1957), p 272; Gibbs, Ms 11,040, vol 4, 23 Oct 1902.

17. Milner, Deps 213, fo 161, 214, fo 45, 215, fo 60, 216, fo 36.

18. Gibbs, Ms 11,040, vol 2, 11 Oct 1894; Richard Roberts, *Schroders: Merchants & Bankers* (1992), pp 122, 526.

19. Stanley Chapman, *The Rise of Merchant Banking* (1984), pp 169–81 gives a critical assessment of 'performance', including p 172 on the specific missed opportunities.

20. This thesis is propounded by Michael Lisle-Williams, 'Beyond the market: the survival of family capitalism in the English merchant banks' in *British Journal of Sociology* (1984).

21. Philip Ziegler, *The Sixth Great Power: Barings, 1762–1929* (1988), p 303; Chapman, *Merchant Banking*, p 88 on 'the mutual insurance system'.

22. This is the analysis at the core of Youssef Cassis, *City Bankers, 1890–1914* (Cambridge, 1994), including p 59 for a table showing merchant bank representation on the boards of joint-stock banks.

23. Chapman, *Merchant Banking*, p 62.

24. Richard Roberts, 'What's in a Name? Merchants, Merchant Bankers, Accepting Houses, Issuing Houses, Industrial Bankers and Investment Bankers' in *Business History* (1993), pp 29–31.

25. Morgan, Ms 21,795, vol 12, 8 Jan 1907; Roberts, 'Name', p 31; Kleinwort, Ms 22,033, vol 1, fo 131.

26. Roberts, *Schroders*, p 151.

27. Ziegler, p 377, Roberts, *Schroders*, p 149.

28. Roberts, *Schroders*, p 115.

29. Ibid, p 131.

30. These imponderables are brought out in Youssef Cassis, 'Merchant bankers and City aristocracy' in *British Journal of Sociology* (1988).

31. Milner, Dep 214, fo 42.

32. Morgan, Ms 21,800, vol 1, 1 Nov 1901 (related by Dawkins); Ziegler, p 285; Hamilton, Add Ms 48,683, 5 Sept 1905. Also, see: Chapman, *Merchant Banking*, pp 22–5; *DBB*, S. D. Chapman, 'Nathan Meyer Rothschild, 1st Lord Rothschild of Tring, Hertfordshire', vol 4, pp 946–53.

33. Hamilton, Add Ms 48,680, 1 Oct 1902; S. D. Chapman, 'Aristocracy and meritocracy in merchant banking' in *British Journal of Sociology* (1986), p 189, quoting *Manchester Guardian*, 1 April 1915; F. H. Cripps, *Life's a Gamble* (1957), pp 53–4; Alfred Wagg, 'Autobiography' (unpublished typescript, *c.*1958, held by Schroders), p 13;

Blanche E. C. Dugdale, *Arthur James Balfour* (1936), vol II, p 135; Meyer, 3 Sept 1901; Hamilton, Add Ms 48,682, 25 Sept 1904.

34. Walter's life is sympathetically narrated in Miriam Rothschild, *Dear Lord Rothschild: Birds, Butterflies and History* (1983), including pp 220–2, 229–31 on the financial disaster.

35. Hamilton, Add Ms 48,670, 18 Oct 1896; James Capel & Co records (Guildhall Library), Ms 15,123, item 6; John Vincent (ed), *The Crawford Papers: The journals of David Lindsay twenty-seventh Earl of Crawford and tenth Earl of Balcarres 1871–1940 during the years 1892 to 1940* (Manchester, 1984), p 105.

36. For fuller characterisations of Revelstoke, see: *DBB*, John Orbell, 'John Baring, 2nd Lord Revelstoke', vol 1, pp 164–7; Ziegler, pp 268–72.

37. Hamilton, Add Ms 48,678, 4 Oct 1901; Christopher Sykes, *Nancy: The Life of Lady Astor* (1972), p 103.

38. Ziegler, p 272.

39. Heather Gilbert, *The End of the Road: The Life of Lord Mount Stephen, volume 2: 1891–1921* (Aberdeen, 1977), p 63; Ziegler, p 281; BB, Deps 33.8, 11 Oct 1904, 33.9, 31 July 1905.

40. This paragraph is largely based on Kathleen Burk, *Morgan Grenfell, 1838–1988: The Biography of a Merchant Bank* (Oxford, 1989), including pp 58–9 on Dawkins.

41. Milner, Deps 313, fo 163, 216, fo 249.

42. In general on Norman, see: Clay; Andrew Boyle, *Montagu Norman: a biography* (1967); *DBB*, Michael Moss, 'Montagu Collet Norman, Lord Norman of St Clere', vol 4, pp 447–58.

43. Aytoun Ellis, *Heir of Adventure: The story of Brown, Shipley & Co, merchant bankers, 1810–1960* (1960), pp 121–2.

44. Clay, p 65.

45. Each firm has been the subject of a scholarly history: S. J. Diaper, 'The History of Kleinwort, Sons & Co in Merchant Banking, 1855–1961' (Nottingham PhD, 1983); Richard Roberts, *Schroders: Merchants & Bankers* (1992). Our knowledge will be further enhanced by Jehanne Wake's forthcoming history of Kleinwort Benson.

46. Diaper, p 69; Roberts, p 121; Henry Andrews, 'Memoir' (unpublished typescript, 1955, held by Schroders).

47. Diaper, pp 72–84; Roberts, pp 123–35.

48. Diaper, pp 72–3, 77; Kleinwort, Ms 22,033, vol 1, fo 2; BB, 200240, 3 Nov 1900.

49. Kleinwort, Ms 22,033, vol 1, fo 85; Baron E. B. d'Erlanger, *My English Souvenirs* (1978), p 203.

50. Morgan, Ms 21,799, fo 106; on Cunliffe, see *DBB*, R. P. T. Davenport-Hines, 'Walter Cunliffe, 1st Lord Cunliffe', vol 1, pp 861–5, A. Lentin, 'Walter Cunliffe, first Baron Cunliffe' in C. S. Nicholls (ed), *The Dictionary of National Biography: Missing Persons* (Oxford, 1993), pp 164–5; *War Memoirs of David Lloyd George, I* (1933), p 101; John Keyworth, 'Mole, weasel and the Old Lady' in *FT*, 3 March 1990.

51. Richard Meinertzhagen, *Diary of a Black Sheep* (1964), pp 46–50; Ziegler, p 271.

52. *BM*, March 1901, pp 376–89. Richard Roberts, ' "Foreign Bankers" of the City of London, c.1850–1930' (paper given at Institute of Historical Research, London, 29 April 1994, publication forthcoming) brings out that foreign exchange dealings prior to 1914 were as much in foreign-denominated bills as in money.

53. This paragraph derives from Roberts, *Schroders*, p 116.

54. Charles Short, *Morgan Guaranty's London Heritage* (1986), pp 7–10; Kleinwort, Ms 22,033, vol 1, fos 61, 155; Midland, M 153/47/3; Morgan, Ms 21,795, vol 12, 12 Dec 1906.

55. R. S. Sayers, *Gilletts in the London Money Market* (Oxford, 1968), p 46; Roberts, *Schroders*, p 131.

56. *BM*, May 1901, p 755; *JIB*, Feb 1900, pp 73–6.

57. On the relative decline of Glyn Mills and Martins, see Roger Fulford, *Glyn's: 1753–1953* (1953), pp 220, 224–8, George Chandler, *Four Centuries of Banking*, vol 1 (1964), p 412; *JIB*, May 1903, pp 267–8.

58. Youssef Cassis, *La City de Londres, 1870–1914* (Paris, 1987), pp 29–30.

59. *FN*, 23 July 1901.

60. Youssef Cassis, 'Management and Strategy in the English Joint-Stock Banks, 1890–1914' in *Business History* (1985).

61. d'Erlanger, p 206; Gibbs, Ms 11,040, vol 4, 22 Oct 1902.

62. Youssef Cassis, 'Financial Elites in Three European Centres: London, Paris, Berlin, 1880s–1930s' in *Business History* (1991), p 55.

63. *JIB*, Oct 1899, pp 418–19; Cassis, 'Financial Elites', p 55; *JIB*, Feb 1900, pp 71–5.

64. *BM*, March 1901, pp 423–7; *DBB*, Youssef Cassis, 'Sir Felix Otto Schuster', vol 5, pp 77–82.

65. Hamilton, Add Ms 48,679, 11 March 1902; Gibbs, Ms 11,040, vol 4, 22 Oct 1902.

66. NW, 4905, Union Bank of London, 12 July 1902; *BM*, Feb 1905, p 233, March 1901, p 423.

67. *DBB*, Edwin Green, 'Sir Edward Hopkinson Holden', vol 3, pp 290–8.

68. A. R. Holmes and Edwin Green, *Midland: 150 years of banking business* (1986), p 133; Midland, M 153/72; Midland, Acc 150/1, 3 Sept 1906, 292/46, 9 Oct 1908.

69. Midland, Acc 26/3, 4 June 1902, Acc 26/5, 22 June 1904, Acc 26/6, 20 Jan 1905, 20 March 1906.

70. Midland, Acc 26/7, 12 April 1907.

71. Midland, Acc 150/1, 19 Jan 1905; Holmes and Green, p 134; *BM*, Oct 1920, p 411, Dec 1907, pp 714–15.

72. C. A. E. Goodhart, *The Business of Banking, 1891–1914* (1972), pp 136–7; Roberts, *Schroders*, p 131.

73. Morgan, Ms 21,795, vol 12, 12 Dec 1906.

74. *JIB*, March 1902, p 113; Goodhart, pp 131–3, 148–9; *BM*, Nov 1903, p 582, Aug 1906, p 246.

75. SSA, Mss 14,894, vol 9, 29 Dec 1899, vol 10, 16–27 March 1900. See also: R. S. Sayers, *The Bank of England, 1891–1944* (Cambridge, 1976), vol 1, pp 33–7; Richard Roberts, 'The Bank of England and the City' in Richard Roberts and David Kynaston (eds), *The Bank of England: Money, Power and Influence, 1694–1994* (Oxford, 1995), pp 159–60.

76. SSA, Ms 14,894, vol 12, 30 May 1902; *BM*, July 1891, p 41. In general on Nugent and Union Discount, see George and Pamela Cleaver, *The Union Discount: A Centenary Album* (1985).

77. K. F. Dixon, *Alexanders Discount Company Limited, 1810–1960* (1960), p 7; Sir John Clapham, *The Bank of England: A History* (Cambridge, 1944), vol II, p 355; W. T. C. King, *History of the London Discount Market* (1936), p 262.

78. *BM*, Feb 1905, pp 259–61; *DBB*, Gordon A. Fletcher, 'Lawrence Henry Seccombe', vol 5, pp 102–6; Midland, Acc 26/6, 30 Jan 1905.

79. Allen, Harvey & Ross scrapbook (Cater Allen records); NW, 4,337, vol 1, Union Bank of London (re Hellings & Co); *Times*, 15 Sept 1926; Allen, Harvey & Ross scrapbook.

80. Midland, M 153/47/3.

81. The story is told in Sayers, *Gilletts*, pp 71–2 and Gillett Brothers & Co records (Guildhall Library), Mss 24,692, 24,704.

82. *JIB*, Oct 1899, p 409.

83. *Economist*, 23 May 1903; *JIB*, April 1904, p 238; D. T. A. Kynaston, 'The London Stock Exchange, 1870–1914: An Institutional History' (London PhD, 1983), p 108.

84. Kynaston, 'Stock Exchange', pp 109–10.

85. R. C. Michie, *The London and New York Stock Exchanges, 1850–1914* (1987), pp 50–2; Michie, *City*, p 134.
86. Charles Duguid, *The Stock Exchange* (1904), p 156.
87. Charles Duguid, *The Story of the Stock Exchange* (1901), pp 304–7.
88. Kynaston, 'Stock Exchange', pp 66–8.
89. Wagg, p 16; Henry Warren, *How to Deal with your Broker* (1905), pp 184–5; Paul Babb and Gay Owen, *Bonzo: The Life and Work of George Studdy* (Shepton Beauchamp, 1988), p 9.
90. Kynaston, 'Stock Exchange', pp 72–5; Michie, *Stock Exchanges*, pp 86, 252–3.
91. Kynaston, 'Stock Exchange', p 99.
92. SE, Ms 17,957, vol 138; *Stock Exchange Journal*, Sept 1969, p 13; M. C. Reed, *A History of James Capel & Co* (1975), p 98; Kleinwort, Ms 22,033, vol 2, fo 173; E. Victor Morgan and W. A. Thomas, *The Stock Exchange: Its History and Functions* (1962), p 170; Eric Street, *The History of the National Mutual Life Assurance Society, 1830–1980* (1980), p 34.
93. *Rialto*, 3 Dec 1892; Elizabeth Hennessy, *Stockbrokers for 150 Years: A History of Sheppards and Chase, 1827–1977* (1978), p 55; Max Karo, *City Milestones and Memories* (1962), p 38; Anon, *Kitcat & Aitken: A Brief Historical Survey* (c.1972), pp 1–2; Gibbs, Ms 11,040, vol 3, 9 June 1899.
94. Kynaston, 'Stock Exchange', pp 101–2, 106–7, 110–15; Pember & Boyle details are from a 1900 partnership agreement, consulted c.1980 at the firm's offices at 30 Finsbury Circus.
95. Kynaston, 'Stock Exchange', pp 118–19 is the source for all these profit figures.
96. Karo, p 29; Hermione Gingold, *How to Grow Old Disgracefully* (1989), pp 19–60.
97. Gibbs, Ms 11,040, vol 4, 24 Aug 1900; Godefroi D. Ingall and George Withers, *The Stock Exchange* (1904), p 72; G. Cornwallis-West, *Edwardian Hey-Days* (1930), pp 161–2; David Higham, *Literary Gent* (1978), pp 2–21.
98. David Kynaston, 'Gerry Weigall' in *Journal of the Cricket Society* (Spring 1993); *Rialto*, 2 March 1904.
99. Ingall and Withers, pp 167–9, 171; *Journal of the Institute of Actuaries*, April 1912, p 164; Warren, p 175.
100. Unpublished reminiscences of Sir George Aylwen, consulted c.1980 at home of Alexander Scrimgeour, retired partner of Scrimgeours.
101. L. E. Jones, *Georgian Afternoon* (1958), pp 135, 137; Shirley Nicholson, *A Victorian Household* (1988), pp 185, 210; Dorothy Moriarty, *Dorothy: A Nurse's Memoirs, 1889–1989* (1989), pp 4–55, FT, 13 Jan 1906.
102. Morgan, Ms 21,795, vol 12, 29 Jan 1907; Kleinwort, Ms 22,033, vol 1, fo 187; Morgan, Ms 21,795, vol 12, 9 March 1906; d'Erlanger, p 240.
103. Wagg, p 104; Burk, p 294; Carole Angier, *Jean Rhys* (1990), p 63.
104. SSA, Ms 14,894, vol 9, 25 Jan 1899; Gibbs, Ms 11,040, vol 4, 14 Sept 1900; Wagg, p 106; Jean Rhys, *Voyage in the Dark* (1969 Penguin edn), p 12; Angier, pp 61–77.
105. *DBB*, D. E. Moggridge, 'Robert Molesworth Kindersley, 1st Lord Kindersley of West Hoathly', vol 3, pp 596–7.
106. *DBB*, R. P. T. Davenport-Hines, 'Alexander Henderson, 1st Lord Faringdon', vol 3, pp 153–8; David Wainwright, *Henderson: A History of the life of Alexander Henderson, first Lord Faringdon, and of Henderson Administration* (1985), pp 65, 71.
107. S. Japhet, *Recollections from my Business Life* (1931). See also Laurie Dennett, *The Charterhouse Group, 1925–1979: A History* (1979), pp 71–83.
108. *Ninety-one Years: being the reminiscences of Falconer Larkworthy* (1924), Anon (Paul Bareau), *Ionian Bank Limited: A History* (1953), pp 31–2, 42–3; *DBB*, P. E. Smart, 'Frederick Crauford Goodenough', vol 2, pp 603–6; *DBB*, Oliver M. Westall, 'Sir Edward Mortimer Mountain', vol 4, pp 361–7, George J. Emanuel,

Memories of Lloyd's, 1890 to 1937 (1937), p 101; *DBB*, Christopher J. Schmitz, 'Sir Cecil Lindsay Budd', vol 1, pp 492–5, Kleinwort, Ms 22,030, vol 1, fo 189, Rees, p 348

109. The best overview of the movement is Youssef Cassis, 'The emergence of a new financial institution: investment trusts in Britain, 1870–1939' in J. J. van Helten and Y. Cassis (eds), *Capitalism in a Mature Economy: Financial Institutions, Capital Exports and British Industry, 1870–1939* (Aldershot, 1990).

110. Mary E. Murphy, 'Sir George Touche: A Memoir' in *Business History Review* (1960), Archibald B. Richards, *Touche Ross & Co, 1899–1981* (1981), *DBB*, A. B. Richards, 'Sir George Alexander Touche', vol 5, pp 539–42; P. N. Davies, 'Business History and the Role of Chance: The Extraordinary Philipps Brothers' in *Business History* (1981), *DBB*, John P. Scott, 'John Wynford Philipps, 1st Viscount St Davids of Lydstep Haven', vol 4, pp 662–7; Cassis, 'Investment Trusts', p 141, BB, Dep 33.10, 30 April 1906.

111. Jehanne Wake's forthcoming history of Kleinwort Benson provides the best portrait of Benson.

112. Grey, 221/4, 22 Jan 1897.

113. *DBB*, P. E. Smart, 'Sir Richard Biddulph Martin', vol 4, pp 169–71; Cassis, *City Bankers*, pp 116–17.

114. On Cassel: Kurt Grunwald, ' "Windsor-Cassel" – The Last Court Jew' in *Leo Baeck Institute, Year Book* (1969); *DBB*, P. Thane, 'Sir Ernest Joseph Cassel', vol 1, pp 604–14. On Ellerman: *DBB*, William D. Rubinstein, 'Sir John Reeves Ellerman', vol 2, pp 248–61.

115. Milner, Dep 214, fo 48; Hamilton, Add Ms 48,680, 22 March 1903; Cornwallis-West, p 122; Esher Papers (Churchill College, Cambridge), 5/15, 31 May 1902.

116. H. Osborne O'Hagan, *Leaves from my Life* (1929), vol I, pp 384–5.

117. Bryher, *The Heart to Artemis: A Writer's Memoirs* (1963), pp 12–30, 103–6, 267.

118. *Post Magazine and Insurance Monitor*, 23 Dec 1916.

CHAPTER SIXTEEN

1. Hamilton, Add Mss 48,678, 13 May 1901, 48,679, 18 April 1902, 48,682, 8 June 1904; Esher Papers (Churchill College, Cambridge), 2/10, 1 April 1901; Maurice V. Brett (ed), *Journals and Letters of Reginald, Viscount Esher* (1934), vol 1, pp 321–3, 338–9; *Dictionary of National Biography, 1922–1930* (1937), p 109.

2. David Cannadine, *The Decline and Fall of the British Aristocracy* (1990), pp 341–7.

3. The concept was pioneered by P. J. Cain and A. G. Hopkins during the 1980s and brought to full fruition in their *British Imperialism* (2 vols, 1993). For another discussion, and bibliography of the wider debate, see David Kynaston, *The City of London, volume I: A World of Its Own, 1815–1890* (1994), pp 380–9, 462.

4. John Buchan, *Francis and Riversdale Grenfell: A Memoir* (1920), pp 19, 28, 38, 72.

5. Gibbs, Ms 11,040, vol 5, 12 Aug 1904.

6. Youssef Cassis, *City Bankers, 1890–1914* (Cambridge, 1994), especially chs 2 and 5–7.

7. D. T. A. Kynaston, 'The London Stock Exchange, 1870–1914: An Institutional History' (London PhD, 1983), p 97; *List of Members of the Stock Exchange* (1896), pp 121–37.

8. Hamilton, Add Ms 48,675, 16 Sept 1899; *Who Was Who, 1929–1940* (1941), p 957; information from Richard Davenport-Hines.

9. Hamilton, Add Ms 48,678, 26 May 1901; G. R. Searle, *Corruption in British Politics, 1895–1930* (Oxford, 1987), pp 49–50; Meyer, 13 Nov 1900.

10. The most suggestive assessment of what remains a surprisingly shadowy process is Ranald C. Michie, 'The Social Web of Investment in the Nineteenth Century' in *Revue Internationale d'Histoire de la Banque* (1979).

11. Richard Roberts, *Schroders: Merchants & Bankers* (1992), p 361; Morgan, Ms 21,800, vol 1, 13 Dec 1901.

12. J. H. Clapham, *An Economic History of Modern Britain, volume 3* (Cambridge, 1938), p 289; *Journal of the Institute of Actuaries*, April 1899, p 421; Foster & Braithwaite records (Guildhall Library), Ms 14,253, vol 31.

13. 'Upstream', Radio Four, 24 March 1969; *Independent*, 9 April 1993; Thea Thompson, *Edwardian Childhoods* (1981), pp 143–65.

14. John Gielgud, *Early Stages* (1953 edn), pp 37–8; David Kynaston, *Cazenove & Co: A History* (1991), pp 78–9; Roberts, pp 359–60. On Wagg, see also L. E. Jones, *Georgian Afternoon* (1958), pp 71–98.

15. Max Karo, *City Milestones and Memories* (1962), pp 1–14.

16. Hurford Janes and H. J. Sayers, *The Story of Czarnikow* (1963), pp 38–9; Elspet Fraser-Stephen, *Two Centuries in the London Coal Trade: The Story of Charringtons* (1952), p 111; Kleinwort, Mss 22,030, vol 1, fo 48, vol 3, fo 45; Anon, *Glover Brothers, 1853–1953* (1953), p 7; Philip Paul, *City Voyage: The Story of Erlebach and Company, Limited, 1867–1967* (1967), pp 46–7; George Bruce, *Poland's at Lloyd's* (1979), p 29.

17. Cecil Beaton, *My Bolivian Aunt: A Memoir* (1971), pp 18–22, 56; Hugo Vickers, *Cecil Beaton: The Authorized Biography* (1985).

18. On Addis in general, see Roberta Allbert Dayer, *Finance and Empire: Sir Charles Addis, 1861–1945* (1988).

19. Addis, 14/23, 17 March – 2 Dec 1905, 14/24, 16 March 1906, 14/25, 4 Jan – 10 March 1907.

20. Addis, 14/26, 23 Nov 1908, 14/261, 6–8 Sept 1910, 14/28, 7 Sept 1910.

21. Addis, 14/260, 17 Aug 1909; James Lomax and Richard Ormond, *John Singer Sargent and the Edwardian age* (1979), p 59.

22. Nicola Beauman, *Morgan: a biography of E. M. Forster* (1993), p 186; *Independent*, 30 May 1992.

23. Gibbs, Ms 11,040, vol 4, 22 Oct 1902; Robert Henriques, *Marcus Samuel, First Viscount Bearsted and founder of The 'Shell' Transport and Trading Company* (1960), pp 121–2; Elizabeth Hennessy, *Stockbrokers for 150 Years: A History of Sheppards and Chase, 1827–1977* (1978), p 28; Beatrice Webb, *Our Partnership* (1948), p 413; Bo Bramsen and Kathleen Wain, *The Hambros* (1979), pp 346–7.

24. Stanley Chapman's work is notably unreductive. See also, on this side of the argument: M. J. Daunton, ' "Gentlemanly Capitalism" and British Industry, 1820–1914' in *Past and Present* (1989); Andrew Porter, ' "Gentlemanly Capitalism" and Empire: The British Experience since 1850' in *Journal of Imperial and Commonwealth History* (1990).

25. Morgan, Ms 21,799, fo 92; S. J. Diaper, 'The History of Kleinwort, Sons & Co in Merchant Banking, 1855–1961' (Nottingham PhD, 1983), pp 66–71. Roberts, pp 113, 119–21, 150 is also suggestive.

26. M. J. Daunton, 'Australian Merchants in the City of London, 1840–1890' in Rob Turrell (ed), *The City and the Empire, Volume 2* (Collected Seminar Papers no 36, Institute of Commonwealth Studies, University of London, 1986), pp 135–6, 141; Graham L. Rees, *Britain's Commodity Markets* (1972), p 348; D. E. W. Gibb, *Lloyd's of London: A Study in Individualism* (1957), p 182; Kynaston, 'Stock Exchange', p 60.

27. Ranald Michie, 'Dunn, Fischer & Co in the City of London, 1906–14' in *Business History* (1988), p 213.

28. W. S. Robinson, *If I Remember Rightly* (Melbourne, 1967).

29. *DBB*, David J. Jeremy, 'Sir Edward David Stern', vol 5, pp 309–12; *Esher*, vol 1, p 396, vol 2, pp 52, 58, 60.

30. G. Cornwallis-West, *Edwardian Hey-Days* (1930), pp 121–2, 158; Addis, 14/166, 19 June 1905.

31. Meyer, 15 Aug 1907; Philip Ziegler, *The Sixth Great Power: Barings, 1762–1929* (1988), p 269; Gibbs, Ms 11,040, vol 5, 21 Sept 1906.

32. Milner, Dep 215, fo 44; M. Arkin, 'Sir Sigismund Neumann', in D. W. Krüger and C. J. Beyers (eds), *Dictionary of South African Biography, vol. III* (Cape Town, 1977), pp 655–6; Kleinwort, Ms 22,033, vol 1, fo 159; Sir Frederick Ponsonby, *Recollections of Three Reigns* (1951), pp 59–60.

33. Hamilton, Add Ms 48,675, 16 Sept 1899; *Society in the New Reign, By a Foreign Resident* (1904), pp 69–70; Ralph Nevill (ed), *The Reminiscences of Lady Dorothy Nevill* (1906), pp 99–100; George W. E. Russell, *Social Silhouettes* (1906), p 281.

CHAPTER SEVENTEEN

1. *Statist*, 5 July 1902; *CCJ*, Feb 1898, p 28; LCC, Ms 16,643, vol 4, 2 Aug 1899; *Royal Commission on the Port of London* (P.P. 1902, XLIII), qq 7925, 8075; *Economist*, 5 July 1902. For a chronological framework of the Port of London saga, see: *CCJ*, April 1904, pp 81–2; Sir Joseph G. Broodbank, *History of the Port of London* (1921), vol II, pp 273–345.

2. *FT*, 28 Oct 1902; *Economist*, 6 Dec 1902; *CCJ*, July 1903, p 157; LCC, Ms 16,643, vol 6, 15 July 1903.

3. LCC, Ms 16,643, vol 6, 15 July 1903, 24 Nov 1903; *CCJ*, Dec 1903, p 284.

4. *Economist*, 29 April 1905; *CCJ*, May 1908, p 128, May 1909, p 136; W. J. Passingham, *London's Markets: Their Origin and History* (1935), p 199.

5. *FT*, 14 Aug 1902; on the Coronation Syndicate, see *Times*, 11 Aug 1902, *Statist*, 16 Aug 1902, R. R. Mabson, *The Statist's Mines of the Transvaal* (3rd edn, 1904), pp 147–51, Maryna Fraser and Alan Jeeves, *All that Glittered: Selected Correspondence of Lionel Phillips, 1890–1924* (Cape Town, 1977), p 137; *FT*, 3 Oct 1902, 10 Nov 1902; *Statist*, 23 Aug 1902.

6. SE, Mss 14,600, vol 70, 28 Jan 1901, vol 71, 1 April 1901, 18 Sept 1901, vol 73, 11 Aug 1902.

7. *DBB*, R. P. T. Davenport-Hines, 'Arthur Morton Grenfell', vol 2, pp 649–55.

8. Kleinwort, Ms 22,033, vol 1, fo 116; Morgan, Ms 21,760, HC 4.7.4, May 1900, 5 June 1900; Kleinwort, Ms 22,033, vol 1, fo 116.

9. Grey, 246/6, 20 Aug 1902, 4 Sept 1902; BB, 200238, 26 Sept 1902; Grey, 190/2, 19 Sept 1902.

10. Eric Bussière, *Paribas, 1872–1992: Europe and the World* (Antwerp, 1992), pp 46–7; Esher Papers (Churchill College, Cambridge), 5/16, 19 Sept 1902; Hamilton, Add Ms 48,680, 1–27 Oct 1902.

11. Toshio Suzuki, *Japanese Government Loan Issues on the London Capital Market, 1870–1913* (1994), pp 75–82. Suzuki's study is the fullest account of Japanese sovereign loans during the period.

12. RAL, XI/111/33, 22 Sept 1902 (letter from Bertie); *Statist*, 4 Oct 1902; BB, 200149, 9 Oct 1902; Sir Fred Warner, *Anglo-Japanese Financial Relations: A Golden Tide* (Oxford, 1991), p 52.

13. Kathleen Burk, *Morgan Grenfell, 1838–1988: The Biography of a Merchant Bank* (Oxford, 1989), pp 104–11.

14. Hambros records (Guildhall Library), Ms 19,178, bundle 3, 24 April 1902; Morgan, Mss 21,800, vol 1, 18 June 1902, 21,800, vol 2, 9 Sept 1902, 21,799, fo 88, 21,800, vol 2, 14 Aug 1903.

15. T. C. Barker and Michael Robbins, *A History of London Transport, Volume II* (1974), pp 61–84.

16. Morgan, Mss 21,800, vol 2, 19 July 1902, 21,760, HC 2.110 (2), box 5, 21 Oct 1902; BS, Ms 20,112, vol 15, 21 Oct 1902; *Times*, 1 Nov 1902; Barker and Robbins, p 84.

CHAPTER EIGHTEEN

1. 'Diary kept by alderman Sir Marcus Samuel during the year of his mayoralty' (Guildhall Library), Ms 10,590, 10–11 Nov 1902; see also Robert Henriques, *Marcus Samuel, First Viscount Bearsted and founder of The 'Shell' Transport and Trading Company* (1960), pp 422–7 for an account of the day's ceremonies.

2. *Lloyd's Weekly Newspaper*, 16 Nov 1902, 28 Dec 1902, 4 Jan 1903, *Illustrated Police News*, 22 Nov 1902, 29 Nov 1902, 6 Dec 1902, 27 Dec 1902, *Economist*, 22 Nov 1902, 'Diary kept by . . . Samuel', 25 Nov 1902.

3. *FT*, 19–22 Nov 1902; *Economist*, 22 Nov 1902; *FN*, 6 Dec 1902.

4. George H. Nash, *The Life of Herbert Hoover: The Engineer, 1874–1914* (1983), pp 245–76, 666–72 tells the story in detail.

5. Herbert Hoover Library (West Branch, Iowa), Presidential Papers, Pre-Commerce Collection, Subject Series, Rowe Defalcation 1902–4, 28 Dec 1902; Nash, p 275.

6. D. E. W. Gibb, *Lloyd's of London: A Study in Individualism* (1957), pp 183–6.

7. *Economist*, 4 July 1903.

8. *Times*, 12 June 1903; *Economist*, 4 July 1903.

9. *FT*, 11 Dec 1902; *Hansard*, 15 Dec 1902, cols 1263, 1273; *FT*, 17 Dec 1902; D. C. M. Platt, *Finance, Trade, and Politics in British Foreign Policy, 1815–1914* (Oxford, 1968), pp 339–46.

10. Accounts of this episode include: Richard M. Francis, 'The British Withdrawal from the Bagdad Railway Project in April 1903' in *Historical Journal* (1973); Pat Thane, 'Financiers and the British State: The Case of Sir Ernest Cassel' in *Business History* (1986), pp 92–3; Philip Ziegler, *The Sixth Great Power: Barings, 1762–1929* (1988), pp 316–17; Kathleen Burk, *Morgan Grenfell, 1838–1988: The Biography of a Merchant Bank* (Oxford, 1989), p 124; Anthony Allfrey, *Edward VII and his Jewish Court* (1991), pp 220–3.

11. BSP, HBC 29, 25 Feb 1901, 11 April 1901, 27 June 1901, 26 March 1902; Morgan, Ms 21,800, vol 2, 12 Sept 1902.

12. BSP, HBC 29, 6 Feb 1903, 13 March 1903, 26 March 1903.

13. Hamilton, Add Ms 48,680, 14 April 1903; BSP, HBC 29, 15 April 1903; Morgan, Ms 21,800, vol 2, 23 April 1903.

14. Hamilton, Add Ms 48,680, 21 April 1903; BSP, HBC 29, 27 April 1903; Francis, p 174; *National Review*, May 1903, p 344.

15. Hamilton, Add Ms 48,680, 17 March – 4 May 1903; *FT*, 7 May 1903.

16. *FT*, 8 May 1903; Hamilton, Add Ms 48,680, 8–11 May 1903; *FT*, 14 May 1903; *Economist*, 16 May 1903; Tritton's justification in *JIB*, Dec 1903, pp 510–11.

17. Hamilton, Add Mss 48,680, 21–2 April 1903, 48,681, 9 Dec 1903; *Economist*, 25 July 1903.

18. *FT*, 22 Nov 1902, *Economist*, 29 Nov 1902 on 'The Jobber's Jeremiad'; SE, Mss 14,600, vol 73, 17 Dec 1902, vol 74, 2 Feb 1903, 16 Feb 1903; *Economist*, 28 March 1903; SE, Ms 14,600, vol 74, 23 April 1903, 21 May 1903.

19. *FT*, 1–4 May 1903.

20. *Statist*, 25 July 1903; *Citizen*, 25 July 1903; *FT*, 7–10 Oct 1903, 7 Nov 1903.

21. 'Diary kept by . . . Samuel', 21 Sept – 10 Nov 1903.

CHAPTER NINETEEN

1. Hamilton, Add Ms 48,679, 13 Feb 1902; *FT*, 14 Feb 1902, 21 March 1903.

2. The larger context to Chamberlain's campaign is lucidly outlined in Scott Newton and Dilwyn Porter, *Modernization Frustrated: The Politics of Industrial Decline in Britain since 1900* (1988), pp 1–22.

3. Ruth Dudley Edwards, *The Pursuit of Reason: The Economist, 1843–1993* (1993), pp 452–3; *FN*, 18 May 1903; *FT*, 18 May 1903; Richard A. Rempel, *Unionists*

Divided: Arthur Balfour, *Joseph Chamberlain and the Unionist Free Traders* (Newton Abbot, 1972), p 43; Hamilton, Add Ms 48,681, 3–5 July 1903; Julian Amery, *Joseph Chamberlain and the Tariff Reform Campaign* (1969), p 301; Maurice V. Brett (ed), *Journals and Letters of Reginald, Viscount Esher* (1934), vol 2, p 3; *BM*, Sept 1903, p 405; *CCJ*, Aug 1903, p 179.

4. *FT*, 19 Sept 1903; Amery, pp 467–8; *FT*, 9 Oct 1903; *JIB*, Dec 1903, pp 503, 509.

5. Gibbs, Ms 11,021, vol 30, 8 Jan 1904; Wolfgang Mock, *Imperiale Herrschaft und nationales Interesse* (Stuttgart, 1982), pp 393–7. For a detailed analysis of how the banking interest lined up, see: Youssef Cassis, *City Bankers, 1890–1914* (Cambridge, 1994), pp 301–7.

6. *JIB*, Feb 1904, pp 55–100, *BM*, Jan 1904, p 56.

7. *JIB*, Feb 1904, pp 101–22.

8. *FT*, 20 Jan 1904; Milner, Dep 216, fo 250.

9. *FT*, 9 Feb 1904; *CCJ*, April 1904, p 83; *BM*, July 1904, p 45.

10. *BM*, Jan 1904, pp 50–1; P. J. Cain and A. G. Hopkins, *British Imperialism: Innovation and Expansion, 1688–1914* (1993), p 220; Roland Quinault, 'Joseph Chamberlain: a Reassessment' in T. R. Gourvish and Alan O'Day (eds), *Later Victorian Britain, 1867–1900* (1988), pp 71–3; *JIB*, Dec 1904, p 534; *BM*, March 1904, p 380.

11. Stimulating discussions of the new dispositions include: Geoffrey Ingham, *Capitalism Divided? The City and Industry in British Social Development* (1984), pp 152–3, 159–62, 169; Newton and Porter, pp 22–9; E. H. H. Green, 'The influence of the City over British economic policy, c. 1880–1960' in Youssef Cassis (ed), *Finance and Financiers in European History, 1880–1960* (Cambridge, 1992), p 200; Cain and Hopkins, pp 214–24.

12. Beatrice Webb, *Our Partnership* (1948), p 269; W. J. Ashley, *The Tariff Problem* (1903), pp 112–13.

CHAPTER TWENTY

1. *FT*, 25 Nov 1903.

2. *BM*, Dec 1903, pp 696–8, March 1904, p 476.

3. *BM*, July 1920, p 43; *FT*, 21 June 1906; *BM*, March 1904, pp 381–2; *JIB*, March 1904, pp 154, 156–7, *BM*, March 1904, p 383.

4. Sir John Clapham, *The Bank of England: A History* (Cambridge, 1944), vol II, p 379.

5. R. S. Sayers, *The Bank of England, 1891–1944* (Cambridge, 1976), vol 1, pp 60–3.

6. *JIB*, Dec 1904, p 533; L. S. Pressnell, 'Gold Reserves, Banking Reserves, and the Baring Crisis of 1890' in C. R. Whittlesey and J. S. G. Wilson (eds), *Essays in Money and Banking in honour of R. S. Sayers* (Oxford, 1968), p 224.

7. 'Diary kept by alderman Sir Marcus Samuel during the year of his mayoralty' (Guildhall Library), Ms 10,590, 27–8 Oct 1903. Helpful accounts of the Japanese loan of May 1904 are: Philip Ziegler, *The Sixth Great Power: Barings, 1762–1929* (1988), pp 311–12; Toshio Suzuki, *Japanese Government Loan Issues on the London Capital Market, 1870–1913* (1994), pp 84–104.

8. BB, 200187, 8 March 1904.

9. Suzuki, pp 93–7; Cyrus Adler, *Jacob H. Schiff: His Life and Letters* (1929), vol I, pp 214–16; Anthony Allfrey, *Edward VII and his Jewish Court* (1991), pp 214–15.

10. *FT*, 4–12 May 1904.

11. Suzuki, pp 99–104; BB, Dep 33.8, 31 Dec 1904.

12. Suzuki, pp 106–13; *FT*, 29 March 1905; Addis, 14/23, 29 March 1905, 31 March 1905.

13. BB, Dep 33.9, 11 July 1905; Suzuki, pp 115–17; Addis, 14/23, 4 Aug 1905.

14. In general on the City and China at this time, see: E. W. Edwards, 'The origins of British financial co-operation with France in China, 1903–6' in *English Historical Review* (1971); E. W. Edwards, *British Diplomacy and Finance in China, 1895–1914* (Oxford, 1987), pp 30–88; P. J. Cain and A. G. Hopkins, *British Imperialism: Innovation and Expansion, 1688–1914* (1993), pp 432–40.

15. Edwards, *Diplomacy and Finance*, p 64; Edwards, 'Financial Co-operation', p 301; Edwards, *Diplomacy and Finance*, p 63; *Statist*, 16 July 1904; Edwards, *Diplomacy and Finance*, p 70; Roberta Allbert Dayer, *Finance and Empire: Sir Charles Addis, 1861–1945* (1988), p 56.

16. *DBB*, R. P. T. Davenport-Hines, 'Sir Edmund Gabriel Davis', vol 2, pp 24–8. The case of Chang Yen-Mao is exhaustively related in George H. Nash, *The Life of Herbert Hoover: The Engineer, 1874–1914* (1983), pp 182–222, 646–59.

17. Davenport-Hines, 'Davis'; *FT*, 2 March 1905; *Times*, 2 March 1905; Lo Hui-Min (ed), *The Correspondence of G. E. Morrison, volume I: 1895–1912* (Cambridge, 1976), p 376.

18. Milner, Dep 216, fo 250; *FT*, 23 Jan 1904; *Hansard*, 17 Feb 1904, cols 53, 55, 59, 71, 85, 94–5, 102; *FT*, 20 Feb 1904.

19. Milner, Dep 216, fos 253, 255; *FT*, 4 July 1904.

20. John Buchan, *Francis and Riversdale Grenfell: A Memoir* (1920), p 46; Godefroi D. Ingall and George Withers, *The Stock Exchange* (1904), p 230; *FN*, 26 March 1904; *Daily Mail*, 28 June 1904; BB, Dep 33.8, 17 Aug 1904; Hamilton, Add Ms 48,682, 29 Aug 1904.

21. *FN*, 23 Jan 1904; *Economist*, 5 March 1904; *DBB*, David T. A. Kynaston, 'Ferdinand Faithfull Begg', vol 1, pp 249–50; *City Punch Bowl*, 13 March 1897; *FN*, 16 March 1904; *Economist*, 26 March 1904.

22. *Economist*, 5 Nov 1904; *FN*, 6–8 Dec 1904.

23. D. T. A. Kynaston, 'The London Stock Exchange, 1870–1914: An Institutional History' (London PhD, 1983), pp 66, 73.

24. SE, Ms 14,600, vol 76, 11 July 1904; *FN*, 20 March 1905.

25. *FN*, 22 March 1905; *Economist*, 25 March 1905; *FN*, 23 March 1905.

26. Kynaston, 'Stock Exchange', pp 61–3.

27. Kynaston, 'Stock Exchange', pp 63–4; *Economist*, 26 Nov 1904, 6 May 1905; *FN*, 3 July 1905.

28. R. C. Michie, *The London and New York Stock Exchanges, 1850–1914* (1987), pp 81–2 offers a partial defence of the managers, mainly on the international side.

29. SE, Mss 19,297, vol 17, 3 Feb 1904, 17 Feb 1904, 14,608, vol 3, 17 April – 23 July 1907, 14,601, vol 1, 5 Nov 1908 – 8 June 1909, 14,600, vol 89, 6 Nov 1911, 19,297, vol 17, 21 Sept 1904.

30. Meyer, 20 Feb 1905; *FT*, 19 Jan 1905; Grey, 202/2, 5 April 1905; Robert V. Kubicek, *Economic Imperialism in Theory and Practice: The Case of South African Gold Mining Finance, 1886–1914* (Durham, NC, 1979), pp 77–9; *Times*, 26 July 1905; Grey, 202/2, 14 Nov 1905.

31. Jane Ridley and Clayre Percy (eds), *The Letters of Arthur Balfour and Lady Elcho, 1885–1917* (1992), p 210; Morgan, Ms 21,800, vol 2, 16 Feb 1904; BB, 200090, 2–9 Feb 1904.

32. BB, Dep 33.8, 15 Aug 1904, 101938, 10 March 1905; Ziegler, p 304.

33. On the putative merger in 1904/5, see: Vincent P. Carosso, *The Morgans: Private International Bankers, 1854–1913* (Cambridge, Mass, 1987), pp 446–8; Ziegler, pp 296–9; Kathleen Burk, *Morgan Grenfell, 1838–1988: The Biography of a Merchant Bank* (Oxford, 1989), pp 59–62. There is evidence (Milner, Dep 214, fo 45) that Revelstoke had been pushing for an alliance in 1901.

34. BB, Dep 33.9, 14 April 1905; Milner, Dep 177, 16 April 1905.

35. Burk, pp 59, 61–2, 64–5.

36. *FT*, 6 Dec 1905; Milner, Dep 222, fos 13–14.

CHAPTER TWENTY-ONE

1. BB, 200164, 9 June – 9 Oct 1905, 200243, 14 Oct 1905, Dep 33.9, 17 Oct 1905; 'Louis XIV' is identified in Duff Hart-Davis (ed), *End of an Era: Letters and Journals of Sir Alan Lascelles, 1887–1920* (1986), p 153. The story is also told in L. E. Jones, *Georgian Afternoon* (1958), p 136.

2. BB, 200164, 22–31 Oct 1905, 200243, 7 Nov 1905.

3. Toshio Suzuki, *Japanese Government Loan Issues on the London Capital Market, 1870–1913* (1994), pp 117–27.

4. *FT*, 28–9 Nov 1905; Addis, 14/23, 14 Dec 1905.

5. R. S. Sayers, *The Bank of England, 1891–1944* (Cambridge, 1976), vol 1, p 40; *Statist*, 16 Dec 1905; Midland, Acc 26/6, 13 Dec 1905; *BM*, March 1906, p 462; SSA, Ms 14,894, vol 15, 13 Dec 1905; Hamilton, Add Ms 48,614, 27 Dec 1905.

6. *FT*, 5 Dec 1905; R. P. T. Davenport-Hines, 'The Ottoman Empire in Decline: The Business Imperialism of Sir Vincent Caillard, 1883–98' in R. V. Turrell and J. J. van Helten (eds), *The City and the Empire* (Collected Seminar Papers no 35, Institute of Commonwealth Studies, University of London, 1985), p 130; *Economist*, 13 Jan 1906; Heseltine, Moss & Co records (consulted at 3 Trump Street c.1980), Heseltine, Powell & Co circular dated 19 Jan 1906; Addis, 14/167, 21 Jan 1906.

7. *FT*, 6 Jan 1906; *Times*, 16–17 Jan 1906.

8. *Times*, 18 Jan 1906; Balfour Papers (British Library), Add Ms 49,858, fo 163; *FT*, 15 Jan 1906; Balfour, Add Ms 49,858, fo 163.

9. Gibbs, Ms 11,039, c.22 Jan 1906; RAL, XI/130A/o, 21 Feb 1906; SE, Ms 14,600, vol 78, 26 Feb 1906.

10. D. Porter, 'The Unionist Tariff Reformers, 1903–14' (Manchester PhD, 1976), pp 464–6; *DBB*, David T. A. Kynaston and R. P. T. Davenport-Hines, 'Frederick George Banbury, 1st Lord Banbury of Southam', vol 1, pp 144–6.

11. RAL, XI/130A/o, 1 Jan 1906; the rest of the paragraph derives from Edgar Jones, *True and Fair: A History of Price Waterhouse* (1995).

12. BB, Dep 33.10, 13 Feb 1906; *Economist*, 27 Jan 1906, 24 Feb 1906; Robert V. Kubicek, *Economic Imperialism in Theory and Practice: The Case of South African Gold Mining Finance, 1886–1914* (Durham, NC, 1979), p 78.

13. *IR*, 3 March 1906.

14. RAL, XI/130A/o, 16–30 March 1906; Beatrice Webb, *Our Partnership* (1948), p 338.

15. On this loan, see: Philip Ziegler, *The Sixth Great Power: Barings, 1762–1929* (1988), pp 313–14.

16. BB, 200214, 19 April 1906; RAL, XI/130A/o, 23 April 1906, 30 April 1906; Morgan, Ms 21,795, vol 12, 1 May 1906; BB, 200214, 11 May 1906.

17. Grey, 202/2, 13 May 1906; Hamilton, Add Ms 48,614, 25 May 1906; RAL, XI/130A/o, 6 June 1906; B of E, G23/88.

18. *BM*, July 1906, pp 64–6.

19. Midland, Acc 150/1, 9 July 1906; BB, Dep 33.8, 2 Nov 1904.

20. ND, Ms 18,211; *FN*, 12 July 1906.

21. Morgan, Ms 21,802, vol 11, 13 July 1906; RAL, XI/130A/o, 16 July 1906; Morgan, Ms 21,795, vol 12, 17 July 1906; BB, 200214, 20 July 1906; SSA, Ms 14,894, vol 16, 19 July 1906; Morgan, Ms 21,802, vol 11, 20 July 1906.

22. BB, Dep 33.10, 3 Aug 1906, 200214, 5 Sept 1906.

23. Grey, 202/2, 26 Aug 1906.

24. Grey, 202/2, 26 Aug 1906; *BM*, Oct 1906, p 460. On finance bills, see: Schuster's exposition in *BM*, Feb 1905, pp 227–8; C. A. E. Goodhart, *The New York Money Market and the Finance of Trade, 1900–1913* (Cambridge, Mass, 1969), pp 54–6; Ranald C. Michie, *The City of London: Continuity and Change, 1850–1990* (1992), pp 77–8.

25. BB, 200214, 27 June 1906, Dep 33.10, 2 Aug 1906; Morgan, Ms 21,795, vol 12, 12 Dec 1906 (Grenfell's $400m estimate); *BM*, Oct 1906, p 460.

26. J. Spencer Phillips in *JIB*, Dec 1906, pp 475–6; R. C. Michie, *The London and New York Stock Exchanges, 1850–1914* (1987), pp 148–9.

27. *Economist*, 6 Oct 1906; *FT*, 11–12 Oct 1906, 19–20 Oct 1906.

28. *FT*, 22–4 Oct 1906.

29. SSA, Ms 14,894, vol 16, 20–4 Oct 1906; *BM*, Dec 1906, pp 745–7; Sayers, vol 1, p 55. In general, Sayers offers a helpful narrative of these difficult weeks.

30. BB, 200214, 29 Nov 1906; Morgan, Ms 21,802, vol 11, 8 Dec 1906; *Economist*, 29 Dec 1906; SSA, Ms 14,894, vol 16, 31 Dec 1906.

31. Grey, 202/2, 29 Nov 1906.

32. B of E, C45/13; L. S. Pressnell, 'Gold Reserves, Banking Reserves, and the Baring Crisis of 1890' in C. R. Whittlesey and J. S. G. Wilson (eds), *Essays in Money and Banking in honour of R. S. Sayers* (Oxford, 1968), p 222.

33. *JIB*, Jan 1907, pp 13, 19–21; RAL, XI/130A/o, 21 Dec 1906.

34. *BM*, Feb 1907, p 233; *JIB*, Feb 1907, pp 66–84.

35. B of E, C40/314; *BM*, April 1907, p 591, Sept 1907, p 417.

36. SE, Ms 14,600, vol 79, 24 Sept 1906, 15 Oct 1906.

37. SE, Mss 14,600, vols 79 and 80, 6 Nov 1906 – 13 Feb 1907.

38. SE, Ms 14,600, vol 80, 21 Feb 1907; *FN*, 22 March 1907, 28 Dec 1916. On Graham, see *The Stock Exchange Memorial of those who fell in The Great War, MCMXIV–MCMXIX* (1920), unpaginated.

39. *Statist*, 12 Jan 1907; *Times*, 31 Jan 1907; *FT*, 1 Feb 1907; *Economist*, 2 Feb 1907; Philip Magnus, *King Edward the Seventh* (1964), p 389; Morgan, Ms 21,795, vol 12, 14 Dec 1906; Kathleen Burk, *Morgan Grenfell, 1838–1988: The Biography of a Merchant Bank* (Oxford, 1989), pp 70, 295.

40. RAL, XI/130A/1, 16 Jan 1907; *Economist*, 19 Jan 1907; SSA, Ms 14,894, vol 17, 31 Jan 1907.

41. RAL, XI/130A/1, 19 Feb 1907.

42. Suzuki, pp 129–39.

43. Addis, 14/25, 5 March 1907; Stanley Chapman, *The Rise of Merchant Banking* (1984), p 89; Morgan, Ms 21,795, vol 12, 6 March 1907 (both Grenfell letters); Addis, 14/25, 9 March 1907.

44. *FT*, 14–15 March 1907; RAL, XI/130A/1, 15 March 1907; Morgan, Ms 21,795, vol 12, 16 March 1907, 23 March 1907.

45. BB, 200216, 27 March 1907; RAL, XI/130A/1, 27 March 1907; Morgan, Ms 21,802, vol 11, 27 March 1907; BB, 200216, 4 April 1907.

46. John Buchan, *Francis and Riversdale Grenfell: A Memoir* (1920), pp 99–101; Morgan, Ms 21,795, vol 12, 19–23 April 1907.

47. BB, 200216, 12 June 1907, 26 June 1907; Addis, 14/168, 23 July 1907.

48. Sayers, vol 1, pp 57–9 is the best guide to the events between August and December 1907.

49. SSA, Ms 14,894, vol 17, 6 Aug 1907; Meyer, 8 Aug 1907; S. J. Diaper, 'The History of Kleinwort, Sons & Co in Merchant Banking, 1855–1961' (Nottingham PhD, 1983), p 83; RAL, XI/130A/1, 4 Sept 1907; *FT*, 26 Sept 1907.

50. Grey, 202/3, 12 Oct 1907; RAL, XI/130A/1, 14 Oct 1907; Goodhart, p 117; Heseltine, Moss & Co records, Heseltine, Powell & Co circular dated 19 Oct 1907.

51. RAL, XI/130A/1, 22 Oct 1907; SSA, Ms 14,894, vol 17, 22 Oct 1907; *FT*, 23 Oct 1907; S. Japhet, *Recollections from my Business Life* (1931), p 98; RAL, XI/130A/1, 23 Oct 1907.

52. *FT*, 29 Oct 1907; RAL, XI/130A/1, 29 Oct 1907; *FT*, 31 Oct – 1 Nov 1907; RAL, XI/130A/1, 1 Nov 1907.

53. Sayers, vol 1, p 59; *FT*, 5 Nov 1907; RAL, XI/130A/1, 4 Nov 1907; *FT*, 6–7 Nov 1907; Morgan, Ms 21,802, vol 11, 6 Nov 1907.

54. Grey, 202/3, 7 Nov 1907; *FT*, 8 Nov 1907; RAL, XI/130A/1, 7 Nov 1907; *FT*, 8 Nov 1907.
55. Morgan, Ms 21,795, vol 13, 13 Nov 1907; *FT*, 16 Nov 1907; Grey, 202/3, 18 Nov 1907; SSA, Ms 14,894, vol 17, 18 Nov 1907; *FT*, 19 Nov 1907; Sayers, vol 1, p 59.
56. Grey, 202/3, 25 Nov 1907.
57. Osbert Sitwell, *The Scarlet Tree* (1947 Reprint Society edn), pp 289–90.

CHAPTER TWENTY-TWO

1. ND, Ms 18,211.
2. The impact of Will Hutton, *The State We're In* (1995), with the City foursquare in the author's sights, is testimony to the debate's hardiness. Important recent contributions to the historical, pre-1914 debate include: P. L. Cottrell, *Industrial Finance, 1830–1914: The Finance and Organization of English Manufacturing Industry* (1980); R. C. Michie, 'Options, Concessions, Syndicates, and the Provision of Venture Capital, 1880–1913' in *Business History* (1981); Geoffrey Ingham, *Capitalism Divided? The City and Industry in British Social Development* (1984); Sidney Pollard, 'Capital Exports: Harmful or Beneficial?' in *Economic History Review* (1985); William P. Kennedy, *Industrial structure, capital markets and the origins of British economic decline* (Cambridge, 1987); Perry Anderson, 'The Figures of Descent' in *New Left Review* (Jan–Feb 1987); Scott Newton and Dilwyn Porter, *Modernization Frustrated: The Politics of Industrial Decline in Britain since 1900* (1988); Sidney Pollard, *Britain's Prime and Britain's Decline: The British Economy, 1870–1914* (1989), especially pp 58–114 on 'The Export of Capital'; M. J. Daunton, ' "Gentlemanly Capitalism" and British Industry, 1820–1914' in *Past and Present* (1989); Ranald C. Michie, 'The Stock Exchange and the British economy, 1870–1939' in J. J. van Helten and Y. Cassis (eds), *Capitalism in a Mature Economy: Financial Institutions, Capital Exports and British Industry* (Aldershot, 1990); Ranald C. Michie, *The City of London: Continuity and Change, 1850–1990* (1992), pp 108–16; P. J. Cain and A. G. Hopkins, *British Imperialism: Innovation and Expansion, 1688–1914* (1993), especially chs 3–7. For two particularly useful – and measured – overviews, see: Youssef Cassis, 'British finance: success and controversy' in van Helten and Cassis; Michael Collins, *Banks and Industrial Finance in Britain, 1800–1939* (1991).
3. *BM*, Dec 1906, pp 747–8; *FT*, 6 March 1907.
4. *CCJ*, May 1907, p 132; *Economist*, 1 June 1907; *BM*, July 1907, pp 18, 25. On Docker in general, see: R. P. T. Davenport-Hines, *Dudley Docker: The Life and Times of a Trade Warrior* (Cambridge, 1984).
5. *CCJ*, Oct 1907, supplement, pp 11–13.
6. Collin Brooks, *Something in the City* (1931), p 62; *JIB*, Dec 1907, pp 575, 582–3.
7. *JIB*, Dec 1908, pp 568–9; National Monetary Commission (Senate doc no 405), *Interviews on the Banking and Currency Systems of England, Scotland, France, Germany, Switzerland, and Italy* (Washington, 1910), p 47; *JIB*, Jan 1908, p 57.
8. Forrest Capie and Michael Collins, *Have the Banks Failed British Industry?* (1992), pp 28–43.
9. Cottrell, *Industrial Finance*, pp 230–6; Youssef Cassis, 'Management and Strategy in the English Joint-Stock Banks, 1890–1914' in *Business History* (1985), pp 304–5; Midland, Acc 26/6, 23 Jan 1905; A. R. Holmes and Edwin Green, *Midland: 150 years of banking business* (1986), pp 115–16.
10. For more on these 'five main criticisms', see: Cottrell, *Industrial Finance*, pp 237–9; P. L. Cottrell, 'The domestic commercial banks and the City of London, 1870–1939' in Youssef Cassis (ed), *Finance and Financiers in European History, 1880–1960* (Cambridge, 1992), pp 53–5; C. A. E. Goodhart, *The Business of Banking, 1891–1914* (1972), p 135; Collins, *Banks and Industrial Finance*, pp 35–42; Cassis, 'Success and Controversy', pp 3–5; Holmes and Green, pp 112–18. The standard history

of the banking system as a whole, with much on these matters, is Michael Collins, *Money and Banking in the UK: A History* (1988).

11. National Monetary Commission, pp 47–8.

12. Cassis, 'Success and Controversy', p 5; Philip Ziegler, *The Sixth Great Power: Barings, 1762–1929* (1988), p 286; BB, 200243, 24 Jan 1905, 101938, 7 Feb 1905; Vincent P. Carosso, *The Morgans: Private International Bankers, 1854–1913* (Cambridge, Mass, 1987), p 497; David Wainwright, *A History of the life of Alexander Henderson, first Lord Faringdon, and of Henderson Administration* (1985), p 47; H. Osborne O'Hagan, *Leaves from my Life* (1929), vol II, pp 82–95, 105; MG, private letter books, no 3, 22 Nov 1910.

13. *JIB*, May 1904, pp 281–2; *Times*, 8 Oct 1909; PRO, BT 55/32.

14. Cottrell, *Industrial Finance*, pp 64–75 is the best guide to the legislative background.

15. *BM*, Feb 1903, pp 209, 211; *Economist*, 2 March 1907. On the continuing prevalence of market-making and related practices, and the inadequate supervision exercised by the Stock Exchange Committee, see D. T. A. Kynaston, 'The London Stock Exchange, 1870–1914: An Institutional History' (London PhD, 1983), pp 142–86.

16. Henry Lowenfeld, *All About Investment* (1909), pp 14–17.

17. Lowenfeld, p 175; Godefroi D. Ingall and George Withers, *The Stock Exchange* (1904), p 89; *Economist*, 27 Aug 1904; James Capel & Co records (Guildhall Library), Ms 15,123, item 36; Kynaston, 'Stock Exchange', p 6.

18. G. Byng, *Protection: The Views of a Manufacturer* (1901), pp 25–6.

19. Kennedy, *Industrial Structure*, pp 134–8; William P. Kennedy, 'Shorting the Future: The Financing of the Electrical Industry in Victorian Britain' (forthcoming). The best overall guide is I. C. R. Byatt, *The British Electrical Industry, 1875–1914: the economic returns to a new technology* (Oxford, 1979).

20. *Statist*, 25 April 1903; Donald Read, *England, 1868–1914: The age of urban democracy* (1979), p 226.

21. Kennedy, *Industrial Structure*, pp 139–40; Roy Church, *The Rise and Decline of the British Motor Industry* (1994), pp 1–7. See also David Thoms and Tom Donnelly, *The Motor-Car Industry in Coventry since the 1890s* (Beckenham, 1985).

22. *Economist*, 24 Jan 1914; J. M. Keynes, *The General Theory of Employment, Interest and Money* (1936), p 155.

23. *Electrician*, 17 Aug 1894; *Electrical Investments*, 8 Oct 1902; *Times*, 27 May 1911; Kynaston, 'Stock Exchange', p 238; *Economist*, 19 Dec 1903.

24. Kennedy, 'Electrical Industry'.

25. Midland, Acc 26/8, 1 Feb 1912; *Electrical Review*, 30 July 1909.

26. The case is made best by Ranald Michie, 'The Finance of Innovation in Late Victorian and Edwardian Britain: Possibilities and Constraints' in *Journal of European Economic History* (1988), pp 509–18.

27. Institution of Electrical Engineers, application of J. B. Braithwaite, 13 Feb 1893; *DBB*, R. P. T. Davenport-Hines, 'Andrew Wilson Tait', vol 5, p 430, J. F. Wilson, *Ferranti and the British electrical industry, 1864–1930* (Manchester, 1988), pp 81–4; Cottrell, *Industrial Finance*, pp 232–3 (Glyns); Midland, Acc 26/4, 29 July 1903, Acc 26/6, 7 March 1905; *DBB*, R. P. T. Davenport-Hines, 'Hugo Hirst, Lord Hirst', vol 3, p 277; Midland, Acc 26/3, 5 Feb 1903, Acc 26/8, 6 June 1913, Acc 26/9, 6 Oct 1913, 17 Nov 1913, 2 Jan 1914; Adam Gowans Whyte and T. C. Elder, *The Underwar* (1914), p 100.

28. *MF*, 1 Jan 1908; Kennedy, *Industrial Structure*, p 140.

29. For exoneration of the City from the motor industry's problems, see: S. B. Saul, 'The Motor Industry in Britain to 1914' in *Business History* (1962); Michie, 'Finance of Innovation', pp 518–26.

30. *DBB*, R. P. T. Davenport-Hines, 'Sir Edward Manville', vol 4, p 109 (Daimler); Standard Motor Co records (Modern Records Centre, University of Warwick), Mss 226/ST/1/1/1–2; *DBB*, J. Lowe, 'Charles Vernon Pugh', vol 4, p 781; Lanchester Private

Papers (Lanchester Polytechnic, now University of Coventry), F. W. Lanchester, 'History of the Lanchester venture', pp 10, 14; Ian Lloyd, *Rolls-Royce: The Growth of a Firm* (1978), pp 14–20; Lloyd, p 6 (*Motor Trader*); *Motor*, 7 May 1907; *CCJ*, Jan 1908, Annual Trade Review, p 7; Roy Church, *Herbert Austin: The British Motor Car Industry to 1941* (1979), p 19.

31. A. E. Harrison, 'Joint-Stock Company Flotation in the Cycle, Motor-Vehicle and Related Industries, 1882–1914' in *Business History* (1981).

32. *MF*, 20 March 1907, 22 April 1908.

33. Wayne Lewchuk, 'The Return to Capital in the British Motor Vehicle Industry, 1896–1939' in *Business History* (1985).

34. Kenneth Richardson, *The British Motor Industry, 1896–1939* (1977), p 38; *MF*, 13 March 1907; Pollitt Papers (University of London Library), 8/34, letter by H. H. Rodwell, 14 Sept 1944; *MF*, 13 March 1907.

35. *DBB*, R. P. T. Davenport-Hines, 'Charles Birch Crisp', vol 1, pp 822–7; *FN*, 15 May 1920; *MF*, 30 Jan 1907, 24 July 1907.

36. T. C. Barker and Michael Robbins, *A History of London Transport, Volume II* (1974), pp 126–36; *Economist*, 24 Jan 1906, 22 Dec 1906, 2 Feb 1907; *MF*, 5 June 1907, 12 June 1907; Midland, Acc 26/8, 13 June 1910; *Times*, 25 Aug 1927.

37. The decline is usefully summarised by Cain and Hopkins, pp 108–13.

38. Richard Roberts, *Schroders: Merchants & Bankers* (1992), p 115.

39. The argument is taken to its extreme limit in W. D. Rubinstein, *Capitalism, Culture, and Decline in Britain, 1750–1990* (1993).

40. Michie, *City*, p 25.

41. See, for example: Michael Barratt Brown, 'Away With All the Great Arches: Anderson's History of British Capitalism' in *New Left Review* (Jan–Feb 1988); Theo Barker, 'Workshop of the World, 1870–1914' in *History Today* (June 1994).

42. *Statist*, 20 Jan 1906; *Financial Review of Reviews*, Nov 1906, p 353; *FN*, 27 Feb 1907; *Economist*, 9 Oct 1909; *Statist*, 29 June 1912.

43. Roberts, p 115.

44. Probably the most user-friendly overview is Collins, *Banks and Industrial Finance*, pp 42–51.

45. Cain and Hopkins, p 196.

46. *FT*, 15 Jan 1906.

47. *Investor's Monthly Manual*, Jan 1910, p 2.

CHAPTER TWENTY-THREE

1. Esher Papers (Churchill College, Cambridge), 2/10, 3 Dec 1907; RAL, XI/130A/2, 12 March 1908; Morgan, Ms 21,795, vol 13, 21 March 1908, 31 March 1908.

2. BB, 200218, 25 April 1908; Morgan, Ms 21,795, vol 13, 26 April 1908; RAL, XI/130A/2, 13 May 1908.

3. Grey, 202/7, 1 July 1908; John Buchan, *Francis and Riversdale Grenfell: A Memoir* (1920), p 122.

4. On Lloyd's in 1908, see: D. E. W. Gibb, *Lloyd's of London: A Study in Individualism* (1957), pp 190–6; Andrew Brown, *Cuthbert Heath* (Newton Abbot, 1980), pp 98–104. On the Stock Exchange and the capacity question in 1908/9, see two detailed, broadly compatible accounts: R. C. Michie, *The London and New York Stock Exchanges, 1850–1914* (1987), pp 14–27, 84–5; D. T. A. Kynaston, 'The London Stock Exchange, 1870–1914: An Institutional History' (London PhD, 1983), pp 236–62.

5. *Times*, 17 July 1908.

6. *FT*, 5 Nov 1908; *Times*, 6 Nov 1908.

7. SE, Ms 14,600, vol 81, 27 Jan – 3 Feb 1908.

8. Kynaston, 'Stock Exchange', pp 256–7.

9. *Morning Post*, 23 March 1908; *FT*, 27 June 1908, 15 Jan 1908; BB, 200243, 11 Dec 1905.

10. *IR*, 27 June 1908; Henry Lowenfeld, *All About Investment* (1909), p 241; Kynaston, 'Stock Exchange', p 220; SE, Ms 14,600, vol 83, 1 March 1909. On Williams, see also Donald Read, *The Power of News: The History of Reuter's, 1849–1989* (Oxford, 1992), pp 114–15.

11. Addis, 14/169, 1 Oct 1908; on the Peking-Hankow loan in general, see Frank H. H. King, *The History of the Hongkong and Shanghai Banking Corporation* (vol II, Cambridge, 1988), pp 388–95; Addis, 14/26, 6–15 Oct 1908; *FT*, 10–13 Oct 1908.

12. Richard Roberts, *Schroders: Merchants & Bankers*, (1992), pp 139–44 tells the story. See also Graham L. Rees, *Britain's Commodity Markets* (1972), p 241.

13. RAL, XI/130A/o, 12 Feb 1906, XI/130A/1, 3 April 1907; Morgan, Ms 21,795, vol 14, 28 Aug 1908.

14. Roberts, p 142 ('swindle'); RAL, XI/130A/2, 8 Nov 1908, 14 Dec 1908.

15. BB, 200167, 7 Jan 1909; Pat Thane, 'Financiers and the British State: The Case of Sir Ernest Cassel' in *Business History* (1986), p 88; Anthony Allfrey, *Edward VII and his Jewish Court* (1991), p 217; BB, 200167, 8 Jan 1909; RAL, XI/130A/3, 14 Jan 1909, 22 Jan 1909; BB, 200168, 1 Feb 1909.

16. Vincent P. Carosso, *The Morgans: Private International Bankers, 1854–1913* (Cambridge, Mass, 1987), pp 578–82; Philip Ziegler, *The Sixth Great Power: Barings, 1762–1929* (1988), pp 307–8; Kathleen Burk, *Morgan Grenfell, 1838–1988: The Biography of a Merchant Bank* (Oxford, 1989), pp 55–7.

17. Morgan, Ms 21,795, vol 14, 16 Sept 1908 – 15 Jan 1909, 24 Feb 1909, 30 Jan 1909.

18. Grey, 202/5, 21 March 1909.

19. Peter Clarke, 'Churchill's Economic Ideas, 1900–1930' in Robert Blake and Wm Roger Louis (eds), *Churchill* (Oxford, 1993), p 87.

20. National Monetary Commission (Senate doc no 405), *Interviews on the Banking and Currency Systems of England, Scotland, France, Germany, Switzerland, and Italy* (Washington, 1910), pp 26–7, 30, 48–9.

21. *BM*, March 1908, p 454; LCC, Ms 16,647, 16 Dec 1908, 13 Jan 1909, 10 Feb 1909, 8 July 1909.

22. *JIB*, Dec 1909, pp 612–15.

23. Midland, Acc 150/1, 23 March 1909; *Statist*, 4 April 1908; R. P. T. Davenport-Hines, 'Lord Glendyne' in R. T. Appleyard and C. B. Schedvin (eds), *Australian Financiers: Biographical Essays* (Melbourne, 1988), p 194; *Economist*, 18 April 1908.

24. RAL, XI/130A/3, 17 March 1909; *Times*, 1 April 1909.

25. Kurt Grunwald, ' "Windsor-Cassel" – The Last Court Jew' in *Leo Baeck Institute, Year Book* (1969), pp 149–50; Maurice V. Brett (ed), *Journals and Letters of Reginald, Viscount Esher* (1934), vol 2, p 295; Morgan, Ms 21,795, vol 14, 23 March 1909.

CHAPTER TWENTY-FOUR

1. John Grigg, *The Young Lloyd George* (1973), p 202; RAL, XI/130A/3, 4 Jan 1909; *BM*, March 1909, p 462; Meyer, 27 April 1909.

2. *FN*, 30 April 1909; RAL, XI/130A/3, 3 May 1909; Grey, 202/5, 5 May 1909; RAL, XI/130A/3, 10 May 1909; Asquith Papers (Bodleian Library), Ms Asquith 12, fos 34–5; Alan Sykes, *Tariff Reform in British Politics, 1903–1913* (Oxford, 1979), p 186; John Buchan, *Francis and Riversdale Grenfell: A Memoir* (1920), p 138.

3. *FT*, 24 June 1909.

4. *FT*, 25 June 1909; RAL, XI/130A/3, 25 June 1909.

5. G. R. Searle, *Corruption in British Politics, 1895–1930* (Oxford, 1987), p 246 (Speyer); *DBB*, John P. Scott, 'John Wynford Philipps, 1st Viscount St Davids of Lydstep

Haven', vol 4, p 666; Searle, p 148 (Kleinwort); José Harris and Pat Thane, 'British and European bankers, 1880–1914: an "aristocratic bourgeoisie"?' in Pat Thane, Geoffrey Crossick and Roderick Floud (eds), *The Power of the Past*: *Essays for Eric Hobsbawm* (Cambridge, 1984), p 225; Morgan, Ms 21,795, vol 16, 30 Nov 1909.

6. *Hansard* (House of Lords), 22 Nov 1909, cols 795–9, 23 Nov 1909, cols 868–9, 29 Nov 1909, col 1153, 30 Nov 1909, col 1277.

7. RAL, XI/130A/3, 1 Dec 1909; *FN*, 6 Jan 1910, 17 Jan 1910; Grey, 202/1, 22 Jan 1910; MG, private letter books, no 1, 21 Jan 1910.

8. *Times*, 13 Jan 1910, 18 Jan 1910.

9. Sykes, p 186.

10. The answer given here follows the persuasive analysis in P. J. Cain and A. G. Hopkins, *British Imperialism*: *Innovation and Expansion, 1688–1914* (1993), pp 220–1.

11. SE, Ms 14,600, vol 87, 28 Nov 1910; Richard Davis, *The English Rothschilds* (1983), p 240; *FN*, 12 Aug 1911; Roy Jenkins, *Asquith* (1964), pp 539–42.

12. Philip Ziegler, *The Sixth Great Power*: *Barings, 1762–1929* (1988), pp 308–9; Richard Roberts, *Schroders*: *Merchants & Bankers* (1992), p 147; *FT*, 8 Feb 1910.

13. *FT*, 1–5 Feb 1910; see also Robert V. Kubicek, *Economic Imperialism in Theory and Practice*: *The Case of South African Gold Mining Finance, 1886–1914* (Durham, NC, 1979), p 156 on the Budapest loan; BB, COF/05/Box 6/File 9, 2 Dec 1909, 1 Nov 1911; *DBB*, R. P. T. Davenport-Hines, 'Charles Birch Crisp', vol 1, pp 822–3.

14. R. P. T. Davenport-Hines, *Dudley Docker*: *The Life and Times of a Trade Warrior* (Cambridge, 1984), pp 33–5; *Manchester Guardian*, 31 Dec 1910; *FN*, 2 Jan 1911; Addis, 14/29, 2 Jan 1911, 5 Jan 1911; MG, private letter books, no 4, 11 Feb 1911.

15. RAL, XI/130A/5, 10 Feb 1911; MG, private letter books, no 5, 6 May 1911; BB, Dep 33.12, 14 Dec 1911.

16. Cain and Hopkins, pp 269–71.

17. On these financiers and their activities, see: Gregory P. Marchildon, 'British Investment Banking and Industrial Decline before the Great War: A Case Study of Capital Outflow to Canadian Industry' in *Business History* (1991); Gregory P. Marchildon, ' "Hands Across the Water": Canadian Industrial Financiers in the City of London, 1905–20' in *Business History* (1992).

18. On Edgar, see Stefanie Diaper, 'The Sperling Combine and the shipbuilding industry: merchant banking and industrial finance in the 1920s' in J. J. van Helten and Y. Cassis (eds), *Capitalism in a Mature Economy*: *Financial Institutions, Capital Exports and British Industry, 1870–1939* (Aldershot, 1990). On Dunn, see: *DBB*, Duncan McDowall, 'Sir James Hamet Dunn', vol 2, pp 210–12; Ranald Michie, 'Dunn, Fischer & Co in the City of London, 1906–14' in *Business History* (1988).

19. Morgan, Ms 21,799, fo 136; NW, 4,337, vol 1, Union Bank of London.

20. Grey, 208/9, 26 Dec 1910, 223/4, 3 Feb 1911, 3 March 1911, 202/5, 26 April 1911.

21. Kleinwort, Ms 22,033, vol 2, fo 80; Grey, 202/5, 1 Aug 1911; John Jolliffe (ed), *Raymond Asquith: Life and Letters* (1980), p 277.

22. On all three areas in this section, see David McLean, 'Finance and "Informal Empire" before the First World War' in *Economic History Review* (1976). On China, see: Clarence B. Davis, 'Financing Imperialism: British and American Bankers as Vectors of Imperial Expansion in China, 1908–1920' in *Business History Review* (1982); E. W. Edwards, *British Diplomacy and Finance in China, 1895–1914* (Oxford, 1987), pp 121–57; Vincent P. Carosso, *The Morgans*: *Private International Bankers, 1854–1913* (Cambridge, Mass, 1987), pp 550–64; Frank H. H. King, *The History of the Hongkong and Shanghai Banking Corporation* (vol II, Cambridge, 1988), pp 395–450; Roberta Allbert Dayer, *Finance and Empire*: *Sir Charles Addis, 1861–1945* (1988), pp 61–4; Cain and Hopkins, pp 436–41. On Persia, see: David McLean, *Britain and Her Buffer State*: *The collapse of the Persian empire, 1890–1914* (1979), pp 87–105; Geoffrey Jones, *Banking and Empire in Iran*: *The History of the British Bank of the*

Middle East, Volume I (Cambridge, 1986), pp 114–31; Cain and Hopkins, pp 411–18. On Turkey, see: Marian Kent, 'Agent of Empire? The National Bank of Turkey and British Foreign Policy' in *Historical Journal* (1975); Pat Thane, 'Financiers and the British State: The Case of Sir Ernest Cassel' in *Business History* (1986), pp 93–4; Anthony Allfrey, *Edward VII and his Jewish Court* (1991), pp 224–37; Cain and Hopkins, pp 407–8.

23. Addis, 14/27, 29 June 1909; Morgan, Mss 21,795, vol 15, 17 Aug 1909, vol 16, 20 Nov 1909; Addis, 14/28, 17 May 1910, 10 Nov 1910; Kathleen Burk, *Morgan Grenfell, 1838–1988: The Biography of a Merchant Bank* (Oxford, 1989), p 66.

24. Midland, Acc 26/8, 29 Dec 1910.

25. McLean, *Buffer State*, p 143 ('leverage'); PRO, FO 371/958; McLean, *Buffer State*, p 100 ('quite decently').

26. McLean, 'Finance', p 294.

27. BSP, HBS 28, 25–6 May 1910, HBS 30, 13 Sept 1910.

28. BSP, HBS 30, 30 Sept 1910; Kent, p 378.

29. BSP, HBS 30, 7 Oct 1910; McLean, 'Finance', p 295; MG, private letter books, no 4, 6 Jan 1911; Kent, p 384.

30. BSP, HBS 31, 16 June 1911, 29 July 1911, HBS 30, 12 Jan 1912.

31. Kent, p 387; RAL, XI/130A/5, 24 Jan 1911.

32. LCC, Ms 16,643, vol 6, 12 Nov 1909.

33. *J. E. Beerbohm's Evening Corn Trade List*, 21 July 1910; London Oil and Tallow Trades Association records (Guildhall Library), Ms 23,234.

34. *Fairplay*, 1 Sept 1910, 8 Sept 1910, 1 Dec 1910.

35. *DBB*, Rory Miller, 'Archibald Williamson, 1st Lord Forres of Glenogil', vol 5, pp 833–6; Stanley Chapman, *Merchant Enterprise in Britain: From the Industrial Revolution to World War I* (Cambridge, 1992), pp 242–3; BW, Box 9, vol 1, 18 May 1909, 18 June 1909 (profits), 8 Sept 1909, 9 Oct 1910.

36. Miller, 'Archibald Williamson', p 834; BW, Box 9, vol 1, 21 Oct 1909; RAL, XI/130A/4, 4 April 1910; Harrisons & Crosfield records (Guildhall Library), Arthur Lampard out-letter book, 1906–11, 2 Feb 1911.

37. Lampard's career is covered in Peter Pugh and others, *Great Enterprise: A History of Harrisons & Crosfield* (1990), pp 28–74.

38. There is, surprisingly, no good account of the rubber boom. A reasonable make-weight is Hubert A. Meredith, *The Drama of Money Making: Tragedy and Comedy of the London Stock Exchange* (?1931), pp 206–16.

39. Zorn & Leigh-Hunt, *A Manual of Rubber Planting Companies* (3rd edn, Jan 1909), pp xiii, ix; Meredith, p 211.

40. Kleinwort, Ms 22,030, vol 3, fo 155; NW, 4,337, vol 1, Union Bank of London; Meredith, p 211.

41. John Arnold Lambert, *Reminiscences of a Financial Venturer* (1955), p 86; W. A. Morgan (ed), *The Stock Exchange Christmas Annual, 1912–13* (1912), p 195; *Quarterly Review*, July 1912, p 98.

42. David Kynaston, *The Financial Times: A Centenary History* (1988), pp 65–6; FN, 22 April 1910.

43. Lampard out-letter book, 1906–11, 25 May – 27 July 1910.

44. Lampard out-letter book, 1906–11, 20 Jan 1911; *Times*, 23 Sept 1916; FT, 19 Oct 1906.

45. SE, Ms 14,600, vol 85, 10 Jan 1910, 17 Jan 1910; *Economist*, 5 Feb 1910; SE, Ms 14,600, vol 85, 31 Jan 1910.

46. SE, Ms 14,600, vol 70, 13 June 1900; Kleinwort, Ms 22,030, vol 3, fo 83; *Times Law Reports*, 14 Nov 1910; Kleinwort, Ms 22,033, vol 2, fo 50.

47. SE, Mss 14,609, vol 3, 25 Nov 1908 – 3 Feb 1909, 14,600, vol 83, 10 Feb 1909.

48. SE, Ms 14,609, vol 3, 3 Feb 1909; David Kynaston, *The City of London, volume I: A World of Its Own* (1994), pp 281–2.

49. *Economist*, 12 June 1909; SE, Mss 14,609, vol 3, 21 April 1909, vol 4, 22 Sept 1909.
50. SE, Mss 14,600, vol 85, 3 Feb 1910, vol 86, appendix (fo 6) and 2 March 1910; *Economist*, 12 March 1910; SE, Ms 14,600, vol 86, 3 May 1910.
51. SE, Ms 14,600, vol 88, 1 March 1911, 20 March 1911; R. C. Michie, *The London and New York Stock Exchanges, 1850–1914* (1987), p 85.
52. James Capel & Co records (Guildhall Library), Ms 15,123, item 25.
53. *Nineteenth Century and After*, March 1911, pp 449–50, 453; *BM*, April 1911, pp 585–7, 541.
54. *BM*, June 1911, pp 811–16, 896, Sept 1911, p 406.
55. RAL, XI/130A/5, 21 July 1911; *FN*, 22 July 1911; *BM*, Sept 1911, pp 402, 404; Winston S. Churchill, *The World Crisis, 1911–1918* (1939 edn), vol 1, p 32; *FN*, 24 July 1911.

CHAPTER TWENTY-FIVE

1. This account follows: Sir John Clapham, *The Bank of England: A History* (Cambridge, 1944), vol II, p 412; A. R. Holmes and Edwin Green, *Midland: 150 years of banking business* (1986), pp 143–5.
2. B of E, G4/134.
3. B of E, G4/134; Tessa Ogden, 'An analysis of Bank of England discount and advance behaviour, 1870–1914' in James Foreman-Peck (ed), *New perspectives on the late Victorian economy: Essays in Quantitative Economic History, 1860–1914* (Cambridge, 1990), p 341; B of E, G4/134.
4. B of E, G4/134; BB, Dep 33.11, 2 Aug 1911, 24 Aug 1911.
5. SSA, Ms 14,894, vol 20, 16 Aug 1911; *Economist*, 19 Aug 1911; Foster & Braithwaite records, consulted c.1980 at 22 Austin Friars, letter by John Braithwaite dated 1 Sept 1911.
6. BS, Ms 20,111, vol 4, 4 Oct 1911, 21 Nov 1911; Sir Henry Clay, *Lord Norman* (1957), pp 56–8, 70.
7. The implications of the inquiry are explored in Paul M. Kennedy, 'Strategy versus Finance in Twentieth-Century Great Britain' in *International History Review* (1981).
8. PRO, CAB 16/18A.
9. *JIB*, Feb 1912, pp 50–83.
10. On the background, see Avner Offer, 'Empire and Social Reform: British Overseas Investment and Domestic Politics, 1908–14' in *Historical Journal* (1983), pp 130–2, linking the decline of Consols to the gold reserves question; more specifically on Lloyd George's enforced initiative and the City's response, see Youssef Cassis, *City Bankers, 1890–1914* (Cambridge, 1994), pp 287–90.
11. *BM*, Sept 1911, p 405; *JIB*, Dec 1911, pp 496, 483; PRO, T 172/92 (Holden); *BM*, March 1912, pp 387–8.
12. PRO, T 172/92.
13. Gibbs, Ms 11,042, vol 1, 25–6 Oct 1911.
14. Gibbs, Ms 11,042, vol 1, 13 March 1912, 22 March 1912.
15. BB, Dep 33.7, 13 Nov – 15 Dec 1911.
16. BB, Dep 33.12, 24 Nov – 1 Dec 1911; RAL, XI/130A/6, 28 Feb 1912.
17. RAL, XI/130A/6, 5 March 1912, R Fam C/12, XI/130A/6, 7 March 1912.
18. *Economist*, 16 Sept 1911; for background to the fixed scale, and the whole question of cost, see D. T. A. Kynaston, 'The London Stock Exchange, 1870–1914: An Institutional History' (London PhD, 1983), pp 270–81.
19. James Capel & Co records (Guildhall Library), Ms 15,123, item 22; *FN*, 2 March 1912, 20 March 1912; Kynaston, 'Stock Exchange', pp 278–9.
20. W. A. Morgan (ed), *The Stock Exchange Christmas Annual, 1912–13* (1912), p 89.

21. Duff Hart-Davis (ed), *End of an Era: Letters and Journals of Sir Alan Lascelles, 1887–1920* (1986), pp 109–20; H. Osborne O'Hagan, *Leaves from my Life* (1929), vol II, p 335; Baron E. B. d'Erlanger, *My English Souvenirs* (1978), p 268. Also on Bevan, see *DBB*, R. P. T. Davenport-Hines, 'Gerard Lee Bevan', vol 1, pp 321–4.

22. *Lascelles*, pp 122–3; *FN*, 16 April 1912.

23. *FN*, 17 April 1912; Ron Chernow, *The House of Morgan: An American Banking Dynasty and the Evolution of the Modern Financial World* (1990), p 146 (Smith); Jehanne Wake's forthcoming history of Kleinwort Benson ('quite the young man'); SE, Ms 19,297, vol 21, 8 May 1912; *FN*, 18–20 April 1912; *DBB*, Oliver M. Westall, 'Sir Edward Mortimer Mountain', vol 4, p 362; RAL, XI/130A/6, 16 April 1912; *Lascelles*, p 123.

24. *Lascelles*, p 125.

CHAPTER TWENTY-SIX

1. In general on the Marconi Scandal, see: Frances Donaldson, *The Marconi Scandal* (1962); G. R. Searle, *Corruption in British Politics, 1895–1930* (Oxford, 1987), pp 172–200; Bentley Brinkerhoff Gilbert, 'David Lloyd George and the Great Marconi Scandal' in *Historical Research* (1989).

2. Donaldson, p 21; Robert Speaight, *The Life of Hilaire Belloc* (1957), p 15.

3. Henry D'Avigdor-Goldsmid, 'The Little Marconi Case' in *History Today* (April 1964); Searle, pp 201–12.

4. John Vincent (ed), *The Crawford Papers: The journals of David Lindsay twenty-seventh Earl of Crawford and tenth Earl of Balcarres 1871–1940 during the years 1892 to 1940* (Manchester, 1984), p 286; RAL, XI/130A/6, 10 Dec 1912.

5. RAL, XI/130A/7, 25 March 1913; *Economist*, 3 May 1913.

6. *Select Committee on Marconi's Wireless Telegraph Company, Limited* (P.P. 1913, VII), qq 3671–4425.

7. RAL, XI/130A/7, 10 April 1913.

8. SE, Mss 14,600, vols 92–3, 9 Oct – 10 Nov 1913; *Economist*, 15 Nov 1913.

9. *FN*, 6 June 1912; RAL, XI/130A/6, 2–3 Oct 1912; *Economist*, 5 Oct 1912, 15 Feb 1913; SE, Ms 19,297, vol 22, 19 March 1913; *Economist*, 27 Dec 1913.

10. Robert V. Kubicek, *Economic Imperialism in Theory and Practice: The Case of South African Gold Mining Finance, 1886–1914* (Durham, NC, 1979), p 73; SE, Ms 14,609, vol 4, 13 June 1912.

11. Duff Hart-Davis (ed), *End of an Era: Letters and Journals of Sir Alan Lascelles, 1887–1920* (1986), pp 144–53.

12. D. T. A. Kynaston, 'The London Stock Exchange, 1870–1914: An Institutional History' (London PhD, 1983), p 101; MG, private letter book, no 10, 18 Oct 1913.

13. Richard Roberts, *Schroders: Merchants & Bankers* (1992), pp 363–4.

14. In general on the Crisp Loan and Reorganisation Loan, see: K. C. Chan, 'British Policy in the Reorganisation Loan to China, 1912–13' in *Modern Asian Studies* (1971); David McLean, 'Finance and "Informal Empire" before the First World War' in *Economic History Review* (1976), pp 302–4; Clarence B. Davis, 'Financing Imperialism: British and American Bankers as Vectors of Imperial Expansion in China, 1908–1920' in *Business History Review* (1982); *DBB*, R. P. T. Davenport-Hines, 'Charles Birch Crisp', vol 1, pp 823–4; Vincent P. Carosso, *The Morgans: Private International Bankers, 1854–1913* (Cambridge, Mass, 1987), pp 564–78; E. W. Edwards, *British Diplomacy and Finance in China, 1895–1914* (Oxford, 1987), pp 158–75; Frank H. H. King, *The History of the Hongkong and Shanghai Banking Corporation* (vol II, Cambridge, 1988), pp 477–509; Roberta Allbert Dayer, *Finance and Empire: Sir Charles Addis, 1861–1945* (1988), pp 64–71; Geoffrey Jones, *British Multinational Banking, 1830–1990* (Oxford, 1993), pp 128–30; P. J. Cain and A. G. Hopkins, *British Imperialism: Innovation and Expansion, 1688–1914* (1993), pp 440–3.

15. Addis, 14/30, 12 March 1912, 21 May 1912; Dayer, p 67.

16. *Times*, 30 Oct 1912; Lo Hui-Min, *The Correspondence of G. E. Morrison, volume II: 1912–1920* (Cambridge, 1978), pp 65, 27; *Times*, 30 Oct 1912; Addis, 14/30, 23 Sept 1912.

17. *FT*, 24–5 Sept 1912; Addis, 14/30, 24 Sept 1912; *FT*, 26 Sept 1912; *Economist*, 28 Sept 1912; RAL, XI/130A/6, 26 Sept 1912; *FT*, 27 Sept 1912; *Economist*, 28 Sept 1912; *FT*, 1 Oct 1912; Carosso, p 572.

18. Addis, 14/30, 18 Oct 1912, 14/173, 23 Oct 1912; Davis, p 253.

19. Addis, 14/30, 30–1 Oct 1912; BB, 200250, 31 Oct 1912.

20. PRO, FO 371/1324; *Times*, 8 Nov 1912; PRO, FO 371/1324; Addis, 14/30, 26 Nov 1912; BB, 200250, 26 Nov 1912; Addis, 14/30, 27 Nov 1912.

21. Midland, Acc 26/8, 28 Nov 1912; PRO, FO 371/1325.

22. BB, 200250, 12 Dec 1912; Addis, 14/31, 4 Feb 1913; BB, 200250, 15 May 1913; Midland, Acc 26/8, 16 May 1913; Addis, 14/31, 20–1 May 1913.

23. McLean, p 303; Meyer, 23 Oct 1913; Cain and Hopkins, p 440, citing King, pp 517–19.

24. RAL, XI/130A/6, 22 May 1912, XI/130A/7, 1 Dec 1913; *BM*, Nov 1913, pp 632–4; Roberts, p 135.

25. RAL, XI/130A/6, 8 July 1912, 15 July 1912, 19 July 1912.

26. RAL, XI/111/57.

27. *FT*, 6 May 1913; RAL, XI/130A/7, 5 May 1913; *FT*, 8 May 1913.

28. *FT*, 8–9 May 1913; RAL, XI/130A/7, 8 May 1913.

29. BB, COF/05/7/4, 28 Aug – 7 Oct 1913; Roberts, p 147.

30. On Norman in 1913, see: Sir Henry Clay, *Lord Norman* (1957), pp 71–5; Andrew Boyle, *Montagu Norman: a biography* (1967), pp 90–5.

31. BS, Mss 20, 111, vol 4, 23 Dec 1912, 4 April 1913, 20,120, vol 1, 12 Nov 1913; Clay, pp 72–3; B of E, ADM 20/1.

32. LCC, Ms 16,648, 7 May 1913.

33. LCC, Ms 16,648, 7 May 1913; RAL, XI/130A/7, 27 May 1913.

34. LCC, Ms 16,648, 11 June 1913, 18 June 1913.

35. On this background, see Marcello de Cecco, *Money and Empire: The International Gold Standard, 1890–1914* (Oxford, 1974), pp 70–5.

36. *Royal Commission on Indian Finance and Currency: Minutes of Evidence, Volume I* (P.P. 1914, XIX), qq 3348, 3351, 3429, 3463, 3465–9.

37. LCC, Ms 16,648, 30 July 1913; *BM*, Sept 1913, p 318.

38. LCC, Ms 16,648, 12 Nov 1913.

39. *DBB*, R. P. T. Davenport-Hines, 'Walter Cunliffe, 1st Lord Cunliffe', vol 1, pp 861–5.

40. Morgan, Ms 21,795, vol 14, 10 Nov 1908; B of E, G15/111.

41. Addis, 14/31, 29 Nov – 4 Dec 1913; Mocatta & Goldsmid records (Guildhall Library), Ms 18,639, 23 Dec 1913.

CHAPTER TWENTY-SEVEN

1. MG, private letter books, no 10, 1 Jan 1914; RAL, XI/130A/8, 7 Jan 1914; BW, Box 9, vol 2, 17 Jan 1914; BB, Dep 33.15, 21 Jan 1914; Philip Ziegler, *The Sixth Great Power: Barings, 1762–1929* (1988), p 277.

2. *Times*, 24 Jan 1914; RAL, XI/130A/8, 26 Jan 1914; B of E, G23/89.

3. MG, private letter books, no 10, 2 Feb 1914; Grey, 197/9, 5 Feb 1914; *DBB*, R. P. T. Davenport-Hines, 'Arthur Morton Grenfell', vol 2, p 651; John Buchan, *Francis and Riversdale Grenfell: A Memoir* (1920), pp 153, 178, 183; Addis, 14/32, 5 Feb 1914.

4. *Times*, 10 Feb 1914.

5. LCC, Ms 16,648, 10 Feb 1914.

6. PRO, T 171/53; R. S. Sayers, *The Bank of England, 1891–1944* (Cambridge, 1976), vol 1, p 64.

7. BS, Ms 20,112, vol 16, 9 March 1914; *FT*, 5 June 1914 refers to Charlie Clarke having 'headed the Stock Exchange in the recent great gathering in Hyde Park to protest against the Home Rule Bill'; RAL, XI/130A/8, 16 March 1914.

8. RAL, XI/130A/8, 30 March 1914; LCC, Ms 16,648, 2 April 1914.

9. RAL, XI/130A/8, 6 April 1914; Richard Roberts, *Schroders: Merchants & Bankers* (1992), p 148; RAL, XI/130A/8, 30 March 1914; BB, Dep 33.15, 30 April 1914; RAL, XI/130A/8, 11 May 1914.

10. LCC, Ms 16,648, 14 May 1914.

11. Davenport-Hines, 'Grenfell', p 651.

12. Grey, 255/2, 30 May 1914; Davenport-Hines, 'Grenfell', p 651; Grey, 255/2, 30 May 1914.

13. Midland, Acc 26/9, 4 June 1914; SSA, Ms 14,894, vol 24, 6 June 1914; RAL, XI/130A/8, 8 June 1914; *Times*, 8 June 1914; Grey, 255/2, 8 June 1914.

14. Midland, Acc 26/9, 4 June 1914; LCC, Ms 16,531, vol 1, fos 49–50.

15. MG, private letter books, no 11, 29 June 1914, 25 June 1914; RAL, XI/130A/8, 29 June 1914; *FT*, 30 June 1914.

16. RAL, XI/130A/8, 1–6 July 1914; *FT*, 6–8 July 1914; RAL, XI/130A/8, 14 July 1914; *FT*, 18 July 1914.

17. *FT*, 20 July 1914.

18. MG, private letter books, no 12, 20 July 1914; *FT*, 21–2 July 1914; BB, Dep 33.15, 21 July 1914; *FT*, 23 July 1914; RAL, XI/130A/8, 22 July 1914.

19. Grey, 255/2, 25 July 1914; *BM*, Sept 1914, p 415; LCC, Ms 16,648, 22 July 1914.

20. Ellis T. Powell, *The Mechanism of the City* (1910), pp 1, 4; *Economist*, 11 Jan 1913; Ranald C. Michie, *The City of London: Continuity and Change, 1850–1990* (1992), p 14; R. Dixon Smith, *Ronald Colman, Gentleman of the Cinema* (Jefferson, NC, 1991), pp 2–3.

21. B of E, G15/111; Sayers, *Bank*, vol 1, p 67; B of E, ADM 30/17 (*Financier* cutting); D. E. W. Gibb, *Lloyd's of London: A Study in Individualism* (1957), pp 247–50; *FN*, 7 July 1914.

22. Anon, *Two Centuries of Lewis & Peat, 1775–1975* (1975), p 20; Frank H. H. King, *The History of the Hongkong and Shanghai Banking Corporation* (vol II, Cambridge, 1988), pp 186–7; Sayers, *Bank*, vol 2, pp 609–10; BW, Box 9, vol 1, 22 May 1912, 1 July 1912.

23. A. J. Wilson, *The Life & Times of Sir Alfred Chester Beatty* (1985), p 133; Peter Brackfield, 'Singer & Friedlander Limited', *Bowring Magazine* (Summer 1978); BB, 200214, 1 March 1906; W. Lionel Fraser, *All to the Good* (1963), pp 34–5, L. E. Jones, *Georgian Afternoon* (1958), pp 146–7.

24. Hartley Withers, *Stocks and Shares* (1910), pp 234–5; Georgiana Blakiston (ed), *Letters of Conrad Russell, 1897–1947* (1987), p 17.

25. For elaboration, see: Marcello de Cecco, *Money and Empire: The International Gold Standard, 1890–1914* (Oxford, 1974), pp 104–6; Roberts, p 115; Michie, pp 42–4, 64–5, 73–5, 78–9, 109–10.

26. Helpful accounts of the 1914 financial crisis include: de Cecco, pp 141–70; 'Sir John Clapham's account', reproduced in Sayers, *Bank*, appendices, pp 31–45; Sayers, *Bank*, vol 1, pp 70–4; Teresa Seabourne, 'The Summer of 1914' in Forrest Capie and Geoffrey E. Wood (eds), *Financial Crises and the World Banking System* (1986).

27. RAL, XI/130A/8, 24 July 1914; MG, private letter books, no 12, 24 July 1914; SSA, Ms 14,894, vol 24, 24 July 1914; BB, Dep 33.15, 24 July 1914; *FT*, 25 July 1914; SSA, Ms 14,894, vol 24, 25 July 1914; BB, Dep 33.15, 7 Aug 1914; Heseltine, Powell & Co records (Guildhall Library), Ms 23,267, vol 2, 26 July 1914.

28. *FT*, 27–8 July 1914; SSA, Ms 14,894, vol 24, 27 July 1914; Gibbs, Ms 11,115, vol 2, 27 July 1914.

29. *FT*, 29 July 1914.

30. *FN*, 29 July 1914; *FT*, 30 July 1914; British Bank of South America records (University College London), E 2/4, 29 July 1914; BS, Ms 20,112, vol 16, 29 July 1914; SSA, Ms 14,894, vol 24, 29 July 1914.

31. *Pall Mall Gazette*, 29 July 1914; BB, Dep 33.15, 7 Aug 1914; de Cecco, pp 142–3; LCC, Ms 16,648, 29 July 1914.

32. *FT*, 31 July 1914; RAL, XI/130A/8, 30 July 1914; SE, Ms 14,600, vol 94, 30 July 1914; SSA, Ms 14,894, vol 24, 30 July 1914; Gillett Brothers & Co records (Guildhall Library), Ms 24,700.

33. Gilletts records, Ms 24,700; SE, Ms 14,600, vol 94, 31 July 1914; Gilletts records, Ms 24,700; SSA, Ms 14,894, vol 24, 31 July 1914; *FT*, 1 Aug 1914.

34. Gibbs, Ms 11,115, vol 2, 31 July 1914; RAL, XI/130A/8, 31 July 1914; Roberts, p 153 analyses the position facing some of the accepting houses; RAL, XI/130A/8, 31 July 1914.

35. Gilletts records, Ms 24,700; SSA, Ms 14,894, vol 24, 1 Aug 1914; R. S. Sayers, *Gilletts in the London Money Market* (Oxford, 1968), p 66.

36. Elizabeth Johnson (ed), *The Collected Writings of John Maynard Keynes: Volume XVI, Activities 1914–1919* (1971), p 3; Ronald Knox, *Patrick Shaw-Stewart* (1920), p 99.

37. PRO, T 170/14.

38. BB, Dep 33.15, 7 Aug 1914; SSA, Ms 14,894, vol 24, 3 Aug 1914; MG, private letter books, no 12, 3 Aug 1914.

39. PRO, T 170/14.

40. SSA, Ms 14,894, vol 24, 4 Aug 1914; MG, private letter books, no 12, 4 Aug 1914 (reply to Huth Jackson); PRO, T 170/55.

41. D. E. Moggridge, *Maynard Keynes: an economist's biography* (1992), pp 238–9.

42. Semi-defences include Sayers, *Bank*, vol 1, pp 72–3, Seabourne, pp 96–101.

43. RAL, XI/130A/8, 30 July 1914; MG, private letter books, no 12, 7 Aug 1914; *War Memoirs of David Lloyd George, I* (1933), pp 111–12.

44. *FT*, 29 July 1914; *The History of The Times* (vol IV, part I, 1952), p 208; *Lloyd George*, p 65; Ruth Dudley Edwards, *The Pursuit of Reason: The Economist, 1843–1993* (1993), pp 537–8.

45. *Lloyd George*, pp 65–6; *FT*, 4 Aug 1914; RAL, XI/130A/8, 4 Aug 1914.

46. BB, Dep 33.15, 7 Aug 1914; Hartley Withers, *War and Lombard Street* (1915), p 1; Anthony Allfrey, *Edward VII and his Jewish Court* (1991), pp 267–8; Baron E. B. d'Erlanger, *My English Souvenirs* (1978), p 238; David Kynaston, *The Financial Times: A Centenary History* (1988), p 75.

Acknowledgements

I am grateful to the following for allowing me to reproduce material: The Bank of England; Baring Brothers; the Bonham Carter family (Asquith papers); Cater Allen; Alan Clodd; Lord Esher; Freshfields (Alfred Wells reminiscences); Hambros; Kleinwort Benson; Macmillan (*The Scarlet Tree*); Matheson & Co; R. R. Meinertzhagen; Sir Anthony Meyer; Midland Bank; Morgan Grenfell; National Westminster Bank; School of Oriental and African Studies and the Addis family; N. M. Rothschild & Sons; The Royal Bank of Scotland; Schroders; University College, London; A. P. Watt Ltd on behalf of Mrs Lavinia Hankinson, The Hon Mrs David Erskine and Duff Hart-Davis (Sir Alan Lascelles journals).

The following kindly supplied illustrations: The Governor and Company of the Bank of England (14); Baring Brothers (endpapers, 16); Guildhall Library, Corporation of London (jacket, 1, 3, 4, 5, 6, 7); N. M. Rothschild & Sons (endpapers, 15); The Royal Bank of Scotland (9). John Fisher at the Guildhall Library was very helpful guiding me to illustrations.

The Guildhall Library itself remains as user-friendly as ever, and I am grateful. In *A World of Its Own* I mentioned archivists and fellow-historians who have been particularly helpful to me, and I continue in their debt. In addition, Melanie Aspey, Forrest Capie, J. M. Fewster, Robert Greenhill and Edgar Jones have all assisted the progress of this volume in various ways. I am grateful to Robin Holland-Martin and Nicholas Meinertzhagen for their continuing interest. For the last two years I have been a Fellow of the Business History Unit at the London School of Economics, and I would like to thank Terry Gourvish for providing me with a congenial academic base. My research for this book in effect dates back to the late 1970s, and I recall with affection Theo Barker's encouragement when I first came to him at the LSE intending to work on the City. One historian I never met was Sydney Checkland. On 1 October 1979 – my first day as a postgraduate student – I read his wonderful article on 'The Mind of the City, 1870–1914', published in *Oxford Economic Papers* (1957). It taught me that the City had no mind – an invaluable lesson, and I wish I could have thanked him personally.

There are other people, at this two-thirds point of my putative trilogy, to whom I would like to express thanks: Amanda Howard and Michael Burns for help at important stages; John Flower for drawing the endpapers; Margaret Sadler for designing the illustrations; Mark Bell and Alison Mansbridge for their copy-editing skills; and everyone at Chatto, especially Jenny Uglow, an editor who understands what I am trying to do and makes me do it better. Deborah Rogers has been my agent for ten years, and her belief in me has meant a lot.

Finally, at home, a 'thank you' to three friendly faces: Laurie, George and (just in time for the endgame) Michael.

London, winter 1994/5

INDEX

Note: in the case of a firm that changed its name, the name given is the one by which it was most usually known during the period.

Index

Campbell, Charles 90
Campbell, Colin 90
Campbell, William 444, 488–9, 582
Campbell-Bannerman, Sir Henry 337
Canada 505–7
Canadian Agency 426, 431, 475–6, 487, 506, 587, 591–2, 595
Canadian Northern Railway 601
Cannan, Edwin 119
Capel, James & Co 305, 547
capital: discount houses 297–8; merchant banks 269–70; merchants 264–6, 520; Stock Exchange firms 305, 401–2
Capital and Counties Bank 249, 534, 566
capital exports 38, 468–71, 498–9, 505
capital market: allotment 368, 485–6; British Government funding 203–7, 209–11, 222–6, 234–6; company financing 2–3, 67–9, 83–4, 109–11, 128–9, 134, 136–49, 173–5, 176–83, 187–8, 211–15, 217, 231–2, 236, 351–2, 435–6, 441, 455–9, 462–8, 487, 505–7, 518, 521–3, 535; company law and Stock Exchange regulation 177–8, 458–9; costs 179–82, 420, 459; distribution 209–10, 315; foreign government and state loans 48–9, 58–9, 62–4, 81, 172–3, 188–9, 349–50, 367–8, 390–4, 405–6, 409–12, 418–20, 437–9, 451, 473–4, 484–7, 491–2, 502–4, 510–14, 544–5, 564–75; foreign railways 394–5, 406, 441, 482–3, 504–5, 508–10, 545; market making 2–3, 67–9, 177–83, 231, 236; underwriting 189, 268, 311, 420, 438, 456, 459, 485, 572–4; see also Stock Exchange
Carey & Browne 14, 23, 251, 258, 264, 328
Carlton Club 182, 324, 378
Carrington, Lord 436
Cassel, Sir Ernest: advice to British government 376; American crisis

473; Anglo-German relations 493; association with Cornwallis-West 335; association with Lord Esher 322–3, 335; Baghdad Railway 365–6; character 127, 318–19, 349; Chinese loans 126–7, 570; closeness to Edward VII 237, 318, 322–3, 349; Consols 204, 206; First World War 610; Japanese loan 391, 393; Lloyd George budget 497–8; Mersey Docks and Harbour Board 456; Moroccan loan 368–9; National Bank of Turkey 511–14; opposition to bimetallism 74; relations with Barings 349; relations with Rothschilds 207, 224, 271; Russian loan 484–5; standing 171–2; tariff reform 379; Transvaal loan 235; underground railway 243; war loan 209, 224, 225–6
Cater & Co 296
Caucasus Copper Company 436
Caudery, Wm. & Co 264–5
Cavan, Earl of 544
Cawston, George 121
Cazenove, Arthur Philip 327
Cazenove & Akroyds 44, 248, 547, 573
Cecil, Lord Robert 556, 558, 559
Central Association of Bankers 153, 191–2
Central Bank of London 39
Central London Railway 243
Central Mining and Investment Corporation 404, 562
Chalmers, Lawrence 166
Chamber of Commerce Journal 33, 344, 465
Chamberlain, Austen 579
Chamberlain, Joseph 116, 190, 194, 196, 351, 366, 375–8, 380, 382–3, 384–5, 416, 471
Chambers's Journal 184–5
Chang Yen-Mao 396
Channel Tunnel Co 24
Chant, Mrs Ormiston 105
Chaplin, Ernest 592
Chaplin, Henry 116, 378
Chaplin, Milne, Grenfell & Co 347, 426, 495, 507, 590, 592
Charleton, Charles 343–4

politics: Chinese labour issue 397–8;
City of London electoral contests
414–16, 500–1; dislike of
Anarchism, Socialism, Radicalism
and Liberalism 101, 104–5, 414,
437, 572; Liberal sympathisers 105,
188, 233, 497, 501, 517; Marconi
Scandal 552–9; opposition to Irish
Home Rule 78–9, 589;
predominant Tory allegiance 49,
377, 384, 542–3; reaction to Lloyd
George's 1909 Budget and ensuing
political crisis 494–502; support for
strong Navy 85–6
Pollack & Bamberger 111
Ponsonby, Frederick 338
port 515
Port of London Bill 343–5
Post Office 354–6, 552
Poston, Charles 332
Povah, John 597
Powell, David 93, 95, 97–8, 99
Powell, Ellis 457, 521, 596, 610
Prance, George 303
Prance, R.H. 303
Prentice, Graham 306
Prescott, Dimsdale, Cave, Tugwell
& Co 283
press 24, 76, 109, 177–82, 409,
459; *see also* individual newspaper
and periodical titles
Prevost, Sir Augustus 224–5, 235,
386
Price, Forbes & Co 252–3
Price & Pierce 506
Price Waterhouse 417
Prince & Whitely 230–1
Prior, Selwyn 534
private banks 38–9, 62, 91, 152–3,
191, 283–4
profits 270, 305–6, 517
Promenade Concerts 352
Public Ledger 23
Pulley, Henry 435
Punch 6, 326

Quilter, Ball & Co 319

racial prejudice 78
Railway Companies Association
313

railways 11, 16, 260: American 50,
227, 317, 469, 474; Argentine 44,
85, 313; Baghdad 364–8;
Brazilian 545; Canadian 601;
Chinese 173, 394–5, 406, 482,
508; commuting 175, 241–2, 326;
Home Rails 50, 59, 61, 64, 123,
313, 498, 562; Japanese 504;
Manila 406; Mexican 59; Prussia
491; Sevenoaks smash 468; South
African 63, 279; stations 205,
596; Turkish 80
Raleigh, Cecil 143, 168
Randlords 81–3, 109–11, 122–3,
128–30, 132–5, 161, 193, 195,
201, 214–15, 333, 337–8, 345,
372, 379, 397–8, 404–5, 503
Randolph, E. & C. 301, 529
Ranjitsinhji, Prince 147
Raphael, Henry 71, 119
Raphael, R. & Sons 117, 151, 228,
229, 230, 474, 495
Raphael, Walter 560
Rayleigh, Lord 323
Reed & Sons, *see* Austin Reed
Reeves, Whitburn & Co 151
Reform Club 324
religions 65–7, 143, 152, 159, 254,
306
Renals, Sir Joseph 122, 130, 161
Revelstoke, John Baring, 2nd Baron:
advice to British government
537–8; ambition 274; Argentine
424–5, 502; assessment of
Rothschilds 271; attitude to Stock
Exchange 336; Baghdad Railway
365–6; character 271, 280;
Chinese loan 567–9, 570–1; First
World War 602; industrial market
456; Japanese loan 350, 390–1,
392; Lloyd George budget 496,
498; National Bank of Turkey
511; Ottoman Bank 513; Port of
London inquiry 342; relations
with Cassel 391, 399, 474;
relations with Schröders 502;
relations with Speyers 405–7;
rescue of Arthur Grenfell 348–9;
role in rehabilitation of Barings
58, 204, 274; Rumanian loan 574;
Russian loan 409–12, 484, 485–6,